12 Albertson's Inc. (NYSE / ABS)
250 Parkcenter Boulevard
Boise, ID 83726
3-Year Sales History:
Fiscal	1995	$12,585,034,000
	1996	$13,776,678,000
	1997	$14,476,000,000

13 Walgreen Co. (NYSE / WAG)
200 Wilmot Road   www.walgreens.com
Deerfield, IL 60015
3-Year Sales History:
Fiscal	1995	$10,395,096,000
	1996	$11,778,408,000
	1997	$13,794,000,000

14 Winn-Dixie Stores, Inc. (NYSE / WIN)
5050 Edgewood Court   www.winndixie.com
Jacksonville, FL 32254
3-Year Sales History:
Fiscal	1995	$12,955,488,000
	1996	$13,218,715,000
	1997	$13,382,000,000

15 The May Department Stores Company (NYSE / MAY)
611 Olive Street   www.maycompany.com
St. Louis, MO 63101
3-Year Sales History:
Fiscal	1995	$10,484,000,000
	1996	$11,650,000,000
	1997	$12,494,000,000

16 Publix Supermarkets Inc. (OTC BB / PUSH)
1936 George Jenkins Blvd.
Lakeland, FL 33815
3-Year Sales History:
Fiscal	1995	$ 9,393,021,000
	1996	$10,431,302,000
	1997	$11,213,000,000

17 Toys-R-Us, Inc. (NYSE / TOY)
461 From Road   www.toysrus.com
Paramus, NJ 07645
3-Year Sales History:
Fiscal	1995	$ 9,426,900,000
	1996	$ 9,932,400,000
	1997	$10,723,000,000

18 The Great Atlantic & Pacific Tea Company, Inc. (NYSE / GAP)
2 Paragon Drive   www.aptea.com
Montvale, NJ 07645
3-Year Sales History:
Fiscal	1995	$10,101,356,000
	1996	$10,089,014,000
	1997	$10,107,000,000

19 Lowe's Companies, Inc. (NYSE / LOW)
P.O. Box 111   www.lowes.com
North Wickesboro, NC 28656
3-Year Sales History:
Fiscal	1995	$ 7,075,442,000
	1996	$ 8,600,241,000
	1997	$ 9,781,000,000

20 Food Lion, Inc. (NASDAQ / FDLNB)
2110 Executive Drive   www.foodlion.com
Salisbury, NC 28145
3-Year Sales History:
Fiscal	1995	$ 8,210,884,000
	1996	$ 9,005,932,000
	1997	$ 9,741,000,000

21 The Limited, Inc. (NYSE / LTD)
The Limited Parkway   www.limited.com
Columbus, OH 43230
3-Year Sales History:
Fiscal	1995	$ 7,881,437,000
	1996	$ 8,644,791,000
	1997	$ 8,887,000,000

22 Circuit City Stores (NYSE / CC)
9950 Mayland Drive   http://circuitcity.pic.net
Richmond, VA 23233
3-Year Sales History:
Fiscal	1995	$ 7,029,123,000
	1996	$ 7,663,811,000
	1997	$ 8,439,000,000

23 Best Buy Company, Inc. (NYSE / BBY)
7075 Flying Cloud   www.bestbuy.com
Eden Prairie, MN 55344
3-Year Sales History:
Fiscal	1995	$ 7,217,448,000
	1996	$ 7,770,683,000
	1997	$ 7,854,000,000

24 Woolworth Corporation (NYSE / Z)
233 Broadway
New York, NY 10279
3-Year Sales History:
Fiscal	1995	$ 8,224,000,000
	1996	$ 8,092,000,000
	1997	$ 7,219,000,000

25 Dillard's Inc. (NYSE / DDS)
1600 Cantrell Road   www.azstarnet.com/dillards
Little Rock, AR 72201
3-Year Sales History:
Fiscal	1995	$ 5,918,038,000
	1996	$ 6,227,587,000
	1997	$ 6,498,000,000

RETAILING
THIRD EDITION

K. DUNNE
F. LUSCH

RETAILING

THIRD EDITION

PATRICK DUNNE
TEXAS TECH UNIVERSITY

ROBERT F. LUSCH
UNIVERSITY OF OKLAHOMA

THE DRYDEN PRESS

HARCOURT BRACE COLLEGE PUBLISHERS

FORT WORTH   PHILADELPHIA   SAN DIEGO

NEW YORK   ORLANDO   AUSTIN   SAN ANTONIO

TORONTO   MONTREAL   LONDON   SYDNEY   TOKYO

Publisher: GEORGE PROVOL

Acquisitions Editor: BILL SCHOOF

Product Manager: LISÉ JOHNSON

Developmental Editors: KAREN HILL, TRACY MORSE

Project Editor: JIM PATTERSON

Art Director: BURL DEAN SLOAN

Production Manager: LOIS WEST

Credits appear on page 605, which constitutes a continuation of the copyright page.
Cover illustration: Photoshop work by Glenn Caldwell.

ISBN: 0-03-024758-6
Library of Congress Catalog Card Number: 97-77645

Address for orders:
The Dryden Press
6277 Sea Harbor Drive
Orlando, FL 32887-6777
1-800-782-4479

Address for editorial correspondence:
The Dryden Press
301 Commerce Street, Suite 3700
Fort Worth, TX 76102

Web site address:
http://www.hbcollege.com

The Dryden Press, Dryden, and the Dryden Press logo are registered trademarks of Harcourt Brace & Company.

Printed in the United States of America

9 0 1 2 3 4 5 6 7   032   9 8 7 6 5 4 3 2

The Dryden Press
Harcourt Brace College Publishers

This book is dedicated to our fathers (Tom Dunne and Frank Lusch), who first gave us an appreciation and love for Retailing, and to Bob Kahn and Bill Davidson who have continued to provide us with their insightful analysis of the current state of Retailing.

THE DRYDEN PRESS SERIES IN MARKETING

Assael
Marketing

Avila, Williams, Ingram, and LaForge
The Professional Selling Skills Workbook

Bateson
Managing Services Marketing: Text and Readings
Third Edition

Blackwell, Blackwell, and Talarzyk
Contemporary Cases in Consumer Behavior
Fourth Edition

Boone and Kurtz
Contemporary Marketing WIRED
Ninth Edition

Boone and Kurtz
Contemporary Marketing 1999

Churchill
Basic Marketing Research
Third Edition

Churchill
Marketing Research: Methodological Foundations
Seventh Edition

Czinkota and Ronkainen
Global Marketing

Czinkota and Ronkainen
International Marketing
Fifth Edition

Czinkota and Ronkainen
International Marketing Strategy: Environmental Assessment and Entry Strategies

Dickson
Marketing Management
Second Edition

Dunne and Lusch
Retailing
Third Edition

Engel, Blackwell, and Miniard
Consumer Behavior
Eighth Edition

Ferrell, Hartline, Lucas, and Luck
Marketing Strategy

Futrell
Sales Management: Teamwork, Leadership, and Technology
Fifth Edition

Grover
Theory & Simulation of Market-Focused Management

Ghosh
Retail Management
Second Edition

Hoffman and Bateson
Essentials of Services Marketing

Hutt and Speh
Business Marketing Management: A Strategic View of Industrial and Organizational Markets
Sixth Edition

Ingram, LaForge, and Schwepker
Sales Management: Analysis and Decision Making
Third Edition

Lindgren and Shimp
Marketing: An Interactive Learning System

Krugman, Reid, Dunn, and Barban
Advertising: Its Role in Modern Marketing
Eighth Edition

Oberhaus, Ratliffe, and Stauble
Professional Selling: A Relationship Process
Second Edition

Parente, Vanden Bergh, Barban, and Marra
Advertising Campaign Strategy: A Guide to Marketing Communication Plans

Rosenbloom
Marketing Channels: A Management View
Sixth Edition

Sandburg
Discovering Your Marketing Career CD-ROM

Schaffer
Applying Marketing Principles Software

Schaffer
The Marketing Game

Schellinck and Maddox
Marketing Research: A Computer-Assisted Approach

Schnaars
MICROSIM

Schuster and Copeland
Global Business: Planning for Sales and Negotiations

Sheth, Mittal, and Newman
Customer Behavior: Consumer Behavior and Beyond

Shimp
Advertising, Promotion, and Supplemental Aspects of Integrated Marketing Communications
Fourth Edition

Talarzyk
Cases and Exercises in Marketing

Terpstra and Sarathy
International Marketing
Seventh Edition

Weitz and Wensley
Readings in Strategic Marketing Analysis, Planning, and Implementation

Zikmund
Exploring Marketing Research
Sixth Edition

Zikmund
Essentials of Marketing Research

Harcourt Brace College Outline Series

Peterson
Principles of Marketing

PREFACE

This Third Edition of *Retailing,* like much of retailing itself, has undergone significant changes from prior editions. Not only do we have a new publisher, but we have added many new and exciting features. Given the impact of the Internet and the many changes in the world's economic systems, there has never been a more exciting time to study retailing. Thus every chapter in this text discusses the impact of the Internet and Global Retailing on retailing concepts and practices. As a result, we believe that students and instructors will like this edition even more than they did the highly-successful first two editions.

The authors have a strong belief that retailing, with one out of every five jobs in today's economy, offers one of the best career opportunities for today's students. Thus, *Retailing* was written to convey that message, not by using boring descriptions of retailers and the various routine tasks they perform, but by making the subject matter come alive by focusing on the excitement that retailing offers its participants, in an easy-to-read conversational style filled with pictures and exhibits. This text demonstrates to the student that retailing as a career choice can be fun, exciting, and challenging. This excitement arises from selecting a merchandise assortment at market, determining how to present the merchandise in the store, developing a promotional program for the new assortment, or planning next season's sales in an ever-changing economic environment. While other texts may make retailing a series of independent processes, this edition, like the first two editions of *Retailing,* highlights the excitement, richness, and importance of retailing as a career choice. *Retailing* provides the student with an understanding of the inter-relationship of the various activities that retailers face daily. To do this we attempted to show how retailers must use both creativity and analytical skills in order to solve the problems of today's fast-paced environment.

In keeping with our goal of maintaining student interest, *Retailing* focuses on the material that someone entering the retailing field would need to know. We were more interested in telling the student what should happen, and what is happening, than in explaining the academic "whys" of these actions. Thus, when knowledge of a particular theory was needed, we generally ignored the reasoning behind the theory for a simple explanation and an example or two of the use of the theory. In presenting these examples we drew from a rich array of literature sources, as well as our combined 75 years of work in retailing.

Students and teachers have responded favorably to the "personality" of *Retailing* because the numerous current examples, both in the text itself and in the Winners & Losers, Global Retailing, and Behind the Scenes boxes, give realistic insights into retailing. One student wrote to say "thanks" for writing a book that was "so interesting and not too long." A faculty member noted she was "so pleased with the writing style because it was easier to understand, and the examples used were very appropriate and helped to present the material in a meaningful and easy-to-grasp manner for students. Still another liked *Retailing* because the writing style was "conversational, thus lending itself to very easy reading," so that she felt confident that her students would read the chapters. "The content coverage was excellent. Terms were explained in easy-to-understand language. And, although most of the topics of an advanced retailing text were presented, the extent and presentation of the material was very appropriate to an introductory course." Another reviewer for this third edition was especially pleased that we used two senior retailing executives (Robert Kahn, the editor of *Retailing Today* and an advisor to many of the nation's top retailers, and David Overton, Vice-President, Strategy and Business Development Home Services for Sears Roebuck & Company) as our first reviewers on each chapter. These reviews enabled us to incorporate so many new, more current examples, as well as the discussion of issues that are only now being discussed in board rooms. Another reviewer asked that we "please keep a few of the examples, especially our boxes, from the earlier editions" because he considered these examples "classics." Well the customer is always right, so we retained a few of these classics, but most examples are new to this edition.

TEXT ORGANIZATION

Retailing, which features an attractive, full-color format throughout the entire text, is divided into five parts, which are in turn divided into 16 chapters, that can easily be covered over the course of the term. Part 1 serves as an introduction to the study of retailing and provides an overview into what is involved in retail planning. Part 2, examines the environmental factors; customers, competitors, channels, and legal system, that impact retailing today. Part 3 examines the role location plays in a retailer's success.

Part 4 deals with the operations of a retail store. This section begins with a chapter on managing the retailer's finances. Special attention in this section is given to merchandise buying and handling, pricing, promotion and advertising, personal selling, and store layout and design. At the end of this section is a chapter on the retailing of services. In Part 5 we discuss retail administration in detail with chapters on managing human resources and retail information systems.

In addition, there is an appendix that includes answers to sample test questions. Also, there are three separate indexes grouped by company, name, and subject. Finally, a brief profile of the nation's largest retailers, along with their last three year's sales, stock exchange symbol, and web site address is on the inside of the front and back covers.

CHAPTER ORGANIZATION

Each chapter begins with an Overview which highlights the key topic areas to be discussed. In addition, a set of Learning Objectives provides a description of what the student should learn after reading the chapter. To further aid student learning, the text material is integrated with the objectives listed at the beginning of the chapters and in the summaries at the end. Numbered Learning Objectives appear in the margins and summaries of the text to mark where each objective was fulfilled. Also, a Top 25 Retailer icon has been placed in the margins so students can quickly find top retailer examples. In addition the text features a prominent placement of key term definitions in the margin to make it easier for students to check their understanding of these key terms. If they need a fuller explanation of any term, the discussion is right there—next to the definition.

The body of text will have photos, exhibits, tables, and graphs presenting the information and relationships in a visually appealing manner. The chapters will have three retailing boxed features covering either the brilliant decisions made by retailers or their mistakes (Winners & Losers), the inside story on a particular retailing event or decision (Behind the Scenes), and what is happening in the international retail market (Global Retailing). These are typically lengthier real-world examples than can be incorporated in the regular flow of text material. Some of these boxed features are humorous, while others present a unique way to solve problems retailers faced in their everyday operations.

At the conclusion of each chapter is a Student Study Guide. The first feature of this new addition to the text is a Chapter Summary by Learning Objective followed by a list of Terms to Remember. These are followed by the traditional Review and Discussion Questions, which are also tied into the learning objectives for the chapter. They are meant to test recall and understanding of the chapter material, as well as provide students with an opportunity to integrate and apply the text material. Another new feature is Sample Test Questions, a set of multiple-choice questions covering each of the chapter's learning objectives. The answers to these questions are at the end of the book.

The second half of the study guide is the Applications section. This section opens with a Writing and Speaking Exercise that is an attempt to aid the instructor in improving the students' oral/written communication skills, as well as their teamwork skills. Here the student, or group of students, is asked to make a one page written report and/or oral presentation to the class incorporating the knowledge gained by reading the chapters. Some instructors may prefer to view these as "mini-cases." A Retail Project is then included that has the student either visiting a library or a web site and finding an answer to a current retail question.

The next feature of each chapter's Application's section is a Case, most of which are drawn from actual retail situations. The authors believe that the ability to understand the need for better management in retailing requires an explanation of retailing through the use of case studies. These cases will cover the entire spectrum of retail operations with cases involving department stores, specialty shops, direct retailing, hardware stores, grocery stores, apparel shops, discount stores, and convenience stores. There is also a casebook available, that features longer and more advanced cases that can be used to accompany this text.

Since many of the students taking this class will one day open their own retail business, the next section is for them. Planning Your Own Retail Business presents a very specific problem based on the chapter's material that a small business manager/owner will face in his or her day to day operations.

SUPPLEMENTARY MATERIALS

Instructor's Resource Manual   This supplement includes an overview of the chapter, several detailed teaching tips for presenting the material, a detailed outline, the answers to questions for review and discussion, suggestions for handling the writing and speaking exercises, retail projects, cases, and planning your own business.

Test Bank   This printed ancillary contains over 2,000 questions for professors to choose from. Varied levels of true-false and multiple-choice questions are organized by chapter and learning objectives. The test bank is available in both printed and microcomputer versions.

Computerized Test Bank   Available in PC-, Windows-, and Macintosh-compatible formats, the computerized version of the printed test bank enables instructors to preview and edit test questions, as well as add their own. The test and answer keys can also be printed in "scrambled" formats.

RequesTest and Online Testing Service   The Dryden Press makes test planning quicker and easier than ever with this program. Instructors can order test masters by question number and criteria over a toll-free telephone number. Test masters will be mailed or faxed with 48 hours. Dryden can provide instructors with software to install their own online testing program, allowing a test to be administered over network or individual terminals. This program offers instructors greater flexibility and convenience in grading and storing test results.

PowerPoint Presentation Software   An innovative, easy-to-use presentation tool that will enable professors to custom design their own multimedia classroom presentations. Organized by chapter, this software will allow professors to use full-color slides of the figures, tables, and graphs from the text, as well as completely new material from outside sources in their classroom presentations.

Casebook   Optional for packaging with the textbook, these cases feature longer and more advanced cases than those found in the textbook. Ask your local Dryden sales representative for packaging options.

Retail Spreadsheet Project   A computer spreadsheet book called "The House" replaces the study guide for this edition. The project is set up for use with a computer, but it is possible to do all the required computations with a calculator or by hand. "The House" is about a small retail apparel shop and has two exercises for each chapter in the third edition of *Retailing*.

Videos   The video package features companies such as Kmart, JCPenney, Pier 1 Imports and Fossil Watches. Each video segment supplements the ideas and concepts illustrated in the textbook.

Web Site   At http://www.hbcollege.com/ go to Dryden Press Marketing to find the Retailing web site that the authors have put together for the students using this text. Included in the web site will be a section on choosing retailing as a career, an advanced case for each of the five parts of the text, a detailed outline of the chapters, and 20 sample questions (10 true-false and 10 multiple-choice) for each chapter. Also, links to other important retail sites on the Web are provided. The authors will update this site regularly with current examples of the various retailing concepts and practices discussed in the text.

ACKNOWLEDGMENTS

Many people contributed to the development of this text. For their helpful suggestions as reviewers of the various editions of this text, we are especially grateful to the following:

Phyllis Ashinger, Wayne State University
Steve Barnett, Stetson University
Barbara Bart, Savannah State College
Holly E. Bastow-Stoop, North Dakota State University
Jerry E. Boles, Western Kentucky University
Mike Bowlin, University of Oklahoma
Louis D. Canale, Genesee Community College
John Clark, California State University—Sacramento
Roger Dickinson, University of Texas at Arlington
Janice Driggers, Orlando College
Joanne Eckstein, Macomb Community College
Sevo Eroglu, Georgia State University
Mort Ettinger, Salem State College
Kenneth R. Evans, University of Missouri
Richard Feinberg, Purdue University
Robert C. Ferrentino, Lansing Community College
Susan Fiorito, Florida State University
Sally L. Fortenbery, Texas Christian University
Jack Gifford, Miami University
D. Elizabeth Goins, University of Illinois at Springfield
Blaine S. Greenfield, Bucks County Community College
Norman E. Hansen, Northeastern University
Shelley S. Harp, Texas Tech University
Joseph C. Hecht, Montclair State University
Stanley Hollander, Michigan State University
Charles A. Ingene, University of Washington
Marian H. Jernigan, Texas Woman's University
Julie Johnson-Hillery, Northern Illinois University
Laura Jolly, University of Kentucky
Mary Joyce, Bryant College
Jikyeong Kang, University of Wisconsin
William Keep, University of Kentucky
Karen W. Ketch, University of Kentucky
Tammy Lamb Kinley, Western Illinois University
Marilyn Lavin, University of Wisconsin—Whitewater
Marilyn Lebahn, Northwest Technical College
Dong Lee, Fairmont State College
Melody L. Lehew, Kansas State University

Deborah Hawkins Lester, Kennesaw State University
Michael W. Little, Virginia Commonwealth University
John W. Lloyd, Monroe Community College
Dolly D. Loyd, University of Southern Mississippi
Paul MacKay, East Central College
Shawna L. Mahaffey, Delta College
Louise Majorey, Cazenovia College
Raymond Marquardt, University of Nebraska—Lincoln
Nancy McClure, Eastern New Mexico University
Nancy J. Miller, Iowa State University
Diane Minger, Cedar Valley College
Michelle A. Morganosky, University of Illinois—Urbana
Mark Mulder, Grand Rapids Junior College
David W. Murphy, Madisonville Community College
Lewis J. Neisner, University of Baltimore
Elaine M. Notarantonio, Bryant College
Katherine A. Olson, Northern Virginia Community College
Jan P. Owens, University of Wisconsin
Charles R. Patton, University of Texas at Brownsville
V. Ann Paulins, Ohio University
Kathryn Payne, Texas Tech University
John Porter, West Virginia University
Dawn Pysarchik, Michigan State University
Jacquelene Robeck, University of Wisconsin—Stout
Marvin J. Rothenberg, Rutgers University
Rod Runyan, University of Wisconsin—Stevens Point
Ben Sackmary, State University College at Buffalo
Duane Schecter, Muskegon Community College
Jean Shaneyfelt, Edison Community College
Shirley Stretch, California State University—Los Angeles
Harriet P. Swedlund, South Dakota State University
William R. Swinyard, Brigham Young University
Jane Boyd Thomas, Winthrop University
James A. Veregge, Cerritos Community College
Irena Vida, University of Tennessee
Mary Walker, Xavier University
Jim Walton, Augusta State University
Mary Margaret Weber, Emporia State University
Scarlett C. Wesley, University of Tennessee—Knoxville
Sarah B. Wise, University of South Carolina
Cengiz Yilmaz, Texas Tech University
Deborah D. Young, Texas Woman's University

A special thanks must go to William R. Davidson, Management Horizons, not only for being a mentor to the authors, but also for providing us with many of the photos for the book.

We also want to thank all those in the retailing industry for their input with the text. We particularly want to thank Paul Adams, Fleming Companies; Steve Wilkinson, Kmart; Suzanne Allford, HEB Grocery Company; W. R. Howell, JCPenney; Doral Chenoweth, USA Dining Network; Marvin Lurie, North American Retail Dealer's Association; John Mount, Mount Marketing Services International; Marvin J. Rothenberg, Marvin J. Rothenberg Retail Marketing Consultants, Inc.; Molly Powers, Nielsen Marketing Research; and Carol J. Greenhut, Schonfeld & Associates, Inc.

To the team at Dryden, we can only say we're glad you let us be a part of the team. These individuals include: Bill Schoof, Acquisitions Editor; Karen Hill and Tracy Morse, Developmental Editors; Bobbie Bochenko, Editorial Assistant; Adele Krause, Art and Literary Rights Editor; Jim Patterson, Senior Project Editor; Lois West, Production Manager; Burl Sloan, Senior Art Director; Lisé Johnson, Executive Product Manager; and Kendall Ray, Marketing Coordinator.

We would be remiss if we didn't acknowledge the many contributions of Randall Gebhardt, our co-author on *Retail Marketing* and Myron (Mike) Gable, our co-author on the earlier two editions of *Retailing*. Many of the ideas in the text are Randy's and Mike's. GOOD LUCK IN RETIREMENT, MIKE.

Finally, we want to take this opportunity to thank our wives for their love and understanding, especially as seemingly endless deadlines approached. Thanks Judy and Virginia.

Patrick Dunne　　Lubbock, TX
Robert Lusch　　Norman, OK

ABOUT THE AUTHORS

PATRICK DUNNE

Patrick Dunne, an Associate Professor at Texas Tech University, received his Ph.D. in Marketing from Michigan State University and his B.S. from Xavier University.

In his 30 years of university teaching, Dr. Dunne has taught a wide variety of marketing and distribution courses at both the undergraduate and graduate levels. His research has been published in many of the leading Marketing and Retailing journals. In addition, he has authored five books. Dr. Dunne was the first academic to receive the Wayne A. Lemburg Award for "conspicuous individual accomplishments" from the American Marketing Association.

Previously Dr. Dunne served as Vice President of both the Publications and Association Developmental Divisions of the American Marketing Association. Professor Dunne is an active consultant to a variety of retailers, ranging from supermarkets to shopping malls.

ROBERT F. LUSCH

Robert F. Lusch holds the Helen Robson Walton Chair in Marketing and is the George Lynn Cross Research Professor at the University of Oklahoma. He received his Ph.D. from the University of Wisconsin and his M.B.A. and B.S. from the University of Arizona.

His expertise is in the area of marketing strategy and distribution systems. Professor Lusch currently serves as the Editor of the *Journal of Marketing*. He is the author of over 150 academic and professional publications including 15 books. In 1997, The Academy of Marketing Science awarded him its Distinguished Marketing Educator Award and the American Marketing Association presented him the Harold Maynard Award.

Professor Lusch has served as President of the Southwestern Marketing Association, Vice President of Education and Vice President Finance of the American Marketing Association, and trustee of the American Marketing Association Foundation.

CONTENTS IN BRIEF

CONTENTS

INTRODUCTION TO RETAILING

PERSPECTIVES ON RETAILING

One of the oldest and most successful retailers in the United States is the JCPenney Company which has regularly updated its stores and merchandising strategies to stay focused on the changing U.S. household.

OVERVIEW

In this chapter, we acquaint you with the nature and scope of retailing. We view retailing as a major economic force in this country and as a significant area for career opportunities. Finally, we introduce the approach to be used throughout this text as you study and learn about the operation of retail firms.

After reading this chapter, you should be able to

LEARNING OBJECTIVES

1. define retailing
2. explain why retailing is undergoing so much change today
3. describe the five methods used to categorize retailers
4. list the major aspects of a retail career, as well as the prerequisites necessary for success in retailing
5. explain the different methods for the study and practice of retailing

LO • I
Define retailing

WHAT IS RETAILING?

It is easy to take for granted the impact retailing has on a nation's economic growth. On your way home from class today, look around you. It is likely that you will see many fast-food restaurants (e.g., Taco Bell, Wendy's, and Dominos Pizza), convenience stores (e.g., 7-Eleven, Circle K, Texaco Star Mart), several car dealerships, or a neighborhood shopping center with a supermarket (e.g., A&P, Kroger, IGA, Albertsons, and Safeway). You also might see a regional shopping mall with several large department stores (e.g., Sears, JCPenney, and Bloomingdale's) and hundreds of specialty stores (e.g., Lens Crafters, Radio Shack, The Limited, The Gap, Foot Locker, and Eddie Bauer). It is even possible that you might pass some retailers that don't sell physical products but instead provide services (e.g., movie rentals from Blockbuster Video or help with your taxes from H&R Block). A variety of locally based retailers may also be observed.

In fact, retailing has made a significant contribution to the economic prosperity that we enjoy so much. The nations that have enjoyed the greatest economic and social progress have been those with a strong retail sector. Retailers have become valued and necessary members of society. Although some may argue that we have too many retailers with too many stores operating today, we must not forget the social benefits that "overstoring" provides an economy. Some of the benefits that a vibrant retailing sector provides are easier access to products, having to settle to a second or third choice less often when shopping for a particular product, greater customer satisfaction, and higher levels of customer service.[1]

However, perhaps the critical role of retailing in a society can best be illustrated when retailing doesn't perform as it should. Our Global Retailing box illustrates one of the reasons that the Eastern European countries experienced a low rate of economic growth when they were under Communist control. Interestingly, when Toys "Я" Us, Wal-Mart, Pizza Hut, and McDonald's opened for business in these countries, they became instant successes. The joy and excitement that these new forms of retailing provided the citizens was amazing, which illustrates very well the value people of all cultures place on retailing that is responsive to their needs and wants.

DOLLAR $ & CENTS

Retailers that enter foreign markets and understand the local cultures and customs will be higher performers than those who don't understand the local cultures and customs.

NOT EVERYBODY OPERATES THE SAME WAY

Although American retailers have made a significant contribution to this country's economic growth, the same can't be said for retailers in other parts of the world. For example, Kmart found a totally different retailing philosophy when it expanded into Eastern Europe during 1992 after the fall of Communism.

Kmart's strategy for entering this market involved the purchase of a 13-store department store chain in the former Czechoslovakia. What they found was a retailing system totally different from the one in the United States. Like other retailers under the Communist system, the newly purchased chain failed to take markdowns or reductions to move older merchandise and use whatever money they got from the sale of this older merchandise to purchase newer and more "exciting" merchandise. Kmart also found that the chain's warehouses were full of decade-old state-manufactured sweaters, dresses, and underwear that offered very limited variations in assortment and price. Kmart was surprised to learn that under the Communist system, when an item didn't sell it was simply sent back to the warehouse and then returned to the shelves a few years later at its original full retail price for another try. This failure to take markdowns was terrifying to the retailer that was famous for unloading slow-moving items at giveaway prices by announcing a "blue-light" special.

If this wasn't enough to make shopping a "boring" event for the Eastern European consumer, Kmart also found another custom in Czechoslovakia that made shopping difficult. Czech customers, if they were unhappy with a product, could bring it back to the store just like Americans. However, whereas Americans are generally given either replacement merchandise, credit toward another purchase, or their money back, Czech customers were only given receipts and told to check back next month. Under the former Communist system, a refund committee, made up of store employees, would meet each month and decide on a case-by-case basis what to do with each returned item. Refund applicants could be denied or given refunds ranging from 10 to 100 percent of the purchase price. Any money left over would be split among the employees on the committee and the store. As a result, Kmart had to educate both the customers and their "new" employees as to what a "full-refund policy" was all about. No wonder retailing didn't contribute to the economic growth of Eastern European countries as it did in the Western world.

SOURCE: Based on a presentation by several top Kmart executives to the American Collegiate Retailing Association, Troy, Michigan, April 23, 1993. As a follow-up, in the spring of 1996 Kmart sold these 13 stores (6 in the Czech Republic and 7 in the Slovak Republic) to Tesco, one of the United Kingdom's largest retailers. The influx of capital from this sale enabled Kmart to focus on its troubled North American operations.

Retailing, as we use the term in this text, consists of the final activity and steps needed to place merchandise made elsewhere in the hands of the consumer or to provide services to the consumer. Quite simply, any firm that sells merchandise or provides services to the final consumer is performing the retailing function. Regardless of whether the firm sells to the consumer in a store, through the mail, over the telephone, through a television infomercial, over the Internet, door to door, or through a vending machine, it is involved in retailing.

Retailing
Consists of the final activity and steps needed to place merchandise made elsewhere in the hands of the consumer or to provide services to the consumer.

LO • 2
Explain why retailing is
undergoing so much
change today

THE NATURE OF CHANGE IN RETAILING

Many observers of the American business scene believe that retailing is the most "staid and stable" sector of business. Although this observation may have been true in the past, quite the contrary is occurring today. Retailing, which accounts for just less than 10 percent of the worldwide labor force and includes every living individual as a customer, is the largest single industry in most nations and is currently undergoing changes in many exciting ways.

Currently, there are 1.9 million retail establishments in the United States with total sales of nearly $2 trillion. Based on U.S. Bureau of Census data, there are 23 retail establishments for every thousand households, with average annual sales of more than $750,000. However, most retailers are smaller than the average. Today, more than 50 percent of retail establishments are small operations with annual sales less than $400,000.

These figures also don't reflect the changes that have occurred behind these dollar amounts. The number of new retail enterprises that have been developed in the past two decades is truly amazing. Most of these new businesses have actually been new institutional forms such as electronic retailing, warehouse retailing, supercenters (which are combination of discount department store and supermarket), and home delivery fast-food businesses. Change is truly the driving force behind retailing today. We now explore some of the trends that are affecting retailing.

DOLLAR $ & CENTS

Retailers that control, better than their competition, the costs incurred after merchandise is acquired will be higher performers.

PRICE COMPETITION

America's current retailing revolution began with the birth of Wal-Mart in Rogers, Arkansas, in 1962. Contrary to popular belief, Wal-Mart was not the nation's first discount department store; there were actually 41 publicly held discount stores already operating at the time.[2]

However, what Sam Walton did, which forever changed the face of retailing, was to realize before everybody else that most of any product's cost gets added after the item is produced and moves from the factory to retailer's shelf and finally to the consumer. Therefore, Walton began enlisting suppliers to help him reduce these costs and increase the efficiency of the product's movement. Also, Walton, who

By using satellite information technology, Wal-Mart is able to keep in constant communication with its suppliers and retail stores, and thus achieve very low distribution costs.

never operated a computer in his life, made a major commitment in the 1980s to computerizing Wal-Mart as a means to reduce these expenses. As pointed out in our Winners & Losers box, this commitment may have been born of necessity, not out of insight. Nevertheless, as a result of the introduction of the computer to retail management, Wal-Mart's selling, general, and administrative costs as a percentage of sales are currently less than 16 percent, while all its competitors' operating expenses are more than 20 percent and sometimes more than 30 percent. For instance, Kmart, operating essentially the same type of stores as Wal-Mart, had operating expenses in the low-to-mid 20 percent range. Simply put, Wal-Mart became the nation's largest retailer by relentlessly cutting unnecessary costs and demanding that their suppliers do the same.

DEMOGRAPHIC SHIFTS

Other significant changes in retailing over the past decade have resulted from changing demographic factors such as the fluctuating birth rate, the aging of baby boomers, the redistribution of income levels, and the increasing number of women in the work force. Many people simply failed to realize how these factors, which had profound effects on our society, could also affect retailing. The high-performance retailers of the 1990s, however, noticed that as a result of these demographic shifts, the customers of the mid-1980s who "shopped 'til they dropped" and made shopping a recreational sport had less time, less money, less energy, and less patience for shopping in the mid-1990s. Successful retailers, in an effort to reduce the pain of shopping, have now become more service-oriented, offering better "value" in price and quality and more promotion.

WAL-MART'S EARLY USE OF COMPUTERS

Although Wal-Mart's success can be attributed to more than just being the first discounter to make a major commitment to service, there is no doubt that its integrated use of the computer changed the way retailers now do business. But was it insight, luck, or a necessity that made Sam Walton make his initial investment of $800 million and 1,000 "associates" into a computer division, when competitors thought that this was too expensive?

Folks who knew Sam Walton claim that his greatest asset was his ability to learn from others, so as not to duplicate their mistakes and to gain from their successes. Others were already using computers in their business. Electronic point-of-sale (EPOS) computer systems had already been used in retailing for close to 10 years by supermarkets but only to check prices. Computers weren't used to gather sales and inventory data as they do today. Walton saw these new uses and installed his first system out of necessity to help manage the distribution centers that he had been forced by the vendors to set up a decade earlier.

In 1970, the year its stock first traded publicly, Wal-Mart established its distribution system. At the time, it had fewer than four dozen stores, and many of the big vendors (Procter & Gamble [P&G], General Foods, Lever Brothers, etc.) didn't always call on that small a retailer in the northwestern corner of Arkansas. And when they did call on Wal-Mart, the vendors would dictate the purchase terms. Walton's distribution system enabled him to buy in volume and equalize the negotiation terms.

A decade later, Wal-Mart's advanced computers enabled it to not only scan sales but also to make certain that in-bound shipments coming in one side of a distribution center were transferred to the correct dock on the other side of the center for shipment to the more than 1,000 stores. The computers not only managed product movement within the distribution centers but connected the stores, distribution centers, and the vendors via Wal-Mart's headquarters in Arkansas via satellite using electronic data interchange (EDI). This made it possible for Wal-Mart to be the first U.S. retailer to benefit from having a just-in-time (JIT) inventory system, as well as knowing what products were moving in which store, which significantly lowered operating costs.

Several years later, Walton proposed to Procter & Gamble the idea of setting up a "partnership" that involved not only sharing sales information through the EDI system but having a real partnership between the companies, whereby P&G would tailor its production and shipments to Wal-Mart's sales. Today, P&G is Wal-Mart's largest supplier, and Wal-Mart is now P&G's largest customer, accounting for more sales than the entire country of Japan. Because of the success of this program, nearly 50 other vendors have not only a partnership relationship with Wal-Mart but with their other major retailing customers.

SOURCE: Based on information supplied by Robert Kahn, editor of *Retailing Today* and a long-time friend of Sam Walton.

Same Store Sales
Compares an individual store's sales to its sales for the same month in the previous year.

Market Share
Is the retailer's sales as a percentage of total market sales for the product line or service category under consideration.

Also, with population growth slowing, retailers are no longer able to sustain their long-term growth projections by just adding new stores as they did in the 1980s and early 1990s. Growth must come by increasing same store sales at the expense of the competition's market share. (*Same store sales* is a retailing term that compares an individual store's sales to its sales for the same month in the previous year.) Market share refers to a retailer's sales as a percentage of total market sales for the product line or service category under consideration. Today, there is a new breed of retailer who uses its efficiencies in the marketplace to drive out the slow, inefficient, and resistant-to-change retailer. As a result, many retailers, selling all lines of

Best Buy, a category killer, is able to obtain a significant market share by concentrating its inventory in the computer and electronic merchandise category.

products and types of services, who haven't adapted to the changing environment are struggling to survive. All that these more efficient retailers have to do is divert a few of the customers that the existing firms need to operate profitably. For example, recently we have witnessed the rapid growth of "category killers," which now account for a third of U.S. retail sales.[3] Essentially, the ultimate in specialty stores, the category killer, got its name from its marketing strategy: carry such a large amount of merchandise in a single category at such good prices that it makes it impossible for the customer to walk out without purchasing what they needed, thus "killing" the competition.

Toys "Я" Us, which began operations in the 1950s, has the distinction of being the first category killer. Today, Toys "Я" Us operates more than 600 toy stores in the United States and more than 300 toy stores in more than 20 countries around the globe. The company also operates more than 200 Kids "Я" Us children's clothing stores in the United States. Beginning in the 1980s, the category killer retail format began to grow explosively. Some well-known category killers include Best Buy, Home Depot, Blockbuster Video, Circuit City, Office Depot, CompUSA, PetsMart, Bed Bath & Beyond, AutoZone, Barnes & Noble Book Superstores, and Sports Authority. Today's modern supermarkets offering banking, fast food, floral arrangements, and pharmaceuticals are also a breed of category killers. These retailers have begun to make their presence felt as they divert business away from the more traditional outlets such as general merchandise and the old-fashioned grocery stores; more than 40,000 such stores have closed since the mid-1980s.[4] Many category killers are also diverting business away from traditional wholesale supply houses. For example, Home Depot appeals to the professional contractor and Office Depot to the business owner who traditionally purchased supplies from hardware wholesalers and office supply and equipment wholesalers.[5]

Category Killer

Is a retailer that carries such a large amount of merchandise in a single category at such good prices that it makes it impossible for the customer to walk out without purchasing what they need, thus killing the competition.

DOLLAR $ & CENTS

Retailers who can spot upcoming demographic changes and adapt and not merely react after the changes occur will have higher performance.

Today, as we enter a new millennium, retail firms are run by seasoned professionals who can look at the changing environment and see opportunities, exert enormous buying power over manufacturers, and anticipate future changes before they affect the market. This is in contrast to the typical retailer in the 1980s who just reacted to these changes after they occurred. However, today not even the experts always agree about what the future will bring.

NEW TECHNOLOGY AND THE INTERNET

Internet

Is a network of computer systems that allows computer users to exchange information electronically with other users; also referred to as the information super highway.

The great unknown for today's retail managers is the often-heralded, not-yet-arrived era of on-line computer shopping. Bill Gates, the legendary founder of Microsoft, believes that with the Internet a person's computer will soon become as indispensable to everyday life as our telephone.[6] The Internet (also referred to as the information superhighway) is a network of computer systems that allows computer users to exchange information electronically with other users and businesses. This consists of e-mail, infomercials, bulletin boards, and discussion groups.[7] Despite a slow start, some retailers are preparing for the soon-to-come day when, as people find the computer more user-friendly, the information superhighway will see sales increase from $518 million in 1997 to $6.9 billion in the year 2000.[8] A possible reason for the Internet's slow start as a retailing venue, however, is that it will take merchants several years to learn not only how to sell effectively on-line but also to find and maintain repeat customers.[9] Others have disregarded these growth claims entirely and point out that the same claims have been made about electronic shopping over the past three decades.[10]

Although the future cannot be predicted with certainty, we attempt to provide you with the tools to meet these upcoming challenges and be a success in retailing. Still, the answer of what the future will bring lies in the disquieting fact that retailers do not operate in a closed environment; they operate in a continuously changing environment. These changes are discussed in greater detail in Chapters 3 through 6. For now, we will concentrate on the following environmental elements: the behavior of consumers, the behavior of competition, the behavior of channel members (the manufacturers and wholesalers that the retailer buys from), the legal and ethical system, the state of technology, and the socioeconomic nature of society. Exhibit 1.1 depicts these elements.

STORE SIZE

Further insight about the changes occurring in retailing today can be obtained by looking at the average store size for various retail categories. The largest increase in store size in recent years has been in drugstores, a reflection of the rapid growth of

EXHIBIT 1.1	EXTERNAL ENVIRONMENTAL FORCES CONFRONTING RETAIL FIRMS

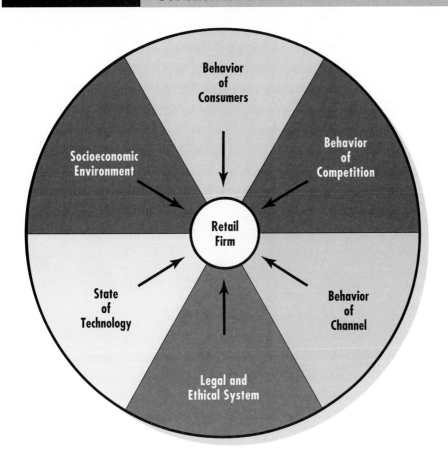

super-discount drugstores (e.g., Drug Emporium and Osco). In addition to drugs, these stores handle many other items such as auto parts, motor oil, food products, office supplies, greeting cards, and even clothing. Handling many different unrelated items by a retailer is called scrambled merchandising. There has also been an increase in the average store size for supermarkets, which in many cases are combining with general merchandise stores to form supercenters. Even these operators are taking lessons from the market leaders by building larger stores and adding more merchandise categories. By contrast, department stores have been shrinking in both size and the range of merchandise carried, reflecting the increased competition from specialty stores. In addition, they have had to make better use of space because rents are rapidly increasing (i.e., many are or already have dropped carrying furniture and other slow-moving, bulky items). Furthermore, the average department store is now smaller because many retailers are closing their downtown stores, which often were their largest stores, because the downtown areas of many cities have become "ghost towns." Thus, retailers in the 21st century are seeing a trend emerge: Retail stores are now either larger or smaller than their counterparts from the past.

Scrambled Merchandising
Exists when a retailer handles many different and unrelated items.

Discount retailers such as Wal-Mart have found scrambled merchandising to be an effective merchandising strategy.

Thus, success in retailing is dependent on retail managers' ability to properly interpret what changes are occurring and what these changes mean to their customers, and to build a strategy to respond to these changes. Therein lies the excitement and challenge of retailing as a career. After all, 30 years ago, the Wal-Mart strategy of building a major retail enterprise in small-town America and offering "everyday low prices" was probably considered foolhardy. This was a time when retailers thought growth could only be achieved by competing in the big cities where large population bases were located. And yet, someone who purchased 100 shares of Wal-Mart when it went public on October 1, 1970, for $16.50 a share would in 1997 be holding more than 104,000 shares worth $3,800,000.[11] A final comment about the changing face of retailing: Remember, business entrepreneurs, not obliged to conform to old legal and social standards, are free to forge new retail approaches that capitalize on emerging market opportunities. In retailing, this is all the more evident when we consider fashion trends that in the past would have lasted for years, now may last only a few months.

LO • 3
Describe the five methods used to categorize retailers

CATEGORIZING RETAILERS

Categorizing retailers can help the reader understand competition and the changes that occur in retailing. However, there is no single acceptable method of classifying retail competitors, although many classification schemes have been proposed. The five most popular schemes are described in Exhibit 1.2

EXHIBIT 1.2	CATEGORIZING RETAILERS			
CENSUS BUREAU	NUMBER OF OUTLETS	MARGIN/ TURNOVER	LOCATION	SIZE
2-digit SIC code	Single unit	Low margin/ low turns	Traditional	By sales volume
3-digit SIC code	2–10 units	Low margin/ high turns	Central shopping districts	
4-digit SIC code	11+ units	High margin/ low turns	Shopping centers	By number of employees
		High margin/ high turns	Free-standing Nontraditional	

CENSUS BUREAU

The U.S. Bureau of the Census, for purposes of conducting the Census of Retail Trade, classifies all retailers using two-digit standard industrial classification (SIC) codes. These SIC codes include

1. building materials, hardware, garden supply, and mobile home dealers (SIC 52)—there are approximately 107,000 of these retailers
2. general merchandise stores (SIC 53)—there are approximately 57,000 of these retailers
3. food stores (SIC 54)—these stores number almost 300,000
4. automotive dealers and gasoline service stations (SIC 55)—there are more than 330,000 of these retailers
5. apparel and accessory stores (SIC 56)—there are nearly 197,000 of these retailers
6. home furniture, home furnishings, and equipment stores (SIC 57)—there are roughly 180,000 of these retailers
7. eating and drinking places (SIC 58)—there are nearly 500,000 of these
8. miscellaneous retail stores (SIC 59)—this is the largest category, with more than 770,000 establishments

Generally, these two-digit SIC codes are too broad to be of much use to the retail analyst. The three-digit SIC codes provide much more information on the structure of retail competition and are easier to work with.

However, SIC 596 is nonstore retailing. There are approximately 66,000 nonstore retailers operating today in the United States. Within this number are 31,000 catalog and mail-order houses (e.g., Spiegel, Lands' End, and L.L. Bean), 24,000 merchandising machine operators that sell everything from snack food to toiletries, and 11,000 direct-selling establishments (e.g., Avon, Amway, Mary Kay Cosmetics, and Encyclopedia Britannica).

In almost all instances, the SIC code reflects the type of merchandise that the retailer sells. The major portion of a retailer's competition comes from other retailers in its SIC category. General merchandise stores (SIC 53) are the exception to this rule, especially department stores (SIC 531), which are listed under three different types (conventional: May Company, Macy's; national: Sears, JCPenney, and Wards; and discount:

Wal-Mart, Target and Kmart). General merchandise stores, due to the variety of merchandise carried, compete with retailers in most other SIC categories. For example, general merchandise stores such as department stores compete with specialty apparel stores such as The Gap and The Limited, mail-order retailers such as Lands' End and L.L. Bean, or off-priced stores such as T.J. Maxx or Ross Dress-for-Less, when someone is interested in buying clothing. In fact, most retailers must compete to a considerable extent with general merchandise stores, because these larger stores probably handle many of the same types of merchandise that smaller, more limited retailers sell. In a very broad sense, all retailers compete with each other because they are all vying for the same limited consumer dollars.

A shortcoming of using SIC codes is that they don't reflect all retailing activity. The Census Bureau definition equates retailing only with the sale of "tangible" goods or merchandise. However, by our definition, selling services to the final consumer is also retailing. And this suggests that retailing can also be applied to businesses such as barber/beauty shops, health clubs, dry cleaners, banks, insurance agencies, funeral homes, movie theaters, amusement parks, maid services, medical and dental clinics, one-hour photo labs, and so on. Remember, anytime the consumer spends money—either on tangibles (merchandise) or on intangibles (services)—retailing has occurred.

NUMBER OF OUTLETS

Another method of classifying retailers is by the number of outlets each firm operates. Generally, retailers with several units are a stronger competitive threat because they can spread many fixed costs such as advertising and top management salaries over a larger number of stores and can achieve economies in purchasing. However, single-unit retailers such as your neighborhood IGA grocery store do have several advantages. They are generally owner- and family-operated and tend to have harder-working, more motivated employees. Also, they can focus all their efforts on one trade area and tailor their merchandise to that area. In the past, such stores were usually able to spot emerging customer desires sooner and respond to them faster than the larger multiunit operations. However, as we point out later in the Behind the Scenes box, this is no longer just an advantage for the small local retailer.

Any retail organization that operates more than one unit is technically a chain, but this is really not a very practical definition. The Census Bureau classifies chain stores into two size categories: 2 to 10 stores and 11 or more. We use the 11 or more units when we discuss *chain stores*.

Chain Stores
Normally refer to operations having 11 or more units.

Exhibit 1.3 shows sales by chain stores, those retail operations having 11 or more units, as a percentage of total U.S. sales for 10 different merchandise lines. The statistics in Exhibit 1.3 reveal that chain stores account for nearly 40 percent of all retail sales (including 96 percent of all department store sales and 63 percent of all grocery store sales). Although large chain operations account for more than 57 percent of nondurable goods sales, they only account for just more than 16 percent of durable goods sales such as autos and furniture.

Not all chain operations enjoy the same advantages. Small chains are local in nature and may enjoy some economies in buying and in having the merchandise tailored to their market needs. Large chains are generally regional or national and can take full advantage of the "economies of scale" that centralized buying, account-

EXHIBIT 1.3	IMPORTANCE OF LARGE CHAIN OPERATIONS

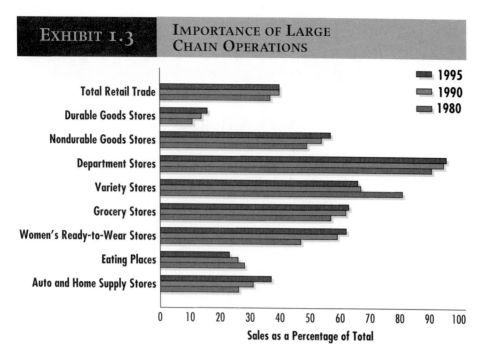

U.S. Bureau of the Census, Statistical Abstract of the United States: 1996 (116th edition), Washington, D.C., 1996. Table No. 1259. Retail Trade Sales of Multiunit Organizations, By Kind of Business: 1980–1995, p. 766.

ing, training, and information systems and a standard stock list can achieve. A standard stock list requires that all stores in a retail chain stock the same merchandise. Other large chains such as JCPenney and May Department Stores, recognizing the variations of regional tastes, use the optional stock list approach, which gives each store the flexibility to adjust its merchandise mix to local tastes and demands. Our Retailing Behind the Scenes box describes how Wal-Mart is able to tailor the merchandise and layout of each store to the market being served. Both of the above-mentioned stock lists provide scale advantages in other retailing activities. For example, promotional savings occur when more than one store operates in an area and can use the same advertisements, even while tailoring specific merchandise to specific stores.

Finally, chain stores have long been aware of the benefits of taking a leadership role in the marketing channel. When a chain store retailer is able to achieve critical mass in purchases, it can get other channel members—wholesalers, brokers, and manufacturers—to engage in activities they might not otherwise engage in and is thus referred to as the channel captain. Some of the things the chain store retailer might get other channel members to do include direct-to-store deliveries, increased promotional allowances, extended payment terms, special package sizes, and so on that allow the retailer to operate in the most efficient manner.

In recent years, chains have relied on their high level of consumer recognition to engage in private branding. Private branding, also sometimes called *store branding,* is when a retailer develops its own brand name and contracts with a manufacturer to

Standard Stock List
Is a merchandising method where all stores in a retail chain stock the same merchandise.

Optional Stock List
Is a merchandising method where each store in a retail chain is given the flexibility to adjust its merchandise mix to local tastes and demands.

Channel Captain
Is the institution (manufacturer, wholesaler, broker, or retailer) in the marketing channel who is able to plan for and get other channel institutions to engage in activities they might not otherwise engage in. Large chain store retailers are often able to perform the role of channel captain.

Private Branding,
Also often called store branding, occurs when a retailer develops its own brand name and contracts with a manufacturer to produce the merchandise with the retailer's brand on it instead of the manufacturer's name.

"TRAITING:" WAL-MART'S METHOD OF INVENTORY MANAGEMENT

Another reason that Wal-Mart has grown into the nation's number 1 retailer is its inventory management system. Wal-Mart's use of sophisticated inventory technologies has permitted the chain to look beyond the more traditional "merchandising by region" to "merchandising by individual store." Wal-Mart uses a system called *traiting* to look at both the customers' makeup and their buying preferences at individual stores.

Traiting indexes the product movement at each store with the store's market traits. This is used to determine not only if a given product should be carried in a particular store given the demographic makeup of the trading area, but also where it should be stocked in the store's layout. Traiting permits a store manager to alter total shelf space allotments based on product flow data. That's why in a rural area Wal-Mart may carry more hardware and do-it-yourself merchandise and in an urban area Wal-Mart will stock more fax paper and other home office supplies. Likewise, a store in one part of a metropolitan area may carry more golf equipment whereas the Wal-Mart just across town carries more swimming pool supplies.

This doesn't mean that only sales data can be used to support carrying a product. If a store manager finds out that Garth Brooks is going to have a concert in the area, it is reasonable to assume that a thousand Garth Brooks T-shirts will not only be in the manager's store but every other store near where Brooks is touring.

produce the merchandise with the retailer's brand on it instead of buying merchandise with the manufacturer's brand name on it. Such private branding goods now account for almost 40 percent of department store sales and 20 percent of total grocery units sold and are expected to reach 30 percent of grocery sales by the year 2000.[12] Other retailers have borrowed from the success of the supermarkets and department stores with their private labels. Barnes & Noble now sells deluxe hardcover editions of many of the classics with its own publishing house imprint.[13] Private labels usually have lower acquisition costs, which can be passed on to the consumer in the form of lower prices, thereby increasing demand. Also whereas private brands have no national advertising costs, the retailer must spend more to develop local demand for the brand. As a result, retailers today are now competing with the national brand manufacturers, as well as the store across the street.

DOLLAR $ & ¢ENTS

Retailers who can develop private-branded merchandise better than their competition will experience higher profitability.

EXHIBIT 1.4	RETAILERS CLASSIFIED BY MARGIN AND TURNOVER

MARGINS VERSUS TURNOVER

Retailers can be classified in regard to their gross margin percentage and rate of inventory turnover as shown in Exhibit 1.4. The gross margin percentage shows how much gross margin (net sales minus the cost of goods sold) the retailer makes as a percentage of sales; this is also referred to as the gross margin return on sales. A 40 percent gross margin indicates that on each dollar of sales the retailer generates 40 cents in gross margin dollars. This gross margin will be used to pay the retailer's operating expenses (the expenses the retailer incurs in running the business other than the cost of the merchandise [e.g., rent, wages, utilities, depreciation, insurance]). Inventory turnover refers to the number of times per year, on average, that a retailer sells its inventory. Thus an inventory turnover of 12 times indicates that, on average, the retailer turns over or sells its inventory once a month. Likewise, an average inventory of $40,000 (retail) and annual sales of $240,000 means the retailer has turned over its inventory six times in one year ($240,000 divided by $40,000), or every two months.

High-performance retailers, those who produce financial results substantially superior to the industry average, have long recognized the relationship between gross margin percentage, inventory turnover, and profit. As was shown in Exhibit 1.4, one can classify retailers into four basic types by using the concepts of margin and turnover.

Typically, the low-margin/low-turnover retailer will not be able to generate sufficient profits to remain competitive and survive. Thus there are no good examples of successful retailers using this approach. However, the low-margin/high-turnover retailer is common in the United States. Perhaps the best examples are the discount department stores (Venture and Target), off-price stores (T.J. Maxx and Marshalls), category killers (Best Buy, Office Depot, Circuit City), or the warehouse clubs (Sam's and Price/Costco). High-margin/low-turnover retailers are also common in the United States. Furniture stores, television and appliance stores, jewelry stores, gift shops, funeral homes, and most of the mom-and-pop stores located in small towns across the country are generally good examples of high-margin/low-turnover operations. Finally, some retailers find it possible to operate on both high margin and high turnover. As you might expect, this strategy can be very profitable. Probably the most popular examples are convenience food stores such as 7-Eleven, Circle K, Stop&Shop, or Quick Mart.

The low-margin/low-turnover retailer is the least able of the four to withstand a competitive attack because this retailer is usually unprofitable or barely profitable, and when competitive intensity increases, profits are driven even lower. However, the

Gross Margin Percentage
Is the gross margin divided by net sales or what percent of each sales dollar is gross margin.

Gross Margin
Is net sales minus the cost of goods sold.

Operating Expenses
Are the expenses the retailer incurs in running the business other than the cost of the merchandise.

Inventory Turnover
Refers to the number of times per year, on average, that a retailer sells its inventory.

High-Performance Retailers
Are those retailers that produce financial results substantially superior to the industry average.

Low-Margin/ Low-Turnover Retailer
Is one that operates on a low gross margin percentage and a low rate of inventory turnover.

Low-Margin/ High-Turnover Retailer
Is one that operates on a low gross margin percentage and a high rate of inventory turnover.

High-Margin/ Low-Turnover Retailer
Is one that operates on a high gross margin percentage and a low rate of inventory turnover.

High-Margin/ High-Turnover Retailer
Is one that operates on a high gross margin percentage and a high rate of inventory turnover.

high-margin/high-turnover retailer is in an excellent position to withstand and counter competitive threats because the high profit it generates enables it to finance price wars with competitors.

LOCATION

Retailers have long been classified according to their location within a metropolitan area, be it the central business district, a mall or strip shopping center, or as a free-standing unit. These traditional locations are discussed in greater detail in Chapter 7. However, the last decade saw a major change in the locations that retailers selected. Retailers are now aware that the opportunities to improve financial performance could result not only by improving the sales per square foot of traditional sites but by operating in new nontraditional retail areas.

DOLLAR $ & C ENTS

Retailers that seek out nontraditional locations to reach customers will increase their chances of being highly profitable.

In the past, rather than expand into untested territories, many retailers simply renovated existing stores. Not today! Now retailers are reaching out for alternative retail sites. American retailers today are testing all types of nontraditional locations to expand their business. For example, to get more people to eat pizza when they rent video tapes, Pizza Hut is testing the use of kiosks in video rental stores with direct telephone lines to the local Pizza Hut. McDonald's is testing locations in service stations along interstate highways as well as in Wal-Marts.

Also, given the high income levels of many airline travelers and the increasing amount of "lay-over time" between flights, many retailers have opened stores in airports, an idea that originated and has long been used by European and Asian retailers. Airports in Pittsburgh and Denver have opened mini-malls, whereas Palm Springs Regional has an outdoor putting green and Seattle's airport has a massage bar.[14]

Dollar General, Jewel/Osco, Pathmark, Von's, and Sears are leaders in opening stores in inner-city neighborhoods.[15] Also, KFC, Pizza Hut, and Taco Bell are opening free-standing units near or on several large universities with all three fast-food chains under one roof where employees and facilities (parking lots, restrooms, etc.) could be shared in this nontraditional location. Other fast-food operators have combined two or more franchises together. One popular example would be to combine a "meal" retailer (KFC) with a "dessert" operator (Haagen-Dazs).

Before ending our discussion on location, it is most important to point out that this is one of those areas of retailing that may undergo significant changes in the next decade. The trend of "retailing without walls" suggests that future locations may be as close as a consumer's computer or telephone. Many retailers of physical products are now able to operate out of their home office or car with a portable telephone/fax

The Body Shop is one rapidly expanding retailer that has not avoided locating stores in inner-city locations.

traveling to the customer. As we noted earlier, although there is some debate about the growth rate for this electronic sector, there is no question that this sector will affect retailing in the future.

SIZE

Many retail trade associations classify retailers by sales volume or number of employees. The reason for classifying by size is that the operating performance of retailers tends to vary according to size. That is, larger firms generally have lower operating costs per sales dollar than smaller firms. For example, the National Retail Federation, which categorizes department stores into three volume groups, found that operating expenses were 38.15 percent for firms having sales between $5 and $20 million, 38.31 percent for stores in the $20 to $100-million range, and only 34.37 percent for larger operations. Most retail trade associations provide similar breakdowns on gross margins, net profits, net markups, sales per square foot of selling space, and so forth. Retailers will find this information meaningful when comparing their results against others of a similar size. The inside covers of this text provide a description, along with the most recent sales figures, for America's Largest 25 Retailers.

A RETAILING CAREER

LO • 4
List the major aspects of a retail career, as well as the prerequisites necessary for success in retailing

Someone once said that "managing a retail store is an easy job. All you have to do is get consumers to visit your store (traffic) and then get these consumers to buy something (convert the traffic into customers) while operating at a lower cost than your competition (financial management)." Assuming this is correct, what type of person is needed to manage a retail store in the 21st century? A(n)

Economist	Yes _____	No _____
Fashion expert	Yes _____	No _____
Marketer	Yes _____	No _____
Financial analyst	Yes _____	No _____
Personnel manager	Yes _____	No _____
Traffic manager	Yes _____	No _____
Information system manager	Yes _____	No _____
Accountant	Yes _____	No _____

In reality, the answer is "yes" to all the above! A retail store manager needs to be knowledgeable in all these areas. As we have pointed out, few industries offer a more fast-paced, ever-changing environment where results are readily seen on the bottom line than retailing. Few job opportunities will train you to become an expert not in just one field, but in all business disciplines. Retailing offers you the economist's job of forecasting sales up to six months in advance, the fashion expert's job of predicting consumer behavior and how it will affect future fashion trends, and the marketing manager's job of determining how to promote, price, and display your merchandise. Further, it offers the financial analyst's job of seeking to reduce the various expenses; the personnel manager's job of hiring the right people, training them to perform their duties in an efficient manner, and developing their work schedules; the traffic manager's job of arranging delivery of a "hot item;" the information system analyst's job of analyzing sales and other data to determine opportunities for improved management practices; and the accountant's job of arriving at a profitable bottom line.

In summary, a retailer is like a master chef. Anyone can buy the ingredients but only a master chef can make a masterpiece. Over the course of a career, you will have to deal with many issues. Among them are

1. what product(s) or service(s) to offer
2. what group of customers to target
3. where to locate the store
4. how to train and motivate your employees
5. what price level to use
6. what levels of customer service (store hours, credit, staffing, parking, etc.) to offer your customers
7. how to lay out the store

If you consider that there are 10,000 possible combinations of products and at least 10 possible combinations of the other six issues, then there are more than 10 billion different possible retailing formats. No other occupation offers the immediate opportunities and challenges that retailing does. Yet many students do not consider retailing when exploring career opportunities.

COMMON QUESTIONS ABOUT A RETAILING CAREER

You may have certain perceptions that turn you away from pursuing retailing as a career. Sometimes this is good, because not all individuals are suited for retailing. However, it can be unfortunate when inaccurate perceptions turn one from a potentially rewarding retailing career to another career that may only appear to be more promising. By examining some of these issues, we will present a more accurate picture of retailing.

COLLEGE EDUCATION
Is a college education a prerequisite to a career in retailing? It depends. For a retail career that would not progress beyond assistant buyer or department manager, the answer is probably *no*. A degree from a four-year or two-year college would be helpful but not required. However, for career advancement with a fast-track, progressive, retailer or a career in top management (buyer, store manager, merchandise manager, vice-president, chief executive officer), a college degree is generally a prerequisite. Most large chain stores today will not consider anyone without a college degree for their training programs.

SALARY
Are salaries in retailing competitive? A recent graduate who is seeking an entry-level position can probably earn a higher salary in business fields other than retailing. In general, retailers offer 5 to 15 percent below what college graduates can earn from manufacturers, insurance companies, and many other fields represented by campus recruiters. Some retailers, however, are making an aggressive attempt to meet the starting salaries of these more traditional employers of college graduates. Generally, starting salaries in executive training programs will be about $24,000 to $30,000 per year. That, however, is only the short-run perspective. In the long run, the retail manager or buyer is directly rewarded on individual performance. Entry-level retail managers or buyers who do exceptionally well can double or triple their incomes in three to five years and often can have incomes twice those of classmates who chose other career fields attained in seven to ten years. For example, it is not uncommon for a person within ten years of their college graduation in the supermarket industry to be made a store director or manager and earn a six-figure annual income.

CAREER PROGRESSION
Can one advance their career rapidly in retailing? Yes. Obviously, this answer depends on both the retail organization and the individual. A person capable of handling more responsibility than he or she is given can move up quickly. However, if individuals work for retail firms that are too small or growing too slowly, they may have to join another retail organization to advance.

GEOGRAPHIC MOBILITY
Does a retailing career allow one to live in the area of the country where one desires? Yes and no. Retailing exists in all geographic areas of the United States where there is sufficient population density. In the largest 300 cities in the United States, there will be sufficient employment and advancement opportunities in retailing. To progress rapidly, a person must often be willing and able to make several moves, all of which may not be attractive in terms of an individual's lifestyle.[16] Rapidly growing chain stores usually find it necessary to transfer individuals to open stores in new geographic areas. Fortunately, these transfers are generally coupled with promotions and salary adjustments. Finally, a person may stay in one geographic area if he or she desires. However, this may cost that person opportunities for advancement and salary increases.

WOMEN IN RETAILING   Retailing has always been viewed as a good career for women. But the role of women in retailing was most often restricted to the sales floor, the buying office, or middle management. Women typically found the door shut when it was time to move into the executive suite. This pattern has begun to change. Today, women constitute more than 50 percent of all department store executives,[17] making it the profession where women have attained the highest level of achievement. Although most female executives are still only at the lower levels of corporate management, breakthroughs into the retail presidential ranks have recently been made. Dayton Hudson was cited by *Business Week* as being a pacesetter in providing advancement opportunities for women.[18] In addition, the Department of Commerce reported that women-owned businesses now represent 40 percent of all retail and service firms. In fact, businesses owned by women generated $1.6 trillion in revenues and employed 13.2 million individuals.[19]

SOCIETAL PERSPECTIVE   Professional merchants are considered respected and desirable members of their community, their state, and their nation. Leading retail executives are well-rounded individuals with a high social consciousness. Many of them serve on the boards of nonprofit organizations, as regents or trustees of universities, as active members of the local chambers of commerce, on school boards, and in other service-related activities. Retailers serve society not only outside their retailing career but within it as well. For example, civic events such as holiday parades are often sponsored by local merchants. In addition, many retail firms support local groups and charities with cash, food, and other goods and services as a means to "reinvest" some of their profits in the communities they serve. Take a moment to envision a world without merchants or retailers. How could any advanced industrial society survive in their absence? It couldn't!

It is the unscrupulous, deceiving merchant that society can do without, not the professional merchant. This happens to be true in all professions. There are unscrupulous lawyers, physicians, and ministers who give their professions a negative image at times. However, there are professional and ethical lawyers, physicians, and ministers who are good for their professions and society as a whole. It is not the profession that dictates one's contribution to society but the soundness of one's ethical principles. Early in your career (preferably as a student), you need to develop a firm set of ethical principles to help guide you throughout your managerial career.

PREREQUISITES FOR SUCCESS

What is required for success as a retail manager? Let's look at several factors that influence a retailer's success.

HARD WORK   Most successful retailers, as will any successful individual, respond to the above question with a simple: "hard work." The work is hard, the hours almost always exceed 40 per week, evening and holiday work is required, and a six-day week is not unusual for a retail manager. However, this is true for any industry. Beginning retailers have long known that they earn their salary 9 to 5 Monday through Friday but earn their advancement on weekends and after 5 o'clock. Also, many entrepreneurs, with little cash but a great idea and the willingness to work hard, have found their fortunes in retailing.

ANALYTICAL SKILLS   The retail manager must be able to solve problems through numerical analysis of facts and data to plan, manage, and control. The retail manager is a problem solver on a day-to-day basis. An understanding of the past and present performance of the store, merchandise lines, and departments is necessary. It is the analysis of these performance data that forms the basis of future actions in the retailing environment. Today's retailer must be able to analyze all the financial data that are available before going to market. In addition, quantitative and qualitative analysis of customers, competitors, suppliers, and other constituencies often helps to identify emerging trends and innovations. Combined with current performance results and market knowledge, continual monitoring of these constituencies provides insight into past performance and alerts the retailer to new directions. Many retailers also get information from reading trade journals such as *Women's Wear Daily, Progressive Grocer,* or *Chain Age,* discuss current happenings with their buying office, visit markets, and even talk to their competitors as a means to keep up.

CREATIVITY   The ability to generate and recognize novel ideas and solutions is known as creativity. A retail manager cannot operate a store totally by a set of preprogrammed equations and formulas. Because the competitive environment is constantly changing, there is no standard recipe for retailing. Therefore, retail executives need to be idea people as well as analysts. Success in retailing is the result of sensitive, perceptive decisions that require imaginative and innovative techniques. For example, a buyer must be able to spot environmental changes and relate these changes to new needs or products in the marketplace.

DECISIVENESS   The ability to make rapid decisions and to render judgments, take action, and commit to a course of action until completion is termed *decisiveness.* A retail manager must be an action person. Better decisions could probably be made if more time were taken to make them. However, more time is frequently unavailable because variables such as fashion trends and consumer desires change quickly. Thus a manager must make decisions quickly, confidently, and correctly to be successful even if perfect information is not always available. For example, buyers often make purchase decisions six months to a year before the merchandise arrives at the store.

FLEXIBILITY   The ability to adjust to the ever-changing needs of the situation calls for flexibility. The retail manager must have the willingness and enthusiasm to do whatever is necessary (although not planned) to get the job completed. Because plans must be altered quickly to accommodate changes in trends, styles, and attitudes, successful retail managers must be flexible. For example, successful chains of prerecorded music were able to change from LP displays to CD and cassette displays almost overnight as a result of having interchangeable display bins.

INITIATIVE   Retail managers are doers. They must have the ability to originate action rather than wait to be told what to do. This ability is called initiative. To be a success, the modern retail manager must monitor the numbers of the business (sales volumes, profits, inventory levels) and seize opportunities for action.

LEADERSHIP   The ability to inspire others to trust and respect your judgment and the ability to delegate, guide, and persuade others calls for leadership. Successfully conducting a retail operation means depending on others to get the work done; in any large-scale retailing enterprise, one person cannot do it all. A manager succeeds when his or her subordinates do their jobs.

ORGANIZATION

Another important quality is the ability to establish priorities and courses of action for yourself and others and to plan and follow through to achieve results. This prerequisite is organization. Retail managers are often forced to deal with many issues, functions, and projects at the same time. To achieve goals, the successful retailer must be good "time managers" and set priorities when organizing personnel and resources.

RISK TAKING

Retail managers should be willing to take calculated risks based on thorough analysis and sound judgment; they should also be willing to accept responsibility for the results. Success in retailing often comes from taking calculated risks and having the confidence to try something new before someone else does. All successful buyers have at one time or another purchased merchandise that could be labeled as "losers." After all, if buyers never made errors, then they were afraid to take "risks" and probably passed up many winners. However, they must have the ability to recognize when they made a mistake.

STRESS TOLERANCE

As the other prerequisites to retailing success suggest, retailing is a fast-paced and demanding career in a changing environment. The retailing leaders of the 21st century must be able to perform consistently under pressure and to thrive on constant change and challenge.

PERSEVERANCE

Because of the difficult challenges that a retail career presents, it is important to have perseverance. All too often retailers may become frustrated due to the many things occurring that they can't control. For example, a blizzard may occur just before Christmas and wipe out the most important shopping days of the year. Others may become frustrated with fellow employees; the long hours, especially the weekends; or the inability to satisfy some customers. The person that has the ability to persevere and take all this in stride will find an increasing number of career advancement opportunities.

ENTHUSIASM

Successful retailers must have a strong warmth of feeling for their job, otherwise they will convey the wrong image to their customers and associates in their department. Retailers today are training their salesforce to smile even when talking to customers on the telephone "because it shows through in your voice."[20] Without enthusiasm, retailing will soon become a boring job in which you count the hours until you "punch out" and you will miss the excitement of the career.

These 12 prerequisites for success in retailing are not intended to scare you off. In fact, if you are a student or a young retail manager, you probably do not yet possess all 12. The important thing for a person beginning a retailing career is to have the desire to acquire them. If you do desire these abilities, this book will help you move toward that goal. If you acquire and develop these abilities, your career in retailing will progress more rapidly.

Retailers that succeed must work hard and have perseverance as did Itchy Popkin, who helped his retail furniture business survive stiff competition from powerful retail chains plus one tornado and two hurricanes.

DOLLAR $ & CENTS

Retail stores that have store managers that possess the 12 prerequisite characteristics of successful retail managers will be more profitable.

THE STUDY AND PRACTICE OF RETAILING

LO • 5
Explain the different methods for the study and practice of retailing

As we have seen, two of the prerequisites to success as a retail manager are analytical skills and creativity. These attributes also represent two methods for the study and practice of retailing.

ANALYTICAL METHOD

The analytical retail manager is a finder and investigator of facts. These facts are summarized and synthesized to make decisions systematically. In making these decisions, the manager uses models and theories of retail phenomena that enable him or her to structure all dimensions of retailing. An analytical perspective can result in a standardized set of procedures, success formulas, and guidelines.

Consider, for example, a manager operating a McDonald's, restaurant, where everything is preprogrammed, including the menu, decor, location, hours of operation, cleanliness standards, customer service policies, and advertising. This store manager needs only to gather and analyze facts to determine whether the preestablished guidelines are being met and to take appropriate corrective action if necessary.

CREATIVE METHOD

Conversely, the creative retail manager is an ideas person. This retail manager tends to be a conceptualizer and has a very imaginative and fertile mind capable of creating a highly successful retail chain. A good example of this is Leslie Wexner, founder and chairman of The Limited. When everyone else in the mid-1960s thought he was crazy (including his father) for selling only a "limited" line of women's apparel focusing on the 18- to 35-year-old professional career women, Wexner had a gut feeling that he was right. Such a retailer uses insight, intuition, and more often implicit knowledge than facts. The result is usually a novel way to look at or solve a retail problem that reflects a deeper understanding of the market.

Is it possible to operate a retail establishment, in most part, with just creativity? YES. However, in the long run, using only creativity will not be adequate. Witness the slow-down in sales of the Body Shop, a retailer with a very creative "pro-environment" focus, as other firms, including The Limited, were able to copy its creative focus.[21] Analytical decision making must also be used so that a manager can profitably respond to unforeseen events in the environment.

A TWO-PRONGED APPROACH

As shown through our McDonald's manager and Leslie Wexner examples, retailing can indeed be practiced from both perspectives. The retailer who uses both approaches is most successful in the long run. Aren't stores like McDonald's successful using only the analytical method? No. The McDonald's franchisee can operate analytically quite successfully. However, behind the franchisee is a franchisor who is creative as well as analytical. On the creative side was the development of McDonald's characters such as Ronald McDonald, the Grimace, and the Hamburglar and selected menu items such as Egg McMuffin, Arch Deluxe, and Big Mac. On the analytical side was the development of standardized layouts, fixtures, equipment, and employee training. It is the combination of the creative with the analytical that has made McDonald's what it is today.

Our Winners & Losers box provides an example of how one small-town retailer successfully combined analytical and creative methods to overcome the arrival of Wal-Mart in its market area.

The synthesis of creativity and analysis is necessary in all fields of retailing. Roger Dickinson, a former retail executive and now retailing professor, has stated that "many successful merchandisers are fast duplicators rather than originators."[22] To decide who or what to duplicate requires not only creativity but also an analysis of the strategies that retailers are pursuing. This is an exercise in weighing potential returns against risks. Dickinson further states that "creativity in retailing is for the sake of increasing the sales and profits of the firm."[23] If creativity is tied to sales and profits, then one cannot avoid analysis; profit and sales statistics require analysis.

Retailers in the 21st century cannot do without either creativity or analytical skills. We attempt to develop your skills in both of these areas. At the outset, however, you should note that the analytical and creative methods for studying retailing are not that different. Whether you use creativity or analytical skills, they will be directed at solving problems.

SMALL-TOWN RETAILERS CAN COMPETE WITH WAL-MART

Many people mistakenly assume that the arrival of a Wal-Mart spells disaster for small-town retailers. This is not the case if the retailer is able to differentiate itself from the competition. One such case occurred in southern Illinois. When a hardware store owner heard that a Wal-Mart was coming to her small town and locating a half-mile away, she was in shock. After all, the hardware store had been in her family for half a century. Her store, which offered a wide arrangement of housewares, sporting goods, appliances, hardware, gifts, and automotive parts, did have one thing going for it as it prepared to battle Wal-Mart. Five years earlier, the store had moved away from the downtown square to a small shopping center on the outskirts of the town of 6,000. This shopping center had a major supermarket chain for an anchor. With the supermarket, at least, Mrs. Bee knew that traffic would still be coming to the shopping center.

After thinking about the problem for a couple of days, Mrs. Bee decided to fight the competitive battle. She drove to Mt. Vernon, the nearest Wal-Mart, and spent a day combing the aisles, visiting with the manager (yes, Wal-Mart will try to help competitors survive when they enter a new market), and filling a whole notebook with comments about Wal-Mart's merchandise, prices, and store layout.

For the next month, Mrs. Bee analyzed the data completely and concluded she could survive with Wal-Mart, but she would have to change her operations. First, she would have to drop her gifts, housewares, sporting goods, and automotive parts lines because she couldn't compete with Wal-Mart on either price or selection. She would now have to specialize in the appliance (which Wal-Mart does not carry) and hardware lines; offering a larger selection and better service, including advice on which products to purchase and how to use them, than Wal-Mart self-service merchandising could offer the customer.

Although she dropped what had been her strongest merchandise lines—they were also Wal-Mart's strongest—Mrs. Bee was soon operating at a higher profit level than before Wal-Mart arrived. However, Mrs. Bee also had to become much more creative with her business. The lack of competition had left her complacent in running the business before Wal-Mart. This has all changed.

SOURCE: The above was based on information provided the authors by Marvin Lurie of the North American Retail Dealers Association.

DOLLAR $ & ¢ENTS

Retailers that practice both analytical and creative management will be consistently more profitable.

A PROPOSED ORIENTATION

The approach to the study and practice of retailing that is reflected in this book is an outgrowth of the previous discussion. This approach has four major orientations: (1) environmental, (2) management planning, (3) profit, and (4) decision making.

Retailers should have an environmental orientation, which will allow them to anticipate and adapt continuously to external forces in the environment. Retailing is not static. With the social, legal and ethical, technological, economic, and other external forces always in flux, the modern retailer finds it necessary both to assess these changes in an analytical perspective and to respond with creative actions.

Retailers should have a planning orientation, which will help them to adapt systematically to a changing environment. Planning is deciding today what to do in the future. A retailer who wants to have the competitive edge must plan for the future. We place special emphasis on the development of creative retail strategies.

Retailers should have a profit orientation, because all retail decisions will have an effect on the firm's financial performance. The profit orientation will therefore focus on fundamental management of assets, revenues, and expenses. Management tools that show how to evaluate the profit impact of retail decisions are discussed.

Retailers should have a decision-making orientation, which will allow them to focus efforts on the need to collect and analyze data for making intelligent retail decisions. To aid in this process, a retail information system is needed to help retail executives program their operations for desired results.

THE BOOK OUTLINE

This book is composed of 16 chapters, each with its own study guide and application section. The end-of-chapter materials provide a way to bring the real world into your studies, by launching you into the kind of situations you might face as a retail manager, and to reinforce text concepts. Through careful analysis of this material and discussion with fellow students, you will discover retailing concepts that can be vividly retained because of the concrete context. Furthermore, this material requires you to think of yourself as a retail decision maker who must sometimes make decisions with less-than-perfect information.

INTRODUCTION TO RETAILING

This book is divided into five parts. The first part, Introduction to Retailing, has two chapters. In Chapter 2, Retail Planning and Management, you are exposed to the basic concepts of strategy, administration, and operations planning and management in retailing that are used in the remaining chapters.

THE RETAILING ENVIRONMENT

The second part, The Retailing Environment, focuses on the external factors that the retailer faces in making everyday business decisions. The four chapters examine, in detail, the factors shown in Exhibit 1.1. Chapter 3, Understanding Customer Behavior, looks at the behavior of the retail consumer and the socioeconomic environment. Chapter 4, Evaluating the Competition in Retailing, examines the behavior of competitors as well as the technological advances taking place in the market. Chapter 5, Understanding Channel Behavior, focuses on the behavior of the various members of the channel of distribution and their effect on the retailer. Chapter 6, Legal and Ethical Behavior, analyzes the effect of the legal and ethical constraints on today's retailer.

MARKET SELECTION AND LOCATION ANALYSIS

It has often been said that the three keys to success in retailing are location, location, and location. In Chapter 7, Market Selection and Location Decisions, we discuss the various elements considered in determining the feasibility of targeting a given market segment and entering a given retail market and then look at site selection.

MANAGING RETAIL OPERATIONS

In the fourth part, Managing Retail Operations, we discuss the merchandising operations of a retail firm. This part deals with the day-to-day decisions facing retailers. Chapter 8, Managing a Retailer's Finances, discusses various financial statements, the key methods of valuing inventory, and the development of merchandise planning budgets by retailers. Chapter 9, Merchandise Buying and Handling, looks at how a retailer determines what to buy for its market and how these purchases are made. The appendix following Chapter 9 discusses the merchandising of apparel goods. Chapter 10, Merchandise Pricing, discusses the importance to the retailer of setting the correct price. In addition to the various markup methods used by retailers, the chapter also looks at markdowns. Chapter 11, Advertising and Promotion, is devoted to a complete discussion (with the exception of personal selling, which is covered along with services offered by retailers in Chapter 12, Customer Services and Retail Selling) of how a retailer can and should promote itself. Chapter 13, Store Layout and Design, discusses the impact of proper layout and design on retail performance. Chapter 14, Retailing of Services, discusses the retailing of services, which require specialized in-store selling strategies due to their intangibility.

RETAIL ADMINISTRATION

In the fifth part, Retail Administration, we are concerned with how to maximize the efficiency of retail operations. Chapter 15, Managing Human Resources, examines the role of human resources in a retail firm. Chapter 16, Retail Information Systems, develops a framework for collecting and gathering information that is needed for optimal planning, administration, and control.

The text concludes with an appendix which includes answers to the sample test questions at the end of each chapter, as well as an index of the retailers mentioned. Also, the inside covers of this text list the nation's Largest 25 Retailing Companies, including their financial performance for three years as well as the their address and the web page listing.

STUDENT STUDY GUIDE

SUMMARY   This chapter seeks to acquaint the reader with the nature and scope of retailing by discussing its impact on the economy, the types of retailers, prerequisites for a successful career in retailing and different approaches to the study and practice of retailing.

LO•1 **WHAT IS RETAILING?**   Retailing consists of the final activities and steps needed to place merchandise in the hands of the ultimate consumer or to provide services to the consumer.

LO•2 **WHY IS RETAILING ALWAYS UNDERGOING SO MUCH CHANGE?**   It is not staid and stable, rather it is an exciting business sector that effectively combines an individual's skills to make a profit in an ever-changing market environment. That is why some retailers are successful and others, who are either unwilling or unable to adapt to this changing environment, fail.

LO•3 **WHAT ARE THE VARIOUS METHODS USED TO CATEGORIZE RETAILERS?**   Retailers can be classified in a variety of ways. Five of the more popular schemes are by SIC code, number of outlets, margins versus turnover, location, and size. None, however, sheds adequate light on competition in retailing.

LO•4 **WHAT IS INVOLVED IN A RETAILING CAREER?**   In the long run, a retailing career can offer salary comparable with other careers, definite career advancement, and geographic mobility. In addition, a career in retailing incorporates the knowledge and use of all the business activities or disciplines (accounting, marketing, finance, personnel, economics, and even fashion). Besides, in retailing "no two days are alike; each offers its own set of opportunities and problems." The prerequisites for success in retailing besides hard work include analytical skills, creativity, decisiveness, flexibility, initiative, leadership, organization, risk taking, stress tolerance, perseverance, and enthusiasm. These are all important, but it is especially important for the retail manager to work at developing an attitude of openness to new ideas and a willingness to learn. After all, the market is always changing.

LO•5 **WHAT ARE THE DIFFERENT METHODS FOR THE STUDY AND PRACTICE OF RETAILING?**   To be successful in retailing, an individual must make use of the analytical and creative methods of operation. The four proposed orientations to the study and practice of retailing in this text are an environmental orientation, which allows the retailer to focus on the continuously changing external forces affecting retailing; a planning orientation, which will help the retailer to adapt systematically to this changing environment; a profit orientation, which will enable the retailer to examine the profit implications of any decision; and a decision-making orientation, which will allow the retailer to focus on the need to collect and analyze data for making intelligent creative retail decisions.

TERMS TO REMEMBER

retailing
same store sales
market share
category killer
Internet
scrambled merchandising
chain stores
standard stock list
optional stock list
channel captain

private branding
gross margin percentage
gross margin
operating expenses
inventory turnover
high-performance retailer
low-margin/low-turnover retailer
low-margin/high-turnover retailer
high-margin/low-turnover retailer
high-margin/high-turnover retailer

REVIEW AND DISCUSSION QUESTIONS

LO•1 WHAT IS RETAILING?

1. Which of the following transactions is considered to be a retailing transaction according to the text's definition? (1) a student buying an airline ticket from a travel agent, (2) a retired farmer setting up a trust account at a local bank, (3) a student buying a Mother's Day card, (4) a homemaker buying a magazine from a door-to-door salesperson, and (5) an appliance repairperson coming to your home to fix a dishwasher.

LO•2 WHY IS RETAILING ALWAYS UNDERGOING SO MUCH CHANGE?

2. Retailing is often said to be a stable and never-changing sector of the economy since a Wal-Mart or McDonald's seldom change their layout or merchandise selection once they enter a market area. Agree or disagree and defend your answer.

3. Many different environmental trends are taking place today that will have an effect on retailing operations over the next decade. Discuss three of these and their effects on retailing.

4. Currently there is a great deal of debate about the future impact of the Internet on retailing. What is your prediction concerning the Internet's impact on retailing in the year 2005? What support do you have for your prediction?

LO•3 DESCRIBE THE FIVE METHODS USED TO CATEGORIZE RETAILERS.

5. How can a retailer operate with a high-margin/high-turnover strategy? Won't customers avoid this type of store and shop at a low-margin store?

6. Isn't it better for a chain store operation to always use a standard stock list? After all, it would confuse the customer if a JCPenney or Target in Portland, Oregon, is different from one in Portland, Maine?

LO•4 WHAT IS INVOLVED IN A RETAILING CAREER?

7. What concepts and/or techniques from economics and/or accounting do you believe would be most useful in retail decision making?

8. Twelve prerequisites for success were given. Which one(s) do you think is (are) the most important? Why? Which ones do you think you already possess? Which ones do you think you need to improve?

LO • 5 BE ABLE TO EXPLAIN THE DIFFERENT METHODS FOR THE STUDY AND PRACTICE OF RETAILING.

9. An individual who is both creative and analytical will definitely succeed in retailing. Do you agree or disagree with this statement? Defend your position.

10. Jim McCann is often given credit for using his analytical skills to make 800-FLOWERS one of the most successful service retailers of the 1990s, with annual sales approaching $400 million. Yet, McCann was not the individual who started the company. McCann purchased the company from the individual who had the creative idea of having one easy-to-remember phone number, as opposed to having to look up a local FTD florist's number. However, before McCann's buyout, 800-FLOWERS had too small an advertising budget, too many managers, and too large a telemarketing center. Does this mean that analytical skills are more important than creative skills for success in retailing? Defend your answer.

11. Visit a local retailer who you would describe as creative and seek to determine which analytical skills that retailer also possesses.

SAMPLE TEST QUESTIONS

LO • 1 RETAILING

a. may be defined as any cash purchase for merchandise
b. is the same the world over
c. the final move in the flow of merchandise from producer to consumer
d. is the sale of an item by the manufacturer to a wholesaler
e. is not necessary to produce economic growth

LO • 2 WHICH OF THE FOLLOWING WORDS IS DESCRIPTIVE OF THE RETAILING INDUSTRY?

a. changing
b. stagnant
c. unexciting
d. staid
e. boring

LO • 3 WHICH OF THE FOLLOWING IS NOT ONE OF THE WAYS BY WHICH RETAILERS ARE CATEGORIZED?

a. number of outlets
b. size
c. margin versus turnover
d. location
e. gender of the manager

LO • 4 WHICH OF THE FOLLOWING CHARACTERISTICS IS IT NOT DESIRABLE FOR A RETAIL MANAGER TO POSSESS?

a. stress tolerance
b. indecisiveness
c. creativity

d. leadership
e. enthusiasm

LO • 5 THE ABILITY TO CONCEPTUALIZE AND BE VERY IMAGINATIVE IS CHARACTERISTIC OF

a. a strong analytical person
b. a creative person
c. a retail manager
d. a good detective
e. an "A" student

APPLICATIONS

WRITING AND SPEAKING EXERCISE   Your family has owned a small convenience store in a resort area community for the past 10 years. Over that time, the store has been profitable, but your parents think that it could be more profitable if they could lower the high rate of employee turnover. Prepare a presentation for your parents listing what you think they should look for in hiring part-time employees. Also, list what employee traits they should seek to avoid.

RETAIL PROJECT   The World Wide Web is a graphical-based version of the Internet, organizing information in an easy-to-use format. Topics are categorized into web sites, whose information can be retrieved by pointing at a word or a picture and clicking a mouse.

Using either your own computer or one at school, select two or three of the Largest 25 Retailers listed on the inside covers of this text. Using their web address, locate their web sites and make a report describing what they have on the web. Which one did you like best? Why? Also, are these sites for use by the retailers' customers, suppliers, employees, or even competitors? Finally, if a retailer is trying to make the most out its Internet site, what should be on the site?

PLANNING YOUR OWN RETAIL BUSINESS   If you think you might want to be a retail entrepreneur, you can use the "Planning Your Own Retail Business" computer exercises at the end of each chapter to assist you in this process. Also, your teacher may have had you purchase *The House: Understanding A Retail Enterprise Using Spreadsheet Analysis* by Robert F. Lusch and Patrick Dunne, which can be used to help you understand the dollars and cents of retailing.

This first exercise is intended to acquaint you with how sensitive your retail business will be to changes in sales volume. Let's assume that you plan that your retail business will generate $400,000 per year in annual sales and that it will operate on a gross margin percentage of 32 percent. If your fixed operating expenses are $80,000 annually and variable operating costs are 10 percent of sales, how much profit will you make? (*Hint:* Sales * Gross margin percentage = Gross margin; Gross margin − Fixed operating expenses − Sales * Variable operating expenses as a % of sales = Net profit.) Use a spreadsheet program on your computer to compute your firm's net profits; next, analyze what happens if sales drop 10 percent and if sales rise 10 percent. Why are bottom line results (net profits) so sensitive to changes in sales volume?

NOTES

1. David Reibstein and Paul Farris, "Do Marketing Expenditures to Gain Distribution Cost the Customer?" *European Management Journal,* March 1995: 31–38.
2. From a list compiled by Robert Kahn from data contained in *1962 Fairchild's Financial Manual of Retail Stores* and published in the Feature Report section of *Retailing Today,* January 1995.
3. "Too Much of a Good Thing?" *Forbes,* June 3, 1996: 115–119.
4. "P&G, Seeing Shoppers Were Being Confused Overhauls Marketing," *Wall Street Journal,* January 15, 1997: A1.
5. Robert F. Lusch and Deborah Zizzo, *Competing for Customers: How Wholesaler-Distributors Can Meet the Power Retailer Challenge,* Washington, DC: Distribution Research and Education Foundation, 1995.
6. "Why the Web Is Still a No-Shop Zone," *Fortune,* February 5, 1996: 127; "Whose INTERNET Is It, Anyway?" *Fortune,* December 11, 1995: 120–142.
7. "Cyberspace Glossary," *Shopping Centers Today,* October 1995: 31.
8. "Wired Kingdom," a special supplement to *Chain Store Age,* January 1997: 3.
9. "Up against the Mall," *Entrepreneur,* February 1996: 26.
10. For a more detailed discussion, complete with the quotes made, on this subject, see "The Myth of QVC," *Retailing Today,* Robert Kahn, editor, December 1993: 1–3.
11. Based on the authors computations using data from Sam Walton with John Huey, *Sam Walton: Made in America, My Story* (New York: Doubleday, 1992: 98).
12. "Private Label Losing Its 'Enemy' Status," *Advertising Age,* October 11, 1993: 27; "No End to March of Private Label," *Advertising Age,* November 1, 1993: S-6.
13. "Big Bookseller Grows Its Publishing Arm," *Wall Street Journal,* November 29, 1994: B1.
14. "Stranded at O'Hare?" *Wall Street Journal,* June 1, 1995: A1–A4; "Are Airports Becoming the New Malls," *Chain Store Age-Executive,* May 1995: 78–80.
15. "Rediscovering the Inner City," *Marketing News,* January 17, 1994: 1–2.
16. "As More Men Become 'Trailing Spouses,' Firms Help Them Cope," *Wall Street Journal,* April 13, 1993: A1–A4.
17. Myron Gable, Susan Fiorito, and Martin Topol, "The Current Status of Women in Department Store Retailing: 1993," *Journal of Retailing,* Spring 1994: 65–71.
18. "Welcome to the Woman-Friendly Company," *Business Week,* August 6, 1990: 48–55.
19. "One-Third of Nation's Businesses Owned by Women," a press release issued by the Department of Commerce for release on January 29, 1996.
20. "Americans Can't Get No Satisfaction," *Fortune,* December 11, 1995: 194.
21. "Can The Body Shop Shape Up?" *Fortune,* April 15, 1996: 118–120.
22. Roger Dickinson, "Creativity in Retailing," *Journal of Retailing* Winter 1969–1970: 4.
23. Ibid.

RETAIL PLANNING AND MANAGEMENT

As a result of SWOT analysis, Sears decided to focus on its historical strength of operating retail stores and divested itself of Coldwell Banker (real estate sales) and Dean Witter (stock brokerage and investments).

In this chapter, we explain the importance of planning in successful retail management. To facilitate the discussion, we introduce a retail planning and management model that serves as a frame of reference for the remainder of the text. This simple model illustrates the importance of strategic planning, operations management, and administration of a retailer's resources. These three activities, if properly conducted, will result in the retail firm achieving results exceeding those of the competition.

OVERVIEW

After reading this chapter, you should be able to

LEARNING OBJECTIVES

1. explain why strategic planning is important and be able to describe the components of strategic planning: statement of mission; goals and objectives; an analysis of strengths, weaknesses, opportunities, and threats; and strategy

2. describe the text's retail planning and management model, which explains the three tasks that a retailer must perform and how they lead to high performance results

LO • 1
Explain why strategic planning is important and be able to describe the components of strategic planning: statement of mission; goals and objectives; an analysis of strengths, weaknesses, opportunities, and threats; and strategy

Planning
is the anticipation and organization of what needs to be done to reach an objective.

Strategic Planning
involves adapting the resources of the firm to the opportunities and threats of an ever-changing retail environment.

COMPONENTS OF STRATEGIC PLANNING

In most endeavors, a well-defined plan of action can mean the difference between success and failure. For example, a traveler does not go from Fargo to Kansas City without a well-defined plan of which highways to use. Political candidates and their advisors develop a campaign plan long before the election. Successful college students plan their assignments so that they are not forced to pull an "all nighter" the night before an assignment is due. Similarly, a clearly defined plan of action is an essential ingredient of all forms of business management. This is especially true in the highly competitive field of retailing in which in the first half of this decade the number of stores has expanded faster than consumer demand, resulting in roughly 15,000 retail bankruptcies in 1995.[1]

Planning is the anticipation and organization of what needs to be done to reach an objective. This sounds simple enough, but as any retail buyer will tell you, it is difficult to know in advance of each upcoming season what styles, quantities, colors, and sizes the customers will want for the upcoming season. Superior planning by retailers enables them to offset some of the advantages that their competition may have, such as a good location. People not familiar with retailing often wonder how retailers can anticipate what consumers are going to want next season. In reality, success for all retailers, large and small, is generally a matter of good planning and then implementing that plan or plans. For example, today some of the nation's top retailers (Wal-Mart, Target, and Kmart) are rapidly building new supercenters across the country. However, because their expertise is in dry goods, they are relying on newly hired food merchants and their suppliers to aid them in developing the strategic plans for these supercenters. Failure to develop good plans can spell disaster for a retailer. Consider Ann Taylor. For years, this chain had been successful selling sensibly priced, fashionable clothes for working professional women. Yet, in the mid-1990s, Ann Taylor in its planning process misread the "needs and wants" of the marketplace. It planned for shorter and tighter skirts than most women wanted for the office, trendy silhouettes, blouses without sleeves, and generally younger styles. This action alienated the traditional Ann Taylor customer, who went elsewhere to shop for more traditional styles.[2]

Meanwhile, the nation's two largest food wholesalers, Fleming and Super-Valu, have worked with their retailers to develop plans to withstand the onslaught of supercenters into their trading area. Only by watching the changing environment and anticipating future changes were the wholesalers able to help the retailers make the necessary strategic plans to survive this new type of competition.

Strategic planning is a type of planning that involves adapting the resources of the firm to the opportunities and threats of an ever-changing retail environment. Through the proper use of strategic planning, retailers achieve and maintain a balance between

DOLLAR $ & CENTS

Retailers who do a better job of strategic planning than their competition can overcome some of the competition's natural advantages.

Ann Taylor has planned its stores and merchandising to appeal to relatively affluent, fashion conscious working women (with limited time to shop) from the ages of 20 to 50 who prefer classic styles, updated to reflect current fashion trends.

resources available and opportunities. Let's take a closer look at the components of the strategic planning process.

Strategic planning consists of four components:

1. development of a mission (or purpose) statement for the firm
2. definition of specific goals and objectives for the firm
3. development of basic strategies that will enable the firm to reach its objectives and fulfill its mission
4. identification and analysis of the retailer's strengths, weaknesses, opportunities, and threats—referred to as SWOT analysis

MISSION STATEMENT

The beginning of a retailer's planning process is the formulation of a mission statement. The mission statement is a basic description of the fundamental nature, rationale, and direction of the firm. It provides the employees and customers with an understanding of where future growth for the firm is coming from. Not every retailer has a mission statement. In fact, only about 50 percent of all businesses have written mission statements.[3] Because so many businesses don't know where they want to go and how to get there, they fail. The lack of a written statement, however, is not a cause by itself for failure if the firm has a clearly understood even if unwritten plan of action. For example, Wal-Mart doesn't have a written mission statement. Wal-Mart does, however, have a clearly defined sense of direction, which Sam Walton based on Marshall Field's idea of "give the customer what she wants."[4]

Although mission statements vary from retailer to retailer, good ones usually include three elements:

1. how the retailer uses or intends to use its resources
2. how it expects to relate to the ever-changing environment
3. the kinds of values it intends to offer to serve the needs and wants of the consumer

Mission Statement
is a basic description of the fundamental nature, rationale, and direction of the firm.

Consider the mission statement that was developed by Record World, a northeastern chain with more than 100 outlets.[5]

> Record World is in business to provide prerecorded entertainment in all modes desired by consumers. Our target market consists of all viable segments of the population shopping in locations, primarily malls, where our stores are situated in the northeast and mideast regions of the United States. In addition to a broad assortment of merchandise, we strive to provide our customers with both value and personal service. In the long-run, we will have the dominant market share in all the market segments we serve. We endeavor to double our sales in the next five years, primarily through improved market and merchandise development and secondarily through market penetration.

As the above illustration points out, a mission statement answers the question: What business should the retailer be in? Record World has used its mission statement not to be a record store leader but to be a "value-oriented" retailer of all prerecorded entertainment. The preceding mission statement illustrates how Record World overcame one of the major shortcomings of most retailers' mission statements—defining one's business too narrowly (i.e., being in the record business and not in prerecorded entertainment). A critical issue in defining a retail business is to do it at the most meaningful level of generalization. This is why most mission statements should be broad and general in nature, yet still provide direction, as well as be motivational. If Ann Taylor had followed its mission of providing sensibly priced, fashionable clothes for the working professional women and had not introduced that too-youthful line of clothing, it may not have experienced all those problems a few years ago. Instead, it appeared to many retail experts that the retailer had lost its sense of direction. By not following its mission, it expanded too rapidly into new markets and introduced a fragrance, personal care products, a separate chain of shoe stores, and a low-priced chain named Loft, all the while forgetting what it does best—selling fashion staples.[6]

DOLLAR $ & CENTS

Retailers that have missions that are broad and general in nature and motivate employees, yet still provide direction, will have higher longer-term performance.

As a further example of what makes a good mission statement and what doesn't, consider how a poor mission statement can be improved. Avon Drive-In Theater claims it is "in the movie business and we shall only show PG13 movies at the lowest prices in our trading area." A better statement might be the following: "We are in the entertainment business and we shall seek to show the movies that customers want at prices that reflect the market's price sensitivity."

Just having a mission statement is not enough in today's business climate; it must be adhered to. As part of Ann Taylor's mission, they focused on a broad customer base comprising primarily relatively affluent, fashion-conscious working women with limited time to shop from the ages of 20 to 50 who prefer classic styles, updated to reflect current fashion trends. However, the failure of Ann Taylor's to sell stylish professional clothes that was described earlier indicates that it may have forgotten its mission.

Some retailers pursue societal objectives by giving (providing) customers the choice of products made from recycled materials such as the Deja Shoe.

STATEMENT OF GOALS AND OBJECTIVES

The second step in the planning process is to define specific goals and objectives for the retailer. These goals and objectives should be derived from, and give precision and direction to, the retailer's mission statement. Goals and objectives should identify the performance results that the retailer intends to bring about through the execution of its major strategies. Goals and objectives serve two purposes. First, they provide specific direction and guidance to the firm in the formulation of its strategy. Second, they provide a standard against which the firm can measure and evaluate its performance results.

   Although these goals and objectives can be expressed in many different ways, usually retailers will divide them into two dimensions: market performance objectives, which compares its actions against its competitors, and financial performance objectives, which analyzes its ability to provide an adequate profit level to continue in business. However, in addition to the market performance and financial performance objectives, some retailers may also establish societal objectives, which are phrased in terms of helping society fulfill some of its needs, and personal objectives, which relate to helping individuals employed in retailing fulfill some of their needs. Let us examine each type of these goals and objectives in more detail.

Goals and Objectives *are the performance results intended to be brought about through the execution of a strategy.*

Market Performance Objectives *represent how a retailer desires to be compared to its competitors.*

Financial Performance Objectives *represent the profit and economic performance a retailer desires.*

Societal Objectives *are those which reflect the retailers' desire to help society fulfill some of its needs.*

Personal Objectives *are those which reflect the retailers' desire to help individuals employed in retailing fulfill some of their needs.*

DOLLAR **$** & **C**ENTS

As retailers increase their market share, their financial performance will also increase in comparison with their competitors.

MARKET PERFORMANCE OBJECTIVES

Market performance objectives establish the amount of dominance the retailer has in the marketplace. The most popular measures of market performance in retailing are sales volume and market share (retailer's total sales divided by total market sales), or the proportion of total sales in a particular market that the retailer has been able to capture. Research has shown that profitability is clearly and positively related to market share.[7] Thus, market performance objectives are not pursued for their own sake but because they are a key profit path.

FINANCIAL OBJECTIVES

Retailers can establish many financial objectives, but they can all conveniently fit into categories of profitability and productivity.

PROFITABILITY OBJECTIVES Profit-based objectives deal directly with the monetary return that a retailer desires from its business. When retailers speak of "making a profit," the definition of profit is often unclear. The most common way to define profit is the total net profit after taxes—the bottom line of the income statement. Another common retail method of expressing profit is as a percentage of net sales. However, most retail owners think that the best way to define profit is in terms of return on investments (ROI).

This method of reporting profits as a percentage of investments is complicated by the fact that there are two different ways to define the term *investment*. Return on assets (ROA) reflects all the capital used in the business whether provided by the owners or by creditors. ROI, also referred to as return on net worth (RONW), reflects only the amount of capital that the owners have invested in the business.

The most frequently encountered profit objectives for a retailer are shown in Exhibit 2.1—the Strategic Profit Model (SPM). The elements of the SPM start at the far left and move right. These five elements include

Net Profit Margin
is the ratio of net profit (after taxes) to total sales and shows how much profit a retailer makes on each dollar of sales after all expenses and taxes have been met.

1. net profit margin, which is the ratio of net profit (after taxes) to total sales and shows how much profit a retailer makes on each dollar of sales after all expenses and taxes have been met. For example, if a retailer is operating on a net profit margin of 2 percent, it is making two cents on each dollar of sales. In general, retailers operate on lower net profit margins than manufacturers. The net profit margin is derived exclusively from income or operating statement data and does not include any measures from the retailer's balance sheet. Thus, it does not show how effectively a retailer is using the capital at its disposal.

Asset Turnover
is total sales divided by total assets and shows how many dollars of sales a retailer can generate on an annual basis with each dollar invested in assets.

2. asset turnover, which is computed by taking the retailer's total sales and dividing by total assets. This ratio tells the retail analyst how productively the firm's assets are being used. Put another way, it shows how many dollars of sales a retailer can generate on an annual basis with each dollar invested in assets. Thus, if a retailer has a rate of asset turnover of 3.0 times, it is generating 3 dollars in sales for each dollar in assets. The asset turnover ratio incorporates key measures from the income statement (total sales) and the balance sheet (total assets) and, as such, shows how well the retailer is using its capital to generate sales. In general, retailers experience higher rates of asset turnover but lower net profit margins than do manufacturers.

Return on Assets
is net profit (after taxes) divided by total assets.

3. ROA, which is net profit divided by total assets and depicts the profit return that the retailer achieved on all assets invested regardless of whether the assets were financed by creditors or the firm's owners. As shown in Exhibit 2.1, return on assets

EXHIBIT 2.1	STRATEGIC PROFIT MODEL

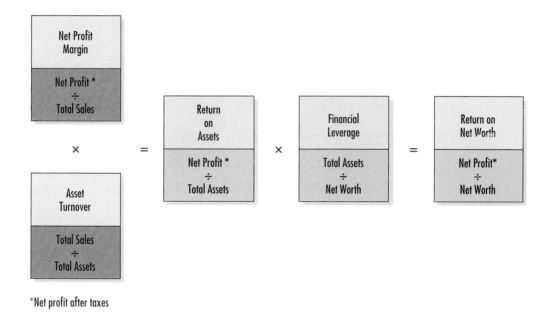

*Net profit after taxes

is the result of multiplying the net profit margin by asset turnover. For example, a retailer with a net profit margin of 2 percent and asset turnover of 4.0 would have an ROA of 8 percent (2 percent times 4 equals 8 percent).

4. financial leverage, which is total assets divided by net worth or owners' equity. This ratio shows the extent to which a retailer is using debt in its total capital structure. The low end of this ratio is 1.0 times and depicts a situation in which the retailer is using no debt in its capital structure. As the ratio moves beyond 1.0, the firm is using a heavier mix of debt versus equity. For example, when the ratio is 2.0 times, the firm has 2 dollars in assets for every dollar in net worth.

5. RONW, which is net profit divided by net worth or owner's equity. RONW is shown at the far right of the SPM and is usually used to measure owner's performance. Note that, as shown in Exhibit 2.1, the ROA multiplied by financial leverage yields return on net worth. Thus if a retailer has a ROA of 8 percent and a financial leverage of 2.0, then it will have a RONW of 16 percent (8 percent times 2.0 equals 16 percent).

Financial Leverage
is total assets divided by net worth or owners' equity and shows how aggressive the retailer is in its use of debt.

Return on Net Worth
is net profit (after taxes) divided by net worth or owner's equity.

The important point to remember from this discussion of profitability is that department or specialty stores (higher gross margin and lower asset turnover rates) compete differently than discounters (generally lower gross margins but higher asset turnover resulting from the need for fewer capital assets outside of inventory). Discounters expect to gain a higher asset turnover by reducing their gross margins, and specialty stores expect a lower asset turnover rate with their higher gross margins.

Likewise, it must also be remembered that attempts to increase asset turnover by merely reducing inventory levels can have serious consequences for a retailer. These lower inventory levels may produce higher turnover rates, but they could also be suicidal if the customers can't find what they want.

Often, business leaders are benefactors for important societal causes, such as when Tommy Hilfiger and Sheryl Crow donated $75,000 to The Breast Cancer Research Foundation.

Managers are usually evaluated on ROA because the amount of debt the firm uses or financial leverage is beyond their control. In addition to the five elements of the SPM, another measure of profitability is the gross margin percentage, which is gross margin (net sales minus cost of goods sold) divided by total sales.

All retailers establish some form of profit objective. The specific profit objectives developed will play an important role in evaluating potential strategic opportunities.

Productivity Objectives *state the sales objectives that the retailer desires for each unit of resource input: floor space, labor, and inventory investment.*

PRODUCTIVITY OBJECTIVES   Productivity objectives state the sales objectives that the retailer desires for each unit of resource input: floor space (sales per square foot of floor space), labor (sales per employee), and inventory (sales per dollar invested in inventory).

Productivity objectives are vehicles by which a retailer can program its business for high profit results. For instance, it would be impossible for a supermarket chain to achieve a respectable ROA while experiencing dismal space, labor, and merchandise productivity. In short, productivity is a key determinant of profit in retailing.

SOCIETAL OBJECTIVES Sometime in the early 1970s, a significant number of retailers began to establish societal objectives. Although generally not as specific or as quantitative as market and financial objectives, societal objectives highlight the retailer's concern with broader issues in our society. The five most frequently cited societal objectives are

1. employment objectives. Employment objectives relate to the provision of employment opportunities for the members of the retailer's community. Many times they are more specific, relating to hiring the handicapped, social minorities, or students.
2. payment of taxes. Paying taxes is the retailer's role in helping finance societal needs that the government deems appropriate.
3. consumer choice. A retailer may have as an objective to compete in such a fashion that the consumer will be given a real alternative. A retailer with such an objective desires to be a leader and innovator in merchandising and thus provide the consumer with choices that previously were not available in the trade area.
4. equity. An equity objective reflects the retailer's desire to treat the consumer fairly. The consumer will not be unnecessarily price-gouged in case of merchandise shortages. Consumer complaints will be handled quickly, fairly, and equitably. The retailer will inform the consumer, to the extent possible, of the strengths and weaknesses of its merchandise.
5. benefactor. The retailer may desire to underwrite certain community activities. For example, many department store retailers make meeting rooms available for civic groups to use for meetings. Other retailers help underwrite various performing arts with either cash donations or by hosting social events that in turn help draw customers to their stores.[8] Still others provide scholarships to help finance the education of the young. One of the best examples of a retailer with this objective is the late Milton Petrie, the founder and majority owner of Petrie Stores. Mr. Petrie had always been a generous individual, often sending checks to hard-luck cases that he learned about in the morning paper. In his will, he not only remembered 383 individuals with gifts ranging from $5,000 to $15 million; but the majority of his $800 million in assets was placed in a trust not to fund charitable institutions but to continue his "passion for helping needy individuals."[9]

PERSONAL OBJECTIVES The final set of objectives that retailers may establish is personal. Personal objectives can relate to the personal goals of any of the employees of the retail establishment. Generally, retailers tend to pursue three types of personal objectives.

1. self-gratification. Self-gratification has as its focus the needs and desires of the owners, managers, or employees of the firm to pursue what they truly want out of life. For example, individuals may have opened up a sporting goods store because they enjoyed being around athletically oriented people. These individuals may also be avid amateur golfers, and by operating a sporting goods store, they are able to combine work with pleasure. Basically, these individuals are experiencing and living the life they really wanted even though the profit potential may be higher in another line of trade.
2. status and respect. All humans strive for status and respect. In stating this type of objective, one recognizes that the owners, managers, or employees need status and respect in their community or within their circle of friends. Recognizing this need,

Personal objectives are often pursued in retailing, such as when a former professional athlete operates an athletic or sportswear store.

the retailer may, for example, give annual awards to outstanding employees. Or when promotions occur, favorable coverage may be sought in local newspapers or trade journals such as *Stores* or *Chain Store Age.*

3. power and authority. Objectives based on power and authority reflect the need of managers and other employees to be in positions of influence. Retailers may establish objectives that give buyers and department managers maximal flexibility to determine their own destiny. They are given the power and authority to allocate scarce resources such as space, dollars, and labor to achieve a profit objective. Having the power and authority to allocate resources makes many of these managers feel important and gives them a sense of pride when they excel because they know they controlled their own destiny.

Exhibit 2.2 is a synopsis of the market performance, financial performance, societal, and personal objectives that retailers can establish in the strategic planning process. Clearly revealed in this exhibit is the fact that all retail objectives, of whatever type, must be consistent with the overall mission of the retailer. The retailer's objectives must reinforce its mission.

To see how objectives relate to an organization's mission, let's now look at Record World's goals and objectives.

1. Open or acquire five to ten new stores over the next year.
2. Remodel six to eight stores over the next year.
3. Increase the operating profit margin in each store by 1 percent for each six-month period.
4. Increase video sales in existing stores by 20 percent over last year.
5. Improve sales in classical music by increasing merchandise productivity by 1 percent over the preceding year.
6. Improve the quality of promotion activities including in-store appearances, publicity, contests, cross-promotions, school promotions, and in-store circulars.

EXHIBIT 2.2	RETAIL OBJECTIVES

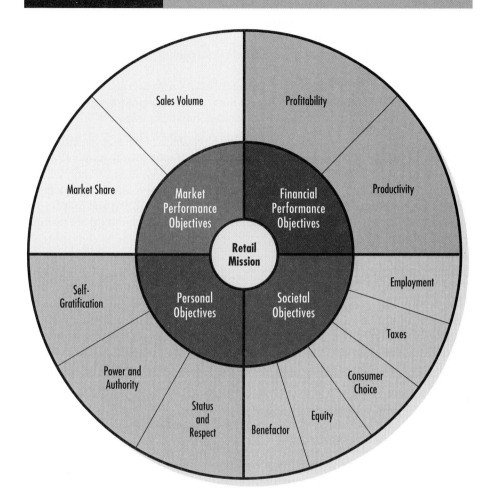

7. Increase awareness/recognition levels of consumers in newer market areas (i.e., Florida) equal to that in the New Jersey/Long Island area.

8. Improve teamwork among top-level executives, especially those at similar management levels.

9. Restructure the buying operation to better interact with other corporate activities.

10. Target 2 percent of each store's profits to the favorite local charity of the store manager.

11. Have handicapped applicants account for 10 percent of all new companywide hires.

12. Maintain labor costs between 7.5 and 9 percent of sales.

Notice how goal 3 did not just say that Record World wanted to increase operating profit margins but stated an amount that it wanted to increase operating profit margins by (1 percent) over each six-month period. To be effective, goals should identify what the company wants to accomplish, the level that it wants to achieve, and the time period involved. In other words, goals should be measurable and schedulable.

Dollar General's objectives and goals are fewer in number but no less directional:

1. To achieve increases in same store sales and, consistent with that primary objective, to open as many productive new stores as possible. There are many opportunities to do so in our 23-state market.
2. To reduce our overhead as a percentage of sales, enabling us to further sharpen our low everyday prices.
3. To increase the return on our largest financial asset—inventory.
4. To develop our "number 1" resource, human assets, to its fullest potential and to provide future management primarily by promotion from within.[10]

As shown above, objectives and goals should be established for each department or performance area in the business. In our example from Record World, goals and objectives 1, 2, 6, 7, 8, and 9 are market performance oriented; 3, 4, 5, and 12 are financial performance oriented; 10 and 11 are societal objectives; and 10 could be a personal objective (self-gratification) for the store managers. Dollar General's first and fourth goals and objectives are market performance oriented and the second and third are financial performance oriented.

STRATEGIES

Strategy

is a carefully designed plan for achieving the retailer's goals and objectives.

After developing a mission statement and establishing goals and objectives, a retailer must develop a strategy. A strategy is a carefully designed plan for achieving the retailer's goals and objectives. It is a course of action that when executed will produce the desired levels of performance. A major retail consulting firm has proposed that retailers can operate with as few as three strategies:[11]

1. Get as many consumers as possible into your store.
2. Convert these consumers into customers by having them purchase merchandise.
3. Do this at the lowest operating costs possible that are consistent with the level of service that your customers expect.

Although the above three strategies may seem too simple to be operational, they actually do summarize the tasks that every retailer must perform. Many retailers go further and use strategies that enable retailers to differentiate themselves from the competition to accomplish these three tasks.

However, one of the greatest failings in retailing entering the next decade is that too many retailers have concentrated on just one means of differentiation—price. Price promotions usually attract, but rarely hold, customers. The customers you gain with these promotions are just as apt to switch to another retailer when it cuts its price below your price. As a result, retailers have taught the consumer that if they wait, and in many cases this wait is only a matter of days, the merchandise desired will go on sale. Unless a retailer has substantially lower operating costs, such as Wal-Mart does in comparison with its competitors, this is a very dangerous strategy to use because it can easily be copied by the competition and will result in reducing profits or causing losses. Some better forms of differentiation for a retailer are

1. *physical differentiation of the product,* such as what Ann Taylor was known for with the high-quality fabric and stitching in its garments or Crate & Barrel for its brilliant and innovative merchandise that really catches the customer's eye.
2. *the selling process,* such as the way Nordstrom and Neiman-Marcus connect with their target customers with their excellent customer service.

Crate & Barrel differentiates itself from the competition by its brilliant and innovative merchandise that really catches the customer's eye.

3. *after-purchase satisfaction,* which some of the major retailers such as L.L. Bean, achieve with their "satisfaction guaranteed" programs that enable customers to return clothing after years of wear for a new one.

4. *locational,* which Dollar General excels at with it small-sized stores (6,000 square feet) in towns too small for the major chains to enter. The small size of their stores also gives the retailer advantages in negotiating leases, thus reducing their operating costs in comparison with those other chains.

5. *never being out of stock,* which means being in stock with regards to the sizes, colors, and styles that the target market expects the retailer to carry. This particularly applies to the category killers.

These means of differentiation will not only get more consumers into your store but will result in their buying more merchandise once they are in the store. Note also that in all these examples, the retailers are able to develop their own unique "niches" in the minds of the consumer and avoid price wars.

DOLLAR $ & ¢ENTS

Retailers that seek to differentiate themselves from the competition on something other than price will be higher performers.

SWOT ANALYSIS SHOWS WHY OUTBACK STEAKHOUSE HAS BEEN SUCCESSFUL

One of the most interesting areas of retailing to observe is the restaurant industry. This industry is highly competitive as restaurants open, shine briefly, and then die as low-wage employees take off while costs spiral and the restaurant's popularity and prices decline. One of the most successful restaurant operators to open during the past decade has been Outback Steakhouse. Here is what their SWOT analysis might look like, which provides an insight as to why Outback has been so successful. Outback positioned itself between the "low-end" 1960s-era "family steakhouses" such as Bonanza and Ponderosa with their $8.00 average tab per person and the white-tablecloth steakhouses with their $50.00-per-person tabs.

STRENGTHS

What are the major competitive advantages we have over the competition?

A "catchy name and atmosphere" that sets us apart from the competition.

Veteran managers at all stores as a result of requiring managers to have an ownership in their restaurant. This enables us to keep an entrepreneurial flame burning inside them. This is also supported by an unconventional decentralize management structure that results in an extremely low manager turnover (5.4 percent vs. a 30 to 40 percent industry average).

High wages for staff because we are only open for dinner. (Average ticket is $16 with bar tab, thus a typical table of four generates a tip of $10.00, or about $30 an hour in tips. This enables the chain to hire and retain only the best.)

What are we good at?

We have one of the highest cash flows in the industry.

What do customers perceive as our strong points?

High-quality steak in a clean atmosphere with excellent service/staff.

WEAKNESSES

What is the major competitive advantage that competitors have over us?

A few competitors that are perceived as being at the higher end of the market, such as Ruth's Chris and Del Frisco's Double Eagle, with a more formal white-tablecloth dining atmosphere. However, their prices really put them out of our market.

SWOT ANALYSIS

*SWOT Analysis
is the assessment of a retailer's strengths, weaknesses, opportunities, and threats.*

So how does a retailer develop a strategy to differentiate itself? This starts with an analysis of the retailer's strengths and weaknesses as well as the threats and opportunities that exist in the environment. This process, which is often referred to as SWOT analysis, involves the following:

STRENGTHS

What is (are) the major competitive advantage(s) we have over the competition? (This could be lower prices, better locations, better store personnel, etc.)

What are we good at? (This might be the ability to anticipate customer demands better than the competition so that the merchandise is there when the customer wants it, etc.)

What are competitors better at than we are?

Some restaurant operators such as Bonanza, Ponderosa, and Golden Corral have lower prices but not our quality and/or service. However, we have added "value items" (i.e., hamburgers) on the regular menu to attract some of these customers.

What are our major internal weaknesses?

Many competing restaurants operate in better locations in comparison with us. However, by not competing for the lunch crowd, we have no need to operate in high-rent areas. We can operate in lower-rent suburban areas where people are at night.

A feeling that some customers have expressed but isn't true—that we are rushing them to turn the tables faster. These customers want to enjoy a leisurely meal with friends and family. This is a problem because many other customers want that type of fast service.

OPPORTUNITIES

What favorable environmental trends exist that may benefit our firm?

The fact that steak remains the country's favorite entree.

A growing trend toward casual dining exists throughout the country.

What is the competition doing in our market?

Many older restaurants will soon be exiting the marketplace, and some may try to copy us as a means of survival.

Others such as Texas Land & Cattle Co., Velandi Ranch, and Lone Star Steakhouse have also targeted our market in recent years.

THREATS

What unfortunate environmental trends exist that may hurt our future performance?

Press reports warning consumers about the dangers of eating too much red meat.

An economic slowdown that has negatively affected sales at higher-end restaurants in recent years but hasn't yet reached the middle-priced types such as ours.

What do customers perceive as our strong points? (Customers might perceive that we offer the "best value for the dollar.")

WEAKNESSES

What is (are) the major competitive advantage(s) that competitors have over us? (Do they have lower prices, better locations, salespersons, etc.?)

What are competitors better at than we are? (Do they do a better job at merchandise selection or demand anticipation?)

What are our major internal weaknesses? (Do we do a poorer job in employee training, are our stores in need of remodeling, etc.?)

O PPORTUNITIES

What favorable environmental trends exist that may benefit our firm? (Is our market size growing, are family income levels rising in our market, is merchandise priced correctly for the target market, etc.?)

What is the competition doing in our market? (Are new firms entering or are existing firms leaving and what is the impact on us?)

What areas of business, that are closely related to ours, are undeveloped? (Is it possible for us to expand into a related field serving the same customers and take advantage of our good name in the marketplace?)

T HREATS

What unfortunate environmental trends exist that may hurt our future performance? (Has inflation caused consumers to become more price sensitive or has it prevented us from raising our prices to pass increasing costs on to consumers, etc.? How could our competitor's actions [price, new products, services, etc.], the entrance of new competitors, or the possible loss of suppliers hurt us.)

What technology is on the horizon that may soon have an impact on our firm? (Will some new electronic equipment soon replace our manual way of performing activities?)

In our Behind the Scenes box, we look at what could be the SWOT analysis for Outback Steakhouse, one of the most successful restaurant chains to open during the past decade. Not all SWOT analyses are so positive for a retailer. When a new management team took over Hardee's, they found a very negative situation.[12]

Now, the retailer is ready to develop some strategies to accomplish its objectives. Again, notice the close relationship between a retailer's goals and objectives and its strategies. Objectives indicate what the retailer wants to accomplish and strategies indicate how the retailer will attempt to accomplish those goals with the resources available.

A retail marketing strategy with strong financial elements must be developed. The retailer should have a fully developed marketing strategy, which should include

1. the specific target market. A target market is the group or groups of customers that the retailer is seeking to serve.
2. a location(s), which could either be a traditional store in a geographic space or a virtual store in cyberspace, that is consistent with the needs and wants of the desired target market.
3. the specific retail mix that the retailer intends to use to appeal to its target market to meet its financial objectives. The retail mix is the combination of merchandise, price, advertising and promotion, customer services and selling, location, and store layout and design that the retailer uses in satisfying the target market.

Target Market
is the group or group of customers that the retailer is seeking to serve.

Location
is the geographic space or cyberspace where the retailer conducts business.

Retail Mix
is the combination of merchandise, price, advertising and promotion, customer services and selling, location, and store layout and design that the retailer uses in satisfying the target market.

LO • 2
Describe the text's retail planning and management model, which explains the three tasks that a retailer must perform and how they lead to high performance results

RETAIL PLANNING AND MANAGEMENT

A retailer must engage in three types of planning and management tasks: (1) strategic planning, (2) operations management, and (3) administration of its resources (Exhibit 2.3). Each of these tasks is undertaken to achieve high performance results. At this point, you should take a few moments to examine this model.

EXHIBIT 2.3   RETAIL PLANNING AND MANAGEMENT MODEL

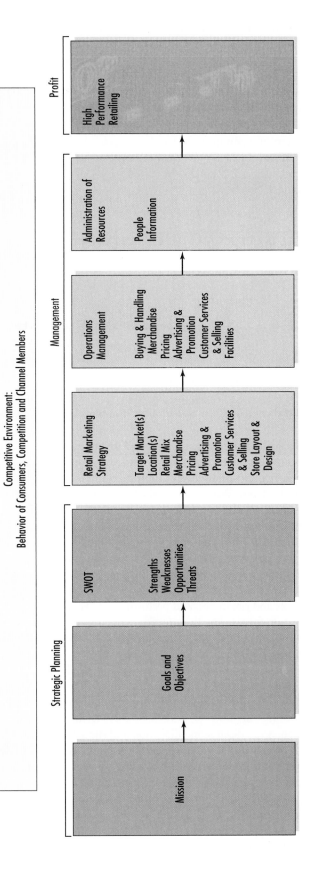

Competitive Environment:
Behavior of Consumers, Competition and Channel Members

Strategic Planning

Mission

Goals and
Objectives

SWOT

Strengths
Weaknesses
Opportunities
Threats

Retail Marketing
Strategy

Target Market(s)
Location(s)
Retail Mix
Merchandise
Pricing
Advertising &
Promotion
Customer Services
& Selling
Store Layout &
Design

Management

Operations
Management

Buying & Handling
Merchandise
Pricing
Advertising &
Promotion
Customer Services
& Selling
Facilities

Administration of
Resources

People
Information

Profit

High
Performance
Retailing

Social and Legal Environment:
Socioeconomic Environment, State of Technology, Legal System, Ethical Behavior

It was pointed out in Chapter 1 that this book would have an environmental orientation, a management planning orientation, a profit orientation, and a decision-making orientation. By looking at Exhibit 2.3, you will note that the environmental orientation is represented by the top and bottom parts of the exhibit; the management planning orientation by the center section (strategic planning, operations management, and administration) of the model that goes left to right; the profit orientation by demand for high performance results at the far right of the model; and the decision-making orientation by the all decisions that the retailer must make throughout this model.

STRATEGIC PLANNING

DOLLAR $ & C ENTS

Retailers who develop strategic plans are better able to withstand competitive onslaughts and thus will have better long-term performance.

Strategic planning, as pointed out at the beginning of the chapter, is concerned with how the retailer responds to the environment in an effort to establish a long-term course of action to follow. In principle, the retailer's strategic planning should best reflect the line(s) of trade in which the retailer will operate, the market(s) it will pursue, and the retail mix it will use. Remember, strategic planning requires a long-term commitment of resources by the retailer. As pointed out in our Winners & Losers box about Sears and Wards, an error in strategic planning can result in a decline in profitability, bankruptcy, or in this case, a loss of competitive position. However, effective strategic planning can help protect the retailer against competitive onslaughts.[13]

The initial steps in strategic planning are to define the firm's mission, establish goals and objectives, and perform a SWOT analysis. The next step is target market selection followed by the selection of an appropriate location(s). Of particular note is the fact that most established retailers have very little control over location decisions. A newly appointed manager for a chain department store could change promotional strategy, personnel, service levels, credit policies, and even prices but would in all likelihood be constrained by a long-term lease agreement. In fact, only the senior management of most chains is ever involved in locational decisions. For the small retailer just starting out, however, or retailers considering expansion, location is an important decision. A full discussion of location and site selection occurs in Chapter 7.

Following the target market selection and location decision is the development of the firm's retail mix. Retailers can best perform this strategic planning only after assessing the external environment. They should be looking for an opportunity to fulfill the needs of a defined group of consumers (i.e., their target market) in a method different from competition. In other words, retailers should strive to seek a differential advantage over the competition. Retailers will rarely discover a means of gaining a differential advantage over their competitors by merely reviewing their own internal

THE GENERAL'S GAMBLE PAYS OFF

Shortly after the end of World War II, the leaders of the nation's two largest general merchandise chains met for lunch at The Chicago Club. They had agreed to a frank discussion of what they saw ahead for their industry.

Sears's Robert E. Wood, a former Army general and supply coordinator during World War I, and Montgomery Wards's Sewell Avery had both spent the morning looking at their depleted warehouses and had to make plans for the future. However, before committing their resources in this highly uncertain time, they decided to consult with each other about their assessment of the economic environment.

Not only were both chains' warehouses empty because of war shortages and rationing programs, but Sears was in a cash bind because it had recently been forced to return $250 million to customers whose mail orders went unfilled due to these shortages.

Yet, based on their completely different assessments of the retailing environment, these two men were about to plot two completely different strategies that would change the course of retailing in the United States as well as the American landscape.

Mr. Avery bet that the American economy was on the verge of a depression. Avery concluded that because WWII was the greatest war ever, he thought that a depression worse than the one that occurred in the 1930s was due. He told "The General" that Wards was going to hunker down, reduce expenses, and build up its cash reserve to withstand the up-coming slowdown.

"The General" was far more optimistic about the economic situation. He sensed enormous pent-up consumer demand; at the time, General Motors was selling 1942 models as "new" because no newer model had been developed during the war. Wood wanted to warehouse merchandise (washing machines, tools, pots, pans, tires, and clothes) for this demand, not cash as Avery and many other smaller "mom and pop" retailers across the country were doing. In fact, Wood was so sure of this coming economic expansion that during the war when Sears couldn't actually do anything because of war-time shortages, he had assigned a top-level strategic planning team to work out an aggressive growth plan for implementation the moment the war ended. That's why he wanted to talk to Avery.

Shortly, after his luncheon meeting Wood made the difficult and risky decision to go full speed ahead with the merchandise replenishment and growth strategy. Not only was he going to fill his warehouses with merchandise but he was going make two other decisions that would soon vault Sears past the Great Atlantic & Pacific Tea Co. as the nation's largest retailer.

First, Sears was going to take a financial stake in its vendors. This would not only provide them with the needed liquidity to get going after the war, but it would ensure a source of future merchandise for Sears. Second, Wood began a major postwar expansion program that relocated more than 200 Sears stores from downtown city centers to the flourishing new suburbs. In addition, he added another 100 new stores in the suburbs. Sears was going to the shopper's homes and the shoppers came by the thousands to Sears's new stores, purchasing household supplies, tools, appliances, apparel, toys, and furniture. America's great baby boom was on, and Sears was the leader of this postwar retail growth.

Within five years Sears had doubled Wards in sales and was to be the nation's retailing leader until being passed by Wal-Mart in 1990. Wards would eventually thrive but never to the extent it had before Avery's fateful decision to play it safe.

SOURCE: For a more complete discussion of this famous event in retailing history, the reader may consult James Worthy, *Shaping An American Institution* (Urbana, IL: University of Illinois Press, 1984): 215–220.

operations or by focusing exclusively on the conventional industry structure. Strategic planning opportunities are to be found in the realities of a constantly changing environment. An effective retail strategy can only result from matching environmental forces with a retail marketing program that satisfies the customer better than anybody else can. For example, Woolworth's Foot Locker division has found success by concentrating on a very narrow segment of the shoe market, and Toys "Я" Us has remodeled its stores to eliminate the earlier warehouse look.

The major environmental forces that should be assessed were also profiled in Exhibit 2.3. Briefly these are

1. consumer behavior. The behavior of consumers will obviously have a significant impact on the retailer's future. Specifically, the retailer will need to understand the determinants of shopping behavior so that likely changes in that behavior can be identified and appropriate strategies developed.
2. competitor behavior. How competing retailers behave will have a major impact on the most appropriate strategy that the retailer should develop. Retailers must develop a competitive strategy that is not easily imitated.
3. channel behavior. The behavior of members of the retailer's distribution channel can have a significant impact on the retailer's future. For example, are certain channel members, such as manufacturers and wholesalers, establishing their own retail outlets to get rid of excess products? Or are wholesalers requiring larger minimum orders and offering less attractive credit terms? Behaviors such as these could have implications for the retailer's strategy.
4. socioeconomic environment. The retailer must understand how economic and demographic trends will influence revenues and costs in the future and adapt its strategy according to these changes.
5. technological environment. The technical frontiers of the retail system encompass new and better ways of performing standard retail functions. The retailer must always be aware of opportunities for improving operating efficiency.
6. legal and ethical environment. The retailer should be familiar with local, state, and federal regulations of the retail system. It must also understand evolving legal patterns to be able to design future retail strategies that are legally defensible. At the same time, the retailer must operate at the highest level of ethical behavior.

Detailed discussions of these forces are provided in Chapters 3 through 6. For now, you should realize that these external forces are uncontrollable by a single retailer but that threats emanating from these forces are often translated into opportunities by successful retailers. For example, Macy's once was an independent operation that catered to the working classes of New York City but now has become a trendy boutique store owned by Federated Department Stores catering to the top 25 percent of families.[14]

After reviewing its mission, objectives, environment, and developing its retail marketing strategy, the retailer should be able to develop alternative uses of resources to obtain the highest performance level. After determining which strategy will yield the best results, the retailer is now able to concentrate on operations and administrative management.

Operations Management *deals with activities directed at maximizing the efficiency of the retailer's use of resources. It is frequently referred to as day-to-day management.*

OPERATIONS MANAGEMENT

Operations management is concerned with maximizing the efficiency of the retailer's use of resources. Operations management converts resources into sales and profits. In other words, its aim is to maximize the performance of current operations.

Most of the retailer's time and energy is devoted to the day-to-day activity of operations management. Our Retail Planning and Management Model (Exhibit 2.3) shows that operations management involves managing the buying and handling of merchandise, pricing, advertising and promotion, customer services and selling, and facilities. All these activities require day-to-day attention. For example, the selling floor must be maintained, customers served, merchandise bought and handled, advertisements run, and pricing decisions made each and every day. In other words, operations management is running the store.

In Part IV, we focus on operations management, the real "guts" of retailing. In the first several years of a retailing career, your primary concern will be almost exclusively with the operations management side of retailing. The strategic planning and the administrative management will be handled by the senior executives. However, if you enter retailing via a small or medium-sized firm, you will be making administrative decisions, and even strategic ones, sooner. Nonetheless, when a retailer is able to do a good job at operations management, that is, efficiently using the resources available, then the retailer is said to be operations-effective.

ADMINISTRATION

Administration of resources involves the acquisition, maintenance, and control of resources that are necessary to carry out the retailer's strategy. It involves the structuring and designing of resources to maximize the retailer's performance potential. As shown in our model, the retailer is concerned with acquiring two primary categories of resources: personnel and informational. Everything is ultimately done by individuals who can do their jobs better with good information. Thus, people and information are the most important resources in retailing.

Part V is devoted to administrative management, with a separate chapter devoted to each type of resource. At this juncture, the essential point to remember is that a retailer can develop a well-conceived strategy with a good operations manager. However, if it does not know how to obtain the personnel or informational resources to put that strategy into practice, then all is wasted.

Administration of resources *involves the acquisition, maintenance, and control of resources that are necessary to carry out the retailer's strategy.*

DOLLAR $ & ¢ENTS

To be a high performance retailer, the retailer needs good strategic planning coupled with good operations and administration of resources.

HIGH PERFORMANCE RESULTS

The far-right portion of the retail planning and management model suggests that the cumulative effect of well-designed and executed strategic, operations, and administration plans will be the achievement of high performance results. Mistakes in any of these three areas will severely hamper the retailer's performance and prevent it from being among the leaders in its industry. For instance, in the 1980s The Limited was

EXHIBIT 2.4	THE SPM FOR SOME OF THE COUNTRY'S TOP RETAILERS				
RETAILER	NET PROFIT*/ NET SALES	TOTAL SALES/ TOTAL ASSETS	NET PROFIT*/ TOTAL ASSETS	TOTAL ASSETS/ NET WORTH	NET PROFIT*/ NET WORTH
CompUSA, Inc.	2.0%	4.2	8.3%	3.2	26.2%
Home Depot, Inc.	5.0%	2.3	11.4%	1.6	18.5%
LIMITED, Inc.	4.8%	2.2	10.5%	2.2	23.4%
May Department Stores	5.9%	1.3	7.6%	2.7	20.2%
McDonalds Corp.	15.0%	0.6	9.6%	2.0	19.5%
Safeway Inc.	2.7%	3.2	8.7%	4.6	39.8%
Walgreen Company	3.2%	3.5	11.1%	1.8	19.9%
Wal-Mart Stores, Inc.	2.9%	2.8	8.0%	2.4	19.3%

* Net Profit After Taxes

Based on corporate annual reports to stockholders of the respective firms and on computations by authors.

hailed as the most successful innovator in the retail apparel industry. However, by the mid-1990s, when middle-aged baby boomers already have all the clothes they need, its largest two divisions, Limited Stores and Lerner, began losing traditional customers. Due to poor strategic planning, another division, Express, started luring Limited's younger shoppers away with its hip sportswear at popular prices. In fact, Express was using the same appeal that made The Limited famous. The Limited also failed to note the change in consumer behavior that saw Lerner's core customer no longer shopping the malls but going to discounters for the same type of merchandise but at lower prices.

However, Sears, after a decade of declining performance, has in recent years been outperforming the competition. Sears attributes its recent success to changes made as a result of research studies of its customers. These studies revealed that despite the retailer's image as a great place to purchase tools and tires, more than 70 percent of its core customer base were women. Catering to this base, Sears remodeled its stores by widening the aisles, introducing softer lighting and fancier display presentation; improved the quality and fashionability of its apparel, and increased the space devoted to these lines by eliminating office and warehouse space; added cosmetics; improved customer service, complete with the introduction of two small employee-training booklets and the elimination of more than 29,000 pages of policies and procedures; and introduced a catchy, cohesive advertising campaign focused on the "softer side of Sears."[15]

The need to strive for high performance results is tied to the extremely competitive nature of retailing. It is still relatively easy to start a retail operation in comparison with starting a business in other industries. Thus new retail entrepreneurs are continually entering the marketplace. As a consequence of this increased competition, profit levels naturally deteriorate with more chains using the same format. A retailer is therefore well advised to set high financial performance objectives, so that if its planned results are not achieved, at least the retailer has a chance of achieving average operating results. The retailer that aims only for average results will often find itself having to confront a rather sobering financial performance. Exhibit 2.4 shows the SPM results for some of the countries' high-performance retailers. As a general rule of thumb, retailers should strive for the following goals when planning their SPM: net profit margin of 2.5 to 3.5 percent; asset turnover of 2.5 or 3.0 times; and financial leverage of 2.0 to 3.0 times. Achieving such goals would produce a return on assets of 8 to 10 percent and a 18 to 25 percent return on net worth.

STUDENT STUDY GUIDE

SUMMARY   This chapter seeks to explain the importance, as well as the use of, planning in retail management. Toward that end, a model of retail planning is introduced.

LO•1 EXPLAIN WHY STRATEGIC PLANNING IS SO IMPORTANT AND DESCRIBE ITS COMPONENTS.   Strategic planning and the financial performance of the retailer are intertwined. High performance results do not just happen; they are engineered through careful planning. Not all retailers can be leaders, but the ones that do will be those that did the best job of planning and managing. The components of strategic planning include development of a statement of purpose or mission for the firm, definition of specific goals and objectives for the firm, an identification of the retailer's strengths, weaknesses, opportunities, and threats, and development of basic strategies that will enable the firm to reach its objectives and fulfill its mission.

LO•2 DESCRIBE THE TEXT'S RETAIL PLANNING AND MANAGEMENT MODEL.   Retailers must engage in three types of planning and management tasks: strategic planning, operations management, and administration of resources. Strategic planning consists of matching the retailer's mission and goals with available opportunities. The retail marketing strategy that results from this consists of a target market, location(s), and retail mix. Operations management consists of planning the efficient use of available resources to manage the day-to-day operations of the firm successfully. Administration of resources involves planning for the acquisition of the human and information resources that will be necessary to carry out the retailer's strategy successfully. When retailers succeed at these three levels, they will achieve high performance results.

TERMS TO REMEMBER

planning
strategic planning
mission statement
goals and objectives
market performance objectives
financial performance objectives
societal objectives
personal objectives
net profit margin
asset turnover
return on assets (ROA)

financial leverage
return on net worth (RONW)
productivity objectives
strategy
SWOT analysis
target market
location
retail mix
operations management
administration of resources

REVIEW AND DISCUSSION QUESTIONS

LO•1 EXPLAIN WHY STRATEGIC PLANNING IS SO IMPORTANT AND DESCRIBE ITS COMPONENTS.

1. Why should a retailer always define its "line or type of business" in the most general terms. Doesn't this make planning more difficult?

2. How do the retail firm's mission statement and goals and objectives statement relate to the retailer's development of competitive strategy?

3. Most college students have unfavorable opinions of their bookstores. Suppose you were asked to advise your bookstore, what items would you consider in your SWOT analysis?

4. Is planning more important for a small retailer than for a large retailer? Explain your answer.

5. Can a mission statement be too narrow in scope? Too broad in scope? Explain your answer.

6. Sewell Motors, a automobile dealer based in Dallas, has the following mission statement: "We will provide the best vehicle sales and service experience for our customers. We will do this in a way that will foster the continuous improvement of our people and our company. We will be top performing, thoroughly professional and genuinely caring organization in all that we do." Would you change this mission statement? If so, why?

LO•2 DESCRIBE THE TEXT'S RETAIL PLANNING AND MANAGEMENT MODEL.

7. What are the major environmental forces that a retailer must face? Is any one more important than the others?

8. Does strategic planning become more or less important as uncertainty in the retailer's market increases?

9. When doing the planning and management tasks described in our model, does the retailer use creative thinking or analytical problem solving?

10. A wise person once said that "a good plan will always overcome poor execution of operations management and administration of resources." Agree or disagree with this statement and explain your reasoning. Use current examples, if possible, in your answer.

11. Why is it so important for a retailer to seek high performance results? Isn't it enough to seek to be above average?

SAMPLE TEST QUESTIONS

LO•1 WHEN A RETAILER SETS GOALS BASED ON A COMPARISON OF ITS ACTIONS AGAINST ITS COMPETITORS, IT IS ESTABLISHING _____ GOALS.

a. competitive analysis
b. market performance
c. geo-market performance
d. societal performance
e. financial performance

LO•2 THE BEST WAY FOR A RETAILER TO DIFFERENTIATE ITSELF IN THE EYES OF THE CONSUMER FROM THE COMPETITION IS TO

a. increase advertising of sale items
b. offer the lowest prices in town
c. always being in stock with the basic items that a customer would expect to find in your store

    d. not sell any of the brand names that the competition is selling

    e. increase its strategic planning effort

APPLICATIONS

WRITING AND SPEAKING EXERCISE

William Lewis owns several copy shops near college campuses, known as Quick Copies. In the past, he has run his shops very informally—he likes to claim that he is successful because he doesn't think too much and that he makes most of his decisions by the "seat of his pants." Over the past five years, profits at each shop have increased between 5 and 7 percent each year, and Lewis hasn't given much thought to changing his original plans for his copy shops. However, competitors are beginning to appear near some of his shops. As a result, Lewis thinks that it is time to develop a more structured approach for his business and asks you as part of your summer internship to research the strategic planning process. You are to prepare a memo on the basic steps and tasks that are involved in developing a strategic plan. Be sure to include in your memo a mission statement and a list of objectives that Quick Copies should seek to achieve.

RETAIL PROJECT

Go to the library and either look at the most recent annual reports for four or five of the Top 25 Retailers listed on the inside covers of this text or locate the 10-Ks of those firms on the Internet. (*Note:* Starting in 1997, all publicly held firms need to file their SEC 10-Ks, a more complete financial analysis of the firms performance, electronically. The address for looking up this information is **www.sec.gov/edgarhp.htm**). Using the SPM described in Exhibits 2.1 and 2.4, calculate your own SPM numbers for these retailers. Finally, after calculating these numbers, which retailer do you believe is the best at achieving financial superiority?

CASE | THE DANCER'S STUDIO

MaryJo Watkowski has always been involved with the performing arts in some manner since childhood. At a young age, she began taking ballet lessons and as a teenager began performing with a local dance troupe. MaryJo eventually auditioned for and was hired by a ballet company that performed throughout the United States. At the age of 24, MaryJo resigned from the company so that she could pursue a degree in arts administration on a full-time basis.

    MaryJo has recently completed her degree and has begun working for The Dancer's Studio, a company that operates seven dance instruction studios throughout Dallas. Before MaryJo's arrival, the owner of the company, Emmitt Helm, had conducted business based purely on intuition. Mr. Helm hired MaryJo in the hope that she could assist him in instituting a more formalized strategic planning process.

    In the past, customers seeking dance lessons from The Dancer's Studio had ranged from two years old to 62 years old. Mr. Helm encouraged the managing instructors at each of his studios not to turn anyone away—he believed that "a customer is a customer" and that the managers should be grateful for any business they could get. Most of the instructors that taught for The Dancer's Studio were trained in ballet, jazz, and to a limited extent, tap dancing. Yet, they often found themselves in situations in which meeting all the needs of the customers forced them to give lessons on types of dancing (e.g., Texas two-step, ballroom, contemporary, and folk) in which they were not skilled.

Over the past several years, approximately 55 percent of the studios' customers have been in the age range of five to 13 and have resided in the somewhat affluent suburbs that surround Dallas. Sales increased last year by $20,000, to a total of $200,000. Patrons seemed to have become aware of the studios primarily through word of mouth or from The Dancer's Studio's advertisement in the classified section of the area telephone books.

Although Mr. Helm has concentrated on his real estate development interests in the past, he now plans to devote his energies to developing the business and reputation of The Dancer's Studio. There are virtually no limitations on the financial resources that Mr. Helm will make available for this purpose.

Develop the following for MaryJo to present to Mr. Helm and the other members of the management team:

1. a mission statement for The Dancer's Studio
2. two possible market performance objectives and two feasible financial performance objectives
3. a statement describing (members of) the market that The Dancer's Studio will be targeting.

PLANNING YOUR OWN RETAIL BUSINESS

In the "planning your own retail business" exercise in Chapter 1, you learned how to estimate the net profits that your business might earn. You saw what would happen if your sales estimate was off by 10 percent. Now, it is time to analyze the dollar investment that you would need in assets to support your business and how you might finance these assets.

Your investment in assets would need to cover inventory, fixtures, equipment, cash, customer credit (i.e., accounts receivable), and perhaps other assets. These assets could be financed with debt or by investments that you make in the business or perhaps other investors.

Compute the strategic profit model ratios under the assumption that your first year sales are $500,000, net profit is $15,000, total investment in assets is $200,000, and the total debt to finance these assets is $100,000. (*Hint:* net worth is equal to total assets less debt.) What would happen to these ratios if net profit rose to $20,000?

NOTES

1. "Gloomy Days Are Here Again," *Business Week,* January 8, 1996: 103.
2. "Can Ann Taylor Dust Itself Off?" *New York Times,* December 2, 1995: 17.
3. "'Visioning' Missions Becomes Its Own Mission," *Wall Street Journal,* January 7, 1994: B1.
4. This was provided to the authors by Robert Kahn.
5. Reprinted with permission of Record World.
6. "A Stitch Too Far," *Forbes,* September 25, 1995: 12, 16.
7. Sidney Schoeffler, "Nine Basic Findings on Business Strategy," in *PIMS Letter, No. 1,* (Boston: The Strategic Planning Institute, 1977).
8. "Charity Begins at the Shopping Center," *Shopping Center Today,* September 1996: 17–18.
9. "He Sure Didn't Take It with Him," *New York Times,* November 20, 1994: F6.
10. *Dollar General,* Annual Report to Stockholders (1992).
11. *Maximizing Store Profitability* (Dublin, OH: Management Horizons, 1990).

12. "Hardee's Sees the Enemy—and It Is Them," *Wall Street Journal,* December 18, 1995: B1, B4.

13. Michael E. Porter, *Competitive Strategy: Techniques for Analyzing Industries and Competitors* (New York: The Free Press, 1980).

14. "Miracle or Mirage on 34th Street," *Fortune,* February 5, 1996: 84–90.

15. "Sears's Softer Side Paid Off in Hard Cash This Christmas," *Wall Street Journal,* January 5, 1996: 4B; "Retailers Call Sales in December Worst since '90–'91 Recession," *New York Times,* January 5, 1996: A1, C4; "Sears: In with the New . . . Out with the Old," *Fortune,* October 16, 1995: 96–98; and conversations with Sears executives.

THE RETAILING ENVIRONMENT

RETAIL CUSTOMERS

Smart Shopping for Busy People

Peapod has developed a retail strategy to appeal to the time-constrained household by offering home delivery of over 30,000 grocery items via an on-line computer system where customers can order from home.

In this chapter, we examine the effects of the socioeconomic environment on retailing. We discuss the effects of recent demographic, economic, and psychographic changes on consumer behavior and the implications of these changes for retailers. We conclude with the development of a consumer behavior model incorporating all these factors to describe overall shopping and buying practices.

OVERVIEW

After reading this chapter, you should be able to

LEARNING OBJECTIVES

1. explain the importance of demographic and household economic trends to the retail manager
2. list the macro-economic factors that retail managers should regularly monitor and describe their impact on retailing
3. explain the changing American lifestyle and its effect on retailing
4. discuss the consumer behavior model, including the key stages in the buying process and how they interact

INTRODUCTION

In the first chapter, we said that retailing consisted of the final activities and steps needed to place goods or services in the hands of the consumer. In the second chapter, we pointed out that to be a high performer, a retailer must make plans to be able to differentiate itself from the competition. In doing this, retail managers must realize, with the one possible exception of a supermarket, that a retailer can't serve all possible customer types. Some consumers will never shop at Wal-Mart and others will never shop at a Nordstrom or Neiman-Marcus. Therefore, before developing any plans, the successful retailer must first target a specific segment(s) of the overall market to serve and study the environmental factors affecting that segment(s), competition, the behavior of the other channel members, and legal and ethical factors. Only then can retailers develop the rest of their retail mix: the combination of location, merchandise assortment, price, promotion, customer services and selling, and selling facilities that best serves the segment(s) targeted by the retailer.

The easiest way for a retailers to differentiate themselves is to satisfy the customer's needs and wants better then the competition. This *customer satisfaction,* as we use the term, is different from customer service. Customer satisfaction is determined by whether the total shopping experience has met or exceeded the customer's expectation. If it has, the customer is said to have experienced a rewarding shopping experience. This is important because it costs four times as much to get a "new" customer into your store as it does to retain a current customer.

However, studies have shown that for most customers, not only in this country but worldwide, shopping experiences haven't always met their expectations, resulting in an unsatisfying experience.[1] A part of the shopping experience, in addition to the physical product or service offered for sale, is the services included as part of the offering. These customer services are the activities performed by the retailer that influence (1) the ease with which a potential customer can shop or learn about the store's offering, (2) the ease with which a transaction can be completed once the customer attempts to make a purchase, and (3) the customer's satisfaction with the purchase. These three elements are the pretransaction, transaction, and posttransaction components of customer service. Some common services provided by retailers, in addition to having the product on hand that satisfies the customer's needs and wants, include alterations, fitting rooms, delivery, bridal registries, check cashing, credit, in-home shopping, extended shopping hours, short check-out lines, gift wrapping, parking, layaway, and merchandise return privileges. It must be remembered that none of these services are actually part of the merchandise or service offered for sale; they merely entice the customers whom the retailer is targeting.

If the customer is dissatisfied with either the product (in the rest of this chapter, we use the term *product* to designate either the physical product or service offered for sale and the term *service* to refer to the services the retailer uses to facilitate that sale) offered or the services provided; then the customer is less likely to choose that retailer in the future, thus decreasing future sales. Knowing what products to carry, as well as determining which customer services to offer is a most challenging experience at best for retailers as they seek ways to improve the shopping experience. Imagine listening to a radio with no tuning or volume knob. The receiver picks up so many different signals, some in harmony, some in conflict, that the result coming through the speaker is noise. You're getting something, but you can't understand it. To make sense of the

---

Customer satisfaction *occurs when the total shopping experience of the customer has been met or exceeded.*

Customer services *include the activities the retailer performs that influence (1) the ease with which a potential customer can shop or learn about the store's offering, (2) the ease with which a transaction can be completed once the customer attempts to make a purchase, and (3) the customer's satisfaction with the purchase.*

Customer services such as this bridal registry department at Burdines Home Store in Miami, Florida, can be both highly profitable and a way to improve customer satisfaction.

confusing array of information, retailers use market segmentation techniques to "tune in" segments of the population, hoping to hear a series of clear messages that can then be constructed into some overall meaning.

Using market segmentation will enable us to examine ways to segment, or break down, America's heterogeneous consumer population into smaller, more homogeneous groups based on demographic, economic, psychographic, and behavioral characteristics. Doing this will help retailers understand who their customers are, how they think, and what they do, respectively, thus enabling them to build a meaningful picture of consumer needs, desires, perceptions, shopping behaviors, and the image these consumers have of the retailer in comparison with its competitors. Only by doing these activities can a retailer hope to satisfy the consumers' needs better than the competition. Failure to spot changes in the marketplace before the competition will result in the retailer only being able to react to what more sensitive retailers have already spotted and adapted to. Thus, although the high performance retailer will have spotted an emerging trend and made the necessary changes in their retail mix, the average retailer can only be a follower or "look-alike" retailer. And what differential advantage does a "me-too" retailer offer a consumer? No wonder so many retailers are currently facing financial difficulties.

Market segmentation *is the dividing of a heterogeneous consumer population into smaller, more homogeneous groups based on demographic, economic, psychographic, and behavioral characteristics.*

DOLLAR $ & ¢ENTS

Retailers who focus on understanding a well-defined customer niche and serving the customers in this niche with a differentiated offer will be higher performers than their competitors.

KEEPING MANAGEMENT IN TOUCH WITH THE CUSTOMER

The sportswear chain Decathlon, which operates more than 100 stores in France, Germany, Spain, and Italy and is a division of Marches Usines Auchan, recently inaugurated its new headquarters in France. The building is approximately 400,000 square feet, with all its divisions and offices—buying, research and development, workshops, staff restaurant, meeting rooms, travel agency etc.—arrayed around a store. There is only one entrance for the customers, the store staff, and the headquarters personnel; the latter of whom cannot avoid being informed as to what is happening in the store's departments. As a result of this setup, the buyers must spend some time on the floor with real live customers, and if they identify themselves to the customers, they most likely receive an earful about what could be improved.

This behavior is especially significant when it is compared with what so many other large retailers have done. They built corporate offices like palaces, full of sculpture, brass, and marble, far removed from their nearest retail outlet. And when top management does visit one of the chain's retail outlets, store management is warned ahead of the visit, thus preventing management from really understanding how the store appeals to the customer every day. Two notable exceptions to this behavior pattern were W.R. Howell of JCPenney's and the late Sam Walton. Both of these CEOs surprised employees with unannounced visits to their stores to make purchases.

SOURCE: Based on visits by the authors to headquarters of major U.S. retailers and on a column in the July 1995 issue of *Retailing Today,* Robert Kahn, editor, and used with his permission.

Our Global Retailing box describes how the management of France's Marches Usines Auchan, one of the world's largest retail chains, has ensured that its employees keep in touch with the customer.

Now, let's begin our study of the changing consumer to see how an understanding of demographic and household economic trends can help a retailer select a market segment to target.

Demographic variables
are those which can be used to describe the composition of a population.

DEMOGRAPHIC AND HOUSEHOLD ECONOMIC TRENDS

Retailers often find it useful to group consumers according to demographic variables, which characterize the composition of a population, such as population growth trends, age distributions, geography, and social trends. This is useful for two reasons: First, demographic data are often linked to marketplace needs, and second, demographic data are readily available and can easily be applied in analyzing markets.

POPULATION GROWTH

We begin by discussing the various population trends that affect retailing.[2] Retailers have long viewed an expanding population base as synonymous with growth in retail markets. Unfortunately, this growth rate in market size has been declining during the past three decades as families have fewer children. From a historical viewpoint, the fertility rate in the United States—the average number of births per woman—has

EXHIBIT 3.1	NUMBER OF BIRTHS BY YEAR

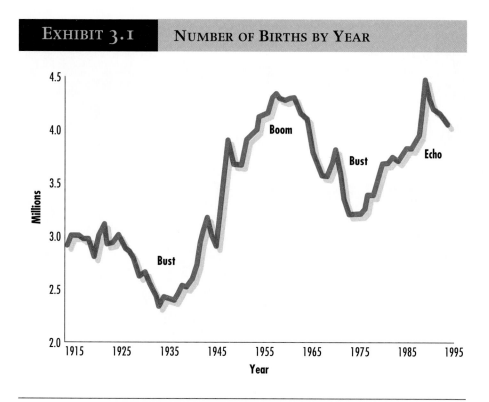

U.S. Bureau of the Census, Current Population Reports, P25-1095, P25-1130; Population Paper Listings PPL-41.

never been as low as its current level. The fertility rate was 2.2 children per woman in the 1930s, rose to 3.6 in the 1950s—the peak of the "baby boom era"—and dropped to 1.9 in 1995. It is expected to remain stable for the next 15 years. Despite this decreased birthrate, the total number of births, as shown in Exhibit 3.1, is still higher than it was a decade ago. This increase in births has been dubbed the "baby boomlet" or "echo." However, as the last stage of baby boomers, those born between 1946 and 1964, move beyond childbearing years, total childbirths are not expected to rise in the future.

Two other important influences on population growth are life expectancy rates and net immigration totals. As Americans live longer, the population base becomes larger. In 1970, the average life expectancies for a male and female at birth were 67 and 75 years, respectively; by year 2005, these figures are projected to increase to 74 and 81 years. Because immigration laws are under the control of Congress and difficult to predict, we will not project their impact on future population other than to report that the current estimate on future net immigration, both legal and illegal, is 880,000 a year, up from the 1989 estimate of 500,000. Of course, the economic conditions existing in this and other countries could greatly influence this figure.

IMPLICATIONS FOR RETAILERS   Overall, population is expected to grow but at a slower rate. If current average projections for the fertility, immigration, and death rates are correct, the U.S. population will increase 15 percent from 262 million in 1995 to 300 million in 2010. An increase in population growth will mean an increased demand for goods and services domestically, but nowhere near the 87 percent increase experienced over the past half century. The key to success will remain increasing productivity of

Live Well stores are capitalizing on the aging population by offering nutritional products and advice.

existing stores, taking market share from competitors, and managing gross margin through selling price and cost control.

AGE DISTRIBUTION

The age distribution of the U.S. population is changing significantly. The most significant change today is the bulge of baby boomers moving into their 40s and 50s. In the 1980s, the baby boomers with incomes and energy to "shop 'til they drop" fueled the rapidly expanding retail sector, especially with regard to apparel sales. But today, as the first wave of boomers reach age 55 and older—a demographic group known as the "gray market"—they are not spending as they did in the past. Many are aggressively saving for retirement because of increasing concern over the long-term viability of social security and uncertainty about corporate downsizing, which has left many mature adults unemployed. In the future, it is assumed that this first wave of boomers will spend less on apparel and clothing and more on medicine and recreation and focus more on security, good health, comfort, their homes, and safety.[3] Today's younger boomers, those between 40 and 55, are paying off mortgages and car loans and saving for their children's educations. Thus, as this large percentage of the country's population ages, it is expected to cut back on its retail spending.

DOLLAR $ & CENTS

Retailers who understand the implications of the country's age distribution will be more apt to identify opportunities to improve their performance.

"Baby busters," "Generation Xers," or "Children of the 80s"—those born between 1965 and 1978—are an often overlooked age group. Unlike the baby boomers, this age group is a declining percentage of the population. Today, there are 46 million of these consumers, yet as we point out later in this chapter, this is the most diverse-behaving age group in U.S. history. No wonder many retailing executives, themselves baby boomers, claim not to be able to understand this age group.

IMPLICATIONS FOR RETAILERS The most significant effect of an aging population is negative for retailers because, especially with regards to boomers, their big spending years are behind them. Retailers must remember what motivates consumers to spend money. Younger adults are by their very nature acquisition-oriented. These first-time renters and home buyers need to acquire material objects and usually judge their progress by such possessions. Older adults tend to conserve what they have already acquired. Thus, as the population ages, a significant driving force for total economic growth dries up.

DOLLAR $ & ¢ENTS

In view of the fact that as consumers age they change their spending habits, the high performance retailers of the next decade will be those that best adapt to these changes.

Also, because different retailers tend to serve different age groups, the changing distribution of the U.S. population poses many challenges and opportunities. Retailers should be aware of what was pointed out above—consumers older than 50, the first wave of baby boomers, tend to focus more on their families and finances than those in other age groups. They also spend more on medical services and travel. Thus, the products and services that appealed to these older consumers as free-spending younger consumers will not necessarily be the ones that appeal to them now as grandparents, managers, and home owners. In addition, this older market is expected to use the services of others more. For example, in announcing the closure of some Western Auto stores, an executive of the chain noted that "the DIY (do-it-yourself) market is probably getting a little soft. There are now more people over 30 than under 30, and as they get older, more of them are becoming 'do-it-for-me's."[4]

The "graying of America" will have enormous consequences for business in general, not just retailing, as most older consumers are skeptical and uninterested in shopping. Retailers must be able to speak the older consumer's language and not talk down to or patronize them, avoid tendencies of "phoney friendliness," and in a tactful manner recognize that as they age, they have a declining ability to deal with spatial relationships.[5]

However, it is doubtful that the baby boomers reaching 50 will behave as their parents did a generation before them. Retailers who assume the baby boomer will behave as their parents will be mistaken. A 50-year-old in 2005 will not act like a 50-year-old in 1985. In fact, they may act like a 30-year-old in 1985 (which is what they were), just older and wiser. Many of these "Pepsi Generation" types will probably enter the gray market kicking and screaming. They will demand that retailers embrace their values, such as youthfulness and invincibility, no matter what the product: food, insurance, or medicine.[6]

Micromarketing involves tailoring merchandise in each store to neighborhood preferences, such as this supermarket in Los Angeles, which is merchandised to appeal to the Hispanic shopper.

Therefore, besides the increase in health care services and travel, restaurants (where the older-than-60 category accounts for more than 30 percent of the breakfast and dinner trade) will have to consider such items as the design of their tables and seats; financial service firms will have to reconsider their product offerings to this fixed-income category of consumers; malls will offer valet parking and lounges with concierge services that not only make shopping easier but make the shopper feel pampered;[7] and retailers in general will have to use bigger print, brighter parking lots, and fewer displays blocking store aisles, as well as rethink the way they portray and target senior citizens in their advertising.

GEOGRAPHIC SHIFTS

The location of consumers in relation to the retailer often affects how they buy. In this section, we take a closer look at the geographic patterns of consumers.

SHIFTING GEOGRAPHIC CENTERS
Retailers should be concerned not only with the number of people and their ages but also with where they reside. Consumers, especially as they get older, will not travel great distances to make retail purchases. Consumers want convenience and will therefore patronize local retail outlets.

Because the U.S. population for the past 200 years has been moving toward the West and the South, growth opportunities in retailing should be greatest in these areas. Over the past half century, the South, now with 35 percent of the country's population versus 31 percent in 1960, and the West, now with 22 percent versus 16 percent, grew as the other two regions, Midwest (24 vs. 29 percent) and Northeast

(20 vs. 25 percent), declined in population share. Demographers expect that this trend will continue.

IMPLICATIONS FOR RETAILERS This changing geographic shift means northeastern and midwestern retailers are experiencing slower growth, and national retailers are adding stores and distribution centers (warehouses) in the South and West. However, one of the biggest mistakes that retailers make is to assume that all the consumers in a certain geographic area have the same purchasing habits. Exhibit 3.2 shows that not all Texans are alike in their product usage. In fact, the same differences have been found to occur in different parts of the same city. As a result, many of the leading retailers, such as Target and Wal-Mart, have developed "micromarketing" merchandising strategies. Micromarketing involves tailoring merchandise in each store to the preferences of its neighborhood.[8] This is made possible by the use of computer software programs that match neighborhood demographics with product demand.

Micromarketing
is the tailoring of merchandise in each store to the preferences of its neighborhood.

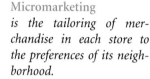
DOLLAR$ & ¢ENTS

Retailers who develop micromarketing merchandising strategies will have higher performance.

URBAN CENTERS Most of the U.S. population resides in freestanding urban population centers with populations greater than 50,000, which the U.S. Census Bureau calls metropolitan statistical areas (MSAs). The proportion of the population residing in these cities has increased dramatically, from 64 percent in 1950 to more than 75 percent today. The 1990 census showed that three-fourths of the U.S. population was concentrated into 3 percent of the land. This migration to MSAs, however, is directed more to suburban than central city areas.

Metropolitan statistical areas
are freestanding urban areas with population in excess of 50,000.

IMPLICATIONS FOR RETAILERS Every shift in population patterns of consumers has major implications for retailers, especially regarding where expenditures are made for household products. Although these recent shifts have resulted in a decline in downtown retail sales, sales increases in malls and free-standing suburban locations have more than made up for any decline.

However, there are opportunities for retailers in the smaller markets. During the past decade, retailers have witnessed a rapid growth in retail activity in secondary markets, areas with populations less than 50,000. Historically, most chain retailers have ignored these markets. Secondary markets are also attractive because of the low level of retail competition, lower building costs, cheaper labor, and fewer building and zoning regulations. But as MSAs began to stabilize, secondary markets became more attractive. Some retailers have been successful in moving into small-town America as our Winners & Losers box indicates.

EXHIBIT 3.2	TEXAS CONSUMERS PERCENTAGE OF NATIONAL AVERAGE USAGE			
PRODUCT	DALLAS FORT WORTH	HOUSTON	SAN ANTONIO CORPUS CHRISTI	WEST TEXAS
Biscuits/Dough	148%	122%	103%	85%
Butter	51%	57%	39%	57%
Fresh Eggs	94%	112%	141%	110%
Juice/RFG	74%	104%	76%	66%
Lard	26%	121%	*	419%
Canned Ham	39%	21%	22%	28%
Sausage	134%	179%	219%	73%
Baked Beans	82%	76%	51%	60%
Cocktail Mixes	118%	79%	82%	112%
Pasta	71%	80%	72%	76%
Rice/Popcorn Cakes	84%	69%	58%	73%
Cosmetics	237%	133%	329%	221%
Cold/Sinus Tab/ Cough Drops	157%	113%	125%	105%
Deodorant	119%	118%	125%	86%
Hair Coloring	137%	122%	238%	130%
Laxatives	152%	116%	164%	117%
Cat Food	88%	73%	81%	67%
Diapers	115%	135%	160%	74%
Facial Tissue	82%	66%	64%	78%
Paper Napkins	71%	74%	78%	68%
Motor Oil	112%	92%	279%	114%
Shoe Polish & Accessories	147%	145%	171%	147%
Tape	163%	105%	175%	149%
Hosiery	164%	126%	156%	110%

* Not measured in this market.

SOURCE: Used with the permission of Information Resources, Inc.

MOBILITY   In many countries, people are born, raised, married, widowed, and die in the same city or immediate geographic area. Although this was once true in the United States, it certainly is not true of contemporary America. Typically, Americans change residence about a dozen times in a lifetime. This is twice the rate as for the British and French and four times as often as the Irish. A major factor for this heightened mobility is the country's divorce rate.[9]

IMPLICATIONS FOR RETAILERS   A recent study regarding mobility has found that in almost half of large families in which the children don't go to college, one child will live within five miles of the parent(s) when the parent(s) reach age 60 and in more than three-quarters of the cases within 50 miles of the parents.[10]

SMALL REGIONAL DISCOUNT CHAINS CAN BE SUCCESSFUL IF THEY CHOOSE THEIR LOCATIONS CAREFULLY

As the national chains expand by entering markets usually held by regional chains, many of these smaller chains have been forced to close their doors. One retailer who hasn't is Omaha-based Pamida. In recent years, Pamida, with annual sales of $750 million, has come to grips with its expenses and prepared itself for the stiffer competition of the national chains. In doing so, the chain has proved that there is still a place for regional discounters in the marketplace if they choose their locations carefully.

With its new prototype 42,500-square-foot stores, which is only a quarter of the size of a national chain's supercenter, Pamida has found success by relocating to rural midwestern towns of 10,000 to 15,000. By choosing such locations, they don't have to face the Wal-Marts, Targets, and Kmarts storefront to storefront. For example, in 1992 Pamida competed with Wal-Mart in 28 percent of its markets versus only 16 percent today. By locating in these smaller markets first, Pamida has developed a base of customer loyalty and made it difficult for a larger chain to enter and fight over market share. With the majority of its sales coming from convenience goods (underwear, hardgoods, toothpaste, socks, snacks, etc.), Pamida, with low prices and national brands, has given its customers a good reason not to drive 20 to 30 miles to a much larger national chain operation.

However, what has made Pamida successful is that it knows how to compete with its limited floor space in small towns. A couple of key illustrations are

1. Because many people are willing to drive great distances to save money on prescription drugs, the chain has in-store pharmacies in 40 stores. These competitive-priced pharmacies give customers a reason to come back consistently, day after day.

2. Without disregarding its more traditional hard-goods lines, Pamida has increased the percentage of floor space devoted to ready-to-wear in its prototypes to 45 from the 25 percent in its older stores. This additional space enabled the firm to stress its selection of daily wear and avoid the more competitive dress wear in which the national chains had an advantage.

3. Home furnishings, with its higher margins, have been moved into the center core of the store with stationery, domestics, and RTA (ready-to-assemble) furniture.

4. Pamida has invested millions in updating its information systems technology, which allows store managers to use information to help them make better decisions. In the past, Pamida had the problem of most regional chains: Their buyers and store managers knew how to buy the right merchandise, and how to display it, and reorder it if it was selling; however, they were lost when it came to reacting to merchandise that wasn't moving. Now, with the new information system they could spot trends and react immediately without calling Omaha.

SOURCE: Based on "Pamida's Focus: Small Towns in a Big Way," *Discount Merchandiser*, December 1995: 20–23 and the author's experience with the firm.

Thus, in view of the recent trends toward higher education, which is discussed next and results in more job variations, retailers can only expect that mobility will increase. This presents a problem because retailers tend to serve local markets and tend to cater to well-defined demographic groups. If the population moves, the retailer may find that its target market no longer resides in its immediate area. Likewise, retailers in areas undergoing population growth will want to be prepared to serve these new consumers as many retail-oriented decisions will have to be made quickly. After a move, consumers must locate new sources for food, clothing, household goods, and recreation. This presents an advantage for chain operations in that a consumer moving from

| EXHIBIT 3.3 | U.S. EDUCATIONAL LEVELS |

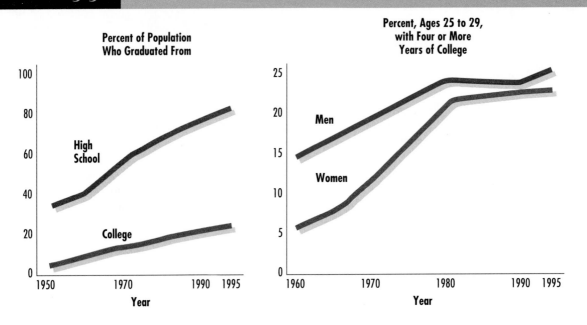

U.S. Bureau of the Census, Statistical Abstract of the United States: 1996 (116th edition) Washington, D.C., 1996. Table 242.

Des Moines, Iowa, to New Orleans, Louisiana, knows what to expect at a Sears, Target, Casual Corner, Foot Locker, or Pizza Hut.

SOCIAL TRENDS

In this section, we continue our examination of demographic factors affecting the modern retailer by looking at several social trends: the increasing level of educational attainment, the state of marriage and divorce, and the makeup of the American household.

EDUCATION   The education level of the average American is increasing. Exhibit 3.3 shows that in 1995, 23 percent of Americans older than age 25 had a college degree. The "baby boomers," those between the ages 36 and 54 in year 2000, are the most educated generation ever. Over one in four has completed four years of college.

IMPLICATIONS FOR RETAILERS   Educational attainment is the single most reliable indicator of a person's income potential, attitudes, and spending habits. Thus, college-educated consumers differ in their buying behavior from other workers of the same age and income levels. They are more alert to price, quality, and advertised claims. However, often overlooked when using education to segment the marketplace are the 27 million Americans older than the age of 25 who have some college experience but not a degree. In many ways, people with some college best describe the term *average* American. They have more money than high school graduates but less than college graduates. They also fall between the groups in their propensity to shop in department stores, spend on apparel, buy new cars, travel, read books, and watch television.[11]

Retailers such as the Pottery Barn appeal largely to single households or young couples without children.

Overall, as shown in Exhibit 3.4, households headed by people with some college spend 16 percent more than those headed by high school graduates and 29 percent less than those headed by college graduates.

Because education levels for the population, in aggregate, are expected to continue to rise, retailers can expect consumers to become increasingly sophisticated, discriminating, and independent in their search for consumer products. They will also demand a sales staff capable of intelligently dealing with their needs and wants.

Education also is a key determinant of the use of the Internet for shopping. Today's middle-aged consumers grew up with the computer and feel comfortable with it. With their higher level of education, they are more prone to electronically shop because they don't need assurances or hand-holding that some retailers provide. This may present problems for many traditional sellers of services. For example, travel agencies may be left out of the loop as cyber shoppers "surf the net" to shop for airline tickets, hotel rooms, rental cars, and cruises.

STATE OF MARRIAGE   A relatively new social phenomenon has occurred during the past quarter century. In 1970, less than 10 percent of the U.S. male population between the ages of 30 and 34 had never married and just more than 6 percent of the female population had never married. In 1995, as shown in Exhibit 3.5, these percentages have increased to 28 and 19 percent, respectively. Married couples are one of the slowest-growing household types, not only in this country but worldwide. Not only are some persons choosing not to marry but many are postponing marriage; some, however, may have postponed marriage too long, to a point at which some won't find a spouse. Even women who have been married once are delaying their remarriages longer than ever.

IMPLICATIONS FOR RETAILERS   For the retailer, this trend toward single individual households presents many opportunities because the need for a larger number of smaller-sized houses complete with home furnishings will occur. This is especially true for the young adult market. The retailer's store hours may also require an adjustment

EXHIBIT 3.4	EDUCATION AND SPENDING

Some college households fall between high school graduates and college graduates in most spending categories, but they spend less than both groups on health care.

(number of consumer units in thousands, after-tax income, and average annual expenditures by category, by education of reference person, 1992)

	ALL	LESS THAN HIGH SCHOOL	HIGH SCHOOL GRADUATE	SOME COLLEGE NO DEGREE	COLLEGE GRADUATE
Consumer units	100,019	24,191	29,622	23,499	22,706
Income after taxes	$30,786	$17,741	$28,115	$30,639	$48,246
Total spending	$29,846	$18,240	$26,924	$31,221	$44,237
Food	$4,273	$3,231	$4,129	$4,353	$5,340
Food at home	2,643	2,403	2,669	2,509	2,950
Food away from home	1,631	828	1,460	1,844	2,391
Housing	9,477	5,920	8,340	9,751	14,393
Shelter	5,411	3,159	4,549	5,678	8,658
Utilities/public services/fuels	1,984	1,693	2,010	1,927	2,318
Household operations	487	201	354	462	990
Housekeeping supplies	433	305	400	448	574
Furnishings/equipment	1,162	561	1,027	1,236	1,852
Apparel and services	1,710	922	1,397	1,877	2,705
Men's and boys'	450	220	344	520	736
Women's and girls'	680	341	564	743	1082
Children under 2	78	62	83	76	87
Footwear	231	177	208	229	311
Other products/services	272	122	198	309	488
Transportation	5,228	3,207	5,188	5,739	6,901
Vehicle purchase (net outlay)	2,189	1,271	2,269	2,494	2,745
Gasoline and motor oil	973	749	1,016	1,027	1,101
Other vehicle expenses	1,776	1,052	1,694	1,912	2,507
Public transportation	290	135	209	306	547
Health care	1,634	1,515	1,521	1,516	2,035
Health insurance	725	689	733	650	833
Medical services	533	393	442	533	801
Drugs and medical supplies	376	432	346	333	402
Entertainment	1,500	680	1,338	1,670	2,398
Personal care	387	237	361	433	515
Reading	162	76	138	169	276
Education	426	119	215	579	868
Alcohol	301	149	252	366	441
Tobacco and smoking supplies	275	306	360	241	165
Miscellaneous*	765	405	684	853	1,155
Cash contributions	958	393	634	905	2,039
Personal Insurance/pensions	2,750	1,081	2,367	2,770	5,006

* Includes accounting, banking, and legal fees, funeral expenses; and other personal services.

SOURCE: 1992 Consumer Expenditure Survey, Bureau of Labor Statistics

EXHIBIT 3.5	THE "NEVER MARRIEDS"				
PERCENT OF MEN NEVER MARRIED			PERCENT OF WOMEN NEVER MARRIED		
YEAR	AGE 20 TO 24	PERCENT	YEAR	AGE 20 TO 24	PERCENT
1970		54.7	1970		35.8
1980		68.8	1980		50.2
1990		79.3	1990		62.8
1995		80.7	1995		66.8
	25 TO 29			25 TO 29	
1970		19.1	1970		10.5
1980		33.1	1980		20.9
1990		45.2	1990		31.1
1995		51.0	1995		35.3
	30 TO 34			30 TO 34	
1970		9.4	1970		6.2
1980		15.9	1980		9.5
1990		27.0	1990		16.4
1995		28.2	1995		19.0
	35 TO 39			35 TO 39	
1970		7.2	1970		5.4
1980		7.8	1980		6.2
1990		14.7	1990		10.4
1995		20.3	1995		12.6

SOURCE: U.S. Bureau of the Census, Statistical Abstract of the United States: 1996 (116th edition) Washington, D.C., 1996. Table 54.

to accommodate the needs of this market. Finally, despite a decline in the number of marriages, the purchasing done by newly married couples will still present significant opportunities for retailers of home furnishings and appliances.

DIVORCE   Since 1960, the divorce rate has increased by 250 percent. It may be interesting at this point to review the findings of Professor Gary Becker of the University of Chicago. Professor Becker was awarded the 1992 Nobel Prize in economics for his 1981 book *A Treatise on the Family*. Becker theorized that families, just like businesses, rationally make decisions that maximize benefits. The theory suggests that in the traditional family, working husbands and stay-at-home wives each performed labor that, when combined, provided the greatest payoff for the time involved. However, as women's wages rose, it became more profitable for them to enter the labor force. As a result, spouses became less dependent on each other and divorces increased.[12]

IMPLICATIONS FOR RETAILERS   When a divorce occurs, many retail purchases are stimulated. A second household, quite similar to that of the never-married individual,

With the rapid growth of women in the labor force and more time constraints, households are finding stores such as Boston Market a good place to shop for home meal replacement.

is formed almost immediately. These new households need certain items such as furniture and kitchen appliances, televisions and stereos, and even linens. Once settled into their new homes, divorce may affect the way individuals shop. Time will become even more critical, as we discuss below.

MAKEUP OF AMERICAN HOUSEHOLDS

Because households are the basic consumer unit for most products, household growth and consumer demand go together. Yet, because of the differing sizes and habits of various generations, the change in the makeup of households is notoriously hard to predict. The number of households without children increased 27 percent in the 1970s, 14 percent in the 1980s, and only 6 percent between 1990 and 1995. As shown by Exhibit 3.6, current estimates are that these households will increase by 11 percent through the year 2000 and remain flat through 2010.

Some interesting trends have occurred over the past two decades. For example, between 1975 and 1995 the number of individuals living alone ("home-aloners") increased by 70 percent. This trend, which represented nearly one-fourth of all households, is the result of an increased desire for privacy, an increase in young adults delaying marriage, an increase in never-marrieds, and a large increase in the number of persons who live alone after the death of a spouse. Also, the number of unmarried couples ("mingles") increased by 82 percent since the mid-1970s. This trend, although it represents only 5 percent of all couple-households, is significant to the retailer because it represents a purchasing unit that is hard to understand by conventional household or family norms. The retailer, as well as the social scientist, has little knowledge of how joint decision making occurs or does not occur in such households.

Finally, there is one more interesting facet about the changing American household formation: the "boomerang effect"—so called because the parents think the

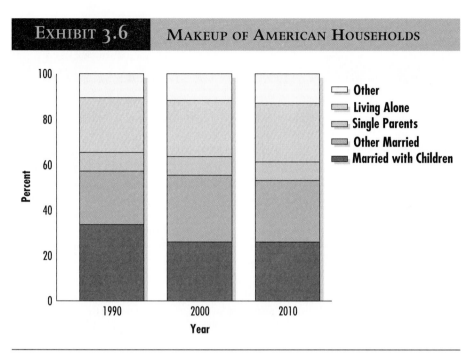

EXHIBIT 3.6 **MAKEUP OF AMERICAN HOUSEHOLDS**

SOURCE: U.S. Bureau of the Census, Statistical Abstract of the United States: 1996 (116th edition) Washington, D.C., 1996. Based on data contained in Tables 60, 61, 66, 67, 68.

children have left for good, but they just keep coming back. Between now and the year 2010, it is estimated that 40 percent of children will return to live with their parents after they have previously left. Although this projection is extremely sensitive to future economic conditions, several factors will account for the projected 7 million boomerang households in 2010: individuals who marry in their twenties are just as likely to divorce as those who marry as teens, high school dropouts will not be able to find permanent work, and finally the length of time needed to complete a college degree has been increasing to nearly 6 years.

IMPLICATIONS FOR RETAILERS Today, the combination of "home-aloners," "mingles," "singles," and "dinks" (dual-income, no-kids households) accounts for nearly 75 percent of all U.S. households. This market is not concerned about "back-to-school" sales and other traditional family-oriented retail activities. This segment of the market is more interested in CD players, high social image, merchandise, and gourmet foods. However, it is important that retailers recognize the differences in this market. Younger women will normally spend more on candy and shoes, and men will spend more on alcohol, cars, and eating out. As they age, women will begin to spend more than men on cars and entertainment and men will remain the best customers for eating out. This older segment of the single household market will require special attention from retailers entering the 21st century. After all, between now and the year 2005, the "wild and crazy single guys" of the 1980s will turn into "tired and pudgy older guys" who no longer live as college students. As a result of better health habits, this group will live longer and develop other special needs.[13]

As you can see in our second Global Retailing box, this changing structure in the makeup of households is not just an American trend but a worldwide trend.

WORLDWIDE CHANGES IN HOUSEHOLD STRUCTURE

The United States isn't the only country in which nontraditional households are becoming mainstream. Retailers in other developed countries are facing similar trends.

For example, the rise in the number of single parents, unmarried couples, and people living alone is common to most countries in the developed world. The difference is in the pace at which these trends are progressing.

Four main factors have changed the makeup of households and families in the past two decades: Women are having fewer children, more women are having children out of wedlock, populations are aging, and marriage is down while divorce is up.

Japan remains the most traditional of the developed nations, with low rates of divorce and low rates of out-of-wedlock births. It also has the largest share of married couples. Sweden and Germany have the largest shares of single-person households, in part because they have older populations.

Scandinavia has been setting the pace for out-of-wedlock births and cohabitation. Sweden and Denmark have the largest shares of births to unmarried women, yet they don't have the highest shares of single parents, because many unmarried mothers in these countries live with partners.

It's not clear which country has the highest shares of mingles, or cohabitating couples, because some countries now include them with married couples in official household statistics. One estimate shows that virtually all young Swedes cohabitate before they marry.

The United States tops the list for single parents, partly because of high divorce rates but also because American single parents are more likely to be young, never-married women on their own, rather than cohabitaters.

HOUSEHOLD ECONOMIC TRENDS

In this section, we look at the effect of income growth, the declining rate of personal savings, the increase in the number of working women on the modern retailer, and the widespread use of credit in our economy.

INCOME GROWTH   In the mid-1990s, the median household income was slightly over $32,000, which after adjusting for inflation was up less than 4 percent since 1980. As incomes rise, more families can afford to spend more on the good things of life. But this income increase has not been shared equally by all age groups. While income for households headed by someone younger than age 25 fell by 30 percent during the 1980s, it grew 15 percent in households headed by people age 25 to 34, just keeping pace with inflation. But income grew rapidly for middle-age households nearing their peak earning years. Income in households headed by 35- to 44-year-olds grew by 51 percent, and just as impressively in households headed by persons aged 44 to 54. Households headed by 55- to 64-year-olds, however, experienced a 2 percent decline over the past decade, a result of the trend toward early retirement caused in part by the recession and wave of corporate downsizing of the early 1990s.

There has also been, as shown in Exhibit 3.7, a shifting of incomes among the various classes of Americans. The upper segments of Americans now have a higher share of the nation's aggregate income in comparison with 1970. Today, the top fifth of all

EXHIBIT 3.7	SHARE OF AGGREGATE INCOME RECEIVED BY EACH FIFTH AND THE TOP 5 PERCENT OF U.S. HOUSEHOLDS, 1970–1994					
YEAR	LOWEST FIFTH	SECOND FIFTH	THIRD FIFTH	FOURTH FIFTH	HIGHEST FIFTH	TOP 5%
1994	4.2	10.0	15.7	23.3	46.9	20.1
1990	4.5	10.7	16.6	24.1	44.2	17.1
1980	5.1	11.6	17.5	24.3	41.6	15.3
1970	5.4	12.2	17.6	23.8	40.9	15.6

SOURCE: U.S. Bureau of the Census, Statistical Abstract of the United States: 1996 (116th edition) Washington, D.C., 1996. Table 714.

households by income level accounts for almost 47 percent, up from 41 percent in 1970, of the nation's income whereas the bottom two-fifths, or lowest 40 percent of the population, are earning only a seventh (14.2 percent) of the nation's income, down from 17.6 percent in 1970. Thus, it appears that the rich are getting richer and the poor are getting poorer. However, this is in part misleading because income mobility in the United States is high. A significant proportion of the lowest income households move up the income scale over a 10-year period, and similarly a significant proportion of the richest households move down the income scale over a 10-year period.

IMPLICATIONS FOR RETAILERS   The imbalance in income growth across households has created increased demand for value-oriented retailers such as discounters and manufacturers' outlets. At the same time this explains why many of the upscale retailers (e.g., Macy's, Nordstrom, and Neiman-Marcus) have also fared well.

Disposable income *is personal income less personal taxes.*

Discretionary income *is disposable income minus the money needed for necessities to sustain life.*

Economists tend to view income from two different perspectives: disposable and discretionary. Disposable income is simply all personal income less personal taxes. For most consumers, disposable income is their "take-home" pay. Discretionary income is disposable income minus the money needed for necessities to sustain life (i.e., minimal housing, minimal food, minimal clothing, etc.). Retailers selling necessities, such as a supermarket, like to see incomes rise and taxes decrease; knowing that while consumers won't spend all their increased disposable income on the retailer's merchandise, they will nevertheless increase spending. Retailers selling luxury goods want to see either disposable income increase and have the costs of necessities either decline or at least increase at a slower rate than income increases. Exhibit 3.8 shows how the changes in the nation's disposable income per household have affected retail sales by product category. Higher taxes, cost of medical care, medical insurance, and other cost of living increases will continue to outpace growth in income. Clothing and food for in-home consumption purchases have declined and will continue to do so.[14]

PERSONAL SAVINGS
A major criticism of the United States' economic system is that it does not reward personal savings. The percentage of disposable income that U.S. citizens save is shown in Exhibit 3.9. Savings that had dwindled from a post–World War II high of 8.8 percent in 1981 to 3.8 percent in 1994, rose to 4.9 percent in 1996. This was the largest two-year increase in two decades. Many economists believe that this rise was the first sign that the savings rate could again approach the

| EXHIBIT 3.8 | CHANGING PURCHASING HABITS OF AMERICAN HOUSEHOLDS |

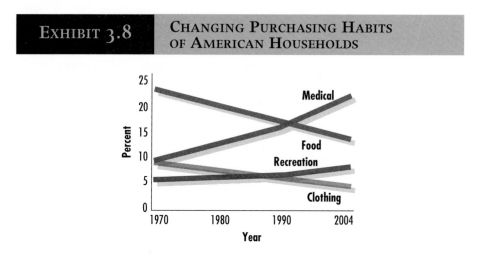

SOURCE: *Vision for the New Millennium* . . . (Atlanta: Kurt Salmon Associates, 1997). Used with permission.

| EXHIBIT 3.9 | ANNUAL PERSONAL SAVINGS RATE |

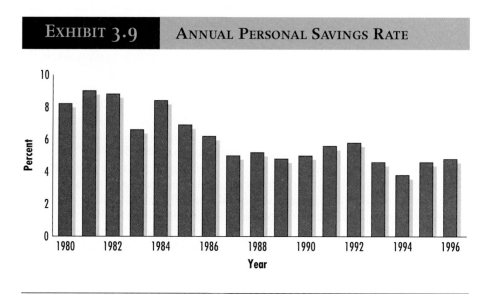

SOURCE: U.S. Bureau of the Census, Statistical Abstract of the United States: 1996 (116th edition) Washington, D.C., 1996. Based on Tables 697, 698.

historic levels before the advent of the baby boomers to middle-age. This is because as the boomers age, they realize the need to plan for retirement. Still, our savings rate is far below that of Japan, Germany, and France, which all are more than 10 percent. With a continually aging population, experts predict that we will soon begin a period of increased savings. Also the Gen Xers are beginning to influence the saving rate. This group has learned that they need to be more self reliant and can't count on social security and/or corporate pensions to be around when they retire. Consequently 65 percent of Gen Xers are already investing for retirement and 19 percent say they have saved more than $50,000.[15]

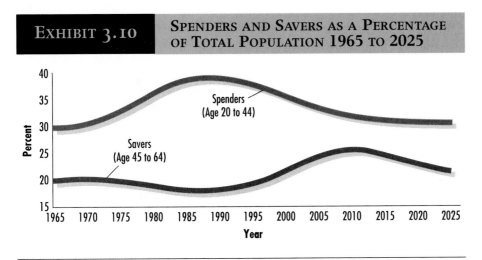

EXHIBIT 3.10	SPENDERS AND SAVERS AS A PERCENTAGE OF TOTAL POPULATION 1965 TO 2025

SOURCE: Based on data from U.S. Bureau of the Census, Population Paper Listings PPL 41, Current Population Reports P25-1130, U.S. Census of Population (1970), volume 1, Part B, Census of Population (1980), volume 1, part B.

IMPLICATIONS FOR RETAILERS   Retailers have enjoyed continued sales growth over the past decade, because even though median household income in fixed dollars has increased only slightly, spending and not saving was the focus of the consumer. However, retailers must be prepared for the next decade with baby boomers planning for retirement by reducing their spending and increasing savings. If the rise in 1996's savings rate is indicative of a new trend, this may keep inflation under control and lead to lower interest rates. Such savings increase would also mean less consumer spending. Exhibit 3.10 shows savers, those aged 45 to 64, and spenders, those aged 20 to 44, as a percentage of the total population. However, every threat is also an opportunity. The next 10 to 20 years promises to be a growth period for investment firms and financial planners that cater to the baby boomers.

Some other economists believe that the recent savings rise represents the third phase of a normal cyclical pattern. During a economic recession, they note, consumer spending on big-ticket durable goods tends to collapse and the savings rate rises smartly. Once a recovery gets going, however, pent-up demand unleashes a surge in durable spending that depresses the savings rate. And finally, when that pent-up demand is exhausted, spending growth slows and the savings rate starts to edge up—as it began doing in the mid-1990s. This is to be followed by another pickup in demand, although with less gusto than the first recovery, before beginning the cycle again. Such a scenario would mean bad times for retailers as they enter the 21st century.[16]

WOMEN IN THE LABOR FORCE   Over the past five decades, women have become a dominant factor in the labor force. Two decades ago, 46 percent of all women older than the age of 16 were in the labor force; this participation is expected to reach 63 percent in the year 2000. This trend is true of all age groups, even women aged 25 to 34, who might be expected to be raising families. Seventy-five percent of all women aged 25 to 34 are currently in the labor force. The percentage of all married women with preschoolers in the labor force increased from 45 to 59 percent in the past decade.

EXHIBIT 3.11	DUAL WAGE EARNERS AND THEIR EFFECT ON HOURS SPENT SHOPPING

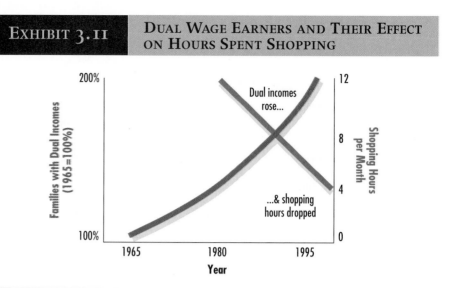

SOURCE: *Vision for the New Millennium* . . . (Atlanta: Kurt Salmon Associates, 1997). Used with permission.

This significant rise in the number of working women has protected many households from inflation and recession. In fact, many economists suggest that the working woman has been the nation's secret weapon against economic hardships.

DOLLAR $ & CENTS

High-performance retailers will be those that realize that the increase of women in the labor force is a two-edged sword. It will increase disposable income for the family, but it will reduce the time available for shopping, making it imperative that the retailer make shopping a pleasant experience as well as add value to the transaction.

IMPLICATIONS FOR RETAILERS   The rise in the number of working women has many retail implications. As shown in Exhibit 3.11, the increase in dual wage-earner families means that many families have less time for shopping and are more prone to look for convenience and services from retailers. Working men and women are often unable to shop "8 AM to 6 PM Monday thru Friday," thus preferring that retailers hold sales and special events in the evening or weekends. Time-pressed shoppers find that price is sometimes less important than convenience, availability, and service. One study found that part-time working mothers of preschoolers tend to do more in-home shopping.[17]

Retailers must develop strategies such as using direct mail, early morning, evening and weekend store hours, and even baby-sitting services for their working customers. These special services will go a long way in capturing the time-pressed shopper's store loyalty.

WIDESPREAD USE OF CREDIT Retailers, especially department stores and those selling big-ticket items, have long offered their own credit to customers. However, today the trend is away from the retailer's store-brand credit cards that can be used only in that store toward third-party (Visa, MasterCard, Discover, American Express, etc.) cards. Spurred on in recent years by an active promotional campaign, these third-party firms are getting customers to rack up credit card debt at four times the increase in their paychecks by giving customers and retailers many reasons for using these cards.[18]

For the customer, it may be offering airline miles or a rebate on a future purchase. For the retailer, it is increased sales and profits as 4 out of 5 retailers claim that acceptance of such cards increases sales and 3 out of 6 think that it increases profits.[19]

As a result, retailers from supermarkets to the family veterinarian are now forced to accept these third-party cards, and other retailers such as Kroger Co., Nordstrom, and Toys "Я" Us, are now co-branding their names with these third-party issuers.

DOLLAR $ & ¢ENTS

The acceptance of third-party credit cards is a way for retailers to improve sales and profits.

IMPLICATIONS FOR RETAILERS Although the use of third-party credit cards has contributed toward the increase in retail sales in the early to mid-1990s, it may lead to problems in the future, especially during any economic slowdown.

In the mid-1990s, total consumer debt including mortgages, home equity lines of credit, car loans, and credit card charges nearly equaled the governments own deficit of $4.9 trillion. Seven in 10 American families with credit cards carry balances over from month to month, with the outstanding balance averaging $3,900. Nearly 20 percent of household disposable income each month is now dedicated to paying off credit card debt.[20]

MACRO-ECONOMIC FACTORS

LO • 2
List the macro-economic factors that retail managers should regularly monitor and describe their impact on retailing

The previous discussion focused on how various demographic and household economic trends have influenced how the retailer should respond to changing consumer behavior. It is also important to understand the broader macro-economic environment that influences retail enterprises.

The macro-economic environment in which retailers operate is complex. Few business managers or government officials fully understand the economic forces shaping society. Consider all the conflicting economic predictions that you have heard

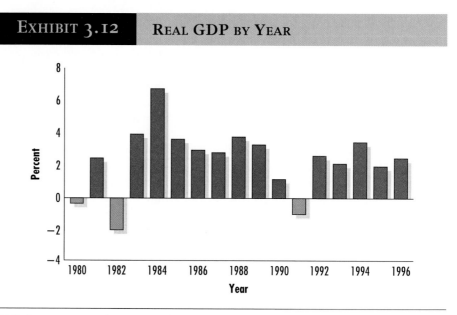

EXHIBIT 3.12   REAL GDP BY YEAR

SOURCE: U.S. Bureau of Economic Analysis, "Survey of Current Business," 1997.

during the past several months. Our brief overview does not pretend to explain the complexities of this environment. Rather, it focuses on six important factors that the retail manager should monitor regularly. They are gross domestic product (GDP), interest rates, economic turbulence, national debt, unemployment, and the underground economy.

GROSS DOMESTIC PRODUCT

Gross domestic product *is the total value of all the goods and services produced in the United States during one year.*

The most important long-range economic indicator is the GDP. Gross domestic product, which in 1991 replaced the gross national product as the government's leading indicator of economic output, is the total value of all the goods and services produced in the United States during one year. Retailers want the GDP to grow at a moderate and steady rate. Too-rapid growth in the GDP will produce inflation (a decline in buying power due to prices rising faster than income) and too-slow growth or no growth will result in reduced consumer spending, which in turn will reduce the need for workers and increase unemployment. GDP figures are useful for projecting future national disposable income levels (the total amount of personal income that all U.S. consumers have left after withholding taxes and social security levies), which in turn can be used to project future retail sales figures. An ideal growth rate is between 2.5 and 5 percent annually. Since the early 1980s, the country's real GDP, which is shown in Exhibit 3.12, has grown at an annual rate of 3.0 percent.

IMPLICATIONS FOR RETAILERS   The growth rate for GDP translates into growth in retail sales. However, although the overall average has been up for the past three decades, GDP has had its ups and downs. That is why it is important for retailers to keep an eye on this indicator in predicting future sales performance.

INTEREST RATES

An interest rate is the price paid for the use of money. Consumers and retailers alike use other individual's money to purchase merchandise. Consumers use credit cards or installment plans to purchase a large number of goods, especially durable goods such as household appliances, furniture, and automobiles. Retailers use bank credit to finance their investment in inventory. For example, the typical new car dealer with a modest inventory of 200 cars has to finance about $3.3 million in inventory investment. At an interest rate of 10 percent, the daily interest expense to carry this inventory would be more than $800.

Because the interest rate is the price of money and because the consumer needs money to buy merchandise, the effective price of merchandise rises each time the interest rate rises. We know from basic economics that as the price of most merchandise rises, the quantity demanded declines. Consider, for example, a young couple contemplating the purchase of three rooms of furniture at a cash price of $4,000. If the total purchase price is financed at 12 percent over 30 months, the monthly payment would be $155, which would work out to a deferred payment price of $4,650 ($155 times 30). If the total purchase price is financed at 18 percent over 30 months, the monthly payment would be $165.96, which would be a deferred payment of $4,978.80 ($165.96 times 30). Thus, because the price of money (the interest rate) went up, the deferred payment price of the furniture also rose. Each time the interest rate rises, more and more potential customers are eliminated from the market because they cannot afford the purchase. Just as rising rates slash the size of the market, declining rates expand it.

IMPLICATIONS FOR RETAILERS Retailers generally must purchase merchandise on credit. As the cost of credit increases, it becomes more expensive to finance and hold inventory. The net result of this higher cost of carrying inventory is that less of the proceeds from sales to customers can be used to pay for the merchandise and make a profit. In view of the high level of credit card debt discussed above, retailers need to be aware of interest rate fluctuations and their resulting impact not only on their financial performance but also on the consumer's behavior. Interest rates can also affect the retailer's capital investment decisions, such as whether to invest in a new store or to upgrade an existing store.

ECONOMIC TURBULENCE

The U.S. economy is characterized by frequent swings in the business cycle. A business cycle, which is the changing pattern of a nation's economic growth over time, consists of three stages: prosperity, recession, and recovery. Consumer spending has typically varied predictably with each stage. Today's consumers are confused—they don't know whether they should purchase an item today because its price might increase or postpone the purchase in the hope of a price decrease. Because the economy is so volatile, consumers have become more pessimistic and conservative in their purchasing activities. Economic turbulence has become one of the realities of retail planning.

Business cycle
captures the changing pattern of a nation's economic growth over time and categorizes it into prosperity, recession, and recovery.

IMPLICATIONS FOR RETAILERS These swings in the business cycle make the retailer's job more difficult. Does the retailer increase inventory in hopes of a good season or keep inventory stable? Because it takes time to order and receive merchandise (usually several days to weeks for domestic goods and up to six months for imported goods), the retailer can easily over- or undercommit inventory stock. For example, a city's economy may be booming in mid-June when a department store buyer begins to order for the Christmas season. However, imagine what would happen if the city's leading employer were to announce major layoffs shortly thereafter.

UNEMPLOYMENT

Unemployment
is the population without jobs who are able, willing, and actively looking for work.

In the past, unemployment (which counts persons who are without jobs and are able, willing, and actively looking for work) data were rather simple to analyze. Retailers wanted to see unemployment rates decrease because that meant more individuals had jobs, jobs produced income, and this income led to retail sales. When unemployment increases, consumer demand decreases and taxes to support the unemployed increase. When unemployment falls below 5 percent, however, many experts think that the economy is nearing a level of full employment, and the shortage in the supply of labor forces wages upward, causing some increases in prices and higher inflation.

IMPLICATIONS FOR RETAILERS   In recent years, the unemployment rate has been declining to below 5 percent in 1997 from more than 7 percent as recently as 1993. Usually when this occurs, retailers have found it necessary to pay higher starting wages to get even semiskilled employees. However, the lower employment levels of today may be hiding a critical problem for retailing's future—underemployment. Underemployment occurs when individuals who would normally qualify for higher-level jobs have to settle for lower-paying jobs to keep from being unemployed. Such behavior affects retailers through

Underemployment
occurs when individuals who would normally qualify for higher-level jobs have to settle for lower paying jobs to keep from being unemployed.

1. reduced sales as a result of the reduced buying of the underemployed
2. increased taxes for both the employed and their employers to support social services needed by the underemployed and unemployed
3. the fear of future employment problems, which will cause many consumers to reduce spending and increase savings

The unemployment issue is further complicated by the fact that as unemployment falls and wages increase, the Federal Reserve may raise interest rates in an attempt to halt inflation.

UNDERGROUND ECONOMY

Each year, as much as $1 trillion of income goes unreported to the government, and this amount appears to be growing. In addition, the bulk of this unreported income isn't due to drug dealers and illegal gambling but to business people large and small. These businesses may, and probably do, include many small retailers, independent service contractors, physicians, lawyers, cabbies, farmers, and innkeepers, as well as illegal immigrants. Even one of the most famous retailers in America, who for years was hailed as having the highest "sales per square feet of selling space" in his industry, recently pleaded guilty to underreporting sales. One can only imagine what this retailer's sales per square foot would have been if all sales had been reported. The most common reason given for this activity is to avoid taxes and/or regulatory costs.

IMPLICATIONS FOR RETAILERS   The very existence of an underground economy affects retailers in two ways: It places a higher tax burden on that large percentage of businesses who pay their fair taxes, and it often leads retailers who rely on government-generated demographic data derived from reported taxes to make wrong decisions.

As taxes continue to increase, this underground economy will continue to grow. Even spending additional sums of money to ensure enforcement of current laws will add a further financial burden to the four of five Americans who pay taxes voluntarily.

PSYCHOGRAPHIC TRENDS

LO • 3
Explain the changing American lifestyle and its effect on retailing

Changing demographic and economic factors are not sufficient to explain changing consumption patterns in the United States; an understanding of psychographics is also fundamental. Psychographics is the examination of the activities, interests, and opinions (AIO) of the population or of a meaningful segment of the population.[21]

Psychographics is sometimes referred to as lifestyle analysis by retailers. *Lifestyle* can be defined as "the patterns in which people live and spend time and money."[22] Several of the major changes in lifestyles that have or will affect retailing in the remaining years of this century are outlined in the sections that follow.

Psychographics
is the examination of the activities, interests, and opinions of the population or of a meaningful segment of the population.

MALE AND FEMALE ROLE FLEXIBILITY

The distinction between male and female roles in society is becoming blurred. Women are entering traditionally male jobs: bus drivers, telephone repair persons, police officers, and business executives. Males are taking traditionally female jobs. The number of male nurses, secretaries or administrative assistants, and airline attendants are all increasing dramatically. More men are deciding to stay home and take care of households as their wives become the major breadwinners, and technology permits "electronic commuting" from home offices.

IMPLICATIONS FOR RETAILERS   With more men at home, supermarkets will have to direct promotions toward their needs and habits, because men tend to focus on getting specific items and then getting out of the store. Likewise, as we pointed out previously, retailers must make specific adjustments for women in the labor force by adjusting store hours, providing more consumer information, and changing the product assortment.

DETERIORATION OF INSTITUTIONAL CONFIDENCE

Recently, the American public has shown an increasing distrust of government, as witnessed by recent national elections that showed a demand for smaller government and a general distrust of other institutions (e.g., Wall Street, the media, religion, and business in general). Much of this distrust is latent, but it surfaced after the various religious scandals, insider-trading scandals on Wall Street, the tobacco companies not being honest about research they had conducted about the health risks of cigarettes, and convictions of numerous public officials. This skepticism is perhaps based on feelings that these institutions are more interested in satisfying their goals than in meeting the public's wants and needs.

IMPLICATIONS FOR RETAILERS   Many established retailers no longer enjoy the customer loyalty that they once had. These retailers still have a loyal following among older adults, but the younger shoppers are a different story. With so many competing stores available today, the successful retailer of the next decade will be the one who does the best job of getting its message out. The deliverance of the "best value for the money" will help retailers reestablish the consumer loyalty they so long enjoyed. Finally, retailers should exemplify the highest ethical and moral conduct in all their dealings with consumers, employees, suppliers, and other retailers. This type of behavior will go a long way toward resolving this deterioration in confidence.

MANAGEMENT OF TIME VERSUS MONEY

There is tremendous time pressure on Americans today, reducing their ability to shop when they please. As a result, many households, especially multiple-income households, are becoming more concerned with the management of time versus money. Given a choice of eight goals for the future in a recent study, the majority of Americans listed "spending time with family" and "job/career satisfaction" as their top priority. The same study found that 51 percent of Americans say that they would rather have more free time even if it meant less money; 35 percent believed the opposite. This feeling of time poverty has made 48 percent of the public attempt to control schedules, seek more conveniences and services when shopping, and spend less time on household chores over the past five years.[23] Despite the fact that Americans currently have more free time at their disposal than in the past, an increasing number thought that they had less free time.[24] Money management obviously cannot be ignored, but households frequently realize that it is time, not money, that determines whether they participate in some activities. Consumers who experience "time poverty" want to reduce the amount of time spent in retail stores. They don't want to wander around for hours or even minutes in search of a particular product. They have too many other things to do.

IMPLICATIONS FOR RETAILERS   In view of this new time management crisis, it is not surprising to find estimates that Internet and mail-order shopping will ring up big sales increases. In addition, any store manager who can ease this time crunch by means of "express checkouts," "phone ahead," or "free delivery" can turn a problem into an opportunity for success.

Supermarkets, probably more than any other retailers, have been dramatically affected by symptoms of "time poverty." In addition to adding delis featuring HMRs (home-meal replacements), supermarket managers are adapting to one-stop shopping by offering goods and services such as postage stamps, banking, and video rentals. In an effort to speed customers through their stores, supermarkets are improving aisle signs, opening more check-out stations, widening their aisles, and offering specialized express check-outs. But most supermarkets still have a lot to do to streamline food shopping. Although they are investing in salad bars and delis, many put these services deep in the store, forcing customers to make a longer stop than they want. More than half of all food shoppers would buy takeout food from supermarkets more often if they could get in and out of the store faster. As a result, new supermarket prototypes have put takeout sections in the front of the store, with a separate entrance, check-out, and/or a drive-through window. The impact of perceived time scarcity extends to all retailers. A store that wastes a person's time is committing competitive suicide.

The combination of technology (i.e., the Internet), new distribution systems, and the perception of time scarcity is changing the concept of convenience. In just a few years, the standards for photo-processing have shifted from seven days to one hour. The same thing is occurring with eyeglass service, furniture delivery, automobile maintenance, and other categories. Convenience is not just a state of mind, it is a dynamic state of mind. It is a "moving target" that savvy retailers should monitor closely.[25] Probably nowhere is this more evident than in the dating process. This lack of time, combined with the increase number of single-person households, has resulted in a new cottage industry—"dating services." In 1997, there were more than 3,000 such businesses.[26]

VALUE AND LIFESTYLE FRAGMENTATION

In what is considered the most advanced study of this nation's lifestyle patterns, SRI International developed its values and lifestyle (VALS) program. VALS, first introduced in 1978, helped marketers predict patterns of consumption based on consumers' values and lifestyles. However, significant changes with both the consumer and the marketplace have led to diversity in the consumer population and value and lifestyle fragmentation, making it increasingly difficult for marketers to predict consumer behavior. SRI developed VALS 2, which is based on more permanent psychological states. Consumers are organized into eight classifications that vary on two dimensions: resources such as money and education available to the consumer, and whether the consumer is oriented toward principles, status, or action. The basic orientations to consumption are

> *Principle-oriented:* persons guided by how they believe the world is or should be.
> *Status-oriented:* persons driven by the opinions of others.
> *Action-oriented:* persons driven by a need for diverse social and physical activity, as well as experimentation

As consumers obtain more resources (money, education, etc.), they are able to achieve more of their goals—or become actualized—within each of these consumption orientations.

IMPLICATIONS FOR RETAILERS   The population is getting older. Financial and other resources tend to accumulate with age. As baby boomers age, obtain greater resources, and consume more goods and services, retailers must understand how to satisfy principle-, status-, or action-oriented goals, as appropriate for their target market.

BABY BUSTERS

Although we briefly discussed baby busters in the first part of this chapter, too many retailers mistakenly still believe that their customer today is the same as a decade or two ago. They have overlooked the fact that the generation just behind the boomers, the so-called baby busters or Generation Xers have an entirely different psychographic makeup. These "post–baby boomers," who were born between 1965 and 1978 and would much rather be called the "Children of the 80s," are just beginning to enter the mainstream of American life. Yet, despite their annual spending power of $125 billion and heavy use of credit,[27] they have to date been ignored by most retailers, especially

Values and lifestyle (VALS)

is a research program by SRI International that analyzes the nation's lifestyle patterns and is used by marketers to predict consumption.

when it comes to promotion and service.[28] Maybe according to Fred Newell,[29] a retail consultant, they failed to realize that

YOUR WORLD HAS CHANGED
YOUR CUSTOMER HAS CHANGED
    98% are not old enough to remember 1913.
    85% are not old enough to remember the first stock market crash in 1929.
    70% don't remember "before TV."
    66% don't remember the Korean War.
    50% don't remember the Kennedy assassination.
    30% don't remember the Arab oil embargo.
    22% don't remember the Bicentennial.
    For 33% of Americans, we have always been on the moon.

Nevertheless, baby busters are a different market and it is important that retailers begin to plan for them now.

Baby busters, whose early members entered and left college during an economic slowdown, are also the first generation of latchkey children; sons and daughters of single-parent homes. This segment is also the first generation of Americans who don't think that they will have as "good a life as their parents." In fact, they feel alienated and angry at the boomers' culture and lifestyle, which they believe placed the economy in such poor shape.[30] This generation is more ethnically diverse than any previous generation, and they are happy with that. The most ironic thing in comparing these two groups is that the boomers had everything for the taking in the 1960s and at first rejected it. The busters, because they were exposed to the temptations of consumer culture at an early age, are a group that would like some of these things. However, because of circumstances beyond their control, they are going to have a hard time getting it.

IMPLICATIONS FOR RETAILERS   This group is not only different in age but it has an entirely alien buying behavior that will be difficult for retailers to reach unless they make a well-considered effort. Busters won't be like the boomers who sought out conspicuous consumption. In fact, as an angry and alienated segment, they are already dressing for the part with the "grunge" look: asexual, antifashion attire that celebrates the outdoors look. They are definitely not mass market material. They seem to be turned off by promotions that take themselves too seriously.[31] Busters will want different promotions that are irreverent, funny, and say "we understand." Retailers dealing with this market can't "fake it."

LO • 4
Discuss the consumer behavior model, including the key stages in the buying process and how they interact

CONSUMER BEHAVIOR MODEL[32]

DOLLAR $ & CENTS

Retailers can use their understanding of their target consumer's buying behavior to improve their performance.

EXHIBIT 3.13	CONSUMER BEHAVIOR MODEL

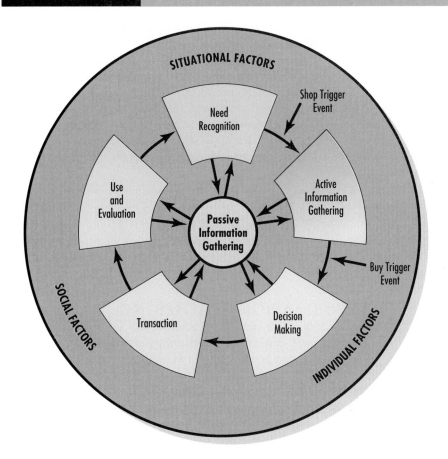

Now that we have examined the demographic, economic, and psychographic factors, we can develop a comprehensive model that describes, and to some degree predicts, how these factors come together to affect consumer buying patterns. We call this the consumer behavior model.

NATURE OF A CONCEPTUAL MODEL

Before presenting and discussing the consumer behavior model, we should clarify the objectives and uses of such conceptual models. Models are developed as a framework for understanding complex phenomena that defy understanding through simple observation. Such phenomena are usually dependent on many input factors, which interact in a complex manner to "cause" certain outcomes. Consumer behavior is so incredibly complex, and the input factors so variable and difficult to measure, that it is virtually impossible to say with certainty what causes consumers to behave as they do. Nonetheless, the consumer behavior model serves as a representation of a typical buying process.

Examine the consumer behavior model in Exhibit 3.13. This model suggests that consumer behavior is a process, with a series of stages or steps occurring against a backdrop of individual, social, and situational factors. Furthermore, the process is cyclic, with the stage of need recognition, active information gathering, decision

Consumer behavior model

is a simplified framework for understanding the complex phenomena of consumer behavior.

making, transaction, and evaluation cycling around the central element of passive information gathering, all feeding back into formation of long-term beliefs about certain shopping alternatives.

We can simplify this model by considering the purchase of a specific item, beginning with need recognition and ending with use and evaluation. This is a highly rationalized, stepwise shopping process, but as we have suggested, human beings often don't behave quite that rationally. The very first stage of need recognition, along with all subsequent stages, is dependent on beliefs formed from all previous purchases and the long-term use of the goods or services purchased, and these beliefs strongly influence future shopping behavior. From the time of a consumer's first purchase, it is difficult to determine which step in the process is the initial step. Our consumer behavior model is therefore made somewhat more complex, although more representative of reality, by viewing it as a cyclic process.

STAGES IN THE BUYING PROCESS

As shown in our model, there are six stages or steps in the buying process: passive information gathering, need recognition, active information, decision making, transaction, and use and evaluation.

Passive information gathering
is the receiving and processing of information regarding the existence and quality of merchandise, services, stores, shopping convenience, pricing, advertising, and any other factors that a consumer might consider in making a purchase.

PASSIVE INFORMATION GATHERING
We begin with passive information gathering, which consists of receiving and processing information regarding the existence and quality of merchandise, services, stores, shopping convenience, pricing, advertising, and any other factors that a consumer might consider in making a purchase. As consumers move through their daily routine, they are constantly exposed to hundreds of messages regarding merchandise and services. Consumers retain some of this information, although perhaps not consciously, through passive information gathering, and this learning subsequently influences all other stages or steps in the buying process.

Need recognition
is the point at which the consumer recognizes a need or desire for a product or service.

NEED RECOGNITION
Need recognition, sometimes called "problem recognition," has traditionally been considered the beginning of the shopping process, and indeed, if every consumer behaved perfectly rational, every buying process would begin here. Need recognition occurs when the consumer recognizes a need or desire for a product or service. The term *need* is inclusive of both absolute survival needs, such as food and clothing, and desires, or items consumers would like to have to enhance the quality of their lives.

Recognition of a need in itself is not enough to cause consumers to begin shopping, for there are many needs and desires consumers have for which consumers don't make a purchase. To move beyond need recognition, the consumer must perceive some type of event or set of circumstances that suggests the degree of need is high relative to the barriers to resolving it. The point at which this "need/barrier quotient" is high enough is called the shop trigger event.

Shop trigger event
occurs when the consumer perceives that the degree of need is high relative to the barriers to resolving it and thus decides to shop for a product or service to fulfill the need.

For instance, consider a consumer who believes her mattress is becoming a bit saggy and isn't giving her as good a night's sleep as before. Clearly, she has recognized a problem, but she wonders whether it is yet time to do something about this situation. That can only be determined relative to the cost—in financial and other terms—of correcting the problem. Perhaps she remembers what a hassle it was to shop for her last mattress. She knows from talking with friends and noticing advertising that a quality king-sized mattress can cost more than $1,000, so she is reluctant to enter the shopping process. She may rationalize to herself that her bed isn't that bad yet. Simply put, the consumer does not currently recognize her need as being acute enough to overcome "need barriers" such as convenience and cost.

Can retailers induce consumers to overcome this barrier? This is a highly debated question, because influencing need recognition theoretically requires changing a consumer's perceptions of needs. A critical factor in the formation of these perceptions is information consumers receive through many sources, and retailers can be one of the richest sources of this information. For customers who have not yet entered the store, retailers can provide information through advertising that alerts customers to the availability of certain merchandise, the convenience of shopping, or the price or savings available.

Recall our consumer whose mattress is becoming worn, who has for now decided her need is not great relative to the costs of solving the need. New information, perhaps provided by the retailer, can change her perception of either the degree of her problem or the barriers to correcting the problem. Watching the local news, for instance, she might see a commercial for a local mattress retailer that demonstrates a test for determining the condition of a mattress. Based on this test, the customer might conclude that her need is greater than she thought. One of the most famous of these "test" programs is the Special K pinch, in which Kellogg's showed consumers a quick, painless, and private test for whether they should lose weight, and by inference, if they could pinch more than an inch of skin around their waistline, perhaps they better start eating Special K cereal.

Alternatively, retailers can send messages that influence consumers' perceptions of the barriers to solving needs. Our consumer might read in a newspaper advertisement that a local mattress retailer is holding a "50 percent off" sale, with free delivery of the new mattress and free disposal of the old mattress. With this new information, she might conclude that although the degree of her problem has not increased, the barriers to correcting it have decreased, and therefore she is triggered into the shopping process.

Retailers can influence consumer perceptions in the store as well. Many needs are "discovered" after the shopper has arrived at a store. In fact, the Point-of-Purchase Advertising Institute (POPAI) reports that nearly 60 percent of all purchases are decided on after the customer has entered the store.[33] This means retailers can influence consumer perceptions regarding the need/barrier quotient through sales associates, visual communications, and most important, the presentation of the merchandise itself.

ACTIVE INFORMATION GATHERING

Once consumers reach the shopping trigger event, they move from need recognition to the active information-gathering step in our process. Active information gathering is when consumers proactively gather and evaluate information that will eventually lead to a decision either to not purchase or which item to purchase and where to purchase the item. Active information gathering typically involves three stages:

1. Development of a set of attributes on which the purchase decision will be based. The set of attributes are the characteristics of the store and its products and services. In fact a store and its products and services can be thought of as a bundle or set of attributes which can include such things as price, product quality, store hours, knowledgeable sales help, convenient parking, after-sale service, and so on. These attributes are often based on general information sources such as preexisting knowledge, advertising, discussions with friends and relatives, and reading of magazines such as *Consumer Reports*. Retailers of high-priced categories, such as cars and large appliances, must train their salespersons to determine whether a

Active information gathering
occurs when consumers proactively gather and evaluate information that will eventually lead to a decision either to not purchase or which item to purchase and where to purchase the item.

Set of attributes
consist of the set of characteristics of the store and its products or services which are evaluated in deciding what to purchase and where to purchase.

customer is in this process of building a set of attributes, in the decision-making stage, or in the transaction stage. Here, the salesforce's approach, as well as the selling environment, must be adjusted in response to the consumer's stage in the buying process. Although in some cases sales pressure or just the right product or price can move customers into the decision-making or transaction stage, too much pressure can intimidate or irritate consumers, causing them not only to leave without purchasing but also to not return once they reach the buying stage.

2. In the second stage, consumers narrow the consideration set to a more manageable number of attributes. Although consumers want to think that they have considered a wide range of options so as to not miss a golden opportunity, they do not want to be confused by a myriad of options. In the second stage, consumers might visit stores to gather more specific information, including price ranges, to narrow their list.

3. In the final stage, consumers directly compare the key attributes of the alternatives remaining on their "short list." Here, consumers are very active in their search for specific information and often begin ascertaining actual prices through store visits or preliminary negotiating when appropriate.

One of the most important variables of active information gathering is the information resources used by consumers. It is important for retailers to understand what information resources their target market prefer to use, then match their communications programs to these vehicles.

DECISION MAKING

Based on information gathered in the previous phase, consumers decide whether they intend to purchase and which product and store they intend to choose.

Of course, a possible outcome of the active information-gathering stage is a decision not to buy or to delay the purchase. A shopper might conclude that an adequate product or service isn't available or that the cost (financial or otherwise) is greater than previously thought. Although a purchase is not made, the information gathered is often mentally recorded and influences future shopping processes.

When active information gathering yields a combination of elements that works for the consumer, he or she reaches the buy trigger event, when the consumer has decided to purchase the good or service and often where to buy the good or service. In some cases, the consumer decides on an item but retains more than one store in the consideration set, leaving the final purchase decision to be made in the transaction stage based on the results of negotiation. Of course, prices for most consumer goods are not negotiable, so in most cases a final decision as to store is made before the transaction stage.

Buy trigger event *occurs when active information gathering results in a combination of elements that works for the consumer and thus they decide to buy or purchase.*

TRANSACTION

The consumer is now ready to enter into the transaction stage, in which the actual purchase is made. The transaction may include final negotiation, application for credit if necessary, and determination of the terms of purchase (cash, credit card, etc.). Sometimes last-minute unexpected factors can intervene during the transaction phase to preempt the purchase. For instance, the consumer can become aware of unanticipated costs such as taxes, delivery charges, or other items and decide not to buy.

The transaction is often used by retailers as an opportunity, as we discuss in Chapter 12, to use suggestion selling to sell add-on or related purchases such as extended service warranties, batteries for toys, and other impulse merchandise. If handled properly, consumers can view this selling practice as a customer service, as if the retailer were "looking out" for the customer's long-term satisfaction. If handled poorly, the customer can view this as an attempt to gouge the unsuspecting consumer. In extreme cases, the consumer may even decide to cancel the initial transaction.

USE AND EVALUATION
The consumer behavior process does not end with the transaction. In fact, according to our model, the process continually cycles on itself. Therefore, successful retailers must concern themselves not just with the activities leading to the transaction but also with what happens after the transaction. Ultimately, consumers are buying solutions to their perceived needs, and successful retailers take an active interest in ensuring that customers feel satisfied over the long term that their need has been resolved. The consumer's use and evaluation is therefore a critical, although sometimes overlooked, stage in the consumer behavior process.

The first important moment in the use and evaluation stage is immediately after the transaction, in the first hours and days in which the consumer uses the product or service. During this critical time, consumers form lasting impressions regarding the soundness of their purchase decision that feed directly into passive information gathering and influence all future purchases. If the consumer is dissatisfied, a condition can emerge known as post-purchase resentment, in which the consumer's dissatisfaction results in resentment toward the retailer.

If post-purchase resentment is not identified and rectified by the retailer, it can have a long-term negative influence on the retailer's ability to recapture the consumer as a satisfied customer because a satisfied customer tells a few friends, whereas a dissatisfied customer tells a dozen.

Fortunately, if the retailer is proactive in its customer satisfaction program and responds quickly to budding resentment, it can be overcome. The problem is that many unhappy consumers do not report their dissatisfaction, so retailers must be vigilant in their monitoring of customer satisfaction. This process begins with the establishment of proactive policies such as full-satisfaction guarantees, which should be boldly communicated to the shopper. This tells consumers that if they do have a problem, the retailer wants to hear about and rectify the problem. Beyond this, many retailers have started customer follow-up programs, such as customer satisfaction reply cards given out at the time of purchase or mailed to the customer several days later. Electronic cash registers have aided in this process by efficiently gathering the names, addresses, and telephone numbers of customers, recording the merchandise purchased, and automatically mailing the customer satisfaction surveys. It is important that retailers seek to find out why some past customers no longer shop their stores.

Many large retailers—especially chains in which individual stores are not under central control, such as franchises and dealerships—have taken this customer satisfaction process one step farther. They have instituted programs that measure customer satisfaction on an ongoing basis and compare customer service ratings of individual retail locations against preestablished benchmarks or a chainwide average.

Post-purchase resentment *arises when after the purchase the consumer becomes dissatisfied with the product, service, or retailer and thus begins to regret that the purchase was made.*

DYNAMIC NATURE OF CONSUMER BEHAVIOR MODEL

It should be apparent from the preceding discussion that the consumer behavior model is a dynamic, interactive process of shopping, learning, purchasing, evaluating, and shopping again. We have placed passive information gathering at the center of this dynamic model because the consumer can jump to and from this point from virtually every other stage in the process. Consumers who reach a decision but fail to purchase in the transaction stage because of new information do not necessarily return to the need recognition stage. Instead, information they have gathered feeds into subsequent purchasing processes. At some later time, perhaps when the customer is approved for a credit card, he or she may jump directly from passive information gathering to transaction, for an item previously considered. One of the richest sources of passive information gathering is the browsing done while shoppers are in the active information-gathering stage for other items. Shopping processes are ongoing, so successful retailers must be constantly attentive to providing information, presenting goods and services that solve perceived needs, and satisfying the customer.

STUDENT STUDY GUIDE

SUMMARY   This chapter has concentrated on how major changes in the socio-economic environment affect consumer demand. It should be clear that the rapid changes occurring in the socioeconomic environment demand both sensitive management and good retail information systems in the retail industry. Retailers need managers who can provide leadership in meeting the challenges of, and likewise profiting from, the opportunities that these changes present.

LO•1 EXPLAIN THE IMPORTANCE OF DEMOGRAPHIC AND HOUSEHOLD ECONOMIC TRENDS ON RETAIL PLANNING.   We began Chapter 3 with a discussion of the major demographic trends occurring in the United States today and their implications for the future of retailing. These trends include a slowing down of the population growth rate, a changing age distribution as America ages, the geographic shifting of the population to the South and West, the growth of large urban centers, the ever-expanding consumer mobility, the increasing educational levels of consumers, the expanding population base of never-marrieds, and the effect of higher divorce rates and the unrelated two-person households on retailing. The chapter also considered the effects of income growth, level of personal savings, women in the labor force, and the widespread use of credit.

LO•2 WHAT MACRO-ECONOMIC FACTORS SHOULD BE MONITORED AND WHAT ARE THEIR IMPACTS ON RETAILING?   Next, we examined the five macro-economic factors that significantly influence both the retailer and the consumer: GDP, interest rates, economic turbulence, unemployment, and the underground economy. Although retailers aren't able to control these factors, their impact on the demand for a retailer's products is significant. For example, as GDP increases, so does consumer spending or demand. A rise in interest rates causes the effective price of retailers' products to increase and a reduction in demand for those products. Economic turbulence, unemployment, and to a smaller degree, the underground economy likewise affect demand.

LO•3 HOW DOES THE CHANGING AMERICAN LIFESTYLE AFFECT RETAILING?   We concluded our examination of the socioeconomic environment with a look at how some of the changing lifestyle trends occurring today will affect retailing into the 21st century. These factors include male and female role flexibility, changes in institutional confidence, the management of time versus money, value and lifestyle fragmentation, and the arrival of the baby busters.

LO•4 WHAT IS INVOLVED IN THE CONSUMER BEHAVIOR MODEL, INCLUDING THE KEY STAGES IN THE BUYING PROCESS?   The consumer behavior model is a cyclical process that was presented to provide an understanding of the consumer's shopping behavior rather than the ability to absolutely predict shopping behavior. The stages or steps involved in this process are passive information gathering, need recognition, active information gathering, decision making, transaction, and use and evaluation, all of which revolve around and are interactive with passive information gathering. The entire model is set against the backdrop of individual, social, and situational influences.

TERMS TO REMEMBER

customer satisfaction	underemployment
customer services	psychographics
market segmentation	values and lifestyle (VALS)
demographic variables	consumer behavior model
micromarketing	passive information gathering
metropolitan statistical areas	need recognition
disposable income	shop trigger event
discretionary income	active information gathering
gross domestic product	set of attributes
business cycle	buy trigger event
unemployment	post-purchase resentment

REVIEW AND DISCUSSION QUESTIONS

LO•1 EXPLAIN THE IMPORTANCE OF DEMOGRAPHIC AND HOUSEHOLD ECONOMIC TRENDS ON RETAIL PLANNING.

1. What type of retailers would be most affected by changes in the age distribution of the population?
2. How does a demographic trend, such as the increasing number of working women, affect women's apparel retailing? recreational retailing? grocery retailing?
3. What strategies should retailers develop in the face of slower population growth?
4. Which age groups are experiencing higher growth rates? Will these changes increase or decrease the chances of success of any particular types of retailers not mentioned in the chapter? Explain your answer.

LO•2 WHAT MACRO-ECONOMIC FACTORS AFFECT A RETAILER?

5. Describe how an increase in interest rates could influence retail performance.
6. Should a retailer care about changing trends in national or local economic factors? After all, does a high unemployment rate in Florida affect a retailer operating only in Michigan and Ohio?
7. Why is it more difficult for retailers to manage their businesses in a roller-coaster economy of economic turbulence?

LO•3 HOW DOES THE CHANGING AMERICAN LIFESTYLE EFFECT RETAILING?

8. What are the implications of consumers' growing concern for time to a retailer?
9. Compare your values and lifestyle with that of your parents. What opportunities do any differences present for different types of retailers?
10. Is it important for a retailer to understand that baby boomers are different from baby busters in shopping behavior? Is there one example from current events that you can use to emphasize your argument?

LO•4 WHAT IS INVOLVED IN THE CONSUMER BEHAVIOR MODEL, INCLUDING THE KEY STAGES IN THE BUYING PROCESS?

11. Why is the consumer behavior model presented in the text called a cyclic model? Explain how this would affect a retailer's actions.
12. Does a consumer begin the buying process at the need recognition stage?
13. Why should a retailer care about a customer after a sale has already been made?

SAMPLE TEST QUESTIONS

LO•1 THE "BOOMERANG EFFECT" IS A RELATIVELY NEW PHENOMENON THAT DESCRIBES

a. the recent trend for firms to seek bankruptcy protection
b. the way styles from years ago come back as today's most popular styles
c. the recent trend of children returning to live with their parents after having already moved out
d. the use of price as the main means to attract new customers
e. the recent trend of having most companies report losses for the current quarter

LO•2 WHICH OF THE FOLLOWING STATEMENTS, CONCERNING MACRO-ECONOMIC FACTORS, IS CORRECT?

a. Retailers need to worry about a rising unemployment rate, but not about under-employment.
b. The U.S. economy is highly stable and seldom undergoes significant changes.
c. The number of college students is useful in projecting future short-term sales figures for the nation.
d. An ideal GDP growth rate is 3 to 5 percent annually.
e. Too-slow a growth in GDP will produce inflation.

LO•3 WHICH OF THE FOLLOWING IS *NOT* A CURRENT PSYCHOGRAPHIC TREND AMONG THE U.S. POPULATION?

a. The distinction between traditional male and female roles is becoming blurred.
b. Most Americans would rather have more money than "free time."
c. Americans are losing confidence in government, business, religious, and educational institutions.
d. The VALS study indicates that as consumers obtain more resources, they will be able to achieve more of their goals.
e. Many established retailers no longer enjoy the strong customer loyalty they once had.

LO•4 THE CENTRAL STAGE OF THE DYNAMIC CONSUMER BEHAVIOR MODEL AROUND WHICH ALL OTHER STAGES REVOLVES IS

a. need recognition stage
b. active information-gathering stage
c. situational stage
d. "have a problem" stage
e. passive information-gathering stage

APPLICATIONS

WRITING AND SPEAKING EXERCISE You have recently been hired as the assistant manager for a large regional mall in Sacramento, California. One of the first things you notice on an early inspection tour of the mall is a lack of benches in the common areas for the elderly and mothers with babies to sit and rest while shopping. This is said to reduce the selling area that the mall can rent to various temporary vendors such as arts-and-crafts shows. You also find a memo from your predecessor banning the early opening of the mall commons so that elderly exercise groups cannot use the mall for walking and exercise classes. Prepare a one-page memo agreeing or disagreeing with the current mall policy and explaining your reasoning.

RETAIL PROJECT
By the time you read this chapter, much of the demographic data mentioned in it will be outdated. You can get up-to-date data one of two ways. You can go to the government document section of your local library and use the most current issue of *Statistical Abstract of the United States.* Or you can use your computer to connect with the Census Bureau's web site. A series of easy directions will guide you to the most current available data for any geographic area—from the entire nation to any county or town in any state. By using your mouse, you can easily specify what kind of information you want. Also because the census does more than just count individuals, you can obtain breakdowns by different variables than the ones used in this chapter, including occupation, home value, and even households with indoor plumbing.

CASE MED-CENTER DRUGSTORE

There are three Med-Center Drugstores operating in Rio Bravo, Texas. Until the past five years, Rio Bravo had basically been a "retirement town," with adults older than the age of 60 accounting for the largest segment of the population. This situation made it fairly simple for Med-Center Drugstores to target and serve the senior citizen market. Recently, though, the area has experienced a migration of young families and middle-aged couples who wanted to escape the city life. Although 50 percent of the population had once been in the 60-years-and-older category, the 35- to 45-year age group and the senior citizens group now each share 35 percent.

Older consumers, originally, had been attracted to Med-Center Drugstores because they did not have to worry about dealing with many children when shopping, they knew that they would not have to wait in long check-out lines, and they would not have difficulty maneuvering themselves and/or their carts in the extra-wide aisles. Many of these attractions no longer exist. Families with young children have become regular customers of the stores, store traffic has been increasing, and aisle widths have shrunk so that additional shelves could be installed as a means of displaying more merchandise and, ultimately, generating more sales.

Albert Clemens, president of the company that owns the drugstores, realizes that if the stores continue to operate as they are presently, there is a distinct possibility that older customers will begin shopping elsewhere. Although he wishes to continue to cater to the loyal senior citizen customers who helped Med-Center Drugstores achieve its current success, he does not want to ignore the potentially lucrative "baby boomer" market that is beginning to form in Rio Bravo. As Mr. Clemens' assistant, you are to consider and answer the following questions:

1. Should Med-Center Drugstores concentrate on only the "baby boomer" or on the senior citizen market? Both? Neither? Explain your position.
2. What types of marketing strategies could Med-Center Drugstores implement that would meet the needs of both age groups?
3. How might the changing marketplace effect Med-Center Drugstores merchandise assortment? What types of merchandise might management want to add, delete, or expand?

PLANNING YOUR OWN RETAIL BUSINESS In this chapter, you learned that how broadly or how selectively you define your market niche is a major determinant of performance in retailing. In planning your retail business, it will be important that you develop your retail marketing strategy to appeal to a particular market—either broadly or narrowly defined. For example, a women's apparel store could cater to all age groups, professional working women, or teens; it could also target various income groups such as low, moderate, or high income. Further, it could target women of different sizes from petite to full figured.

Assume that for the store you are planning there are 20,000 households in your community and these are within a reasonable driving distance to your store. You have determined that if you broadly define your store's market, 75 percent of households in the community would be shoppers at the store and shop there an average of 2.7 times per year. However, if you define your market much more selectively by focusing on a well-defined niche, you estimate only 28 percent of households would shop at the store but they would shop an average of 9.2 times annually.

In this situation, would a broadly or more narrowly defined market create more customer visits to the store? [*Hint:* Total store visitors, also referred to as traffic, is equal to the total number of households in the market multiplied by the proportion that would shop the store multiplied by their average shopping frequency.] What other factors should you consider in deciding how narrowly or broadly to define your market?

NOTES

1. "Customer Satisfaction Falls Broadly, Paced by Complaints about Insurers," *Wall Street Journal,* November 7, 1995: A16; "Shoppers Tell Marketers To Save Breath on Offers," *Ad Age International,* January 15, 1996: 2.
2. The material in this section is taken from the most recent data and estimates available from various government publications.
3. *Vision for the New Millennium . . . Evolving to Consumer Response,* (Atlanta: Kurt Salmon Associates, 1996).
4. "Western Auto Shuts Area Stores," *Dallas Morning News,* February 1, 1997: 1F–2F.
5. "Older Consumers Don't Believe You," *Advertising Age,* August 14, 1995: 14.
6. "Making Generational Marketing Come of Age," *Fortune,* June 26, 1995: 110–114.
7. "Tapping the Graying Market," *Shopping Centers Today,* February 1996: 1, 22.
8. "Target 'Micromarkets' Its Way to Success; No 2 Stores Are Alike," *Wall Street Journal,* May 31, 1995: A1, A9.
9. "Americans on the Move," *U.S. News & World Report,* April 15, 1996: 18.
10. "A Bigger Family Stays Closer to the Nest," *Wall Street Journal,* April 1, 1994: B1.
11. "The Real Middle Americans," *American Demographics,* October 1994: 28–35.
12. "Family Values," *U.S. News & World Report,* October 20, 1992: 24.
13. "People Living Alone," *American Demographics,* December 1993: 38–39.
14. *Vision for the New Millennium.*
15. "Generation $ Is More Like It" *Business Week,* November 3, 1997: 44.
16. For a more complete discussion of this topic, see William Strauss and Neil Howe, *The Fourth Turning* (New York: Broadway Books, 1997).
17. Jean C. Darian, "In-Home Shopping: Are There Consumer Segments?" *Journal of Retailing,* Summer 1987: 163–186.
18. "A Hard Blow for Easy Credit," *Business Week,* March 31, 1997: 39; Ernst & Young "Survey of Retail Payment Systems," *Chain Store Age,* January 1996: 3A.
19. "Survey of Retail Payment Systems,": 6A.
20. Ibid: 3A.
21. For a detailed discussion of the general use of psychographics in business, the reader is referred to Peter W. Bernstein, "Psychographics Still an Issue on Madison Avenue," *Fortune,* January 16, 1978: 78–84.

22. James F. Engel and Roger D. Blackwell, *Consumer Behavior,* 4th ed. (Chicago: The Dryden Press, 1982): 188.

23. "Time Out," *U.S. News & World Report,* December 11, 1995: 85–95.

24. "Are We Having Fun Yet?" *American Demographics,* October 1997: 28–30.

25. The above was based on Leonard L. Berry, "Market to the Perception," *American Demographics,* February 1990: 32–33.

26. "Heart Trouble," *U.S. News & World Report,* February 10, 1997: 16.

27. "In Debt All the Way Up to Their Nose Rings," *U.S. News & World Report,* June 9, 1997: 38–39.

28. "Two for Me, None for You," *Business Week,* August 11, 1997: 35; "Most Generation X-ers," *Wall Street Journal,* August 7, 1997: A1.

29. Kenneth Banks, "Does Anyone See Our Ads?" *Arthur Andersen Retailing Issues Letter,* November 1992.

30. "In a Portland Hot Tub, Young Grads' Anxiety Bubbles to the Surface," *Wall Street Journal,* July 28, 1993: A1, A6; "Young America's Rally Cry: 'Dis the Deficit'," *Business Week,* August 9, 1993: 37.

31. "Two for Me, None for You," *Business Week,* August 11, 1997: 35.

32. The authors want to acknowledge the contribution of Randall Gebhardt, our co-author on *Retail Marketing,* for his contribution to this section.

33. "Supermarket Sweepstakes," *Marketing & Media Decisions,* November 1988: 33–38.

EVALUATING THE COMPETITION IN RETAILING

Competition has become so intense in the United States that even supermarkets and discount department stores, such as MEIJER, are selling gasoline in order to generate more traffic.

OVERVIEW

The behavior of competitors is an important component of the retail planning and management model. Effective planning and execution in any retail setting cannot be accomplished without the proper analysis of competitors. In this chapter, we begin by reviewing the various models of retail competition. The types of competition in retailing are described next. We then discuss the evolution of retail competition and look at the upcoming retail revolution in nonstore retailing. We next look at some new retailing formats. Finally, we look at some trends in international retailing.

LEARNING OBJECTIVES

After reading this chapter, you should be able to

1. explain the various models of retail competition
2. distinguish between various types of retail competition
3. describe the three theories used to explain the evolution of retail competition
4. describe the changes that could effect retail competition
5. discuss how trends in international retailing can affect U.S. retailers

LO • 1
Explain the various models of retail competition

MODELS OF RETAIL COMPETITION

In this chapter, we look at the effects of competition on a retailer's performance. As we noted in Chapter 1, retailing was once a growth industry that was able to increase profits solely on the basis of an increasing population base. Today's slower economic and population growth rates have matured retailing into a business in which successful regional and national retailers can only grow by taking sales away from competitors. This is not always true, however, when discussing retail competition at the local level. Here, as a result of the makeup of the area's economy, the area's population and disposable income could be growing even while the country's is slowing. Consider, for example, the growth occurring in Orlando, Florida, with its major tourist attractions. In such trading areas, a retailer could grow without having to take sales away from a competitor. Just the opposite would occur in those areas experiencing an economic slowdown.

Nevertheless, a high-performance retailer must always be on the offensive by studying the changing competitive environment, especially its local competition, and differentiating itself from that competition. Only by establishing a pace that is extremely difficult in terms of time and money for others to follow will a retailer reap all the rewards that the industry offers. Prime examples of such differentiation are category killers, such as CompUSA or Office Depot, with their large selection, Nordstrom with its excellent customer service, and Wal-Mart with a technologically advanced distribution system that enables it to operate with significantly lower operating costs than its competitors. A retailer's performance will be substandard if it is always forced to copy the actions of others and isn't able to differentiate itself. This, however, does not mean that a retailer should not pay close attention to what the competition is doing. Only by visiting the neighboring Wal-Mart, Target, or Kmart will the small local retailer know what items the discounters are carrying and what they are not. These large discounters usually carry only a limited selection within a product category. Rather than saying that he or she would never be caught dead in a Wal-Mart, it is to the small appliance store owner's benefit to know which televisions the discounter is carrying. This is the only way he or she can match the price on similar units and offer better services and a more complete range of units.

It is important to remember that no retailer, however clever, can design a strategy, that will totally insulate it from the competitive actions of others. This is true despite the fact that the retailer may have done an excellent job in developing and following its mission statement, setting its goals and objectives, and conducting its (SWOT) analysis. After all, some merchandising innovations can be easily copied and cannot be patented. Furthermore, the relatively low cost of entry into a retail business, in comparison with other businesses, means that retailers can count on being copied by others when they unveil a profitable strategy. The rapid growth of fast-food restaurants, discount department stores, one-hour photo shops, and convenience stores attest to this fact.

If you plan to become a retailer, you must develop the talent for designing and implementing innovative competitive strategies. Furthermore, you need to recognize that in retailing, competition is the fact of life.

Competition in retailing, as in any other industry, involves the interplay of supply and demand. One cannot appreciate the nature and scope of competition in retailing by studying only the supply factors (i.e., the type and number of competing retailers that exist). One must also examine consumer demand factors spoken of in Chapter 3. Let's examine a formal framework for describing and explaining the competitive environment of retailing.

THE COMPETITIVE MARKETPLACE

When retailers compete for customers, they generally compete on a local level unless they are catalog or electronic retailers. Households will typically not travel beyond local markets to purchase the goods that they desire. When they do travel beyond local markets, however, it is usually because their city or town is too small to support retailers with the selection of merchandise that they desire. Although some customers will always want to shop out of town, most cities with a population of more than 50,000 can provide the consumer with sufficient selection in almost all lines of merchandise. And in cities of less than 50,000, households may need to travel to another town or city only for large purchases such as a new automobile, television, furniture, or for a special item of clothing, such as a wedding dress.

DOLLAR $ & ¢ENTS

Retailers that attempt to study and respond to the local retail competition will be higher performers than retailers who don't understand that national competitive trends don't always affect every market.

MARKET STRUCTURE

Economists use four different economic terms to describe the competitive environment in the retailing industry: pure competition, pure monopoly, monopolistic competition, and oligopolistic competition.

Pure competition occurs when a market has

1. homogeneous (similar) products
2. many buyers and sellers, all having perfect knowledge of the market
3. ease of entry for both buyers and sellers (i.e., new retailers can start up with little difficulty and new consumers can easily come into the market)

In pure competition, each retailer faces a horizontal demand curve and must sell its products at the going "market" or equilibrium price. To sell at a lower price would be foolish, because you could always get the "market" price. Of course, you could not sell your merchandise at a higher price.

The second type of economic environment does not occur too often in real life. In pure monopoly, the seller is the only one selling the product under question and will set its selling price accordingly. Nonetheless, as the retailer seeks to sell more units, the retailer must lower the selling price. This is because if consumers already have one unit, they will tend to place a lower value on an additional unit. This is called "the law of diminishing returns" or of "declining marginal utility." After all, a hot fudge sundae

Pure competition
occurs when a market has homogeneous products and many buyers and sellers, all having perfect knowledge of the market, and ease of entry for both buyers and sellers.

Pure monopoly
occurs when there is only one seller for a product or service.

Retailers such as Macy's use its own I.N.C. private label of apparel to avoid direct price competition on identical merchandise.

would taste great right now, but would the second, third, or tenth one, purchased and consumed today, be as satisfying as the first?

Monopolistic competition is a market situation that develops when a market has

Monopolistic competition *occurs when the products offered are different, yet viewed by buyers as substitutable for each other and the sellers recognize that they compete with sellers of these different products.*

1. different (heterogeneous) products in the eyes of the consumers that are still substitutable for each other. Here, two or more retailers may be selling the same product, but one retailer is able to differentiate itself by providing better service. Thus, the consumers perceive them to be selling different products
2. sellers who think that even though they may be the only ones selling a particular brand, they do face competition from other retailers selling similar goods

The word *monopolistic* means that each seller is trying to control its own segment of the market. However, the word *competition* means that there are substitutes for the product available (e.g., a Compaq computer as a substitute for an IBM). The degree of the seller's control is dependent on the similarity of the competitor's product. This is why with monopolistic competition the retailer attempts to try to differentiate itself by the products and/or services that it offers. Some of the common means of achieving this are better customer service, offering credit, more convenient parking, larger merchandise selection, cleanliness, free setup and delivery, etc., as well as the brand or store image created and developed through advertising.

Oligopolistic competition occurs when a market has

Oligopolistic competition *occurs when relatively few sellers, or many small firms who follow the lead of a few larger firms, offer essentially homogeneous products and any action by one seller is expected to be noticed and reacted to by the other sellers.*

1. essentially homogeneous products, such as gasoline
2. relatively few sellers or many small firms who always follow the lead of the few large firms
3. any action by one is expected to be noticed and reacted to by the others

As in pure competition, oligopolists face a long-run trend toward selling at the equilibrium price, because everybody knows what each other is doing. Nonprice competition, relying on product or service differences other than price, is extremely difficult because consumers view the products and services as essentially similar. This is why when selling retail airline tickets, the major airlines such as American and Delta almost always match each other's prices on identical travel routes.

Retailing can be characterized as monopolistic or, in rare cases, oligopolistic competition. The distinction between monopolistic competition and oligopolistic competition lies in the number of sellers. An oligopoly means there are few sellers, so any action by one is noticed and reacted to by the others. Conventional economic thought suggests that for oligopoly to occur, the top four firms have to account for more than 60 to 80 percent of the market. Although, as we pointed out in our discussion of "category killers" in the first chapter, some national retailers do have large market shares, oligopolistic competition does not actually occur on a national level. However, it is not uncommon at a local level, especially for smaller communities, for food stores and department or discount department stores to operate as oligopolists. However, if prices become too high, merchandise selection too limited, or services too poor, residents of these communities will travel to larger communities to shop. This is known as outshopping. However, even when retailing becomes concentrated at the local level, there are several checks on the retailers' power:

> The country is full of automobiles, so most customers have large numbers of alternatives. Moreover, many modern retailers are becoming less specialized. The supermarket that sells nylons and the drugstore where you cannot find the drug counter are famous. Any seller who tries to maintain high prices is apt to find the grocers or the gas stations or someone equally far removed trying to take over his profitable lines. At any rate, there seems to be a continuous supply of new shopkeepers, ready to appear whenever prospects are good, and often even when they are not. It takes a good deal more to break into such fields as food retailing than it once did, but the cost of entry is still much lower than in most concentrated segments of manufacturing.[1]

In addition, another check on a retailer at a local level is mail-order shopping or shopping over the Internet. If prices at department and specialty stores were to become too excessive, then local shoppers may increase their use of nonstore shopping alternatives.

DEMAND SIDE OF RETAILING

Since most retailers face monopolistic competition, we will assume such a market structure in the remainder of the text. In a monopolistically competitive market, the retailer will be confronted with a negatively sloping demand curve. That is, consumers will demand a higher quantity as price is lowered. The typical retailer thus faces a demand function as shown in Exhibit 4.1.[2]

Higher prices in most cases will result in less quantity demanded, because households have limited incomes and many alternatives to allocate those dollars to. If a retailer raises prices and all else remains unchanged, then households will try to shift some of their purchasing power to other retailers with lower prices. This should suggest to you that retailers cannot be profitable by setting prices at the highest possible levels. Retailers will find it necessary to set prices somewhere below the maximum possible price but above zero. As prices approach zero, the retailer will sell large quantities but may not generate sufficient revenue to cover costs. This implies that they will not sell the maximum quantity. But where should they set prices? It seems reasonable that the retailers would want to set prices to maximize profits over the long run. To do so,

Outshopping occurs when individuals in one community travel usually to a larger community to shop.

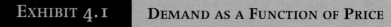

EXHIBIT 4.1   DEMAND AS A FUNCTION OF PRICE

however, they need knowledge of their costs, and this involves an examination of supply factors.

SUPPLY SIDE OF RETAILING

Retailers cannot operate without incurring costs, which can be classified as fixed or variable. These costs are portrayed graphically in Exhibit 4.2. Fixed costs are those that the retailer incurs regardless of the quantity of goods or services sold. These costs are in most part related to the size of the store and the costs of maintenance and finance, regardless of whether the store is open or closed. Examples of fixed costs in retailing include insurance, taxes, rent or lease payments, and security guards. Variable costs are those that increase proportionately with sales volume. The two largest variable costs in retailing are the cost of the goods or services sold and salaries and wages, especially for commissioned employees.

Without a doubt, not all the costs of operating a retail store can be categorized strictly into fixed and variable costs. Semifixed costs are constant over a range of sales volume, but past a crucial point they increase to a higher plateau and then again remain constant at another higher sales volume range. For example, labor may be viewed as semifixed. Before the doors of the store can be opened each day, a staff of employees must be on hand, but as store traffic volume rises past a crucial point, more employees would need to be added, because the existing staff would be inadequate.

Regardless of the exact form of the retailer's cost function, these costs must be examined to set a profit-maximizing price.

PROFIT-MAXIMIZING PRICE

A profit-maximizing price seeks to get as much profit as possible from the sale of goods and services. In this situation, the retailer seeks to charge a price in which the marginal revenue (the change in total revenue that results from the sale of one more unit) is equal to the marginal costs (the change in total costs that results from the sale of one more unit). If the marginal revenue (MR) is greater than the marginal cost (MC) for a grocery store selling milk, then the store will increase total profits by selling one more

---

Fixed costs
are those that the retailer incurs regardless of the quantity of goods or services sold.

Variable costs
are those that increase proportionately with sales volume.

Semifixed costs
are constant over a range of sales volume, but past a crucial point they increase to a higher plateau and then again remain constant at another higher sales volume range.

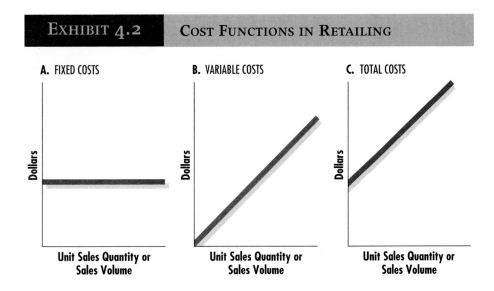

EXHIBIT 4.2 — COST FUNCTIONS IN RETAILING

A. FIXED COSTS

B. VARIABLE COSTS

C. TOTAL COSTS

unit, or gallon, of milk. Likewise, if MC is greater than MR for that extra gallon of milk, then the store will reduce total profits by selling it. This doesn't mean the store will lose money by selling that extra gallon, only that profits will be lowered. Part of the reason for this phenomenon is that the store can't sell milk at different prices to different customers. If the store wants to sell extra milk, it has to lower the price not just for a single customer but for all customers, or at least for a segment (e.g., giving senior citizen or student discounts, using special coupons).

NONPRICE DECISIONS

The retailer has more than just price to influence the quantity it will sell and the profit level it will achieve. If store location is fixed (the retailer has a long-term lease), some of the more important nonprice variables are merchandise mix, advertising, special promotions, personal selling, and store atmosphere (e.g., width of aisles). These and all other nonprice variables are directed at enlarging the demand that the retailer faces. Here are some ways a retailer could make use of nonprice competition:

DOLLAR $ & CENTS

Retailers that are able to remove themselves from price competition by using some other means of differentiating themselves will be higher performers than those that aren't able to do this.

1. The retailer could alter its merchandise mix in the direction of higher-quality goods or having large sizes. This would increase the maximum price that consumers will pay and also increase the distance consumers would travel to shop for

THESE STORES HAVE A RETURN POLICY THAT IS UNBEATABLE

In the highly competitive world of retailing, Nordstrom and L.L. Bean have turned exacting standards of customer service into something legends are made of.

Retailers across the country agree that Nordies, as Nordstrom employees are called, are better paid and trained than the competition and are encouraged to do almost anything within reason to satisfy customers. One sales clerk personally ironed a customer's newly purchased shirt so it would look fresher for an upcoming meeting. Another example of Nordstrom excellent service was when the store refunded $6,500 to a customer for a fur coat because they forgot to give instructions on how to care for the coat during the summer. This insistence on servicing the customer starts at the top with the president's, James Nordstrom, orders to "replace anything on demand, no matter how expensive, no questions asked." Although the policy is sometimes abused by shoppers (who may, for example, order an expensive dress, wear it to a party and then return it), it made Nordstrom a symbol of customer satisfaction. There is even a story—which the company doesn't deny—about a customer who got his money back on a tire. Because Nordstrom doesn't sell tires, it was a testament to James Nordstrom's dictum of "no questions asked."

L.L. Bean, however, recently did something few other retailers aspired to: It wanted to grow more slowly. Bean, long a mecca for yuppies and outdoorsmen, prided itself on its service and promised 100 percent satisfaction or your money back. The problem was, lots of customers weren't satisfied. Dismayed, Bean launched a new service campaign: "Get it right the first time" and scaled back expansion goals to ensure greater care in inspecting and shipping goods.

Bean's focus on improving service isn't to say it wasn't pleasing many customers. The main reason for the returns was because clothes don't fit—common

in the $35 billion U.S. catalog-company business. Only a small percentage of merchandise is returned because of defects, Bean says. The company once recalled 25,000 of its oxford shirts because the yoke in a few shirts ripped. Only a handful of shirts were returned after the recall. Nonetheless, everyone received a new shirt—on the house.

However, the Bean employees are as much a legend as the Nordies are when it comes to service. Often, Bean's employees meet vacation-bound customers at highway tollbooths to deliver hiking or camping equipment. That's why it should not be surprising when a Bean employee goes out of his or her way to help somebody. Take, for example, the story of Loretta Green.

At 6 A.M. on Sunday morning, Loretta got a call from a New York policeman who found a dazed elderly woman wandering the streets clutching a small terrier. The dog's tag read "My name is Tiger. Return to Mary Will, Bethesda, Maryland." No such listing was found. Luckily, the woman was wearing an L.L. Bean field watch.

Ms. Green, after failing to find any Mary Will in her New York zip codes, tried using Maryland zips. She found one with a discontinued telephone number who had last ordered a watch and a 25-inch dog bed. Figuring that the woman now lived alone in New York, Ms. Green next searched her records to see if Mary Will had ever sent gifts to a relative. Within the hour, Mary's son in Pennsylvania was located. It seemed his mother had been missing for three days after leaving New York on her way to visit him.

When it comes to great customer service, lifesaving is hard to beat.

SOURCE: Based on the authors' experiences with these retailers and Denise Goodman, "Mail-Order Rescue," *Redbook,* March 1993: 160.

When communities become overstored, price competition will become more intense and some retailers, in an attempt to increase sales, will offer 2-for-1 specials.

these goods, thereby enlarging the retailer's trade area. Marshall Field's, Neiman-Marcus, Nordstrom, and L.L. Bean have done an excellent job of removing themselves from price competition by offering private-label merchandise that customers consider to be very high quality, in combination with excellent service. However, the service described in the Behind the Scenes box is probably a little extraordinary, even for these retailers.

2. The retailer could provide customers with free parking and/or gas, which would effectively lower transportation costs for customers; for example, one West Texas car dealer promotes the fact that he will fill any out-of-town shopper's gas tank, up to 20 gallons. The lower transportation costs would increase the distance that the customer would be willing to travel, thereby increasing the retailer's trade area.

3. The retailer could engage in an extensive advertising campaign directed at persuading consumers to purchase more of the goods it sells. The net effect could be an increase in the maximum quantity demanded.

Most retail decision variables, whether price or nonprice, are directed at influencing demand. Of course, the profitability of the decisions depends on the marginal cost of the action versus the marginal revenue it generates.

COMPETITIVE ACTIONS

We just saw that most retailers attract customers from a limited geographic area and that as prices are lowered this area expands. But even at a zero price, households can only afford to travel a certain distance to get the goods and services retailers offer. Therefore, in most cities there are several, if not many, retailers in each line of retail trade.

When there are too many retail establishments competing in a particular city, the profitability of all the retailers will suffer. Eventually, some retailers may leave the market. If there are too few retailers, profits may be high enough to attract new retail competitors, or existing retailers may be enticed to expand. A market is in equilibrium in terms of number of retail establishments if the return on investment is high enough to justify keeping capital invested in retailing, but not so high to invite more competition.

A good measure of competitive activity in a market is the number of retail establishments of a given type per thousand households. If the stores are of the same approximate size, then as the number of stores per thousand households increases, the degree of competition intensifies. This intensified competition will tend to decrease the retailer's profit. When the number of stores per household gets too large, the market can be characterized as overstored. However, if there is only a small number of stores per thousand household, in comparison with other markets, the market will be characterized as understored. Importantly, in overstored markets the average return on investment that retailers earn in that market is below what is needed to keep all of them doing business in that market, and some will thus eventually exit the market. However, in understored markets the average return on investment that retailers earn in that market is above what is needed to keep all of them doing business in that market. This will, in fact, be an invitation for some retailers in the market to expand by opening more stores or for other retailers to enter this market.

Competition is most intense in overstored markets, because many retailers are achieving an inadequate return on investment. These retailers face a major performance imperative and will implement both price and nonprice actions in an all-out attempt to increase sales and profit levels. Because retailers operate in a relatively closed geographic market, with a fixed number of households and a limited number of dollars to compete for, any action by one retailer to increase its sales or profit level will warrant an action from competitors.

Overstored

is a condition in a community where the number of stores in relation to households is so large that to engage in retailing is usually unprofitable or marginally profitable.

Understored

is a condition in a community where the number of stores in relation to households is relatively low so that engaging in retailing is an attractive economic endeavor.

LO • 2
Distinguish between various types of retail competition

TYPES OF COMPETITION

It is possible to merge the preceding discussion of competition in retailing with the classification schemes used by the Department of Commerce in conducting the Census of Retail Trade.

INTRATYPE AND INTERTYPE COMPETITION

Intratype competition

occurs when two or more retailers of the same type, as defined by SIC codes in the Census of Retail Trade, compete directly with each other for the same households.

Intratype competition occurs when two or more retailers of the same type, as defined by SIC (Standard Industrial Classification) codes in the Census of Retail Trade, compete directly with each other for the same households. This is the most common type of retail competition: Circuit City competes with Best Buy, H&R Block competes with The Tax Place, Avon competes with Mary Kay, Mail Boxes Etc competes with Pack & Mail, Family Dollar competes with Dollar General, and MCI competes with AT&T for your telephone service. Due to the changing nature of the retailing environment, retailers are often forced to change their strategy as their competition changes. For example, Sears, in the early 1990s, wanted to compete head-on with low-priced discounters such as Wal-Mart and Kmart. Today, after doing its own SWOT analysis and concluding that you don't push shopping carts through malls, where most of its stores are located, it successfully targeted instead the middle-of-the-road merchants JCPenney and May Department Stores by appealing to women and emphasizing apparel.

Recently, as we noted in the first chapter, many retailers have been moving toward scrambled merchandising (i.e., carrying any merchandise line that can be sold profitably). Some examples include

1. Discount department stores (e.g., Kmart, Target, and Wal-Mart) handling more cosmetics and fragrances, which were historically the province of the traditional department stores. In addition, these discounters are now handling computers and computer equipment as well as fast-food, groceries, and produce items.

2. Supermarkets (e.g., Albertsons, Kroger, and Food Giant) handling video cassette rentals. Supermarkets today are estimated to have 11 percent of this market. Supermarkets also have taken market share away from fast-food restaurants with their HMRs (home-meal replacements). In addition, their banks and pharmacies have also changed the competitive landscape.

3. Convenience food stores (e.g., 7-Eleven) not only selling motor oil and related auto care products, but adding fast-food, lottery tickets, and automated teller machines (ATMs).

Every time different types of retail outlets sell the same lines of merchandise and compete for the same limited consumer dollars, intertype competition occurs. In each of the preceding examples, as intertype competition expanded, gross margins on the respective merchandise lines declined. For example, mail-order pharmacies have gained a growing share of prescription drugs. Their market share is now close to 20 percent, and the impact on the locally operated or chain-operated retail drugstore has been dramatic. Consequently, the average gross margin return on sales of drugs has declined due to this increased competition. This increased competition has caused both types of drug retailers to seek the lowest priced drugs available, because different drug manufacturers produce virtually identical medicines for arthritis, ulcers, and other common ailments. As a result, the inflation rate for prescription drugs is the lowest of any medical category. This same thing may soon happen in the grocery industry. Our Winners & Losers box explains how Wal-Mart's, along with Kmart and Target, introduction of supercenters is presenting the traditional grocers (i.e., the supermarkets) with an intertype challenge.

Intertype competition *occurs when two or more retailers of a different type, as defined by SIC codes in the Census of Retail Trade, compete directly by attempting to sell the same merchandise lines to the same households.*

DIVERTIVE COMPETITION

Another concept that helps to explain the nature of competition in retailing is divertive competition. This occurs when retailers intercept or divert customers from competing retailers. For example, an individual may recognize that she needs to get a birthday card for a relative and will probably do this the next time she visits the local shopping mall, which has a very well-stocked Hallmark card store. However, one day while picking up a prescription at the drugstore she walks by the card stand and decides to purchase the greeting card at the drugstore. The drugstore retailer has intercepted this customer from the Hallmark store. One retailer with a high potential for using this concept for increasing sales is Kmart. When Floyd Hall replaced Joseph Antonini as CEO in 1995, he was shocked to find that 49 percent of shoppers drove past a Kmart to shop at a Wal-Mart.[3] Many of these shoppers

Divertive competition *occurs when retailers intercept or divert customers from competing retailers.*

SHOULD GROCERS FEAR A DISCOUNTER?

Over the past three decades, the Wal-Mart juggernaut has rolled over scores of smaller inefficient discount stores as it covered North America. Wal-Mart now has set its sights on the one-stop shopper for both grocery and general merchandise.

Wal-Mart has been opening more than 100 supercenters, with an average size of 150,000 square feet, a year. More than one-third of that space, which is devoted to produce, meat, and other foods, competes with the traditional supermarket. And this doesn't count the paper products, cleaning supplies, light bulbs, etc., that are part of the general merchandise category. For two-wage earner or single-parent families, a supercenter allows convenient one-stop shopping; for Wal-Mart, it generates additional sales of general merchandise. Supercenters have general merchandise sales up to 30 percent greater than the older 110,000-square-foot Wal-Mart "boxes" without groceries. Thus, Wal-Mart could operate its grocery business at break-even and still make money with the additional general merchandise sales. In all reality, that appears to be what is occurring, as many grocery experts believe that Wal-Mart is operating just above break-even on the grocery side while it learns the business. Nevertheless, at the end of 1996, Wal-Mart's Supercenters were ranked third in U.S. supermarket sales—behind only Kroger and Safeway, which just acquired Von's. Kmart, with its smaller number of supercenters, also broke into the grocer's Top 25.

This couldn't come at a worse time for supermarket operators. Over the past five years, grocery sales have been flat, as the inflation level for food products has been in the 1 to 3 percent range and more and more time-pressed consumers are eating out, thus reducing their grocery needs. Therefore, supermarkets have been operating at razor-thin margins and have only remained profitable by taking market share away from weaker competitors or by adding nonfood items. Today, many smaller, less efficient retailers doubt whether they can compete with Wal-Mart. However, forewarned, the larger more efficient ones are preparing for the onslaught. H.E. Butts (H.E.B.) is probably doing the best job of reclaiming their distinctive place in the grocery segment. The San Antonio retailer is the nation's largest privately held grocery chain, with sales exceeding $5 billion. In addition to expanding the fresh-food, meat, deli, bakery, and produce areas of its business, H.E.B. recently opened a new grocery store concept. Central Market, a grocery store without Coca-Cola, Pampers, and other general merchandise items, is instead loaded with fresh and prepared foods. The 63,000-square-foot market's produce section features two dozen different kinds of citrus, nine varieties of mushrooms, and two dozen types of potatoes. The first store, which is located in an upper-class San Antonio neighborhood, also stocks more than 2,000 wines, 300 beers, 500 cheeses, and 100 types of mustard. Other grocers ready for the upcoming battle include Food4Less in northern California with its price-impact/warehouse stores. Winn-Dixie, the nation's sixth largest grocer, has begun to increase the size of its stores, using some of the newer space to feature items that the supercenters generally lack—fresh seafood and gourmet meat counters. IGA's independently owned operators are working closer with their vendors to increase their efficiency. At the same time, AWG (Associated Wholesale Grocers), a food wholesaler co-owned by 850 supermarkets, is trying to copy Wal-Mart by squeezing its vendors—something Wal-Mart taught them. AWG has recently opened its own warehouse to carry HBA (health, beauty aids) and general merchandise.

Still, with the continuing advance of Wal-Mart, as well as the expansion of Super K's and Super Target Supercenters, thousands of smaller, less efficient supermarkets will probably close in the next few years while a price war continues in the grocery business.

were Kmart customers before Wal-Mart arrived, but too many "out-of-stock" items combined with poor service and old dirty stores drove them to Wal-Mart. Although Kmart's new strategy calls for rediverting these customers back to Kmart, one can be sure that Wal-Mart will fight to retain them.

To comprehend the significance of divertive competition, which can be either intertype or intratype competition, one needs to recognize that most retailers operate very close to their break-even point (the point at which total revenues equal total expenses) but aren't really aware of this fact. For instance, supermarkets with their extremely low gross margin percent tend to have high break-even points, ranging from 94 to 96 percent of current sales. General merchandise retailers with a higher gross margin percent face lower break-even points of 85 to 92 percent of their current sales. In either case, a modest drop in sales volume could make these retailers unprofitable and fuel the growth of scrambled merchandising.

Break-even point
is where total revenues equals total expenses and the retailer is making neither a profit nor loss.

DOLLAR $ & ¢ENTS

Retailers should attempt to operate at a sales volume of 20 percent above their break-even point because this will allow them to weather major competitive assaults and thus be able to achieve a high long-run performance.

DEVELOPING A PROTECTED NICHE

As competition intensifies in retailing, the retail manager will find it harder to be protected from competitive threats on the basis of the merchandise offered. Why? Because all retailers have access to the same merchandise. Therefore, retailers in the future will find it rewarding to develop a protected niche in the marketplace. Careful store positioning can be used to accomplish this. In store positioning, one identifies a well-defined market segment using demographic or lifestyle variables and appeals to this segment with a clearly differentiated approach. A retailer that has done an especially good job at store positioning is Talbot's, which appeals to the upscale, older-than-30, high-fashion women's market. The merchandising, store atmosphere, price points, customer services, and retail personnel are all positioned to appeal to this segment. Because it is difficult to find unique merchandise, many retailers have developed their own store brands to help set them apart from the competition and develop a protected niche. Some of the major retailers and a few of their private labels include JCPenney (Stafford, Hunt Club, and The Original Arizona Jean Co.), Saks Fifth Avenue (SFA Collections and The Works), Nordstrom (Norsport, Faconnable, and Baby N), Macy's (Charter Club and Austin Grey), Wal-Mart (Sam's American Choice), and Sears (Fieldmaster, Craftsman, and Kenmore). Most retail analysts contend that positioning will be an even more important competitive strategy in the future.

Store positioning
is when a retailer identifies a well-defined market segment using demographic or lifestyle variables and appeals to this segment with a clearly differentiated approach.

EVOLUTION OF RETAIL COMPETITION

Several other theories have developed to explain and describe the evolution of competition in retailing. We review three of them briefly.

WHEEL OF RETAILING

Wheel of retailing theory
*describes how new types
of retailers enter the market
as low-status, low-margin,
low-price operators; how-
ever, as they meet with success, these new retailers
gradually acquire more sophisticated and elaborate
facilties, and thus because
of higher costs become vulnerable to new types of low-
margin retailer competitors
who progress through the
same pattern.*

The wheel of retailing theory, illustrated in Exhibit 4.3, is one of the oldest descriptions of the patterns of competitive development in retailing.[4] This theory states that new types of retailers enter the market as low-status, low-margin, low-price operators. This is the entry phase and allows these retailers to compete effectively and take market share away from the more traditional retailers. However, as they meet with success, these new retailers gradually acquire more sophisticated and elaborate facilities, thereby becoming less efficient, in a trading-up phase. This creates both a higher investment and a subsequent rise in operating costs. Predictably, these retailers will enter the vulnerability phase and must raise prices and margins, becoming vulnerable to new types of low-margin retail competitors who progress through the same pattern. This appears to be the case today with outlet malls. Once bare-bones warehouses for manufacturers' imperfect or excess merchandise, outlet malls have quickly evolved into fancy, almost up-scale malls where retailers try to outdo each other's accent lighting, private dressing rooms, and generous return policies. As a result, with the cost of operating at such locations increasing and with the regular department stores becoming more competitive, there is now little difference in the outlet's prices and the department store's sale prices. Holiday Hospitality Corporation recognizing that it can become vulnerable by constantly upgrading its lodging units has developed three distinct hotel/motel formats. Holiday Inn Select is targeted at the penny-pincher and keeps its costs low by providing spartan lodging, Holiday Inn Express is targeted at the middle market and provides some higher cost features such as swimming pools and continental breakfasts, and Holiday Inn Crowne Plaza is targeted at the more upscale or serious business traveler and features, luxurious furnishings and restrautants, health spas, business services, conference rooms, and other amenities.[5]

RETAIL ACCORDION

Several observers of the history of retailing have noted that retail institutions evolve from outlets that offer wide assortments to specialized stores that offer narrow assortments to its customers and then return to the wide assortment stores to continue through the pattern again and again. This contraction and expansion suggests the term retail accordion.[6]

Retail accordion
*describes how retail institu-
tions evolve from outlets
that offer wide assortments
to specialized stores that offer narrow assortments,
then return to the wide assortment stores and con-
tinue repeatedly through
the pattern.*

Retail historians have observed that in the United States, retail trade was dominated by the general store until 1860. The general store carried a broad assortment of merchandise ranging from farm implements to textiles to food. After 1860, due to the growth of cities and roads, retail trade became more specialized and was concentrated in the central business districts of cities. By 1880–1890, department and specialty stores were the dominant competitive force. Both carried more specialized assortments than the general store. In the 1950s, retailing began to move again to wider merchandise lines. Typical was the supermarket, which added produce and dairy products, nonfood items such as kitchen utensils, health and beauty aids, and small household

McDonald's has increased its cost of store operations over the last 40 years by adding indoor seating and indoor playgounds and thus has fallen victim to the wheel of retailing.

EXHIBIT 4.3	WHEEL OF RETAILING

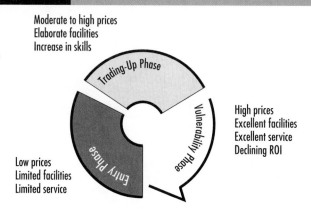

Moderate to high prices
Elaborate facilities
Increase in skills

Trading-Up Phase

Vulnerability Phase

High prices
Excellent facilities
Excellent service
Declining ROI

Entry Phase

Low prices
Limited facilities
Limited service

Retail life cycle

describes four distinct stages that a retail institution progresses through: introduction, growth, maturity and decline.

appliances. By the 1990s, specialization in merchandise categories once again became a dominant competitive strategy. Witness, for example, the recent success of Woolworth's Athlete's Foot division, Barnes & Noble Bookstores, B Dalton Booksellers, and the spin-offs from The Limited of Intimate Brands (the Victoria's Secret division) and Abercrombie & Fitch Co.

RETAIL LIFE CYCLE

The final framework that we examine in the evolution of retail competition is the retail life cycle. Some experts argue that retailing institutions pass through an identifiable cycle. This cycle includes four distinct stages that starts with (1) *introduction,* (2) proceeds to *growth,* (3) then *maturity,* and ends with (4) *decline.* Each stage is briefly discussed.

INTRODUCTION   The introduction stage begins with an aggressive, bold entrepreneur who is willing and able to develop a different approach to retailing of certain products. Most often the approach is oriented to a simpler method of distribution and passing the savings on to the customer. Other times, it could be centered on a distinctive product assortment, shopping ease, locational convenience, advertising, or promotion. For example, quick oil change businesses offered "while you wait" service at more convenient locations with lower prices than conventional service stations and automobile dealers. During this stage, profits are low, despite the increasing sales level, due to amortizing developmental costs.

GROWTH   During the growth stage, sales, and usually profits, explode. Many others begin to copy the idea. Toward the end of this period, cost pressures that arise from the need for a larger staff, more complex internal systems, increased management controls, and other requirements of operating large, multiunit organizations overtake some of the favorable results. Consequently, late in this stage both market share and profitability tend to approach their maximum level.

MATURITY   In maturity, market share stabilizes and severe profit declines are experienced for several reasons. First, managers have become accustomed to managing a high-growth firm that was simple and small, but now they must manage a large

EXHIBIT 4.4	RETAIL INSTITUTIONS IN THEIR VARIOUS STAGES OF THE RETAIL LIFE CYCLE

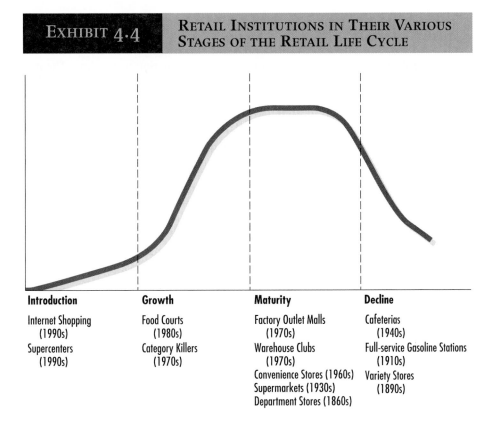

Introduction	Growth	Maturity	Decline
Internet Shopping (1990s)	Food Courts (1980s)	Factory Outlet Malls (1970s)	Cafeterias (1940s)
Supercenters (1990s)	Category Killers (1970s)	Warehouse Clubs (1970s)	Full-service Gasoline Stations (1910s)
		Convenience Stores (1960s)	Variety Stores (1890s)
		Supermarkets (1930s)	
		Department Stores (1860s)	

complex firm in a nongrowing market. Second, the industry has typically overexpanded. Third, competitive assaults will be made on these firms by new retailing formats (a bold entrepreneur starting a new retail life cycle).

DECLINE Although decline is inevitable, retail managers will try to postpone it by changing the retail mix. These attempts can postpone the decline stage, but a return to earlier attractive levels of operating performance is not likely. Sooner or later a major loss of market share will occur, profits fall, and the once promising idea is no longer needed in the marketplace.

The retail cycle is accelerating today. New concepts now move quickly from introduction to maturity as the leading operators will have aggressive growth goals and their investors demand a quick return on equity. In addition, many entrepreneurs will be acquired by larger retailers with the capital and expertise in concept roll-out.[7] Exhibit 4.4 lists the various stages of the retail life cycle for many of our current retail institutions.

FUTURE CHANGES IN RETAIL COMPETITION

LO • 4
Describe the changes that could effect retail competition

As we prepare to enter the 21st century, retailers can expect an increase in competition from both nonstore retailers and the advent of new retailing formats.

NONSTORE RETAILING

Several industry analysts contend that nonstore retailing—sometimes called direct retailing or direct marketing—will become the next revolution in retailing. The mechanics for such a revolution are already in place as a variety of established selling techniques permit consumers to purchase goods and services without having to leave home. With accelerated communications technology and changing consumer lifestyles, the growth potential for nonstore retailing is explosive. Traditional retailers need to continuously monitor developments in nonstore retailing.

The Census of Retailing classifies nonstore retailers into three major types:

Mail-order houses
are retail establishments that primarily engage in the sales of products to housheholds by catalog and mail order.

1. Mail-order houses: establishments primarily engaged in the retail sale of products by catalog and mail order. In 1997, 130 million Americans used direct mail to purchase $390 billion of goods and services.[8] Included are book and CD and tape clubs, jewelry firms, novelty merchandise firms, and specialty merchandisers (e.g., sporting goods—L.L. Bean; children apparel retailers—Right Start; and kitchenware—Williams-Sonoma).

Automatic merchandising machine operators
are retailers engaged in the retail sale of products by means of automatic merchandising units or vending machines.

2. Automatic merchandising machine operators: establishments primarily engaged in the retail sale of products by means of automatic merchandising units, or vending machines. This industry does not include coin-operated service machines such as music machines and amusement and game machines, lockers, or scales.

   Although not exactly vending machines, stand-alone kiosks, are often provided by vendors in high-traffic areas, so that consumers without home computers can buy goods on-line. There is a possible problem with these kiosks, however: Vendors want users to browse and purchase, but other customers will probably not want to wait in line. They will seek out the nearest store. Retailers are also using in-store kiosks to give customers product information without having them locate a salesperson.

Direct selling establishments
are engaged in the retail sale of merchandise on an in-person basis, through party plans, or one-on-one in the home or workplace.

3. Direct selling establishments: primarily engaged in the retail sale of merchandise on an in-person basis, through party plans (Tupperware Home Parties) or one-on-one in the home or workplace (Avon Products), away from a fixed place of business. In the United States, sales from direct selling total about $13 billion annually and are made by more than 4 million individuals who are not employed by the organization they represent but are independent contractors. Worldwide direct selling sales are $50 billion, with Japan being the largest direct selling country. Major products sold include personal care items (Mary Kay Cosmetics), decorative home products (Princess House, Home Interiors and Gifts), cookware (West Bend, CUTCO), encyclopedias (World Book, Encyclopedia Britannica). Today, with women increasingly out of the home, little "cold canvassing" is done, with many companies telephoning to make appointments to show the merchandise. In addition, traditional direct selling techniques are being merged with newer marketing channels, such as mail order and catalogs, and merchandise is being shown and sold anywhere people gather, such as at state fairs, in shopping malls, and at airports. The major attributes of direct selling remain the same; support for the independent contractor, knowledge and demonstration of the product by the salesperson, excellent warranties and guarantees, and the person-to-person component.

The preceding classification is quite archaic, having been developed by the Department of Commerce before 1930. Nonetheless, the government persists in its use,

Target, which has been traditionally in the discount department store business, has added supermarkets to its new stores to create 140,000 square foot, one-stop supercenters.

despite the fact that such nonstore retailers as electronic shopping is not included. A more complete discussion will be presented in Chapter 7 when we look at how retailers set up nonstore locations.

Many retail analysts predict that, as a result of several key forces at work today, nonstore sales (especially those that use the Internet) will experience significant growth into the 2000s. Kurt Salmon Associates expects that by the year 2005, nonstore retailing will account for 55 percent of total GAF (general merchandise, apparel, and furniture) sales up from 15 percent in 1995.[9] Some of the forces contributing to this growth are

consumers' need to save time
erosion of fun in the shopping experience
lack of qualified sales help in stores to provide information
explosive development of the telephone, the computer, and telecommunications
consumers' desire to eliminate the middleman's profit as a means of reducing prices

However, as we noted in the first chapter, not everybody is convinced that nonstore retailing's prospects for growth are unlimited. Critics contend that the consumers' loss of discretionary income, the lack of the personal touch in nonstore shopping, not all products being appropriate for sale this way as very often the color in a print ad or on television doesn't match the product, lack of standardized sizes, lack of computer skills by many older than the age of 40, failure by manufacturers to take control of this channel of distribution, and the reactions of those store retailers threatened with exclusion from this channel will limit nonstore growth. These critics believe that the nonstore revolution, especially via the Internet, will still take place, but because of the factors cited above, it will be slower than expected. This is all the more reason why the successful retail manager for the 21st century must continue to monitor the environmental changes taking place, especially technological changes that enable all the other environmental forces to change.

One of the keys to success in retailing is developing the ability to monitor the environmental changes taking place, especially those pertaining to technology, and adopting the technology that can be used to improve the retailer's performance.

NEW RETAILING FORMATS

The practice of retailing is continually evolving. New formats are born and old ones die. Innovation in retailing is the result of constant pressure to improve efficiency and effectiveness in a continual effort to better serve the consumer. The pressure to better serve has also resulted in a shortened life cycle for retail formats. However, just as retailers find it extremely difficult to predict what will be the "hot new item" for an upcoming season, especially Christmas, they have the same trouble predicting the success of new retail formats.

For example, in the late 1980s, most retail experts agreed that hypermarkets would be retailing's success story of the 1990s. However, despite their overwhelming success in Europe and their limited success in the United States with Meijer's in Michigan and Fred Meyer's in the Northwest; these "super-large" stores, which were designed like today's supercenters but were one and a half times as large, making them look like airplane hangars, were instead retailing's biggest failure for the 1990s. What happened?

Probably, customers thought that any store that had "rest areas" and stockers wearing roller skates was just too big to shop. Also, shoppers were unnerved by ceilings and shelves that rose several stories high. In addition, category killers, such as Toys "Я" Us and Sports Authority, offered greater selection, wholesale clubs offered better prices, and supermarkets and discounters offered more convenient locations.

Another retail format that didn't achieve the success predicted was the off-price retailers. Off-price retailers are similar to discounters with one important difference. Although discounters offer continuity of brands, that is carrying the same brands day-in and day-out, off-pricers, which were more opportunistic, carried only brands that they were able to get on special deals from the manufacturer. Thus, the off-price retailers failed for many of the same reasons that we discussed earlier in this chapter with the outlet malls: They just couldn't compete once the regular merchants, including discounters, became more price competitive.

Although the above retailing formats have not lived up to expectations, four formats brought about in part by the poor economic conditions of the mid-1990s are expected to be successful during the remainder of the decade: supercenters; stores focusing on recycling of good condition, usable merchandise; liquidators; and electronic retailing.

SUPERCENTERS   One of the newest forms of retail competition is the supercenter, which is about two-thirds the size of a hypermarket. These cavernous, one-stop combination supermarkets and discount department stores, which were discussed earlier in this chapter, carrying more than 80,000 to 100,000 products that range

Off-price retailers
sell products at a discount but do not carry certain brands on a continuous basis. They carry those brands they can buy from manufacturers at close-out or deep one-time discount prices.

Supercenters
combine a discount store and grocery store and carry 80,000 to 100,000 products in order to offer one-stop shopping.

from televisions to peanut butter to fax machines should number more than 1,000 by 1998. These stores do, however, offer the customer one-stop shopping (and as a result, are capable of drawing customers from up to a 60- to 80-mile radius in some rural areas) and lower the customer's total cost of purchasing in terms of time and miles traveled without sacrificing service and variety. This is exactly what the time-pressed consumer of the 1990s needs. However, although Wal-Mart, Kmart, and Target are banking their future on this new format, some retail analysts question if older consumers can get around in these stores, if the younger ones will take the time to shop these mammoth stores, or if folks will buy tires, apparel, and tomatoes on the same shopping trip.[10] This appears to be the case, as one recent study of the shopping habits of a Kmart's Supercenter customers found that only 55 percent are now shopping both the grocery and general merchandise sections and 40 percent are now shopping only groceries.[11]

It is difficult to predict if the supercenter will be able to overtake the conventional supermarket as discussed in the Winners & Losers box earlier in this chapter. The study cited above found that grocery shoppers value convenience over price and tend to live closest to the store where they shop.[12] If this is true, then the success of the supercenter is still in doubt. However, in the end, the consumer will be the judge. Although with Target, Kmart, and Wal-Mart (the acknowledged leader in computerized distribution) placing major emphasis on supercenters as their vehicle for growth over the next 5 to 10 years, it is difficult to predict failure. Nevertheless, it is doubtful that the supermarket operators will surrender peacefully to the Big 3 in discounting (Kmart, Wal-Mart, and Target).[13]

Supermarkets, which have always operated with paper-thin net profit margins of 1 to 2 percent, will be forced to match the supercenters by gaining better control over their inventory to achieve cost savings. In the past, unlike Wal-Mart and Kmart, supermarkets mostly allowed their buying plans to be dictated by the food manufacturers' promotional programs. Now, they are joining the discounters in letting the customers' purchasing habits make their purchasing and inventory decisions. By using "just-in-time" (JIT) methods, grocers are now reordering only when and what their computer, which is connected to their in-store bar-code scanners, deems necessary. This way, grocers will be able to reduce costs and meet Wal-Mart, Target, Kmart, and the others' prices head-on. Still, it takes a different type of retailing skill to sell meat and produce than it does to sell general merchandise. After all, when was the last time a sporting goods manager had to wash, wax, and arrange by freshness his merchandise like a produce manager does?

The supercenter concept has even branched out into the automobile market. Glitzy computerized auto superstore chains, such as AutoNation, Driver's Mart Worldwide, and CarMax Auto Superstores, are giving nightmares to the nation's 22,000 traditional car dealers.[14] Since their beginning in the mid-1990s, this new breed of retailer has streamlined an industry in which 30 percent of a car's price had covered the retailer's expenses and has made shopping easier for the customer. These massive publicly traded chains sell new and used cars by using "cheap" Wall Street money to finance, sell, rent, lease, and repair cars. Just like the supercenters in the grocery industry, these auto superstores are making competition tougher for other retailers.[15]

RECYCLED MERCHANDISE RETAILERS

Recycled merchandisers have experienced renewed growth. Originally a product of the Great Depression, recycled merchandise retailers—selling castoff clothes, furniture, sporting goods, and even computers—include pawn shops, thrift shops, consignment shops, and even flea markets. Even as a record number of retailers was seeking bankruptcy

Recycled merchandise retailers *are establishments that sell used and reconditioned products.*

protection in 1996, these recycled merchandise retailers were growing by 10 percent a year. No longer is conspicuous consumption chic. With the advent of the baby busters, this is a period of time when consumers would rather gloat about a good buy than an expensive product. Besides, selling clothes that are no longer needed increases an individual's income.

Shoppers today find it difficult to distinguish between today's recyclers and small specialty shops. Because so much of the merchandise is new or nearly new,[16] the old appearance of looking like a Salvation Army Thrift Store is no longer appropriate. Recyclers have been developed to serve specific markets, such as pregnant women, large sizes, and children, or even specific merchandise, such as toys, sporting goods including camping and backpacking, outerwear, or jewelry. The apparel group accounting for the fewest resale and thrift store sales—men's clothing. It seems that men hang onto their clothes longer than women and children, leaving much less available for resale.[17]

LIQUIDATORS
With more than 15,000 retailers seeking the protection of the bankruptcy courts annually, a new growth industry (albeit from a very, very small starting point) has developed: liquidators. Often called retailing's undertakers or vultures, this small and all-but-invisible retail format comes in and liquidates leftover merchandise when an established retailer shuts down or down-sizes. Firms such as Schottenstein Professional Asset Management, which is part of the Value City family, purchase the entire inventory of the existing retailer and run the "going-out-of-business" (GOB) sale. They make their money by seldom paying more than 30 cents on the dollar for the closeout merchandise. This handful of firms does almost $5 billion in sales annually.

Some might question why retailers do not do this job themselves. Well, for starters, they usually have problems—or else they wouldn't need the liquidator's service in the first place. Second, most liquidators pay cash for the merchandise—a plus for the strapped retailer—and then they take all the risks and gain the rewards. Other liquidators will only conduct the sale but guarantee a minimum payout to the retailer. Finally, by having outsiders run the closeouts, management can focus on the continuing stores.

Running closeouts requires some very special retailing skills. Liquidators have a talent for pricing merchandise and estimating the expense of everything from ad budgets and payrolls to utility bills. And because most of the employees know they will be out of a job as soon as the liquidation is complete, liquidators have to develop special incentive plans to make it more profitable for store personnel to stay and work rather than quit or walk off with merchandise.[18]

ELECTRONIC SHOPPING
The general feeling among retail experts is that electronic, interactive, at-home shopping will definitely take off in the next few years. Every major player in the retail industry, computer industry, telecommunications industry, and the transaction processing industry is committed to this growth. In addition to providing true colors, standardized sizes, and an easy means for returns, which nonstore retailers are already working on, the only prerequisite needed for the Internet's success is having enough homes with PCs. Already 11 percent of the population is taking up this new activity for more than 5 hours a week and estimates are already calling for retail revenues on the net to reach $7 billion ($14 billion if web

site advertising and subscriptions are included) in the year 2000. And if the price of machines and on-line services continues to drop, then the numbers can only grow geometrically.[19]

DOLLAR $ & CENTS

Retailers can improve their long-run performance potential if they begin today to experiment with selling in the virtual world.

Still, what is happening today is only the beginning of the explosion that is about to occur.[20] As the Internet grows to allow access to text and graphics that brings us information packaged in two-dimensional real time and fully immersive three-dimensional video, Americans will spend more of their time in cyberspace.

This in turn will cause a whole new shopping experience. The shoppers of the next millennium will opt for the convenience and heighten experience of virtual shopping. Browsing will be even easier and the choices more extensive. Consumers will still want social activity outside the home; however, this won't be shopping but real entertainment—attending a ball game or concert. The net will allow us to shop with family and friends, even if they live half the world away.

However, before this net explosion can occur, several roadblocks must be overcome:

1. Cost of being on-line: Currently, most consumers must pay a fee to a commercial provider for access to the Internet. What mall could exist if an admission fee was required before a customer could enter to make a purchase?
2. Payment fraud: Even though the risk of credit card fraud is no higher for on-line customers than for traditional retailing, most consumers are reluctant to shop and pay on-line.
3. Too many men, too few women: More than two-thirds of current Internet users are males, who are not the predominate shoppers in the United States. This will especially be a problem for one prediction that electronic shopping will capture 10 percent of food store sales by the year 2005.[21]
4. Loss of a cultural tradition: For many consumers, shopping remains a form of entertainment and social interaction. Although on-line services provide some of this with chat rooms, just plain "people-watching" and meeting for coffee are not possible on-line.
5. Inadequate delivery services: Current delivery service companies may be incapable of handling the volume forecasted. Even if this is overcome, with the growing number of two-wage households, who will be home to accept delivery?
6. Slow transmission rates and poor graphics: Without expensive high-speed modems, the long waiting periods required to download a photograph onto a computer and slow transmission rates will hinder the graphic performance of all retailers using web sites.
7. Possible channel conflicts: Will vendors open their own on-line shopping stores to compete with their existing traditional retailers?

LO • 5
Discuss how trends in
international retailing
can affect U.S. retailers

TRENDS IN INTERNATIONAL RETAILING

The rate of change in retailing around the world appears to be directly related to the stage and speed of economic development in the countries concerned, but even the least-developed countries are experiencing dramatic changes. Retailing in other countries, however, exhibits greater diversity in its structure than it does in the United States. In some countries, such as Italy, retailing is composed largely of specialty houses carrying narrow lines. Finnish retailers generally carry a more general line of merchandise. The size of the average retailer is also diverse, from the massive Harrod's in London and Mitsukoshi Ltd. in Japan, both of which serve more than 10,000 customers a day, to the small one- or two-person stalls in developing African and Latin American nations.

The United States is not alone, however, in developing new retail formats. New types of retailing have emerged from all countries. These changing formats can be attributed to a variety of economic and social factors that are the same worldwide: a widespread concern for health, a steady increase in the number of working women and two-income families, the consequent upsurge in price levels, consumerism, and so forth. These factors, and their effects on consumer lifestyles, encouraged high-performance retailers around the world to seek new market segments, make adjustments in the retail mix, alter location patterns, and adopt new multisegment strategies. In the process, many new retail concepts and formats have emerged and spread. Four outstanding examples of foreign retailing formats that have been transferred to other countries are IKEA (Sweden), Carrefour (France), Benetton (Italy), and ALDI (Germany).

Ingar Kamprad, president of IKEA, was the first to successfully develop a warehouse retailing format that could be followed around the world. IKEA, the home furnishings specialty operation that is based on economies of scale in the areas of marketing, purchasing, and distribution and that uses customer participation in the assembly and transportation of the merchandise, generates almost 90 percent of its revenues from global operations, more than any other major worldwide retailer.[22]

Daniel Bernard, the president of the Paris-based global hypermarket giant, Carrefour, was quoted as saying: "If people think that going international is a solution to their problems at home, they will learn by spilling their blood. Global retailing demands a huge investment and gives no guarantees of a return."[23] Bernard should know. As we noted earlier, Carrefour was a big loser with its hypermarkets in Philadelphia and is currently in a big battle with Wal-Mart in Brazil; yet these same stores are highly successful in Mexico and other South American countries. Here, Carrefour packs so many diverse products into its stores that silk underwear is often found next to toilet seats and children's videos are next to the caviar. As a result, these stores have universal appeal.[24]

Ironically, Benetton is really not a retailer but a franchisor. Long ago, the family decided to just do what it does best:

design stores geared to the aggressive utilization of retail space, no-nonsense selling environment, and slick interiors

efficiently monitor demand for the coolest colors, dyes, and styles

use computer-aided design system to keep merchandise cost and prices down

ALDI, a post–World War II German food retail phenomenon, was the first to show the rest of the world how to be "price driven." Most of their merchandise is private label. They have added some produce and frozen food items, as well as a limited

EXHIBIT 4.5	FOREIGN OWNERSHIP OF U.S. RETAILERS	
U.S. RETAILERS	**FOREIGN OWNER**	**COUNTRY**
7-Eleven	Ito-Yokado	Japan
A&P	Tengelmann	Germany
ALDI	ALDI	Germany
Benetton	Benetton	Italy
BI-LO	Koninklijke Ahold	Netherlands
Brooks Brothers	Marks & Spenser	Britain
Burger King	Grand Metropolitan	Britain
Eddie Bauer*	Otto Versand	Germany
F-A-O Schwarz	Koninklijke Bijenkeorf Beheer	Netherlands
First National Supermarkets	Koninklijke Ahold	Netherlands
Food Lion (50%)	Delhaize "Le Lion"	Belgium
Grand Union	General Occidentale	France
Giant Food	Ahold USA	Netherlands
IKEA	IKEA	Sweden
International House of Pancakes (IHOP)	Weinerwald	Switzerland
Oshman's	Ito-Yokado	Japan
Smart & Final	Casino Gulchard-Perrachon	France
Spiegel (90%)	Otto Versand	Germany
Topps Markets	Koninklijke Ahold	Netherlands
Zales	Peoples Jewelers Ltd & Swarovski Holdings	Canada Switzerland

* Eddie Bauer is 100 percent owned by Spiegel, which is 90 percent owned by Otto Versand.

apparel selection. The stores are ranked among the "dullest" in the world, and their employees have little interchange with the customer. Some say that ALDI isn't really a chain of stores but a formula with price the overriding objective. They are so profitable because they buy at the lowest price, sell at the lowest price, and keep expenses at the bare minimum.[25] This is one operation in which the wheel of retailing has stepped in.

As the world's most competitive retail market, the United States has a well-deserved reputation as a graveyard for foreign retailers, especially nonfood Europeans. Yet as shown in Exhibit 4.5, some well-known American retailers are actually foreign owned.

Also, other countries have done a better job at taking a simple retailing concept and using it to advance into other major marketplaces in the world. Take, for example, franchising. Franchising was developed in the United States as a result of the car—the manufacturers needed a way to obtain outlets to reach consumers, the consumers needed gasoline once they started traveling, and of course, with all the traveling we needed fast-food. Today auto dealers, service stations, and fast-food retailers account for almost 80 percent of franchise sales in the United States. However, franchising is being used by the Western European retailers, not American retailers, as the

WHERE ARE THE "NEW RUSSIANS" SHOPPING?

In Russia, where retail stores have long been characterized as having limited product assortments, a depressing atmosphere, and grim, rude salespersons, three types of retail ownership are emerging: former state-owned stores (the majority of which have now been privatized), new start-up private stores, joint ventures, and franchises. As a result, retailing in Russia is being rejuvenated, and customer needs are becoming an important consideration.

Former state-owned stores are being challenged to become self-sufficient. Years of poor management have left these underfinanced stores in a state of disrepair. The merchandise assortments are broad and shallow, making visual merchandising techniques difficult to implement.

New "start-up" private stores have changed their setup by implementing a smaller store, but space is primitive with few aesthetic enhancements, and there is little use of technology. Owners are entrepreneurial and have chosen to reinvest profits to expand inventory, resulting in scrambled merchandising and the attraction of different customers.

Joint ventures and franchises, with the benefit of foreign investment, are the most technologically advanced retailers. These retailers are collecting data by using computers to track sales and stock levels and are developing highly trained staff members with a more western philosophy. Merchandise is more upscale than in the other store types, and store interiors are aesthetically pleasing.

These start-up and joint-venture/franchise retailers are, for the most part, drawing customers who are typically upper-middle class and higher classed. As this extremely affluent market segment emerges, their consumption behavior is conspicuous. They prefer shopping at foreign joint ventures for western goods. However, the shopping preferences of the "mass consumer" remain unexplained.

Researchers from Michigan State University have explored the buying behavior and customer characteristics of private versus state-owned stores to see how they differed. Those patronizing former state-owned stores displayed higher levels of ethnocentrism, indicating consumers preferred purchas-

best method to enter the Eastern European countries now that the Cold War is over. American retailers are being held back because of their insistence on using joint-venture partners. This doesn't appear to work in these countries with weak economic systems. It is always difficult to understand the retailing culture of a foreign country, especially one undergoing major changes in its economic system as shown by our Global Retailing box on the changing face of retailing in Russia.

Another key difference in retailing behavior between different countries is the use of private labels. Retailers in Canada and Europe, especially Great Britain, use private label merchandise differently than retailers in the United States have traditionally used them. In these countries, private label products, in many cases, dominate the quality and assortment offered by the manufacturers. The strength of private labels in these countries is presumably the consequence of a number of factors. Smaller national markets tend to favor fewer national competitors and higher retail concentration. One study found that the imagination and management talent devoted to private labels in Europe tended to be higher than in the United States.[26] Recently, some American retailers have begun experimenting in test markets with private labels that emphasize quality over price.

ing domestic goods that are cheaper and of good quality. These older customers have lower incomes and tend to be married. However, customers of private stores are younger, have higher incomes (by 60 percent), and are predominantly single.

Shoppers, in the study, were found to have different pricing expectations of retailers. Price estimates of former state-store customers were at least 25 percent lower than those of the private store customers, although there were no differences in quality evaluations.

Two customer profiles have important implications for retailers competing in Russia. The first is of the traditional customers, purchasing from the former state-run retail firms, who are more price sensitive and expect to find quality, lower-priced products. This shopper is moderately ethnocentric and is more patriotic than the private store customer. However, this did not translate into a preference for Russian-made goods, although some of them may be perceived as better quality than imported items. To promote the sale of Russian-made goods, marketing strategies focusing on the "Made In" attribute may or may not be effective. Retailers must also provide customers with product information to justify price differences and modify unrealistic expectations.

Second, the private store customers expect to pay higher prices for comparable quality goods as buyers take higher markups and stock more upscale products. This younger and single customer may be more willing to buy fashion-forward merchandise than the state-store customer.

Brand loyalty is beginning to emerge among Russian consumers. Early in the transition to a market economy, store buyers saw an increase in product selection, but that selection was inconsistent. Neither customers nor the store buyers developed expectations concerning product quality based on a consistent product offering. With the Russian economy becoming more stable, which, therefore, creates a stronger price-sensitive consumer climate, marketers are developing and generating advertising strategies that focus on branded merchandise. National brand strategies are helping develop consumer confidence and enhance store patronage behavior. As a result, consumer brand expectations are emerging.

SOURCE: Based on a research study by Patricia Huddleston, Linda K. Good, and Leslie Stoel; College of Human Ecology, Michigan State University.

Frustrated by a mature, slow growth domestic market, many U.S. retailers have recently tested global expansion. Wal-Mart went to Mexico along with Tandy, Pier 1, and JCPenney. Canada lured Wal-Mart, The Gap, Home Depot, and others. Toys "Я" Us earlier entered Japan with some difficulty. Although Mexico was the most popular destination, Canada, Europe, South America, and Japan also attracted the attention of expansion-minded retailers. Nevertheless, with the possible exception of Wal-Mart's recent establishment of 250 stores in Canada, Mexico, Colombia, Brazil, Argentina, China, and Indonesia, American retailers met more disappointments than successes in entering foreign markets.

This lack of success in foreign markets is evident in looking at the "Top 10" worldwide retailers in Exhibit 4.6. Notice that the American retailers get only a very small percentage of their revenues from international sales. And those that do have a large amount of international sales are actually getting these sales only from nearby countries. For example, many Western European retailers are getting the vast majority of their international sales from other members of the European Community. That is similar to Sears selling in every state but only having a small percentage of their sales from their international operations.

EXHIBIT 4.6	THE "TOP 10" WORLDWIDE RETAILERS				
RANK	NAME	COUNTRY	RETAIL FORMATS	SALES ($)	% INTERN.
1.	Wal-Mart	U.S.	Dis./Sup.Cen./ Food/Whse.Club	104,859*	3.6%
2.	Metro	Germany	Diversified/ Shopping Centers	57,506	24.0%
3.	Tengelmann	Germany	Supermarket	34,735	50.3%
4.	Promodes	France	Supermarket/ Hypermarket/Conv.	32,022	39.1%
5.	Sears	U.S.	Department/Specialty	31,974*	1.2%
6.	Rewe Zentrale	Germany	Supermarket	30,503	N/A
7.	Kmart	U.S.	Discount/Specialty	30,378*	2.9%
8.	Carrefour	France	Hypermarket/Convenience	29,486	37.1%
9.	Daiei	Japan	Supermarket/Drug/ Specialty	28,461	24.3%
10.	Edeka Zentrale	Germany	Department/Supermarket	28,051	N/A

* 1996 Sales Figures, otherwise 1995 Sales Figures.

SOURCES: Company records, trade publications, trade association estimates, and authors' calculations. Note that sales in dollars for foreign retailers will fluctuate greatly with currency fluctuations.

DOLLAR $ & CENTS

U.S. retailers that wish to globally expand and assume that success in one country will follow in all countries they enter will be lower performers than those who recognize that success in one country is not necessarily transferable to success in another country.

Success in one country doesn't always mean success in all countries. As we discussed earlier, the hypermarket was an overwhelming success in Europe, Mexico, and Latin America but a failure in the United States. This may have been caused by the fact that they were introduced in these other countries before the advent of shopping malls and large discount stores. Other causes for failure in one country after success in another is an economic system that isn't set up for the new retail format.

The biggest cause, however, for failure in entering foreign markets is failing to understand the culture of the new market. Although globalization is the buzzword for business in the 21st century, going global is a lot tougher than it looks. Wal-Mart, for example, forgot that Quebec was French-speaking and initially issued English-speaking circulars. The chain also had to learn that a six-pack of soda in China is "bulk packaging."[27] Thus, although Stockholm, where most Swedes speak English, might appear very similar to an American city, it has very different cultural habits. Swedes will bristle at having to write detailed market plans, whereas Americans, without an understanding of the Swedes' culture, will get upset at the Swedes taking off the entire month of July for vacation.[28]

STUDENT STUDY GUIDE

SUMMARY   The behavior of competitors is an important component of the retail planning and management model. Effective planning and management in any retail setting cannot be accomplished without the proper analysis of competitors.

LO•1   WHAT ARE THE VARIOUS MODELS OF RETAIL COMPETITION?   Competition in retailing, as in any other industry, involves the interplay of supply and demand. Various models of retail competition were described to aid in illustrating certain principles of retail competition. These models suggested that retail competition is typically local; the retail industry is monopolistically competitive and not a pure monopoly, pure competition, or oligopoly. In developing price and nonprice strategies, a retailer must look at the supply as well as the demand side of retailing. Key factors in determining supply are costs and competitive actions.

LO•2   WHAT ARE THE VARIOUS TYPES OF RETAIL COMPETITION?   Competition is most intense in retailing, and various classification schemes were used to describe this intensity. Intratype and intertype competition descriptions were used to explain if the retailers competing against each other were in the same line of retail trade or if they were in different lines of retail trade but still competing for the same customer with similar merchandise lines. Divertive competition was used to describe retailers who sought to intercept customers planning to visit another retailer. And the struggle to develop protected niches in retailing, whereby retailers protect themselves from competitive threats on the basis of the merchandise offered, was discussed. One increasingly popular way to do this is by a store positioning strategy.

LO•3   WHAT ARE THE THREE THEORIES USED TO EXPLAIN THE EVOLUTION OF RETAIL COMPETITION?   Retail competition is both revolutionary and evolutionary. Three theories of viewing changing competitive patterns in retailing were reviewed. The wheel of retailing proposes that new types of retailers enter the market as low-margin, low-price, less efficient operators. As they succeed, they become more complex, increasing their margins and prices and becoming vulnerable to new types of low-margin competitors, who, in turn, follow the same pattern. The retail accordion theory suggests that retail institutions evolve from outlets offering wide assortments to specialized narrow assortment stores and then return to wide assortments to repeat the pattern. Finally, the retail life cycle theory views retail institutions, like the products they distribute, as passing through an identifiable cycle during which the basics of strategy and competition change.

LO•4   WHAT FUTURE CHANGES COULD AFFECT RETAIL COMPETITION?   We followed with a discussion of changes that could effect retail competition. Industry analysts contend that nonstore retailing may be a major competitive force in the future. The various types of nonstore retailing were discussed. We also looked at four examples of possible new retailing formats that evolved as an outgrowth of the economic slowdown at the beginning of this decade: supercenters, recycled merchandise retailers, liquidators, and electronic retailing.

LO•5   HOW CAN TRENDS IN THE INTERNATIONAL RETAILING AFFECT U.S. RETAILERS?   Just as the introduction of new retailing formats in one part of the United States will affect retailers in other parts of the country, so it is for international retailing. Retailing in other countries exhibits even greater diversity in its structure than retailing in the United States. The rate of change in retailing appears to be directly related to the stage and speed of economic development in the countries concerned, but even the least-developed countries are experiencing dramatic changes in retailing activities as newer formats are introduced.

In fact, new retail formats are emerging in countries all over the world, not just in the United States. This can be attributed to a variety of economic and social factors: a widespread concern for health, a steady increase in the number of working women and two-income families, long and persistent energy shortages, and the consequent upsurge in price levels, consumerism, and so forth. These factors, and their effects on consumer lifestyles, encouraged retailers to seek new market segments, make adjustments in the retail mix, alter location patterns, and adopt new multisegment strategies. In the process, many new retail concepts and formats have emerged and spread, not only from firm to firm but from country to country.

However, success in one country doesn't always mean success in all countries. This is because every country's economic system isn't set up for every new retailing format.

TERMS TO REMEMBER

pure competition	break-even point
pure monopoly	store positioning
monopolistic competition	wheel of retailing theory
oligopolistic competition	retail accordion
outshopping	retail life cycle
fixed costs	mail-order houses
variable costs	automatic merchandising machine
semifixed costs	operators
overstored	direct selling establishments
understored	off-price retailers
intratype competition	supercenter
intertype competition	recycled merchandise retailers
divertive competition	

REVIEW AND DISCUSSION QUESTIONS

LO • 1 WHAT ARE THE VARIOUS MODELS OF RETAIL COMPETITION?

1. Can a retailer ever operate in a pure monopoly situation? If you agree with the question, provide an example and explain what dangers this retailer faces? If you disagree, explain why not.
2. Develop a list of expenses or costs for a department store and categorize them as fixed, variable, and semifixed.

LO • 2 WHAT ARE THE VARIOUS TYPES OF RETAIL COMPETITION?

3. Provide an example of intratype competition that was not mentioned in the text. Provide an example of intertype competition that was not mentioned in the text. Can a retailer face both intratype and intertype competition at the same time? Explain your response.

4. Can divertive competition only occur in intertype competition (i.e., where two different types of retailers compete with each other with a similar product)?
5. Why is it so important for a retailer to develop a protected niche?

LO•3 WHAT ARE THE THREE THEORIES USED TO EXPLAIN THE EVOLUTION OF RETAIL COMPETITION?

6. Describe the wheel of retailing theory of retail competition. What is the theory's major strength and weakness? Does this theory do a good job of explaining what has happened to retailers in your hometown?
7. Describe the retail accordion theory of competition. What is this theory's major strength and weakness?
8. Would strategies for retailers differ in the four stages of the retail life cycle? What strategies should be emphasized at each of the four stages?
9. A friend told you this afternoon that it was almost impossible to find just an ordinary cheeseburger on the menu anymore. That the elegant simplicity of the original McDonald's has given to a smorgasbord of menu items that are too complicated to comprehend. What evolution theory of retailing does this suggest?

LO•4 WHAT FUTURE CHANGES COULD AFFECT RETAIL COMPETITION?

10. Will nonstore retailing continue to grow? Provide a rationale for your response.
11. What future trends do you see taking place in retail competition over the next decade?
12. Many experts disagree over the future of shopping via the Internet. What is your opinion on the subject?

LO•5 HOW CAN TRENDS IN THE INTERNATIONAL RETAILING AFFECT U.S. RETAILERS?

13. If a new retail format is a "hit" in one country, it generally will be successful in all countries. Agree or disagree.
14. Why have retailers been so slow in their international expansion efforts? What is driving them to grow internationally now?

SAMPLE TEST QUESTIONS

LO•1 WHAT TYPE OF COMPETITIVE STRUCTURE ARE MOST RETAIL FIRMS INVOLVED IN?

a. horizontal competition
b. monopolistic competition
c. vertical competition
d. pure competition
e. oligopolistic competition

LO•2 WHEN WAL-MART COMPETES WITH KROGER CO., ALBERTSONS, AND SAFEWAY BY ADDING GROCERIES TO ITS GENERAL MERCHANDISE PRODUCTS IN ITS NEW SUPERCENTERS, WHAT TYPE OF COMPETITION IS THIS?

a. extended niche
b. intratype
c. scrambled
d. intertype
e. category killer

LO•3 WALKING BACK TO THE DORM AFTER CLASS, YOUR ROOMMATE COMPLAINS THAT SHE WISHES THERE WAS A FAST-FOOD PLACE OR A PLAIN OLD-FASHION HAMBURGER JOINT SHE COULD GO TO FOR A SIMPLE HAMBURGER, NOT A FANCY TRIPLE-DECKER OR ONE WITH 17 SECRET SAUCES, AND NOT ONE WITH A PLAYGROUND FOR 50 KIDS. HER DILEMMA DESCRIBES THIS THEORY OF RETAIL EVOLUTION.

a. retail violin
b. retail life cycle
c. bigger-n-better
d. wheel of retailing
e. compound growth

LO•4 WHICH OF THE FOLLOWING IS NOT A NEW RETAIL FORMAT THAT IS EXPECTED TO BE SUCCESSFUL IN THE COMING YEARS?

a. recycled merchandise retailers
b. supercenters
c. Internet shopping
d. door-to-door selling
e. shopping via the computer

LO•5 WITH REGARD TO INTERNATIONAL TRENDS IN RETAILING, WHICH OF THE FOLLOWING STATEMENTS IS TRUE?

a. Because of its sheer size, retailing in the United States is more diverse in its structure than any other country.
b. Success with a retailing format in one country usually guarantees success in all countries.
c. Retailers around the world use private labels as a means to compete on the basis of price over quality.
d. U.S. retailers haven't been as successful as their European counterparts in entering former Iron Curtain countries, partly as a result of their insistence on doing joint-venture deals and not using franchising.
e. No new successful retailing format has been developed outside of the United States in the past half century.

APPLICATIONS

WRITING AND SPEAKING EXERCISE As a summer intern at a locally owned Ford dealership in a city of 120,000 population, you have been asked to develop an outline of what the firm should do as it competes against a new type of competition. Within the past 18 months, AutoZone has opened two new stores, a new Kmart Supercenter has a complete automotive service department, and Pep Boys has opened a 23,000-square-foot automotive parts supermarket that appeals to both the do-it-yourself auto enthusiast and the person who wants auto service done by others. This latter person can purchase parts and accessories at a Pep Boys at discount prices and have them installed by Pep Boys technicians. During this time period, service sales at your dealership has declined by 20 percent. Previously, sales had been growing 10 percent annually. Don Ruberg, the owner of the dealership, has asked you what strategies can be implemented to combat this increased competition and put the dealership back on a sales growth curve in service sales. He wants your report by Friday morning so he can have the weekend to think it over.

RETAIL PROJECT   You are thinking about buying a Ford Explorer after you graduate this semester. Let's use the Internet to see if we can get a better deal. All you will have to do is make three on-line connections, all free, to get that better deal.

Start by calling DealerNet (www.dealernet.com/), created by Reynolds & Reynolds, which provides computer services to dealers. You can see a picture of the Explorer and find out how it compares with competitors such as the Jeep Grand Cherokee in such key areas as trunk space, fuel economy, and price.

Suppose that you settle on a four-door, four-wheel-drive XLT model. Key over to the prices posted by Edmund Publications (www.enews.com/magazines/edmunds), a longtime compiler of such information. There you discover what the current sticker price is for XLT as well as what the dealer pays. You also learn a little-known fact: The XLT carries a 3 percent holdback—essentially a rebate for each Explorer that Ford pays to the dealer at the end of the year. This may help you in evaluating the price your dealer quotes.

When you're ready to order, type in http://www.autobytel.com/. There are several buying services on the web, but Auto-By-Tel is free. A few days after you've placed your order, you'll get a call from a nearby dealer. He will charge you a fixed amount over the invoice and deliver the car. Now, you have saved enough to buy a copy of this text for all your friends.

CASE TOUGH TIMES FOR GROCERS

In search of new ways to woo shoppers, the nation's 30,000 supermarkets have become a marketing test ground. The industry is still struggling to fight new competition and demographic changes that have been building for years. Baby boomers, one of the largest and most affluent groups of shoppers, have aged and now eat out frequently and shop on the run. The evidence of their lifestyle is ubiquitous: Convenience stores and pharmacies now carry an array of groceries, and purveyors of prepared foods are flourishing.

The liberal spending by baby boomers has helped cause food sales to soar. But supermarket shopping sprees have not weighed heavily in the increase. Since 1965, food spending in America has climbed 46 percent, in real terms, to $490.5 billion in 1997, according to the Agriculture Department. But over that period, spending on food to be consumed at home—purchased mainly from supermarkets—grew by only 20 percent, to $267.2 billion. Spending on food eaten away from home—at fast-food restaurants, delis, and other retailers that prepare food—shot up by 89 percent, to $223.3 billion according to the agency.

In addition, the increased competition from the Big 3 discounters' supercenters has forced at least 1,000 weaker supermarkets a year to shut down. And in an attempt to be as attentive to customers' needs as the corner grocers of the past, supermarkets are stocking twice as many products as they did a decade ago, further increasing their costs. Many have added conveniences such as in-store restaurants, banks, pharmacies, and delis with hot prepared foods. They are using computer scanners to track individual purchases and to improve their marketing. And some are holding events such as sampling extravaganzas to make shopping more exciting.

Service, value, convenience, and quality, rather than price, are the carrots that lure time-pressed shoppers today. "Retailers are moving away from featured sales," said Philip Lempert, president of the Lempert Company, an advertising agency that specializes in the food industry. "No longer do you pile it high and sell it cheap."

1. What strategies can supermarkets adopt to fight off competition from fast-food and mini-marts?
2. Do you believe the trend in spending for food that is eaten away from home will continue in the future? Explain your response.
3. Can supermarkets compete with supercenters?

STARTING YOUR OWN RETAIL BUSINESS

As a knowledgeable retail entrepreneur, you recognize how harmful new retail competitors entering the market can be to your business. You opened your bookstore only 18 months ago and already you have experienced healthy sales. In the year just ended, sales reached almost $870,000. You have estimated of the 41,000 households in your market 38 percent visit your store an average of 4.1 times a year. Due to your excellent merchandising and retail displays, 90 percent of visitors to your store make a purchase (referred to as closure) for an average transaction size of $13.59. Unfortunately, last week you learned that Borders (a category killer bookstore that also sells music tapes and CDs and serves coffee and refreshments and pastries) has signed a lease to be part of a new shopping mall in a city of 405,000 located 20 miles to the north of your store. In this mall, there will also be a Home Depot and Office Max.

Predictably, you are quite concerned about how Borders will take customers from your store. It is hard for you to predict the impact of this new competition, and at least they are 20 miles away. Nonetheless, you believe that the percentage of households in your market that will shop your store will decline from 38 percent to 34 percent and average shopping frequency will decline from 4.1 times per year to 3.9 times per year. You believe you can maintain your excellent closure rate and average transaction size. What is the estimated sales impact of Borders becoming your competitor? (*Hint:* Annual sales can be obtained by multiplying the number of households in the market by the percentage that patronize your store multiplied by their average shopping frequency or number of visits per year; this can then be multiplied by the closure rate and this result multiplied by the average transaction size.)

NOTES

1. Leonard W. Weiss, *Case Studies in American Industry* (New York: John Wiley and Sons, 1971): 222–223.
2. However, in real life retailers are not confronted by such a curve because they face a three-dimensional demand function. The three dimensions are (1) quantity demanded per household, (2) price at the retail store, and (3) distance from the individual's residence or place of work to the store. The quantity demanded by a household is inversely related to the price charged and distance to the store. This discussion is, however, beyond the scope of this text.
3. "Kmart: Who's in Charge Here?" *Business Week,* December 4, 1995: 104, 108.
4. Malcolm P. McNair, "Significant Trends and Developments in the Postwar Period," in A.B. Smith (ed.), *Competitive Distribution in a Free High-Level Economy and Its Implications for the University* (Pittsburgh, PA: University of Pittsburgh Press, 1958).
5. "Sleepless Nights at Holiday Inn" *Business Week,* November 3, 1997: 66–67.
6. Stanley C. Hollander, "Notes on the Retail Accordion," *Journal of Retailing,* Summer 1966: 29–40, 54.
7. *Retailing 2000* (Columbus, OH: Management Horizons, 1995): 4.

8. "Junk Mail," *U.S. News & World Report,* January 12, 1998: 4.

9. *Vision For The New Millennium . . .,* (Atlanta: Kurt Salmon Associates, 1996).

10. "Discount Supercenters Sell Almost Everything, but Some Folks on Wall Street Aren't Buying," *Wall Street Journal,* February 9, 1996: C2.

11. Frederick Langrehr and Sandra Strasser, "Who Is and Is Not the Discounter Supercenter? A Study in One Market," working paper at Valparaiso University, 1995.

12. Ibid.

13. "Trying to Bag Business," *U.S. News & World Report,* February 26, 1996: 53–54.

14. "Hurricane Huizenga," *Business Week,* February 24, 1997: 88–93; "Will he own the road?" *U.S. News & World Report,* October 20, 1997: 45–54.

15. "Suddenly, Detroit Stops Fighting the Future," *Business Week,* January 27, 1997: 34.

16. "Second-Hand Rows: These Thrift Shops Are Classy—and Doing a Booming Business," *Wall Street Journal,* January 20, 1997: A1, A6.

17. Ibid.

18. "Everything Must Go—to the Liquidators," *Business Week,* January 15, 1996: 52.

19. "Wired Kingdom," a special supplement to the January 1997 issue of *Chain Store Age,* 1997: 3; "A Way Out of the Web Maze," *Business Week,* February 24, 1997: 94–104.

20. The following is based on Michael Rollens, "Shopping in the Virtual World," *Arthur Andersen Retailing Issues Letter,* January 1996.

21. *Retailing 2005* (Columbus, OH: Management Horizons, 1995): 13.

22. For a complete discussion of IKEA, see "IKEA: Create a Better Everyday Life for the Majority of People," *International Trends in Retailing,* December 1995: 45–65.

23. "Retailers Go Global," *Fortune,* February 20, 1995: 102–108.

24. Ibid.

25. Michael J. O'Connor, "Price, Employees or Customers?" *International Trends in Retailing,* July 1995: 37–48.

26. Stephen Hoch and Shumeet Banerji, "When Do Private Labels Succeed?" *Sloan Management Review,* Summer 1993: 57–67.

27. "Global Powers of Retailing," a special section to the December 1996 issue of *Chain Store Age,* 1996: 9B.

28. "Cross-Border Merger Results in Headaches for a Drug Company," *Wall Street Journal,* February 4, 1997: A1, A12.

CHAPTER 5

CHANNEL BEHAVIOR

Wayne Huizenga is threatening established marketing channels for used cars by building a national chain of used car superstores which sell nearly new cars at no-haggle prices.

OVERVIEW

In this chapter, we examine the retailer's need to analyze and understand the marketing channel in which it operates. We begin by discussing how all the activities in the marketing system must be performed by either the retailer or another channel member. Next, we review the various types of marketing channels and the benefits they offer the retailer. We conclude with some practical suggestions to improve channel relationships.

At the outset of this text, we stated that retailing is the final movement in the progression of merchandise from producer to consumer. Many other movements occur through time and geographic space, and all of them need to be executed properly for the retailer to achieve optimum performance.

LEARNING OBJECTIVES

After reading this chapter, you should be able to

1. discuss the retailer's role in the larger marketing system
2. describe the institutions involved and the functions that must be performed in every marketing system
3. describe the difference between the two types of marketing channels: conventional and vertical
4. explain the terms *dependency* and *channel power* and why cooperation is so important in channel management

LO • 1
Discuss the retailer's role
in the larger marketing
system

THE MARKETING SYSTEM

Consider the following example. The final movement of a retail item occurred on November 17 at 10:47 A.M. when the customer of a specialty store in a suburban Chicago mall purchased a new coat for the winter season. At some prior time (probably six months to a year earlier), that coat was manufactured. Later, it was warehoused and then placed on display in the manufacturer's showroom. Next, a large quantity of these coats were purchased by the specialty retailer to be sold throughout the country. This particular coat was shipped by the manufacturer to the retailer to be placed on display in the store in the Chicago mall.

In the above example, manufacturing occurred in Taiwan, a Japanese freighter was used to transport the coats to the United States, and after going through Customs, the coat was warehoused in Los Angeles before being shipped to Chicago. Thus, before the final retail transaction could take place, many physical movements were needed, involving many firms other than the retailer. Retailers cannot properly perform their roles without these other firms. Retailers are part of a complex marketing system—an important component, but not the only one.

Marketing channel
is a set of institutions that moves goods from the point of production to the point of consumption.

To understand the retailer's role in this larger marketing system, it should be viewed as a member of one or even several marketing channels. A marketing channel is a set of institutions that moves goods from the point of production to the point of consumption. For example, the marketing channel might include manufacturers, wholesalers, and retailers. The manufacturer could sell directly to an individual for household usage, sell to a retailer for sale to the individual, or sell to a wholesaler(s) for sale to the retailer, who then sells to the individual. As such, marketing channels consist of all the institutions and all the marketing activities (e.g., storage, financing, purchasing, transporting) that are spread over time and geographic space in the marketing process. If the retailer is a member of the marketing channel that collectively does the best job, it will be better able to compete with other retailers.

Why should the retailer view itself as part of a larger marketing system? Why can't it simply seek out the best assortment of goods for its customers, sell the goods, make a profit, go to the bank, and forget about the system? In reality, the world of retailing isn't that easy. Profits sufficient for survival and growth will be difficult, if not impossible, to achieve if the retailer ignores the channel. This doesn't mean that the system can never be changed. Sometimes an innovative channel member, like a retailer, might break out of the existing system and replace it with a new system. For example, discounters established a new relationship with vendors by buying in large quantities, warehousing the merchandise in efficiently run distribution centers, and shipping to their own stores as a means of obtaining lower prices. Today, a revolution is occurring in the channel for automobiles. Car shoppers are now logging on to the Internet (e.g., Microsoft's CarPoint [www.carpoint.com], Edmund's Automobile Buyer's Guides [www.edmunds.com], and IntelliChoice [www.intellichoice.com]) to pursue information on almost every make and model of car, product reviews, specifications, buyers' advice, and prices. Shoppers are using auto brokers such as Auto-By-Tel (www.autobytel.com) to negotiate the best price for them. They are visiting giant auto malls carrying several different lines of cars. And when they finally decided on a particular model, the total transaction time has now been cut to 90 minutes or less.[1] No wonder that many experts expect that 25 percent of all car buyers will shop on-line by the year 2000.[2] Already the number of auto dealers has dropped from more than 30,000 in 1970 to fewer than 23,000 today, despite all the new franchises

Some manufacturers sell directly to consumers as does Inglenook Winery with this wine tasting room and direct sales facility at its Napa Valley location.

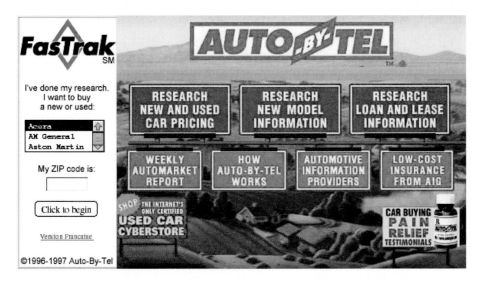

Auto-By-Tel, an auto broker that operates on the Internet, will help you purchase the car you desire by negotiating with auto dealers for the best price.

awarded by Japanese and Korean automakers.[3] And if the various state franchise laws are ever changed to allow discounters (e.g., Price-Costco and Wal-Mart's Sam's Club) to sell new cars, the numbers could be cut in half. Nevertheless, many experts believe that the recent birth of mega-dealerships such as AutoNation, CarMax, Driver's Mart Worldwide, and United Auto Group will soon streamline the existing channel for cars, which with its many small, family-owned dealerships is as ineffective, inefficient, and antiquated as the general merchandise channel was 30 years ago.

One of the leaders in consolidating the largely locally owned automobile business is Wayne Huizenga who helped to build Blockbuster Video. Huizenga is building the

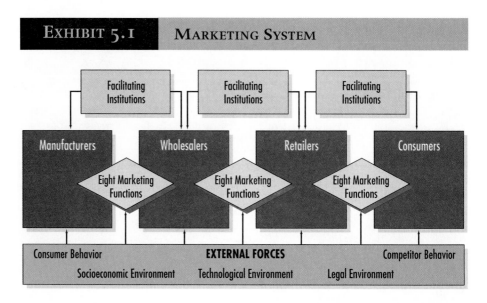

EXHIBIT 5.1   MARKETING SYSTEM

AutoNation chain of used car supersotres. AutoNation sells nearly new cars at a no haggle price. The major source of these nearly new cars is Alamo and National rental car firms which Huizenga also controls. Recently Huizenga began acquiring new car dealerships and plans to further revolutionize auto retailing by having a national chain of new car dealerships carrying all major makes of autos. His potential ability to control a large volume of business will give him huge negotiation power with auto manufacturers, something that locally owned auto dealers have not had.[4]

Marketing system

is the set of institutions performing marketing functions (activities), the relationships between these institutions, and the functions that are necessary to create exchange transactions with target populations or consumers.

The marketing system consists of institutions performing marketing functions (activities), the relationships between these institutions, and the functions that are necessary to create exchange transactions with target populations or consumers. We will view the marketing system as largely synonymous with the marketing channel.

Exhibit 5.1 illustrates the marketing system. Study it closely. This exhibit portrays many of the links between institutions and functions that are necessary to bring about final exchange with some target populations. Note that the marketing system is affected by five external forces: (1) consumer behavior, (2) competitor behavior, (3) the socioeconomic environment, (4) the technological environment, and (5) the legal and ethical environment. These external forces cannot be completely controlled by the retailer or any other institution in the marketing system but need to be taken into account when retailers make decisions. For example, a change in the minimum-wage law will usually increase the retailer's cost of doing business. A retailer can't ignore these external forces. The retail management and planning model (Exhibit 2.3) also dramatizes the importance of these external forces in retail decision making.

MARKETING FUNCTIONS

What marketing functions need to be performed in the marketing system? Eight functions are necessary: buying, selling, storing, transporting, sorting, financing, information gathering, and risk taking. Each will be discussed briefly, but the retailer need not perform all these functions. They can be performed by any member of the channel.

BUYING   Before a retailer can sell merchandise to the final consumer, the retailer must purchase the merchandise from a supplier, either the manufacturer or a wholesaler who gets it from the manufacturer. Buying the merchandise is as important to the retailer's overall success as is selling merchandise. Sometimes, the buying function isn't as easy to perform as it seems. Consider our Behind the Scenes box, which describes the experiences of a recent graduate selling recycled merchandise, a developing retailing format that was highlighted in the previous chapter and for which there isn't a well-organized source of supply.

DOLLAR $ & CENTS

Because cost of merchandise is a major expense area for all retailers, the highest performing retailers will be those that best manage the buying function.

SELLING   Selling is the function that most consumers associate with retailing, and it obviously is important. It involves all activities that are necessary and incidental to contacting customers and persuading them to purchase. Selling activities include advertising, personal selling, and sales promotions. One controversial practice that occurs in today's retail marketing channels is when some retailers sell merchandise they purchased from the vendor not to the final consumer but to diverters or off-price discount operations. A diverter is an unauthorized member of a channel who buys and sells excess merchandise to and from authorized channel members. For instance, suppose a retailer could buy a name-brand appliance intended to retail for $389 at $185 if it purchases 100 units. However, if the retailer orders 500 units, it can purchase the item at $158. What does the retailer do? Some retailers will purchase 500 units even though they only need 100. They in turn sell the 400 extra units at a slight loss (e.g., at $155) to an off-price discount store, which may retail the item for $219. The net result is that the retailer loses $3 a unit on 400 units, or $1,200; however, it has the remaining 100 units at $27 a unit less, for a savings of $2,700. The retailer is $1,500 ahead on the transaction; however, the manufacturer is upset because the appliance has been diverted into a retail channel that it did not intend.

Diverter
is an unauthorized member of a channel who buys and sells excess merchandise to and from authorized channel members.

STORING   Storage is necessary because there is usually a difference between the time when products are manufactured and the time consumers purchase them. For example, an apparel manufacturer may produce 1,000 blue dresses within two days, but because the demand for those dresses is not immediate, storage becomes necessary. The storage function involves many expenses such as rent for the warehouse, insurance, fixtures, wages, and ticketing the floor-ready merchandise with retailer-specific price tags.

TRANSPORTING   Transportation is necessary when production occurs in geographic locations different from where consumers need the product and as a result the merchandise needs to be transported. Transportation of merchandise from the store to the customer is also considered to be a part of the transportation function.

TOYS*LIKE*NU

Toys*Like*Nu, a retail store selling *used* toys, games, dolls, and related items, opened in a working-class suburb of Pittsburgh in May 1993. Since the store has opened, sales have exceeded all expectations. The owner, Liz Bright, and her husband had a baby earlier that year. Because of the need for baby toys, she visited many toy retailers and was surprised at the high prices, even at a discount retailer such as Toys "Я" Us.

The more Liz thought of it, the more she became intrigued with toy retailing. After speaking to a retired retailing professor and family friend, she became aware of the way channels for toys operated and of the perils of trying to compete with Toys "Я" Us, Target, Wal-Mart, and Kmart. As a result, Liz decided that operating a single store competing with these retailers would not enhance her chances of success.

Then Liz had a brainstorm. Why not change the channel and become a "used" or "recycled" toy retailer. Because she resided in a blue-collar suburb of Pittsburgh and unemployment was high, Liz thought that there was a niche for a used toy retailer if a secure and constant source of merchandise could be obtained. Having made the decision to become a retailer, a location was secured near a string of tax preparers in a small shopping center.

Liz realized the fundamental task was securing an adequate assortment of used toys, games, dolls, and related items. As her professor-advisor had pointed out, supply is usually not a problem for most retailers, especially those as big as Toys "Я" Us, etc., as there are a multitude of vendors. For someone selling used toys, however, suppliers would be a problem.

Thus, Liz took the following steps to develop her own channel of distribution:

1. She placed small, inexpensive ads in several local weekly shopper–type newspapers indicating her willingness to buy used, not broken, toys. A telephone number was given. If callers only had a few toys, they were asked to come by the store. If they had a large number of items, Liz made arrangements to visit the seller's home and would offer a price for the entire lot.
2. She would visit all garage sales and yard sales in her neighborhood. Again, she would seek to buy the entire lot, not just individual items.
3. She developed a working relationship with local service organizations such as the Girl Scouts. These organizations would run "fund raisers" to secure large assortments for Liz.
4. Her parents, who lived in a different part of the state, would also visit garage sales near their home. In fact, they became so successful at getting merchandise that they soon bought a van to carry the merchandise to Liz's store.

Despite all these efforts to secure merchandise, Liz was still looking for other means to improve her channel as her sales continued to grow.

SORTING

Sorting occurs because both demand for and supply of products are heterogeneous or different from each other. Matching these very dissimilar demands and supplies involves four sorting processes: sorting out, accumulation, allocation, and assortment. Exhibit 5.2 uses the glass of orange juice you drink in the morning as an example of the sorting process.

The first step in the sorting process is sorting out, which involves separating large heterogeneous supplies into smaller, more homogeneous groups. For example, if you go to an orange grove, you will quickly realize that not all oranges are suitable for processing into orange juice. Some will be too ripe, some will be diseased, others may not be ripe enough, and still others may be better suited to be sold as eating oranges. Sorting out occurs with eggs, wheat, and many other crops and raw materials. Many

EXHIBIT 5.2   SORTING PROCESS

SORTING OUT

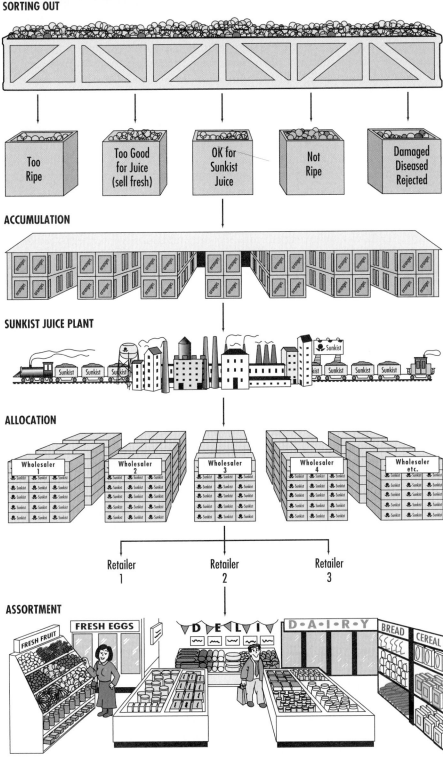

ACCUMULATION

SUNKIST JUICE PLANT

ALLOCATION

ASSORTMENT

SOURCE: Virginia Newell Lusch, used with permission.

manufacturers, especially with apparel goods, do a similar process with imperfects or seconds.

The second step in the sorting process is accumulation. Accumulation consists of assembling groups of homogeneous supplies from many different sources in sufficient quantity for mass production or mass marketing. Sunkist, for example, must accumulate large quantities of high-quality oranges for its orange juice. There is a class of wholesalers who will buy in small quantities to accumulate the large quantities that food processors such as Sunkist desire.

The third step in the sorting process is allocation, which consists of separating large amounts of processed goods into smaller quantities suitable for resale to retailers and wholesalers. Once again, the wholesaler enters the picture. A food wholesaler will buy Sunkist orange juice by the truckload (approximately 2,000 cases) and then sell it in smaller quantities to various supermarkets.

Assortment is the final step in the sorting process. Assortment occurs when someone, usually the retailer, assembles diverse supplies in a single place to meet customer demand. Surely, you do not want to go to separate stores for the bacon, eggs, bread, and butter you eat with your juice! All retailers are in the business of building assortments that match the demands of the consumers who shop at their stores.

FINANCING

If we recognize that there are discrepancies between the time demand occurs and the time supplies are created and also between geographic points of production (supply) and geographic points of consumption (demand), then it becomes clear that someone needs to finance these discrepancies. Ideally, the final consumer pays the retailer for the merchandise before the retailer must pay its supplier, but this generally doesn't happen. For example, most retailers have to pay for their Christmas merchandise before the Christmas selling season is over. Retailers would find it difficult to operate without credit from manufacturers. Many manufacturers, especially the smaller ones, that sell to retailers cannot afford or do not care to finance the inventory, and in these cases, they sell their receivables (what the retailers owe the manufacturer) to what are referred to as "factors." Factors buy receivables from channel members (manufacturers, wholesalers, or retailers) at a discount and then assume the risk of collecting these accounts. Sometimes, manufacturers are urged by credit rating agencies to show caution in shipping new merchandise on credit to certain retailers. This happened to Kmart during the 1995 Christmas season when many analysts were worried that the retailer's weak performance over the past three years and heavy debt load might cause the firm to seek bankruptcy protection. Kmart didn't seek court protection, but the damage was done as some suppliers did cut back on Christmas shipments.[5] Kmart's financial problems have continued to plague the retailer. In 1997, it was listed as number 3 in *Fortune*'s list of "the least admired" companies. *Fortune* sighted the chain desperate need for revenue growth to obtain new financing to improve stores and merchandise selection but noted that it couldn't lower prices without damaging its earnings picture.[6]

Factors

are institutions in the marketing system that buy receivables from channel members (manufacturers, wholesalers, or retailers) at a discount and then assume the risk of collecting these accounts.

INFORMATION GATHERING

Retailers must find out not only what their customers want and need but also the best available source of supply. In addition, without an exchange of information, the retailer can't tell the consumers that it has the merchandise that will satisfy their needs. Information is essential to match suppliers properly with the demands of the retailer's market. It is not useful for suppliers to produce designer jeans when the marketplace no longer wants these jeans.

RISK TAKING   It is obvious that demand cannot be forecast precisely. Products will be produced or purchased for resale for which a demand might not materialize. In that case, the retailer can incur a loss. Consider, for example, the case of toy retailers. If they incorrectly forecast the demand for certain toys at the "Christmas toy show" in June and July, they may under- or overstock certain toys. Either way, a loss will occur. No wonder retailers say "risk taking's reward is profit."

NONELIMINATION OF THE FUNCTIONS

Whether the economic system is capitalistic, socialistic, or communistic, these eight marketing functions will exist. They cannot be eliminated. They can, however, be shifted or divided among the different institutions and the consumer in the marketing system.

All forms of retailing were created by rearranging the marketing functions among institutions and consumers. For example, department stores were created specifically to build a larger and better assortment of goods. They capitalized on the opportunity to perform more of the sorting process. No longer was it necessary to travel to one store for a shirt, another for slacks, and yet another for shoes; the necessary assortment was available in a single store. Supermarkets increased consumer participation by shifting more of the information-gathering, buying, and transporting functions to them. Before supermarkets, consumers could have the corner grocer select items and deliver them. But with the supermarket came self-service. Consumers had to locate the goods within the store, select them from an array of products, and transport them home. For performing more of these marketing functions, the consumer was compensated with lower prices.

A marketing function does not have to be shifted in its entirety to another institution or to the consumer but can be divided among several entities. For example, the manufacturer who does not want to perform the entire selling function could have the retailer perform part of the job through in-store promotions and local advertising. At the same time, the manufacturer could assume some of the task through national advertising.

DOLLAR $ & CENTS

Retailers who understand the importance of the eight marketing functions and use the abilities of other channel members to most efficiently operate the channel will tend to be higher performers than those who don't understand their dependency on other channel members.

No member of the marketing channel would want, or be able, to perform completely all eight marketing functions. For this reason, the retailer must view itself as being dependent on others in the marketing system.

Primary marketing institutions
are those channel members that take title to the goods as they move through the marketing channel. They include manufacturers, wholesalers, and retailers.

Facilitating marketing institutions
are those that do not actually take title but assist in the marketing process by specializing in the performance of certain marketing functions.

Freelance broker
is a broker who has no permanent ties with any manufacturer and may negotiate sales over any territory for a large number of manufacturers.

Manufacturer's agent
act as the sales force for several manufacturers at the same time within a prescribed market area.

MARKETING INSTITUTIONS

What institutions are involved in performing the eight marketing functions? There are many more than you might initially think. These institutions can be meaningfully broken into two categories: primary and facilitating. Primary marketing institutions are those channel members that take title to the goods. Facilitating marketing institutions are those that do not actually take title but assist in the marketing process by specializing in the performance of certain functions. Exhibit 5.3 is a classification of the major institutions participating in the marketing system.

PRIMARY MARKETING INSTITUTIONS

There are three types of primary marketing institutions: manufacturers, wholesalers, and retailers.

Often, we don't think of manufacturers as marketing institutions because they produce goods. But manufacturers cannot exist by only producing goods; they must also sell the goods produced. They often need the assistance of other institutions in performing the eight marketing functions. There are more than 380,000 manufacturers in the United States.

A second type of primary marketing institution is the wholesaler. Wholesalers buy merchandise from manufacturers and resell to retailers, other merchants, industrial institutions, and commercial users. There are nearly 400,000 wholesalers in the United States, each performing some of the eight marketing functions.

The third type of primary institution is the retailer. There are 1.9 million retail stores or establishments/institutions and more than 1.8 million service establishments in the United States. Retailers can perform portions of all eight marketing functions.

It is possible that some firms (e.g., the membership warehouse clubs [Sam's or Price-Costco]) can act as both a wholesaler, selling to small businesses, and as a retailer, selling to households. However, for statistical purposes, the Census Bureau considers all membership warehouse clubs to be wholesalers, because that activity accounts for more than 50 percent of their sales.

FACILITATING MARKETING INSTITUTIONS

A variety of institutions facilitate the performance of the marketing functions. Most of these institutions specialize in one or two functions; none of them takes title to the goods. Institutions that facilitate buying and selling in the marketing system include

1. The freelance broker who has no permanent ties with any manufacturer and may negotiate sales for a large number of manufacturers. There is no limit on the territory in which sales may occur, but the broker is strictly bound by the manufacturer specifications on prices, terms, and conditions of sale.

2. The manufacturer's agent acts as the sales force for several manufacturers at the same time within a prescribed market area. The manufacturer's agent has a rather loose arrangement with the manufacturer that is seldom permanent beyond a year. This arrangement is usually renewed but can also be terminated on notice. The manufacturer's agent, like the freelance broker, is strictly bound by the

| EXHIBIT 5.3 | INSTITUTIONS PARTICIPATING IN THE MARKETING SYSTEM |

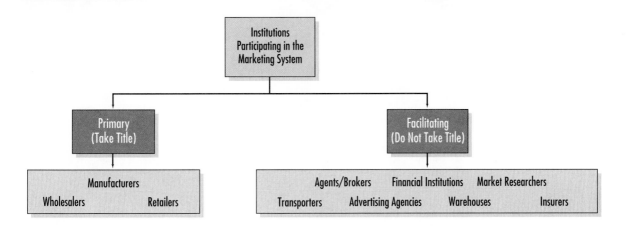

manufacturer regarding prices, terms, and conditions of sale but is additionally bound by territory. Manufacturer's agents usually have jurisdiction over only a part of the manufacturer's total output. Manufacturer's agents are extremely important in product lines such as furniture, dry goods, clothing, and accessories.

3. The sales agent has long-term arrangements with one or a very few manufacturers. The sales agent sells the entire output for the manufacturer and has no limitation on territory, prices, terms, or conditions of sale. The sales agent also frequently finances the manufacturer. The sales agent is generally used in such product lines as home furnishings, textiles, and canned goods.

4. Purchasing agents specialize in seeking out sources of supply for some members of the channel. They operate on a contractual basis for a limited number of customers and receive a commission just as sales agents do. Purchasing agents, who are sometimes known as resident buyers, which once was a way of life for retail buyers, especially in the apparel industry, usually operate in the central market headquarters. They were the buying arm and intelligence service for out-of-town retailers on the availability of products; whose showrooms to shop and whose to not shop, the reliability of suppliers; present and future market trends; and special deals, prices, shipping, and other considerations involving the purchase of merchandise. Today, however, because of advances in communication and the advent of mega-retailers, there are only a few major resident buying offices remaining.[7]

These facilitating agents and brokers are independent business persons who receive a commission or fee when they are able to bring buyer and seller together to negotiate a transaction. Seldom do agents or brokers take physical possession of the merchandise. The purchasing agents assist in buying and the others assist in selling for manufacturers.

Advertising agencies also facilitate the selling process by designing effective advertisements and advising management on where and when to place these advertisements. Institutions that facilitate the transportation function are motor, rail, and air carriers and pipeline and shipping companies. These firms offer differing advantages in terms of delivery, service, and cost. Generally, the quicker the delivery, the more costly it is. Transporters can have a significant effect on how efficiently goods move through the

Sales agent
has long-term arrangements with one or a very few manufacturers to sell their entire output and has no limitation on territory, prices, terms, or conditions of sale.

Purchasing agent
operates on a contractual and commission basis for a limited number of customers and specializes in seeking out sources of supply for some members of the channel.

Resident buyers
are a type of purchasing agent which reside in the central market for a particular line of merchandise and represent several retailers in that market.

Home Depot performs some of the selling functions for Kohler, a manufacturer of plumbing fixtures, by its use of in-store displays and sales promotion.

marketing system. They can be a major source of conflict when they fail to perform their jobs properly.

The major facilitating institution involved in storage is the public warehouse. A public warehouse stores goods for safekeeping for any owner in return for a fee. Fees are usually based on cubic feet used per time period (month or day). Frequently, retailers take advantage of special promotional buys that manufacturers offer but often have no space for the goods in their stores or warehouses. As a result, they find it necessary to use public warehouses.

Public warehouse

is a facility which stores goods for safekeeping for any owner in return for a fee, usually based on space occupied.

A growing number of retailers are turning over all their distribution functions (warehousing and transportation) to facilitating institutions. For example, Laura Ashley has handed over all its global distribution functions for its 540 worldwide stores to a division of Federal Express. The FedEx division will manage all aspects of Laura Ashley's flow of merchandise. This will include the routing and transportation of global inventory from suppliers to all stores.[8]

A variety of facilitating institutions also assists in providing information in the marketing system. For example, the role of the computer specialists, referred to as "system integrators," in setting up computer systems for transmitting information is evident throughout the business world. Retailers can now order many types of merchandise by using an on-line computer. In fact, many retail analysts believe that Wal-Mart's leap into the number 1 spot in retail sales stems directly from the deployment of sophisticated electronics to run a huge supply and distribution network. JCPenney and Wal-Mart require all their vendors be linked electronically to retailer's computer, permitting the vendors to automatically ship replacements without purchase orders that were paid by electronic funds transfers.[9] As a result of this, the majority of business mergers occurring today are to improve distribution and not to gain production advantages.[10]

There are also facilitating institutions that aid in financing (e.g., commercial banks, merchant banks, savings and loan associations, stock exchanges, and venture capital firms). These institutions can provide or help the retailer obtain funds to finance marketing functions. Retailers frequently need short-term loans for working capital requirements (to handle increased inventory and accounts receivables) and long-term loans for continued growth and expansion (adding new stores or remodeling).

Finally, insurance firms facilitate by assuming some of the risks in the marketing system. Insurance firms can insure inventories, buildings, trucks, equipment and fixtures, and other assets for the retailer and other primary marketing institutions. They can also insure against employee and customer injuries.

Having reviewed the various functions and institutions in the marketing system, we are now ready to examine how the primary marketing institutions are arranged into a marketing channel.

TYPES OF MARKETING CHANNELS

LO • 3
Describe the difference between the two types of marketing channels: conventional and vertical

A large part of the marketing system consists of the marketing functions and the primary marketing institutions that perform them. But how are these functions and institutions arranged into a marketing channel? There are two basic channel patterns: the conventional marketing channel and the vertical marketing system. Exhibit 5.4 provides an illustration of these major channel patterns.

CONVENTIONAL MARKETING CHANNEL

A conventional marketing channel is one in which each member of the channel is loosely aligned with the others and takes a short-term orientation. Predictably, each member's orientation is toward the next institution in the channel and "what is happening today" as opposed to "what will happen in the future." Thus the manufacturer interacts with and focuses efforts on the wholesaler, the wholesaler focuses efforts on the retailer, and the retailer focuses efforts on the final consumer. In short, all the members focus on their immediate desire to "close" the sale or create a transaction. Thus the conventional marketing channel consists of a series of pairs in which the members of each pair, or dyad, recognize each other but not necessarily the other members of the system.

The conventional marketing channel, although historically predominant in the United States, is a sloppy and inefficient method of conducting business. It fosters intense negotiations within each pair of institutions in the channel. In addition, channel members do not see the possibility of shifting or dividing the marketing functions among all channel participants. Therefore, it is an unproductive method for marketing goods and has been on the decline in the United States since the early 1950s.

Conventional marketing channel
is one in which each channel member is loosely aligned with the others and takes a short-term orientation.

VERTICAL MARKETING SYSTEMS

Vertical marketing systems are capital-intensive networks of several levels that are professionally managed and centrally programmed to realize the technological, managerial, and promotional economies of a long-term relationship orientation. The basic premise behind the idea of managing a channel is that because of their very nature, channels are never able to operate at 100 percent efficiency. This is because although channel members are dependent on each other to reach goals, they are still, for the

Vertical marketing systems
are capital-intensive networks of several levels that are profesionally managed and centrally programmed to realize the technological, managerial, and promotional economies of a long-term relationship orientation.

EXHIBIT 5.4	MARKETING CHANNEL PATTERNS

Quick response (QR) systems *also known as* efficient consumer response (ECR) systems *are integrated information, production, and logistical systems that obtain real-time information on consumer actions by capturing sale data at point of purchase terminals and then transmitting this information back through the entire channel to enable efficient production and distribution scheduling.*

Stock-keeping-units (SKU) *are the lowest level of identification of merchandise.*

Category management (CM) *is a process of managing all SKUs within a product category and involves the simultaneous management of price, shelf space, merchandising strategy, promotional efforts, and other elements of the retail mix within the category based on the firm's goals, the changing environment, and consumer behavior.*

most part, independently owned. Therefore, a vertical system is an attempt to "minimize the suboptimization" of the channel.

DOLLAR $ & ¢ENTS

Almost every high performance retailer in the U.S. economy is part of a vertical marketing system.

Formerly adversarial relationships between retailers and their suppliers are now giving way to new vertical channel programs of channel partnership to minimize such inefficiencies.[11] Because vertical channel members now realize that it is impossible to offer consumers "value" without being the low-cost, high-efficiency channel, they have developed either quick response (QR) systems or efficient consumer response (ECR) systems.[12] These systems, which are the same despite the different names adopted by various retail industries, are designed to obtain real-time information on consumers' actions by capturing stock-keeping-units (SKU, the lowest level of identification of merchandise) data at point of purchase terminals and then transmitting this information back through the entire channel. This information is used to develop new or modified products, manage channelwide inventory levels, and lower total channel costs. Category management is an important part of ECR. Category management (CM) is a process of managing all SKUs within a product category, not a single SKU or alternatively the entire store's merchandise. CM involves the simultaneous management of price, shelf space, merchandising strategy, promotional efforts, and other elements of the retail mix within the category based on the firm's goals, the changing environment, and consumer behavior. CM is accomplished in a channel establishing a team, made up of channel members who in a conventional channel would have acted independently, to apply the ECR concept to an entire category of merchandise.

For most CM-oriented retailers, their goal is to optimize the operations of each part of the store by allocating space that maximizes gross margin dollars produced per unit of space. For a supplier working with a CM retailer, the goal is to become the lead supplier for that category. The names of the channel members who are active in CM reads like a "who's who" list: on the retail side—Wal-Mart, H.E.B. Grocery, Dominick's, and Schnuck's; on the supplier side—General Electric, Procter & Gamble, Kraft/General Foods, M&M/Mars, Quaker Oats, VF Corp. (manufacturer of Lee Jeans), and Hallmark.[13]

There are three types of vertical marketing systems—corporate, contractual, and administered—each of which has grown significantly in the past 40 years.

CORPORATE SYSTEMS

Corporate vertical marketing systems typically consist of either a manufacturer that has integrated vertically to reach the consumer or a retailer that has integrated vertically to create a self-supply network. The first type includes manufacturers such as Sherwin Williams (paint), Hart, Schaffner and Marx (men's apparel), and Famolare (shoes), which have created their own warehousing and retail outlets. The second type includes retailers such as Holiday Inns. For example, Holiday Hospitality Corp has vertically integrated to control a carpet mill, furniture manufacturer, and numerous other suppliers needed to build and operate its hotels and motels.

Another example of this trend is manufacturers such as Liz Claiborne, London Fog, Guess, Bass, and Esprit opening factory outlet stores that sell direct to the public at 50 to 70 percent off regular retail prices. These outlets traditionally were located near a manufacturer's factory, but now the trend is to open these stores in factory outlet malls. This practice has angered traditional retailers that buy from these manufacturers and has created channel conflict.

In corporate systems, it is much easier to program the channel for productivity and profit goals, because a well-established authority structure already exists. Independent retailers that have aligned themselves in a conventional marketing channel are at a significant disadvantage when competing against a corporate vertical marketing system.

CONTRACTUAL SYSTEMS

Contractual vertical marketing systems, which include wholesaler-sponsored voluntary groups, retailer-owned cooperatives, and franchised retail programs, are channel systems that use a contract to govern the working relationship between the members. Each of these channel types allows for a more coordinated and systemwide perspective than conventional marketing channels. However, they are more difficult to manage than corporate vertical marketing systems because the authority and power structures are not as well defined. Channel members must give up some autonomy to gain system economies of scale and greater market impact.

WHOLESALER-SPONSORED VOLUNTARY GROUPS   Wholesaler-sponsored voluntary groups are created when a wholesaler brings together a group of independently owned retailers (*independent retailers* is a term embracing anything from a single mom-and-pop store to a

Corporate vertical marketing systems
exist where one channel institution owns multiple levels of distribution and typically consists of either a manufacturer that has integrated vertically to reach the consumer or a retailer that has integrated vertically to create a self-supply network.

Contractual vertical marketing systems
use a contract to govern the working relationship between channel members and include wholesaler-sponsored voluntary groups, retailer-owned cooperatives, and franchised retail programs.

Wholesaler-sponsored voluntary groups
involve a wholesaler that brings together a group of independently owned retailers and offers them a coordinated merchandising and buying program that will provide them with economies like those their chain store rivals are able to obtain.

Buying is a critical marketing function that retailers perform. Here we see Jody Spiera of Peter Luger's Steakhouse with Gachot & Gachot Wholesale meat market supervisor, John Buono of New York City.

small local chain), grocers, for example, and offers them a coordinated merchandising and buying program that will provide them with economies like those their chain store rivals are able to obtain. In return, the independent retailers agree to concentrate their purchases with that wholesaler. It is a voluntary relationship (i.e., there are no membership or franchise fees). The independent retailer may terminate the relationship whenever they desire, so it is to the wholesaler's advantage to build competitive merchandise assortments and offer other services that will keep the voluntary group satisfied. Nonetheless, some retailers will reach a level of sophistication and sales volume at which they believe they can handle their own distribution. Fleming Companies (the nation's largest food wholesaler and an early pioneer in voluntary group wholesaling with annual sales in excess of $18 billion) lost customers such as Smith Food & Drug, who decided to build their own warehouse and transportation systems.

The voluntary group wholesaler commonly offers the retailer the following services: store design and layout, store site and location analysis, inventory management systems, accounting and bookkeeping systems, insurance services, pension plans, trade area studies, advertising and promotion assistance, and employee-training programs. The better the services and merchandising programs offered by the wholesaler, the more loyal the retailer and the more the wholesaler can direct and organize the channel's activities. Associated Wholesale Grocers, for example, has developed a special program for its retailers facing competition from supercenters entering their trading area. A year in advance of the supercenter's arrival, Associated helps its retailers adjust prices, remodel or relocate stores, add bakeries and delis, and develop other strategies to successfully combat the supercenters.[14]

In the past, local food wholesalers got practically all their business from independent grocers. Recently, however, as transportation costs have risen, major chains operating over a wide geographic area have also started using local or national wholesalers.

COTTER & COMPANY'S TRUE ADVANTAGE PROGRAM

In 1995, Cotter & Company, a retailer-owned hardware cooperative, affiliated with True Value hardware stores offered its retailers the True Advantage program. True Advantage is a commitment between the True Value retailer and Cotter & Company in which both parties agree to take actions that will be mutually beneficial. The True Value retailer agrees to implement 12 retail standards, which include exterior True Value identification, competitive store hours, purchasing of core merchandise categories, pinpoint pricing promotion, advertising participation, adoption of the True Help return policy, computerization of the store, retail training, participation in Cotter's communication satellite network,

utilization of the charge card and gift certificate promotion, retail data reporting, and attendance at the semiannual hardware market. If the True Value retailer implements these 12 standards within 24 months, then it qualifies for the following incentives: a retail marketing and operational analysis at no charge (valued at $20,000), a volume discount of 5 percent of the increase in purchases over the prior year, and a below-market rate financing package that can be used to finance store remodeling or other capital expenditures.

SOURCE: Company brochure describing the True Advantage program and conversations with Dan Cotter.

While welcoming this new business, wholesalers have tried to keep their independents happy (because they still account for more than 40 percent of their business) by offering them even more services.

Wholesaler-sponsored voluntary groups have been a major force in marketing channels since the mid-1960s. They are now prevalent in many lines of trade. Independent Grocers' Alliance (IGA) and National Auto Parts Association (NAPA) are both examples of wholesaler-sponsored voluntary groups.

RETAILER-OWNED COOPERATIVES   Another common type of contractual vertical marketing system is retailer-owned cooperatives, which are organized and owned by retailers and are most common in hardware retailing, and include such wholesalers as Ace, Cotter & Company, Handy Hardware, SERVISTAR, and Sodisco-Howden. They offer scale economies and services to member retailers, allowing their members to compete with larger chain-buying organizations. Our second Behind the Scenes box provides a detailed look at Cotter & Company's True Value Advantage program, which it offers its retail members.

Finally, in theory, wholesale-sponsored groups should be easier to manage because they have only one owner, the wholesaler, versus the many owners of the retailer-owned group. In retailer-owned wholesale cooperatives, individual members tend to want to keep their autonomy and depend less strongly on their supplier-partner for support and direction. In reality, however, just the opposite has been true. A possible explanation for this is that retailers belonging to a wholesale co-op may make greater transaction-specific investments in the form of stock ownership, vested supplier-based store identity, and end-of-year rebates on purchases that combine to erect significant exit barriers.[15]

Retailer-owned cooperatives
are wholesale institutions, organized and owned by member retailers, which offer scale economies and services to member retailers that allows them to compete with larger chain-buying organizations.

Ace Hardware stores, although independently operated, are part of a vertical marketing system where the Ace Hardware wholesale buying cooperative is the channel leader.

Franchise

is a form of licensing by which the owner of a product, service, or business method (the franchisor) obtains distribution through affiliated dealers (franchisees).

FRANCHISES   The third type of contractual vertical marketing system is the franchise. A franchise is a form of licensing by which the owner of a product, service, or business method (the franchisor) obtains distribution through affiliated dealers (franchisees). In many cases, the franchise operation resembles a large chain with trademarks, uniform symbols, equipment, storefronts, and standardized services, products, and practices as outlined in the franchise agreement.

Franchising is a convenient and economic means of fulfilling the desire for independence that many individuals have with a minimum amount of risk and investment and maximum opportunities for success. This is possible through the use of a proven product or service and marketing method. However, the owner of a franchise gives up some freedom in business decisions that the owner of a nonfranchised business would have. To maintain uniformity of service and to ensure that the operations of each outlet will reflect favorably on the organization as a whole, the franchisor usually exercises some degree of control over the operations of franchisees, requiring them to meet stipulated standards of product and service quality and operating procedures.

Franchisors can be found at any position in the marketing channel. The franchisor could be a manufacturer, such as Chevrolet and Midas Mufflers; a service specialist, such as Kelly Girl, Mail Boxes Etc, AAMCO Transmissions, H&R Block, Jenny Craig Weight Loss Centers, Supercuts, and Century 21 Real Estate; a retailer that rents formalwear, such as Gingiss Formalwear, or a fast-food retailer, such as McDonald's, Dunkin Donuts, Subway, Domino's Pizza, and KFC. Exhibit 5.5 lists some of the major advantages and disadvantages of owning a franchise.

DOLLAR $ & CENTS

Franchisors that focus their expansion efforts internationally will experience higher performance.

EXHIBIT 5.5	ADVANTAGES AND DISADVANTAGES OF FRANCHISE OWNERSHIP

ADVANTAGES TO FRANCHISEE

1. Franchisor provides managerial skills that are taught to franchisee.
2. Franchisee can begin a business with a relatively small capital investment.
3. Franchisee can acquire a relatively well-known or established line of business.
4. Franchisee can acquire rights to a well-defined geographic area.
5. The standardized marketing programs and operating procedures enable the franchisee to be competitive immediately.
6. Franchisees, because they own a piece of the action, tend to be more motivated and "bottom-line" oriented than managers.

DISADVANTAGES TO FRANCHISEE

1. Too many franchises can be located in a geographic area.
2. Too many franchisors make promises they cannot keep (e.g., overstating income potential of a franchise).
3. Franchisors can include a buy-back agreement whereby the franchisee must sell back the franchise at a given point in time or the franchise agreement is for a short duration.
4. Under most franchise agreements, payments to the franchisor are a percentage of sales regardless of a franchisee's profitability.
5. Franchise systems may be too inflexible in terms of operating procedures (i.e., hours, product selection, etc.) for the franchisee. In short, the franchisee must surrender its freedom to make many decisions.

Currently, only one-third of U.S. franchisors are operating in foreign countries; however, another third are looking to expand internationally within the next five years. After all, why compete in overcrowded U.S. markets when many foreign markets are available? Although franchising is seen as an economic-development tool for poor countries, the most widely considered foreign markets are Canada, Japan, Mexico, Germany, the United Kingdom, and more recently, Southeast Asia—Philippines, Thailand, Taiwan, Singapore, and Indonesia.

ADMINISTERED SYSTEMS

The final type of vertical marketing system is the administered system. Administered vertical marketing systems are similar to conventional marketing channels, but one of the channel members takes the initiative to lead the channel by applying the principles of effective interorganizational management, which is the management of relationships between the various organizations in the channel. Administered systems, although not new in concept, have grown substantially in recent years. Frequently, administered systems are initiated by manufacturers because they have historically relied on their administrative expertise to coordinate the retailers' marketing efforts. Suppliers with dominant brands have predictably experienced the least difficulty in securing strong support from retailers and wholesalers. But many manufacturers with "fringe" items have been able to elicit such cooperation only through the use of liberal distribution policies that take the form of attractive discounts (or discount substitutes), financial assistance, and various types of concessions that protect resellers from one or more of the risks of doing business.[16]

Administered vertical marketing systems exisit when one of the channel members takes the initiative to lead the channel by applying the principles of effective interorganizational management.

Some of the concessions manufacturers offer retailers are liberal return policies, display materials for in-store use, advertising allowances, extra time in paying for the merchandise, employee training programs, assistance with store layout and design, inventory maintenance, computer systems support, and even free merchandise.

Manufacturers that use their administrative powers to lead channels include General Electric (on both major and small appliances), Sealy (on its Posturepedic line of mattresses), Villager (on its dresses and sportswear lines), Scott (on its lawn care products), Norwalk (on its upholstered furniture), Keepsake (on diamonds), and Stanley (on hand tools). Retailers can also dominate the channel relationship. For example, Wal-Mart, one of the earliest adopters of ECR and CM systems, administers their relationships with almost all their suppliers by asking that all advertising allowances, slotting fees, end of aisle display fees, etc., be taken off the price of goods.

LO • 4

Explain the terms *dependency* and *channel power* and why cooperation is so important in channel management

MANAGING RETAILER-SUPPLIER RELATIONS

Retailers who are not part of a contractual system or corporate channel will probably participate in several marketing channels, because they will need to acquire merchandise from many suppliers. Predictably, these marketing channels will either be conventional or administered. If retailers want to improve their performance in these channels, they must understand the principal concepts of interorganizational management. In this case, it involves a retailer managing its relations with wholesalers and manufacturers.

What are the basic concepts of interorganizational management that a retailer needs to understand? They are dependency, power, and managing cooperative relations.

DEPENDENCY

Dependency
occurs when one channel member must rely on another channel member to achieve an objective.

As we mentioned earlier, all marketing systems need to perform eight marketing functions. These functions are performed by a multitude of institutions in the marketing channel. None of the respective institutions can isolate itself; each has a dependency on the others to do an effective job.

Retailer A is dependent on suppliers X, Y, and Z to make sure that goods are delivered on time and in the right quantities. Conversely, suppliers X, Y, and Z depend on retailer A to put a strong selling effort behind the goods, displaying the merchandise and helping to finance consumer purchases. If retailer A does a poor job, each supplier can be adversely affected; if even one supplier does a poor job, retailer A can be adversely affected. In all channel alignments, each party depends on the others to do a good job.

When each party is dependent on the others, we say that they are interdependent. Interdependency is at the root of cooperation and conflict in marketing channels. To better understand cooperation and conflict between retailers and suppliers, an understanding of power is necessary.

POWER

Power
is the ability of one channel member to influence the decisions of the other channel members.

We can use the concept of dependency to explain power; but first, we must define *power*. Power is the ability of one channel member to influence the decisions of the other channel members. The more dependent the supplier is on the retailer, the more power the retailer has over the supplier. For example, a small manufacturer of grocery products would be very dependent on a large supermarket chain if it wanted to reach the most consumers. Or many suppliers to Wal-Mart are very dependent on it because Wal-Mart is their biggest customer. For example, Toastmaster, a manufacturer of home appliances, sells 30 percent of its annual sales to Wal-Mart, making it highly dependent on Wal-Mart.[17]

There are five sources of power:

1. Reward power is based on the ability of A to provide rewards for B. For instance, a retailer offers a manufacturer a prominent display area in exchange for additional advertising monies and promotion support.

2. Expertise power is based on B's perception that A has some special knowledge. For example, Midas Muffler (a franchisor) has developed an excellent training program for store managers. Thus franchisees view the franchisor as an expert.

3. Referent power is based on the identification of B with A. B wants to be associated or identified with A. Examples of this would be the auto dealers that want to handle BMWs or Mercedes because of the cars' status or a manufacturer that wants to have its product sold in Neiman-Marcus because of the image that retailer projects.

4. Coercive power is based on B's belief that A has the capacity to punish or harm B if B doesn't do what A wants. A franchisor, Burger King, for example, has the right to cancel a franchisee's contract if it fails to maintain standards concerning restaurant cleanliness, food, hours of operation, and employees.

5. Legitimate power is based on A's right to influence B, or B's belief that B should accept A's influence. The appearance of legitimate power is most obvious in contractual marketing systems. A manufacturer may, for example, threaten to cut off a retailer's supply if the retailer doesn't properly display the manufacturer's products. Also, if the retailer accepts co-op advertising dollars, the manufacturer may control the minimum retail price, because this subject is usually covered in the agreement. Otherwise, the retailer is free to set the selling price. To do otherwise, without an agreement specifically covering retail price, would be a violation of certain federal antitrust laws, which we discuss in the next chapter.

Retailers and suppliers that use reward, expertise, and referent power can foster cooperation. For example, Liz Claiborne was recently forced to play catch-up after several years of offering what could best be described as "basic, boring, and heavy on polyester."[18] To get retailers back, it increased the cash discount, from 8 percent to 10 percent, to retailers that paid for merchandise within 10 days of delivery. This was an attempt by the women's apparel manufacturer to gain additional sales from those retailers that were in poor or weak financial condition, as well as to make sure that they were paid first, before other manufacturers. In addition, Liz Claiborne made a major investment in computer technology to manage inventory. The retailer's computerized information system (LizRIM) relied on state-of-the-art bar-coding to let it track and stock hot items, replenish them during the early part of the selling season, and avoid merchandise losers by spotting poor sellers.[19] Liz Claiborne realized that many of the nation's department stores needed to increase their profits and were dependent on manufacturers that offered some reward, expertise, and referent (having a hot seller's brand in stock) power.

However, the use of coercive and legitimate power tends to elicit conflict and destroy cooperation. For example, although the franchisor has the legitimate right to set standards for items covered in the franchise agreement, such as store cleanliness,

Reward power
is based on the ability of A to provide rewards for B.

Expertise power
is based on B's perception that A has some special knowledge.

Referent power
is based on the identification of B with A.

Coercive power
is based on B's belief that A has the capacity to punish or harm B if B doesn't do what A wants.

Legitimate power
is based on A's right to influence B, or B's belief that B should accept A's influence.

signage, store hours, and retail price, many franchisees still think that they should be consulted on all these issues before decisions are made unilaterally.

MANAGING COOPERATIVE RELATIONS

DOLLAR $ & CENTS

Those retailers who treat their fellow channel members as partners and not as the enemy will tend to have better long-term performance than those who don't.

Although all channels experience conflict, the dominant behavior in most retail channels is cooperative. Cooperation is necessary and beneficial because of the interdependency of retailers and suppliers and because most retailers and suppliers must develop a partnership if they want to deal with each other on a long-term and continuing basis. As a result, many channel members have begun to follow a new set of Ten Commandments listed in Exhibit 5.6. This vendor partnership is often a critical factor for the retailer who doesn't want to confuse the final consumer with constant adjustments in product offerings that result from always changing suppliers.

The management of cooperative relations is facilitated by three important types of behaviors and attitudes. These are mutual trust, two-way communication, and solidarity.[20]

Mutual trust

occurs when both the retailer and its suppliers have faith that each will be truthful and fair in their dealings with the other.

MUTUAL TRUST
Mutual trust occurs when the retailer trusts the supplier and the supplier trusts the retailer. In continuing relations between retailer and suppliers, mutual trust is critical because it allows for short-term inequities to exist. If mutual trust is present, then each party will tolerate these inequities because they know that in the long term things will be fairly treated. For example, a retailer may receive a shipment of swimwear that is not precisely what was ordered. The retailer could immediately ship the unordered merchandise back or immediately begin to merchandise the swimwear knowing that the supplier can be trusted to make an appropriate adjustment on the invoice amount, provide markdown money, or that the supplier will make up this inequity in the future.

Without mutual trust, retail supply channels would disintegrate. However, if trust exists it will be contagious and allow the channel to grow and prosper. This occurs because of reciprocity. If a retailer trusts a supplier to do the right thing and the supplier treats the retailer fairly, then the retailer develops more trust and the process of mutual trust continues to build. Trust in retail channels grows over time.

Two-way communication

occurs when both retailer and supplier communicate openly thier ideas, concerns and plans.

TWO-WAY COMMUNICATION
As noted earlier, conflict is inevitable in retail channels. Consequently, two-way communication becomes the pathway for resolving disputes, which allows the channel relation to continue. Two-way communication occurs when both parties communicate openly their ideas, concerns, and plans. Because of the interdependency of the retailer and supplier, two-way communication becomes necessary to coordinate actions. For example, when Jockey decides to have a national promotion on its underwear it needs to coordinate this

EXHIBIT 5.6	TEN COMMANDMENTS FOR CHANNEL PARTNERS

1. Thou shalt know and celebrate the "retail customer" who makes all things possible.
2. Thou shalt love and trust thy partner for richer or poorer, in cash bind or cash health.
3. Thou shalt not seek a new partner at the first sign of trouble.
4. Thou shalt work together in developing an honest pricing policy for honest products.
5. Thou shalt not negotiate from positions of strength but from an understanding of thy partner's needs.
6. Thou shalt not covet thy partner's just profit.
7. Thou shalt not have too many partners for the same merchandise line so as to dilute the value of the relationship with existing partners.
8. Thou shalt use the highest ethical standards every day, so as to be an example to others.
9. Thou shalt make seasonal plans together. Only when this fails should one consider breaking up the partnership.
10. Thou shalt strive for a relationship when you would be just as happy if you were your own channel partner.

promotion with its retail channels so that when customers enter stores to shop for the items nationally advertised they will find them displayed and in stock. This requires coordination, and two-way communication is critical to accomplishing this coordination. For example, Wal-Mart's computer system has improved total channel efficiency by allowing manufacturers to know inventory levels for their products at Wal-Mart's stores and warehouses. Before developing trust, such a communication system would have been impossible.

Communication is not independent of trust. Disputes can be resolved by good two-way communication, and this improves trust. Furthermore, trust facilitates communication. The process is circular and builds over time.

SOLIDARITY

Solidarity exists when a high value is placed on the relationship between a supplier and retailer. Solidarity is an attitude and thus is hard to explicitly create. Essentially, as trust and two-way communication increase, a higher degree of solidarity develops. Solidarity results in flexible dealings in which adaptations are made as circumstances change. When solidarity exists, each party will come to the rescue of the other in time of trouble. For example, in the mid-1990s when the economy was weak, many retailers, already operating under intense competitive pressure and operating on thin margins, sought and obtained assistance such as advertising or building in-store displays from suppliers with whom they had developed strong relationships in the past. Usually, these activities are the responsibility of the retailer, but given the business climate, the vendor was able to assist. However, when solidarity does not exist each party will abandon the other in time of trouble. This has often occurred when retailers have developed poor relationships and conflict with their suppliers. If the retailer then experiences a liquidity crisis, suppliers are likely to refuse shipment of needed merchandise. This is what happened to Kmart in 1995. However,

Solidarity
exists when a high value is placed on the relationship between a supplier and retailer.

KEYS TO DEVELOPING AND BUILDING A HIGHLY SUCCESSFUL CHANNEL PARTNERSHIP

by Drayton McLane
Chairman, McLane Group

- A close, personal friendship based on mutual trust, admiration, and respect.
- The development of an interdependency in establishing and maintaining the same high standards to achieve common goals and objectives.
- Creating and maintaining a business climate based on cooperation, fairness, and mutual success.
- Open, honest, and constant communication of ideas, concerns, needs, and plans.

- A total focus on quality and outstanding customer service and satisfaction must be a part of every decision and action taken.
- Performance plays a major role in maintaining a long-term relationship, but it is equally important to utilize innovative, visionary leadership in identifying opportunities and ways to assist one another. Collectively plan your strategies for the future and always stay at least one step ahead of the competition!

by late 1997 a new management team at Kmart, working closely with its suppliers, was able to overcome this problem and develop a positive working relationship with them the following year.[21]

In our Winners & Losers box, we describe in more detail the 15-year relationship between Sam Walton and Drayton McLane of the McLane Company, Inc., the nation's largest distributor of food and nonfood items to convenience stores, as well as to other retailers such as Wal-Mart. As you can see, this was truly a cooperative partnership built on trust, two-way communication, and solidarity. This was further highlighted in the early 1990s when McLane sold the family business to Wal-Mart. Instead of having lawyers spend weeks, if not months, drawing up the contract involving hundreds of millions of dollars, Walton and McLane sat down and, using a yellow legal pad, which Sam always carried with him, worked out the details of the sale. They then shook hands and called in their lawyers and told them this was the deal and not to change anything.

When asked to say what made his relationship with Sam Walton so special, Drayton McLane stated that he and Sam shared the same vision, the same business philosophy, and certainly, the same code of business ethics. That the above list of values and standards made up the cornerstone of not only his and Sam's relationship with each other, but their relationship with all channel partners. This is the only way to build a strong and lasting foundation of teamwork to make a channel system work.

MANAGING CONFLICT

Although channel conflict is inevitable, it does have the benefit of reminding channel members of their interdependency. The level of conflict must, however, be controlled so that the channel can perform its functions efficiently. Ideally, conflict should be anticipated and controlled before it breaks down channel relationships. Typically, however, conflict is detected only after it becomes evident. At this point, the conflict may have done its damage and become difficult to control, manage, and resolve.

One way to resolve conflicts before they worsen a channel relationship is to anticipate potential conflict situations by periodically reviewing the relationship. A channelwide committee composed of representatives from channel members performs such reviews most effectively. In the fast-food industry, for example, committees consisting of representatives of the franchisor and franchisees periodically review channel relationships on all levels of activity from menu selection to promotional campaigns. Because it includes representatives of both groups, the committee can take all perspectives into account in making channelwide decisions. Maybe it is just finding out that the biggest complaint among retailers is late deliveries or that vendors want better communications, especially in the case of BAD news, so they can correct the problem before it festers.[22]

To avoid conflict, the channel committee must arrive at a set of goals that benefit both groups, along with systemwide performance standards. Channel functions must be properly distributed among channel members, taking into consideration the resources of each.

Recently, Procter & Gamble (P&G), long accustomed to conflict in its dealings with retailers, began a new program of partnerships with its customers. No longer at war with retailers, P&G sought to reduce conflict in the channel. P&G started setting its sales program based on the retailers' needs, as well as its own, with its "partnering" program. P&G started setting up sales offices near major retailers' central buying offices, such as Wal-Mart's in northwest Arkansas. In addition, P&G eliminated incentive programs that prompted retailers to overstock slow-selling products such as Gleem and Spic & Span or forgo merchandising money. Now, P&G won't penalize retailers for not meeting order quotas on these products, which represent 20 percent of the P&G line.[23] Retailers across the country now find P&G to be a true working partner.[24]

STUDENT STUDY GUIDE

SUMMARY

LO•1 **WHAT IS THE RETAILER'S ROLE IN THE LARGER MARKETING SYSTEM?** The marketing system must be viewed as the solution. If the retailer ignores the marketing system to maximize short-run profits, then in the long run the system will work against the retailer. And if the system overlooks the retailer, profits sufficient for survival and growth will vanish. In learning to work within the marketing system, the retailer needs to recognize the eight marketing functions necessary in all marketing systems: buying, selling, storing, transporting, sorting, financing, information gathering, and risk taking.

LO•2 **WHAT ARE THE INSTITUTIONS INVOLVED AND FUNCTIONS THAT MUST BE PERFORMED IN EVERY MARKETING SYSTEM?** The retailer can seldom perform all eight functions: buying, selling, storing, transporting, sorting, financing, information gathering, and risk taking and therefore must rely on other primary and facilitating institutions in the marketing system. Although the marketing functions occur throughout the marketing system, they can be shifted or divided among the institutions in the marketing system.

LO•3 **WHAT IS THE DIFFERENCE BETWEEN THE TWO TYPES OF RETAIL CHANNELS?** The institutions in the marketing system can be arranged into two primary marketing channel patterns—conventional and vertical. A conventional marketing channel is one in which each member of the channel is loosely aligned with the others, each member recognizing only those it directly interacts with and ignoring all others. Conventional marketing channels are on the decline in the United States, and vertical marketing systems are becoming dominant. In the vertical marketing system, all parties to the channel recognize each other, and one party programs the channel to achieve technological, managerial, and promotional economies. Three types of vertical marketing systems are corporate, contractual, and administered.

LO•4 **HOW DOES DEPENDENCY, POWER, COOPERATION, AND CONFLICT INFLUENCE CHANNEL RELATIONS?** The retailer, to operate efficiently and effectively in any marketing channel, must depend on other channel members for assistance. When a retailer becomes highly dependent on other channel members, the other channel members gain power over the retailer. However, other channel members (manufacturers and wholesalers) are also dependent on the retailer, resulting in interdependency and a sharing of power. Although power and interdependency can lead to conflict, it actually is more likely to create a high desire for cooperative relationships. Cooperation is critical to performing marketing functions effectively and efficiently and to managing the marketing channel for the benefit of the consumer.

TERMS TO REMEMBER

marketing channel

marketing system

category management (CM)

corporate vertical marketing systems

diverter
factors
primary marketing institutions
facilitating marketing institutions
freelance broker
manufacturer's agent
sales agent
purchasing agent
resident buyers
public warehouse
conventional marketing channel
vertical marketing systems
quick response (QR) systems
efficient consumer response
 (ECR) systems
stock-keeping-units (SKU)
contractual vertical marketing
 systems

wholesaler-sponsored voluntary
 groups
retailer-owned cooperatives
franchise
administered vertical marketing
 systems
dependency
power
reward power
expertise power
referent power
coercive power
legitimate power
mutual trust
two-way communication
solidarity

REVIEW AND DISCUSSION QUESTIONS

LO•1 WHAT IS THE RETAILER'S ROLE IN THE LARGER MARKETING SYSTEM?

1. Why must a retailer, to be successful in the 21st century, view itself as a member of a larger marketing system?
2. Define the sorting process and its four steps. Give an example of each step in your answer that was not used in the chapter.
3. Must a retailer be involved in performing all the marketing functions? If it can rely on other members of the channel, what are the functions they can perform and who else can perform them?

LO•2 WHAT ARE THE INSTITUTIONS INVOLVED AND FUNCTIONS THAT MUST BE PERFORMED IN EVERY MARKETING SYSTEM?

4. Facilitating marketing institutions are powerless in the marketing channel. Agree or disagree with this statement and explain your reasoning.
5. Some say that it is easy to see how a facilitating institution such as a manufacturer's agent helps manage a channel without taking title to the goods. However, they question the contribution of other institutions such as advertising agencies and computer specialists. How would you resolve this dilemma?

LO•3 WHAT IS THE DIFFERENCE BETWEEN THE TWO TYPES OF RETAILING CHANNELS?

6. What is a vertical marketing system? What is the primary difference between a conventional marketing channel and a vertical marketing system?
7. How do wholesaler-sponsored voluntary groups benefit independent retailers?
8. Can a retailer lead the marketing channel? Why or why not? Give an example of a retailer who might lead a channel.

9. Why are retailers so dependent on other channel members? Couldn't they simply perform all eight marketing functions themselves?
10. Define and give an example of the five sources of power that can be used by a retailer in the marketing channel.
11. Why must conflict be controlled in managing a channel?
12. Looking over the list of "Ten Commandments for Channel Partners," which of these commandments is the most important for all the channel members to follow if they want to improve channel cooperation? Why?

SAMPLE TEST QUESTIONS

LO•1 **WHICH ONE OF THE FOLLOWING MARKETING FUNCTIONS IS ONE THAT A RETAILER COULD NOT PERFORM?**

a. selling
b. sorting
c. location analysis
d. buying
e. financing

LO•2 **FACILITATING INSTITUTIONS MAY BEST BE DESCRIBED AS SPECIALISTS THAT**

a. take title but not possession of the merchandise
b. take title to the merchandise to facilitate the transaction
c. manage the channel so as to increase over-all efficiency above 100 percent
d. facilitate the transaction by performing all eight marketing functions
e. perform certain marketing functions, in which they have an expertise, for other channel members

LO•3 **A MARKETING CHANNEL IN WHICH EACH MEMBER IS LOOSELY ALIGNED WITH THE OTHERS IS A(N)**

a. highly efficient system
b. contractual system
c. marketing channel capable of achieving 100 percent efficiency
d. marketing channel based on the ideals of cooperation and partnership
e. conventional marketing channel

LO•4 **THE BASIC ROOT OF ALL CONFLICT IN A MARKETING CHANNEL IS**

a. that each member wants all the power
b. that each member is dependent on the other members of the channel
c. that each member is fully capable of performing all eight marketing functions
d. that partnership agreements tend to expire after a year
e. the fact that everybody wants to work independent of the other members

APPLICATIONS

WRITING AND SPEAKING EXERCISE   Your sister and her husband opened a sports trading card store in downtown Dayton 10 years ago. Since then, they have added four more stores, two more in the Dayton suburbs and one each in Cincinnati and Columbus. Up to now, your sister has handled almost all the marketing functions internally. Because of the success of the stores and the growth in business, it seems unfeasible for this practice to continue. However, your sister doesn't believe that she has adequate "manpower" to perform all the related duties, nor does she think that she is carrying out the functions at the highest level of efficiency and effectiveness. During a discussion with her on a recent trip home, you promise to send her a one-page memo making some suggestions concerning what to do and what marketing functions she could have other marketing institutions perform.

RETAIL PROJECT   Last chapter, in our discussion on divertive competition, we introduced the topic of break-even point, or the point at which total revenues equal total expenses. Let's see how this topic aids us in determining whether to join a franchise system or to stay independent.

Assume that you own a sandwich shop. In looking over last year's income statement, you see that the annual sales were $250,000 with a gross margin of 50 percent, or $125,000. The fixed operating expenses were $50,000; the variable operating expenses were $50,000 or 20 percent of sales; and your net profit was $25,000, or 10 percent of sales.

In discussions with your spouse, you wonder whether joining a franchise operation such as Subway or Blimpie will improve your results. Your research has determined that Subway requires a $10,000 licensing fee in addition to an 8 percent royalty on sales and a 2.5 percent advertising fee on sales. Blimpie, although requiring an $18,000 licensing fee, only charges a 6 percent royalty and a 3 percent advertising fee.

Assuming that you wanted to break even, what is the amount of sales you would have to generate with each system because both your fixed and variable expenses would increase?

Remember the break-even point (BEP) is where sales equals cost of merchandise sold plus total operating expenses, or in equation form,

$$\text{Sales} = \text{Cost of merchandise sold} + \text{Fixed operating expenses}$$
$$+ \text{Variable operating expenses}$$

Thus with Subway, your fixed expenses would increase from $50,000 to $60,000 and your variable operating expenses would increase from 20 percent of sales to 30.5 percent (20 percent + 8 percent + 2.5 percent). Blimpie's would increase fixed expenses by $18,000 and variable expenses by 9 percent. Using the equation, we can calculate the BEP for both.

Subway's BEP

$$\text{net sales} = 50\%(\text{net sales}) + \$60,000 + 30.5\% (\text{net sales})$$
$$\text{Net sales} = \$307,692$$

Blimpie's BEP

$$\text{net sales} = 50\%(\text{net sales}) + \$68,000 + 29\% (\text{net sales})$$
$$\text{Net sales} = \$323,809$$

As a result of the increased expenses, by joining a franchise just to break even, you would have to increase sales more than 20 percent. To make the same profit you already are making, you would have to add that profit figure to the equation.

$$\text{net sales} = \text{Cost of merchandise sold} + \text{Fixed operating expenses}$$
$$+ \text{Variable operating expenses} + \text{Profit}$$

Subway's BEP with a $25,000 profit

$$\text{net sales} = 50\%(\text{net sales}) + \$60,000 + 30.5\%\,(\text{net sales}) + \$25,000$$
$$\text{Net sales} = \$435,897$$

Blimpie's BEP with a $25,000 profit

$$\text{net sales} = 50\%(\text{net sales}) + \$68,000 + 29\%\,(\text{net sales}) + \$25,000$$
$$\text{Net sales} = \$442,857$$

Thus, to keep the same profit as you currently have, a franchise would have to help you increase sales by more than 75 percent. There is no doubt that the image of the franchise will draw additional customers and its management may even help cut some of your other expenses. However, as the above numbers point out, joining a franchise system is not always a "sure-fire" guarantee of success.

Now, either by using a franchise directory in the library (i.e., the Worldwide or International Franchise Directory) or by using a franchisor's web site home page on the Internet, look up two competing franchise systems in the same line of retail trade. After locating the information about these franchises, do the same cost analysis we just did and determine whether, based on these figures, joining a franchise is a good investment.

CASE LockerRooms

Matt Mettler owns and operates five LockerRooms sporting stores in the St. Louis market. The layout and atmosphere of Mettler's stores is more upscale than that of other area sporting goods stores, which seems to be a key feature for attracting new customers and maintaining customer loyalty.

Although Mettler is pleased with his sales volume, he is unhappy with the fact that his cost of goods sold and operating expenses are reducing profits below what he has determined to be a satisfactory level. Mettler is responsible for ordering all the merchandise for the stores. However, he is frustrated because he has been unable to negotiate significant price breaks and promotional packages, similar to what Woolworth's gets with its Foot Locker stores, from many of the manufacturers and wholesalers he uses.

Recently, Mettler has been approached by the vice-president of a wholesaler-sponsored voluntary group of sporting goods stores based in Chicago about the possibility of LockerRooms becoming part of the chain. Mettler was strongly reassured by the vice-president that he could operate LockerRooms as he has in the past. However, in addition to savings on merchandise, the group would provide him information on services, bookkeeping, and layout that could improve sales and reduce operating expenses. However, he would not be required to make use of any of these benefits.

Mettler has many hesitations about letting others tell him how to run his business. He is also worried that joining the group would cause him to relinquish control of the stores he worked so hard to develop, especially when the stores are experiencing such success. Yet, he thinks that he must somehow lower his operating cost if he is to maximize profits.

1. What negative consequences might Mettler experience if he joins the group? How might Mettler's current situation improve if he were to join?
2. Would it be better for Mettler to just join a franchising chain instead, even if it meant having to drop his name for theirs?

PLANNING YOUR OWN RETAIL BUSINESS

You are in the process of planning a giftshop to be located in a tourist area of the downtown section of your city. This area has been recently renovated and includes a large number of restaurants, a theater, an art museum, and a sports arena that hosts a minor league baseball franchise. Your preliminary sales forecasts lead you to believe that your first year's sales will be $220,000. You have identified two major giftware wholesalers from which to purchase merchandise. One wholesaler is in a distant city and is able to promise seven-day delivery on orders more than $5,000. The second wholesaler is located in a city 80 miles to the south and provides next-day delivery on orders of $500 or more placed by 1 P.M. Unfortunately, the nearby wholesaler has slightly higher prices. Consequently, you estimate that by purchasing through this source your gross margin percent would be 42 percent versus 44 percent by purchasing from the more distant retailer. However, because the nearby wholesaler is able to provide more frequent and smaller deliveries you estimate that your average inventory would be $21,000 versus $25,500 if you used the more distant wholesaler as a supply source. Each wholesaler sells on terms of 2 percent/10 net 30. This means that if the invoice is paid within 10 days a 2 percent discount can be taken and if not the net invoice is due in 30 days. Which supply source should you select? (*HINT*: Compute the gross margin return on inventory investment, which is defined as the gross margin dollars divided by average inventory investment.)

NOTES

1. "Cruising the Internet," *Forbes*, March 24, 1997: 198–199; "U.S. Car-Buying Practices Are Getting a Big Overhaul," *Wall Street Journal*, January 31, 1997: B4.
2. "The Hottest Web IPO You Never Saw," *Business Week*, April 14, 1997:37.
3. "How To Buy a Car on the Internet," *Fortune*, March 4, 1996: 164–168.
4. "Will He Own the Road?" *U.S. News & World Report*, October 20, 1997: 45-54.
5. "Kmart, in Letter, Seeks to Reassure Its Suppliers," *Wall Street Journal*, February 16, 1996: A3, A6.
6. "America's Most Admired Companies," *Fortune*, March 3, 1997: 68.
7. "Buying Offices: Once a Staple, Now Few Exist," *Shopping Center Today*, May 1997: 76, 86.
8. "Laura Ashley Outsources Distribution," *Chain Store Age Executive*, August 1993: 80–82.
9. "Wiring Small Business," *Business Week*, November 25. 1996: 164–172.
10. "Improved Distribution, Not Better Production, Is Key Goal in Mergers," *Wall Street Journal*, August 29, 1995: A1, A2.
11. For a more complete discussion on this subject, the reader should consult Robert Buzzell and Gwen Ortmeyer, "Channel Partnerships Streamline Distribution," *Sloan Management Review*, Spring 1995: 85–96.
12. For a more detailed discussion on this topic, see Management Horizon's "Critical Issue Report, Efficient Assortment," January 1997.
13. For more details on this topic, see "Category Insights Bonds Marketers To Retailers," *Advertising Age*, October 16, 1995: 24–26; "Category Management Gains, but Confusion Still Reigns," *Chain Store Age*, January 1996: 112–116; "Rationalizing SKUs," *Progressive Grocer*, February 1996: 43–46.
14. "How Grocers Are Fighting Giant Rivals," *Wall Street Journal*, March 27, 1997: B1, B18.

15. F. Robert Dwyer and Sejo Oh, "A Transaction Cost Perspective on Vertical Contractual Structure and Interchannel Competitive Strategies," *Journal of Marketing,* April 1988: 21–34.
16. Bert C. McCammon, Jr., "Perspectives for Distribution Programming," in Louis P. Bucklin, ed., *Vertical Marketing Systems* (Glenview, IL: Scott, Foresman, 1970): 45. Reprinted with permission of the author.
17. "The Big Squeeze," *Forbes,* March 11, 1996: 45–46.
18. "Liz Claiborne Gets Dressed for Success," *U.S.News & World Report,* February 20, 1996: 55–56.
19. ibid.
20. Jan B. Heide and George John, "Do Norms Matter in Marketing Relationships?" *Journal of Marketing,* April 1992: 32–44; James C. Anderson and James A. Narus, "A Model of Distributor Firm and Manufacturer Firm Working Partnerships," *Journal of Marketing,* January 1990: 42–58.
21. "Kmart, in Letter, . . ." ibid.
22. "Degrees of Separation," *Discount Merchandise,* July 1994: 48–55.
23. "P&G to Stores: Keep the Dented Crisco Cans," *Wall Street Journal,* March 21, 1997: B1.
24. "Behind the Tumult at P&G," *Fortune,* March 7, 1994: 74–82.

LEGAL AND ETHICAL BEHAVIOR

In 1997, Staples attempted to merge with Office Depot. However, the federal government prevented the merger because of the combined strength of these two large chains and the potential impact on competition.

OVERVIEW

In this chapter, we discuss how the legal and ethical environment affects the retailer in making decisions. The discussion revolves around the legal aspects of decisions made on pricing, promotion (including the use of credit), products or merchandise, and marketing channels and concludes with a discussion of the major ethical decisions facing a retailer today.

LEARNING OBJECTIVES

After reading this chapter, you should be able to

1. explain how legislation constrains a retailer's pricing policies
2. differentiate between legal and illegal promotional activities
3. explain the retailer's responsibilities regarding the products sold
4. discuss the impact of governmental regulation on a retailer's behavior with other channel members
5. describe how various state and local laws, in addition to other federal regulations, must also be considered in developing retail policies
6. explain how a retailer's code of ethics will influence its behavior

In addition to studying the changing consumer, competition, and channel environments, the dynamic nature of retailing requires that the legal environment also be monitored. Most large retailers maintain legal departments and lobbyists to keep abreast of, interpret, and even influence government regulations. Such activities are usually beyond the resources of small businesses. However, the government and the business press do a reasonably good job of keeping retailers informed of pending and new legislation. In addition, there are retailer associations in most states that keep retailers abreast of proposed changes in state laws and attempt to protect the retailers' interests.

We will now explore the final set of external constraints that have an effect on retail decisions: legal and ethical decision making. These forces are shown in Exhibit 6.1. Consider the impact on convenience stores when the Food and Drug Administration (FDA) required a photo ID from any person younger than 27 years of age who wanted to buy cigarettes or smokeless tobacco. Think about the impact of various state laws that allow only retailers to conduct one yearly promotional game of chance. What about the cities that regulate garage sales? What about those cities that have "sign ordinances" regulating the retailer's use of billboards and even the sign on the retailer's building? What about state regulations restricting the retailer's use of product samples? All these laws control the ability of retailers to serve the needs of their target market. In addition, retailers will be affected by ethical issues when making decisions that will determine their behavior.

DOLLAR $ & ¢ENTS

Retailers who are familiar with the various laws regulating business will be less apt to make costly mistakes and thus more likely to be higher performers.

To avoid costly blunders, the retailer needs to understand its legal and ethical constraints. Knowledge in this area can aid the retailer in profitably managing the retail firm. Retailers cannot freely make decisions without regard for the laws that society has established to regulate all business trade. This legal environment consists of those federal, state, and local laws that limit the retailer's flexibility and freedom in making business-related decisions.

This chapter deals mainly with the various federal constraints that can affect the retailer's decision-making process with regard to pricing, promotion, products, and channel relationships.

Due to their complexity, we are not able to discuss all the other federal laws that affect retailers in this chapter. In addition, because state and local laws are quite varied, we only make general comments on some state and local laws. For the most part, we leave it up to you and your class discussions to investigate the impact of state and local laws on retail activities in your state and community.

As shown in Exhibit 6.2, most federal laws affecting retailing seek to "promote competition." These fall into several categories. First, the Sherman Act, the Clayton Act, the Federal Trade Commission (FTC) Act, the Celler-Kefauver Antimerger Act, and the

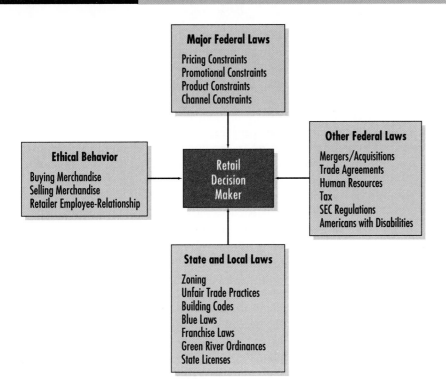

EXHIBIT 6.1 — **ETHICAL AND LEGAL CONSTRAINTS INFLUENCING RETAILER**

Major Federal Laws

Pricing Constraints
Promotional Constraints
Product Constraints
Channel Constraints

Ethical Behavior

Buying Merchandise
Selling Merchandise
Retailer Employee-Relationship

Retail Decision Maker

Other Federal Laws

Mergers/Acquisitions
Trade Agreements
Human Resources
Tax
SEC Regulations
Americans with Disabilities

State and Local Laws

Zoning
Unfair Trade Practices
Building Codes
Blue Laws
Franchise Laws
Green River Ordinances
State Licenses

Hart-Scott-Rodino Act were passed to ensure a "competitive" business climate. Second, the Robinson-Patman Act was designed to regulate pricing practices. Third, the Wheeler-Lea Act was created to control false advertising. Although some may question whether all these regulations are bleeding the economy, many do believe that they sometimes boost competitiveness.

Other laws have been passed to protect consumers and innocent third parties. A sampling of these consumer protection laws is shown in Exhibit 6.3.

Note that all aspects of retailing—price, promotion, product, and channel membership—are regulated. We begin our discussion of how federal laws affect a retailer's decision-making ability by looking at pricing regulations.

PRICING CONSTRAINTS

LO • 1
Explain how legislation constrains a retailer's pricing policies

Retailers continuously establish prices for the many items that they offer to consumers. Retailers are also influenced by pricing laws in determining what price they should pay for a product. In making these decisions, they have considerable, but not total, flexibility. The major constraining factors are summarized in Exhibit 6.4.

EXHIBIT 6.2	PRIMARY U.S. LAWS THAT AFFECT RETAILING
LEGISLATION	**IMPACT ON RETAILING**
Sherman Act, 1890	Bans (1) "monopolies or attempts to monopolize" and (2) "contracts, combinations, or conspiracies in restraint of trade" in interstate and foreign commerce
Clayton Act, 1914	Adds to the Sherman Act by prohibiting specific practices (e.g., certain types of price discrimination, tying clauses) "whereas the effect . . . may be to substantially lessen competition or tend to create a monopoly in any line of commerce"
Federal Trade Commission Act, 1914	Establishes the Federal Trade Commission, a body of specialists with broad powers to investigate and to issue cease-and-desist orders to enforce Section 5, which declares that "unfair methods of competition in commerce are unlawful"
Robinson-Patman Act, 1936	Amends the Clayton Act, adds the phrase "to injure, destroy, or prevent competition." Defines price discrimination as unlawful (subject to certain defenses) and provides the FTC with the right to establish limits on quantity discounts, to forbid brokerage allowances except to independent brokers, and to band promotional allowances or the furnishing of services or facilities except when made available to all "on proportionately equal terms"
Wheeler-Lea Amendment to the FTC Act, 1938	Prohibits unfair and deceptive acts and practices regardless of whether competition is injured
Lanham Act, 1946	Establishes protection for trademarks
Celler-Kefauver Antimerger Act, 1950	Amends Section 7 of the Clayton Act by broadening the power to prevent corporate acquisitions where the acquisition may have a substantially adverse effect on competition
Hart-Scott-Rodino Act, 1976	Requires large companies to notify the government of their intent to merge

HORIZONTAL PRICE FIXING

Horizontal price fixing
occurs when a group of competing retailers (or other channel members operating at a given level of distribution) establishes a fixed price at which to sell certain brands of products.

Horizontal price fixing occurs when a group of competing retailers establishes a fixed price at which to sell certain brands of products. For example, all retail grocers in a particular trade area may agree to sell eggnog at $1.79 a quart during the Christmas season. Regardless of its actual or potential impact on competition or the consumer, this price fixing by the retailers would violate Section 1 of the Sherman Antitrust Act, which states, "Every contract, combination in the form of trust or otherwise, or conspiracy, in restraint of trade or commerce among the several states, or with foreign nations is declared to be illegal."[1] It is also illegal for retailers to reach agreements with one another regarding the use of double (or triple) coupons, rebates, or other means of reducing price competition in the marketplace.

Occasionally, retailers have argued that the Sherman Act does not apply to them, because they operate locally, not "among the several states"—the definition of interstate commerce. However, because the merchandise retailers purchase typically originates in another state, the courts view retailers as involved in interstate commerce even if all their customers are local. Also, most states have laws similar to the Sherman Act, prohibiting such restraints of trade as horizontal price fixing on a strictly local level.

EXHIBIT 6.3	EXAMPLES OF LAWS DESIGNED TO PROTECT CONSUMERS
LEGISLATIVE ACTION	**IMPACT OR CHANGE IN CONSUMER ENVIRONMENT**
Mail Fraud Act, 1872	Makes it a federal crime to defraud consumers through use of the mail
Pure Food & Drug Act, 1906	Regulates interstate commerce in misbranded and adulterated foods, drinks, and drugs
Flammable Fabrics Act, 1953	Prohibits interstate shipments of flammable apparel or material
Automobile Information Disclosure Act, 1958	Requires auto manufactures to post suggested retail prices on new cars
Fair Packaging and Labeling Act, 1966	Regulates packaging and labeling; establishes uniform sizes
Child Safety Act, 1966	Prevents the marketing and selling of harmful toys and dangerous products
Truth in Lending Act, 1968	Requires lenders to state the true costs of a credit transaction; established a National Commission on Consumer Finance
Fair Credit Report Act, 1970	Regulates the reporting and use of credit information; limits consumer liability for stolen credit cards to $50
Consumer Product Safety Act, 1972	Creates the Consumer Product Safety Commission
Magnuson-Moss Warranty/ FTC Improvement Act, 1975	Empowers the FTC to determine rules concerning consumer warranties and provides for consumer access to means of redress, such as the "class action" suit; expands FTC regulatory powers over unfair or deceptive acts or practices
Equal Credit Opportunity Act, 1975	Prohibits discrimination in credit transactions because of gender, marital status, race, national, origin, religion, age, or receipt of public assistance

VERTICAL PRICE FIXING

Vertical price fixing occurs when a retailer collaborates with the manufacturer or wholesaler to resell an item at an agreed-on price. This is also often referred to as resale price maintenance or "fair trade." These agreements are illegal and have been viewed as a violation of Section 1 of the Sherman Act. This does not mean that manufacturers cannot recommend to retailers a price at which they would like to see an item sold, but they cannot establish a price at which the retailer must sell the product, unless, as discussed in the last chapter, the retailer has signed a "co-op" advertising agreement requiring a specific price. Nor can manufacturers legally threaten retailers with supply cutoffs if they do not sell at the recommended price. Resale price maintenance agreements were legal between 1937 and 1975 and were established as a means for small retailers to combat the price advantages of the chain stores during the depression of the 1930s. They were banned by President Ford, with the consent of Congress, in 1976. Although their use is being urged by some manufacturers and retailers as a means to combat the inroads of discounters such as Wal-Mart and Kmart and the warehouse

Vertical price fixing occurs when a retailer collaborates with the manufacturer or wholesaler to resell an item at an agreed-on price.

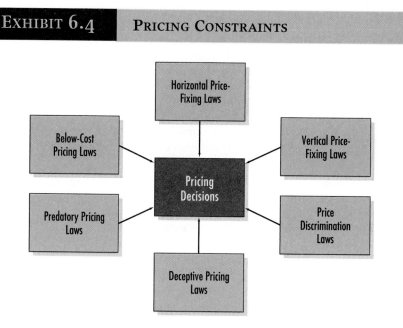

EXHIBIT 6.4   PRICING CONSTRAINTS

clubs, the Clinton administration has vowed to "treat vertical price fixing as per se illegal." Stride Rite, the maker of Keds, and Reebok recently agreed to pay $7.2 million and $9.5 million, respectively, to the FTC to settle claims that it attempted to fix the retail price of their shoes.[2] Such action was an attempt to make sure that their shoes were never discounted.

Although manufacturers or franchisors cannot require that their retailers or franchisees sell their products at an established price, the U.S. Supreme Court recently ruled that they are allowed to cap retail prices. This is not identical to strict vertical price fixing because retailers or franchisees can sell at lower than the capped retail price that manufacturers or franchisees establish. Also the U.S. Supreme Court decided that alleged violations will be decided by a "rule of reason" analysis which means that each price cap should be evaluated on its own merits to determine if it unreasonably restrains competition.[3]

PRICE DISCRIMINATION

Price discrimination

occurs when two retailers buy an identical amount of "like grade and quality" merchandise from the same supplier but pay different prices.

Laws can also influence the price that the retailer has to pay for the merchandise it wants to sell. Price discrimination occurs when two retailers buy an identical amount of "like grade and quality" merchandise from the same supplier but pay different prices. However, these laws do not mean that the retailer can't sell identical products (e.g., a new car) to two different customers at different prices. These laws are meant to protect competition by making sure that the retailers are treated fairly by suppliers.

Not all forms of price discrimination are illegal, however. Federal legislation addressed the legality of price discrimination in the Clayton Act, which made certain forms of price discrimination illegal. The Clayton Act was amended and strengthened by the passage of the Robinson-Patman Act. This act had two primary objectives: (1) to prevent suppliers from attempting to gain an unfair advantage over their competitors by discrimination among buyers either in price or in providing allowances or services and (2) to prevent buyers from using their economic power to gain discriminatory prices from suppliers so as to gain an advantage over their own competitors.

For price discrimination to be considered illegal, it must meet three conditions. First, the transaction must occur in interstate commerce. Trade between states, which is the definition of interstate commerce, covers all retailers, because the items they produce or market typically originate in another state. Second, the actual competition does not have to be lessened, only the potential of a substantial lessening of competition must exist. Third, the buyer who knowingly receives the benefit of discrimination is just as guilty as the supplier granting the discrimination.

Considerable attention has been given to the phrase *commodities of like grade and quality.* What does this phrase mean? To begin with, commodities are goods and not services. This implies that discriminatory pricing practices in the sale of advertising space or the leasing of real estate are not prohibited by the act. For example, shopping center developers frequently charge varying rates for equal square footage depending on the tenant and the type of merchandise to be sold.

Like grade and quality has been interpreted by the courts to mean identical physical and chemical properties. This implies that different prices cannot be justified merely because the labels on the product are different. Therefore, private labeling of merchandise does not make it different from identical goods carrying the seller's brand. However, if the seller can establish that an actual physical difference in grade and quality exists, then a differential in price can be justified.

The preceding discussion may have led you to believe that the illegality of price discrimination is clear-cut and that retailers no longer have to fear being discriminated against. This is not always the situation. A variety of defenses are available to buyers and sellers that enable some types of price discrimination to occur. These defenses include cost justification, changing market conditions, and meeting competition in good faith.

DOLLAR $ & ¢ENTS

Retailers who are aware that not all price discrimination is illegal may be able to purchase merchandise at more favorable prices than competitors and thus be higher performers.

COST JUSTIFICATION DEFENSE
The cost justification defense would attempt to show that a differential in price can be accounted for on the basis of differences in cost to the seller in the manufacture, sale, and/or delivery arising from differences in the method or quantities involved.

CHANGING MARKET CONDITIONS DEFENSE
The changing market conditions defense would attempt to justify the price differential on the danger of imminent deterioration of perishable goods or on the obsolescence of seasonal goods.

ALL LAWS GOVERNING RETAILING ARE NOT THE SAME

Each nation's regulations reflect and reinforce its brand of capitalism—predatory in the United States, paternal in Germany, and protected in Japan—and its social values. As a result, sometimes government regulations in foreign nations can drive retailers crazy.

Take the case of Yasuyuki Nambu's Designer Collezione shops in Tokyo, Osaka, and Sapporo. These Japanese shops have been importing cosmetics and designer apparel directly from the manufacturers, thus undercutting the very long and multilayered, in-efficient distribution channels operating in Japan. As a result, the shops offered Armani and Versace suits for 30 to 70 percent less than the department stores. In the fall of 1995, Nambu announced plans to open a six-story shopping and entertainment complex fea-turing not only low-price cosmetics, food, and ap-parel but automobiles as well.

Soon afterward, Japan's Ministry of Health and Welfare closed the Designer Collezione store in Tokyo's posh Ginza district for selling "improperly labeled" cosmetics that allegedly pose a threat to pub-lic health. It seems the products in question didn't have an "official" ingredient label as prescribed by law. This regulation is part of a PROTECTIONIST pro-gram in Japan to ensure high margins for the tradi-tional channels of distribution.

Nambu reopened the next month and sold $110,000 worth of merchandise in two days before being closed down again. This time for selling cos-metics containing both prohibited and "excessive" amounts of certain ingredients. Noting that Japanese women have been bringing in foreign cosmetics for years without any ill effects, Nambu says he'll keep fighting. "The current law makes it impossible for newcomers to sell cosmetics in Japan," he charges.

SOURCE: Based on "Recession Is My Friend," *Forbes*, October 23, 1995, pp. 47–48, "Attention Tokyo Shoppers," *Forbes*, January 22, 1996, p. 14, and "To All U.S. Managers Upset by Regulations: Try Germany or Japan," *Wall Street Journal*, December 14, 1995, pp. A1 & A5.

MEETING COMPETITION IN GOOD FAITH
DEFENSE
The seller can attempt to show that its lower price to a purchaser was made in good faith to meet an equally low price of a competitor provided that this "matched price" did actually exist and was lawful in itself.

Therefore, it is legally possible that one retailer, a large warehouse club purchasing 10,000 cases, for example, might have a lower cost per case than a smaller retailer pur-chasing only 15 cases. However, the retailer that knowingly receives a discriminatory price from a seller (assuming the goods are of like grade and quality) should be rela-tively certain that the seller is granting a defensible discrimination based on any of the three preceding criteria. Fleming Company, the nation's largest food wholesaler, re-cently retained its Megafoods account by agreeing to match, not beat, the lower prices that Safeway had offered Megafoods.

Sellers are not only prohibited from discrimination in price; they are also banned from providing different services and payments to different retailers. These services and payments frequently include advertising allowances, displays and banners to promote the goods, in-store demonstrations, and distribution of samples or premiums. The Robinson-Patman Act deals specifically with these practices and states that such services and payments or consideration must be made available on proportionately equal terms to all competing customers. Finally, most of the United States' trading partners don't have laws such as the Robinson-Patman Act that ban price discrimination, as well as

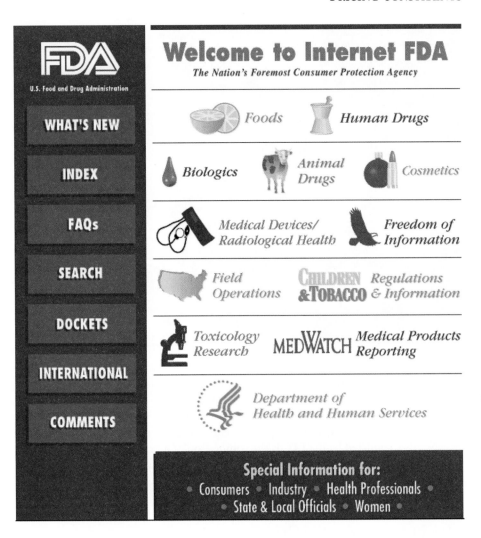

The FDA's Internet site (www.fda.gov) can provide useful regulatory information to retailers that sell food and drug products.

many of the other regulations discussed in this chapter. As a result, many U.S. retailers have been shocked by what they perceived as an "unfair" playing field when they entered foreign markets. Drayton McLane, whom we discussed in Chapter 5, stated that the lack of laws such as Robinson-Patman was one of his major concerns when his distribution firm entered Spain earlier this decade. Price and quality of product are not always the most important issue when setting up a channel in some foreign countries. In fact, as our Global Retailing box indicates, the laws of each nation can drive retailers crazy. However, they do present some interesting opportunities for the retailer who is alert enough to take advantage of the situation.

DECEPTIVE PRICING

Retailers should avoid using a misleading price to lure customers into the store. Advertising an item at an artificially low price and then adding hidden charges is a deceptive pricing practice, which is an unfair method of competition. The Wheeler-Lea Amendment of the FTC Act made illegal all "unfair or deceptive acts in commerce," such as when the retailer has no intention of selling the product. Not only is the retailer's

Deceptive pricing
occurs when a misleading price is used to lure customers into the store; usually there are hidden charges or the item advertised may be unavailable.

When U.S. firms enter foreign markets, such as Warner Bros. with this studio store in Singapore, they must become aware of the local laws governing doing business in that country.

customer being unfairly treated when the retailer uses deceptive pricing, but the retailer's competitors are being potentially harmed because some of their customers may deceitfully be diverted to that retailer. In addition, FTC Guide 233.1 prohibits the advertisement of an inflated former price to emphasize a price reduction (a clearance or sale). Also, regulated by the FTC is the comparison of a price lower than a competitor's price for the same product and use of additional "free" merchandise to be given to a customer when purchasing a particular product at the price usually offered by the retailer.

PREDATORY PRICING

Predatory pricing
exists when a retail chain charges different prices in different geographic areas to eliminate competition in selected geographic areas.

Predatory pricing exists when a retail chain charges different prices in different geographic areas to eliminate competition in selected geographic areas. This is in violation of the Robinson-Patman Act, which also forbids the sale of goods at lower prices in one area for the purpose of destroying competition or eliminating a competitor, or the sale of goods at unreasonably low prices for such purpose. Generally, predatory pricing charges are difficult to prove in federal court.

LO • 2
Differentiate between legal and illegal promotional activities

PROMOTION CONSTRAINTS

The ability of the retailer to make any promotion decision is constrained by two major pieces of federal legislation, the FTC Act and the Wheeler-Lea Amendment of the FTC Act. The retailer should be familiar with three promotional areas that are potentially under the domain of the FTC Act and the Wheeler-Lea Amendment. These areas

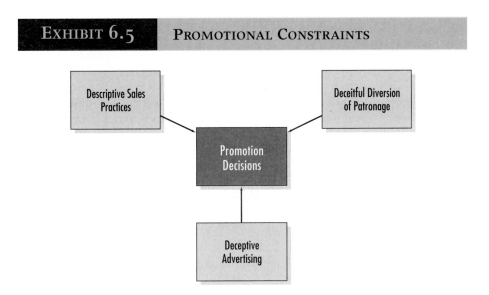

| EXHIBIT 6.5 | PROMOTIONAL CONSTRAINTS |

are deceitful diversion of patronage, deceptive advertising, and deceptive sales practices. Exhibit 6.5 depicts these three areas of constraint.

DECEITFUL DIVERSION OF PATRONAGE

If a retailer publishes or verbalizes falsehoods about a competitor in an attempt to divert patrons from that competitor, the retailer is engaging in an unfair trade practice. The competitor would be afforded protection under the FTC Act but also could receive protection by showing that the defamatory statements were libel or slander. In either case, the competitor would have to demonstrate that actual damage had occurred.

Another form of deceitful diversion of patronage that occurs in retailing is palming off. Palming off occurs when a retailer represents that merchandise is made by a firm other than the true manufacturer. For example, an exclusive women's apparel retailer purchases a group of stylish dresses at a bargain price and replaces their labels with those of a top designer. This is deception as to source of origin, and litigation can be brought under the FTC Act and the Wheeler-Lea Amendment. Also, if the designer's dress label is a registered trademark, protection would also be afforded under the major piece of federal trademark legislation—Lanham Act (1946).

U.S. firms lose $200 billion a year as a result of the counterfeiting of trademarked U.S. products.[4] Hundreds of different products—all fakes—have been copied overseas and shipped to the United States for retail sale. The top categories for fake products are video games and other electronic software, apparel, watches, and golf clubs.[5] Not all the blame for such actions should be placed on retailers. After all, a great deal of the merchandise sold in the United States is made in many Third World countries. For many of these foreign countries, trademark law is relatively new, and the concept of such protection isn't always clear to the workers. In fact, most of the $200 billion in sales was probably unwittingly sold by U.S. retailers and when informed they will cease. Recently, Columbia Sportswear Co. noted a suspect item in one of Sears' last catalogs. When Sears was contacted, it canceled the order while the ship bringing the merchandise from a Taiwanese factory was still at sea.

Palming off
occurs when a retailer represents that merchandise is made by a firm other than the true manufacturer.

DECEPTIVE ADVERTISING

Deceptive advertising *occurs when a retailer makes false or misleading advertising claims about the physical makeup of a product, the benefits to be gained by its use, or the appropriate uses for the product.*

Deceptive advertising occurs when a retailer makes false or misleading advertising claims about the physical makeup of a product, the benefits to be gained by its use, or the appropriate uses for the product. Deceptive advertising is illegal. However, it is often difficult to distinguish between what is false or misleading and what is simply "puffery," which retailers can legally use. Puffery occurs when a retailer, or its spokesperson, states what is considered to be an opinion or a judgment about a product, not a statement of fact. For example, saying that "this is an excellent buy, and you can't afford to pass it up" would probably be viewed as puffery, because the product may not be an excellent buy by all standards, and the consumer should pass it up! Probably most important for the retailer to recognize is that the FTC's concern is not with the intent of the advertiser but with whether the consumer was misled by the advertising. When the FTC challenges any claim contained in advertising or promotional material, several requirements must be met before the commission can find actionable deception: (1) the FTC must prove that the challenged claim is contained in the advertisement; (2) the claim must be deceptive; and (3) the deceptive claim must be material.[6] Although there is disagreement over whether this was a change in, rather than a summary of, FTC policy toward deception, it appears that an example of a case that would not be judged deceptive would be an ad for "Danish pastry." This advertisement would not be considered deceptive because "a few misguided souls believe . . . that all 'Danish pastry' is made in Denmark."

DOLLAR $ & CENTS

Retailers who engage in any type of deceptive promotional activities will damage their reputations and harm their ability to achieve long-term high-performance results.

Bait-and-switch advertising *is promoting a product at an unrealistically low price to serve as "bait" and then trying to "switch" the customer to a higher-priced product.*

Bait-and-switch advertising is another type of deceptive advertising. Bait-and-switch advertising is promoting a product at an unrealistically low price to serve as "bait" and then trying to "switch" the customer to a higher-priced product. However, the scope of the FTC's ban on bait-and-switch is much broader than the typical bait-and-switch scenario, and this strictness could, at least theoretically, pose problems for many retailers. For example, federal regulations outlaw all acts or practices of an advertiser that would discourage the purchase of the advertised merchandise as part of a bait scheme to sell other merchandise. Among those forbidden acts or practices are

1. refusing "to show, demonstrate, or sell the product offered . . ."
2. disparaging, by word or deed, the advertised product or the "guarantee, credit terms, availability of service, repairs or parts, or in any other respect, in connection with it"
3. failing to have sufficient quantities of the advertised product to meet "reasonable anticipated demands" at all outlets listed in the advertisement, unless the ad clearly discloses that supply is limited or available only at certain locations

YOU BE THE JUDGE

After reading all the facts, you decide whether this retailer was guilty of using bait-and-switch advertising.

A Wisconsin television and appliance dealer, whom we will call XYZ, ran the following radio advertisement:

> There are lots of good-quality washers and dryers on the market. But when you ask which ones are the best automatic washers and dryers, well, it's simple. There's Speed Queen, Maytag, and all the rest . . . at XYZ we have both of them and they're on sale for our January white sale. A clearance sale on the finest washers and dryers you can buy. This week a Speed Queen washer and dryer set is reduced to $499 . . . you can buy the finest for less than $500 . . . Why pay more at Sears?

The court determined that the dealer

1. Lost money on each sale of the advertised set
2. Ordered only 20 of the sale sets, but 133 additional more expensive Speed Queen sets
3. Didn't pay a sales commission on the advertised sets
4. Accepted credit cards for the purchase of the more expensive sets, but not on the advertised sets
5. Only sold four of the advertised sets

Whether the managers of XYZ actually did intend to "bait-and-switch" was never proven. However, they were found guilty.

SOURCE: Based on *State of Wisconsin v. American TV & Appliance of Madison, Inc.,* 140 Wis. 2d 353, 410 N.W.2d 596 (Wis. Ct. App. 1987).

4. "the refusal to take orders for the advertised merchandise to be delivered within a reasonable period of time"
5. the "use of a sales plan or method of compensation for salesmen . . . designed to prevent or discourage them from selling the advertised product."[7] In our Behind the Scenes box you can decide whether a retailer was involved in bait-and-switch advertising.

DECEPTIVE SALES PRACTICES

There are basically two deceptive sales practices that are illegal. These practices are (1) failure to be honest or to omit key facts in either an ad or the sales presentation and (2) using deceptive credit contracts.

With regard to deceptive credit, federal laws attempt to "assure a meaningful disclosure of credit terms so that the consumer will be able to compare more readily the various credit terms available to him and avoid the uninformed use of credit."[8] These laws were the result of unscrupulous practices on the part of retailers attempting to hide the true cost of merchandise in unrealistically (and sometimes illegal) high credit terms. For example, the retailer might sell a car at a very low price but then tack on a high (and often hidden) finance charge. In many states, these hidden charges are limited by law.

To ensure that the consumer can make informed purchases when using credit, federal law requires that the customer receive information on

1. the total amount financed
2. the finance charge as an annual percentage rate (APR)
3. the finance charge in dollars

This street vendor in Jakarta, Indonesia, is selling counterfeit branded merchandise which is a major legal issue in foreign trade.

4. information on payments (number, amount, due dates, early repayment, etc.)
5. disclosure of any other fees or charges (late payment, insurance, etc.)

If the credit agreement involves merchandise bought on time, creditors are also required to provide

1. a description of the merchandise
2. the cash price
3. the "deferred payment" price (price plus total interest)
4. the amount of any down payment and/or trade-in

These credit disclosure rules apply not only to in-store selling but also to all promotional activities of the retailer.

LO • 3
Explain the retailer's responsibilities regarding the products sold

PRODUCT CONSTRAINTS

A retailer's major goal is to sell merchandise. To accomplish this goal, the retailer must assure customers that the products they purchase will not be harmful to their well-being and will meet expected performance criteria. Three areas of the law have a major effect on the products that a retailer handles: product safety, product liability, and warranties. They are highlighted in Exhibit 6.6.

PRODUCT SAFETY

Retailers are in a difficult position when it comes to product safety. Most retailers do not produce the goods that they offer for sale but purchase them from wholesalers or manufacturers. Basically, retailers have little to say about product quality or safety.

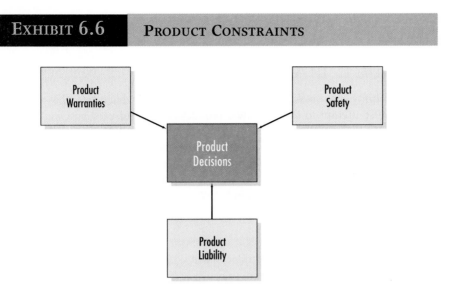

| EXHIBIT 6.6 | PRODUCT CONSTRAINTS |

Their only weapon is deciding to use reputable suppliers so as not to carry merchandise that they consider to be unsafe. You might therefore believe that retailers are not responsible for the safety of products that they sell; this is definitely not the case.

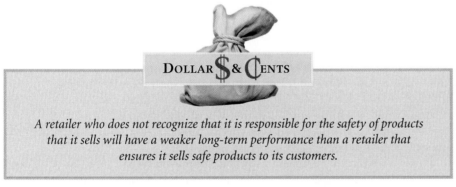

DOLLAR $ & CENTS

A retailer who does not recognize that it is responsible for the safety of products that it sells will have a weaker long-term performance than a retailer that ensures it sells safe products to its customers.

According to the Consumer Product Safety Act (1972), the retailer has specific responsibilities to monitor the safety of consumer products.[9] Specifically, retailers (as well as manufacturers, other intermediaries, and importers) are required by law to report to the Consumer Product Safety Commission any possible "substantial product hazard." Furthermore, included in the description of substantial hazards is any failure to comply with an existing safety standard. Thus a retailer may unknowingly violate the law by reselling products that do not conform to existing safety standards, such as a stuffed doll with "button eyes" that may come off and be swallowed by a child. In addition, a retailer may violate the law by not cooking its meals to a required temperature. Retailers may further violate the law by failing to repurchase from customers nonconforming products sold after the effective or expiration date of a health standard or for a number of other reasons. For example, a supermarket might sell a product after the expiration date marked on the product. Also, an appeals court recently substantially reduced a lower court award of $2.9 million against McDonald's for serving a "too hot" cup of coffee. Finally, for years the famous "30-minute delivery guarantee" was part of the Domino's product. The company discarded the guarantee in fear for being sued as a result of any traffic accidents involving a delivery person.

PRODUCT LIABILITY

Product liability laws
deal with the seller's responsibility to market safe products. These laws invoke the "foreseeability" doctrine, which states that a seller of a product must attempt to foresee how a product may be misused and warn the consumer against the hazards of misuse.

Product liability laws invoke the "foreseeability" doctrine, which states that a seller of a product must attempt to foresee how a product may be misused and warn the consumer against the hazards of misuse. The courts have interpreted this doctrine to suggest that retailers must be careful in how they sell their products. This is of particular importance to restaurant, nightclub, and bar owners who fail to consider the consequences of serving a consumer one more drink "for the road." In addition to the federal laws covering product liability, all states have their own regulations.

WARRANTIES

Retailers are also responsible for product safety and performance under conventional warranty doctrines. Under the current warranty law, the fact that the ultimate consumer may bring suit against the manufacturer or processor in no way relieves the retailer from its responsibility for the fitness and merchantability of the goods. The disheartening fact that confronts the retailer is that in many states the buyer has been permitted to sue both the retailer and the manufacturer or processor in the same legal suit.

Expressed warranties
are either written or verbalized agreements about the performance of a product and cover all attributes of the merchandise or only one attribute.

Retailers can offer expressed or implied warranties. Expressed warranties are the result of negotiation between the retailer and the customer. They may be either written into the contract or verbalized. They can cover all characteristics or attributes of the merchandise or only one attribute. An important point for the retailer (and its salespeople) to recognize is that an expressed warranty can be created without the use of the words *warranty* or *guarantee*. For example, a car salesperson might tell a buyer, "Everybody we've sold this type of car to has gone at least 60,000 miles with no problems whatsoever, and I see no reason why you can't expect the same. I wouldn't be surprised if you are able to go 100,000 miles without any mechanical problems." This statement could create an expressed warranty, particularly if someone is with the buyer. The court would, however, be concerned with whether this was just sales talk (puffery) or a statement of fact or opinion by the salesperson.

Implied warranties are not expressly made by the retailer but are based on custom, norms, or reasonable expectations. There are two types of implied warranties (which overlap a bit): an implied warranty of merchantability and an implied warranty of fitness for a particular purpose.

Implied warranty of merchantability
is made by every retailer when they sell goods and imply that the merchandise sold is fit for the ordinary purpose for which such goods are typically used.

An implied warranty of merchantability is made by every retailer selling goods. By offering the goods for sale, the retailer implies that they are fit for the ordinary purpose for which such goods are typically used. The notion of implied warranty applies to both new and used merchandise. For example, imagine that a sporting goods retailer located close to a major lake resort sells used inner tubes for swimming and a customer purchases one. The tube bursts while the person is floating on it, and the person subsequently drowns. This retailer may be held liable. Because of the potential legal liability that accompanies an implied warranty, many retailers will expressly disclaim at the time of sale any or all implied warranties. This is not always legally possible; some retailers will not be able to avoid implied warranties of merchantability.

Implied warranty of fitness
is a warranty that implies the merchandise is fit for a particular purpose and arises when the customer relies on the retailer to assist or make the selection of goods to serve a particular purpose.

The implied warranty of fitness for a particular purpose arises when the customer relies on the retailer to assist or make the selection of goods to serve a particular purpose. Consider a customer who is about to make a cross-country moving trip and

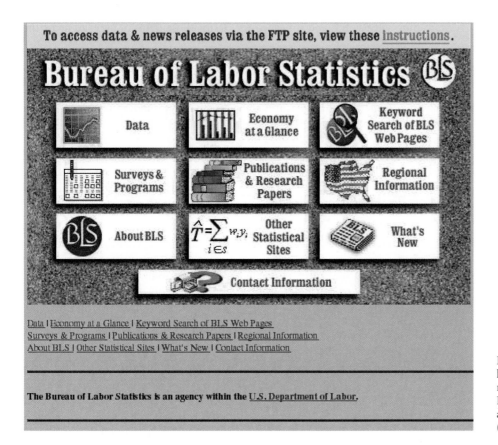

Employment practices are highly regulated and thus retailers might find the U.S. Department of Labor to be a useful information source. (See www.stats.bls.gov)

plans to tow a $4' \times 4'$, two-wheel trailer behind her automobile. She needs a pair of tires for the rear of the automobile and thus goes to a local tire retailer and asks the salesperson for a pair of tires that will allow her to tow the loaded trailer safely. The customer in this regard is ignorant and is relying on the expertise of the retailer. If the retailer sells the customer a pair of tires not suited for the job, then the retailer is liable for breach of an implied warranty of fitness for a particular purpose. This is true even if the retailer did not have in stock a pair of tires to safely perform the job but instead sold the customer the best tire in stock.

Consumer product warranties frequently have been confusing, misleading, and frustrating to consumers. As a consequence, the Magnuson-Moss Warranty Act was passed. Although nothing in federal law requires a retailer to warrant a product under this act, anyone who sells a product costing the consumer more than $15 and gives a written warranty (although only written warranties are covered by federal laws, many types of warranties are subject to state laws) to the consumer is required to provide the consumer with the following information:[10]

1. the identity of the persons to whom the warranty is extended
2. a clear description of the products, parts, characteristics, components, and properties covered by the warranty; if necessary for clarity, those items excluded from the warranty must be described
3. a statement of what the warrantor will do in the event of a defect, malfunction, or failure to conform with the written warranty, including those items or services the

warrantor will pay for, and if needed for clarity, those items or services he or she will not pay for

4. the point in time when the warranty begins (if it begins on a date other than the purchase date) and its duration

5. a step-by-step explanation of the procedure that the consumer should follow to obtain performance of the warranty obligation and information regarding any informal dispute-settling mechanisms that are available

6. any limitations on the duration of implied warranties or any exclusions or limitations on relief (e.g., incidental or consequential damages) together with a statement that under some state laws the exclusions or limitations may not be allowed

7. a statement that the warranty gives the consumer certain legal rights, in addition to his or her other rights under state law, which may vary from state to state

It is the retailer's responsibility to provide the prospective buyer with the written terms of the warranty for review before the actual sale. In this regard, the retailer has two options: clearly and conspicuously displaying the text of the written warranty near the product or making warranties available for examination by consumers on request and posting signs advising consumers of the presale availability of warranties.

LO • 4
Discuss the impact of governmental regulation on a retailer's behavior with other channel members

CHANNEL CONSTRAINTS

Retailers are restricted in relationships and agreements that they may develop with channel partners. These restrictions can be conveniently categorized into four areas as shown in Exhibit 6.7.

TERRITORIAL RESTRICTIONS

Territorial restrictions *are attempts by a supplier, usually a manufacturer, to limit the geographic area in which a retailer may resell its merchandise.*

As related to retail trade, territorial restrictions can be defined as attempts by a supplier, usually a manufacturer, to limit the geographic area in which a retailer may resell its merchandise. The courts have viewed territorial restrictions as potential contracts in restraint of trade and in violation of the Sherman Antitrust Act. Thus even though the retailer and manufacturer may both favor territorial restrictions, because of the lessening of competition between retailers selling the brand in question, the courts will often frown on such arrangements. The law does not, however, prevent manufacturers and retailers from establishing territorial responsibilities as long as they do not exclude all other retailers and restrict the sale of the manufacturer's products. Franchise agreements have long had territorial restrictions that provide a protected zone for the franchisee. Because of these zones, the franchisee is to develop a primary demand for the product without fear of cannibalization by another entry in the protected zone. For example, franchise contracts with KFC prevent the chain from authorizing new units within 1.5 miles of an existing unit.[11] Nevertheless, this does not guarantee that customers will not drive by a nearby KFC to visit one that they believe provides better service.

DUAL DISTRIBUTION

Dual distribution *occurs when a manufacturer sells to independent retailers and also through its company owned retail outlets.*

A manufacturer that sells to independent retailers and also through its own retail outlets is engaged in dual distribution. Thus the manufacturer manages a corporately

EXHIBIT 6.7	CHANNEL CONSTRAINTS

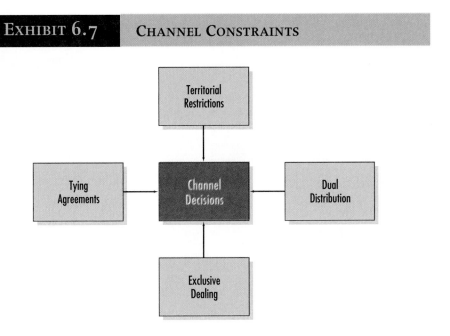

owned vertical marketing system that competes with independent retailers, which it also supplies through a conventional, administered, or contractual marketing channel. Retailers tend to become upset about dual distribution when the two channels compete at the retail level in the same geographic area. For example, Levi Strauss is currently seeking approval from the FTC to turn aside a 1976 complaint against it for engaging in anticompetitive practices so that it may operate its own retail outlets. Likewise, Ralph Lauren has wholly owned retail outlets and, in addition, uses major independent retailers as outlets, and many manufacturers are opening their own retail stores in so-called factory outlet malls. This can have an adverse effect on manufacturer–retailer relationships. Independent retailers will argue that dual distribution is an unfair method of competition and thus is in violation of the Sherman Act. Dual distribution also takes place when manufacturers sell similar products under different brand names for distribution through different channels. This kind of dual distribution is common in the retailing of private labels.

DOLLAR $ & C ENTS

Retailers who view the channel as a partnership and abide by the law in their relations with their partners will have higher long-term performance.

The courts have not viewed dual-distribution arrangements as antitrust violations. In fact, they have reasoned that dual distribution can actually foster competition. For example, the manufacturer may not be able to find a retailer to represent it in all trade

Ralph Lauren has a dual distribution strategy where they market their Polo branded apparel through manufacturer-owned retail stores as shown in this photo and also through traditional department stores, such as Macy's and Marshall Field's.

areas or the manufacturer may find it necessary to operate its own retail outlet to establish market share and remain competitive with other manufacturers. The courts will apply a rule-of-reason criterion. Thus the independent retailer suing a manufacturer for dual distribution will have to convince the court that it was competed against unfairly and competition was damaged. The retailer's best bet would be to show that the manufacturer-controlled outlets were favored or subsidized (for instance, with excess advertising allowances or lower prices) to an extent that was detrimental to the independent retailer.

EXCLUSIVE DEALING

One-way exclusive dealing occurs when the supplier agrees to give the retailer the exclusive right to merchandise the supplier's product in a particular trade area.

Two-way exclusive dealing occurs when the supplier offers the retailer the exclusive distribution of a merchandise line or product if in return the retailer will agree to do something for the manufacturer such as not handle competing brands or heavily promote the supplier's products.

Retailers and their suppliers occasionally enter into exclusive dealing arrangements. In one-way exclusive dealing, the supplier agrees to give the retailer the exclusive right to merchandise the supplier's product in a particular trade area. The retailer, however, does not agree to do anything in particular for the supplier; hence the term *one-way.* For example, a weak manufacturer will often have to offer one-way exclusive dealing arrangements to get shelf space at the retail level. Truly one-way arrangements are legal.

With two-way exclusive dealing the supplier offers the retailer the exclusive distribution of a merchandise line or product if in return the retailer will agree to do something for the manufacturer. For example, the retailer might agree not to handle certain competing brands. Two-way agreements violate the Clayton Act if they substantially lessen competition or tend to create a monopoly. Specifically, the courts have generally viewed exclusive dealing as illegal when it excludes competitive products from a large share of the market and when it represents a large share of the total sales volume for a particular product type.

TYING AGREEMENTS

When a seller with a strong product or service forces a buyer (the retailer) to buy a weak product or service as a condition for buying the strong one, a tying agreement exists. For example, a large national manufacturer with several very highly demanded lines of merchandise may try to force the retailer to handle its entire merchandise assortment as a condition for being able to handle the more popular merchandise lines. This is called a full-line policy. Alternatively, a strong manufacturer may be introducing a new product, and to get shelf space or display space at the retail level it may require retailers to handle some of the new product before they can purchase better established merchandise lines.

Tying arrangements have been found to be in violation of the Clayton Act, the Sherman Act, and the FTC Act. Tying is not viewed as a violation per se, but it will generally be viewed as illegal if a substantial share of commerce is affected. The most serious problems involving tying arrangements are those associated with franchising. Quite often, franchise agreements contain provisions requiring the franchisee to purchase all raw materials and supplies from the franchisor. The courts generally consider tying provisions of a franchise agreement legal as long as there is sufficient proof that these arrangements are necessary to maintain quality control. Otherwise, they are viewed as unwarranted restraints of competition.[12]

> **Tying agreement**
> *exists when a seller with a strong product or service requires a buyer (the retailer) to purchase a weak product or service as a condition for buying the strong product or service.*

OTHER FEDERAL, STATE, AND LOCAL LAWS

LO • 5
Describe how various state and local laws, in addition to other federal regulations, must also be considered in developing retail policies

Several other federal laws also affect retailers, but their impact is beyond the scope of this text. One such set of these laws, which is shown in Exhibit 6.1, is extremely important today because it deals with mergers and acquisitions. As retailers seek to either consolidate their operations by selling off some unprofitable stores or by acquiring the outlets of other retailers to expand into new markets, they must consider the impact on the competitive environment.[13]

Our country's various trade agreements regulating the amount of importing and exporting American firms can conduct with firms in various countries, sometimes limits, if not totally forbids, a retailer's ability to purchase merchandise from certain foreign countries. Witness, for example, our country's current ban on all merchandise from Cuba, Iraq, and Libya and at the same time our membership in NAFTA. This problem can be particularly acute for some retailers as described in the case at the end of Chapter 9. Also, because labor is a retailer's largest operating expense, retailers must be aware of the laws that deal with minimum wages and hiring practices. Chapter 15, Human Resources, covers the major laws affecting employment and personnel decisions. Tax laws and Security & Exchange Commission (SEC) rules and regulations that deal with the legal form of ownership (sole proprietorship, partnership, or corporation) and shareholder disclosure requirements are also not covered in this text. Chapter 13 considers how the Americans with Disabilities Act affects the layout and design of the retailer's store.

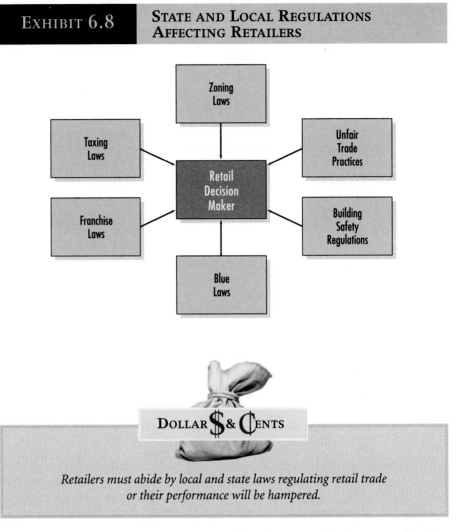

| EXHIBIT 6.8 | STATE AND LOCAL REGULATIONS AFFECTING RETAILERS |

Retailers must abide by local and state laws regulating retail trade
or their performance will be hampered.

In addition to federal laws, many state and local municipalities have passed legislation regulating retail activities. Exhibit 6.8 illustrates how state and local laws affect the retailer. Zoning laws, for example, prohibit retailers from operating at certain locations and require building and sign specifications to be met. Many retailers have found these codes to be highly restrictive, especially because some existing firms have been able to influence this type of legislation, thereby protecting their already established local business.

With regard to unfair trade practices laws, most states have established their own set of laws that prevent one retailer from gaining an unfair advantage over another retailer. As a general rule, "unfair trade practices" laws regulate the competitive behavior (usually relating to pricing, advertising, merchandise stocked, and employment practices) of retailers. For example, 22 states have laws against predatory pricing. The specific content of these laws varies, but usually they prohibit the retailer from seeking unfair advantages from vendors, selling merchandise below cost (or at cost plus some fixed percentage markup—6 percent is typical) with the intent of using profits from another geographic area or from cash reserves to destroy or hurt competition. These state laws are generally unclear in their definitions of selling below cost and as to the actions that can be taken (i.e., whether the retailer can give merchandise away or offer prizes or premiums without increasing an item's price as a form of price reduction).

A number of states have also introduced laws preventing both "zero down" car leases and "zero percent" financing programs that they claim mislead consumers. Also, the franchise laws in many states, for example, assume that, unless otherwise spelled out in the franchise agreement, there is an implied agreement not to locate another outlet near a current location without the current franchisee's permission. These state laws are often in conflict with federal regulations. As a result, in many instances, state laws regulating retailers have either been declared unconstitutional or amended to meet federal guidelines.

Many localities have strong building codes that regulate construction materials, fire safety, architectural style, height and size of building, number of entrances, and even elevator usage. Some local ordinances are attempts to aid retailers, such as the attempt by traffic engineers in some cities to reduce downtown traffic to less than 20 miles per hour so that the consumers can observe local businesses and their promotions being displayed. It is not uncommon for local communities to have sign ordinances which regulate the size and nature of signs. Recently many retailers, especially auto dealers, have begun using large inflatable signs such as gorilla balloons or blue elephants. These large balloons have been quite effective at drawing attention to the retailer and increasing store traffic. However, many local communities have begun to ban them because of their negative visual impact on neighborhoods and communities.[14] Other states enforce blue laws restricting the sale of certain products, such as automobiles, on Sundays. Many states have passed strong regulations on topics not covered by federal regulations governing the relationship between franchisors and franchisees to protect the individual business persons of their states. These laws basically require a full disclosure of all the pertinent facts involved in owning a local franchise. Many experts believe that these state franchise laws protect the current antiquated and inefficient automobile dealerships from newer, more efficient forms of competition because dealers provide 20 percent of sales tax revenues and are usually the largest advertisers in the local media. With such political clout, most state governments will make it difficult for discounters and Internet sellers to enter the new-car business or for Detroit to control the pricing and promotion of its own products. However, what is occurring is that the Internet businesses are developing which serve as brokers. These businesses bring together purchasers with franchised dealers, who will sell the car to the purchaser at a price that the Internet broker negotiates. Finally, many state and local governments have recently started viewing the Internet as a cash cow. With projected sales of $7 billion and on-line advertising revenues of $5 billion by year 2000,[15] as well as the Internet access fees themselves, these taxing authorities see the Internet as a new source of tax revenue. The two pressing issues that could affect a retailer's future strategies are

Blue laws *are local laws which ban the sale of certain products or merchandise lines on Sundays.*

1. who's responsible for collecting these taxes
2. what constitutes a sufficient presence in a area that would obligate a retailer to pay taxes to that jurisdiction

The court systems in many states sometimes make rulings that will affect retailers across the country. For example, supreme courts of two states are deciding whether to hear cases involving injury to a customer when the retailer's employee didn't follow a robber's demands as directed by the retailer's rules. Also, various cities have passed laws governing retailing, such as the "Green River Ordinances"—named after the town in Wyoming that first passed them—restricting door-to-door selling. Other communities restrict the excessive use of garage sales, lottery promotions, and sale of obscene

SOME OF THE "FUNNY" LAWS REGULATING RETAILERS AROUND THE WORLD

In Japan, local merchants can legally demand concessions when a new store opens nearby. This can often delay construction for years.

In Germany, comparative advertising is banned; also local authorities can—and do—bar new stores if they believe existing stores will be hurt.

Still, although it is more difficult to open new retail outlets in these two countries than in the United States, it is easier to open a bank branch in those countries than it is to open one in all but a few states in the United States. However, this is rapidly changing as more and more banks are merging, thus creating the need for branch banking.

Quebec, a Canadian province that is 80 percent French speaking, allows English on commercial signs only if French words dominate.

In Italy, retailers may operate 44 hours per week provided that they close on Sunday.

Retailers in Germany were recently granted permission to "expand" the number of hours they may be open. The new law allows the store to stay open until 8 P.M. on weekdays and 4 P.M. on Saturday, but not to be open on Sunday. Bakeries may be open for three hours on Sunday. These expanded hours, which were a cultural revolution in a country where unions are first and consumers are last, were an attempt to give employees regular hours and not disrupt family time. In addition, the sale of any item in Germany costing more than 500 deutschemarks ($300) requires the registration of the customer's name and address.

In Mexico, the clock on cash discounts, discounts given to retailers by vendors for early payment, doesn't start ticking until the retailer receives the bill and determines it is acceptable.

In Japan, under a law designed to protect small retailers, giant retailers can stay open until 8 P.M. but are required to close their stores at least 20 days a year for "holidays." In addition, self-service gas stations, and any discounter who might want to introduce them, are banned in Japan on the grounds that they are a fire hazard.

In Australia, store hours are regulated separately by each state, resulting in confusion across the country. Also, supermarkets in Australia having conveyor belts on their check-outs must pay an annual $25 "weights and scaffolding" fee for each one.

The Netherlands sets minimum selling prices for goods produced within the country, but none for imported items.

The size of a store in France is limited to 1,000 square meters if it is located in a city with a population of less than 40,000. If the city is larger, the size may increase to 1,500 square meters.

In France, the funeral business until recently was treated as a public utility. Retailers had to bid for the right to operate in a certain city at fixed prices.

Retailers in the United Kingdom, the country from which our "blue laws" were copied, have to cope with laws that make it legal to buy food for a mule on Sunday but not for your baby. Also, pornographic material may be sold on Sunday but not a Bible to take to church. British retailers do get around these laws. One British furniture dealer, for example, sells a box of matches for 1,000 British pounds ($1,650), then gives the customer a "free" suite of furniture.

Finally, an international retailer seeking to open a store in the United States must be prepared for some of our unusual local laws. For example, a law in Kansas City prohibits the sale of capguns to children but not shotguns.

materials and dangerous products. In addition, states and cities might require licenses to operate certain retail businesses such as liquor stores or massage parlors. Although all these federal, state, and local laws governing a retailer's behavior are sometimes confusing, consider the plight of the international retailer. Global Retailing describes some real "funny" laws regulating retailers.

For further information about these various laws, a retailer should consult the local Better Business Bureau, the National Retail Federation, state and local retail trade associations, or state and local regulatory agencies.

ETHICS IN RETAILING

LO • 6
Explain how a retailer's code of ethics will influence its behavior

Ethics is a set of rules for moral human behavior. These rules or standards of moral responsibility often take the form of dos and don'ts. Some retailers have an explicit code of ethics, which are written policies that state what is ethical and unethical behavior. However, most often an implicit code of ethics exists. An implicit code of ethics is an unwritten but well-understood set of rules or standards of moral responsibility. This implicit code is learned as employees become socialized into the organization and the corporate culture of the retailer.

Ethics
is a set of rules for human moral behavior.

Explicit code of ethics
consist of a written policy that states what is ethical and unethical behavior.

Implicit code of ethics
is an unwritten but well understood set of rules or standards of moral responsibility.

DOLLAR **$** & **C**ENTS

Retailers who abide by a strong set of ethical guidelines are more likely to be higher performers.

Regardless of whether the code of ethics is explicit or implicit, it is an important guideline for making retail decisions. We will review some retail decision areas in which ethical considerations are common. However, before doing so, it should be pointed out that legal and ethical behavior are not necessarily the same. Unethical actions may be legal. Laws, after all, represent a formalization of behavioral standards through the political process into rules or laws. Therefore, a retailer needs to behave legally because laws represent a "formalized" set of ethical rules. In addition, retailers need to look beyond laws and engage in practices that are also ethical. One problem, though, is that "reasonable" people may disagree as to what is "right" and "wrong" behavior. For this reason, retailers should develop explicit codes of ethical behavior for their employees so that they might have a sense of what is right and wrong.

Let's look at three decision areas in which ethical considerations are needed in retailing:

1. buying merchandise
2. selling merchandise
3. retailer–employee relationship

In each of these situations, the retailer faces an ethical dilemma. Note that in each of these situations what is legal may not necessarily represent the best ethical guideline.

ETHICAL BEHAVIOR IN BUYING MERCHANDISE

When buying merchandise, the retailer can face at least four ethical dilemmas, which relate to product quality, sourcing, slotting fees, and bribery.

PRODUCT QUALITY

Should a retailer inspect merchandise for product quality or leave that to the customer? Although the law doesn't require such inspections, most retail buyers are concerned that their merchandise meet the expectations of the store's customers. As a result, some retailers have developed laboratory testing programs to verify quality of not only their private label products but of manufacturers' brands as well.

SOURCING

Should a retailer verify the source of merchandise? A State Department document revealed that the Chinese may be exporting up to $100 million of merchandise made by prisoners, including many political prisoners, as well as counterfeiting some $800 million a year in videotapes, compact discs, and books.[16] The importation of such merchandise violates American laws, yet most U.S. importers are unaware of this problem. In addition, although not against U.S. laws, some foreign merchandise sources use child labor or fail to pay a fair level of wages. The only way U.S. retailers can be sure that they aren't buying illegal merchandise is to inspect all suppliers, down to the smallest subcontractors. However, some retailers are also having troubles with American suppliers. A program of careful vigilance to overcome such activities can be expensive, and it is doubtful whether American consumers would be willing to bear the cost. Seeking to overcome such complaints, Kmart has begun to use private investigators to check out vendors to make sure that they are not buying from unsavory characters.[17] Many other major American retailers have agreed to allow independent observers, including human rights officials, to monitor working conditions in their foreign factories. Consumers can check the U.S. Department of Labor's web site (http://www.dol.gov/dol/esa/public/nosweat/trends.htm) to see if a particular retailer is involved in the program.

SLOTTING FEES

Should a retailer accept money, commonly called slotting fees, from a manufacturer for agreeing to add a new product to its inventory? Slotting fees (also called slotting allowances) are fees paid by a vendor for space, or a slot, on a retailer's shelves, as well as having its UPC number given a slot in the retailer's computer system. After all, if its UPC code isn't in the system, individual stores couldn't stock the item. Retailers claim that such fees are actually a means of defraying their added expenses of adding warehouse space, replacing existing items in the store, placing the new items in the inventory control system, and as a form of insurance, or a way of guaranteeing at least some profit from carrying the new item. The FTC has ruled that slotting fees, although making a lot of vendors unhappy, are not discriminatory or anticompetitive. In fact, the Internal Revenue Service (IRS) even issued an "audit-issue" paper on reporting such fees for both the retailer and manufacturer.

Slotting fees
are fees paid by a vendor for space, or a slot, on a retailer's shelves, as well as having its UPC number given a slot in the retailer's computer system.

BRIBERY   Should a retailer, or its employees, be allowed to accept a bribe? Bribery occurs when a retail buyer is offered an inducement (which the IRS considers to have a value greater than $25) for purchasing a vendor's products. Such inducements, it should be noted, are legal in many foreign countries. Recently, a JCPenney's buyer admitted to taking $1 million in bribes over several years, even though the products under question made money for JCPenney. Many retailers currently have no formal policy on this subject. The negative consequences of this behavior have lead some retailers to ban employees from accepting anything from a supplier. Wal-Mart, which by being the world's largest retailer is also the largest purchaser, has probably the strictest employee standard in the industry. Wal-Mart's employees are not allowed to accept any gifts (including samples) from vendors, not even if it is just a cup of coffee or soft drink when visiting a supplier's showroom. Kmart has gone a step farther by requiring not only all its managers and buyers but also its VENDORS to sign an integrity pledge.

ETHICAL BEHAVIOR IN SELLING MERCHANDISE

Ethics can also influence the selling process with regard to the products sold and the various selling practices that salespersons use.

PRODUCTS SOLD   Should a retailer be allowed to sell any product, so long as it is not illegal? For example, should a convenience store operator located near a high school be allowed to sell wine coolers? Should the same stores carry cigarette paper for those few customers who prefer to roll their own and risk selling the paper to high schoolers who might use the paper for smoking marijuana? Many retailers have developed policies restricting the sale of legal products. For example, Wal-Mart has stopped selling handguns in its U.S. stores and tobacco items in its Canadian stores.

Sometimes such decisions can add to a retailer's profit. For example, Trader Joe's, a California specialty food retailer, recently analyzed all its cigarettes carried by company and brand and found only Marlboro merited the space allocated. Therefore, rather than just carry that one brand, the retailer dropped all cigarettes.[18]

SELLING PROCESS PRACTICES   Can a salesperson, while not saying anything wrong, be allowed to conceal from the customer all the facts? Also, should selling the "wrong" product for the customer's needs be permitted? Many retailers have ethical standards against such practices. However, as long as salespersons are paid on commission, we can expect such behavior to occur. Some highly successful retailers, such as Home Depot's Bernie Marcus, have sought to overcome this dilemma by never putting their employees at odds with their own code of ethics. Marcus has been quoted as saying: "The day I'm laid out dead with an apple in my mouth is the day we'll pay commissions. If you pay commissions, you imply that the small customer isn't worth anything."[19] It should be pointed out, however, that paying commissions would be difficult in a self-service operation such as Home Depot.

ETHICAL BEHAVIOR IN THE RETAILER–EMPLOYEE RELATIONSHIP

Ethical standards can also influence the retailer–employee relationship in three ways: misuse of company assets, job switching, and employee theft.

MISUSE OF COMPANY ASSETS
Most people would agree that the stealing of merchandise is illegal; but what about other types of stealing? What about an employee taking home a company notebook or pen? Also, what about taking an extra break or using the retailer's telephone for a personal long-distance call? All these, although not subject to criminal prosecution, are forms of employee theft and should be considered when an employee develops his or her code of ethics.

JOB SWITCHING
Does an employee have the right to work for whom they want? Employees have a responsibility to their previous employer. The employer provided them with training and access to confidential information such as vendor costs, customer lists, and future plans. When an employee leaves one retailer for another, the employee should respect the previous employer's right to retain the confidentiality of this information.

At the same time, the retailer should not seek to replace an employee, usually a manager or executive, just because the employee reaches the so-called 20-40-60 plateau (20 years or more with the firm; 40 years or older; and making more than $60,000 a year) and replace the employee with a lower-paid younger employee.

EMPLOYEE THEFT
Just as employers have a responsibility to be fair to their employees, employees must do likewise. However, many workers admit to "stealing" from their employers. Employee theft is most prevalent in food stores, department stores, and discount stores. Considering that these types of stores are usually larger in size, sales volume, and number of employees, the lack of close supervision might contribute to this problem. Some retailers, such as Wal-Mart, are trying to address this problem by offering cash bonuses just before Christmas if the store makes not only its profit goal but keeps shrinkage under a predetermined limit.

The above discussion was not meant to be an all-inclusive list of the ethical dilemmas facing retailing today. It does, however, provide the reader with a big picture of the role of ethics in retailing.

STUDENT STUDY GUIDE

SUMMARY   We began this chapter by describing the multifaceted legal environment that confronts retailers in the United States. We identified constraints on retailers' activities in six broad categories: (1) pricing, (2) promotion, (3) products, (4) channel relations, (5) other federal laws, and (6) state and local regulations. Within each of these broad constraints, we summarized some specific activities that are regulated.

LO•1   DOES LEGISLATION CONSTRAIN A RETAILER'S PRICING POLICIES?   With regard to pricing, which is the issue that most frequently confronts retailers, the retailer should first be familiar with two methods of price fixing: with other retailers (horizontal) and with channel members (vertical). In addition, the retailer must consider all the ramifications of price discrimination when purchasing merchandise. In setting retail prices, two other areas of concern are deceptive pricing and predatory pricing.

LO•2   IS THERE A DIFFERENCE BETWEEN LEGAL AND ILLEGAL PROMOTIONAL ACTIVITIES FOR A RETAILER?   Regarding promotion constraints, the retailer should focus on three areas: deceitful diversion of patronage, which includes selling counterfeit or fake products; deceptive advertising, including making false claims about a product and using bait-and-switch tactics; and deceptive sales practices, not being completely honest in discussions about merchandise and use of deceptive credit contracts.

LO•3   WHAT RESPONSIBILITIES DOES A RETAILER HAVE REGARDING THE PRODUCTS SOLD?   With regards to product constraints, the retailer should be aware of legislation dealing with product safety, product liability, and both expressed and implied warranties requirements as they relate to retailing.

LO•4   HOW DOES GOVERNMENTAL REGULATION INFLUENCE A RETAILER'S BEHAVIOR WITH OTHER CHANNEL MEMBERS?   Because all retailers are members of some type of channel, it is important to understand channel relationships in terms of the legality of territorial restrictions, dual distribution, exclusive dealing, and tying agreements.

LO•5   WHAT IS THE IMPACT OF VARIOUS STATE AND LOCAL LAWS, IN ADDITION TO OTHER FEDERAL REGULATIONS, IN DEVELOPING RETAIL POLICIES?   In addition to the federal laws discussed in the chapter, the retailer must be aware of the impact of the various state and local laws on retailers. These laws include regulations on zoning, unfair trade practices, building safety, blue laws, franchises, and taxes.

LO•6   HOW DOES A RETAILER'S CODE OF ETHICS INFLUENCE ITS BEHAVIOR?   Laws and regulations don't cover every situation that a retailer might face in the day-to-day operations of a business. In such cases, the retailer's and its employees' codes of ethics will provide guidance. This is particularly important in buying merchandise, selling merchandise, and in the retailer–employee relationship.

TERMS TO REMEMBER

horizontal price fixing	implied warranty of fitness
vertical price fixing	territorial restrictions
price discrimination	dual distribution
deceptive pricing	one-way exclusive dealing
predatory pricing	two-way exclusive dealing
palming off	tying agreement
deceptive advertising	blue laws
bait-and-switch advertising	ethics
product liability laws	explicit code of ethics
expressed warranties	implicit code of ethics
implied warranty of merchantability	slotting fees

REVIEW AND DISCUSSION QUESTIONS

LO•1   HOW DOES LEGISLATION CONSTRAIN A RETAILER'S PRICING POLICIES?

1. Deceptive pricing harms not only the consumer but also competition. Agree or disagree and explain your reasoning.
2. A federal grand jury argues that because all major supermarkets in a town are selling milk at the same price, there must be a conspiracy to fix prices. Agree or disagree and explain your reasoning.
3. Why should a retailer be familiar with the Robinson-Patman Act?

LO•2   WHAT IS THE DIFFERENCE BETWEEN LEGAL AND ILLEGAL PROMOTIONAL ACTIVITIES FOR A RETAILER?

4. Describe what is meant by the term *bait-and-switch*. Is this a legal or illegal retailing tool?
5. What is deceitful diversion of patronage? Comment on its legality.
6. Explain what is meant by the term *palming off*. Does palming off hurt competing retailers, consumers, or both?

LO•3   WHAT RESPONSIBILITIES DOES A RETAILER HAVE REGARDING THE PRODUCTS SOLD?

7. If a retail salesperson makes a misleading statement to a customer, can the retailer be held liable? Even if the retailer instructed the salesperson never to make such statements?
8. What should a retailer do so that it does not violate the customer's rights under the Magnuson-Moss Warranty Act?

LO•4   HOW DOES GOVERNMENTAL REGULATION INFLUENCE A RETAILER'S BEHAVIOR WITH OTHER CHANNEL MEMBERS?

9. How could two-way exclusive dealing arrangements be harmful to the consumer and competition?
10. Discuss the concept of exclusive dealing. Are exclusive dealing arrangements in the retailer's best interest? Are they in the consumer's best interest?

LO•5 **WHAT IS THE IMPACT OF VARIOUS STATE AND LOCAL LAWS, IN ADDITION TO OTHER FEDERAL REGULATIONS, IN DEVELOPING RETAIL POLICIES?**

11. Are state predatory laws usually effective? Why?
12. In a free market system, such as the one we have in the United States, should states be allowed to use zoning to regulate the architectural style of a retailer's building?

LO•6 **HOW DOES A RETAILER'S CODE OF ETHICS INFLUENCE ITS BEHAVIOR?**

13. Retailers should abide by the philosophy that "as long as it is legal, it is ethical." Agree or disagree and explain your reasoning.
14. A local supermarket operator, desiring to build store traffic, contracted with the operator of a bungee cord. Is there an ethical problem, even though not a legal one, for this retailer?
15. A drugstore manager is approached by a salesperson from a major pharmaceutical firm. The salesperson has a sick sister, and she needs an expensive prescription drug that is manufactured by another company. Could the drugstore manager ethically trade off the free samples he has of the expensive drug that the sister needs for twice their value in free samples of products that the salesperson handles? After all, because they are free samples anyway, who would be hurt by such an arrangement? Agree or disagree with the above and explain your reasoning.

SAMPLE TEST QUESTIONS

LO•1 **TED BABAIN'S PONTIAC CHARGES TWO DIFFERENT CUSTOMERS (ONE A MAN, THE OTHER A WOMAN) TWO DIFFERENT PRICES FOR IDENTICAL AUTOMOBILES. THIS IS IN ALL PROBABILITY A PER SE VIOLATION OF THE**

a. Clayton Act
b. your state's Unfair Trade Practices Act
c. Robinson-Patman Act
d. Sherman Act
e. This is not illegal because it involved a sale to a final consumer, not just sales between channel members

LO•2 **AN EXAMPLE OF DECEITFUL DIVERSION OF PATRONAGE WOULD BE**

a. spreading rumors about a competitor, even if the rumors do not hurt the competitor's business
b. telling the truth about a competitor that will hurt the competitor's business
c. advertising a product at a very low price then adding hidden charges
d. putting extra large signs in your store's front window offering lower prices than your competitor next door
e. illegally using another company's trademark or brand name, which results in the loss of sales for the other company

LO•3 WHEN A CUSTOMER RELIES ON THE RETAILER TO ASSIST THE CUSTOMER OR TO SELECT THE RIGHT GOODS TO SERVE A PARTICULAR PURPOSE, THE RETAILER IS ESTABLISHING

a. an implied warranty of fitness
b. an implied warranty of merchantability
c. a price discrimination defense
d. an expressed warranty of fitness
e. an expressed warranty of merchantability

LO•4 D-A PET PRODUCTS COMPANY HAS AN EXTREMELY POPULAR LINE OF CAT FOOD. THE COMPANY HAS RECENTLY STARTED INSISTING THAT RETAILERS WHO CARRY ITS CAT FOOD MUST ALSO CARRY ITS RATHER OVERPRICED CAT LITTER. DUE TO ITS PRICE, THE LITTER IS NOT A BIG SELLER, AND IT TAKES AWAY SHELF SPACE FROM MORE PROFITABLE PRODUCTS. REQUIRING STORES THAT STOCK THE CAT FOOD TO ALSO STOCK THE LITTER IS AN EXAMPLE OF

a. a consent agreement
b. a tying contract
c. unfair advertising
d. monopolistic competition
e. power marketing

LO•5 THE MOST STRINGENT LAWS GOVERNING FRANCHISES ARE TYPICALLY ENACTED AT WHAT LEVEL?

a. federal
b. state
c. county
d. local
e. international

LO•6 WHICH OF THE FOLLOWING IS NOT AN ETHICAL DILEMMA THAT A RETAILER FACES WHEN BUYING MERCHANDISE?

a. whether the buyer believes that he or she can sell the merchandise
b. the source of the merchandise
c. the issue of product quality
d. whether to ask for a slotting fee
e. whether to ask for a bribe

APPLICATIONS

WRITING AND SPEAKING EXERCISE As manager for a fast-food restaurant chain, you have been approached by your counterpart at a rival chain. He wants to raise the prices of his soft drinks by a nickel for all sizes. He wants to know if you would follow suit in this attempt to cover the increase in operating expenses that has affected not only soft drinks but all other food items. After all, you both are paid a bonus, in addition to your salary, if you exceed your profit quota for the year. Prepare a response to the other manager outlining your position on this subject.

RETAIL PROJECT   Each year, the U.S. government's Consumer Information Center publishes the *Consumer's Resource Handbook*. This book is designed to help consumers make informed decisions and address any problems they may have if they think they were cheated, swindled, or treated unfairly. In addition, the book lists other pamphlets and the telephone numbers for all government agencies dealing with consumer issues (i.e., credit, door-to-door selling, car repairs [including what to do if you purchased a "lemon"], and insurance).

You can order a copy of the handbook and get a list of all other pamphlets by writing the CIC at P.O. Box 100, Pueblo, CO 81002 or by Internet at "cic.info @pueblo.gsa.gov" and type in the words "SEND INFO" for your message. Better yet, why not just go to the CIC's home page (http://www.gsa.gov/staff/pa/cic/cis.htm) and see what you can find.

CASE   THE NEW ADVERTISING CAMPAIGN*

O'Haran's Furniture is located in north central Dallas, Texas. The store was founded by Thom O'Haran, an Irish immigrant, in 1901 and has been operated since 1977 by his granddaughter, Ruth Reel, and her husband, Dick. As one of the area's most successful merchants, last month Ruth was elected to replace Mort Ettinger, the owner of several local Dairy Queen franchises, as president of the North Central Business Roundtable (NCBR). Due to the close-knit relationship of the area's business community that Ettinger developed over the past decade, the job of president has until recently been largely ceremonial.

The event that has changed the nature of the job was a series of advertisements that ran on local television stations featuring the area's only hospital, General Medical, and its prenatal program.

For nearly 15 months, the residents of the entire Dallas/Fort Worth Metroplex have watched and shared the joy as Billy Ray Smith and his wife, MaryJo, first found out they were going to have a baby, and with the proper prenatal care at General Medical the baby was born a healthy eight-pound boy. Not only did the ads show General Medical in a favorable light, but it also reflected on the neighboring business community.

The ads that began last year were first-person accounts of the pregnancy. The first ad had MaryJo telling the viewers how she told Billy Ray that he was about to become a father. Later ads, which were updated monthly, showed the physician at General Medical telling MaryJo the baby was going to be a healthy boy, the couple painting the baby's room at their home, the couple taking birthing classes, and doing all the other things new parents do. Finally, earlier this year, the entire Metroplex rejoiced as the ads showed little Bubba Smith being born. In fact, more than 100 residents sent cards and gifts to the couple and baby in care of the hospital.

Now, however, the ads are a source of problems for Ruth and the other NCBR officers. While planning the Roundtable's Annual Business Awards Dinner, the officers decided to honor Medical General for its contributions to the area's business community. As part of the award ceremony, the Roundtable also wanted to present Billy Ray, MaryJo, and little Bubba with gift certificates from local merchants.

That's when the bad news first hit. Bubba was really a baby girl named Jennifer Ann and Billy Ray and MaryJo weren't a couple but actors from Waco. In fact, MaryJo not only wasn't married to Billy Ray, she never was pregnant. One of the local radio stations picked up on the false pregnancy story, and soon all the television and radio stations, as well as the newspaper, were saying "Shame on you, General Medical." One radio station went so far as to call the ads deceptive and asked for the Attorney General to investigate. Others began questioning General Medical's ethics. More than a dozen expecting mothers who had planned to use General Medical for their delivery asked their physicians whether they could switch hospitals.

Now, some of the local merchants were worrying that the unfavorable publicity being cast on General Medical would reflect on them. A few even wanted General Medical kicked out of the NCBR.

1. Were the ads deceptive?
2. Were the ads unethical?
3. What should Ruth Reel do to handle this situation?

* The names and events in this case are fictional and not to be confused with any other events.

PLANNING YOUR OWN RETAIL BUSINESS

You are the general manager/partner for a local Ford dealership with a net worth of $1,800,000, and at your regular Friday morning meeting with the salesforce, you congratulate them on being ahead of their sales quota for the year.

Things couldn't be better you thought to yourself as you left the meeting and returned to your office. You were going to exceed your $8.5 million sales goal for the year. Your cost of merchandise sold was expected to average 88 percent of sales and your fixed operating costs were being held to $30,000 a month. With variable cost averaging 5 percent of sales, you are expecting to produce almost a quarter million dollars in profit before taxes this year.

Just when things looked so great, your partner calls to ask if your read the article in the morning newspaper about last night's city council meeting. It seems that to reduce local property taxes and keep voters happy, a council member has suggested that the city increase the sales tax by 1 percent. This tax would cover everything sold in the city, including automobiles.

Although you hate to see any type of sales tax increase, because it raises the price of your automobiles, this one in particular could present your dealership with a major problem. Just last year, several dealers representing most major domestic and foreign car manufacturers moved to a nearby suburban location, creating a sort of "car mall" where shoppers could easily move from one dealership to another and compare the various dealer offerings. One of those "car mall" dealers was the city's other Ford dealer. This dealer's customers wouldn't have to pay this additional sales tax because it appeared that the suburb's government planned to keep local sales taxes at the current level and reap the benefits of seeing total retail sales increase as consumers flocked to suburban merchants to get lower prices.

What should you do? Should you absorb the additional tax to keep your prices competitive? What would this do to your profits?

Or should you lobby city hall to get it to see the errors of its proposed tax increase?

Notes

1. Sherman Act, 26 Stat, 209 (1890) as amended, 15 U.S.C. articles 1–7.
2. "Stride Rite Agrees to Settle Charges It Tried to Force Pricing by Retailers," *Wall Street Journal,* September 28, 1993: A12; "Reebok and FTC Settle Price-Fixing Charges," *Wall Street Journal,* May 5, 1995: B1.
3. "Manufacturers Allowed to Cap Retail Prices," *Wall Street Journal,* November 5, 1997: A1, A4.
4. "Farewell, My Love," *Fortune,*May 27, 1996: 128–140.
5. "Fake King Cobras Tee Off the Makers of High-End Clubs," *Wall Street Journal,* February 11, 1997: A1, A17.
6. Fred W. Morgan and Allen B. Saviers, "Retailer Responsibility for Deceptive Advertising and Promotional Methods," paper presented at the Retail Patronage Conference, Lake Placid, NY, May 1993.
7. *Id.*Ibid.
8. *N. C. Freed Co., Inc. v. Board of Governors of Federal Reserve System* (CA2 NY) 473 F.2d 1210.
9. United States Public Law 92-573, Consumer Product Safety Act (1972).
10. Magnuson-Moss Warranty Federal Trade Commission Act, Public Law 93-637, 93rd Congress (1975).
11. "PepsiCo's KFC Unit Reinstates Territorial Protection," *Wall Street Journal,* February 27, 1996: B2.
12. *Eastman Kodak Company v. Image Technical Services* (1992), 112 S. Ct. 2072.
13. For a detailed analysis of the changes taking place in this area of government regulation, the reader should consult "Antitrust Enforcers Drop the Ideology, Focus on Economics," *Wall Street Journal,* February 27, 1997: A1, A8.
14. "Retailers Love Big Balloons, But Others Try to Pop Them," *Wall Street Journal,* October 7, 1997: B1.
15. "Virtual Growth," *Wall Street Journal,* March 20, 1997: R4; "Internet Stocks Are on Track to a Comeback, . . . ," *Wall Street Journal,* February 19, 1997: C2.
16. "Will China Scuttle Its Pirates?" *Business Week,* August 15, 1995: 40–41; "Copyright Pirates Prosper in China Despite Promises," *New York Times,* February 20, 1996: A1.
17. "The Detectives," *Fortune,* April 14, 1997: 123.
18. "To Those Still Selling Cigarettes," *Retailing Today,* February 1997: 1–2.
19. "Companies That Serve You Best," *Fortune,* May 31, 1993: 74–88.

MARKET SELECTION AND LOCATION ANALYSIS

MARKET SELECTION AND LOCATION DECISIONS

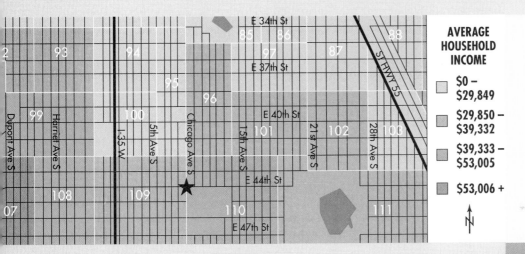

AVERAGE HOUSEHOLD INCOME

☐ $0 – $29,849

▨ $29,850 – $39,332

▨ $39,333 – $53,005

▨ $53,006 +

N↑

The location of retail stores is heavily influenced by where households in a retailer's target market live.

OVERVIEW

In this chapter, we review how retailers select and reach their target market through the location decision. The two broad options for reaching your target market are store-based and nonstore-based locations. Our major focus is on the decision process for selecting store-based locations. We describe the various demand and supply factors that must be evaluated in each geographic market area under consideration. We end with a discussion of alternative locations that retailers consider as they select a specific site.

LEARNING OBJECTIVES

After reading this chapter, you should be able to

1. explain the criteria used in selecting a target market
2. identify the different options, both store-based and nonstore-based, for effectively reaching the retailer's target market and identify the advantages and disadvantages of business districts, shopping centers, and free-standing units as sites for retail location
3. define geographic information systems (GIS) and discuss their potential uses in a retail enterprise
4. describe the various factors to be considered in identifying the most attractive geographic market for a new store
5. discuss the various attributes considered in evaluating retail sites within a retail market
6. explain how to select the best geographic site for a store

SELECTING A TARGET MARKET

Many retailing experts consider deciding who you want to sell to and deciding how to reach these potential customers as the most critical determinants of success in retailing. This involves the selection of a target market and evaluating alternative ways to reach this target market. Traditionally, for retailers desiring to reach a given target market this has meant selecting the best location for a store. In fact, one wise retailing executive once said that the three major decisions in retailing are location, location, and location. Although the other elements of the retail mix are also important, if the customer can't reach your store conveniently, these elements become secondary. The easier it is to reach the store, the more traffic a store will have, and this will lead to higher sales.

Today, however, location is much broader than simply store-based location because retailers are finding alternatives to the customer traveling to a fixed based store to purchase goods and services. For example, MacWarehouse sells computers and peripherals to households through the mail, the University of Phoenix offers an MBA on-line via a computer in the student's home or place of business, the Home Shopping Network and QVC sell $2 billion annually in merchandise via television, and Tupperware continues to sell most of its kitchenware via parties.

It is projected by some experts that the Internet will become a major retailing format over the next decade. The equivalence of a store on the Internet is a retailer's World Wide Web (WWW) site. When visiting a retailer's WWW site, it is the home page that is first viewed, and it is equivalent to a store front. From this home page, a person visiting the retailer can be linked to other pages that provide more and more detailed information about merchandise, credit, warranties, terms of trade, etc. The total collection of all the pages of information on the retailer's WWW site has become known as its virtual store. Whereas a traditional store is located in geographic space, a virtual store is located in cyberspace.

The counterpart to location on the Internet is linkage or "to whom or what you are connected." For example, a retailer's home page may be accessed through the home pages of other businesses or institutions, which provides customers visiting the retailer's WWW site with locational convenience. Some argue that success on the Internet will be determined by linkage, linkage, linkage.[1]

This suggests that the critical issue that determines convenience of a virtual store is how many different other web sites are linked to your virtual store. This determines the traffic for your virtual store and as is well known in retailing traffic is a critical determinant of success.

Home page
is the introductory or first material a viewer sees when they access a retailer's Internet world wide web (WWW) site. It is the equivalent to a retailer's storefront in the physical world.

Virtual store
is the total collection of all the pages of information on the retailer's WWW site.

Linkage
is to whom or what are you connected on the WWW.

DOLLAR $ & ¢ENTS

Retailers who select geographic or cyberspace sites for their stores that have high traffic will be able to generate high-performance results.

Regardless of whether you plan a traditional store in geographic space or a virtual store in cyberspace, your first step is to develop a cost-effective way to reach the household and individual consumer that you clearly identify as your target market. Importantly, failure to clearly identify the target market will result in a large amount of wasted marketing expenditures.

MARKET SEGMENTATION

In Chapter 3, market segmentation was defined as the dividing of large heterogeneous consumer populations into smaller, more homogeneous groups based on demographic, economic, psychographic, and behavioral characteristics. Because any single retailer cannot serve all potential customers, it is important that it segment the market and select a target market(s). A target market is that segment of the market that the retailer decides to pursue through its marketing efforts. Retailers in the same line of retail trade often pursue different target markets (e.g., Ann Taylor appeals to the higher-income woman, The Limited appeals to the moderate-income woman, and Ross Dress for Less appeals to the budget-conscious female shopper).

We are combining the topics of target market selection and location analysis because a retailer should identify its target market(s) before it decides how to best reach that target market(s). Reaching the target market can be obtained through a store-based location in which the consumer travels to the store or through a non-store retailing format in which products and services are offered to the consumer at a location more convenient or accessible by the consumer. These are related topics because individuals of different characteristics are not randomly spread over geographic space; in fact, what has been repeatedly demonstrated is that persons of similar backgrounds live nearby each other and have similar media habits, consumption habits, and activities, interests, and opinions. Because of this, retailers such as Nordstrom know where to geographically locate its stores and retailers such as Williams-Sonoma, with a very successful mail-order catalog for high-quality kitchenware, knows which zip codes or geographic areas or specific households to mail its catalog.

Market segmentation *is the dividing of a heterogeneous consumer population into smaller, more homogeneous groups based on demographic, economic, psychographic, and behavioral characteristics.*

Target market *is the group of customers that the retailer is seeking to serve.*

IDENTIFYING A TARGET MARKET

To successfully reach a target market, three criteria should be met. First, the selected market segment should be measurable or able to be described by using objective measures on which there are data available, such as age, gender, income, education, ethnic group, and religion. The most commonly available objective data are demographic, which the U.S. Census Bureau provides for business at little cost. Conversely, a subjective variable such as personality is more difficult to determine. For example, how can a retailer reasonably or cost-effectively measure the number of compulsive individuals in the United States?

A second criterion is accessibility, or the degree to which the retailer can target its promotional or distribution efforts to a particular market segment. Do individuals in the target market watch certain television programs, listen to certain radio programs, frequently visit certain WWW sites (i.e., cluster in cyberspace) or do they cluster together in geographic space. As we see in this chapter, the location decision is largely determined by identifying the most effective way to reach a target market.

Finally, successful target marketing requires that the segment be substantial enough to be profitable for the retailer. Clearly, a retailer could develop a store to appeal to any market segment regardless of size, such as fans of the Green Bay Packers;

however, the retailer would have to ask itself whether there were a sufficient number of Packer fans living within its trade area to make the store profitable. If not, perhaps a virtual store composed of a WWW site on the Internet may be a more cost-effective way to market to fans of the Green Bay Packers.

DOLLAR $ & CENTS

Retailers that select markets that are measurable, accessible, and substantial will be able to generate high-performance results.

Store-based retailers
operate from a fixed store location that requires customers to travel to the store to view and select merchandise and/or services.

Nonstore-based retailers
intercept the customer at home or at work or at a place other than a store where they might be susceptible to purchasing.

Central business district (CBD)
usually consists of an unplanned shopping area around the geographic point at which all public transportation systems converge; it is usually in the center of the city and often where the city originated historically.

REACHING YOUR TARGET MARKET

As was suggested earlier, once a retailer identifies its target market it must identify the most effective way to reach this market. In Exhibit 7.1, the different retail formats that can be used to reach target markets are illustrated. Essentially, there are store-based and non-store-based retailers. Store-based retailers operate from a fixed store location that requires customers to travel to the store to view and select merchandise and/or services. Essentially, the retailer requires that the consumer perform part of the transportation function, which was one of the eight marketing functions discussed in Chapter 5. However, nonstore-based retailers intercept the customer at home or at work or at a place other than a store where they might be susceptible to purchasing. As hinted earlier, many retailers are beginning to intercept customers on the Internet.

LOCATION OF STORE-BASED RETAILERS

As shown in Exhibit 7.1, there are four basic types of locations from which a store-based retailer can select: business districts, shopping centers/malls, free-standing units, and nontraditional locations. No one type of location is inherently better than the others. Many retailers such as McDonald's have been successful in all four location types. Each type of location has its own characteristics relating to the composition of competing stores, parking facilities, affinities with nonretail businesses (e.g., office buildings, hospitals, universities), and other factors.

BUSINESS DISTRICTS
Historically, many retailers were located in the central business district (CBD), usually an unplanned shopping area around the geographic point at which all public transportation systems converge. Many traditional department stores are located in the CBD along with a good selection of specialty shops. Recently, Kmart opened its first Big Kmart (99,000 square feet) in downtown Philadelphia. This is significant since most discount department stores stayed away from high cost central business district locations and located in lower cost suburbs. The makeup or the mix of retailers in a CBD is generally not the result of any advance

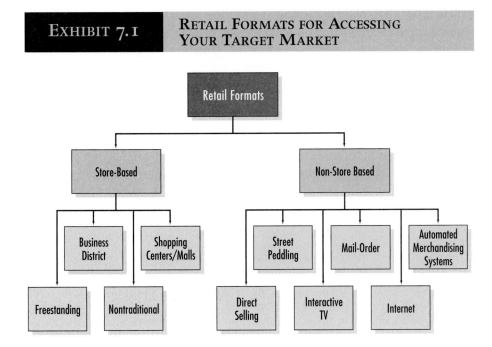

| EXHIBIT 7.1 | RETAIL FORMATS FOR ACCESSING YOUR TARGET MARKET |

planning but depends on history, retail trends, and luck. This is beginning to change today as some communities have tried to reinvigorate the center cities. To date, however, these efforts haven't been too successful.

However, some small New England towns want to protect their town center from nonlocal retailers that want to locate there. In Litchfield, Connecticut, the birthplace of Ethan Allen and Harriet Beecher Stowe, many local residents protested Talbot's planned entry into their town. However Talbot's, an upscale fashionable women's clothing store, despite the local opposition was successful in opening a store in a two-story Colonial revival building.[2]

The CBD has several strengths and weaknesses to consider. Among its strengths are easy access to public transportation, wide product assortment, variety in images, prices, and services, and proximity to commercial activities. Some weaknesses to consider are inadequate (and usually expensive) parking, older stores, high rents and taxes, traffic and delivery congestion, potentially high crime rate, and the general decaying conditions of many inner-cities. However, despite these disadvantages, in 1996 Kmart deviated from its historical suburban location policy to open two discount department stores in New York City (Manhattan). Despite the high costs and other disadvantages of such a location they believed that the high traffic and the expectation of more than $50 million in annual sales was an irresistible incentive.[3]

Often, the weaknesses of CBDs have resulted in a retail situation known as inner-city or ghetto retailing, which occurs when only the poorest citizens are left in an urban area. Traditionally, product and service offerings in these areas have decreased, while prices have held steady or even increased. However, good merchandise selection, careful security, and heavy public relations have enabled some retailers such as Dollar-General, Von's, Stop&Shop, Supermarkets General, Jewel/Osco, Kroger, First National Supermarkets, A&P, American Stores, and Pathmark,[4] to find success by opening stores

in inner-city areas. Even Ben & Jerry's, The Gap, and The Disney Store operate in Harlem and the Body Shop in south central Los Angeles. These retailers are successful in these markets because they tailored their inventories to the special needs and tastes of inner-city residents.

In larger cities, secondary business districts and neighborhood business districts have developed. A secondary business district (SBD) is a shopping area that is smaller than the CBD and that revolves around at least one department or variety store at a major street intersection. A neighborhood business district (NBD) is a shopping area that evolves to satisfy the convenience-oriented shopping needs of a neighborhood. The NBD generally contains several small stores, with the major retailer being either a supermarket, super drugstore, or a variety store, and is located on a major artery of a residential area. An increasing number of national retail chains are finding the neighborhood business district an attractive location for new stores. This includes retailers such as Ann Taylor, the Body Shop, Starbucks, Liz Claiborne, Williams-Sonoma, and Pottery Barn.[5]

The single factor that distinguishes these business districts from a shopping center/mall is that they are basically unplanned. Like CBDs, the store mixture of SBDs and NBDs usually evolve partially by planning, partially by luck, and partially by accident. No one plans, for example, that there would be two department stores, four jewelry stores, two camera shops, three leather shops, 12 apparel shops, and one theater in an SBD.

SHOPPING CENTER/MALL
A shopping center, or mall, is a centrally owned and/or managed shopping district that is planned, has balanced tenancy (the stores complement each other in merchandise offerings), and is surrounded by parking facilities. A shopping center has one or more anchor stores (a dominant large-scale store that is expected to draw customers to the center) and a variety of smaller stores. To ensure that these smaller stores complement each other, the shopping center often specifies the proportion of total space that can be occupied by each type of retailer. Similarly, the center's management places limits on the merchandise lines that each retailer may carry. A unified cooperative advertising and promotional strategy is followed by all the retailers in the center. A shopping center location can offer a retailer several major advantages over a CBD location. Among them are

1. heavy traffic resulting from the wide range of product offerings
2. nearness to population
3. cooperative planning and sharing of common costs
4. access to highway and availability of parking
5. lower crime rate
6. clean, neat environment
7. more than adequate parking space

Despite these favorable reasons for locating in a shopping center, the retailer does face several disadvantages. Among the limitations are

1. inflexible store hours (the retailer must stay open the hours of the center and can't be open at other times)
2. high rents
3. restrictions as to the merchandise that the retailer may sell
4. inflexible operations and required membership in the center's merchant organization

The Mall of America in Bloomington, Minnesota, with over four million square feet of space is the largest mall in the United States.

5. possibility of too much competition and the fact that much of the traffic is not interested in a particular product offering
6. dominance of the smaller stores by the anchor tenant

Shopping center image, shopping center preferences, and shopping center personality all attract various subsets of consumers, giving retailers located at these centers a
competitive advantage over other retailers. Therefore, it is extremely important that a
retailer considering a shopping center location be aware of the makeup, image, preferences, and personality of the center under question.

There are eight different types of shopping centers, each with a distinctive function.

1. A neighborhood shopping center provides for the sale of convenience goods
   (foods, drugs, and sundries) and personal services (laundry and dry cleaning, barbering, shoe repairing, etc.) to satisfy the day-to-day living needs of the immediate
   neighborhood. In the past, it was built around a supermarket as the principal tenant. Now, however, the supermarket is being replaced by home improvement centers, discount department stores, and so forth. The neighborhood center is the
   smallest type of shopping center and as a rule of thumb will have approximately
   100,000 to 150,000 square feet in gross leasable space. A neighborhood center has a
   primary trade area of three miles.
2. The community shopping center is next in size. In addition to the convenience
   goods and personal services of the neighborhood center, community centers provide a wider range of facilities for the sale of soft good lines (clothing for men,
   women, and children) and hard good lines (hardware, furniture, and appliances).
   Community centers are also built around either a junior department store (not a
   full-line one), a variety store, a category killer, or discount department store as the
   major tenant, in addition to a supermarket. In theory, the typical size is 150,000
   square feet of gross leasable area, but in practice the size may vary and approach

**Neighborhood shopping
center**
*provides for the sale of con-
venience goods (food, drugs,
and sundries) and personal
services (laundry and dry
cleaning, barbering, shoe
repairing, etc.) to satisfy the
day-to-day living needs of
the immediate neighbor-
hood.*

**Community shopping
center**
*is larger than a neighbor-
hood shopping center and
in addition to the conve-
nience goods and personal
services of the neighborhood
center, it provides a wider
range of facilities for the
sale of soft good lines and
hard good lines.*

Faneuil Hall in Boston is a festival marketplace that offers on-going entertainment, such as street performers and concerts, which adds to the visitors' shopping and dining experience.

Regional center
is larger than a community shopping center and thus has a trade area of 5 to 15 miles and provides a wide range of general merchandise, apparel, furniture, and home furnishings, as well as a range of services and recreational facilities.

upward of 350,000 square feet. About two-thirds of all shopping centers in the United States are neighborhood or community types, and they account for about one-third of all retail sales in the United States. A community center has a trade area of three to six miles.

3. The regional center provides for a wide range of general merchandise, apparel, furniture, and home furnishings, as well as a range of services and recreational facilities. The regional center is built around one or more full-line department stores of generally not less than 100,000 square feet. In theory, its typical size is considered to be 750,000 to 1,000,000 square feet of gross leasable area. The regional

center is the second-largest type of shopping center. As such, the regional center provides services typical of a business district yet not as extensive as the super-regional center. Regional centers have trade areas of five to 15 miles.

4. The super-regional center provides for an extensive variety of general merchandise, apparel, furniture, and home furnishings, as well as a variety of services and recreational facilities. Because it is larger than a regional center, it also has greater depth of merchandise. The super-regional center is built around at least three major department stores of generally not less than 100,000 square feet each. The typical size of a super-regional center is between 1,000,000 and 1,500,000 square feet of gross leasable area. A super-regional center has a trade area of 5 to 25 miles. The *Guinness Book of World Records* ranks the 110-acre West Edmonton Mall (Alberta, Canada) as the world's largest, with more than 800 shops, several dozen restaurants, 34 theaters, an 18-hole miniature golf course, a 10-acre water park for swimming and sunning under tanning lamps, two dozen amusement rides, and a 360-room hotel for extended stays. It's all indoors, under one roof. Next on the list is the 4.2-million-square-foot Mall of America in Bloomington, Minnesota (the twin cities area of Minneapolis/St. Paul). This center, which opened in 1992, has a seven-acre amusement park, a two-level miniature golf course, more than 400 stores, many restaurants and night clubs, and 14 movie theaters.

5. Fashion/Specialty centers are comprised primarily of upscale apparel stores, boutiques, and craft shops carrying high-quality fashion-oriented merchandise at high price levels. They can also have restaurants and entertainment. These centers are typically 100,000 to 250,000 square feet and are richly appointed and beautifully landscaped. A fashion/specialty center has a trade area of 5 to 15 miles.

6. Power centers are dominated by several anchors including category killers, warehouse clubs, off-price stores, and discount department stores. A power center is typically from 300,000 to 500,000 square feet and has a trade area of 5 to 10 miles. Power centers experienced explosive growth throughout the early to mid-1990s. Recently, however, as power centers saturated the retail landscape their growth has begun to decline significantly.[6]

7. Theme centers are shopping centers located in places of historical interest and where a lot of tourist traffic is generated. An example of a theme center is Faneuil Hall Marketplace in Boston. This festival marketplace offers ongoing entertainment such as street performers and concerts, which adds value to visitors' shopping and dining experiences. Theme centers vary in size but are usually at least 100,000 square feet and less than 500,000 square feet. Another example is MCA's City Walk, which is a two-block entertainment and shopping center designed to have the feel of a problem-free Los Angeles. It is located in San Fernando Valley, California, next to Universal Studios. It has a faux Venice beach, billboards and neon lights of Sunset Boulevard, neo-Mexican facades of Olvera Street, and the chic shops of Melrose Avenue. Theme centers often consist of specialty stores and have no anchor tenant such as a department store. Merchandise is heavily concentrated on intercept merchandise and especially the type of items that individuals will purchase on vacation, such as T-shirts, low- to moderate-priced jewelry and giftware, sports clothing, and specialty foods.

8. Outlet centers specialize in manufacturer's outlets that dispose of overproduction of current merchandise lines, factory seconds (which are clearly marked), and leftovers from last season. Recently, outlet centers have included retailers such as Barneys, The Gap, Ann Taylor, and Saks Fifth Avenue as tenants. These retailers use these outlets to dispose of slow-selling merchandise or overstocks. Traditionally,

Super-regional center *is larger than a regional center and has a trade area of 5 to 25 miles and offers an extensive variety of general merchandise, apparel, furniture, and home furnishings, as well as a variety of services and recreational facilities.*

Fashion/Specialty center *is a shopping center comprised of primarily upscale apparel stores, boutiques, and craft shops carrying high quality fashion oriented merchandise at high price levels.*

Power center *is a shopping center that is dominated by several anchors including category killers, warehouse clubs, off-price stores, and discount department stores.*

Theme center *is a shopping center located in places of historical interest and where high tourist traffic is generated. These centers often consist of specialty stores and have no anchor tenant and merchandise is heavily concentrated on intercept merchandise and especially the type of items that individuals will purchase on vacation.*

Outlet center *is a shopping center specializing in manufacturer's outlets that dispose of overproduction of current merchandise lines, factory seconds, and leftovers from last season.*

SHOPPING MALLS IN ASIA

In Asia, living quarters are small and communal life is important. Consequently, shopping malls as public places play an important social role. Whereas a North American shopper may spend a few hours in a shopping mall, the Asian consumer will spend the entire day at the mall. The appeal is social interaction, entertainment, and air conditioning, which can be a big draw in the warm and humid climate of Asia. Because of the high population density and the high price of land, these malls are built vertically versus horizontally as in the United States.

The growth of shopping malls in Asia is quite logical. For the past two decades, these countries have been the manufacturers for the world. Now, these workers have money to spend and are becoming the consumers of the world.

Fun and entertainment are especially important draws. And the amusement aspects can be quite lavish. Consider the following examples:

- Bangna Central City in Bangkok, Thailand, has 200,000 square feet of amusement attractions; including roller coasters, water slides, and cable cars.
- Alabang Festival Supermall in Manila, Philippines, has 34 bowling lanes and an eight-screen cinema.
- A new 2-million-square-foot center in Berjaya Star City, Kuala Lumpur, Malaysia, adjoins an ice rink and a theme park featuring laser bumper cars.
- Times Square in Shanghai includes a 400,000-square-foot eight-level retail/entertainment center, as well as a 34-story office tower.
- Bangkok Dome in Bangkok contains 7.7 million square feet, 2.3 million of which is retail, restaurants, food court, and entertainment complexes. There is also a hotel, condominium complex, aquarium, and a rooftop sports arena.

factory outlet stores were freestanding locations near their respective manufacturer's factory. However, in 1972, they began to gather together in specially designed malls located away from the factories. By 1980, there were two dozen factory outlet malls in the United States. Today, there are more than 400. A typical center will have 20 to 80 stores and will be located away from major retail centers to avoid competing with other retailers selling the manufacturers' products. Of the different types of shopping centers, the factory outlet centers have the largest trade areas, which range from 25 to 75 miles.

Shopping centers and their latter-day counterpart, the mall, have become a fixture of American life, social and economic, and are popular locations for retailers. Shopping centers and malls now account for one-half of all retail sales, excluding automobile dealerships, in the United States. Seniors take their daily exercise, families find malls a good source of low-cost entertainment, and teens seek out mates in malls. In many cases, the loyalties of shoppers toward a specific center/mall have over time become equal to or greater than their loyalties to a particular retailer. The following Global Retailing discusses the role shopping malls play in Asian social life.

All these malls also have a large amount of space devoted to restaurants and refreshment centers. Some food courts are designed to hold 2,000 persons and cineplexes to hold 15,000. Clearly, the shopping mall experience is an important part of Asian social life.

FREE-STANDING LOCATION

Another location option is to be free-standing. A free-standing retailer generally locates along major traffic arteries, without any adjacent retailers to share traffic. Free-standing retailing offers several advantages:

1. lack of direct competition
2. generally lower rents
3. freedom in operations and hours
4. facilities that can be adapted to individual needs
5. inexpensive parking

Free-standing retailing does have some limitations:

1. lack of drawing power of complementary stores
2. difficulties in attracting customers for the initial visit
3. higher advertising and promotional costs
4. operating costs that cannot be shared with others
5. stores that may have to be built rather than rented
6. zoning laws that may restrict some activities

Free-standing retailer generally locates along major traffic arteries, without adjacent retailers to share traffic.

The difficulties of drawing, and then holding, customers to an isolated or free-standing store is the reason only large, well-known retailers should attempt it. Small retailers may be unable to develop a loyal customer base because customers may be unwilling to travel to a free-standing store that does not have a wide assortment of products and a local or national reputation. Kmart and Wal-Mart, as well as many convenience stores and gasoline stations, have used a free-standing location strategy successfully in the past. Discount appliance stores such as Best Buy and wholesale clubs such as Sam's Club are using them today. However, when these large national chains acquire land for a free-standing store they often acquire more than they need and then "out-parcel" (i.e., sell) the remaining land to smaller retailers. Some astute local retailers or small regional chains have found it attractive to buy this excess land and build stores, even at a premium price, because of the traffic a large discounter such as Wal-Mart generates.

NONTRADITIONAL LOCATIONS

Increasingly, retailers are identifying nontraditional locations for their stores that offer more place utility or locational convenience. Perhaps one of the oldest and best-known nontraditional retail locations is the Army and Air Force Exchange Services (AAFES), which operates more than 10,000 stores in the United States and around the world on U.S. military bases. The largest of these stores are the 172 post or base exchange stores, which handle 42,000 SKUs of general merchandise.[7] Stores in airports are increasing and now not only include cafeterias and restaurants but also apparel, giftware, jewelry, luggage, and bookstores. Due to the success of these stores, some airports are making retail a major part of their offering. For example, the Denver International Airport has more than 100 retail tenants and Pittsburgh International Airport has 80,000 square feet of retail space.[8] Some prominent retailers expanding their airport presence include The Nature Company, Sunglass Hut, Tie Rack, the Body Shop, Bally, and Athlete's Foot. These retailers are recognizing that a significant number of travelers spend several hours in airports and can use this time to purchase merchandise that they may otherwise purchase in their local community. On college campuses, there are an increasing number of food courts in student unions, truck and travel stops along interstate highways also are

Many retailers, such as The Body Shop, are finding it lucrative to locate stores in major airports where travelers have spare time between flights and find shopping a convenient and productive way to spend their time.

incorporating food courts, and some franchisees such as Taco Bell and Dunkin Donuts are putting in small food service units in convenience stores. Hospitals are building emergency care clinics near where people live in the suburbs and away from the hospital, lawyers are putting in store front offices wherever there is high pedestrian traffic, and copying services such as Kinkos are locating in major office buildings. In banking, Wells Fargo is planning on putting drugstores in its branches.[9]

DOLLAR $ & CENTS

Retailers that seek to develop stores in nontraditional locations will enhance their opportunities for achieving high-performance results.

A NOTE ON SERVICE RETAILERS

The location decision is just as important to service retailers as it is to the retailers of tangible products. Some service retailers are an exception, however, because their products are delivered to the consumer at their home. For example, plumbers, house painters, repair services, maid services, carpet cleaners, and lawn care firms may not be concerned with their location. Travel time to the consumer's location might be the only consideration involved.

Most service retailers, however, are visited by the consumer, and location is important. Car washes, dry cleaners, shoe repair stands, and rental retailers such as Taylor Rentals are all examples of service retailers that must be concerned about the convenience of their locations. For example, full-service car wash operators, selling a service most consumers can easily put off, need between 20,000 and 30,000 cars a day passing by at speeds of not more than 25 miles an hour to break even. Similarly, many shoe repair stores are beginning to pay a premium to locate in busy shopping malls, just as car rental agencies pay airport managements to locate on premise. Most American consumers do not want to go out of their way to have their shoes repaired. Another innovative service retailer in the laundry and dry cleaning business has recognized that a high number of tollway users are business persons who have their clothes dry cleaned and laundered but don't have time to take their clothes into a dry cleaner. This retailer has proposed to the Tollway Authority that it be permitted to put up a booth to collect clothes as people go to work, have them cleaned within a few hours, and available at the toll booth for pickup as travelers return home from work.

NONSTORE-BASED RETAILERS

There is a great diversity and variety of nonstore-based retailers. Perhaps the oldest form is the street peddler who peddles their merchandise from a push-cart or temporary stall set up on a street. Street peddling is still common in some parts of the world such as Mexico, Turkey, Pakistan, India, and many parts of Africa and South America. But it is also seen in the United States in such places as New York City and San Francisco, where peddlers sell T-shirts, watches, books, magazines, tobacco, candy, hot dogs, and other products on street corners.

In Chapter 4, we discussed several popular forms of nonstore retailing, which are depicted in Exhibit 7.1 (mail-order houses, automatic merchandising machine operators, direct selling establishments, interactive TV shopping, and shopping on the Internet). Because retailing in the United States for the next 20 years and perhaps beyond will continue to be predominantly store-based, we focus our attention on location analysis for these retailers. However, some innovative retailers are using multiple retail formats to reach their target markets. For example, JCPenney not only continues to build traditional stores but also has an extensive mail catalog operation in which different catalogs are developed to target different customer segments as well as developing and enhancing its World Wide Web site for retail shopping. In fact, most experts predict that by the year 2002 virtually all traditional store-based retailers will have developed multiple retail formats to reach their target market(s). For Starbucks, this has already occurred. Starbucks not only has its traditional stores, it has Internet sites that sell coffee direct to the customer, and they have kiosks in airports. In addition, they are the coffee provider for United Airlines.

DOLLAR $ & ¢ENTS

Retailers who understand the need for multiple retail formats to reach their target market will be the star performers of the next decade.

LO • 3
Define geographic information systems (GIS) and discuss their potential uses in a retail enterprise

Geographic information systems (GIS)

are computerized systems that combine physical geography with cultural geography.

Culture

is the buffer that people have created between themselves and the raw physical environment and includes the characteristics of the population, humanly-created objects, and mobile physical structures.

GEOGRAPHIC INFORMATION SYSTEMS

One recent technological innovation in retailing is geographic information systems. Geographic information systems (GIS) are computerized systems that combine physical geography with cultural geography. Physical geography is the latitude (the north/south) and longitude (east/west) of a specific point in physical space and its related physical characteristics (i.e., water, land, temperature, annual rainfall, etc.). Cultural geography consists of the things that humankind has put in place on that space. To understand this, one needs to appreciate that culture is the buffer that humans have created between themselves and the raw physical environment. It includes the characteristics of the population, such as its age, gender, and income and of the human-created objects placed on that space, such as fixed physical structures (factories, stores, apartment building, schools, churches, houses, highways, railroads, airports, etc.) and mobile physical structures (e.g., cars and trucks). In reality, it includes anything that humans can put onto a physical space that then becomes an attribute of the physical space. For example, some areas such as Scottsdale, Arizona, become known for their very high density of golf courses but these golf courses were not put there by nature but by humans. Other areas become known as high crime areas but nature did not put crime there, humans did. Recent advancements in GIS have allowed the retail analyst to also describe the lifestyle (activities, interests, opinions) of the residents of a geographic areas. This can be helpful in selecting locations for stores that are highly lifestyle sensitive, such as Galyan's Trading Company. Galyan's, which is owned by The Limited, is a 100,000-square-foot category killer in the sporting goods area.[10] In Exhibit 7.2, we show the key components of GISs.

THEMATIC MAPS

Thematic maps

use visual techniques such as colors, shading, and lines, to display cultural characteristics of the physical space.

Historically, it was not unusual for a retailer to push pins into a map of a city where it was located. Each pin represented where a customer lived. An even more sophisticated retailer may have even colored the map to represent different areas of the city in terms of income levels or ethnic composition. This was an early form of thematic mapping. Thematic maps are maps of areas that use visual techniques such as colors, shading, and lines to display cultural characteristics of the physical space. Thematic maps can be very useful management tools for retailers. They can help the retailer visualize a tremendous amount of information in an easy-to-understand format. Today, thematic maps are an important feature of GISs and are fully computerized, making them easy for retailers to develop.

USES OF GIS

GIS as a management technology has a variety of important uses in retailing. Some of these more popular uses are identified below.

1. *Market selection.* A retailer with a set of criteria in mind such as the demographics of its target market and the level of over- or understoring in a market can have the

EXHIBIT 7.2   GIS COMPONENTS

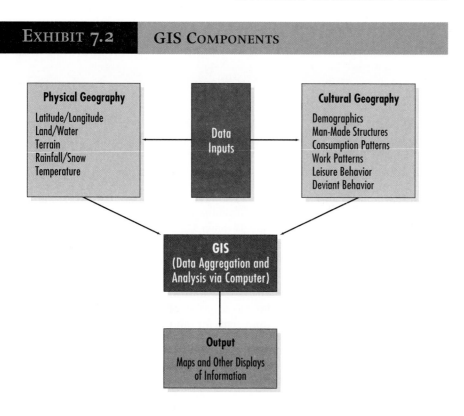

GIS identify and rank order the most attractive cities or counties or other geographic areas to consider for expansion.

2. *Site analysis.* With a particular community in mind, GIS can identify the best possible site or evaluate alternative sites for their expected profitability.

3. *Trade area definition.* If the retailer develops a database of where its customers reside, GIS can automatically develop a trade area map and update this daily, weekly, monthly, or annually.

4. *New store cannibalization.* GIS can help the retailer evaluate how the addition of another store in a community can cannibalize sales of its existing store(s).

5. *Advertising management.* GIS can help the retailer allocate its advertising budget to different stores based on the market potential in their respective trade areas. Similarly, GIS can help the retailer develop a more effective direct-mail campaign to prospective customers.

6. *Merchandise management.* GIS can help the retailer develop an optimal mix of merchandise based on the characteristics of households and individuals within its trade area.

7. *Evaluation of store managers.* GIS can provide an important human resource function. It can help assess how well a store manager is performing based on the trade area characteristics. Consider that two stores of the same size could be performing differently because of the demographics and competitive conditions in the two trade areas. Thus it would be inappropriate to either reward or punish a manager for things they have no control over.

HONDA USES GIS TO IMPROVE SALES

The Japanese company, Honda, has long targeted the United States to sell its automobiles and motorcycles. In the United States, it has developed an extensive network of franchised dealers through which it sells its products. One of the growth opportunities Honda has identified is motorcycle sales, and it has targeted the aging baby boomers. In the 1960s, individuals that rode motorcycles were younger than 30 years of age, non-college-educated, lower-income, blue-collar workers. Today, that has changed, and more than half are older than the age of 30, 40 percent are college-educated, 21 percent earn more than $50,000, and 25 percent are white-collar workers. And surprisingly, a large number are retirees who use their bikes for recreation and vacationing. Honda is using a GIS developed by Map-Info Corp. of Troy, New York, to help it better penetrate the motorcycle market. The Honda GIS includes many databases provided by groups such as the Motorcycle Industry Council, competitive dealer data captured by field managers; demographic and economic databases from Claritas,

Inc., Equifax National Decision Systems; and customer data gathered from warranty registration information.

What follows are some of the uses that Honda is making of its GIS:

- identification of geographic areas where additional Honda Motorcycle dealers are needed.
- identification of which dealers are performing up to potential and those that are not and need business or marketing assistance.
- analyzing advertising campaigns and identifying how to combine cable television and direct-mail campaigns for more effective advertising.

With the use of GIS, Honda has been able to add new retail dealers where needed and grow its sales of Honda motorcycles at substantially greater than the industry average rate of growth.

SOURCE: Based in part on information provided in Roxanne Hoerning, "American Honda Jump-Starts Sales Geographically," *Business Geographics* (March 1996): 24–26.

DOLLAR $ & ¢ENTS

Retailers that use GIS will be able to improve their performance in a number of areas.

If you wish to learn more about GIS, you might look at some of the home pages on the Internet for firms that provide GIS services. These include

Integration Technologies at http://www.integtech.com
Equifax National Decision Systems at http://www.ends.com
Environmental Systems Research Institute, Inc., at http://www.esri.com

In the Behind the Scenes box, we see how American Honda has used GIS to improve its sales of motorcycles in the United States.

MARKET IDENTIFICATION

The location decision for store-based retailers involves three sequential steps. First, the retailer must identify the most attractive markets in which to operate. Some retailers such as Woolworth, Toys "Я" Us, Wal-Mart, Sears, and Benetton are international, and thus when they think of adding new locations, they consider the attractiveness of geographic expansion into foreign countries. Perhaps the most global of all retailers is McDonald's with more than 20,000 locations throughout the world and with plans to add more than 1,000 stores a year over the next decade. Over the past decade, retailers such as Wal-Mart, JCPenney, Kmart, Pier 1, and Sharper Image have identified Mexico as an attractive market for expansion. But most retail analysts contend that the most lucrative market in the early 21st century will be China with the largest population of any country. China's economic status is growing rapidly, as well as its technological infrastructure. Already such U.S. retailers as Wal-Mart, IGA, and Home Depot have entered China and have aggressive expansion plans.[11] Other retailers such as County Seat, Kroger, and many smaller ones concentrate on a single country, the United States, and thus when considering new locations they evaluate the attractiveness of locations in the United States. Whereas, other retailers concentrate on a small region of the United States, possibly a single state or city.

The second step in the retail location decision is to evaluate the density of demand and supply within each market and identify the most attractive sites that are available within each market. Essentially, this means identifying the sites most consistent with the retailer's target market(s) and then identifying those for which the market is not already overstored or in which competition is not overly intense. The third step is the selection of the best site (or sites) available. This stage involves estimating the revenue and expenses of a new store at various locations and then identifying the most profitable new locations. These three steps are illustrated in Exhibit 7.3.

A good retail location decision thus begins by identifying the most attractive market or trading area, the geographic area from which a retailer, group of retailers, or community draws its customers, in which the retailer could locate. For instance, Dollar-General has been very successful in concentrating its expansion in small towns of generally less than 10,000 in population where there is less competition, easier zoning and building regulations, and lower wages and operating costs.

Trading area
is the geographic area from which a retailer, group of retailers, or community draws its customers.

RETAIL LOCATION THEORIES

The most attractive retail markets are not necessarily the largest retail markets. A variety of other factors need to be considered in identifying attractive markets. But to begin with, a trio of methods are especially useful for identifying the best markets.

RETAIL GRAVITY THEORY
Research on store location goes back to the post-World War I era. A marketing professor, William J. Reilly, believed that there were underlying consistencies in shopping behavior that would yield to mathematical analysis and prediction based on the notion or concept of gravity. Reilly, who described himself as a sometime marketing specialist as well as a professor, published the first of

Identifying foreign markets to enter is risky. Wal-Mart entered Indonesia in the mid-1990s. However, in 1998, due in part to the Asian financial crisis, Wal-Mart decided to exit Indonesia.

Reilly's law of retail gravitation,
based on Newtonian gravitational principles, explains how large urbanized areas attract customers from smaller rural communities.

the trading area models in 1929.[12] Reilly's law of retail gravitation dealt with how large urbanized areas attracted customers from smaller communities serving the rural hinterland. As its name implies, Reilly's law had Newtonian gravitational principles as its core. In effect, it stated that two cities attract trade from an intermediate place approximately in direct proportion to the population of the two cities and in inverse proportion to the square of the distance from these two cities to the intermediate place. That is, people will tend to shop in the larger city if travel distance is equal, or even somewhat farther, because they believe that the larger city has a better product selection, and it will be worth the extra traveling.

Two decades later, Paul Converse revised Reilly's original law to determine the boundaries of a city's trading area or to establish a point of indifference between two cities.[13] This point of indifference is the breaking point at which customers would be indifferent to shopping at either city. Converse's formulation of Reilly's law can be expressed algebraically as

Point of indifference
is the extremity of a city's trading area where households would be indifferent between shopping in that city or in an alternative city in a different geographical direction.

$$D_{ab} = \frac{d}{1 + \sqrt{\dfrac{P_b}{P_a}}}$$

EXHIBIT 7.3	SELECTING A RETAIL LOCATION

where D_{ab} is the breaking point from city A, measured in miles along the road to city B;

   d is the distance between city A and city B along the major highway;
   P_a is the population of city A; and
   P_b is the population of city B.

For example, if Levelland and Norwood are 65 miles apart and Levelland's population is 100,000 and Norwood's is 200,000, then the breaking point of indifference between Levelland and Norwood would be 26.9 miles from Levelland and 38.1 miles from Norwood. This means that if you lived 25 miles from Levelland and 40 miles from Norwood, you probably would choose to shop in Levelland because it is within your zone of indifference for Levelland and is beyond your zone of indifference for Norwood. (You might want to figure this out yourself, using Norwood as city A and Levelland as city B.)

Converse's revision of Reilly's law allows the retailer to determine the distances from which each of the smaller cities will be able to attract customers or to determine the size of the trading area for any city under consideration for a retail site. Thus the retailer now has a clear definition of who and where a city's trading area will be if it elects to locate there. Exhibit 7.4 shows how Reilly's law can be used to determine a community's trading area. As shown in Exhibit 7.4, city A has a population of 240,000. City B, with a population of 14,000, is 18 miles north of city A, and its breaking point is 14.5 miles north of city A (point X on Exhibit 7.4). City C, with a population of 21,000, is 14 miles southwest of city A, and its breaking point is 10.8 miles southwest of city A (point Z on Exhibit 7.4). Finally, city D, with a population of 30,000, is 5 miles southeast of city A, and its breaking point is 3.7 miles southeast of city A (point Y on Exhibit 7.4).

EXHIBIT 7.4	TRADING AREA FOR CITY A

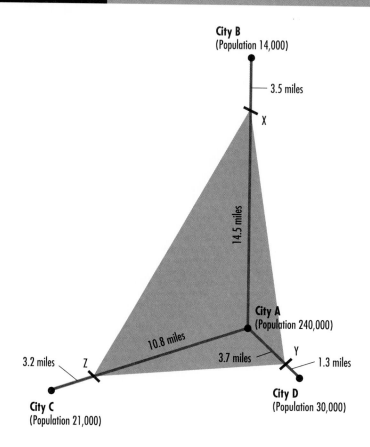

Reilly's law and Converse's revision rest on two assumptions: (1) the two competing cities are equally accessible from the major road and (2) population is a good indicator of the differences in the goods and services available in different cities. Consumers are attracted to the larger population center, not because of the city's size but because of the larger amount of store facilities and product assortment available, thereby making the increased travel time worthwhile.

The law of retail gravitation was an important contribution to trading area analysis because of its ease of calculation. It is easy to use when other data are not available or when the costs of obtaining these data are too high. However, in its simplicity, Reilly's law does have several limitations. First, city population doesn't always reflect the available shopping facilities. For example, two neighboring cities, each with a population of 10,000 and similar demographics, would not be reflected equally in Reilly's law if one of the cities had a Wal-Mart-based shopping center and the other didn't. Second, distance is measured in miles, not the time involved for the consumer to travel that distance or the consumer's perception of that distance or time involved. Given our present highway system, this limitation is extremely important. Traveling 20 miles on an interstate to a mall located at an exit may be easier than the stop-start travel involved in going six miles through downtown traffic. Therefore, some retailers, when using Reilly's law, will substitute travel time for mileage. Finally, although the law works reasonably well in rural areas, where distance is a major decision factor, it isn't flawless.

Recent research on outshopping, that is, leaving your community to shop, from rural areas suggests that factors other than those considered by retail gravity theory are important. For example, in 1992 Canada enacted such high sales taxes that millions of Canadians living near the border, which 70 percent of Canadians do, began to shop in the United States. As a result, the Canadian government was forced to repeal the tax.

Some other factors that the retail gravity theory fails to consider include perceived differences between local and other trading centers, variety-seeking behavior, and other services provided including medical services and/or entertainment facilities. Also, gravity theory is less useful in metropolitan areas where consumers typically have a number of shopping choices available within the maximum distance they are willing to travel.

SATURATION THEORY

Another method for identifying attractive potential markets is based on retail saturation. Called the saturation theory, it enables the retailer to see how the demand for goods and services of a potential trading area is being served by current retail establishments in comparison with other potential markets. Such analysis produces three possible outcomes:

1. Retail store saturation is a condition under which existing store facilities are used efficiently and meet customer needs. Retail saturation exists when a market has just enough store facilities for a given type of store to serve the population of the market satisfactorily and yield a fair profit to the owners.
2. When a market has too few stores to satisfactorily meet the needs of the customer, it is understored. In this setting, average store profitability is really high.
3. When a market has too many stores to yield a fair return on investment, it is overstored.

Saturation theory, therefore, implies a balance between the amount of existing retail store facilities (supply) and their use (demand). As indicated in Chapter 4, one typically measures saturation, overstoring, and understoring in terms of the number of stores per thousand households. The consensus among retail location experts is that the United States is currently highly saturated or overstored with retail stores and thus retailers are taking a second look at some long-ignored markets such as older downtown areas.[14]

A possible indicator of understored versus overstored markets is the index of retail saturation (IRS),[15] which is the ratio of demand for a product or service divided by available supply. The IRS can be measured as follows:

$$IRS = (H \times RE)/RF$$

where *IRS* is the index of retail saturation for an area; *H* is the number of households in the area; *RE* is the annual retail expenditures for a particular line of trade per household in the area; and *RF* is the square footage of retail facilities of a particular line of trade in the area (including square footage of proposed store). If you multiply the two terms in the numerator together (households and retail expenditures per household), you obtain dollar sales. Recalling that the denominator is square footage of retail space, it is easy to see that the IRS is essentially the sales per square foot of retail space in the marketplace for a particular line of retail trade.

Outshopping
occurs when a resident of a community travels to another community to shop.

Retail store saturation
is a condition where there is just enough store facilities for a given type of store to efficiently and satisfactorily serve the population and yield a fair profit to the owners.

Understored
is a condition in a community where the number of stores in relation to households is relatively low so that engaging in retailing is an attractive economic endeavor.

Overstored
is a condition in a community where the number of stores in relation to households is so large that to engage in retailing is usually unprofitable or marginally profitable.

Index of retail saturation (IRS)
is the ratio of demand for a product (households in the geographic area multiplied by annual retail expenditures for a particular line of trade per household) divided by available supply (the square footage of retail facilities of a particular line of trade in the geographic area).

DOLLAR $ & CENTS

Retailers who identify and locate in markets where the index of retail saturation is high will be able to achieve higher performance.

When the IRS takes on a high value in comparison with the line of trade in other cities, it indicates that the market is understored and therefore a potentially attractive opportunity exists. When it takes on a low value, it indicates an overstored market, which precludes the potential of a significant opportunity. Home Depot monitors its sales per square foot for a store because it recognizes that if this ratio is too high, customers may not be well served and competition may be invited into the market. In fact, if sales per square foot is more than $400, it believes it is advantageous to close a thriving store and open two smaller stores. Although this cannibalizes the existing store, it better serves customers and avoids competition entering the market.[16] In a similar strategy, McDonald's will open more restaurants in a growing area as a proactive strategy to discourage competitors such as Hardees and Burger King from building new outlets. This also enables McDonald's to protect its market share.

As an example of how the index of retail saturation is used, consider an individual planning to open a dry cleaner in either city A or city B. This individual has the following information: Residents of both cities spend $6.28 per month on dry cleaning. The total number of households in both cities is also the same 17,000. City A, however, has 2,000 square feet of dry cleaning facilities, and city B has 2,500 square feet; and our proposed square footage is 500 square feet. Given this information and using our formula for IRS, we can find the IRS for each city:

$$IRS \text{ (City A)} = 17,000 \times 6.28/(2,000 + 500) = 42.70$$
$$IRS \text{ (City B)} = 17,000 \times 6.28/(2,500 + 500) = 35.59$$

Thus, based solely on these two factors of demand (number of households and average expenditure for products by each household) and one factor of supply (the square footage of retail space serving this demand), the individual would choose to locate in city A, because its value of $42.70 is higher than city B's $35.59.

As nonstore-based retailing continues to grow, retailers need to recognize that the index of retail saturation may become less useful. That is because it only incorporates store-based retailing in the supply component of the index. This is not a problem for the preceding dry cleaner example but may be a problem for apparel retailing and computer retailing, in which many households are using mail-order catalogs.

BUYING POWER INDEX   *Sales & Marketing Management* magazine annually publishes its Survey of Buying Power. This survey reports on current data for metropolitan areas, cities, and states. It provides some data that are not readily available from other sources such as the Census Bureau. These data include retail sales by specific merchandise categories, effective buying income, and total retail sales by area, population, and retail sales.

The population, retail sales, and buying income data provide the retail manager with an overview of the potential of various trading areas. By comparing one trading area to another, the retailer can develop a relative measure of each market's potential. For each area, the retailer will develop a buying power index (BPI), which is a single weighted measure combining effective buying income (personal income, including all nontax payments such as social security, minus all taxes), retail sales, and population size into an overall indicator of a market's potential. Generally, business firms use a formula for BPI that was developed by *Sales & Marketing Management*. The BPI is weighted in the following manner:

BPI = 0.5 (the area's percentage of U.S. effective buying income) + 0.3 (the area's percentage of U.S. retail sales) + 0.2 (the area's percentage of U.S. population)

It is obvious that effective buying income is the most important factor, followed by retail sales and population. This formula can be further refined by breaking down these general figures into more specific figures geared toward the consumers of the retailer's products.

For example, XYZ Corporation, a retail chain specializing in general merchandise goods, is considering expansion into one of two different trading areas. The proposed trading areas are the Alton-Granite City, Illinois, or Hamilton-Middletown, Ohio, markets. XYZ aims its general merchandise at the 25- to 34-year-old market with incomes greater than $35,000. Therefore, the 25- to 34-year-old group will substitute for population, the general merchandise sales will substitute for total retail sales, and households with income greater than $35,000 will replace effective buying income.

Using data that can be easily obtained from *Sales & Marketing Management*, the retailer can develop the BPI for each city:

$$BPI \text{ (Alton-Granite City)} = 0.5(0.000386) + 0.3(0.00083) + 0.2(0.00012)$$
$$= 0.000466$$

$$BPI \text{ (Hamilton-Middletown)} = 0.5(0.000717) + 0.3(0.00063) + 0.2(0.000112)$$
$$= 0.000570$$

As you can see, the BPI of Hamilton-Middletown is almost 25 percent greater than that of Alton-Granite City although the cities are nearly equal in size. Therefore, XYZ would probably choose to expand its Ohio market over the Illinois market.

Remember that the BPI is broad in nature and only reflects the demand levels for the two proposed trading areas and not the supply level. Therefore, it does not reflect the saturation levels of these two markets. This can be easily taken care of by dividing the BPI for each area by the area's percentage of U.S. retail selling space for general merchandise (the supply factors) to determine each area's attractiveness:

$$IRS \text{ (Alton-Granite City)} = 0.000466/0.000452 = 1.03$$
$$IRS \text{ (Hamilton-Middletown)} = 0.000570/0.000483 = 1.18$$

In this case, the Ohio trading area is again chosen. This IRS formula does not reflect the availability of competing products or stores in nearby larger cities: Cincinnati, in the case of Hamilton-Middletown, and St. Louis, Missouri, in the case of Alton-Granite City.

Buying power index (BPI) *is an indicator of a market's overall retail potential and is comprised of weighted measures of effective buying income (personal income, including all nontax payments such as social security, minus all taxes), retail sales, and population size.*

High annual household income is a key factor in locating Land Rover dealerships.

OTHER DEMAND AND SUPPLY FACTORS   In addition to using Reilly's law, the index of retail saturation, and the buying power index in evaluating various potential markets, the successful retailer will also look at some other demand and supply factors for each market.

MARKET DEMAND POTENTIAL

In analyzing the market potential, retailers identify certain criteria that are specific to their product line or services they are selling. The criteria chosen by one retailer might not be of use to a retailer selling a different product line. The major components of market demand potential are

1. *Population characteristics.* Population characteristics are the most often used criteria to segment markets. Although total population figures and their growth rates are of primary importance to a retailer in examining potential markets, the successful retailer can obtain a more detailed profile of a market by examining school enrollment, education, age, sex, occupation, race, and nationality. Retailers should seek to match a market's population characteristics to the population characteristics of people who desire their goods and services.

2. *Buyer behavior characteristics.* Another useful criterion for analyzing potential markets is the behavioral characteristics of buyers in the market. Such characteristics include store loyalty, consumer lifestyles, store patronage motives, geographic and climatic conditions, and product benefits sought. These data, however, are not as easily obtainable as population data.

3. *Household income.* The average household income and the distribution of household incomes can significantly influence demand for retail facilities. Further insight into the demand for retail facilities is provided by Engel's laws. These laws

imply that spending increases for all categories of products as a result of an income increase but that the percentage of spending in some categories increases more than for others. Thus, as average household income rises, the community will exhibit a greater demand for luxury goods and a more sophisticated demand for necessity goods.

4. *Household age profile.* The age composition of households can be an important determinant of demand for retail facilities. In communities where households tend to be young, the preferences for stores may be different from communities where the average household is relatively old. For example, older consumers spend almost four times as much at drugstores as do 30-year-olds.

5. *Household composition.* If we hold income and age constant and change the composition of the household, we will be able to identify another determinant of the demand for retail facilities. After all, households with children have different spending habits than childless households with similar incomes.

6. *Community life cycle.* Communities tend to exhibit growth patterns over time. Growth patterns of communities may be of four major types: rapid growth, continuous growth, relatively stable growth, and finally decline. The retailer should try to identify the communities that are in a rapid or continuous growth pattern, because they will represent the best long-run opportunities.

7. *Population density.* The population density of a community equals the number of persons per square mile. Research suggests that the higher the population density, the larger the average store should be in terms of square feet and thus the fewer the number of stores that will be needed to serve a population of a given size.

8. *Mobility.* The easier it is for individuals to travel, the more mobile they will be.[17] When individuals are mobile, they are willing to travel greater distances to shop. Therefore, there will be fewer but larger stores in the community. Thus in a community where mobility is high, there will be a need for fewer retailers than in a community where mobility is low.

The most attractive market areas are those in which the preceding criteria are configured in such a way that they represent maximum market potential for a particular retailer. This will vary by the type of retailer and the product lines it handles. In assessing different market areas, a retailer should first establish the market demand potential criteria that characterize the desired target market it would like to attract. Exhibit 7.5 illustrates this concept with a fast-food drive-in chain that sells hamburgers, hot dogs, and drinks. This fast-food chain is a 1950s-style drive-in where people usually order burgers and drinks in their autos and car-hops provide service.

Exhibit 7.5 shows that the chain has determined that there are seven demographic factors that have a positive impact on fast-food restaurant sales. One of these factors may need explanation. Through research, the chain has determined that its restaurants do better when at least 75 percent of the work force travels less than 14 minutes to work. When individuals have to travel longer to work, they get tired and frustrated about being in their cars and thus are not likely to be interested in eating in their auto at a drive-in restaurant. You might examine the other six demographic factors and develop an explanation for why they would be related to the success of a fast-food drive-in restaurant. The information in Exhibit 7.5 shows the desired target market and data on the seven demographic factors for two possible communities. From analyzing these data, you should conclude that community B is the most attractive market to enter from a demand potential basis.

EXHIBIT 7.5	IDENTIFYING COMMUNITIES WITH HIGH DEMAND POTENTIAL FOR A FAST-FOOD DRIVE-IN RESTAURANT		
DEMOGRAPHIC CHARACTERISTIC	DESIRED TARGET MARKET	COMMUNITY A	COMMUNITY B
Population per Square Mile	over 400	375	423
Median Family Income	over $31,000	$28,024	$32,418
% Population 14–54	over 60%	48%	63%
% White Collar	over 50%	38%	54%
% People Living in 1–3 Person Units	over 70%	61%	72%
% Workforce Traveling 0–14 Minutes to Work	over 75%	49%	74%
Average Annual Household Expenditure on Eating Out	over $600	$521	$619

MARKET SUPPLY FACTORS

In deciding to enter a new market, the successful retailer will spend time analyzing the competition. The retailer should consider square feet per store and square feet per employee, store growth, and the quality of competition.

1. *Square feet per store.* It will be helpful if the retailer has data on the square feet per store for the average store in the communities that are being analyzed. These data will indicate whether the community tends to have large- or small-scale retailing. And, of course, this is important in terms of assessing the extent to which the retailer's standard type of store would blend with the existing structure of retail trade in the community.

2. *Square feet per employee.* A measure that combines two major supply factors in retailing, store space and labor, is square feet of space per employee. A high number for this statistic in a community is evidence that each employee is able to handle more space. This could be due to either a high level of retail technology in the community or more self-service retailing. Because retail technology is fairly constant across communities, any difference in square feet per employee is most often due to the level of service being provided. In communities currently characterized by retailers as offering a high level of service, there may be a significant opportunity for new retailers that are oriented toward self-service.

3. *Growth in stores.* The retailer should look at the rate of growth in the number of stores over the past one to five years. When the growth is rapid, then, on average, the community will have better located stores with more contemporary atmospheres. More recently located stores will coincide better with the existing demographics of the community. Their atmosphere will also better suit the tastes of the marketplace, and they will tend to incorporate the latest in retail technology. All these factors hint that the strength of retail competition will be greater when the community has recently experienced rapid growth in the number of stores. Retailers, as well as entrepreneurs, can obtain the information needed for computing the square feet per store, square feet per employee, and growth in stores from the Urban Land Institute's *Dollars and Cents of Shopping Centers,* the National Mall Monitor's *Store Retail Tenant Directory,* and Lebhar-Friedman's *Chain Store Guide.*

4. *Quality of competition.* The three preceding supply factors have reflected the quantity of competition. Retailers also need to look at the strength or quality of competition. They should attempt to identify the major retail chains and local retailers in each market and evaluate the strength of each. Answers to questions such as the following would be insightful: What is their market share or profitability? How promotional- and price-oriented are they? Are they customer-oriented? Do they tend to react to new market entrants by cutting price, increasing advertising, or improving customer service? A retailer would think twice before competing with Wal-Mart and Kmart on price, Dillard's on cost control, Bloomingdale's on fashion, and Nordstrom on service.

Quite often when a large discount retailer such as Wal-Mart enters a small community with an extra 80,000 to 100,000 square feet of retail space, existing small town retailers think that they can't compete and must close down. This is undoubtedly true of the weaker of these retailers, but despite Wal-Mart's enormous buying advantages, small-town retailers can compete head-on with Wal-Mart by providing better customer service, adjusting prices on products carried by Wal-Mart, and remaining open Sundays and evenings. Customers will appreciate the increased standard of living that Wal-Mart's prices make possible, and as a result the trading area will increase. The apparel retailer, for example, will have to cut down on basic stock items such as socks and underwear but increase its inventory of specialty or novelty items. The sales lost on basic items will be overcome with these newer items and the larger trading area Wal-Mart provides.

SITE ANALYSIS

LO • 5
Discuss the various attributes considered in evaluating retail sites within a retail market

Once retailers have identified the best potential market, the next task is to perform a more detailed analysis of the market. Only after the market is carefully analyzed can the retailer choose the best site (or sites) available. Site analysis consists of an evaluation of the density of demand and supply within each market. It should be augmented by an identification of the most attractive sites that are currently available within each market. The third and final step, site selection, will be the selection of the best possible site.

Site analysis begins by evaluating the density of demand and supply of various areas within the chosen market by census tract, ZIP code, or some other meaningful

Site analysis
is an evaluation of the density of demand and supply within each market with the goal of identifying the best retail site(s).

geographic factor and then identifying the most attractive sites, given the retailer's requirements, available for new stores within each market. One of the advantages of using census tract data is the availability of data for census tracts published by the Census Bureau.

Census tracts are relatively small statistical subdivisions that vary in population from about 2,500 to 8,000 and are designed to include fairly homogeneous populations. They are most often found in cities and in counties of metropolitan areas (i.e., the more densely populated areas of the nation).

SIZE OF TRADING AREAS

Earlier we discussed the general trading area of a community. Our attention now shifts to how to determine and evaluate the trading area of specific sites within markets. In short, we attempt to estimate the geographic area from which a store located at a particular site will be able to attract customers.

At the same time that Reilly was developing his theory to determine the trading area for communities, William Applebaum designed a technique specifically for determining and evaluating trading areas for an individual store. Applebaum's technique was based on customer spottings. For each $100 in weekly store sales, a customer was randomly selected or spotted for an interview. These spottings usually didn't require much time because the interviewer only requested demographic information, shopping habits, and some pertinent consumer attitudes toward the store and its competitors. After the home addresses of the shoppers were plotted on a map, the analyst could make some inferences about trading area size and the competition.[18] Exhibit 7.6 is an example of a map generated by using customer spottings.

Thus it is relatively easy to define the trading area of an existing store. All that is necessary is to interview current customers of the store to determine where they reside. For a new store, however, the task is not so easy. There is a fair amount of conventional wisdom that has withstood the test of time about the correlation of trading area size, which can be summarized as follows:

1. Stores that sell products that the consumer wants to purchase in the most convenient manner will have a smaller trading area than so-called specialty products.
2. As consumer mobility increases, the size of the store's trading area increases.
3. As the size of the store increases, its trading area increases, because it can stock a broader and deeper assortment of merchandise, which will attract customers from greater distances.
4. As the distance between competing stores increases, their trading areas will increase.
5. Natural and synthetic obstacles such as rivers, mountains, railroads, and freeways can abruptly stop the boundaries of a trading area.

DESCRIPTION OF TRADING AREA

Retailers can access at relatively low cost information concerning the trading area for various retail locations and the buyer behavior of the trading area. If you go to the web sites for any of the firms providing GISs that were mentioned on p. 228, you will be able to see how readily available this information is to the typical retailer. For example, see Equifax/National Decision Systems (http://www.ends.com).

EXHIBIT 7.6	CUSTOMER SPOTTING MAP FOR A SUPERMARKET

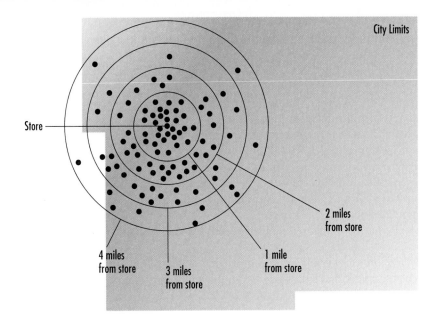

MicroVision is a product of Equifax/National Decision Systems, which is one of the nation's premier market research firms specializing in developing psychographic or lifestyle analyses of geographic areas. MicroVision is based on the old adage that birds of a feather flock together. In other words, even though the total makeup of the American marketplace is very complex and diverse, neighborhoods tend to be just the opposite. People tend to feel most comfortable living in areas with others who are like them. Think for a moment of the place where you are living now as a student and of your parent's home and you will most likely see the truth of the adage mentioned previously.

There are many possible reasons that consumers may live in homogeneous neighborhoods. One may be income because people must be able to afford the homes. However, income alone is probably not the answer, because many types of neighborhoods have similar income levels. Factors such as age, occupation, family status, race, culture, religion, population density, urbanization, and housing types can all distinguish between very different types of neighborhoods that have similar incomes. Therefore, these other factors are usually more important for the retailer to consider than income alone.

In distinguishing between neighborhood types, MicroVision and similar products use two basic criteria. First, each type of neighborhood must be different enough from all the others to make it a distinct marketing segment. Second, there must be enough people living in each type of neighborhood to make it a worthwhile segment to retailers. Using a variety of databases including U.S. Census data and proprietary computer software, MicroVision found 50 neighborhood types in the United States. These types are distinguished from each other in many ways. Some are based primarily on income, some are family-oriented, some are race-oriented, some are urban, some suburban, and some rural. Most combine two or more distinguishing demographic characteristics. Exhibit 7.7 identifies 10 of the 50 neighborhood types.

EXHIBIT 7.7	TEN EXAMPLES OF MICROVISION NEIGHBORHOOD TYPES
NEIGHBORHOOD TYPES	**DESCRIPTORS**
Upper Crust	*Demographics:* Very high income married couples, age 40 to 69, with one or more children *Lifestyles:* Go casino gambling, attend live theater, play golf, write elected officials, and contribute to PBS *Retail:* Buy precious jewelry, home furnishings and improvements, coffee grinders, ice cream makers and golf clubs *Financial:* Have an asset management account, US bonds, whole life and individual medical insurance, and own a business *Media:* Read *Consumer Reports,* airline, business and science magazines; listen to classical music and news radio stations; and watch "Nightline" and news specials *Geography:* Suburbs of New York, Chicago, San Francisco, Washington, D.C.
Movers and Shakers	*Demographics:* Very high income singles, age 25 to 54, with no children, one or two adults *Lifestyle:* Recycle products, phone radio stations, do fund-raisers, participate in environmental causes and lift weights *Retail:* Order flowers by wire, purchase greeting cards, soft contact lenses, laptop PC, Honda automobile and light beer *Financial:* Have asset management account, VISA, accidental D&D, use financial planner, and has publicly held stock *Media:* Read Money, Consumer Reports and Epicurean magazines; listen to album-oriented rock stations; and watches Seinfeld *Geography:* Suburban areas such as Raleigh Durham, NC; Austin, TX; Madison, WI; and Gainesville, FL
Home Sweet Home	*Demographics:* High income married couples, age 40 to 69, with one or two children *Lifestyle:* Get oil changed at quick lube shops, participate in home energy audit, go snow skiing, frequent flyer member *Retail:* Buy racquetball equipment, men's business suit, snow blower, wallpaper, gas dryer, doll accessories *Financial:* Have savings bonds, home equity line of credit, municipal bond fund, $200K in investable assets, obtained an IRA from broker *Media:* Read daily newspaper; listen to soft contemporary stations between 3 and 6 P.M.; and watch the World Series *Geography:* Suburban areas across the country, especially Hartford, CT
Great Beginnings	*Demographics:* Moderate income singles, age 18 to 39, with no children *Lifestyle:* Play billiards, go bowling, play softball, drink beer, belong to a health club, make infomercial purchases *Retail:* Buy sub-compact car, pager, water purifier, PC for on-line services, Toyota or Nissan automobile *Financial:* Have an education loan, overdraft protection, passbook account, and uses ATM card to buy goods *Media:* Read People magazine listen to album-oriented rock stations; watch primetime sitcoms, Entertainment This Week, The Simpsons and Star Trek — Next Generation (Syndicated) *Geography:* Along the East and West Coasts, especially Boston, Miami, and Seattle
Country Home Families	*Demographics:* Moderate income married couples, age 35 to 50, with two or more children

NEIGHBORHOOD TYPES	DESCRIPTORS
	Lifestyle: Do crafts, own a dog or cat, go bowling, camping, fishing, gardening and change their own car's oil
	Retail: Buy chain saw, electric drill, riding lawn mower, separate freezer, video camera, infant or preschooler toys
	Financial: Have a home equity line of credit, auto loan through a bank, IRA from an insurer, use teller and drive-through teller
	Media: Read *Popular Mechanics,* fishing and hunting magazines; listen to country stations; and watch Home Improvement, Roseanne and entertainment specials
	Geography: Northern areas, especially Bend, OR and Harrisburg, PA
Settled In	*Demographics:* Moderate income married couples, over 55, with no children
	Lifestyle: Collects coins, play the lottery, veterans club member, uses utility's balanced billing program, go bowling
	Retail: Buy light beer, heavy coupon user, QVC customer, added kitchen plumbing and attic and wall insulation
	Financial: Have variable payment annuity, obtain financial advice from broker, and purchases Prudential life insurance
	Media: Read daily newspaper and Ladies Home Journal; listen to middle-to-the-road radio stations; and watches This Old House, Wings, The Weather Channel and Lifetime
	Geography: Primarily suburban areas around Great Lakes and Midwest
Books and New Recruits	*Demographics:* Low income singles, age 18 to 24, with no children, two to four adults
	Lifestyles: Go to barber shop, use laundromat, entertain at home, play basketball, go hunting, to the movies, and play cards
	Retail: Buy sub-compact car, designer jeans, men's sweatpants, and heavy convenience store shopper
	Financial: Bank by mail, let life insurance policy lapse, have renter's insurance, maintain a stock fund
	Media: Read Newsweek, Glamour and Sports Illustrated; listen to contemporary hits station on weekends; and watch Hard Copy, Home Improvement and Headline News
	Geography: Urban and suburban areas across the country
On Their Own	*Demographics:* Low income singles, age 18 to 39, with no children, one or two people
	Lifestyles: Go dancing, jogging, get oil changed at quick lube centers, frequently refer to the Yellow Pages, drink bourbon
	Retail: Buy compact car, women's pants suits, soft contact lenses, dress boots, answering machine, and home delivery meals
	Financial: Have renter's insurance, get financial advice from a broker, never have done business with an insurance agent
	Media: Read men's magazines; and watch primetime dramas, The Tonight Show, MTV, and Night Court (Syndicated)
	Geography: Warm weather suburbs in Nevada, Arizona, and Florida
Trying Metro Times	*Demographics:* Very low income singles, age 18 to 24 and over 70, with no children
	Lifestyle: Heavy video renters, smoke cigarettes, listen to cable radio, and play video games daily
	Retail: Eat Mexican fast-food, purchase women's designer jeans, never purchase from mail order catalog

continued

EXHIBIT 7.7	CONTINUED
NEIGHBORHOOD TYPES	**DESCRIPTORS**
University USA	*Financial:* Get financial advice from family and friends, never used a broker, and have a loan from a consumer finance company
	Media: Read National Enquirer, and watch The Simpsons, Married With Children, Cops, Cheers (Syndicated), Nickelodeon, The Nashville Network
	Geography: Urban parts of Oklahoma City; Buffalo, NY; Colorado Springs
	Demographics: Very low income singles, age 18 to 24, with no children
	Lifestyle: Go to health club, dancing, night clubs, use quick copy services, and participate in environmental causes
	Retail: Buy imported car, heavy convenience store shopper, light grocery store shopper, eat a lot of fast-food
	Financial: Have no-interest checking account, education loan, renter's insurance, VISA card, and use phone to transfer funds
	Media: Read science, automotive, sports, music and women's fashion magazines; listen to progressive rock stations; and watch The Simpsons, Beverly Hills 90210, MTV
	Geography: College towns: Columbus, OH; Lubbock, TX; Eugene, OR

SOURCE: MicroVision web site [http://www.ends.com]

The names of the neighborhoods try to capture the essence of the neighborhood and provide an easy way of remembering distinctions. Also associated with the neighborhoods are demographics, lifestyle, retail opportunities, and financial and media habits. Consider, for example, MicroVision segment "Country Home Families." This segment represents retail opportunities for chain saws, electric drills, riding lawn mowers, freezers, video cameras, and infant and preschooler toys. However, the more affluent MicroVision segment, "Upper Crust," represents retail opportunities for precious jewelry, home furnishings and improvements, coffee grinders, ice cream makers, and golf clubs.

DEMAND DENSITY

Demand density
is the extent to which the potential demand for the retailer's goods and services is concentrated in certain census tracts, ZIP code areas, or parts of the community.

The extent to which potential demand for the retailer's goods and services is concentrated in certain census tracts, ZIP code areas, or parts of the community is called demand density. To determine the extent of demand density, retailers need to identify what they believe to be the major variables influencing their potential demand. One such method of identifying these variables is by examining the types of customers who already shop in the retailer's present stores. The variables identified should be standard demographic variables, such as age, income, and education, because readily available data will exist on them. Let us construct an example.

A retailer is evaluating the possibility of locating in a community that has geographic boundaries as shown in Exhibit 7.8. It is comprised of 23 census tracts. The community is bordered on the west by a mountain range, on the north and south by major highways, and on the east by railroad tracks. The retailer has decided that three

EXHIBIT 7.8   DEMAND-DENSITY MAP

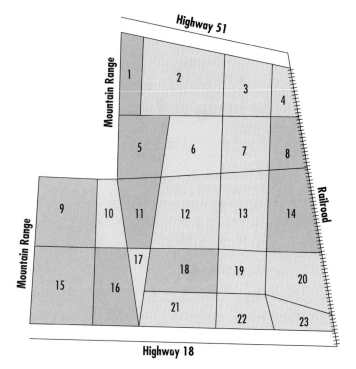

Three-Variable Demand-Density Map
Variable 1 = Median income over $22,000
Variable 2 = Households per square mile greater than 1,200
Variable 3 = Average growth in population over last 3 years
    in excess of 3 percent per year
Number of Variables Met

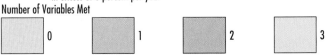

variables are especially important in determining the potential demand: median household income of more than $22,000, households per square mile in excess of 1,200, and average growth in population of at least 3 percent per year over the past three years. In Exhibit 7.8, a thematic map is presented that shows the extent to which these three conditions are met for each of the 23 census tracts in the community undergoing evaluation. Thus you can easily visualize the density of potential demand in each tract. You should note that only three tracts (6, 10, 17) meet all three conditions.

Another method of looking at potential demand for a retailer's product could incorporate the data mentioned earlier when discussing neighborhood types. In this example, suppose a retail computer chain wanted to enter the Los Angeles market. The chain would first determine, from its own records, which MicroVision neighborhood types accounted for the largest sales in comparison with the national average of its product categories. In this case, household neighborhood types Movers and Shakers and Great Beginnings would be attractive locations for a computer store (see Exhibit 7.7).

EXHIBIT 7.9	STORE DENSITY AND SITE AVAILABILITY MAP

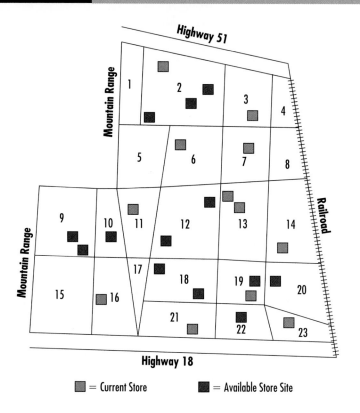

= Current Store   ■ = Available Store Site

SUPPLY DENSITY

Supply density
is the extent to which retailers are concentrated in different geographic areas of a community.

Although the demand-density map allows you to identify the area within a community that represents the highest potential demand, the location of existing retail establishments should also be mapped. This will allow you to examine the supply density (i.e., the extent to which retailers are concentrated in different areas of the market under question).

Exhibit 7.9 shows the density of stores in the community that we saw in Exhibit 7.8. Exhibit 7.9 reveals that two census tracts (10 and 17) of the three most attractive ones have a lack of stores. Also, in two of the four census tracts with fairly attractive demand density (two of the three conditions met), there are currently no retail outlets (see tracts 1 and 5).

SITE AVAILABILITY

Just because demand outstrips supply in certain geographic locations does not immediately imply that stores should be located in those locations. Sites must be available.

A map should be constructed of available sites in each community being analyzed. We have done this in conjunction with the supply-density map in Exhibit 7.9. The only available site in the top seven census tracts (in terms of demand density) is in census

EXHIBIT 7.10   **CHECKLIST FOR SITE EVALUATIONS**

Local Demographics
  Population and/or household base
  Population growth potential
  Lifestyles of consumers
  Income potential
  Age makeup
  Educational makeup
  Population of nearby special markets, that is, daytime workers, students, and tourists, if applicable
  Occupation mix

Traffic Flow and Accessibility
  Number and type of vehicles passing location
  Access of vehicles to location
  Number and type of pedestrians passing location
  Availability of mass transit, if applicable
  Accessibility of major highway artery
  Quality of access streets
  Level of street congestion
  Presence of physical barriers that affect trade area shape

Retail Competition
  Number and types of stores in area
  Analysis of "key" players in general area
  Competitiveness of other merchants
  Number and location of direct competitors in area
  Possibility of joint promotions with local merchants

Site Characteristic
  Number of parking spaces available
  Distance of parking areas
  Ease of access for delivery
  Visibility of site from street
  History of the site
  Compatibility of neighboring stores
  Size and shape of lot
  Condition of existing building
  Ease of entrance and exit for traffic
  Ease of access for handicapped customers
  Restrictions on sign usage
  Building safety code restrictions
  Type of zoning

Cost Factors
  Terms of lease/rent agreement
  Basic rent payments
  Length of lease
  Local taxes
  Operations and maintenance costs
  Restrictive clauses in lease
  Membership in local merchants association required
  Voluntary regulations by local merchants

The authors acknowledge the contribution of Mr. Christopher D. Boring of Retail Planning Associates, Columbus, Ohio.

tract 10. In tracts 1, 5, and 17, which currently have no retail outlets, no sites are available, which may explain the present lack of stores in these areas. Perhaps these tracts are zoned totally for residential use.

Although Exhibit 7.9 seems to show only one good potential site, several more may exist. Census tract 9 borders the high-density tract 10, in which there are no stores and in which only one site is available for a new store. Tract 9, however, has two available sites. Furthermore, tract 12 has an available site that is close to the borders of tracts 11 and 17, which are both attractive but lack available sites. This same kind of analysis can be done with our high-fashion chain in looking over the Los Angeles market. Some retailers have developed a checklist of all the items they want to consider during the site analysis stage. One such list is shown in Exhibit 7.10.

LO • 6
Explain how to select the best geographic site for a store

SITE SELECTION DECISION PROCESS

On completing the analysis of each segment of the desired market and having identified the best available sites within each market, retailers are now ready to make the final decision regarding location: selecting the best site (or sites) available. Retailers are well advised to use the assistance of a real estate professional in this stage. Even if the retailers or their staff have done all the analysis to this point, the assistance of a real estate professional still should be used here. In fact, more and more large retail firms set up separate corporations to handle only their real estate transactions.

100 percent location
is when there is no better use for a site than the retail store that is being planned for that site; it is the best possible use of the site.

In principle, all retailers should attempt to find a 100 percent location for their stores. A 100 percent location is a location where there is no better use for the site than the retail store that is being planned. Retailers should remember that what may be a 100 percent site for one store may not be for another. The best location for a supermarket may not be the best location for a discount department store.

How is the 100 percent location or site identified? Unfortunately, there is no best answer to this basic question. There is, however, general agreement on the types of things that the retailer should consider in evaluating sites: the nature of the site, traffic characteristics, type of neighbors, and the terms of purchase or lease.

NATURE OF SITE

Is the site currently a vacant store, a vacant parcel of land, or the site of a planned shopping center? Many of the available retail sites will be vacant stores. This is because 10 to 15 percent of stores go out of business each year. This does not mean that just because a men's apparel store failed in a location, that a bookstore would do likewise. However, sometimes a piece of property becomes known as jinxed because of the high number of business failures that have occurred there. Such was the case, as pointed out in Winners & Losers box on page 250, of some property in Skokie, Illinois, in the late 1980s.

When the retail site that appears to be most suited to the retailer's needs is a vacant parcel of land, the retailer needs to investigate why it is vacant. Why have others passed up the site? Was it previously not for sale or was it priced too high? Or is there some other reason? For instance, many supermarkets abandon 20,000-square-feet locations to move to newer 65,000-square-feet sites. These abandoned sites usually are available at lower costs and are not necessarily bad locations. Wal-Mart identified a vacant plot

of land on which to build a store in Falmouth, Virginia, but on announcing its plans to build on the site ran into major opposition. The land was the boyhood home and farm that President George Washington grew up on and local preservations and the National Trust for Historic Preservation did not want the place disturbed.[19]

Finally, the site may be part of a planned shopping center. In this case, the retailer can usually be assured that it will have the proper mix of neighbors, adequate parking facilities, and good traffic. Sometimes, of course, the center has not been properly planned, and the retailer needs to be aware of these special cases. It is difficult to succeed in a shopping center in which a high percentage of space is not rented.

TRAFFIC CHARACTERISTICS
The traffic that passes a site, whether it is vehicular or pedestrian, can be an important determinant of the potential sales at that site. However, more than traffic flow is important. The retailer must also determine whether the population and traffic are of the type desired. For example, a retailer of fine furs and leather coats may be considering two alternative sites. One site might be in the CBD and the other in a group of specialty stores in a small shopping center in a very exclusive residential area. The CBD site may generate more total traffic, but the alternative site may generate more of the right type of traffic.

The retailer should evaluate two traffic-related aspects of the site. The first is the availability of sufficient parking, either at the site or nearby. One of the advantages of shopping centers is the availability of adequate parking space. If the site is not a shopping center, then the retailer will need to determine if the parking space will be adequate. It is difficult to give a precise guideline for the space that will be needed. Generally, it is a function of four factors: size of the store, frequency of customer visits, length of customer visits, and availability of public transportation. As a rule of thumb, shopping centers estimate that there should be five spaces for every 1,000 square feet of selling space in medium-sized centers and 10 spaces per 1,000 square feet in large centers.

A second traffic-related aspect the retailer should consider is the ease with which consumers can reach the store site. Are the roadways in good shape? Are there traffic barriers (rivers with a limited number of bridges, interstate highways with limited crossings; one-way streets, and heavy street use resulting in congestion limiting exits to the site)? Remember that customers will normally avoid heavily congested shopping areas and shop elsewhere to minimize driving time and other difficulties.

TYPE OF NEIGHBORS
What are the neighboring establishments that surround the site? There can be good and bad neighbors. What is a good or bad neighbor depends on the type of store that one is considering operating at the site. Suppose that you plan to open a children's apparel store and are considering two alternative sites. One site has a toy store and a gift shop as neighbors. The other site has a bowling alley and an adult book store as neighbors. Obviously, you know what the good and bad neighbors are.

However, determining the good and bad neighbors may not always be that easy, especially for an entrepreneur. A good neighboring business will be one that is compatible with the retailer's line of trade. When two or more businesses are compatible, they can actually help generate business for each other. For example, a paint store, hardware store, and auto parts store located next to one another may increase total traffic and thus benefit them all.

Research has found that retailers experience a benefit from store compatibility. That is, when two compatible, or very similar, businesses (i.e., two shoe stores) locate

Store compatibility *exists when two similar retail businesses locate next to or nearby each other and they realize a sales volume greater than what they would have achieved if they were located apart from each other.*

SKOKIE'S JINXED LOCATION

The retailer has done all the correct things. He or she has double-checked every item on the list, and the location seems perfect. It has it all: pleasant facade, ample parking, heavy traffic passing it every day, easy access, and a rent that is within budget. In short, it is a prime business site. Yet time after time, it seems, some new enterprise there is struggling to make a go of it. Or the place stands empty. In Skokie, Illinois, a north Chicago suburb, 3445 W. Dempster is just that spot. Despite being an ideal location on everybody's checklist, 10 restaurants have come and gone in the past two decades. It's become an eyesore because it's empty so constantly, said a nearby competitor. Individuals say it's jinxed. Jinxed? Real estate experts scoff at such talk. Curses don't cause retailers to fail. Poor management does. Still, experts agree that once several businesses fold in the same spot, a stigma can develop. Customers start avoiding the place. A psychology of failure takes hold. A look at 3445 W. Dempster shows how repeated failures at the same spot can develop, sometimes for unexpected reasons. When different businesses flounder on the same site, the finger naturally points to location. But the tale of woe at 3445 W. Dempster shows how managerial mistakes and plain bad luck can follow a jinxed location more than location itself. As failure follows failure, new owners need ever greater skill to overcome the stigma. Few locations seem more jinxed than 3445 W. Dempster. Restaurants have tried one strategy after another. Menus have run the gamut: French, American, kosher, Greek. There have been steak houses, fish houses, and glorified snack shops. For years, rumors have circulated that a customer choked to death in the jinxed location and that a body was found hanging in the basement. Neither story is true, but truth doesn't always stop rumors. From the early 1940s until 1962, Isbell's Nautical Inn was a success there. However, since Mr. Isbell's death in 1962, no restaurant at 3445 has approached the inn's tenure. Some people believe Isbell put a curse on the place. Recent proprietors, lacking Mr. Isbell's feel for the business, have been overwhelmed by troubles. One had little understanding of the neighborhood when he bought the property in 1978, eager to open a disco there. Residents, however, complained a disco would attract a trashy element, and Skokie officials denied his plans. A year later, the place was leased to three men who aspired to start a chain. Their restaurant, Reel People, made a name for itself quickly. But within a year it failed. Then, others tried to run another fish restaurant, Just for the Halibut. At noon on opening day, a fire extinguisher suddenly went off in the kitchen, forcing

near each other, they will achieve a sales volume greater than what they would have achieved if they were located apart from each other.[20]

Some retailing experts claim that this clustering of similar retailers together dates back to the 1950s, when the choicest location for a gas station was believed to be an intersection that already had three other stations. Today, we see it with shoe stores in malls, auto dealerships, furniture stores, and restaurants. Clustering of stores allows customers to walk from store to store, comparing prices, products, and service.

The Behind the Scenes box on page 252 points out an interesting fact about who retailers want to locate next to when they sign leases for space in shopping centers anchored by large discounters and/or off-price chains. They are hoping to draw from these larger store's customers; however, what is interesting is the combination of stores and their preferred neighbors.

them to close and mop up. It happened again a week later. The new owners had to close again not long afterward when the block lost electrical power for 36 hours. The next tenant was a hotel banquet waiter with dreams of running his own place. He did some market research by having someone check out the menus and prices of the competition. He mailed out 6,000 menus to area residents. And at the outset, customers complimented him on the fish he served. But the cursory research hadn't uncovered the fact that many elderly customers spent their winters in the South. By November 1986, three months after opening, monthly sales fell far short of the break-even point. Soon afterward, the tenant suffered a mild heart attack and is now a waiter at another restaurant. Next came a Greek restaurateur. He aimed to compete with a Jewish deli across the street by offering a broader menu and charging more. At the suggestion of a local resident, he called his place Ess-N-Fress, a Yiddish expression for eating a lot. But the name backfired with some Jewish residents. Meanwhile, other unexpected events occurred. Road construction decreased business. Many waitresses quit as they feared the restaurant would fail like its predecessors. Shortly before Christmas 1987, just eight months af-

ter opening, heavy rains caused the ceiling to collapse. Another failure. On top of all the mistakes and bad luck, location itself may have played some role in the 3445 W. Dempster woes. Some restaurant experts say the site lies outside the habitual traffic pattern of Skokie residents, even though it is full of commuters during rush hours. Sometimes businesses suffer because they are just outside the flow of traffic, not quite visible from the road or one block away from success. But location is often less a villain than it might seem. In Dun & Bradstreet surveys, poor location is cited as a reason for only 0.1 percent of business failures. Even in the retail trade category, which includes restaurants, the figure is only 0.6 percent. Restaurant consultants still rate the location as an above-average B site. Family incomes are well above average in Skokie. Several veteran establishments nearby on the street demonstrate the market's strength.

DO YOU WANT TO RENT 3445 W. DEMPSTER?

SOURCE: Author's visit to site and "In Skokie, Hapless Habitat Fights a Jinx," *Wall Street Journal*, November 3, 1989: B2. Dow Jones & Company, Inc. All Rights Reserved Worldwide. Reprinted by permission of *Wall Street Journal*.

TERMS OF PURCHASE OR LEASE

One consideration for the retailer at this point is the lease terms. The retailer should review the length of the lease (it could be too long or too short), the exclusivity clause (whether or not the retailer will be the only one allowed to sell a certain line of merchandise), the guaranteed traffic rate (a reduction in rent if the shopping center fails to achieve a targeted traffic level), and an anchor clause (which would also allow for a rent reduction if the anchor store in a developing center doesn't open on time or when you open). Lease arrangements generally call for either a fixed payment, in which the rental charge is usually based on a fixed amount per month, or a variable payment, in which rent is a specified percentage of sales with a guaranteed minimum rent. It is important for the retailer to choose the one that is best.

IF RETAILERS COULD SELECT THEIR NEIGHBORS

If retailers could select their neighbors when they lease space in a mall, here's who they would "want to be next to."

Retailer	Next To
A Pea In The Pod (apparel)	Talbot's, Ann Taylor, Williams-Sonoma, Neiman-Marcus, Saks Fifth Avenue
Just Closeouts/It's a Dollar	Wal-Mart, Kmart
Menard's Home Improvement	Wal-Mart, T.J. Maxx, Kmart, Lord & Taylor
Orchard Supply Hardware	Price-Costco, Sam's Club, Kmart
Corey's Jewelry	Sears, JCPenney, Hudson's
Imposters Copy Jewels	Nordstrom, Ann Taylor

Retailer	Next To
Record Giant	Wal-Mart, Kmart
Fay's Drug Stores	T.J. Maxx, Kmart, Lord & Taylor
Dollar Tree	Kmart, Wal-Mart
Cato Fashion	Kmart, Wal-Mart
Benetton	Nordstrom, Bloomingdale's, Saks Fifth Avenue
Frank's Nursery and Crafts	Toys "Я" Us, Circuit City, T.J. Maxx, Marshalls
Welcome Home	Liz Claiborne, Polo, Nike, Wal-Mart
A&P	Wal-Mart, Kmart, T.J. Maxx

SOURCE: Based on *The Dealmaker* (PO Box 429, Belle Mead, NJ 08502), December 18, 1992. Used with Permission.

When the retailer decides to locate in a shopping center, it usually has no other choice than to lease. However, in the case of a free-standing location, an outright purchase is often possible. Let's consider the purchase alternative.

In considering a site for purchase, the retailer should look at the purchase price, how that price relates to a fair value, and the terms of financing. Regarding financing, one should consider the term of the loan (5, 15, or 30 years) and whether the interest rate is fixed or varies each year based on the general level of interest rates. The retailer should have a structural engineer check the building to make certain that it is safe for the purposes intended; the building should also be certified to be free of termites and asbestos. In addition, it is wise to check the condition of the heating and cooling system. Finally, an environmental impact assessment of the land should be made to determine if it is free of hazardous contamination. This is especially true for old gasoline service station building sites with leaky gasoline storage tanks. Incidentally, the person or firm that holds legal title to the land is legally responsible for any hazardous waste cleanup on the site regardless of who deposited the waste at the site.

At last, the site is a reality, and the store is open and operating. In the early weeks of operation, careful attention needs to be given to sales performance. Are sales materializing at the level anticipated? If not, what is the cause? Is it a management or merchandising failure or is it due to poor site selection? If the performance is attributable to poor management or merchandising, corrective action needs to be taken as soon as possible. If a poor site was selected, then the retailer can only hope to learn from its error. However, if retailers carefully plan new locations (as we have suggested), then errors in site selection should be minimal. It should be pointed out that chains can usually learn from their past errors, whereas individual store owners usually go out of business. This is but one reason for the high number of retail failures each year.

EXPECTED PROFITABILITY

The final step in site selection analysis is construction of a pro forma (expected) return on asset model for each possible site. The return on asset model comprises three crucial variables: net profit margin, asset turnover, and return on assets.

For purposes of evaluating sites, the potential return on equity is not relevant. This is because the financial leverage ratio (total assets divided by equity) is a top management decision, which represents how much debt the retail enterprise is willing to assume. Most likely, the question of how to finance new store growth has already been answered or at least contemplated. The retailer should already have determined that it has or can obtain the capital to finance a new store. It is therefore reasonable and appropriate to evaluate sites on their potential return on assets and not return on equity.

If the retailer is to evaluate sites on their potential return on assets, it will need at least three estimates: total sales, total assets, and net profit. Each of these is likely to vary depending on the site. Sales estimates will be different for alternative sites because each will have unique trade area characteristics such as the number and nature of households and the level of competition. Estimated total assets could vary because the alternative sites will likely have different prices and the cost of construction could also vary. Finally, estimated profits could vary not only due to varying sales for the different sites but different operating costs. For example, some sites may be in areas where labor expenses are higher, taxes are higher, or insurance rates are higher.

STUDENT STUDY GUIDE

SUMMARY   Selection of a target market and determining which retail format to use to most effectively reach this market are two of the most important decisions a retailer will make. The retailer can reach potential customers through both store-based retail locations and nonstore retail formats. GISs can help the retailer gain knowledge of its potential customers and where they reside and how they behave. This can help the retailer better know how to reach its target market.

Most of the chapter discussed how to select a location for a store-based retailer. The choice of retail location involves three decisions: (1) market identification, identifying the most attractive markets; (2) site analysis, evaluating the demand and supply within each market; and (3) site selection, selecting the best site (or sites) available.

LO•1 EXPLAIN THE CRITERIA USED IN SELECTING A TARGET MARKET.   We began this chapter by stating that an effective target market must be one that is measurable, accessible, and substantial. Measurability deals with if objective data exists on the attributes of the target market. Accessibility deals with the extent to which marketing efforts can be uniquely targeted at a particular segment of the market. Substantiability deals with the extent to which the target market is of sufficient size that it is economically worth pursuing.

LO•2 IDENTIFY THE DIFFERENT OPTIONS, BOTH STORE-BASED AND NONSTORE-BASED, FOR EFFECTIVELY REACHING THE RETAILER'S TARGET MARKET AND IDENTIFY THE ADVANTAGES AND DISADVANTAGES OF BUSINESS DISTRICTS, SHOPPING CENTERS, AND FREE-STANDING UNITS AS SITES FOR RETAIL LOCATION?   We next reviewed the four store-based location alternatives available to the retailer: the business district, the shopping center/mall, the free-standing unit, and the nontraditional store location. The business district is generally an unplanned shopping area around the geographic point where most cities originated and grew up. As the cities have grown, we witnessed an expansion of two newer types of business districts: the SBD and the NBD.

A shopping center or mall is a centrally owned and/or managed shopping district that is planned, has balanced tenancy, and is surrounded by parking facilities. It has one or more anchor stores and a variety of smaller stores. Because of the many advantages shopping centers can offer the retailer, they are a fixture of American life and account for 55 percent of all retail sales in the United States.

A free-standing retailer generally locates along major traffic arteries. There are usually no adjacent retailers selling competing products with which the retailer will have to share traffic.

The retailer also has six nonstore-based options: street peddling, mail-order, automatic merchandising machines, direct selling methods, interactive TV, and the Internet.

LO•3 DEFINE GEOGRAPHIC INFORMATION SYSTEMS (GIS) AND DISCUSS THEIR POTENTIAL USES IN A RETAIL ENTERPRISE.   Higher-quality market selection and retail location decisions can be made with the use of GISs, which are computerized systems that combine physical geography with cultural geography. The GIS technology cannot only be used for market selection, site analysis, and trade area definition but also to evaluate new store cannibalization, advertising management, merchandise management, and the evaluation of store managers.

LO • 4 **WHAT ARE THE VARIOUS FACTORS TO BE CONSIDERED IN IDENTIFYING THE MOST ATTRACTIVE RETAIL MARKET?** We began our analysis of market selection by looking at a trio of theories that can aid in the location decision. Reilly's law of retail gravitation assumes that the population of a community serves as a drawing power for the community and draws customers into its business district. The index of retail saturation reflects the total demand for the product under question with the availability of retailers to service or supply that product. The buying power index enables us to develop an overall indicator of a market's potential. We concluded our discussion on market identification by looking into other factors that could influence community supply (square feet per store, square feet per employee, growth in stores, and quality of competition) or demand (market population, buyer behavior, household income, age, and composition, community life cycle, density, and mobility) for goods and services.

LO • 5 **WHAT ARE THE VARIOUS ATTRIBUTES CONSIDERED IN EVALUATING RETAIL SITES WITHIN A RETAIL MARKET?** After reviewing the above three location alternatives, we discussed the second of our three steps in the location process site analysis, which consists of an evaluation of the density of demand and supply within each possible market. This process begins by determining the size, description, and density of demand and supply of various areas within the chosen market and then identifying the most attractive sites, given the retailer's requirements, available for new stores within each market.

LO • 6 **HOW IS THE BEST GEOGRAPHIC SITE SELECTED?** Finally, the retailer should conduct a site selection analysis of the top-ranking sites in each market. The goal is to select the best site or sites. Retail site analysts suggest that the following should be considered at this stage: nature of the site, traffic characteristics, type of neighbors, terms of lease or purchase, and finally the expected profitability or return on assets.

TERMS TO REMEMBER

home page
virtual store
linkage
market segmentation
target market
store-based retailers
nonstore-based retailers
central business district
secondary business district
neighborhood business district

shopping center
culture
thematic maps
trading area
Reilly's law of retail gravitation
point of indifference
outshopping
retail store saturation
understored
overstored

anchor stores
neighborhood shopping center
community shopping center
regional center
super-regional center
fashion/specialty center
power center
theme center
outlet center

free-standing retailer
geographic information systems (GIS)
index of retail saturation (IRS)
buying power index (BPI)
site analysis
demand density
supply density
100 percent location
store compatibility

REVIEW AND DISCUSSION QUESTIONS

LO • 1 WHAT ARE THE CRITERIA USED IN SELECTING A TARGET MARKET?

1. Why are the concepts of target market selection and location related?
2. What are the three criteria that should be met to successfully target market?

LO • 2 IDENTIFY THE DIFFERENT OPTIONS, BOTH STORE-BASED AND NONSTORE-BASED, FOR EFFECTIVELY REACHING THE RETAILER'S TARGET MARKET AND IDENTIFY THE ADVANTAGES AND DISADVANTAGES OF BUSINESS DISTRICTS, SHOPPING CENTERS, AND FREE-STANDING UNITS AS SITES FOR RETAIL LOCATION.

3. What types of retailers would be best suited for a neighborhood shopping center?
4. Why are discount stores, such as Wal-Mart and Kmart, usually not located in shopping centers or malls?
5. Because more than one-half of all retail sales, excluding automobile and gasoline, occur in shopping centers and malls, can we assume that their future is bright? Support your answer.
6. What lines of retail trade do you believe will be most affected by the growth of retailing on the Internet and interactive television?

LO • 3 DEFINE GEOGRAPHIC INFORMATION SYSTEMS (GIS) AND DISCUSS THEIR POTENTIAL USES IN A RETAIL ENTERPRISE.

7. Why do GISs include both physical and cultural geography? Give examples of physical and cultural data that may be included in a GIS.
8. Identify and discuss the seven uses of GISs in retailing.

LO • 4 WHAT ARE THE VARIOUS FACTORS TO BE CONSIDERED IN IDENTIFYING THE MOST ATTRACTIVE RETAIL MARKET?

9. Is it more important for a retailer to select the proper trading area in which to locate or the correct site within the market? Explain your answer
10. What is the index of retail saturation? How is it used in making a location decision?
11. What is the buying power index? How is it used in making a location decision?
12. Calculate the Buyer Power Indexes for the following three cities:

CITY	PERCENTAGE OF U.S. EFFECTIVE BUYING INCOME	PERCENTAGE OF U.S. RETAIL SALES	PERCENTAGE OF U.S. POPULATION
Arkon City	0.005	0.006	0.004
Binghamtown	0.006	0.004	0.005
Cochran	0.004	0.005	0.007

13. Compute the index of retail saturation for the following three markets.

The data for department stores is

MARKET	A	B	C
Retail expenditures per household	$510	$575	$610
Square feet of retail space	600,000	488,000	808,000
Number of households	112,000	91,000	147,000

Based on these data, which market is most attractive? What additional data would you find helpful in determining the attractiveness of the three markets?

14. What are the two important factors in the retail gravity theory?

LO•5 WHAT ARE THE VARIOUS ATTRIBUTES CONSIDERED IN EVALUATING RETAIL SITES WITHIN A RETAIL MARKET?

15. Identify the factors you would consider as most important in locating a fast-food restaurant. Compare these factors with the factors you would use in selecting a site for a furniture store.
16. Explain the concepts of demand density and supply density. Why are they important to retail decision making?
17. Agree or disagree with the following statement and support your answer. When demand outstrips supply in a certain trading area, a retailer should locate there as soon as possible.

LO•6 HOW IS THE BEST GEOGRAPHIC SITE SELECTED?

18. What does store compatibility suggest about retail stores locating next to each other?
19. Why is it important to consider the terms of a lease in selecting a specific site?
20. Why is the customer such an important factor in selecting the best site for a retail location?

SAMPLE TEST QUESTIONS

LO•1 WHICH OF THE FOLLOWING IS NOT A CRITERION USED TO SUCCESSFULLY REACH A TARGET MARKET?

a. The market segment should be measurable.
b. Promotional efforts can be directed at the market segment.
c. The market segment should create high sales.
d. The market segment should be profitable.
e. Distribution efforts can be directed at the market segment.

LO•2 FREE-STANDING RETAILERS OFFER THE FOLLOWING ADVANTAGES:

a. lack of direct competition
b. high drawing power from nearby complementary stores

   c. higher traffic than shopping malls
   d. lower advertising costs
   e. longer store hours

LO • 3 GISs CAN BE USED FOR THE FOLLOWING PURPOSES:

   a. site analysis
   b. trade area definition
   c. advertising management
   d. merchandise management
   e. all the above

LO • 4 THE THREE SEQUENTIAL STAGES INVOLVED IN SELECTING A LOCATION FOR A STORE BASED RETAILER ARE

   a. Identify the most understored markets, identify the most attractive sites that are available within each market, select the best site(s).
   b. Identify most attractive markets, identify the most attractive sites that are available within each market, select the best site(s).
   c. Identify most attractive markets, identify the vacant parcels of real estate within each market, select the best site(s).
   d. Identify the most understored markets, identify the vacant parcels of real estate within each market, negotiate terms for best site.
   e. Identify most attractive markets, identify the most attractive sites that are available within each market, negotiate for the lowest-priced site.

LO • 5 SITE ANALYSIS CONSISTS OF

   a. analysis of density of demand and supply within a market
   b. consideration of the type of neighbors
   c. analyzing sources of financing for the site (i.e., debt or equity financing)
   d. determining the expected profitability from operating a store at the site
   e. considering the ease with which consumers can reach the site

LO • 6 WHICH OF THE FOLLOWING IS NOT AN IMPORTANT CONSIDERATION IN SELECTING THE BEST SITE FOR A NEW RETAIL STORE?

   a. nature of the site
   b. traffic characteristics of the site
   c. potential return on equity
   d. terms of purchase or lease
   e. potential return on assets

APPLICATIONS

WRITING AND SPEAKING EXERCISE   You are doing a summer internship with Rowley Jewelers, a family-held concern located in the CBD of a resort community in southwest Missouri, with a summer population of 200,000. Mac Rowley, the owner, has a problem and wants you to help him solve it. Around 10 o'clock this morning, a street vendor showed up in front of the store and began selling fake famous-name brand watches (Rolex, Ebel, Piaget) from a pushcart and suitcase for $10 to $20 each. After first asking the vendor to find another street corner and being told no, Mr. Rowley called the police to have the vendor removed. However, the police informed Mr. Rowley that street vending was not illegal. Rowley then called his city council representative, Jane Berry, explaining that he believes that it was unfair for him to pay city taxes and have to compete with someone who paid no taxes. Ms. Berry told Rowley to send her a memo explaining the situation and proposing a solution(s). Now, Mr. Rowley wants you to write the memo for him.

RETAIL PROJECT

Small, as well as large, retailers can benefit immensely from knowing the trade area of their store. Identify a small local retailer such as a florist, pet store, gift store, or restaurant. Contact the store owner or manager and tell them you are studying retailing and would like to volunteer to construct a map of their trade area. To do this, you need to obtain the addresses of a sample of the patrons over a one-week period and plot these on a map. Review the customer spotting map in Exhibit 7.6 on page 241. Develop a method to collect the needed data and construct the map of the trade area. What percentage of customers are within one mile of the store, within three miles, within five miles?

CASE THE OUTLET MALL

Over the past decade, Anne Wahl had watched with interest the development of factory outlet malls. As a store manager of a regional department store chain operating in a mall, she knew that she would some day have to contend not only with the discount department store chains but also with the manufacturers who were supplying her store as well as the outlets from some of the leading national chains. After all, Saks Fifth Avenue now has Saks Off Fifth stores, Nordstrom has the Rack, and even Neiman-Marcus has their Last Call outlet stores to get rid of their excess and unwanted merchandise. However, what surprised her was the rapid development of the outlet malls in recent years.

Before the Civil War, manufacturers began to sell at retail by either operating directly from their plants or by introducing small outlet stores near their plants. Still, it was more than 100 years before manufacturers banded together and opened the first outlet shopping center near Reading, Pennsylvania, in 1972. For the next decade, only two or three outlets were added each year.

Given this slow growth pattern, these outlet centers didn't upset the retailers selling the manufacturers' products. Besides, the early outlet centers generally sold only "seconds," or imperfect or flawed goods, as well as overproduced merchandise. However, the economic slowdown caused manufacturers to begin opening dozen of outlets each year to the point almost 400 outlet centers have opened since the mid-1980s. And today's outlet malls no longer are satisfied to only sell seconds and overproduced merchandise. Now, they are selling flawless products, deep in sizes and selections.

The outlet mall offers manufacturers who open stores in these malls three major advantages. First, it allows them to reach customers who normally wouldn't purchase their brand-name products. Second, it is more profitable for a manufacturer to sell at a reduced "retail price" to the general public than it is to sell at wholesale to stores such as Ms. Wahl's. Finally, with their plants operating at less than full capacity, the manufacturers could use outlet sales to increase their production and reduce average costs.

Now, Anne Wahl got the bad news in her morning paper: A land developer announced that he was beginning construction on an outlet mall featuring more than 80 manufacturers 40 miles north of Modesto on an interstate highway near a resort area. Included in the press release was a list of just some of the manufacturers planning on opening stores in the new mall: Nike, London Fog, Liz Claiborne, Esprit, Van Heusen, Reebok, Levi's, Jordache, Fieldcrest Cannon, Chaus, and Eddie Bauer.

That night, Wahl decided that early the next morning she would drive up the interstate to visit the site of the new mall. Just as she was getting out of her car at the new mall site, the land developer, Curtis Niehoff, drove up and parked beside her. Anne went over and introduced herself to Niehoff. After some pleasantries, Niehoff stated that he assumed that the reason behind Ms. Wahl's trip was that she was worried about the competition the new mall was going to provide. Anne admitted that she was indeed worried. Niehoff then invited Wahl into his office for coffee and a chat about his plans.

Niehoff began by saying, "First, you have to understand, Anne, that we are not really going after the same target market. You are targeting the population of Modesto. We are targeting an entirely different market. For one thing, our customers will have a higher income than your market. We fully expect that by locating in this resort area, over a third of our customers will have incomes higher than $75,000. In addition, most of our customers will spend one or two full days at our mall. That's why we have triple the parking spaces of a regional mall, so that RVs and charter buses can park. In fact, our market will draw from a radius of 300 miles."

Wahl noted that this was fine and good, but she was still worried about getting into a "price war" with her suppliers. Once again, Niehoff tried to reassure her. "Our prices here will not be as low as you think. In fact, the 'wheel of retailing' is taking place in all of today's new outlet malls. No longer are our stores 'bare-bones' operators. They have added services to match that of any department store. This in turn has caused prices on this season's merchandise to rise to a point somewhere lower than your prices but above the discounters' price that you are already competing against. What our stores will offer is selection, even if some of the merchandise is last season's, and the 'thrill of the hunt.' Also, your customers will have to consider travel time and costs when comparing your prices to ours. That's why our primary emphasis will be on the resort-area vacationer with a secondary emphasis on the interstate highway traveler." With that Mr. Niehoff stated that he was late for a meeting and had to leave.

Driving back to Modesto, Anne was somewhat relieved at what she found out on her trip. She also felt confident that her store could compete with the outlet center. However, on arriving back at her office, she found a note stating that there would be a "special meeting" of all the regional mall's store managers tomorrow morning. It seems that a couple of the managers wanted everyone in the mall to ban together and "reduce, if not totally eliminate, purchases from any manufacturer who was going to open a store in the new outlet mall."

What should Ms. Wahl do?

PLANNING YOUR OWN RETAIL BUSINESS   The retail store that you are planning has an estimated circular trade area with a radius of five miles. Within this five-mile area, there is an average of 1,465 households per square mile. In a normal year, you expect that 47 percent of these households would visit your store (referred to as penetration) an average of 3.8 times (referred to as frequency). Based on the preceding, what would you expect to be the traffic (i.e., number of visitors to your store per year)? (*Hint:* Traffic can be viewed as the square miles of the trade area multiplied by the household density multiplied by penetration, which is in turn multiplied by frequency.)

Once you answer this question, do some sensitivity analysis, which is an assessment of how sensitive store traffic is to changes in your assumptions about penetration and frequency. What happens if penetration drops to 40 percent or rises to 50 percent? What happens if frequency drops to three times annually or rises to 4.5 times annually? In this analysis, only change one thing at a time and hold all other assumptions constant.

NOTES

1. Fred Schneider, "Retailing on the Internet," *International Trends in Retailing,* December 1995: 67–80; "How to Buy a Car on the Internet," *Fortune,* March 4, 1996: 163–168.
2. "Of a Talbots in Litchfield (the Horror?)," *New York Times,* January 28, 1996: Section 1, p. 16.
3. "A Special K," *Discount Merchandiser,* November 1996: 24–27.
4. "Supermarket's Inner-City Success," *New York Times,* February 19, 1997: A15.
5. "More Stores Spurn Malls for the Village Square," *Wall Street Journal,* February 16, 1996: 5.
6. "Power Shortage for 'Big Box' Retailers," *Wall Street Journal,* February 7, 1997: B14.
7. "AAFES: A $7 Billion Military Enterprise," *Discount Merchandiser,* March 1996: 70–76.
8. "Are Airports Becoming the New Malls?," *Chain Store Age Executive,* May 1995: 78, 80.
9. "Wells Fargo Plans to Put Drugstores in Banks," *Wall Street Journal,* July 8, 1996: C19.
10. "A Sporting Venture," *Business Geographics,* January 1997: 23–25.
11. *Retailing in China: Assessing the Opportunity* (Columbus, OH: Management Horizons, Price Waterhouse LLC, August 1996).
12. William J. Reilly, *Methods for the Study of Retail Relationships* (Austin, TX: Bureau of Business Research, The University of Texas, 1929): Research Monograph 4.
13. P.D. Converse, "New Laws of Retail Gravitation," *Journal of Marketing,* January 1949: 379–384.
14. "Location Strategies: An Overbuilt Retail Market," *Discount Merchandiser,* February 1993: 76–77.
15. Bernard LaLonde, "The Logistics of Retail Location," in *American Marketing Proceedings,* William D. Stevens, ed. (Chicago: American Marketing Association, 1961): 572.
16. "Home Depot," *Business Week,* February 13, 1995: 65.
17. Mobility can be viewed as both a household characteristic and a community characteristic. We chose to treat it as a community characteristic because the design of the community, the availability of public transportation, and the cost of operating an auto in any given area are determinants of mobility and are themselves characteristic of the community.
18. The essence of Applebaum's work, plus contributions from several of his students, can be found in "William Applebaum and Others," in *Guide to Store Location Research with Emphasis on Supermarkets,* Curt Korhblau, ed., sponsored by the Supermarket Institute (Reading, MA: Addison-Wesley, 1968).
19. "Protesters Fight a Plan for Washington's Home," *New York Times,* March 13, 1996: A9.
20. Richard L. Nelson, *The Selection of Retail Locations* (New York: F.W. Dodge, 1958): 66.

PART 4

MANAGING RETAIL OPERATIONS

CHAPTER 8

MANAGING A RETAILER'S FINANCES

Unpredictable cold weather which hurts sales for many retailers, such as this Sears Hardware store, makes accurate merchandise budgeting difficult.

OVERVIEW

In this chapter, we begin by looking at how a merchandise budget is prepared and how it is used in making plans for an upcoming merchandise season. Next, we describe the basic differences among an income statement, balance sheet, and statement of cash flow, as well as how a retailer uses these accounting statements in controlling its merchandising activities. Finally, we discuss the accounting inventory systems and pricing methods available to value inventory.

LEARNING OBJECTIVES

After reading this chapter, you should be able to

1. describe the importance of a merchandise budget and know how to prepare a six-month merchandise plan
2. explain the differences among and the uses of these three accounting statements: income statement, balance sheet, and statement of cash flow
3. explain how the retailer is able to value inventory

Merchandising
*is the planning and control
of the buying and selling of
goods and services to help the
retailer realize its objectives.*

Merchandise budget
*is a plan of projected sales
for an upcoming season,
when and how much mer-
chandise is to be purchased,
and what markups and re-
ductions will likely occur.*

THE MERCHANDISE BUDGET

In the last chapter, we described the role location plays in a retailer's success. Location is important and was discussed before the other elements of the retail mix because for most new retailers, it is the first decision made. Also, once the location decision is made, it is difficult to change.

Another important retail mix element is merchandising, including pricing. Some experts agree that it is around merchandising that all the other retail mix elements revolve, especially if we consider chain store operators. After all, the merchandise in a Wal-Mart or Kmart store in Muskegon, Michigan, looks much the same as in one in Sacramento, California. Only after these merchandising decisions are made can retailers concern themselves with the other retail mix elements: promotion, store layout and design, and customer service. However, before we can explain how to make these merchandise decisions, we must discuss the retailer's means of controlling these activities.

Many individuals believe that the terms *retailing* and *merchandising* are synonymous. They are not. Retailing includes all the business activities that are necessary to sell goods and services to the final consumer. Merchandising is only one of these activities and is concerned with the planning and control involved in the buying and selling of goods and services to help the retailer realize its objectives. Success in merchandising requires total financial planning and control. This chapter is divided into three sections: the merchandise budget, retail accounting statements, and inventory valuation.

Successful retailers must have good financial planning and control of their merchandise. The retailer invests money in merchandise for profitable resale to others. A poor choice of merchandise will result in low profits, or maybe even a loss. Therefore, to be successful in retailing, as in any other activity, an individual must have a plan of what is to be accomplished. In retailing, this plan of operation is called the merchandise budget. A merchandise budget is a plan of projected sales for an upcoming season, when and how much merchandise is to be purchased, and what markups and reductions will likely occur. The merchandise budget forces the retailer to develop a formal outline of merchandising objectives for the upcoming selling season.

DOLLAR $ & ¢ENTS

*Retailers who thoroughly analyze and project all the factors in developing a
merchandise budget for an upcoming season will be more profitable.*

In developing the merchandise budget, the retailer must make five major merchandising decisions:

1. What will be the anticipated sales for the department, division, or store?
2. How much stock on hand will be needed to achieve this sales plan, given the level of inventory turnover expected?

A specialty retailer like Tower Records cannot develop its merchandise budget too far in advance because it is virtually impossible to predict the top selling musical artists and new releases. These are only known by buyers about one month before release.

3. What reductions, if any, from the original retail price must be made to dispose of all the merchandise brought into the store?
4. What additional purchases must be made during the season?
5. What gross margin (the difference between sales and cost of goods sold) should the department, division, or store contribute to the overall profitability of the company?

When preparing the merchandise budget, a retailer must follow these four rules.

First, a merchandise budget should always be prepared in advance of the selling season. The original plan is often prepared by the buyer for a particular department to be approved by the divisional merchandising manager and/or the general merchandising manager. Therefore, most retail firms selling apparel and hardgoods begin the process of developing the merchandise budget three to four months in advance of the budget period. This is not always the case with some specialty stores such as record shops. A new record release is only known to the buyer about one month in advance and can be easily reordered if it goes to the top of the charts. These specialty stores also don't have to worry about markdowns because excess quantities can be returned to vendors for full credit. Generally, a firm has only two seasons a year: (1) spring/summer, usually February 1 through July 31, and (2) fall/winter, August 1 through January 31. The buyer for a particular department will usually begin to prepare merchandise budgets on or about March 1 and September 1 for the upcoming seasons.

Second, because the budget is a plan that management expects to follow in the upcoming merchandise season, the language must be easy to understand. The merchandise budget illustration contained in this chapter has only 11 items, although the number of items contained in a budget may vary by companies due to their own merchandise and market characteristics. Remember, the budget serves no useful purpose if it cannot be understood by all the decision makers. Also, it must contain all the information needed for that particular retailer.

MUSIC STORES USE A SHORTER TIME SPAN IN BUDGETING

A prerecorded music store's (e.g., Musicland, Sam Goody, Camelot, Record World) merchandise budget is somewhat different than budgets for other types of retailers. The prerecorded music business is a perfect example of a retailer experiencing the 80-20 principle. This principle maintains that 80 percent of sales are generated by 20 percent of inventory. Conversely, 20 percent of sales are generated by 80 percent of inventory. In a prerecorded music store, these percentages can be even more pronounced. The "Top 50 Best-Sellers" on the Billboard chart can produce up to 90 percent of a store's sales. A store can stock thousands of items, and 50 of them will produce 70 to 90 percent of that retailer's sales. In fact, years ago, an album by Bruce Springsteen and the E Street Band generated more than 80 percent of a chain's sales for a six-week period.

Therefore, no store can be without "the best-sellers." Because merchandise can be received in a relatively short period of time, stores do not have to maintain inventory for longer than estimated sales of a three-week period. There is the need, however, to never run out of key merchandise. Therefore, stores have to anticipate an accelerated rate of sales, rather than a declining sales pattern. For example, if you expect to sell 100 units of an item during one week for the next few weeks, plan to have an inventory of 500 units. If 200 sell in a week, a reorder of 200 can be placed, and it will be received before you run out of the 300 units you have on hand. However, if sales slow down, you can have inventory on hand for a longer period than three weeks.

Prerecorded music retailers must also have merchandise assortments. Young persons do not like to shop in stores with best-sellers only. Customers not only want an artist's latest hit but they are also interested in other cassettes or CDs made by that artist. As long as a store has an assortment, it will not lose customers. It does not have to inventory every album that a best-selling artist (e.g., Celine Dion, Pearl Jam, Garth Brooks) has recorded.

In addition, there is a need to maintain inventory in artists who enjoyed popularity in the past (e.g., Grateful Dead, Beatles, Elvis Presley). Further, stores need assortments of classical, juvenile, and jazz albums. Although inventories of best-sellers have to be checked a minimum of once weekly, many high-volume stores (e.g., Tower, Sam Goody, Blockbuster Music) do this with greater frequency. Other merchandise can be checked periodically. For example, a store can inventory its classical album assortment monthly, the same being true for other categories.

Although the money available to make new inventory purchases can be curtailed for almost all categories, there must always be money available to purchase best-sellers or a new album that is coming out that will be "taking off." If customers cannot find that album in one store, they will go elsewhere. There is a need for flexibility in the merchandise budget because there might be three new items "hitting the best-seller" charts in one week.

Third, since the economy is constantly changing, the merchandise budget must be planned for a relatively short period of time. Six months is the norm used by most retailers, although some retailers, as shown in the Behind the Scenes box, use a three-month, or even shorter, plan. Forecasting future sales is difficult enough without complicating the process by projecting for a time period too far into the future. The firm's general management should be concerned with long-term trends and effects on store and personnel needs. The firm's buyers are involved in the more short-term trends and effects that may influence the merchandise budget.

EXHIBIT 8.1	SAMPLE SIX-MONTH MERCHANDISE BUDGET

SIX-MONTH MERCHANDISE BUDGET
Housewares Department

		FEBRUARY	MARCH	APRIL	MAY	JUNE	JULY	Total
BOM Stock	Last Year							
	Plan							
	Revised							
	Actual							
Sales	Last Year							
	Plan							
	Revised							
	Actual							
Reductions	Last Year							
	Plan							
	Revised							
	Actual							
EOM STOCK	Last Year							
	Plan							
	Revised							
	Actual							
RETAIL PURCHASES	Last Year							
	Plan							
	Revised							
	Actual							
PURCHASES COST	Last Year							
	Plan							
	Revised							
	Actual							
INITIAL MARK-UP	Last Year							
	Plan							
	Revised							
	Actual							
GROSS MARGIN DOLLARS	Last Year							
	Plan							
	Revised							
	Actual							
BOM STOCK/SALES RATIO	Last Year							
	Plan							
	Revised							
	Actual							
SALES PERCENTAGE	Last Year							
	Plan							
	Revised							
	Actual							
RETAIL REDUCTION PERCENTAGE	Last Year							
	Plan							
	Revised							
	Actual							

STOCKTURN: Last Year _____ Plan _____ Actual _____
ON ORDER – BEGINNING OF SEASON _____ Plan _____ Actual _____
EOM INVENTORY FOR LAST MONTH _____ Plan _____ Actual _____
REDUCTION PERCENTAGE _____ Plan _____ Actual _____
MARKUP PERCENTAGE _____ Plan _____ Actual _____

EXHIBIT 8.2	TWO-SEASONS DEPARTMENT STORE, DEPT. 353, SIX-MONTH MERCHANDISE BUDGET						
	FEBRUARY	**MARCH**	**APRIL**	**MAY**	**JUNE**	**JULY**	**TOTAL**
1. Planned BOM Stock	$225,000	$300,000	$300,000	$250,000	$375,000	$300,000	—
2. Planned Sales	75,000	75,000	100,000	50,000	125,000	75,000	$500,000
3. Planned Retail Reductions	7,500	7,500	5,000	7,500	6,250	16,250	50,000
4. Planned EOM Stock	300,000	300,000	250,000	375,000	300,000	250,000	—
5. Planned Purchases at Retail	157,500	82,500	55,000	182,500	56,250	41,250	575,000
6. Planned Purchases at Cost	86,625	45,375	30,250	100,375	30,937.50	22,687.50	316,250
7. Planned Initial Markup	70,875	37,125	24,750	82,125	25,312.50	18,562.50	258,750
8. Planned Gross Margin	63,375	29,625	19,750	74,625	19,062.50	2,312.50	208,750
9. Planned BOM Stock-to-Sales Ratio	3	4	3	5	3	4	—
10. Planned Sales Percentage	15%	15%	20%	10%	25%	15%	100%
11. Planned Retail Reduction Percentage	10%	10%	5%	15%	5%	21.67%	10%

Planned Total Sales for the Period	$500,000
Planned Total Retail Reduction Percentage for the Period	10%
Planned Initial Markup Percentage	45%
Planned BOM Stock for August	$250,000

Fourth, the budget should be flexible enough so that changes are possible. All merchandise budgets are plans and estimates of predicted future events. However, competition and the consumer are not always predictable, especially in regard to fashion preferences. Thus any forecast is subject to error and will need revisions.

Keeping in mind the preceding discussion of merchandising decisions and rules, a blank six-month merchandise budget for the housewares department of a major department store is shown in Exhibit 8.1. Don't be alarmed or confused if Exhibit 8.1 is not clear to you at this time. In the following discussion, as well as in the next chapter, we describe why the budget is set up in this form. Additionally, we explain all the analytical tools used by the retailer to calculate the numbers required in developing a six-month merchandise budget or plan.

Exhibit 8.1 appears to be more confusing than it really is because each element is broken into four parts: last year, plan for the upcoming season, revised plan, and actual. This is merely a means to provide the decision maker with complete information. Last year refers to last year's sales for the period; plan for the upcoming season is what the original plan projected; revised plan is the result of any revisions caused by changing market conditions after the plan is accepted; and actual is the final results.

Exhibit 8.2 presents the same material in a simpler form. Here, we only attempt to show you how and why a retailer develops a six-month merchandise plan. Exhibit 8.3 is a summary of how all the numbers in the merchandise budget are determined.

EXHIBIT 8.3	FORMULAS FOR THE SIX-MONTH MERCHANDISE BUDGET

DETERMINING PLANNED SALES FOR THE MONTH

(Planned Sales Percentage for the Month) × (Planned Total Sales)
= (Planned Sales for the Month)

DETERMINING PLANNED BOM STOCK FOR THE MONTH

(Planned Sales for the Month) × (Planned BOM Stock-to-Sales Ratio for the Month) = (Planned BOM Stock for the Month)

DETERMINING PLANNED RETAIL REDUCTIONS FOR THE MONTH

(Planned Sales for the Month) × (Planned Retail Reduction Percentage for the Month) = (Planned Retail Reductions for the Month)

DETERMINING PLANNED EOM STOCK FOR THE MONTH

(Planned BOM Stock for the Following Month)
= (Planned EOM Stock for the Current Month)

DETERMINING PLANNED PURCHASES AT RETAIL FOR THE MONTH

(Planned Sales for the Month) + (Planned Retail Reductions for the Month)
+ (Planned EOM Stock for the Month) − (Planned BOM Stock for the Month)
= (Planned Purchases at Retail for the Month)

DETERMINING PLANNED PURCHASES AT COST FOR THE MONTH

(Planned Purchases at Retail for the Month)
× (100% − Planned Initial Markup Percentage)
= (Planned Purchases at Cost for the Month)

DETERMINING PLANNED INITIAL MARKUP FOR THE MONTH

(Planned Purchases at Retail for the Month) × (Planned Initial Markup Percentage) = (Planned Initial Markup for the Month)
or
(Planned Purchases at Retail for the Month)
− (Planned Purchases at Cost for the Month)
= (Planned Initial Markup for the Month)

DETERMINING PLANNED GROSS MARGIN FOR THE MONTH

(Planned Initial Markup for the Month)
− (Planned Retail Reductions for the Month)
= (Planned Gross Margin for the Month)

Exhibit 8.2 shows the spring/summer season, February 1 to July 31, for the Two-Seasons Department Store, Department 353, with projected sales of $500,000, planned retail reductions of $50,000 or 10 percent of sales, planned initial markup of 45 percent, and a planned gross margin on purchases made of $208,750.

RETAIL REPORTING CALENDAR

Retailers, when comparing this year's sales with last year's sales, don't always compare with the exact date (i.e., comparing February 1, 1999, sales with February 1, 1998) because the dates could fall on different days of the week. For instance, February 1 in 1998 was on a Sunday, when the retailer might be closed, and on a Monday in 1999. Rather, retailers use a retail reporting calendar, which divides the year into two seasons, each with six months as shown on the next page. Thus, February 1, 1999, the first Monday of the spring season, would be compared with February 2, 1998, which will be the first Monday of 1998's spring season. In the year 2000, the first Monday of the spring season will be January 31.

By using this calendar, retailers will have problems in making direct comparison only once a season. Fashion retailers will be affected by movement of Easter (April 12 in 1998, April 4 in 1999, and April 23 in 2000) when making comparisons in the spring season. Thus in 1999, because Easter is the first day of April on the reporting calendar, the big apparel sales will be reported in the retailer's March sales. The following year, 2000, will see March's sales suffer in comparison. However, April apparel sales will be better because Easter will be 22 days into the retailers' month of April and the weather will also help increase sales. During the fall season, the period between Thanksgiving and Christmas can vary in length by as much as one week. Because Thanksgiving is the fourth Thursday of November, it can fall between November 22 and 28, and as a result the number of days in the Christmas shopping season will differ from year to year. For example, in 1998 and 1999 there are four weekends and 28 and 29 days, respectively, between Thanksgiving and Christmas, whereas in 2000 there will be five weekends and 31 days between November 23 and Christmas Day.

DETERMINING PLANNED SALES

The initial step in developing a six-month merchandise budget is to estimate planned sales for the entire season and for each individual month. The buyer begins by examining the previous year's sales records. Adjustments are then made in the planning of sales for the upcoming merchandise budget. Retailers, when comparing this year's sales with last year's sales, often make these comparisons by using a retail reporting calendar discussed in the Behind the Scenes box.

One retailer with an excellent record of forecasting sales is San Francisco-based Williams-Sonoma, best known for its Catalog for Cooks. Williams-Sonoma's secret for forecasting sales rests on its highly automated mailing lists. Its database of 4.5 million customers tracks up to 150 different pieces of information per customer. With a few simple keystrokes, the retailer can tell you what you've bought from each of its five annual catalogs (an estimated 60 percent of customers have bought from more than one), what time of the year you tend to buy, how often you buy, what category of merchandise you lean toward, and so forth. Through a complex cross-referencing of the data, Williams-Sonoma's two full-time statisticians are able to project, to plus or minus 5 percent accuracy on average, each catalog's sales.

To return to the example in Exhibit 8.2, after reviewing the data available, the buyer for Department 353 forecasted that $500,000 was a reasonable total sales figure for the future season. June, with a projected 25 percent of total season's sales, and April,

1998 RETAIL REPORTING CALENDAR

SPRING 1998

Feb

S	M	T	W	T	F	S
	1	2	3	4	5	6	7
8	9	10	11	12	13	14
15	16	17	18	19	20	21
22	23	24	25	26	27	28

Mar

S	M	T	W	T	F	S
1	2	3	4	5	6	7
8	9	10	11	12	13	14
15	16	17	18	19	20	21
22	23	24	25	26	27	28
29	30	31	1	2	3	4

Apr

S	M	T	W	T	F	S
12	13	14	15	16	17	18
5	6	7	8	9	10	11
19	20	21	22	23	24	25
26	27	28	29	30	1	2

May

S	M	T	W	T	F	S
3	4	5	6	7	8	9
10	11	12	13	14	15	16
17	18	19	20	21	22	23
24	25	26	27	28	29	30

June

S	M	T	W	T	F	S
31	1	2	3	4	5	6
7	8	9	10	11	12	13
14	15	16	17	18	19	20
21	22	23	24	25	26	27
28	29	30	1	2	3	4

July

S	M	T	W	T	F	S
5	6	7	8	9	10	11
12	13	14	15	16	17	18
19	20	21	22	23	24	25
26	27	28	29	30	31	1

FALL 1998

Aug

S	M	T	W	T	F	S
2	3	4	5	6	7	8
9	10	11	12	13	14	15
16	17	18	19	20	21	22
23	24	25	26	27	28	29

Sep

S	M	T	W	T	F	S
30	31	1	2	3	4	5
6	7	8	9	10	11	12
13	14	15	16	17	18	19
20	21	22	23	24	25	26
27	28	29	30	1	2	3

Oct

S	M	T	W	T	F	S
4	5	6	7	8	9	10
11	12	13	14	15	16	17
18	19	20	21	22	23	24
25	26	27	28	29	30	31

Nov

S	M	T	W	T	F	S
1	2	3	4	5	6	7
8	9	10	11	12	13	14
15	16	17	18	19	20	21
22	23	24	25	**26**	27	28

Dec

S	M	T	W	T	F	S
29	30	1	2	3	4	5
6	7	8	9	10	11	12
13	14	15	16	17	18	19
20	21	22	23	24	**25**	26
27	28	29	30	31	1	2

Jan

S	M	T	W	T	F	S
3	4	5	6	7	8	9
10	11	12	13	14	15	16
17	18	19	20	21	22	23
24	25	26	27	28	29	30

1999 RETAIL REPORTING CALENDAR

SPRING 1999

Feb

S	M	T	W	T	F	S
31	1	2	3	4	5	6
7	8	9	10	11	12	13
14	15	16	17	18	19	20
21	22	23	24	25	26	27

Mar

S	M	T	W	T	F	S
28	1	2	3	4	5	6
7	8	9	10	11	12	13
14	15	16	17	18	19	20
21	22	23	24	25	26	27
28	29	30	31	1	2	3

Apr

S	M	T	W	T	F	S
4	5	6	7	8	9	10
11	12	13	14	15	16	17
18	19	20	21	22	23	24
25	26	27	28	29	30	1

May

S	M	T	W	T	F	S
2	3	4	5	6	7	8
9	10	11	12	13	14	15
16	17	18	19	20	21	22
23	24	25	26	27	28	29

June

S	M	T	W	T	F	S
30	31	1	2	3	4	5
6	7	8	9	10	11	12
13	14	15	16	17	18	19
20	21	22	23	24	25	26
27	28	29	30	1	2	3

July

S	M	T	W	T	F	S
4	5	6	7	8	9	10
11	12	13	14	15	16	17
18	19	20	21	22	23	24
25	26	27	28	29	30	31

FALL 1999

Aug

S	M	T	W	T	F	S
1	2	3	4	5	6	7
8	9	10	11	12	13	14
15	16	17	18	19	20	21
22	23	24	25	26	27	28

Sep

S	M	T	W	T	F	S
29	30	31	1	2	3	4
5	6	7	8	9	10	11
12	13	14	15	16	17	18
19	20	21	22	23	24	25
26	27	28	29	30	1	2

Oct

S	M	T	W	T	F	S
3	4	5	6	7	8	9
10	11	12	13	14	15	16
17	18	19	20	21	22	23
24	25	26	27	28	29	30

Nov

S	M	T	W	T	F	S
31	1	2	3	4	5	6
7	8	9	10	11	12	13
14	15	16	17	18	19	20
21	22	23	24	**25**	26	27

Dec

S	M	T	W	T	F	S
28	29	30	1	2	3	4
5	6	7	8	9	10	11
12	13	14	15	16	17	18
19	20	21	22	23	24	**25**
26	27	28	29	30	31	1

Jan

S	M	T	W	T	F	S
2	3	4	5	6	7	8
9	10	11	12	13	14	15
16	17	18	19	20	21	22
23	24	25	26	27	28	29

2000 RETAIL REPORTING CALENDAR

SPRING 2000

Feb

S	M	T	W	T	F	S
30	31	1	2	3	4	5
6	7	8	9	10	11	12
13	14	15	16	17	18	19
20	21	22	23	24	25	26

Mar

S	M	T	W	T	F	S
27	28	29	1	2	3	4
5	6	7	8	9	10	11
12	13	14	15	16	17	18
19	20	21	22	23	24	25
26	27	28	29	30	31	1

Apr

S	M	T	W	T	F	S
2	3	4	5	6	7	8
9	10	11	12	13	14	15
16	17	18	19	20	21	22
23	24	25	26	27	28	29

May

S	M	T	W	T	F	S
30	1	2	3	4	5	6
7	8	9	10	11	12	13
14	15	16	17	18	19	20
21	22	23	24	25	26	27

June

S	M	T	W	T	F	S
28	29	30	31	1	2	3
4	5	6	7	8	9	10
11	12	13	14	15	16	17
18	19	20	21	22	23	24
25	26	27	28	29	30	1

July

S	M	T	W	T	F	S
2	3	4	5	6	7	8
9	10	11	12	13	14	15
16	17	18	19	20	21	22
23	24	25	26	27	28	29

FALL 2000

Aug

S	M	T	W	T	F	S
30	31	1	2	3	4	5
6	7	8	9	10	11	12
13	14	15	16	17	18	19
20	21	22	23	24	25	26

Sep

S	M	T	W	T	F	S
27	28	29	30	31	1	2
3	4	5	6	7	8	9
10	11	12	13	14	15	16
17	18	19	20	21	22	23
24	25	26	27	28	29	30

Oct

S	M	T	W	T	F	S
1	2	3	4	5	6	7
8	9	10	11	12	13	14
15	16	17	18	19	20	21
22	23	24	25	26	27	28

Nov

S	M	T	W	T	F	S
29	30	31	1	2	3	4
5	6	7	8	9	10	11
12	13	14	15	16	17	18
19	20	21	22	**23**	24	25

Dec

S	M	T	W	T	F	S
26	27	28	29	30	1	2
3	4	5	6	7	8	9
10	11	12	13	14	15	16
17	18	19	20	21	22	23
24	**25**	26	27	28	29	30

Jan

S	M	T	W	T	F	S
31	1	2	3	4	5	6
7	8	9	10	11	12	13
14	15	16	17	18	19	20
21	22	23	24	25	26	27

Williams-Sonoma is able to accurately forecast sales by statistically analyzing sales data from its stores and direct mail catalog.

with 20 percent, are expected to be the busy months. May, with only 10 percent, is expected to be the slowest month. The remaining months will have equal sales. Because April, May, and June account for 55 percent of total sales, then February, March, and July's total must be 45 percent, or 15 percent per month, because they are equal. The buyer is able to determine planned monthly sales by multiplying the planned monthly sales percentage by planned total sales. Because we know that February's planned monthly sales are 15 percent of the total planned sales of $500,000, February's planned sales must be $75,000 (15 percent × $500,000 = $75,000).

It is important to use recent trends when forecasting future sales. All too often, some retailers in a no-growth market merely use last season's figures for this season's budget. This method overlooks two major influences on projected sales volume: inflation and competition. If inflation was 10 percent and no other changes occurred in the retail environment, then the retailer planning on selling the same physical volume as during the previous year should expect a 10 percent increase in this season's dollar sales. Similarly, if the exit of a competitor across town is expected to increase the number of customer transactions by 5 percent, this increase should be reflected in the budget. Suppose that last year's sales were $100,000, inflation is 10 percent, and the retailer expects its market share to increase by 8 percent, while the total market remains stable. What should projected sales be? A simple equation used in retail planning is

$$\text{Total sales} = \text{Average sale} \times \text{Total transactions}$$

In the preceding example, average sales would increase by the 10 percent level of inflation to 1.10 times last year's sales and total transactions would increase by the 8 percent gain in market share to 1.08 times last year's total transactions, for an increase in total sales of 1.188 times (or 1.10 × 1.08), resulting in a total sales increase of $18,800 or a budgeted total sales of $118,800.

DETERMINING PLANNED BEGINNING-OF-THE-MONTH AND END-OF-THE-MONTH INVENTORIES

Once the buyer has estimated the season and monthly sales for the upcoming season, plans can be made for inventory requirements. To achieve projected sales figures, the merchant will generally carry stock or inventory in excess of planned sales for the period, be it a week, month, or season. The extra stock or inventory provides a merchandise assortment deep and broad enough to ensure customer sales. A common method of estimating the amount of stock to be carried is the stock-to-sales ratio. This ratio depicts the amount of stock to have on hand at the beginning of each month to support the forecasted sales for that month. For example, a stock-to-sales ratio of 5.0 would suggest that the retailer have $5 in inventory (at retail price) for every $1 in forecasted sales. Planned average beginning-of-the-month (BOM) stock-to-sales ratios can also be calculated directly from a retailer's planned turnover goals. For example, a retailer wants a target turnover rate of 4.0. By dividing the annual turnover rate into 12 (the number of months in a year), the average BOM stock-to-sales ratio for the year can be computed. In this case, 12 divided by 4.0 equals 3.0. Thus the average stock-to-sales ratio for the season is 3. Generally, stock-to-sales ratios will fluctuate month to month as sales tend to fluctuate monthly. Nevertheless, it is important to always review these ratios because if they are set too high or too low, too much or too little inventory will be on hand to meet the sales target.

Retail trade associations such as the National Retail Federation (NRF) conduct surveys and publish industry average stock-to-sales ratios. This information can be found at the NRF web site (http://www.nrf.com/pub). Based on available data, the buyer for Department 353 in Exhibit 8.2 used a planned stock-to-sales ratio of 3.0 for February, April, and June, a ratio of 4.0 for March and July, and a ratio of 5.0 for May. The buyer was able to determine that $300,000 worth of merchandise was needed beginning March 1 due to a planned stock-to-sales ratio of 4.0 and planned sales of $75,000 (line 1). Two things should be noted. First, stock-to-sales ratios always express inventory levels at retail, not cost. Second, the BOM inventory for one month is the end-of-the month (EOM) inventory for the previous month. This relationship can be easily seen by comparing the BOM figures (line 1) for one month with the EOM figures for the previous month (line 4). Remember, July EOM stock is the same as the BOM stock for August, as shown in Exhibit 8.2.

Stock-to-sales ratio *depicts the amount of stock to have on hand at the beginning of each month to support the forecasted sales for that month.*

DETERMINING PLANNED RETAIL REDUCTIONS

All merchandise brought into the store for sale to consumers is not actually sold at the planned initial markup price. Therefore, when preparing the six-month budget, the buyer should make allowances for reductions in the levels of stock not due to sales. Generally, these planned retail reductions fall into three types: markdowns, employee discounts, and stock shortages. These reductions must be planned because as the dollar value of the inventory level is reduced, the BOM stock that is planned to support next month's forecasted sales will be inadequate unless adjustments are made this month. Therefore, a buyer must remember that reductions are part of the cost of doing business.

DOLLAR $ & CENTS

Retailers who recognize that reductions are part of the cost of doing business and plan appropriately will be higher performers.

A small number of retailers don't include planned reductions in their merchandise budgets. They simply treat them as part of the normal operation of the store and think that they should be controlled without being part of the total budget. This gives management an understated, conservative planned-purchase figure, thereby having the effect of holding back some purchase reserve until the physical inventory reveals the exact amount of reductions. We have included planned reductions here for two reasons: (1) to reflect the additional purchases needed for sufficient inventory to begin the next month and (2) to point out that taking reductions is not bad. Too often, inexperienced retailers believe that taking a reduction is an admission of error and therefore fail to mark down merchandise until it is too late in the season. Therefore, a buyer must remember that reductions are part of the cost of doing business. Methods available to the retail buyer for minimizing retail reductions caused by retailer mistakes are discussed in Chapter 10.

The reductions in our six-month budget are listed as a percentage of planned sales. The buyer in our example has estimated monthly retail reduction percentages as shown on line 11. To determine planned retail reductions for March (line 3), planned monthly sales are multiplied by the planned monthly retail reduction percentage to yield the planned monthly retail reduction of $7,500 ($75,000 × 10 percent = $7,500).

Reductions are one of the major items in the merchandise budget subject to constant change. One reason is that the planned reductions may prove inadequate in the light of actual conditions encountered by the retailer. If retailers delay too long in taking reductions, they may be forced to take even larger price cuts later as the merchandise style depreciates even more in value. Alternatively, consider what happens when the department manager does such an effective merchandising job that not all the reduction money is needed for the period. The solution to both these dilemmas is found in the rules for developing a budget, namely, keeping it so flexible that it can be intelligently administered.

DETERMINING PLANNED PURCHASES AT RETAIL AND COST

We are now ready to determine whether additional purchases must be made during the merchandising season. The retailer will need inventory for (1) planned sales, (2) planned retail reductions, and (3) planned EOM inventory. Planned BOM inventory represents purchases that have already been made. In the six-month merchandise budget example shown in Exhibit 8.2, the March planned purchases at retail for Department 353 are $82,500 (line 5). This figure was derived by (1) adding planned sales, planned retail reductions, and planned EOM inventory and (2) subtracting planned BOM inventory:

$$\$75,000 + \$7,500 + 300,000 - 300,000 = \$82,500$$

Once planned purchases at retail are determined, planned purchases at cost can be easily calculated. The retail price always represents a combination of cost plus markup. If the markup percentage is given, the portion of retail attributed to cost or the cost complement can be derived by subtracting the markup percentage from the retail percentage of 100 percent. Given the markup percentage is 45 percent of retail for Department 353, the cost complement percentage must be 55 percent (100 percent − 45 percent = 55 percent). Planned purchases at cost for March (line 6) must be 55 percent of planned purchases at retail or $45,375 ($82,500 × 55 percent = $45,375). Planned initial markup for March (line 7) must be 45 percent of planned purchases, or $37,125 ($82,500 × 45 percent = $37,125).

DETERMINING THE BUYER'S PLANNED GROSS MARGIN

The buyer is accountable for the purchases made, the expected selling price of these purchases, the cost of these purchases, and the reductions that are involved in selling merchandise that the buyer has previously purchased. Therefore, the last step in developing the merchandise budget is determining the buyer's planned gross margin for the period. As already discussed, the buyer, in making plans, recognizes that the initial selling price for all the products will probably not be realized and that some reductions will occur. Referring to Exhibit 8.2, the buyer's planned gross margin for February (line 8) is determined by taking planned initial markup (line 7) and subtracting planned reductions (line 3) ($70,875 − $7,500 = $63,375).

DOLLAR $ & ¢ENTS

It is important for retailers to remember that the planned gross margin for a month in a merchandise budget, which is based on the purchases made that month, will not equal that month's gross margin on the retailer's financial statements, which is based on sales.

RETAIL ACCOUNTING STATEMENTS

Successful retailing also requires sound accounting practices. The number and types of accounting records needed depend on management's objectives. Large retailers generally require more detailed information usually based on merchandise lines or departments. Smaller retailers may be able to make first-hand observations on sales and inventory levels and make decisions before financial data are available. Still, the small retailer should consult the accounting records to confirm personal observations.

Properly prepared financial records provide measurements of profitability and retail performance. In addition, they show all transactions occurring within a given time period. However, these financial records must also provide the manager not only with a "look at the past" but also a "look into the future" so the manager can plan. Financial records not only indicate whether a retailer has achieved good results, they also indicate what growth potential and problem areas lie ahead:

1. Is a merchandise line outperforming or underperforming the rest of the store?
2. Is the inventory level adequate for the current sales level?
3. Is the firm's debt level too high (does the firm owe too much money)?
4. Are reductions, including markdowns, too high a percentage of sales?
5. Is the gross margin adequate for the firm's profit objectives?

These are a few of the questions that the financial data must answer for the retailer. The authors know of one company in which merchandise line "X" was generating an annual profit of $800,000 and merchandise line "Y" was losing money at the rate of $600,000. Management was totally unaware of the situation, just happy to be making $200,000! Management was astounded when a little accounting work revealed the true situation.

Let's look at the three financial statements most commonly used by retailers: the income statement, the balance sheet, and the statement of cash flow.

Income statement
is a financial statement that provides a summary of the sales and expenses for a given time period, usually a month, quarter, season, or year.

Gross sales
are the retailer's total sales including sales for cash or for credit.

Returns and allowances
are refunds of the purchase price or downward adjustments in selling prices due to customers returning purchases, or adjustments made in the selling price due to customer dissatisfaction with product or service performance.

INCOME STATEMENT

The most important financial statement that a retailer prepares is the income statement (also referred to as the profit and loss statement). The income statement provides a summary of the sales and expenses for a given time period, usually monthly, quarterly, seasonally, or annually. Comparison of current results with prior results allows the retailer to notice trends or changes in sales, expenses, and profits. Income statements can be broken down by departments, divisions, branches, and so on, enabling the retailer to evaluate each subunit's operating performance for the period. Exhibit 8.4a shows the basic format for an income statement, and Exhibit 8.4b shows the income statement for TMD Furniture.

Gross sales are the retailer's total sales including sales for cash or for credit. Returns and allowances are reductions from gross sales. Here, the retailer made a financial adjustment for customers because they have become dissatisfied with their purchases and returned the merchandise to the retailer. Because these reductions represent cancellations of previously recorded sales, the gross sales figure must be reduced to reflect these cancellations.

EXHIBIT 8.4A	RETAILERS' BASIC INCOME STATEMENT FORMAT	

Gross Sales		$_____
— Returns and Allowances	$_____	
Net Sales		$_____
— Cost of Goods Sold	$_____	
Gross Margin		$_____
— Operating Expenses	$_____	
Operating Profit		$_____
± Other Income or Expenses	$_____	
Net Profit Before Taxes		$_____

Net sales, gross sales less returns and allowances, represent the amount of merchandise the retailer actually sold during the time period.

Cost of goods sold is the cost of merchandise that has been sold during the period. Although this concept is easy to understand, the exact calculation of the cost of goods sold is somewhat complex. For example, like their own customers, retailers may obtain some return privileges or receive some allowances from vendors. Also, there is the issue of determining how inventory levels will be carried on the company's books. This is fully discussed in the next section of this chapter.

Gross margin is the difference between net sales and cost of goods sold or the amount available to cover operating expenses and produce a profit.

Operating expenses are those expenses that a retailer incurs in running the business other than the cost of the merchandise (e.g., rent, wages, utilities, depreciation, and insurance).

Operating profit is the difference between gross margin and operating expenses.

Other income or expenses includes income or expense items that the firm incurs although not in the course of its normal retail operations. For example, a retailer might have purchased some land to use for expansion and, after careful deliberation, postponed the expansion plans. Now, the retailer rents that land. Because renting land is not in the normal course of business for a retailer, the rent received would be considered other income.

Net profit is operating profit plus or minus other income or expenses. Net profit is the figure on which the retailer pays taxes and thus is usually referred to as net profit before taxes.

Most retailers actually divide the income statement into two sections: the first, or top half, being those elements above the gross margin total and the second, or bottom half, being those elements below the gross margin total. Sales and cost of goods sold are essentially controllable by the buying functions of the retail organization. In more and more retailing operations today, the buying organization is separated from the management of the operating expenses that are shown below gross margin. Some retailers use the terms *top line* (sales), *gross* (gross margin), and *bottom line* (profit) when referring to the key elements of their income statement.

Finally, generally accepted accounting principles (GAAP) allow for variations in how retailers report certain expenses. Pre-opening expenses, for example, can be

Net sales
is gross sales less returns and allowances.

Cost of goods sold
is the cost of merchandise that has been sold during the period.

Gross margin
is the difference between net sales and cost of goods sold.

Operating expenses
are those expenses that a retailer incurs in running the business other than the cost of the merchandise.

Operating profit
is gross margin less operating expenses.

Other income or expenses
includes income or expense items that the firm incurs which are not in the course of its normal retail operations.

Net profit
is operating profit plus or minus other income or expenses.

EXHIBIT 8.4B   SAMPLE INCOME STATEMENT

TMD Furniture, Inc.
Six Month Income Statement
July 31

				PERCENTAGE
Gross Sales			$393,671.79	
Less: Returns and Allowances			16,300.00	
Net Sales			$377,371.79	100%
Less: Cost of Goods Sold				
Beginning Inventory		$ 98,466.29		
Purchases		218,595.69		
Goods Available for Sales		$317,061.98		
Ending Inventory		103,806.23	213,255.75	56.5%
Gross Margin			$164,116.04	43.5%
Less: Operating Expenses				
Salaries & Wages:				
Managers	$18,480.50			
Selling	17,755.65			
Office	7,580.17			
Warehouse & Delivery	6,685.99	50,502.31		
Advertising		$ 15,236.67		
Administration and Warehouse Charge		800.00		
Credit, Collections and Bad Debts		1,973.96		
Contributions		312.50		
Delivery		1,434.93		
Depreciation		5,398.56		
Dues		23.50		
Employee Benefits		566.26		
Utilities		3,738.74		
Insurance		3,041.75		
Legal and Auditing		1,000.00		
Mds. Service & Repair		1,439.16		
Miscellaneous		602.00		
Rent		9,080.00		
Repairs & Maintenance		1,576.99		
Sales Allowances		180.50		
Supplies, Postage		1,135.40		
Taxes:				
City, County & State	$ 2,000.00			
Payroll	3,902.90	5,902.90		
Telephone		1,520.09		
Travel		404.92		
Warehouse Handling Charges		12,216.86	118,088.00	31.3%
Operating Profit			$ 46,028.04	12.2%
Other Income:				
Carrying Charges		$ 3,377.48		
Profit on sale of parking lot		740.47	4,117.95	1.1%
Net Profit Before Taxes			$ 50,145.99	13.3%

Natural disasters, such as this earthquake in Northridge, California, can cause major damage to a retailer's physical facilities and thus hurt the retailer's financial performance.

expensed as they occur, during the month the store opens, or capitalized and written off over several years. Advertising can be written off when the ad runs or when payment is made. Store fixtures can be depreciated over 5 years or 40 years. Thus, when comparing the financial statements of different retailers, it is important to know how each retailer treated these and other expenses.

BALANCE SHEET

The second accounting statement used in financial reporting is the balance sheet. A balance sheet shows the financial condition of a retailer's business at a particular point in time, as opposed to the income statement, which reports on the activities over a period of time. The balance sheet identifies and quantifies all the firm's assets and liabilities. The difference between assets and liabilities is owner's equity or net worth. Comparison of a current balance sheet with that from a previous time period enables a retail analyst to observe changes in the firm's financial condition.

A typical balance sheet format is illustrated in Exhibit 8.5. As Exhibit 8.5a shows the basic equation for a balance sheet is

$$\text{Assets} = \text{Liabilities} + \text{Net worth}$$

Hence both sides always must be in balance with each other. Exhibit 8.5b shows the balance sheet for TMD Furniture.

An asset is anything of value that is owned by the retail firm. Assets are broken down into two categories: current and noncurrent.

Current assets include cash and all other items that the retailer can easily convert into cash within a relatively short period of time (generally one year). Besides cash, current assets include accounts receivable, notes receivable, prepaid expenses, and inventory. Accounts and/or notes receivable are amounts that customers or others owe the retailer for goods and services. Frequently, the retailer will reduce the total receivables by a fixed percentage (based on past experience) to take into account those customers who may be unwilling or unable to pay. Prepaid expenses are those items such as trash collection or insurance for which the retailer has already paid but the service has not been completed. Retail inventories comprise merchandise that the retailer has in the store or in storage and is available for sale.

Balance sheet
is a financial statement that shows the financial condition of a retailer's business at a particular point in time and quantifies the retailer's assets and liabilities.

Asset
is anything of value that is owned by the retail firm.

Current assets
are assets that can be easily converted into cash within a relatively short time (usually a year or less).

Accounts and/or notes receivable
are amounts that customers or others owe the retailer for goods and services.

Prepaid expenses
are those items for which the retailer has already paid, but the service has not been completed.

Retail inventories
comprise merchandise that the retailer has in the store or in storage and is available for sale.

EXHIBIT 8.5A   RETAILERS' BASIC BALANCE SHEET FORMAT

Current Assets			Current Liabilities		
Cash	$_____		Accounts Payable	$_____	
Accounts Receivable	$_____		Payroll Payable	$_____	
Inventory	$_____		Current Notes Payable	$_____	
Prepaid Expenses	$_____		Taxes Payable	$_____	
Total Current Assets		$_____	Total Current Liabilities		$_____
Noncurrent Assets			Long-term Liabilities		
Building (less depreciation)	$_____		Long-term Notes		
Fixtures and Equipment			Payable	$_____	
(less depreciation)	$_____		Mortgage Payable	$_____	
Total Noncurrent Assets		$_____			
Goodwill		$_____	Total Long-term Liabilities		$_____
			Net Worth		
			Capital Surplus	$_____	
			Retained Earnings	$_____	
			Total Net Worth		$_____
			Total Liabilities and		
Total Assets		$_____	**Net Worth**		$_____

EXHIBIT 8.5B   SAMPLE BALANCE SHEET

TMD Furniture
Balance Sheet
July 31

Current Assets			Current Liabilities		
Cash	$ 11,589		Accounts Payable	$57,500	
Accounts Receivable	71,517		Payroll Payable	$ 1,451	
Inventory	103,806		Current Notes Payable	$14,000	
			Taxes Payable	$ 1,918	
Total Current Assets		186,912	Total Current Liabilities		$ 74,869
Noncurrent Assets			Long-term Liabilities		
Building (less depreciation)	$ 61,414		Long-term Notes Payable	$52,750	
Fixtures and Equipment			Mortgage Payable	$38,500	
(less depreciation)	$ 11,505				
Total Noncurrent Assets		72,919	Total Long-term Liabilities		$ 91,250
Goodwill		100	Net Worth		$ 93,812
Total Assets		$259,931	**Total Liabilities** and		
			Net Worth		$259,931

Nordstrom has created a high degree of brand equity for the Nordstrom name by focusing on high levels of personalized customer service. Nonetheless, accounting standards in the United States do not allow this brand equity to be recorded on Nordstrom's balance sheet.

DRESSING UP THE BALANCE SHEET

Retailers, especially small retailers, learned a long time ago that lenders judge the worth and creditability of a business by the firm's financial statements. Thus, many retailers make their statements look as good as possible. Listed below are a number of questionable activities retailers do to window-dress their books.

First, because ratio analysis is probably the most common way lenders analyze a balance sheet, retailers try to improve their ratios by doing the following.

Some attempt to improve the current ratio (current assets divided by current liabilities) by paying off current debt before the review. For example, suppose a retailer has $20,000 in cash, $30,000 in other current assets, and $25,000 in current liabilities, for a current ratio of 2 : 1. If $12,500 of the cash is used to reduce

debt, however, the ratio improves significantly to 3 : 1. The same thing occurs when a retailer exchanges long-term debt for short-term debt.

Another method is to have the retailer borrow against receivables from a bank or a finance company. Retailers normally issue a payment to the lender for any collection on these receivables. As a result, on the day the retailer collects from a customer, the retailer's bank balance is impressive. The next day, however, it is anemic again.

Another method troubled retailers use to improve their balance sheet is to have the lending institution agree to a slower repayment schedule, enabling the retailer to build up its cash balance.

Are the methods legal? Are they ethical? Would you use them?

Noncurrent assets are those assets that cannot be converted into cash in a short period of time (usually 12 months) in the normal course of business. These noncurrent or long-term assets include buildings, parking lots, the land under the building and parking lot, fixtures (i.e., display racks), and equipment (i.e., air conditioning system). These items are carried on the books as cost less accumulated depreciation on everything except the land. Depreciation is necessary because most noncurrent assets have a limited useful life; the difference between the asset and depreciation is intended to provide a more realistic picture of the retailer's assets and prevent an overstatement or understatement of these assets. However, as every retailer has learned, the value of real estate property can fluctuate greatly over time. When Kmart had its financial problems in 1996, many retail analysts disagreed over the value of noncurrent assets carried on Kmart's books, especially with regards to the real estate in the northeastern part of the United States. Some argued that the value was greater than book value because some locations were in prime urban locations in major cities where property values had increased over the 20 to 30 years since Kmart purchased the property. Others noted that it might be true for some locations, but that in many locations the value had decreased as the neighborhood had declined. Thus, one should always recognize that the value recorded on the retailer's books for noncurrent assets is probably not reflective of their actual value.

DOLLAR $ & CENTS

Although noncurrent assets are important in retailing, the high-performance retailer recognizes that current assets (primarily inventory) are usually more critical to achieving outstanding performance.

Some retailers also include goodwill as an asset. Goodwill is an intangible asset, usually based on customer loyalty, that a retailer pays for when buying an existing business. Usually, the dollar value assigned to goodwill is minimal.

Total assets equal current assets plus noncurrent assets plus goodwill.

The other part of the balance sheet reflects the retailer's liabilities and net worth. A liability is any legitimate financial claim against the retailer's assets. Liabilities are classified as either current or long-term.

Current liabilities are short-term debts that are payable within a year. Included here are accounts payable, notes payable that are due within a year, payroll payable, and taxes payable. Accounts payable are amounts owed vendors for goods and services. Payroll payable is money due employees on past labor. Taxes due the government (federal, state, or local) are also considered a current liability. Some retailers also include interest due within the year on long-term notes or mortgages as a current liability.

Long-term liabilities include notes payable and mortgages not due within the year. Total liabilities equal current liabilities plus long-term liabilities.

Net worth, also called owner's equity, is the difference between the firm's total assets and total liabilities and represents the owner's equity in the business. The figure

Retailers not only need to invest in merchandise, but also land, store facilities, and parking lots.

reflects the owner's original investment plus any profits reinvested in the business less any losses incurred in the business and any funds that the owner has taken out of the business.

In actuality, the balance sheet doesn't reflect all the retailer's assets and liabilities. Specifically, such items as store personnel can be an asset, or a liability, to the business. These items might not appear on the balance sheet but are extremely important to the success of a high-performance retailer. Other items that could be either assets or liabilities, although not in the strict accounting sense, are goodwill, customer loyalty, and even vendor relationships. Each of these items can contribute to the success or failure of a retailer.

The mere fact that a retailer reports increased earnings each year and the balance sheet looks great should not lead one to believe that everything is fine. As the Winners & Losers box on page 283 points out, in very rare cases, financial statements can be fraudulent. However, a careful analysis of the statements should have warned individuals about one of the largest frauds in retailing history.

STATEMENT OF CASH FLOW

A third financial statement that retailers can use to help understand their business is the statement of cash flow. A statement of cash flow lists in detail the source and type of all revenue (cash inflows) and the use and type of all expenditures (cash outflows) for a given time period. When cash inflows exceed cash outflows, the retailer is said to have a positive cash flow; when cash outflows exceed cash inflows the retailer is said to be experiencing a negative cash flow. Thus the purpose of the statement of cash flow is to enable the retailer to project the cash needs of the firm. Based on projections, plans may be made to either seek additional financing if a negative flow is projected or to make other investments if a positive flow is anticipated. Likewise, a retailer with a positive cash flow for the period might be able to take advantage of "good deals" from vendors.

Statement of cash flow *is a financial statement that lists in detail the source and type of all cash inflows and the use and type of all cash outflows for a given time period.*

Maybe We Should Have Examined the Books a Little Closer

Since its beginnings in the early 1980s, retail analysts believed that Phar-Mor Inc., a Youngstown, Ohio, operator of 310 deep-discount drugstores, could do no wrong. Phar-Mor's concept of relying on sharp buyers to pounce on manufacturer's special deals was well positioned for the value-conscious consumer of the 1990s. Bargain hunters flocked to its stores and sales exceeded $3 billion in 1991. Consequently, most retail analysts expected them to continue their rapid growth into the 21st century. Even Sam Walton wondered how they could make money with the prices they charged.

However, everything changed in July 1992 when the company fired two key executives and announced that its books had been falsified by $500 million—the largest retail fraud ever uncovered. The fraud began as a scheme to inflate lower-than-expected earnings by overstating payments, reportedly as much as $25 million, made by large vendors such as Gibson Greetings Inc. and Rubbermaid Inc. The vendors made these payments in exchange for an "exclusive supply agreement" covering specific time periods. For example, Rubbermaid created a large "Everything Rubbermaid" department for each store, and Gibson, as an exclusive supplier, was promised an expanded greeting card department.

Actually, this was just one of the ways retailers can improve their performance by "cooking the books," and with the computer, it may actually be easier to do than when all accounting was done manually. For example, buyers have always been under great pressure to produce profits. The following is an illustration to show how easy an unscrupulous retailer, such as Phar-Mor, can take advantage of the firm's use of the computer to produce phony profits. Such behavior would have been difficult to do in the past, before the advent of the computer.

Most retailers appreciate the computer's help in tracking sales, controlling inventory, and developing work schedules; what many are not aware of is their ability to produce nonexisting profits, which Phar-Mor was able to do. Consider the following two cases.

Under the Old System (Precomputer): A buyer purchases 1,000 camper shorts at $15 to sell at $29.95. After the first week, the buyer notices that none of the shorts were sold, so the buyer realizes his or her mistake and marks them down to $13.88 and has the stockers mark each pair of shorts with the new price. On the general ledger, the buyer takes a reduction of $16,070 (1,000 × $16.07). During the first week at the new price, 100 shorts are sold. The price of $13.88 would remain until the buyer lowered the price again. (Remember, it would be difficult to have the buyer increase the price, because the $13.88 stickers would probably still show. In addition, the labor costs would be high.) Anyway, the inventory on hand for the shorts would now be $12,492 (900 × $13.88).

With a New Computer System: The same facts as above, except that after selling the 100 pairs of shorts, the buyers realizes that the "annual inventory" is about to be taken.

"Oh my, what should I do if I want a bonus?" How about "cooking the books"?

Simply re-enter the original selling price of $29.95 in the computer and change the price on the shelf. (Remember, with the new computer system, the buyer doesn't have to re-mark each item. Now, our inventory would be $26,955 (900 × $29.95).

By simply changing the price in the computer, the buyer increased profits by $14,463 (900 × the markdown of $16.07), and there is no way an outside auditor would detect the "phony profit." After all, the auditors will check the count and the price in the computer's PLU (price look-up) and find both to be correct.

The buyer/department manager/store manager and even the divisional merchandise manager would all get a bigger bonus based on the phony computer entry.

Now they have to find a way to make up for this phony entry before next year's inventory. This was Phar-Mor's undoing.

SOURCE: Based on an idea given the authors by Bob Kahn.

A statement of cash flow is not the same as an income statement. In a statement of cash flow, the retailer is only concerned with the movement of cash into or out of the firm, whereas an income statement reflects the profitability of the retailer after all revenue and expenses are considered. Consider the example of TMD Furniture for the month of August as shown in Exhibit 8.6a.

August is a slow month for furniture sales as many customers are taking vacations, and as a result TMD is expecting sales of only $40,000 for the month. However, only $15,450 of that amount will be for cash, and TMD expects to collect $24,998 on its account receivables. Along with a tax refund check due from the state for $97, TMD has projected a cash inflow of $40,545 for August. However, because August is the month that several notes and accounts payable are due, TMD Furniture is expecting to have to pay out $48,372 during August. This will result in a negative cash flow for the month of $7,827. TMD has prepared for this by having cash on hand (as reported on the July 31 balance sheet) of $11,589. However, many retailers forget about cash and realize the difference between cash flow and profit only after the coffers are empty. In the case of TMD Furniture, paying off the notes and accounts payable had no effect on the income statement. Likewise, the statement of cash flow only considered that part of purchases that were paid for with cash, not those placed on account. These credit purchasers had no direct effect on the cash flow. Exhibit 8.6b lists the typical retailer's cash inflow and outflow items. Retailers that decide to use major credit cards, instead of handling their own credit operations, are able to convert sales much more quickly to cash because they don't need to wait for customers to pay for their purchases—some other party such as a bank assumes this financing function.

Although the statement of cash flow is generally not considered as important as the income statement, more and more retailers are becoming aware of its importance. In fact, the number 1 cause of retailing bankruptcies in recent years has been cash flow problems. A retailer can be growing quickly and be profitable but yet fail due to inadequate cash flow.

The lack of a sufficient cash flow isn't limited to those large troubled chains you hear about on television. Many a small entrepreneur came up with a brilliant idea for a retail operation only to fail. The entrepreneur's problems usually started by overestimating revenues and underestimating costs, resulting in a negative cash flow. By not making sure they had enough cash on hand to withstand a rocky two years of starting up a business, most retailers are ensuring themselves failure. No wonder more than a quarter of all new retail operations fail during the first two years. As a result, as shown in our Winners & Losers box on page 286, some of these unsuccessful retailers often resort to questionable tactics to improve their financial statements.

Current ratio
is current assets divided by current liabilities.

EXHIBIT 8.6A	SAMPLE CASH FLOW STATEMENT

TMD Furniture, Inc.
Cash Flow Statement
July 31

Cash Sales	$15,450	
Collection of Accounts Receivable	24,998	
Refund on State Taxes	97	
Total Cash Inflow		$40,545
Cash Outflow		
Rent	$1,513	
Purchases at Cash	5,750	
Salaries	8,483	
Utilities	1,450	
Advertising	2,300	
County Taxes	173	
Supplies	921	
Telephone	150	
Paying Off Accounts Payable	20,632	
Paying Off Notes Payable	7,000	
Total Cash Outflow		$48,372
Total Cash Flow		($7,827)

EXHIBIT 8.6B	TYPICAL CASH INFLOW AND OUTFLOW CATEGORIES

CASH INFLOW	CASH OUTFLOWS
Cash sales	Paying for merchandise
Collecting accounts receivable	Rent expenses
Collecting notes receivable	Utilities expenses
Collecting other debts	Wages and Salary expenses
Sale of fixed assets	Advertising expense
Sale of stock	Insurance premiums
	Taxes
	Interest expenses
	Supplies and other expenses
	Purchase of other assets
	Paying off accounts payable
	Paying off notes payable
	Buying back company stocks
	Paying dividends

INVENTORY VALUATION

LO • 3
Explain how the retailer
is able to value inventory

Due to the many different merchandise lines carried, inventory valuation is complex. Yet the retailer must have information such as sales, additional purchases not yet received, reductions for the period, gross margin, open-to-buy, stock shortages, and inventory levels to operate profitably.

There are two major decisions that a retailer must make with regard to valuing inventory: (1) the accounting inventory system and (2) the inventory pricing method to use.

ACCOUNTING INVENTORY SYSTEM

Two accounting inventory systems are available for the retailer: (1) the cost method and (2) the retail method. We describe both methods on the basis of the frequency with which inventory information is received, difficulties encountered in completing a physical inventory and maintaining records, and the extent to which stock shortages can be calculated.

THE COST METHOD
The cost method of inventory valuation provides a book valuation of inventory based solely on the retailer's cost including freight. It looks only at the cost of each item as it is recorded in the accounting records when purchased. When a physical inventory is taken, all the items are counted, the cost of each item is taken from the records or the price tags, and the total inventory value at cost is calculated.

One of the easiest methods of coding the cost of merchandise on the price tag is to use the first 10 of the alphabet to represent the price. Here A = 1, B = 2, C = 3, D = 4, E = 5, F = 6, G = 7, H = 8, I = 9, J = 0. A product with the code HEAD has a cost of $85.14. The cost method is useful for those retailers who sell big-ticket items and allow price negotiations by customers. Sales personnel can know from the code how much room there is for negotiation to cover the cost of the merchandise plus operating expenses.

The cost method of inventory valuation does have several limitations:

1. It is difficult to do daily inventories (or even monthly inventories).
2. It is difficult to cost out each sale.
3. It is difficult to allocate freight charges to each item's cost of goods sold.

The cost method is generally used by those retailers with big-ticket items and a limited number of sales per day (i.e., a jewelry store selling expensive rings or an antique furniture store), in which there are few lines or limited inventory requirements, infrequent price changes, and low turnover rates.

THE RETAIL METHOD
The retail method of inventory values merchandise at current retail prices. It overcomes the disadvantages of the cost method by keeping detailed records of inventory based on the retail value of the merchandise. The fact that the inventory is valued in retail dollars makes it a little more difficult for the retailer to determine the cost of goods sold when computing the gross margin for a time period.

Cost method
is an inventory valuation technique which provides a book valuation of inventory based solely on the retailer's cost of merchandise including freight.

Retail method
is an inventory valuation technique that values merchandise at current retail prices which is then converted to cost based on a formula.

EXHIBIT 8.7	INVENTORY AVAILABLE FOR WHITENER'S SPORTING GOODS SALE, FALL SEASON, 199X	
	COST	RETAIL
Beginning Inventory	$199,000	$401,000
Net Purchases	70,000	154,000
Additional Markups		5,000
Freight-in	1,000	
Total Inventory Available for Sale	$270,000	$560,000

There are three basic steps in computing an ending inventory value by using the retail method: calculation of the cost complement, calculation of reductions from retail value, and conversion of the adjusted retail book inventory to cost.

STEP 1.   CALCULATION OF THE COST COMPLEMENT   Inventories, both beginning and ending, and purchases are recorded at both cost and retail levels when using the retail method. Exhibit 8.7 shows an inventory statement for Whitener's Sporting Goods for the fall season.

In Exhibit 8.7, the beginning inventory is shown at both cost and retail. Net purchases, which are the total purchases less merchandise returned to vendors, allowances, and discounts from vendors, are also valued at cost and retail. Additional markups are the total increases in the retail price of merchandise already in stock that were caused by inflation or heavy demand and are shown at retail. Freight-in is the cost to the retailer for transportation of merchandise from the vendor and is shown in the cost column.

By using the information from Exhibit 8.7, the retailer can calculate the average relationship of cost to the retail price for all merchandise available for sale during the fall season. This calculation is called the cost complement:

$$\text{Cost complement} = \text{Total cost valuation/Total retail valuation}$$
$$= \$270,000/\$560,000 = 0.482$$

Because the cost complement is 0.482, or 48.2 percent, 48.2 cents of every retail sales dollar is comprised of merchandise cost.

STEP 2.   CALCULATION OF REDUCTIONS FROM RETAIL VALUE   During the course of day-to-day business activities, the retailer must take reductions from inventory. In addition to sales that lower the retail inventory level, retail inventory levels can be lowered by retail reductions. These reductions include markdowns (sales, reduced prices on end-of-season, discontinued, or shopworn merchandise); discounts (employee, senior citizen, student, religious, etc.); and stock shortages (employee and customer theft, breakage). Markdowns and employee discounts can be recorded throughout an accounting period, but a physical inventory is required to calculate stock shortages.

In Exhibit 8.7, it was shown that Whitener's had a retail inventory available for sale of $560,000 for the upcoming fall season. This must be reduced by actual fall season

EXHIBIT 8.8	WHITENER'S SPORTING GOODS ENDING BOOK VALUE AT RETAIL, FALL SEASON, 199X		
		COST	RETAIL
Inventory Available for Sale at Retail			$560,000
Less Reductions:			
Sales		$145,000	
Markdowns		12,000	
Discounts		$ 2,000	
Total Reductions			159,000
Ending Book Value of Inventory at Retail			$401,000

EXHIBIT 8.9	WHITENER'S SPORTING GOODS, STOCK SHORTAGE (OVERAGE) ADJUSTMENT ENTRY, END OF FALL SEASON, 199X		
		COST	RETAIL
Ending Book Value of Inventory at Retail			$401,000
Physical Inventory (at retail)			398,000
Stock Shortages			$ 3,000
Adjusting Ending Book Value of Inventory at Retail			$398,000

sales of $145,000, markdowns of $12,000, and discounts of $2,000. This results in the ending book value of inventory having a retail level of $401,000. This is shown in Exhibit 8.8.

Once the ending book value of inventory at retail is determined, a comparison can be made to the physical inventory to compute the actual stock shortages; if the book value is greater than the physical count, a stock shortage has occurred. If the book value is lower than the physical count, a stock overage has occurred. Shortages are due to thefts, breakages, overshipments not billed to customers, and bookkeeping errors, the most common cause. These errors result from the failure to properly record markdowns, returns, discounts, and breakages. Many retailers have greatly reduced their original shortage estimate by reviewing the season's bookkeeping entries. A stock overage, an excess of physical inventory over book inventory, is usually the result of bookkeeping errors, either miscounting during the physical inventory or improper book entries. Exhibit 8.9 shows the results of Whitener's physical inventory and the resulting adjustment.

Because a physical inventory must be taken to determine shortages (overages) and retailers only take a physical count once or twice a year, shortages (overages) are often estimated in merchandise budgets as shown in Exhibits 8.1 and 8.2. As a rule of thumb, retailers may estimate monthly shortages between 1/2 to 3 percent.

EXHIBIT 8.10	WHITENER'S SPORTING GOODS INCOME STATEMENTS AUGUST 1–JANUARY 31		
		COST	RETAIL
Sales			$145,000
Less: Cost of Goods Sold:			
Beginning Inventory (at Cost)		$200,000	
Purchases (at Cost)		70,000	
Goods Available for Sale		$270,000	
Ending Inventory (at Cost)		191,836	
Cost of Goods Sold			78,164
Gross Margin			$66,836
Less: Operating Expenses			
Salaries		$ 30,000	
Utilities		1,000	
Rent		19,000	
Depreciation (Fixtures + Equipment)		2,200	
Total Operating Expenses			52,200
Net Profit Before Taxes			$14,636

STEP 3. CONVERSION OF THE ADJUSTED RETAIL BOOK INVENTORY TO COST   The final step to be performed in using the retail method is to convert to cost the adjusted retail book inventory figure to determine the closing inventory at cost. The procedure involved here is to multiply the adjusted retail book inventory ($398,000 in the case of Whitener's) by the cost complement (0.482 in the Whitener's example):

$$\text{Closing inventory (at cost)} = \text{Adjusted retail} \times \text{Cost complement book inventory}$$
$$= \$398,000 \times 0.482 = \$191,836$$

Although this equation does not yield the actual closing inventory at cost, it does provide a close approximation of the cost figure. Remember that the cost complement is an average. Now that ending inventory at cost has been determined, the retailer can determine gross margin, as well as net profit before taxes, if operating expenses are known. We discuss expenses in more detail later. In the Whitener's example, let's use $30,000 for salaries, $1,000 for utilities, $19,000 for rent, and $2,200 for depreciation. This is shown in Exhibit 8.10.

The retail method has several advantages over the cost method of inventory valuation. Among these advantages are

1. Accounting statements can be drawn up at any time. Inventories need not be taken for preparation of these statements.
2. Physical inventories using retail prices are less subject to error and can be completed in a shorter amount of time.
3. The retail method provides an automatic, conservative valuation of ending inventory as well as inventory levels throughout the season. This is especially useful in cases in which the retailer is forced to submit insurance claims for damaged or lost merchandise.

A major complaint against the retail method is that it is a "method of averages." This refers to the fact that closing inventory is valued at the average relationship between cost and retail (the cost complement) and that large retailers offer many different classifications and lines with different relationships. This disadvantage can be overcome by computing cost complements for individual lines or departments.

Another limitation is the heavy burden placed on bookkeeping activities. The true ending book inventory value can be correctly calculated only if there are no errors in recording beginning inventory, purchases, freight-in, markups, markdowns, discounts, returns, transfers between stores, and sales. As noted earlier, many of the retailers' original shortages have later been determined to be bookkeeping errors.

INVENTORY PRICING SYSTEMS

Two methods of pricing inventory are first in, first out (FIFO) and last in, first out (LIFO). The FIFO method assumes that the oldest merchandise is sold before the more recently purchased merchandise. Therefore, merchandise on the shelf will reflect the most current replacement price. During inflationary periods, this method allows "inventory profits" (caused by selling the less expensive earlier inventory rather than the more expensive newer inventory) to be included as income.

The LIFO method is designed to cushion the impact of inflationary pressures by matching current costs against current revenues. Cost of goods sold is based on the costs of the most recently purchased inventory, whereas the older inventory is regarded as the unsold inventory. The LIFO method results during inflationary periods in the application of a higher unit cost to the merchandise sold and a lower unit cost to inventory still unsold. In times of rapid inflation, most retailers use the LIFO method, resulting in lower profits on the income statement but also lower income taxes. Most retailers also prefer to use LIFO for planning purposes, because it accurately reflects replacement costs. In addition, the Internal Revenue Service only permits a retailer to change its method of accounting once. Due to these limitations, most retailers today use the retail method of inventory valuation, which was created in the early 1900s.

Let's study an example of the effect of the LIFO and FIFO methods of inventory valuation on the firm's financial performance. Suppose that you began the year with a total inventory of 15 fax machines that you purchased on the last day of the preceding year for $300 each. Thus, if the fax machines were the only merchandise you had in stock, your beginning inventory was $4,500 (15 × $300). Suppose also that during the year you sold 12 fax machines for $700 each for total sales of $8,400, that in June you purchased eight new fax machines (same make and model as your old ones) at $325, and that in November you bought four more at $350. Thus, your purchases were $2,600 in June and $1,400 in November, for a total of $4,000, and you would still have 15 fax machines in stock at year-end. Under the LIFO inventory approach, your ending inventory would be the same as it was at the beginning of the year ($4,500), because we would assume that the 12 fax machines sold were the 12 purchased during the year. However, using the FIFO approach, we would assume that we sold 12 of the original $300 fax machines and had three left. These three fax machines, along with June's and November's purchases, result in an ending inventory of $4,900 [(3 × $300) + (4 × $350)]. Now, let's see how these approaches can affect our gross margins.

FIFO

stands for first in, first out and values inventory based on the assumption that the oldest merchandise is sold before the more recently purchased merchandise.

LIFO

stands for last in, first out and values inventory based on the assumption that the most recently purchased merchandise is sold first and the oldest merchandise is sold last.

	LIFO	FIFO
Net sales	$8,400	$8,400
Less: Cost of goods sold		
Beginning inventory	$4,500	$4,500
Purchases	4,000	4,000
Goods available	$8,500	$8,500
Ending inventory	4,500	4,900
Cost of goods sold	4,000	3,600
Gross margin	$4,400	$4,800

STUDENT STUDY GUIDE

SUMMARY

LO•1 **WHY IS A MERCHANDISE BUDGET SO IMPORTANT IN RETAIL PLANNING AND HOW IS A MERCHANDISE BUDGET PREPARED?**
The purpose of this chapter has been to introduce you to the major financial statements and their importance in retail planning. We began our discussion with the six-month merchandise budget. This statement projects sales, when and how much new merchandise should be ordered, what markup is to be taken, what reductions are to be planned, and the target or planned gross margin for the season. The establishment of such a budget has several advantages for the retailer:

1. The six-month budget controls the amount of inventory and forces management to control markups and reductions.
2. The budget helps to determine how much merchandise should be purchased so that inventory requirements can be met.
3. The budget can be compared with actual or final results to determine the performance of the firm.

We concluded our discussion of the six-month merchandise budget by showing how each of the figures is determined. We illustrated how to estimate sales, inventory levels, reductions, purchases, and gross margin.

LO•2 **WHAT IS THE DIFFERENCES AMONG, AND THE USES OF, THESE THREE ACCOUNTING STATEMENTS: INCOME STATEMENT, BALANCE SHEET, AND STATEMENT OF CASH FLOW?** The second section of this chapter explained how the retailer uses three important accounting statements: the income statement, the balance sheet, and the statement of cash flow. The income statement gives the retailer a summary of the income and expenses incurred over a given time period. A balance sheet shows the financial condition of the retailer at a particular point in time. The statement of cash flow lists in detail the source and types of all revenue and expenditures for a given time period.

LO•3 **HOW DOES A RETAILER VALUE ITS INVENTORY?** The final section of this chapter described two decisions that a retailer must make with regard to inventory record keeping: the accounting system (cost or retail) and whether to use the LIFO or FIFO pricing method.

The cost system is the simplest, but the retail system is the most widely used because of these advantages:

1. Accounting statements can be drawn up at any time.
2. Physical inventories using retail prices are less subject to error and can be completed in a shorter amount of time.
3. The retail method provides an automatic, conservative valuation of ending inventory as well as inventory levels throughout the season.

The FIFO method assumes that the oldest merchandise is sold before the more recently purchased merchandise, making merchandise on the shelf more accurately reflect the replacement price. During inflationary periods, this method allows "inventory profits" to be included as income. The LIFO method is designed to cushion the impact of inflationary pressures by matching current costs against current revenues. Cost of goods sold are based on the costs of the most recently purchased inventory, whereas the older inventory is regarded as the unsold inventory. In times of rapid inflation, most retailers use the LIFO method, resulting in lower profits on the income statement but also lower income taxes. Most retailers also prefer to use LIFO for planning purposes, because it accurately reflects replacement costs.

TERMS TO REMEMBER

merchandising	prepaid expenses
merchandise budget	retail inventories
stock-to-sales ratio	noncurrent assets
income statement	goodwill
gross sales	total assets
returns and allowances	liability
net sales	current liabilties
cost of goods sold	accounts payable
gross margin	long-term liabilities
operating expenses	total liabilities
operating profit	net worth
other income or expenses	statement of cash flow
net profit	current ratio
balance sheet	cost method
asset	retail method
current assets	FIFO
accounts and/or notes receivable	LIFO

REVIEW AND DISCUSSION QUESTIONS

LO•1 WHY IS A MERCHANDISE BUDGET SO IMPORTANT IN RETAIL PLANNING AND HOW IS A MERCHANDISE BUDGET PREPARED?

1. What are the components of a merchandise budget?
2. What rules should be used in developing a merchandise budget?
3. Retailers must carry an amount of inventory in excess of planned sales for an upcoming period. Why?
4. What is a stock-to-sales ratio?
5. Why should a retailer be allowed to change its merchandise budget after the start of a season? Shouldn't plans be made so that they aren't changed?
6. A retailer, who last year had sales of $120,000, plans for an inflation rate of 5 percent and a 4 percent increase in market share. What should planned sales for this year be?
7. The number of transactions is expected to decline 5 percent, but owing to rising prices, the value of the average sale will be increased 5 percent. If sales last year were $100,000, what will they be this year?

LO•2 WHAT ARE THE DIFFERENCES AMONG, AND THE USES OF, THESE THREE ACCOUNTING STATEMENTS: INCOME STATEMENT, BALANCE SHEET, AND STATEMENT OF CASH FLOW?

8. In what ways are the balance sheet and the income statement different? How do retailers use these two financial statements?
9. What is the difference between a statement of cash flow and an income statement?
10. The Toy Shoppe is trying to determine its net profit before taxes. Use the following data to find The Toy Shoppe's net profit.

Rent	$ 25,000	Salaries	$ 60,000
Purchases	$150,000	Sales	$420,000
Ending inventory	$120,000	Utilities	$ 40,000
Beginning inventory	$110,000		

11. A hardware store with sales for the year of $200,000 and other income of $23,000 has operating expenses of $80,000. Its cost of goods sold is $95,000. What is its gross margin, its operating profit, and its net profit in dollars?

LO•3 HOW DOES A RETAILER VALUE ITS INVENTORY?

12. List the advantages and disadvantages that the retail method of inventory valuation has over the cost method.
13. Define FIFO and LIFO and the reasons for using one or the other.
14. Why is it difficult to determine the exact value of inventory when preparing financial statements?

SAMPLE TEST QUESTIONS

LO•1 WHICH ONE OF THE FOLLOWING FACTORS IS NOT FOUND ON A SIX-MONTH MERCHANDISE BUDGET?

a. planned gross margin
b. current liabilities
c. planned sales percentage
d. planned BOM stock
e. planned purchases at retail

LO•2 THE _____ PROVIDES THE RETAILER WITH A PICTURE OF THE ORGANIZATION'S PROFIT AND LOSS SITUATION.

a. expense report
b. index of inventory valuation
c. statement of cash flow
d. income statement
e. statement of gross margin

LO•3 THE TOTAL COST VALUATION OF A RETAILER'S INVENTORY IS $120,000, WHEREAS THE TOTAL RETAIL VALUATION OF SALES WAS $200,000. APPROXIMATELY HOW MUCH OF EVERY RETAIL SALES DOLLAR IS MADE UP OF MERCHANDISE COST?

a. 12 cents
b. 40 cents
c. 60 cents
d. $1.20
e. $1.50

APPLICATIONS

WRITING AND SPEAKING EXERCISE   Over the past few years, the inflation rate has been about 3 percent. However, new economic forecasts predict that the inflation rate will double next year to 6 percent. The cost of goods sold at your family owned men's wear shop mirrors the country's inflation rate, so you expect your cost to increase by 6 percent. Your father asks you to prepare a memo detailing how this new information will affect the profitability of the business if it continues to use a FIFO method of valuing inventory.

RETAIL PROJECT   Go to the library or the internet [www.sec.gov/edgarhp.htm] and look at the most recent annual reports for four or five of the Top 25 Retailers listed on the inside front and back covers of this book. Using the financial data from these reports, compare the net cash flow to the net income for each of the retailers you chose and explain the reason for the differences.

CASE DOLLY'S PLACE

Last year, after years of teaching retailing/merchandising at the local university, Dolly Loyd decided to retire and return to her first love—running an intimate apparel store. Because she used to run such a department for a major retail chain before teaching, she kept up with the current trends in the industry. Dolly gained the support of several ex-students, who soon joined her in her new endeavor.

Today, Dolly is beginning to make plans for the upcoming fall season. Dolly anticipates planned sales of $300,000 for the fall season based on a planned initial markup of 50 percent. Within the season, planned monthly sales are projected to be as follows: 15 percent in August and September, 10 percent in October, 20 percent in November, 30 percent in December, and 10 percent in January. To ensure a profitable season, trade association records were consulted. The records indicated (1) the stock-to-sales ratios need to be 3.5 for August, 3.0 for September, 4.0 for October, 3.0 for November, 2.5 for December, and 4.0 for January; (2) reductions can be planned at 10 percent for the first four months, 20 percent for December, and 30 percent for January; and (3) with Valentine's Day approaching, an inventory of $180,000 will be necessary to begin the spring season. Complete a six-month merchandise budget for Dolly.

PLANNING YOUR OWN RETAIL BUSINESS   You are unsure of what level of sales to forecast for your new drugstore, which you plan to open on New Years Day. Consequently, you have decided to make some assumptions. You believe that it is reasonable to assume that your trade area will encompass about 25 square miles. The city planning department has told you that within this area the population density is 2,857 individuals per square mile. You conservatively estimate that 20 percent of these individuals will visit your store an average of four times annually and that 85 percent will purchase something on a typical visit. You expect them to purchase an average of $25 per visit to your store. Information you have available from industry sources suggests that drugstores do more business in the Fall and Winter. In fact, you expect sales during each of November, December, January, and February to be 10 percent of your annual volume. The remaining eight months will share equally the

DOLLY'S PLACE SIX-MONTH MERCHANDISE BUDGET	DATE MAY 15 TH SEASON FALL						
FALL/WINTER	AUGUST	SEPT	OCT	NOV	DEC	JAN	SEASON TOTAL
1. Planned BOM[a] Stock							
2. Planned Sales							
3. Planned Retail Reductions							
4. Planned EOM[b] Stock							
5. Planned Purchases @ Retail							
6. Planned Purchases @ Cost							
7. Planned Initial Markup							
8. Planned Gross Margin							
9. Planned BOM Stock/Sales Ratio	3.5	3.0	4.0	3.0	2.5	4.0	—
10. Planned Sales Percentage	15%	15%	10%	20%	30%	10%	100%
11. Planned Retail Reduction Percentage	10%	10%	10%	10%	20%	30%	15%

Planned total sales for the period $300,000
Planned total retail reduction percentage for the period   15%
Planned initial markup percentage for the period   50%
Planned BOM stock for February $180,000

Note: All dollar signs have been deleted from the merchandise budget grid.
[a] BOM refers to beginning-of-the-month.
[b] EOM refers to end-of-the-month.

60 percent of remaining sales. You believe for your business to be profitable you need to have a BOM inventory-to-sales ratio of 3.0 for October through November and 2.5 for the remaining months. You want to plan your BOM inventory for each of the next 12 months. You also want to begin the first month of your second year of business with $50,000 in inventory at retail prices.

CHAPTER 9

MERCHANDISE BUYING AND HANDLING

Toys "Я" Us, which is the largest toy retailer in the world with stores in over a dozen countries, has developed a high level of expertise in the toy buying preferences of children, parents, and grandparents.

OVERVIEW

In this chapter, we explain the planning that retailers must do regarding their merchandise selection. We also analyze how a retailer controls the merchandise to be inventoried. The selection of and negotiations with vendors are also discussed, as well as the security measures used when handling the merchandise.

LEARNING OBJECTIVES

After reading this chapter, you should be able to

1. explain the differences between the four methods of dollar merchandise planning used to determine the proper inventory stock levels needed to begin a merchandise selling period

2. explain how retailers use dollar merchandise control and describe how open-to-buy is used in the retail buying process

3. describe how a retailer uses unit stock planning and model stock plans in determining the makeup of a merchandise mix

4. describe how a retailer selects proper merchandise sources

5. describe what is involved in the vendor–buyer negotiation process and what terms of the contract can be negotiated

6. discuss the various methods of controlling loss through shrinkage, vendor collusion, and theft

Merchandise management *is the analysis, planning, acquisition, handling, and control of the merchandise investments of a retail operation.*

DOLLAR MERCHANDISE PLANNING

There is an old retailing adage that "goods well bought are half sold." In this chapter, we look at merchandise management (i.e., the merchandise buying and handling process and its effect on a store's performance).

Merchandise management is the analysis, planning, acquisition, handling, and control of the merchandise investments of a retail operation. Analysis is used in our definition because retailers must be able to correctly identify their customers before they can determine the needs and wants of the consumer in order to buy the correct merchandise. Planning occurs because merchandise must be purchased six to 12 months in advance of the selling season. The term acquisition is used because the merchandise needs to be bought from others, either distributors or manufacturers. Proper handling ensures that the merchandise is where it is needed and in the proper shape to be sold. Control of the large dollar investments in inventory is important to ensure an adequate financial return on the retailer's merchandise investment. In fact, many retailing experts agree that it was the failure to properly manage merchandise that caused The Limited, one of the most successful retail operations for more than a decade, to stumble in the mid-1990s. First, the chain failed to change its merchandise as the consumer changed. Second, and most damaging, consumers failed to notice any difference between the fashions offered at the various Limited divisions (e.g., Limited Express and The Limited).

Whatever career path that you decide to take in retailing, you cannot avoid some contact with the firm's merchandising activities. This is because merchandising is the day-to-day business of all retailers. As inventory is sold, new stock needs to be purchased, displayed, and sold once again. Clearly then, as we explained in Chapter 8, merchandising, although only a subfunction of retailing, is its heart beat. Therefore, retailers that do a superior job at managing their inventory investment will be the most successful. If a retailer's inventory continues to build up, then either the retailer has too much money tied up in inventory or is not making the sales that it was expecting and is heading for trouble. Likewise, a retailer who is frequently out of stock will quickly lose customers. Now, you know why the business trade press and retailers take such an interest in retail inventory levels as retailers approach different seasons, with a special emphasis on the Christmas season. Christmas, which traditionally accounts for 25 to 30 percent of annual sales, can be ruined by the lack of inventory to support sales. If the inventory isn't sold, the costs involved in carrying excess inventory can force the retailer into taking extra markdowns, besides having to pay interest on the inventory investment.

Gross margin return on inventory

is gross margin divided by average inventory at cost; alternatively it is the gross margin percent multiplied by net sales divided by average inventory investment.

Because inventory is the largest investment that retailers make, high-performance retailers use the gross margin return on inventory (GMROI) model when analyzing the performance of their inventory. Gross margin return on inventory incorporates into a single measure both inventory productivity and profit. It can be computed as follows:

(Gross margin/Net sales) × (Net sales/Average inventory at cost)

= (Gross margin/Average inventory at cost)

Here, the gross margin percentage (gross margin/net sales) is multiplied by net sales/average dollars invested in inventory to get the retailer's gross margin dollars generated for each dollar invested in inventory. Net sales is typically computed on an annual or 12-month basis. (Note, net sales/average dollars invested in inventory is not the

The Limited and Limited Express need to carefully consider their merchandising and buying practices so these two stores, which are commonly owned, have differentiated offerings and target markets.

same as inventory turnover. Inventory turnover measures net sales/average inventory at retail. In the GMROI equation, we are using inventory at cost to reflect our investment in carrying the merchandise.) Thus, if a particular merchandise line has a gross margin of 45 percent and sales per dollar of inventory investment of 6.0, its GMROI would be $2.70 ($0.45 $\times$ 6). That is, for each dollar invested in inventory, on average the retailer obtains $2.70 in gross margin annually. Gross margin dollars are used to first pay the store's operating expenses, with the remainder being the retailer's profit.

DOLLAR $ & ¢ENTS

Retailers that use the GMROI model when planning inventory and evaluating inventory decisions will be higher performers.

Before we continue our discussion of merchandise management, you may want to review a couple of our earlier chapters. Because all retailing activities are aimed at serving the customer's needs and wants at a profit, you may want to review Chapter 3 on the customer. Likewise, because merchandise management is concerned with the acquisition of inventory, you may also want to review Chapter 5 on the behavior of the different channel members.

As we pointed out in Chapter 8, successful merchandise management revolves around planning and control. Because it takes time to buy merchandise, have it delivered, record the delivery in the company records, and properly display the merchandise, it becomes essential to plan. Buyers need to decide today what their stock requirements will be weeks, months, a merchandising season, or even a year in advance.

As planning occurs, then it is only logical that control be exercised over the merchandise dollars or units that the retailer plans on purchasing. A good control system is vital. After concluding our discussion on the dollar amount of inventory needed for stock requirements, the remainder of this chapter looks at the other merchandising decisions facing the retailer: the dollar amount available to be spent, the unit or type of goods to be purchased, choosing and evaluating merchandise sources, handling vendor negotiations, handling the merchandise in the store, and evaluating merchandise performance.

Buyers, working with upper management, are responsible for the dollar planning of merchandise requirements. In the previous chapter, we described the various factors that must be considered in making the sales forecast, the first step in determining inventory needs. Once planned sales for the period in question have been projected, buyers are then able to use any one of four different methods for planning dollars invested in merchandise: basic stock, percentage variation, weeks' supply, and the stock-to-sales ratio method.

Although our discussion in this chapter focuses on retailers who sell tangible goods, the same basic principles may be applied to service retailers with one exception. Whereas tangible products are first produced, then sold, and then consumed, services are first sold, then produced and consumed simultaneously. Thus service retailers are prevented from stockpiling their inventories in anticipation of future demand. Still, service retailers must be able to forecast demand and make preparations, most likely with regards to personnel, to satisfy that demand.

BASIC STOCK METHOD

Basic stock method (BSM) is a technique for planning dollar inventory investments and allows for a base stock level plus a variable amount of inventory that will increase or decrease at the beginning of each sales period in the same dollar amount as the period's expected sales.

The basic stock method (BSM) is used when retailers believe that it is necessary to have a given level of inventory available at all times. It requires that the retailer always has a base level of inventory investment regardless of the predicted sales volume. In addition to the base stock level, there will be a variable amount of inventory that will increase or decrease at the beginning of each sales period (one month in the case of our merchandise budget) in the same dollar amount as the period's expected sales. The BSM can be calculated as follows:

Average monthly sales for the season
= Total planned sales for the season/Number of months in the season

Average stock for the season
= Total planned sales for the season/Estimated inventory turnover rate for the season

Basic stock = Average stock for the season − Average monthly sales for the season

Beginning-of-month (BOM)stock at retail
= Basic stock + Planned monthly sales

To illustrate the use of the basic stock method, let's look at the planned sales for Department 353 of Two-Seasons Department Store shown in Exhibit 8.2. Assume that the inventory turnover rate for the six months, or the number of times the average inventory is sold, for the season is 2.0.

Average monthly sales for the season
= Total planned sales/Number of months
= $500,000/6 = $83,333

Average stock for the season
= Total planned sales/Inventory turnover
= $500,000/2 = $250,000

Basic stock = Average stock − Average monthly sale
= $250,000 − $83,333 = $166,667

BOM @ retail (Feb.) = Basic stock + Planned monthly sales
= $166,667 + $75,000 = $241,667

BOM @ retail (Mar.) = $166,667 + $75,000 = $241,667

BOM @ retail (Apr.) = $166,667 + $100,000 = $266,667

BOM @ retail (May) = $166,667 + $50,000 = $216,667

BOM @ retail (Jun.) = $166,667 + $125,000 = $291,667

BOM @ retail (Jul.) = $166,667 + $75,000 = $241,667

It is obvious that $166,667 of basic stock is added to each month's planned sales to arrive at the BOM stock. In those cases in which actual sales either exceed or fall short of planned sales for the month, the retailer can easily adjust the amount of overage or shortfall to bring the next month's BOM stock back in line by buying more or less stock. Therefore, the basic stock method works best when a retailer has a low turnover rate (i.e., less than six times a year) or if sales are erratic.

PERCENTAGE VARIATION METHOD

A second commonly used method for determining planned stock levels is the percentage variation method (PVM). This method is used when the retailer has a high yearly turnover rate (i.e., six or more times a year). The percentage variation method assumes that the percentage fluctuations in monthly stock from average stock should be half as great as the percentage fluctuations in monthly sales from average sales.

BOM stock = Average stock for season
× ½ [1 + (Planned sales for the month/Average monthly sales)]

Because the PVM uses the same components as the BSM, we can use the data from the previous example.

BOM (Feb.) = $250,000 × ½ [1 + ($75,000/$83,333)] = $237,500

BOM (Mar.) = $250,000 × ½ [1 + ($75,000/$83,333)] = $237,500

BOM (Apr.) = $250,000 × ½ [1 + ($100,000/$83,333)] = $275,000

BOM (May) = $250,000 × ½ [1 + ($50,000/$83,333)] = $200,000

BOM (Jun.) = $250,000 × ½ [1 + ($125,000/$83,333)] = $312,500

BOM (Jul.) = $250,000 × ½ [1 + ($75,000/$83,333)] = $237,500

WEEKS' SUPPLY METHOD

A third method for planning inventory levels is the weeks' supply method (WSM). Generally, the WSM formula is used by retailers such as grocers in which inventories are planned on a weekly, not monthly, basis, and in which sales do not fluctuate substantially. It states that the inventory level should be set equal to a predetermined

Percentage variation method (PVM) is a technique for planning dollar inventory investments that assumes that the percentage fluctuations in monthly stock from average stock should be half as great as the percentage fluctuations in monthly sales from average sales.

Weeks' supply method (WSM) is a technique for planning dollar inventory investments that states that the inventory level should be set equal to a predetermined number of weeks' supply which is directly related to the desired rate of stock turnover.

number of weeks' supply. The predetermined number of weeks' supply is directly related to the stock turnover rate desired. In the WSM, stock level in dollars varies proportionally with forecast sales. Thus, if forecast sales triple, then inventory in dollars will also triple.

To illustrate the WSM, let's return to our earlier problem and use the following formulas:

$$\text{Number of weeks to be stocked} = \text{Number of weeks in the period}/\text{Stock turnover rate for the period}$$

$$\text{Average weekly sales} = \text{Estimated total sales for the period}/\text{Number of weeks in the period}$$

$$\text{BOM stock} = \text{Average weekly sales} \times \text{Number of weeks to be stocked}$$

Thus,

$$\text{Number of weeks to be stocked} = 26/2 = 13$$

$$\text{Average weekly sales} = \$500{,}000/26 = \$19{,}231$$

$$\text{BOM stock} = \$19{,}231 \times 13 = \$250{,}000$$

Having determined the number of weeks' supply to be stocked (13 weeks) and the average weekly sales ($19,231), stock levels can be replenished on a frequent or regular basis to guard against stock-outs.

STOCK-TO-SALES METHOD

Stock-to-sales method (SSM)

is a technique for planning dollar inventory investments where the amount of inventory planned for the beginning of the month is a ratio (obtained from trade associations or the retailer's historical records) of stock-to-sales.

The final method for planning inventory levels, and the one we used in Chapter 8, is the stock-to-sales method (SSM). This method is quite easy to use but requires the retailer to have a BOM stock-to-sales ratio. This ratio tells the retailer how much inventory is needed at the beginning of the month to support that month's estimated sales. A ratio of 2.5, for example, would tell retailers that they should have two and one-half times that month's expected sales on hand in inventory at the beginning of the month.

Stock-to-sales ratios can be obtained from internal or external sources. Internally, the statistics can be obtained if the retailer has designed a good accounting system and has properly stored historical data so that they can be readily retrieved. Externally, the retailer can often rely on retail trade associations such as the National Retail Federation or the Menswear Retailers Association. These and other trade associations collect stock-to-sales ratios from participating merchants and then compile, tabulate, and report them in special management reports or trade publications.

However, these ratios should only be used as a guide to how much inventory to have on hand at the beginning of each month. Successful chain store retailers have long known that even stores located nearby each other require not only different merchandise mixes but also different inventory levels per sales dollars. This is a reflection of the store's trading area, layout, and competition. However, inventory turnover remains a key factor in a retailer's financial performance. Planned average BOM stock-to-sales goals can be easily calculated by using turnover goals. If you divide the number of months in the season by the desired inventory turnover rate, an average BOM stock-to-sales ratio for the season can be computed. For example, if you desired an inventory turnover rate of 2.0 (4.0 annually) for the upcoming six-month season, your average BOM stock-to-sales ratio would be 3.0 (6/2.0 = 3.0).

DOLLAR MERCHANDISE CONTROL

LO • 2
Explain how retailers use dollar merchandise control and describe how open-to-buy is used in the retail buying process

Once the dollar merchandise to have on hand at the beginning of each month (or season) is planned by the buyer, it becomes essential to ensure that the buyer does not make commitments for merchandise that would exceed the dollar plan. In short, the dollars planned for merchandise need to be controlled. This control is accomplished through a technique called open-to-buy (OTB). The open-to-buy represents the dollar amount that a buyer can currently spend on merchandise without exceeding the planned dollar stocks discussed previously. When planning for any given month (or season), the buyer will not necessarily be able to purchase a dollar amount equal to the planned dollar stocks for that month (or season). This is the case because there may be some inventory already on hand or on order but not yet delivered. To illustrate this point more succinctly, let's compute the OTB for an upcoming month.

Open-to-buy
is the dollar amount that a buyer can currently spend on merchandise without exceeding the planned dollar stocks.

Assume that at the beginning of February the buyer for Department 353 of the Two-Seasons Department Store (Exhibit 8.2) has already ordered, but had not yet received, $15,000 worth of merchandise at retail. Keeping planned EOM stock at $300,000 and planned reductions for February at 10 percent of planned sales, the buyer's planned purchases for February will remain $157,500. However, the OTB for the month will only be $142,500 at retail because we are now accounting for that $15,000 of merchandise already ordered but not yet received. The computations would look like this:

1.	Planned sales for February	+75,000
2.	Plus planned reductions for February	+7,500
3.	Plus end-of-month (EOM) planned retail stock	+$300,000
4.	Minus BOM stock	−225,000
5.	Equals planned purchases at retail	$157,500
6.	Minus commitments at retail for current delivery	−15,000
7.	Equals OTB	$142,500

The OTB figure should not be set in stone because it can be exceeded. Consumer needs are the dominant consideration. If sales exceed planned sales, additional quantities should be ordered above those scheduled for purchase according to the merchandise budget. This should, however, not be a common occurrence. If this is the case, the sales planning process is wrong. Either the buyers are too conservative in estimating sales or they are buying the wrong merchandise. In any case, the buyer, along with management, should always determine the causes of OTB adjustments. Some common buying errors include

1. buying merchandise that is either priced too high or too low for the store's target market
2. buying the wrong type of merchandise (i.e., too many tops and no skirts) or buying too much "trendy fashion" merchandise
3. having too much or too little basic stock on hand
4. buying from too many vendors
5. failing to identify the season's hot items early enough in the season
6. failing to let the vendor assist the buyer by adding new items and/or new colors to the mix. (All too often, the original order is merely repeated, resulting in a limited selection.)

Merchandise planning is a dynamic process subject to many changes. Consider the implications that could arise in planning your stock levels as a result of (1) sales for the previous month being lower or higher than planned, (2) reductions being either higher or lower than planned, and (3) shipments of merchandise being delayed in transit. Understanding the consequences of each of these situations can show you the interrelationship of merchandising activities with the merchandise budget. In addition, such occurrences serve to make retailing a challenging and exciting career choice.

DOLLAR $ & CENTS

Retailers who realize that their OTB, which is an important planning tool, can be adjusted to meet extraordinary circumstances will be high performers.

LO • 3
Describe how a retailer uses unit stock planning and model stock plans in determining the makeup of a merchandise mix

UNIT STOCK PLANNING

The dollar merchandise plan is only the starting point in merchandise management. Once the retailer has decided how many dollars can be invested in inventory, the dollar plan needs to be converted into a unit plan. On the sales floor, items, not dollars, are sold. The assortment of items that will comprise the merchandise mix must then be planned.

OPTIMAL MERCHANDISE MIX

Exhibit 9.1 shows the three dimensions of the optimal merchandise mix: variety, breadth, and depth. Each of these dimensions needs to be defined; however, we need

EXHIBIT 9.1	DIMENSIONS OF AND CONSTRAINTS ON OPTIMAL MERCHANDISE MIX

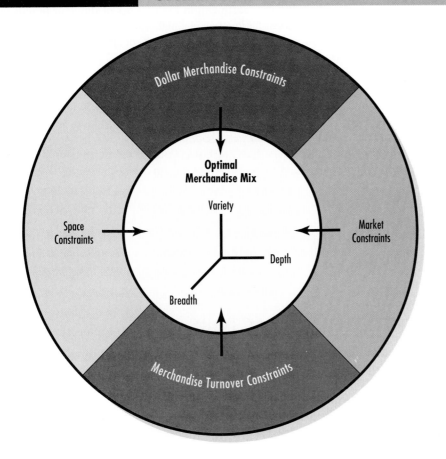

first to define merchandise line. A merchandise line consists of a group of products that are closely related because they are intended for the same end use (all televisions); are sold to the same customer group (junior miss clothing); or fall within a given price range (budget women's wear).

VARIETY

The variety of the merchandise mix refers to the number of different merchandise lines that the retailer stocks in the store. For example, department stores have a large variety of merchandise lines. Some have more than 100 departments, carrying such lines as men's wear, women's wear, children's clothing, infant's wear, toys, sporting goods, appliances, cosmetics, and household goods.

However, Office Max, a specialty chain, carries only two basic merchandise lines: office supplies and office equipment. In the middle of these two would be a retailer such as Sportsmart, selling a complete range of merchandise lines in the sporting goods field.

Merchandise line
is a group of products that are closely related because they are intended for the same end use (all televisions); are sold to the same customer group (junior miss clothing); or fall within a given price range (budget women's wear).

Variety
refers to the number of different merchandise lines that the retailer stocks in the store.

BREADTH

Breadth, also called assortment, refers to the number of merchandise brands that are found in the merchandise line. For example, a supermarket will have a large amount of breadth, or assortment, in the number of different brands of mustard that it carries: six or seven national or regional brands, a private brand, and a generic brand. A 7-Eleven convenience store, however, will offer very little breadth in that it will generally carry only one, or two at the most, brand(s) in any merchandise line. In fact, many retail analysts believe that the factors that led to Circle K's downfall were not just management's inability to pay debt incurred as Circle K expanded into new markets, but also its inability to control breadth. When Circle K filed for bankruptcy in early 1990, it was found to be carrying six brands of dog food, seven brands of aspirin, and a large selection of hair nets, despite the fact that women made up only a small percentage of its customers. This much selection was entirely inappropriate for a retailer selling convenience goods and already heavily in debt.

DEPTH

Merchandise depth refers to the average number of stock keeping units (SKUs) within each brand of the merchandise line. In our preceding example, the supermarket manager must decide on which sizes and types of French's mustard to carry. The convenience store will probably only carry the regular nine-ounce jar of French's and thus have little depth whereas the supermarket may carry many different sizes and flavors of French's mustard and thus have large depth.

CONSTRAINING FACTORS

With these definitions in mind, we can now refer to Exhibit 9.1 to observe the four constraining factors that influence the design of the optimal merchandise mix. Remember, just as the trading areas for each store in a chain are different, the optimal mix will be different for every store. Merchandise mix decisions are a blend of financial plans, that consider the retailer's dollar and turnover constraints, combined with the store's space constraints as well as the constraints caused by the actions of competitors and consumers that exist in the relevant market.[1]

DOLLAR MERCHANDISE CONSTRAINTS

There seldom will be enough dollars to emphasize variety, breadth, and depth. If the decision is made to emphasize variety, it would be unrealistic to expect also to have a lot of breadth and depth.

For instance, assume for the moment that you are the owner/manager of a local gift store. You have $70,000 to invest in merchandise. If you decide that you want a lot of variety in gifts (jewelry, crystal, candles, games, cards, figurines, ashtrays, clocks, and radios), then you obviously could not have much depth in any single item such as crystal glassware.

Some retailers try to overcome this dollar constraint by shifting the expense of carrying inventory back on the vendor. When a retailer buys a product on consignment, the vendor retains the ownership of the goods, usually establishes the selling price, and is paid only when the goods are sold. Or the retailer might try to get extra dating, in which the vendor allows the retailer some extra time before paying for the goods. For example, most textbook publishers either sell their books on consignment or give the bookstores an extra 60 days in which to pay. In this way, your campus bookstore orders its books in early July for an early August delivery. The bookstore then sells the books in late August or early September. However, because the books were sold on

Because sales of specific units are difficult to predict, especially for fashion merchandise and toys, many retailers found themselves out of stock on Tickle Me Elmo dolls during the 1996 holiday season.

consignment, or with extra dating, the bookstore doesn't have to pay the publisher until October.

SPACE CONSTRAINTS

The retailer must also deal with space constraints. If depth or breadth is wanted, space is needed. If variety is to be stressed, it is also important to have enough empty space to separate the distinct merchandise lines. For example, consider a single counter containing cosmetics, candy, fishing tackle, women's stockings, and toys. This would obviously be an unsightly and unwise arrangement. As more variety is added, empty space becomes necessary to allow the consumer to clearly distinguish among distinct product lines.

Some retailers, especially in the grocery business, have been able to turn this space constraint into an advantage by charging the manufacturers the "slotting fees," which are discussed in the Ethics section in Chapter 6, to carry their products.

MERCHANDISE TURNOVER CONSTRAINTS

As the depth of the merchandise is increased, the retailer will be stocking more and more variations of the product to serve smaller and smaller segments. Consequently, inventory turnover will deteriorate and the chances of being out of stock will increase. One does not have to minimize variety, breadth, and depth to maximize turnover, but one must know how various merchandise mixes will affect inventory turnover.

MARKET CONSTRAINTS

Market constraints should also affect decisions on variety, breadth, and depth of the merchandise mix. The three dimensions have a profound effect on how the consumer perceives the store and, consequently, on

the customers the store will attract. The consumer perceives a specialty store as one with limited variety and breadth of merchandise lines but considerable depth within the lines handled. An individual searching for depth in a limited set of merchandise lines such as formal men's wear will thus be attracted to a men's wear retailer specializing in formal wear. However, the consumer perceives the general merchandise retailer such as Wards or Target as a store with lots of variety and breadth in terms of merchandise lines but with more constrained depth. Therefore, someone who needs to make several purchases across several merchandise lines, and who is willing to sacrifice depth of assortment, would be more attracted to the general merchandise retailer.

The constraining factors make it almost impossible for a retailer to emphasize all three dimensions. However, if you are going to lose customers, lose the less profitable ones by properly mixing your merchandise in terms of variety, breadth, and depth within the dollar, space, turnover, and market constraints.

DOLLAR $ & CENTS

High-performance retailers are those who realize that it is impossible to emphasize all three dimensions of the merchandise mix and as a result seek to satisfy the merchandise needs of the most profitable segments.

MODEL STOCK PLAN

Model stock plan

is a unit stock plan that shows the precise items and quantities that should be on hand for each merchandise line.

After you decide the relative emphasis to be placed on the three dimensions of the merchandise mix, you need to decide what merchandise lines and items to stock. Units are planned by using a model stock plan. The model stock plan gives the precise items and quantities that should be on hand for each merchandise line. A separate model stock plan needs to be compiled for each line of merchandise.

Exhibit 9.2 shows a hypothetical men's wear retailer attempting to develop a unit plan for men's shirts. It has already conducted a dollar plan and has allocated $28,000 at retail for men's shirts. Because the average retail price of a shirt for the store is $28, 1,000 shirts will be stocked. The model unit plan will reveal how many shirts of each kind the retailer should keep in stock. Although the exhibit only shows the breakdown within one attribute (casual shirts), the same procedure would be followed for all types of shirts.

IDENTIFY ATTRIBUTES   The first thing that the men's wear retailer should do is attempt to identify what attributes the customer considers in purchasing shirts. Exhibit 9.2 shows that the retailer has identified six attributes: (1) type of shirt (dress, casual, sport, or work), (2) size, (3) sleeve length, (4) collar type, (5) color, and (6) fabric. Are any key attributes left out? What about price? If customers shop for shirts by price, then price should also be a product attribute.

| EXHIBIT 9.2 | PARTIAL MODEL UNIT PLAN FOR MEN'S SHIRTS |

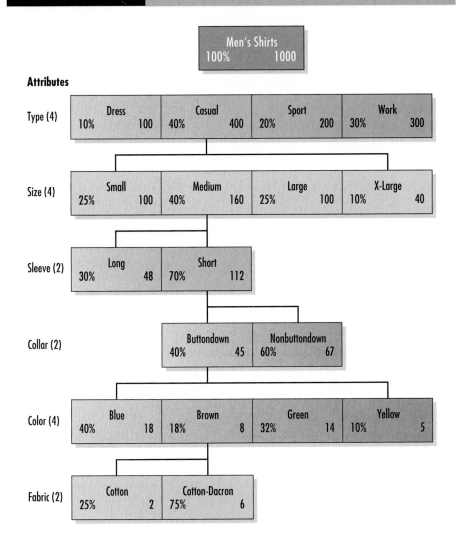

IDENTIFY LEVELS The second step is to identify the number of levels under each attribute. The retailer in Exhibit 9.2 has selected four types of shirts to stock, four sizes, two sleeve lengths, two collar types, four colors, and two fabrics.

In relation to the first two steps in the construction of a model stock plan, a basic principle of merchandise management can be identified: Stocking requirements will grow explosively as more product attributes and expanded levels are offered on each attribute. If the retailer offers four shirt types, four sizes in each type, two sleeve lengths, two collar styles, four colors, and two fabrics, then it will have to stock 512 shirts (4 × 4 × 2 × 2 × 4 × 2), just to stock one unit of each. More important, if the retailer now decides to offer two price points instead of one, the stocking requirements double to 1,024 items. But this example assumes that only 1,000 shirts can be stocked.

Obviously, the retailer has a problem if it wants to feature six or seven attributes and several levels on each attribute.

The preceding discussion illustrates the need for a basic trade-off in merchandise management. As more attributes are featured, the probability is increased that a product on hand will match the customer's needs and purchasing power. However, there is a cost associated with increasing this probability, the cost of carrying the additional inventory. At some point, the carrying cost of the additional inventory required to increase the probability of purchase is greater than the profit obtained from those additional unit sales. Successful retailers know that they will have to allow some customers to walk out of their store empty-handed.

ALLOCATE DOLLARS OR UNITS

The third step in developing the model stock plan is to allocate the total dollars or units to the respective item categories. There is an optimum allocation if the model unit plan has recommended quantities for each item that are in direct proportion to market demand patterns. If the plan reflects this optimum, then by comparing actual stocks with model stocks, one can easily determine whether the stocks are out of balance. The more actual stocks mirror the model stock plan, the more the stocks will be in balance; and balanced stocks maximize sales potential. Stocks that are out of balance will cause customers to walk out of the store without the item they came to purchase. Worse yet, they might purchase a product that is not well suited to their needs. Over the long run, this may hurt the retailer's business.

But how can a retailer determine that the recommended quantities for each item are in direct proportion to market demand patterns? The most useful thing to do is to analyze past sales records. Exhibit 9.3 shows the sales experience of our hypothetical men's wear retailer in reference to the last 500 shirts sold. This exhibit, derived from past sales records, shows the demand density for different types and sizes of shirts. This simple analysis forms the basis of planning unit stocks in the model plan. Changing the data in Exhibit 9.3 to percentage form, we can see that 10 percent of our shirt sales were dress, 40 percent casual, 20 percent sport, and 30 percent work. Furthermore, of the casual shirts, 25 percent were small, 40 percent medium, 25 percent large, and 10 percent extra large. The percentage derived from such a sales analysis can then be used in the model stock plan (Exhibit 9.2). Thus, in this example, past sales will be used to indicate future demand density. Therefore, of the 1,000 shirts that we plan to stock, 100 will be dress, 400 casual, 200 sport, and 300 work. These numbers are obtained simply by multiplying the 1,000 shirts by the percentage obtained in the sales analysis. In the past, 10 percent of the shirts sold were dress shirts, so we will plan to stock 100 dress shirts, which is 10 percent of 1,000. A similar procedure is conducted to determine how many to stock in each size, sleeve length, collar type, color, and fabric.

DOLLAR $ & ¢ENTS

Retailers who realize that in addition to past sales records they must also be aware of changing market conditions when purchasing merchandise will be more profitable.

EXHIBIT 9.3   SALES ANALYSIS OF MEN'S SHIRTS

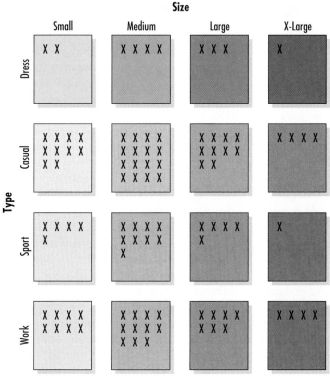

KEY: Each X = 5 shirts

As Behind the Scenes points out, one should not always allow past sales results to determine future stocking patterns.

SPECIAL PROBLEMS WITH NEW STORES So far, we have ignored the problems of individuals opening their first store. Such individuals will have no past sales records to rely on. In this situation, does one only use intuition and creativity in developing a model stock plan? Certainly not! Of the three analytical steps discussed above, the first two pertain as much to the new entrepreneur as to any existing retailer. However, for the third step, one will not have any historical sales records to study. Here, the retailer can still use analytical skills by obtaining trade or other external sources on consumer purchasing patterns. For example, in the food industry, the retailer could consult the Towne-Oller Index, which measures actual sales and the sales rank of each product and shows the number of different products needed to meet the demand of a certain percentage of the buying public for that particular product line. For instance, one might see that if 80 percent of the demand preferences for mouthwash is the desired goal, the four leading brands would need to be stocked.

In addition, creative skills are as important for entrepreneurs opening their first store as they are for buyers going back to the market to restock existing stores. The creative buyer, for example, would recognize that there might be savings gained by

Past Sales Records Are Sometimes Meaningless

When using past sales to determine merchandise orders, the buyer should remember that in the past, quantities not in proportion to demand patterns may have been stocked. As a result, they may have been sold—but probably at a loss. Just using past sales statistics will not reveal this. In addition, new products that come into the market may feature attributes previously not stocked, and the demand for these may be so high that the item must be stocked to compete. However, probably the biggest reason that strict analysis of past statistics should never completely dictate a buyer's model stock plan is changing consumer tastes.

Consider, for example, how such strict analysis would have played havoc with a buyer for men's tailored clothing. Since 1995, the nearly $50 billion market (at retail) has been growing more than 7 percent a year, reversing a declining sales trend over the first half decade. At the same time, relying on past records to determine what sizes to purchase would have produced another problem because men's waistline sizes showed an increase in recent years.

The increase in the men's tailored clothing market is nothing, however, compared to what has happened in the market for plus-sized women's clothing. In fact, the only women's apparel sizes to experience a sales growth in recent years were in the larger sizes. Retailers, manufacturers, and even fashion magazines realize that more than one-third of all women wear a size larger than 14. Plus sizes now generate $25 billion in annual sales as these customers want style and quality. Retailers no longer hide "baggy, cheaply made tent-like smocks" in a "fat ladies" selection in the basement. Today's successful retailers are disregarding past sales records and offering larger selections of plus sizes featuring the latest looks, including the same designer-made fitted dresses and coats that slimmer women wear. Retailers such as Saks, Bloomingdale's, and Macy's are experiencing record sales for this market by lavishing prime floor space and advertising dollars on the plus sizes.

stocking fewer brands of a product, such as canned green beans, that doesn't really evoke strong brand preferences and carrying a greater selection of products, such as ice cream, that evokes strong preferences. Here, even though the retailer doesn't have the desired brand of green beans and the customer is forced to purchase a less-preferred brand, the customer will forgive the retailer when he or she sees the large selection of the more important product category—ice cream. Likewise, the creative retailer is more apt to not follow the "prescribed" rules-of-thumb that all its competitors follow and come up with new ideas to gain an advantage over the competition.

Dollar $ & ¢ents

Retailers who use analytical and creative skills when selecting merchandise for resale will be more profitable.

Lane Bryant has avoided some conflicts in unit stock planning by focusing on plus-size clothing for women and consciously ignoring other merchandise opportunities.

CONFLICTS IN UNIT STOCK PLANNING

Unit stock planning is an exercise in compromise and conflict. The conflict is multidimensional because not everything can be stocked. The conflicts are summarized as follows:

1. Maintain a strong in-stock position on genuinely new items while trying to avoid the 90 percent of new products that fail in the introductory stage. The retailer will want to have on hand the types of new products that will satisfy customers. If the consumer is sold a poor product, it hurts the retailer as much as, if not more than, the manufacturer. The problem becomes one of screening out poor products before they reach the customer. Any screening device, however, has error; the retailer might end up stocking some losers and turning down winners. Thus a basic conflict arises, but even the best of buyers will make a mistake sometimes and be forced to use markdowns to unload slow-selling merchandise.

2. Maintain an adequate stock of the basic popular items while having sufficient inventory dollars to capitalize on unforeseen opportunities. Many times, if the retailer fills out the model stock with recommended quantities, there is little, if any, money left over for the super buy that is just around the corner. For example, the opportunity that occassionally occurs to buy exclusive production runs (such as with Hasbro toys), which can be used to differentiate yourself from the competition.[2] But, if the retailer holds out that money and cuts back on basic stock, customers may be lost, and that super buy may never surface.

3. Maintain high merchandise turnover goals while maintaining high margin goals. This is perhaps the most glaring conflict. Usually, items that turn over more rapidly have thinner profit margins. Therefore, trying to build a unit plan that will accomplish both objectives will surely be challenging.

4. Maintain adequate selection for customers while not confusing them. If customers are confronted with too many similar items, they will not be able to make up their

minds, and they may leave the store empty-handed and frustrated. However, if the selection is inadequate, the customer will again leave empty-handed. Thus a delicate balance needs to be struck between too little and too much selection.

5. Maintain space productivity and utilization while not congesting the store. Take advantage of buys that will use the available space, but avoid buys that cause the merchandise to spill over into the aisles. Unfortunately, some of the best buys come along when space is already occupied.

As should be readily evident at this point, unit stock planning is no easy task. Equally challenging is the selection of vendors from whom to buy the merchandise.

LO • 4
Describe how a retailer selects proper merchandise sources

SELECTION OF MERCHANDISING SOURCES

After deciding on the type and amount of inventory to be purchased, the next step is to determine where the retailer is to obtain the merchandise. All too often, individuals have misconceptions about how retailers choose and negotiate with vendors. In all probability, before you began this course you perceived retail buying as a glamorous job. Many individuals say, "I would love to be a buyer. After all, I have been told I have good taste and I love to travel." Well, buying isn't that simple. However, with proper planning and control, it can be a very rewarding experience, especially when your customers react positively to your merchandise selection. No matter how rewarding your buying experience is, it will also be grueling. Not only must you determine what merchandise lines to carry, but you also must select the best possible vendor to supply you with these items and then you must be able to negotiate the best deal possible with that vendor.

When selecting a merchandise source, the retailer must consider many criteria, depending on the type of store and merchandise sold. Generally, the following criteria, which may vary across merchandise lines, should always be considered: selling history; product quality; consumers' perception of the manufacturer's reputation; reliability of delivery; trade terms; projected markup; quality of merchandise; after-sale service; transportation time; distribution center processing time; inventory carrying cost; country of origin; fashionability; and net-landed cost.[3] Country of origin is becoming a more important issue everyday, as governments use trade agreements to limit the amount of merchandise that can be imported from various countries (one such regulation is the subject of the case at the end of this chapter) and consumers rebel against sweatshops and the use of child labor in certain countries. Often, retailers check out the Council on Economic Priorities web site (www.accesspt.com/cep), which ranks more than 200 consumer product manufacturers on workplace issues, in addition to product safety, quality, and price. However, as discussed in our Behind the Scenes section, some people are beginning to question retailing's role in policing this sourcing problem, which was also covered in the Ethics section in Chapter 6.

In cases in which a manufacturer offers to co-op some expense (e.g., advertising or display support), the amount of price reduction has been shown to have a significant effect on the purchase decision.[4] Some retailers also check to see whether the same merchandise will be made available to a nearby competitor; in such cases, it may be advantageous for the retailer to consider using a private label or not purchasing the

SHOULD RETAILERS POLICE THEIR SUPPLIERS?

For years, American regulators have worried that the low-cost merchandise that was so popular with consumers was being made by political prisoners in China. However, the real worry may be closer to home. Many of this country's garment manufacturers supplying the biggest retailers rely on small subcontractors to cut and assemble the clothing that they sell to the retailers. Competitive pressures from countries with lower labor costs, as well as slow economic growth at home, has caused a resurgence in what was once thought to be a turn-of-the-century problem: sweatshop conditions to keep costs down. Highly publicized raids on small factories have turned up unsafe conditions, subminimum wages, and violations of overtime requirements across the country. For example, in late 1997 Kathie Lee Gifford was facing allegations that her clothing line was made in New York City sweatshops by Chinese workers paid below the minimum wage and sometimes forced to work 24 hours at a time. The state's top prosecutor said the working conditions "resembled something out of a Charles Dickens novel."[6]

The goods manufactured were headed for such major retailers as Sears, Wards, and Dayton Hudson. The Labor Department called on retailers to combat sweatshop conditions by policing their suppliers and the suppliers' subcontractors. With more than 20,000 domestic subcontractors and declining budgets, the government is hard pressed to police these small firms that often open and close, and rename their operations, with great speed to avoid detection.

However, under President Clinton's 1997 directive, retailers are not legally responsible for labor violations of their suppliers' subcontractors. They may legally sell such goods. The Labor Department is hoping that bad publicity such as the announcement of the major retailers selling items manufactured in these plants will get retailers involved and asked retailers to make unannounced spot checks on these firms. Unfortunately, the announcement of such a "hit list" didn't seem to affect consumer behavior. Besides, the cost would be too great for all size retailers. Sears alone uses 10,000 direct suppliers, each with their own subcontractors. This complex network makes it difficult to determine which firm actually makes goods for a retailer. Retailers also claim to lack the legal expertise to detect labor code violations, and their contracts are not written to perform these factory inspections. In addition, tough competition makes the expense of this supervision difficult to pass along to customers.

Although conceding the cost factor, the Labor Department still wants retailer cooperation. Contracts, they claim, can be written to include random spot checks. Experts can be hired. The Labor Department thinks that retailers with large orders from manufacturers should be able to force subcontractor compliance.

merchandise. Toys "Я" Us was recently accused by the Federal Trade Commission (FTC) of stifling price competition by threatening not to stock certain toys if the vendors also sold them to discounters. The discounters, which try to offer lower prices by only carrying the "hottest" toys, claim that some vendors won't sell them the "hot" toys for fear of losing business to Toy "Я" Us, which has just less than 20 percent of toy sales in the United States. The FTC claims that such action allows Toys "Я" Us to maintain high margins.[5]

One of a retailer's greatest assets when dealing with a vendor is the retailer's past experiences with that vendor. Whether you are a small retailer doing all the buying yourself or a new buyer for a large chain, you should always approach vendors with two important pieces of information: the vendor profitability analysis statement and the confidential vendor analysis. The vendor profitability analysis statement (Exhibit 9.4)

Vendor profitability analysis
is a tool used to evaluate vendors and shows all purchases made the prior year, the discount granted, transportation charges paid, the original markup, markdowns, and finally the season-ending gross margin on that vendor's merchandise.

| EXHIBIT 9.4 | TWO-SEASONS VENDOR PROFITABILITY ANALYSIS |

| VENDOR NAME | PURCHASES | | DISCOUNT AND ANTICIPATION % | FREIGHT % | MARKUP % LANDED LOADED | MARKDOWN | | GROSS MARGIN PERCENTAGE | VENDOR NO. |
	COST	RETAIL				$	%		
Anderson Sports	62,481	129,861	7.1	1.4	50.7	20,211	15.6	46.2	273359
Jack Frost, Inc.	26,921	53,962	8.0	1.3	49.4	3,233	6.0	50.5	818922
Sue's Fashions	25,572	51,930	8.1	1.8	49.9	6,667	12.8	47.1	206284
Jana Kantor Asso.	14,022	29,434	8.0	.8	52.0	481	1.6	55.1	050187
Pierce Mills	12,761	25,438	9.5	1.7	49.8	7,858	30.9	33.1	132886
Ray, Inc.	2,196	4,416	8.0	1.8	49.4	754	17.1	43.8	148296
Dusty's Place	2,071	4,332	8.0	1.3	51.6			55.4	662411
Lady Carole	1,050	2,100	8.0	2.1	48.9			52.9	676841
Jill Petites	740	1,584	10.4	.5	54.2	640	40.5	29.2	472977
Andrea's	198	410	8.0	.8	51.1			55.0	527218

Cost: your cost
Retail: your original selling price
Discount and anticipation %: discount received for early payments
Freight %: your shipping expenses
Markup % Landed Loaded: [Retail selling price − (Cost + Freight)]/Retail selling price
Markdown: Amount original selling price is reduced
Gross Margin %: [Actual selling price − (Cost + Freight)]/Actual selling price

Confidential vendor analysis
is identical to the vendor profitability analysis but also provides a three-year financial summary as well as the names, titles, and negotiating points of all the vendor's sales staff.

lists the record of all purchases you made last year, the discount granted you by the vendor, transportation charges paid, the original markup, markdowns, and finally the season-ending gross margin on that vendor's merchandise. The confidential vendor analysis (Exhibit 9.5) lists the same companies as in the profitability analysis statement but also provides a three-year financial summary as well as the names, titles, and negotiating points of all the vendor's sales staff. This last piece of information is based on the notes taken by the buyer after the previous season's buying trip.

DOLLAR $ & CENTS

Retailers who maintain and review both a vendor profitability analysis and a confidential vendor analysis statement before going to market will be more profitable.

Based on the information obtained in the previous two reports, some retailers classify vendors into five categories.

EXHIBIT 9.5 — CONFIDENTIAL VENDOR ANALYSIS, RETAIL

Trip Dates __Fall Market__ City __Dallas__ Buyer's Name __Cooper__ Dept. Name __Women's Wear__ Dept. No. __491__

Vendor/Address Phone No./Floor No.		Volume History 199X	199X	199X	Markup History 199X	199X	199X	Markdown History 199X	199X	199X	Vendor Executives & Titles	Remarks
West Texas Blouse	Spring	590.5	719.4	330.8	47.5	47.7	46.7	2.4	5.3	4.4	Name: Larry Wilcox (VP)	Cash Discount
	Fall	1002.8	706.7		47.3	47.5		3.4	7.8		Julie Davin	Prone to co-op ads
	Year	1593.3	1426.1		47.4			3.1			Ted Rombach	
	Objectives:											
	Results As of 5/22:											
Flatland Fashions	Spring	224.5	230.2	210.8	47.7	50.0	47.2	6.5	8.5	3.8	Name: Joe Hall (P)	
	Fall	175.8	230.5		47.3	47.6		17.0	9.0		Richard Reel	Will deal on
	Year	400.3	460.7		47.5	48.8		11.1	8.7			transportation
	Objectives:											
	Results As of 5/22:											
Southern	Spring	-0-	42.3	50.7		48.4	45.4	-0-	9.1	4.2	Name: Jackie Poteet (SM)	
	Fall	37.0	69.2		47.1	42.3		7.7	7.8		Boonie Hanley	"Quantity"
	Year	37.0	112.5		47.1	44.7		7.7	8.2		Carol Little	
	Objectives:											
	Results As of 5/22:											
Gallo	Spring	21.7	195.0	55.6	46.9	50.0	48.3	1.3	0.2	1.2	Name: Ruth Wilson (P)	
	Fall	-0-	13.9		-0-	46.7		-0-	2.0		John Murphy	Easier of the two
	Year	21.7	33.4		46.9	48.6		1.3	0.9			
	Objectives:											
	Results As of 5/22:											

Class A vendors: These are the vendors from whom the retailer purchases large and profitable amounts of merchandise. The retailer may distinguish these vendors from others by purchasing a certain minimum quantity from them. These vendors and the retailer work together as partners.

Class B vendors: These are the vendors who generate satisfactory sales and profits for the retailer. They occasionally develop a strong product offering for the retailer.

Class C vendors: These are the vendors who carry outstanding lines but do not currently sell to the retailer. This is the type of vendor that the store buyer desires as a supplier.

Class A vendors *are those from whom the retailer purchases large and profitable amounts of merchandise.*

Class B vendors *are those that generate satisfactory sales and profits for the retailer.*

Class C vendors *are those that carry outstanding merchandise lines but do not currently sell to the retailer.*

Class D vendors
are those from whom the retailer purchases small quantities of goods on an irregular basis.

Class E vendors
are those with whom the retailer has had an unfavorable experience.

Class D vendors: These are the vendors from whom the retailer purchases small quantities of goods on an irregular basis. Because of the expense of the small orders, it is doubtful if the purchases from these vendors produce any profits for either the retailer or the vendor.

Class E vendors: These are the vendors with whom the retailer has had an unfavorable experience. Only after the approval of top store officials can orders be placed with these vendors.

Even buyers who do not go to market but have the vendors come to them evaluate their vendors. For years, many grocers thought that firms such as Procter & Gamble (P&G) treated retailers poorly. These grocers needed the many products that P&G manufactured, but they didn't like P&G's "we win, you lose" attitude, which forced retailers to purchase the complete line of P&G products to earn merchandising money. P&G was a Class B vendor, at best. Recently, however, P&G has developed a program in which it helps all its customers in developing their merchandise plans for the next months and no longer requires grocers to purchase slow-moving products.[7] This new attitude of "let's both win" has seen many supermarket managers reevaluate P&G as a class A vendor. P&G knows that it can only be as successful as its retailers let it be.

After selecting the vendor(s), the retailer still must make a decision on the specific merchandise to be bought. Some products, such as the basic items for the particular department in question, are easy to purchase. Other products, especially new items, require more careful planning and consideration. Retailers should concern themselves with several key questions. Among them are

1. Where does this product fit into the strategic position that I have staked out for my department?
2. Will I have an exclusive with this product or will I be in competition with nearby retailers?
3. What is the estimated demand for this product in my target market?
4. What is my anticipated gross margin for this product?
5. Will I be able to obtain reliable, speedy stock replacement?
6. Can this product stand on its own, or is it merely a "me-too" item?
7. What is my expected turnover rate with this product?
8. Does this product complement the rest of my inventory?

LO • 5
Describe what is involved in the vendor-buyer negotiation process and what terms of the contract can be negotiated

VENDOR NEGOTIATIONS

The climax of a successful buying plan is the active negotiation, which involves finding mutually satisfying solutions for parties with conflicting objectives, with those suppliers whom you have identified as suitable supply sources. The effectiveness of this buyer–vendor relationship depends on the negotiation skills of the buyer and the economic power of the firms involved.

Negotiation
is the process of finding mutually satisfying solutions when the retail buyer and vendor have conflicting objectives.

The retail buyer must negotiate price, delivery dates, discounts, shipping terms, and return privileges. All these factors are significant because they affect both the firm's profitability and cash flow.

Manufacturers, as well as retailers, have in recent years become increasingly aware of the cost of carrying excess inventory. Likewise, both parties have also become more concerned with the time value of money and its resulting effect on the firm's cash flow. Because both parties to the negotiation process are aware of these cost factors and are trying to shift these costs to the other party, most negotiations do produce some conflict. However, successful negotiation is usually accomplished when buyers realize that the vendors are really their partners in the upcoming merchandising season. Both the buyer and vendor are seeking to satisfy the retailer's customers better than anybody else. Therefore, buyers and vendors must resolve their conflicts and differences of opinion, remembering that negotiation is a two-way street and a long-term profitable relationship is the goal. After all, the vendor wants to develop a long-term relationship with the retailer as much as the retailer does with its customers.

What can be negotiated? There are many factors to be negotiated (prices, freight, delivery dates, method of shipment and shipping costs, exclusivity, guaranteed sales, markdown money, promotional allowances, return privileges, and discounts), and life is simplest when there aren't surprises. Therefore, the smart buyer leaves nothing to chance and discusses everything with the vendor before purchase orders are signed. The buyer and seller, together, work out the upcoming merchandising plans by using the buyer's merchandise budget and planned turnover. Therefore, the buyer and seller should seek to make negotiations a "win-win" situation, in which both sides win and neither feels like a "loser," such as P&G and its retailers are doing today. The essence of negotiation is to trade what is cheap to you but valuable to the other party for what is valuable to you but cheap to the other party.

DOLLAR $ & CENTS

The retailer who puts all the upcoming areas of negotiations and previous agreements with the vendor in writing before going to market will be more profitable.

The smart buyer puts all the upcoming areas of negotiations and previous agreements in letter form and sends it out before going to market. This helps to eliminate any misunderstandings afterward. Price, of course, is probably the first factor to be negotiated. Buyers should attempt to purchase the desired merchandise at the lowest possible net cost. But remember that although the vendors are your partners, the buyer should not expect unreasonable discounts or price concessions. However, the buyer can try to bring about a price concession that is legal under the Robinson-Patman Act.

The buyer must be familiar with the prices and discounts allowed by each vendor. This is why your past records are so important. However, the buyer must remember that his or her bargaining power is a result of his or her planned purchases from the vendor. As a result, a large retailer may be able to purchase goods from a vendor at a lower price than a small "mom-and-pop" retailer. There are five different types of discounts to be negotiated.

TRADE DISCOUNT

A trade discount, sometimes referred to as a functional discount, is a form of compensation that the buyer may receive for performing certain wholesaling and/or retailing services for the manufacturer. In as much as this discount is given for the performance of some service, the size of the discount will vary with that service. Thus variations in trade discounts are legally justifiable on the basis of the different costs associated with doing business with various buyers.

Trade discounts are often expressed in a chain, or series, such as "list less 40-20-10." Each figure in the chain of discounts represents a percentage reduction from the list price of an item. Assume that the list price of an item is $1,000 and that the chain of discounts is 40-20-10. The buyer who receives all these discounts would actually pay $432 for this item. The computations would look like this:

List price	$1,000
Less 40%	−400
	600
Less 20%	−120
	480
Less 10%	−48
Purchase price	$ 432

To illustrate how the various chains of discount permit a vendor to compensate the members of the distribution channel for their marketing activities, let's look at the preceding example. Assume that the manufacturer sells through a channel system that includes manufacturers' agents, service wholesalers, and small retailers. The purchase price of $432 is accorded to the manufacturers' agent who negotiates a sale between the manufacturer and the service wholesaler. The manufacturers' agent then charges the service wholesaler $480 for the item, thus realizing $48 for rendering a number of marketing activities. The service wholesaler, in turn, charges a retailer $600 for the item, thus making $120. The retailer then sells the item at the suggested list price of $1,000, thus making $400 in gross margin to cover operating expenses and a profit.

Trade discounts are legal when they correctly reflect the costs of the intermediaries' services. Sometimes, large retailers want to buy directly from the manufacturer and pay only $432, instead of $600. This action would enable the large retailer to undercut the competition and would be illegal, unless one of the three defenses of the Robinson-Patman Act explained in Chapter 6 can be applied.

QUANTITY DISCOUNT

A quantity discount is a price reduction offered as an inducement to purchase large quantities of merchandise. There are three types of quantity discounts available:

1. noncumulative quantity discount: a discount based on a single purchase
2. cumulative quantity discount: a discount based on total amount purchased over a period of time
3. free merchandise: a discount whereby merchandise is offered in lieu of price concessions

Noncumulative quantity discounts can be legally justified by the manufacturer if costs are reduced because of the quantity involved or if the manufacturer is meeting a competitor's price in good faith. Cumulative discounts are more difficult to justify, because many small orders may be involved, thereby reducing the manufacturer's savings.

TAKE A CLOSE LOOK AT THOSE QUANTITY DISCOUNTS

Quantity discounts might not always be in the seller's best interest and should always be viewed by the buyer as an invitation for further negotiations. Consider the following price schedule published by IBM for a computer:

QUANTITY	UNIT PRICE
1–19	$5,795
20–49	$5,099
50–149	$4,636
150–249	$4,486

Let's say that as a buyer for a retail chain you want 18 of these computers and your cost is $104,310 (18 × $5,795). But 20 would only cost $101,980 (20 × $5,099). What do you do?

You actually have four choices:

1. Tell IBM to ship 20 computers at $5,099, and you keep the extra two.
2. Tell IBM to ship you 18 computers at $5,099 and have them keep the other two.
3. Order 20 but tell IBM to ship you only 18 and to credit you for two computers at $5,099 each.
4. Negotiate a purchase price.

Whenever quantity discounts are offered, buyers should always check to see if by ordering more, the total purchase price may be lower.

Many times, retailers can make a quick profit from using quantity discounts by selling the extra merchandise to a diverter. The diverter, which is not an authorized member of the marketing channel but still functions as an intermediary, will be able to purchase these goods cheaper from the retailer than it can from the manufacturer and sell this excess merchandise to other retailers. Also, such discounts allow the manufacturer to have its products sold in discount stores without offending its authorized retailers. Witness Kmart, in which most of its cosmetics are diverted from authorized retailers.

Consider the previous retailer that needed only 18 computers and purchased 20 computers. Here, the retailer sold the two computers to a diverter for $3,500 each. As a result, the retailer was better off by $9,330 than it would have been had it bought only 18 computers at $5,795 each (18 × $5,795 = $104,310; 20 × 5,099 = $101,980 − $7,000 = $94,980). The diverter could now profit by selling these two computers to another retailer for $4,000 each.

Today, diverters are important members of the retailer's channel, especially in the grocery and computer fields. However, not all manufacturers feel the same way about them. Nonetheless, it was the manufacturers' pricing policies that enabled diverters to function economically.

Based on an example in "Unauthorized Channels of Distribution: Gray Markets," by Roy Howell, Robert Britney, Paul Kuzdrall, and James Wilcox, *Industrial Marketing Management* (1986): 257–263. Used with the permission of the authors.

For an example of how a quantity discount works, consider the following schedule:

ORDER QUANTITY	DISCOUNT FROM LIST PRICE
1 to 999	0%
1,000 to 9,999	5%
10,000 to 24,999	8%
25,000 to 49,999	10%

If a retailer, which had already purchased 500 units, wanted another 800 units, it would have to pay list price if the vendor uses a noncumulative policy. The retailer would receive a 5 percent discount on all purchases, however, if the vendor uses a cumulative pricing policy. The Winners & Losers box gives an example of how smart retailers can sometimes turn these quantity discount schedules into their advantage.

Promotional discount
is a discount provided for the retailer performing an advertising or promotional service for the manufacturer.

Seasonal discount
is a discount provided to retailers if they purchase and take delivery of merchandise in the off-season.

Cash discount
is a discount offered to the retailer for the prompt payment of bills.

End-of-month (EOM) dating
allows the retailer to take a cash discount and the full payment period to begin on the first day of the following month instead of on the invoice date.

Middle-of-month (MOM) dating
allows the retailer to take a cash discount and the full payment period to begin on the middle of the month.

Receipt of goods (ROG) dating
allows the retailer to take a cash discount and the full payment period to begin when the goods are received by the retailer.

PROMOTIONAL DISCOUNT

A third type of discount available is a promotional discount, which is given when the retailer performs an advertising or promotional service for the manufacturer. For example, a vendor might offer a retailer 50 extra jeans if (1) the retailer purchases 1,250 jeans during the season and (2) runs two newspaper advertisements featuring the jeans during the season. One of the main reasons that manufacturers offer such discounts is because the rates newspapers charge local retailers are often lower than the rates charged national manufacturers. These discounts are legal as long as they are available to all competing retailers on an equal basis.

SEASONAL DISCOUNT

A seasonal discount can be earned by the retailers if they purchase and take delivery of the merchandise in the off-season (e.g., buying swimwear in October). However, this does not mean that all seasonal discounts result in the purchase of merchandise out of season. Retailers in resort areas often take advantage of these discounts because swimwear is never out of season for them. As long as the same terms are available to all competing retailers, seasonal discounts are legal.

CASH DISCOUNT

The final discount available to the buyer is a cash discount for prompt payment of bills. Cash discounts are usually stated as 2/10, net 30, which means that a 2 percent discount is given if payment is received within 10 days of the invoice date and the net amount is due within 30 days.

Although the cash discount is a common method for encouraging early payment, it can also be used as a negotiating tool by delaying the payment due date. This future-dating negotiation may take many forms. Several of the most common are

1. End-of-month (EOM) dating allows for a cash discount and the full payment period to begin on the first day of the following month instead of on the invoice date. EOM invoices dated after the 25th of the month are considered to be dated on the first of the following month.
2. Middle-of-month (MOM) dating is similar to EOM except the middle of the month is used as the starting date.
3. Receipt of goods (ROG) dating allows the starting date to be the date goods are received by the retailer.

Retailers that purchase in large quantities can earn quantity discounts.

4. Extra dating (Ex) merely allows the retailer extra or interest free days before the period of payment begins.
5. A final discount form to be considered but that is not widely used today is anticipation. Anticipation allows a retailer to pay the invoice in advance of the expiration of the cash discount period and earn an extra discount. However, anticipation is usually figured at an annual rate of 7.0 percent, which is below the current cost of money.

Many vendors have eliminated the cash discount because retailers, especially department stores, have been taking 60 to 120 days to pay and still deduct the cash discount. In fact, many vendors are requiring new accounts to pay up front, until credit is established.

DELIVERY TERMS

Delivery terms are another factor to be considered in negotiations. They are important because they specify where title to the merchandise passes to the retailer and whether the vendor or buyer will pay the freight charges and who is obligated to file any damage claims. The three most common shipping terms are

1. Free on board (FOB) factory. The buyer assumes title at the factory and pays all transportation costs from the vendor's factory.
2. FOB shipping point. The vendor pays the transportation to a local shipping point, but the buyer assumes title at this point and pays all further transportation costs.
3. FOB destination. The vendor pays all transportation costs and the buyer takes title on delivery.

Extra dating (Ex) *allows the retailer extra or interest free days before the period of payment begins.*

Anticipation *allows the retailer to pay the invoice in advance of the end of the cash discount period and earn an extra discount.*

Free on board (FOB) factory *is a method of charging for transportation where the buyer assumes title to the goods at the factory and pays all transportation costs from the vendor's factory.*

FOB shipping point *is a method of charging for transportation where the vendor pays the transportation to a local shipping point where the buyer assumes title and then pays all further transportation costs.*

FOB destination *is a method of charging for transportation where the vendor pays all transportation costs and the buyer takes title on delivery.*

LO • 6

Discuss the various methods of controlling loss through shinkage, vendor collusion, and theft

IN-STORE MERCHANDISE HANDLING[8]

The retailer will need to have some means of handling incoming merchandise. For some types of retailers (e.g., a grocery store), this need will be significant and frequent; for others (e.g., a jeweler), it will be relatively minor and infrequent. A retailer with a frequent and significant amount of incoming merchandise needs considerable planning of merchandise receiving and handling space. To illustrate, consider that a full-line grocery store will need to build receiving docks to which 40-to-60-foot semitrailers can be backed up. Similarly, space may be needed for a small forklift to drive between the truck and the merchandise receiving area to unload the merchandise. Subsequently, the merchandise will need to be moved from the receiving area, where it will be counted and marked, to a storage area, either on the selling floor or in a separate location.

The point at which incoming merchandise is received can be a high theft point. The retail manager needs to design the receiving and handling area to minimize this problem. Several types of theft will be mentioned in the following discussion. Some involve the retail employees themselves; others involve outsiders.

Vendor collusion includes the types of losses that occur when the merchandise is delivered. Typical losses involve the delivery of less merchandise than is charged for, removal of good merchandise disguised as old or stale merchandise, and stealing other merchandise from the stockroom or off the selling floor while making delivery. This type of theft often involves both the delivery persons and the retail employee who signs for the delivery, with the two splitting the profit.

Employee theft occurs when employees steal merchandise where they work. Although no one knows for sure how much is stolen annually from retailers as many as 30 percent of American workers admit to stealing from their employers, even if it is only small items such as a pen or pencil. Although some of the stolen goods come from the selling floor, a larger percentage is taken from the stockroom to the employee lounge and lockers, where it is kept until the employees leave with it at quitting time. Employee theft, which amounts to more than $800 per apprehension, is most prevalent in food stores, department stores, and discount stores. Considering that these types of stores are usually larger in size, sales volume, and number of employees, the lack of close supervision might contribute to this problem. Exhibit 9.6 shows 50 ways that an employee can steal from a bar.

Customer theft is also a problem; in fact, more than a dozen shoppers are caught for every case of employee theft, although the average amount of merchandise recovered is less than $50. Stealing merchandise from the stockroom and receiving area may be easier than taking it from the selling floor for several reasons. First, much of the stockroom merchandise is not ticketed, so it is easier to get it through electronic anti-shoplifting devices. Second, once the thief enters the stock area, there is very little antitheft security. Most security guards watch the exits and fitting rooms. Third, there is usually an exit in the immediate area of the stockroom through which the thief can carry out the stolen goods. Recently, these exits have been wired to set off an alarm when opened without a key, helping to reduce thefts somewhat.

The retailer must be aware that there is an excellent opportunity for receiving, handling, and storage thefts to occur. Therefore, steps should be taken to help cut down on these crimes. The retailer cannot watch the employees every minute to see

Vendor collusion

occurs when an employee of one of the retailer's vendors steals merchandise as it is delivered to the retailer.

Employee theft

occurs when employees of the retailer steal merchandise where they work.

Customer theft

is also known as shoplifting and occurs when customers or individuals disguised as customers steal merchandise from the retailer's store.

EXHIBIT 9.6	50 THINGS BAR OWNERS SHOULD BE ON THE LOOKOUT FOR

1. The "Phantom Register" trick: just set up an extra register in bar for use only during busy times. The income from this register is not totaled on master tape and funds are skimmed by the bartender.
2. Serve and collect while register is being read between shift changes.
3. Claim a phony walk-out and keep money received from customer.
4. Pick up customer's cash when he or she isn't paying attention.
5. Fake a robbery of the night deposit on way to bank. It is difficult for owners to prove this fake occurred.
6. Add phantom drinks to a customer's "running tab."
7. The "Phantom Bottle" ploy: here the bartender brings his or her own bottle of liquor onto shift and pockets cash from its sale.
8. The "Short Pour" trick: just pour less than shot to cover "give away" liquor costs.
9. Don't ring up any sale and keep the cash.
10. The "Short-ring" trick: here the bartender under-rings the correct price of item and pockets the difference.
11. The "Free-Giveaway" trick: bartender gives drinks to friends in anticipation of larger tips.
12. Misled the owner regarding the number of draft beers that can be poured from a keg.
13. Undercharge for drinks with the anticipation of a larger tip.
14. Reuse register drink receipts.
15. Trade drinks to the cook for meals.
16. Add water to liquor bottle to maintain inventory.
17. Substitute lower-priced liquor when asked for call brands.
18. Being in collusion with the delivery person, selling "stolen" products that he or she provides, and splitting the profit.
19. Ask for kickbacks from liquor distributor.
20. Dispensing and registering one shot on computerized dispenser system, while short-shoting the liquor into two glasses.
21. Short-changing a customer when he or she is a "little under the weather" and claim it was a "honest" mistake if caught.
22. Claim a returned drink: extra drink produced and can be sold by bartender.
23. When bar is selling both liquor to go and by the drink, count missing bottles as "to go sale."
24. The "Owner Is a Jerk" ploy: here, the bartender is the only person in charge of liquor pick-up, check-in, and stocking.
25. Complimentary cocktail or wine coupons from hotel room sold by maids to bar personnel, which they can place in register for cash.
26. Add two different customer drinks together and charge both, claiming mis-understanding in who was purchasing the round.
27. Ringing food items on liquor key to cover high liquor cost percent.
28. Selling "after-shift drinks" to customers, not having them consumed by other employees.

continued

EXHIBIT 9.6	CONTINUED

29. Not pouring enough liquor into blended fruit drinks to cover other shortages.
30. Having customer sign credit card voucher in advance and then overcharge the ticket.
31. Claiming opening bank was short.
32. Total out register in midshift. Start new tape. Cashier keeps both new tapes and cash.
33. Incorrect "over-ring" or "void" of register.
34. Making sales during tape changes.
35. Mistotaling the amount on the credit card or change the amount after customer leaves.
36. Taking money from the game machines or jukeboxes.
37. Accumulating the guest checks to ring up after customer leaves so as to change the amount or leave out items.
38. Run credit card through twice.
39. Selling empty kegs and returnable bottles to an off-premise retailer.
40. Place the tip jars next to cash register—easy to place cash in tip jar and ring "no sale" for register activity.
41. Falsifying cumulative register readings and "losing" tape.
42. Adding extra hours to your time card and splitting it with the shift manager.
43. Help the shift manager claim a fictitious employee on payroll.
44. Taking home food or liquor or fake a burglary.
45. Taking funds from vending machines.
46. Ringing up sales at happy hour prices, but charging regular bar prices to the customer when he or she is keeping receipts.
47. Servers charging for happy hour hors d'oeuvres and bar snacks.
48. Holding back bank deposits for a couple days and investing or borrowing money or just don't deposit money (or lesser amount) and keep difference.
49. Bartender handwriting bar tabs and ringing up lesser amounts on the register.
50. Wrapping booze into garbage can for later retrieval.

whether they are honest, but some surveillance is helpful. However, the retailer must consider the employee's and customer's right to privacy versus the retailer's right to security. Legislation is currently being considered by several states that would, if approved, only allow the use of electronic monitoring, by video and audio systems, when advance notice is given. In effect, workers and shoppers must be informed when they are being monitored. Many retailers find this disturbing because theft from retailers has been increasing at least 5 percent per year over the last decade and exceeds $10 billion annually in the United States. The customer ultimately pays for this and one source in the United Kingdom estimates that retail theft adds the equivalent of $152 each year to the household bill of every family.[9]

Merchandise theft is a major problem in stores.

The amount of storage space needed will be related to the physical dimensions of the merchandise and the safety stock level needed to maintain the desired rate of stock turnover. For example, furniture is bulky and requires considerable storage space; grocery items turn over frequently, so more merchandise is needed than can be displayed on the shelves. This excess inventory causes retailers to have to stack boxes and cartons on the floor of the stockroom. In most cases, however, this scenario would be fairly inefficient and also costly when the retailer is probably paying those employees anywhere from $5 to $15 per hour. Thus, in most cases, some type of equipment will be used to increase productivity in this area. For instance, rather than having the employees carry incoming merchandise, there are numerous types of carts especially made for this purpose. Also, instead of stacking the cartons and boxes directly on the floor of the stockroom where they must remain packed and risk being damaged, the merchandise can be unpacked, checked, inventoried, and ticketed, then placed on shelves or in bins until needed. By doing this, one can increase the amount of merchandise stored per square foot by decreasing the amount of packing material. As noted earlier, a tidy, well-ordered stock area is less tempting to dishonest employees. Trash compactors can be helpful by compressing the packing clutter.

STUDENT STUDY GUIDE

SUMMARY   Merchandise management is the analysis, planning, acquisition, and control of inventory investments and assortments in a retail enterprise. An understanding of the principles of merchandise management is essential to good retail management. A major part of merchandise management is planning. The retailer needs to plan, first, the dollars to invest in inventory and, second, the units of merchandise to purchase with these dollars. These two forms of planning are called dollar merchandise planning and unit stock planning.

LO•1   WHAT IS THE DIFFERENCE BETWEEN THE FOUR METHODS OF DOLLAR MERCHANDISE PLANNING USED TO DETERMINE THE PROPER INVENTORY STOCK LEVELS NEEDED TO BEGIN A MERCHANDISE SELLING PERIOD?   In the section on dollar merchandise planning, we discussed how the basic stock, percentage variation, weeks' supply, and stock-to-sales inventory methods can be used in retailing today.

LO•2   HOW DOES A RETAILER USE DOLLAR MERCHANDISE CONTROL AND OPEN-TO-BUY IN THE RETAIL BUYING PROCESS?   Once the dollar merchandise to have on hand at the beginning of each month (or season) is planned by the buyer, it becomes essential to ensure that the buyer does not make commitments for merchandise that would exceed the dollar plan. In short, the dollars planned for merchandise need to be controlled by a technique called open-to-buy. OTB represents the dollar amount that a buyer can currently spend on merchandise without exceeding the planned dollar stocks discussed previously.

The OTB figure should not be set in stone because it can be exceeded. Consumer needs are the dominant consideration. If sales exceed planned sales, additional quantities should be ordered above those scheduled for purchase according to the merchandise budget.

LO•3   HOW DOES A RETAILER USE UNIT STOCK PLANNING AND MODEL STOCK PLANS IN DETERMINING THE MAKEUP OF A MERCHANDISE MIX?   The dollar merchandise plan is only the starting point in determining a merchandise line, which consists of a group of products that are closely related because they are intended for the same end use; are sold to the same customer group; or fall within a given price range. Once the retailer has decided how many dollars can be invested in inventory, the dollar plan needs to be converted into a unit plan.

However, there seldom will be enough dollars to emphasize all three inventory dimensions: variety, breadth, and depth. Therefore, retailers must select a merchandise mix that appeals to the greatest number of profitable market segments.

LO•4   HOW DO RETAILERS SELECT PROPER MERCHANDISE SOURCES?   In addition to deciding what and how much to purchase, successful merchandise management must also consider vendor selection and negotiations. In this section, we reviewed what factors are important in the selection of a vendor and how a buyer prepares for a buying trip.

LO·5 WHAT IS INVOLVED IN THE VENDOR—BUYER NEGOTIA-
TION PROCESS AND WHAT TERMS OF THE CONTRACT CAN BE NE-
GOTIATED? The retail buyer must negotiate price, delivery dates, discounts (trade,
quantity, promotional, seasonal, and cash), delivery term, and return privileges. All
these factors are significant because they affect both the firm's profitability and cash
flow.

LO·6 WHAT METHODS ARE AVAILABLE TO THE RETAILER FOR
CONTROLLING LOSS THROUGH SHRINKAGE, VENDOR COLLUSION,
AND THEFT? These include the proper design of receiving and handling areas,
better employee supervision, and methods of watching customers as they shop the
store.

We concluded the chapter with a discussion on in-store merchandise handling, as
a means to control losses by theft.

TERMS TO REMEMBER

merchandise management
gross margin return on inventory
basic stock method (BSM)
percentage variation method (PVM)
weeks' supply method (WSM)
stock-to-sales method (SSM)
open-to-buy
merchandise line
variety
breadth
depth
consignment
extra dating
model stock plan
vendor profitability analysis
confidential vendor analysis
class A vendors
class B vendors
class C vendors
class D vendors
class E vendors

negotiation
trade discount
quantity discount
non-cumulative quantity discount
cumulative quantity discount
free merchandise
promotional discount
seasonal discount
cash discount
end-of-month (EOM) dating
middle-of-month (MOM) dating
receipt of goods (ROG) dating
extra dating (Ex)
anticipation
free on board (FOB) factory
FOB shipping point
FOB destination
vendor collusion
employee theft
customer theft

REVIEW AND DISCUSSION QUESTIONS

LO·1 WHAT ARE THE DIFFERENCES BETWEEN THE FOUR
METHODS OF DOLLAR MERCHANDISE PLANNING USED TO
DETERMINE THE PROPER INVENTORY STOCK LEVELS NEEDED TO
BEGIN A MERCHANDISE SELLING PERIOD?

1. If your annual turnover rate is 10 times, which inventory stock level method
would you use and why?

2. Herb's Hardware is attempting to develop a merchandise budget for the next 12 months. To assist in this process, the following data have been developed. The target inventory turnover is 4.8 and forecast sales are

MONTH	FORECAST SALES
1	$27,000
2	26,000
3	20,000
4	34,000
5	41,000
6	40,000
7	28,000
8	27,000
9	38,000
10	39,000
11	26,000
12	28,000

Develop a monthly merchandise budget using the basic stock method (BSM) and the percentage variation method (PVM).

LO•2 HOW DOES A RETAILER USE DOLLAR MERCHANDISE CONTROL AND OPEN–TO–BUY IN THE RETAIL BUYING PROCESS?

3. What problems can occur to buyers "open-to-buy" if they misjudge planned sales?
4. What does the term *open-to-buy* mean? How can it be used to control merchandise investments?
5. A buyer is going to market and needs to compute the open-to-buy. The relevant data are as follows: planned stock at end of March, $319,999 (at retail prices); planned March sales, $149,999; current stock-on-hand (March 1), $274,000; merchandise on order for delivery, $17,000; planned reductions, $11,000. What is the buyer's open-to-buy?

LO•3 HOW DOES A RETAILER USE UNIT STOCK PLANNING AND MODEL STOCK PLANS IN DETERMINING THE MAKEUP OF A MERCHANDISE MIX?

6. What are the major constraints in designing the optimal merchandise mix?
7. How can merchandise lines have too much breadth, yet not enough depth?

LO•4 HOW DOES A RETAILER SELECT PROPER MERCHANDISE SOURCES?

8. What do you think is the most important criterion in selecting a vendor? Why?
9. Why should a new buyer look over the previous buyer's "confidential vendor analysis" before going to market?

LO•5 WHAT IS INVOLVED IN THE VENDOR–BUYER NEGOTIATION PROCESS AND WHAT TERMS OF THE CONTRACT CAN BE NEGOTIATED?

10. If a vendor ships you $1,000 worth of merchandise on April 27 with terms of 3/20, net 30 EOM, how much should you pay the vendor on June 8?
11. How does a cash discount differ from a trade discount?
12. A retailer purchases goods that have a list price of $5,000. The manufacturer allows

a trade discount of 40-25-10 and a cash discount of 2/10, net 30. If the retailer takes both discounts, how much is paid to the vendor?

13. How can cumulative quantity discounts be considered to be anticompetitive?

LO•6 WHAT METHODS ARE AVAILABLE TO THE RETAILER FOR CONTROLLING LOSS THROUGH SHRINKAGE, VENDOR COLLUSION, AND THEFT?

14. Why is the receiving room such a high theft area for retailers?
15. Should retailers' right to security take precedent over the employee's and the customer's right to privacy when retailers set up an electronic monitoring system in their stores to curb losses from theft?

SAMPLE TEST QUESTIONS

LO•1 DETERMINE THE BUYER'S BOM FOR AUGUST, USING THE PERCENTAGE VARIATION METHOD, BASED ON THE FOLLOWING INFORMATION: PLANNED SALES FOR AUGUST = $170,000; AVERAGE MONTHLY SALES = $142,000; AVERAGE STOCK FOR THE SEASON = $425,000.

a. $466,900
b. $390,000
c. $254,400
d. $425,000
e. $453,800

LO•2 THE OPEN-TO-BUY CONCEPT PROVIDES INFORMATION ABOUT HOW MUCH THE BUYER CAN ORDER AT

a. the beginning of a merchandising period
b. the middle of a merchandising period
c. the end of a merchandising period
d. anytime during the merchandising period
e. anytime a vendor fails to ship merchandise on time

LO•3 WHICH OF THE FOLLOWING FACTORS IS NOT A CONSTRAINT ON THE RETAILER'S OPTIMAL MERCHANDISE MIX?

a. space
b. merchandise turnover
c. legal
d. dollar merchandise
e. market

LO•4 A VENDOR PROFITABILITY ANALYSIS STATEMENT:

a. is a vendor's financial statement that is made available to all retailers
b. is a retailer's analysis of the profitability of the different vendors and their lines from the prior year
c. is a schedule maintained by the retailer that shows each vendor's initial data for new lines, shipment of orders, and gross margins
d. is a retailer's financial statement used by the vendor for determining credit limits
e. contains a list of who provided the retailer with discounts during the prior three years

LO•5 A CUMULATIVE QUANTITY DISCOUNT IS BASED ON

a. a single purchase
b. the total amount of merchandise purchased over a period of time
c. the total amount of merchandise purchased since you began dealing with a vendor
d. the amount of free merchandise that a vendor is offering
e. cumulative discounts are only offered if a buyer is purchasing more than 50,000 units

LO•6 WHICH TWO PARTIES ARE USUALLY INVOLVED IN LOSSES DUE TO VENDOR COLLUSION?

a. delivery people and customers
b. retail employee signing for the delivery and delivery person
c. vendor sale representative and retail employee signing for the delivery
d. customers and vendor sales representative
e. vendor sales representative and the retailer's accountant

APPLICATIONS

WRITING AND SPEAKING EXERCISE One of your firm's vendors has been slipping in service lately. Just last week, your shipping room noticed that on an invoice marked 96 units, the vendor only shipped 86. Last month it was a late delivery, and the month before one of your orders from this vendor had the wrong merchandise.

Now, your firm has been contacted by a competitor offering to ship you similar merchandise at similar prices. The problem is that both vendors use a cumulative quantity discount policy, and you have six months remaining on the original vendor's time period. Your past purchases have qualified for the highest discount available from the original vendor, and you would have to start over with the new vendor. Nevertheless, you do not like the problems that you have been having recently with your current vendor.

Prepare a memo to the divisional merchandise manager with your recommendation.

RETAIL PROJECT In the chapter, we mentioned that before going to market you can check out the Council on Economic Priorities (CEP) web site (www.accesspt.com/cep), which ranks consumer products manufacturers, as well as retailers, on several workplace issues. In addition, the web site also looks at several other issues relating to corporate social responsibility: charitable giving, community outreach, disclosure of information, environment, family benefits, and the advancement of minorities and women.

Go to this web site and examine for yourself how the CEP grades each one of these issues. Do you agree or disagree with the statement that retail buyers should examine this web site before going to market so as to not purchase merchandise from manufacturers on the Dishonor Roll? Or should retailers merely check out this web site to be prepared for any future problems involving manufacturers of products that they are selling? Finally, are some of these issues more important than others?

CASE TWO COUNTRIES; TWO DIFFERENT REGULATIONS

In 1997, Wal-Mart, as a result of its expansion into Canada, faced a problem that no American retailer had ever faced. Should it follow a U.S. law and violate a Canadian law or should it follow a Canadian law and violate a U.S. law?

In 1996, after Cuban MiG fighters shot down two small private U.S. planes off the Cuban coast, President Clinton signed the Helms-Burton Act, codifying Washington's embargo on Cuba that actually began four decades before. This law included an additional provision to punish some foreign firms who profit from doing business with Cuba, so that Americans who lost property when Castro took over could be compensated for their loses.

Canada, however, had never joined the embargo against Cuba nor prevented its citizens from traveling to Cuba. Thus, an array of Cuban goods—including rum, inexpensive apparel items, and of course, Havana's prized cigars—were widely available in Canada. Canada had become a major trading partner with Cuba and a major investor in Cuba's staggering economy. Nevertheless, Canada's annual trade with Cuba amounted to only about half of what Canada traded with the United States in a single day.

Wal-Mart maintains separate buying, merchandising, and logistic centers for its foreign operations at its corporate headquarters in Bentonville. The chain's international buyers, however, serve a different function than its domestic buyers. Their main purpose is to serve as liaisons with their "mirrors" in each foreign country. Thus, the chain's problems began when the resident Wal-Mart Canada buyer purchased some Cuban-made pajamas to retail for C$12.96 (US$9.53), and the international buyer back in Arkansas didn't catch the possible legal hassles. These pajamas, after all, were just one of about 80,000 items in a typical Canadian Wal-Mart store. When Wal-Mart became aware that it was possibly violating the Helms-Burton Act, which prohibited U.S. companies and their subsidiaries from trading with Cuba, they quietly removed the garments from its shelves. However, customer complaints about the removal of these inexpensive pj's to local Canadian newspapers and their subsequent coverage of Wal-Mart's behavior forced Wal-Mart to publicly acknowledge its action.

By removing the Cuban-made merchandise, Wal-Mart probably violated a law in Canada designed to prevent Canadian subsidiaries of U.S. firms from complying with any U.S. trade law that conflicted with Canadian policy. Canada, which has only one-tenth of the U.S.'s population and is highly sensitive to any threat to its sovereignty, soon pressured Wal-Mart Canada into putting back the 75 cotton pajamas that each store carried before the uproar back on the shelves. This placed the retailer in a potential breach of a U.S. law that was already at the center of a U.S. dispute with the World Trade Organization for being "fundamentally wrong." In addition, several free-trade groups in Canada threatened Wal-Mart with a public relations nightmare if they failed to adhere to Canadian laws.

Given that the pajamas were already purchased and placed on the store shelves before anyone became aware of the conflicting laws, how would you handle this problem if you were to advise the head of Wal-Mart Canada?

PLANNING YOUR OWN RETAIL BUSINESS Judy Cox is in

the process of developing the merchandise budget for her family clothing store, which she will be opening next year. She has decided to use the basic stock method of merchandise budgeting. Planned sales for the first half of next year are $635,000, and this is divided as follows: February = 9 percent, March = 10 percent, April = 15 percent, May = 21 percent, June = 22 percent, and July = 23 percent. Planned total retail reductions are 9 percent for February and March, 4 percent for April and May, and 12 percent for June and July. The planned initial markup percentage is 48 percent. Judy desires the rate of inventory turnover for the season to be two times. Also, she wants to begin the second half of the year with $400,000 in inventory at retail prices.

Develop a six-month merchandise budget for Judy.

NOTES

1. "A Blueprint for Local Assortment Management," *Chain Store Age,* February 1997: 27–34.
2. "Toy Stores Spur Buying Frenzies with Exclusives," *Wall Street Journal,* December 2, 1997: B1.
3. "Finding Gold in the Supply Chain Stream," *Chain Store Age,* January 1997: 164.
4. Rockney G. Walters, "An Empirical Investigation into Retailer Response to Manufacturer Trade Promotion," *Journal of Retailing,* Summer 1989: 253–272.
5. "Can Toys "Я" Us Get on Top of its Game?" *Business Week,* April 7, 1997: 124–128; "Is Toys "Я" Us Playing Fair?" *U.S. News & World Report,* March 17, 1997: 53.
6. "Gifford Up Against New Sweatshop Allegations," *Dallas Morning News,* December 6, 1997: 2F.
7. "P&G to Stores: Keep the Dented Crisco Cans," *Wall Street Journal,* March 21, 1997: B1.
8. For a more complete discussion of loss prevention, the reader should consult "The Ernst & Young/IMRA Survey of Retail Loss Prevention Expenses and Trends" in the most recent January issue of *Chain Store Age.*
9. "Retailers Get No Respite from Crime," *Shopping Centers Today,* September 1997: 5.

APPAREL MERCHANDISING'S UNIQUE ROLE IN RETAILING

by Dr. Mary Ann Eastlick

University of Arizona

One of the most exciting and lucrative areas of retailing is ready-to-wear apparel. This is evidenced by the variety of retailers that offer fashion apparel ranging from traditional department and specialty retailers such as Macy's, Neiman-Marcus, and The Gap to discounters such as Wal-Mart and Kmart.

Individuals interested in working in apparel retailing should be familiar with the differences involved in retailing fashion and non-fashion merchandise. Although fundamentals of retailing are the same across product and service classes, several characteristics of fashion goods can create a need for distinct approaches in conducting business. For example, special planning and control methods are used to monitor constant changes in fashion trends and predict consumer demand.

The purpose of this appendix is to describe several approaches used by apparel retailers to deal with unique characteristics of fashion products. In doing so, fashion is defined and described in relation to its life cycle and factors that influence its adoption and diffusion.

WHAT CHARACTERIZES APPAREL AS FASHION?

The term fashion is often associated with apparel and accessories. In reality, it can be applied to a variety of products, services, and forms of human behavior[1] such as apparel, furniture, architectural styles, tastes in food and restaurants, and preferences for different video games.

Two guidelines are used to identify objects as *fashion:*

1. whether aesthetic and emotional appeals are used in evaluating the object
2. whether the object is accepted by a sizeable segment of consumers

One characteristic common to fashion objects is that sensory subjective criteria including visual images, scents, tastes, sounds, and tactile feelings influence purchase and use decisions. Excellent examples of these aesthetic and emotional appeals are provided

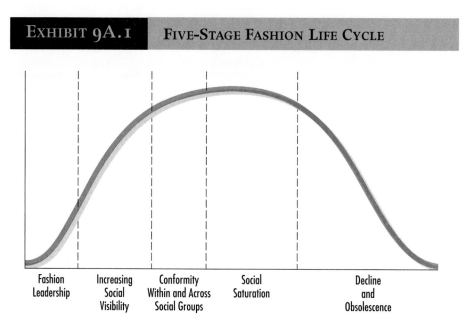

| EXHIBIT 9A.1 | FIVE-STAGE FASHION LIFE CYCLE |

Fashion Leadership · Increasing Social Visibility · Conformity Within and Across Social Groups · Social Saturation · Decline and Obsolescence

in messages communicated by fashion advertisements. Whereas a company such as Calvin Klein promotes apparel that conveys a sensual or daring image, another such as DKNY or Armani emphasizes a sophisticated, refined appeal. Image-creating properties such as these can be important considerations when retailers predict product demand. Compared with functional properties such as quality and price, these subjective characteristics are more difficult to observe, measure, and quantify.

Objects are not technically defined as "fashion" until they begin to experience acceptance by a sizeable group of consumers. Acceptance implies that the use of a product is considered socially appropriate by one's reference groups (i.e., friends, family, co-workers, classmates, fraternity brothers, etc.). Given the variety of consumer segments that exist, what might be perceived as fashion by some groups will not be by others. Retailers need to recognize which products are considered fashionable by consumers in their target market.

STAGES OF FASHION ADOPTION: THE FASHION LIFE CYCLE

The process by which fashion is introduced, reaches widespread consumer acceptance, and then eventually falls from popularity and becomes obsolete is an important consideration when predicting product demand. Although these stages correspond closely to the introduction, growth, maturity, and decline stages of retail life cycle theory, the description of each phase for fashion stresses the important influence of social acceptance on the duration and shape of the life cycle. With fashion-oriented merchandise the five-stage lifecycle shown in Exhibit 9A.1 is used:

1. fashion leadership
2. increasing social visibility
3. conformity within and across social groups

4. social saturation
5. decline and obsolescence[2]

In the first phase of the fashion life cycle, a new fashion is introduced to the consumer via change agents. Change agents are typically leaders of social groups such as prominent personalities, celebrities, or members of the social elite. Following initial introduction, acceptance of the fashion within and across social groups continues to grow until reaching a state of mass conformity and then saturation. At this time, consumers start to lose interest in the fashion, its acceptance begins to decline, and it eventually becomes obsolete.

FASHION LIFE CYCLE AND A STORE'S FASHION IMAGE

One way that retailers establish their fashion image is by associating their store with merchandise at one or more stages of the life cycle. For example, those retailers that sell fashion apparel in the first two stages of the cycle make up the *"high fashion market,"* which consists of both one-of-a-kind and ready-to-wear designer apparel created by prominent European, U.S., and East Asian design houses such as those of Armani, Dior, and Mizrahi. Specialty department stores such as Saks Fifth Avenue and Neiman-Marcus and designer boutiques are examples of upscale U.S. retailers selling high fashion. These stores can command premium prices for their merchandise because of the status associated with the prestige brand-name lines carried and superior quality and service offered. In recent years, however, consumer demand for expensive, high-fashion apparel has been declining. High-fashion design houses and retailers are turning to new, affluent consumer markets in parts of the world such as Asia and to ready-to-wear apparel and other fashion products for new business opportunities.[3]

The majority of apparel sold in the United States is *mass fashion,* which is made up of apparel in the middle of the life cycle (i.e., conformity within and across social groups). These styles are often adaptations or "knock-offs" of those offered by prominent designers. Examples of retailers involved in the mass fashion business include most traditional department and specialty chain stores such as Dillard's, JCPenney, Bloomingdale's, The Limited, and Ann Taylor; promotional department stores such as Mervyn's; and discounters like Target and Kmart. Competition among retailers in the mass fashion market is intense because these retailers are currently operating at overcapacity, the consumers they target have become very value- and price-oriented, and the costs of raw materials used to make the apparel are increasing.[4]

Mass fashion retailers attempt to differentiate themselves from their competitors by their product, price, and service offerings. A few mass fashion retailers including upscale department and specialty stores such as Lord & Taylor and Talbot's are able to position themselves to appeal to upper-end, affluent consumers by offering "bridge" and better fashion lines and specialized customer services. *Bridge* lines have a fashion image somewhere between those of high and better fashions and are often the ready-to-wear lines of high-fashion design houses such as DKNY and

DKNY focuses its fashion design efforts on the high-fashion market and thus retailers that carry DKNY fashion can project a high-fashion image.

Ann Klein II. *Better lines* have an image just above that of mass fashion and include lines such as Tommy Hilfiger, Liz Claiborne, and Jones New York. Considering the fashion life cycle, elements of bridge and better fashions (i.e., style, design details, color, and/or fabric) place these fashion lines in growth phases of their life cycles (i.e., stages that correspond to the fashion life stage of increasing social visibility).

Mass fashion retailers also seek to differentiate themselves from their competitors by developing private label merchandise to be sold exclusively by their stores. They either work with designers or celebrities and product developers from resident buying offices and apparel manufacturing firms or employ their own development and design personnel to create this merchandise. For example, Wal-Mart and Kmart have successfully used celebrity private labels such as the Kathie Lee Gifford and Jaclyn Smith lines, respectively, to increase their market share in the mass fashion business. Others such as Talbot's maintain the image of their own Talbot's brand.

Fashion apparel in the social saturation stage of the life cycle is usually sold by close-out retailers, which specialize in buying the entire inventory or excess inventory of manufacturers or retailers going out of business. Sometimes, in addition to selling excess production of current styles and/or sizes, outlet stores also offer slow-selling fashions from previous seasons at extremely low prices.

Merchandise in the last stage, decline and obsolescence, has little demand, even at extremely low prices. Therefore, such merchandise is usually given away to charitable organizations and thrift shops.

FASHION ADOPTION AND DIFFUSION

The extent of consumer acceptance determines the manner and speed at which fashion moves through the stages in its life cycle. Acceptance rates are influenced by economic, social, political, psychological, and lifestyle factors, and it is important that retailers understand these theories. Several theories are used to explain how these factors affect fashion adoption and diffusion.[5]

DOWNWARD FLOW THEORY

Advocates of the *downward flow (or "trickle-down") theory* claim that fashion is first introduced by exposure from the upper socioeconomic classes. Diffusion occurs as the fashion is adopted by successively lower social classes who are attempting to imitate social classes above them and compete for social status. As adoption gradually diffuses to lower classes, the upper class differentiates itself by turning to new fashions. This theory is not widely used to explain contemporary fashion adoption and diffusion because it proposes that wealthy fashion clientele and their fashion designers dictate fashion to consumers.

COLLECTIVE SELECTION THEORY

The *collective selection theory* proposes that most fashion diffuses horizontally across social groups through social interactions and interpersonal influences. It states that initial adoption and acceptance of a fashion can occur almost simultaneously across socioeconomic classes because of both mass production and the mass communication of consumer information.

This theory is widely accepted as being most applicable to contemporary fashion adoption. It is often used to explain why similar fashion styles are offered by diverse groups of retailers at a variety of price ranges. Collective selection also explains the increased speed at which fashion travels through its life cycle. For example, communication technologies such as the Internet have enabled some mass fashion retailers to copy designer fashions and make them available for sale before the designers' originals are even produced.[6]

SUBCULTURAL LEADERSHIP THEORY

Another common theory of fashion adoption and diffusion is the *subcultural leadership theory,* which recognizes the influence of subcultural groups such as youth, street gangs, and ethnic groups on the mass population. The theory advocates that fashion may flow in an upward direction through the social classes or from a subcultural group to the mass population. This manner of fashion adoption was highly evident in the 1960s and 1970s as fashions worn by youth (e.g., the use of jeans for everyday apparel) were accepted by the mass population. The adoption of the "grunge" look introduced by 1990's rock groups to youth is also explained by the subcultural leadership theory.

The grunge fashion look evolved from a distinctive subculture.

COMMUNICATION MODELS

Another important group of theories used to describe fashion adoption are known as communication models. These *communication models* describe the influence of mass media and interpersonal communications on the adoption process. Communication models also recognize the role of fashion change agents including innovators, opinion leaders, and innovative communicators, who provide visual and verbal communication about new fashions.

One communication model emphasizes the symbolic meanings that consumers attach to their possessions.[7] This approach is consistent with an emerging theme of contemporary research on consumer behavior called hedonic or symbolic consumption. When applied to fashion products, this model focuses on relationships between an individual's self-image, social identity, and the images communicated through use of various fashion objects.

Other similar research proposes that retail patronage motives for hedonically consumed products such as fashion rely more on symbolic than on tangible features of such products.[8] As information is gained from this field of research, fashion retailers may benefit from a better understanding of the symbolic and aesthetic product characteristics that motivate fashion consumers.

UNDERSTANDING FASHION ADOPTION

Just as changes in social, economic, technological, and political conditions cause changes in the retailer's strategies, operations, and/or managerial decisions, these environmental factors also stimulate new fashion trends. Knowledge of fashion adoption theories can be useful for predicting how new fashions will diffuse through society and making retail mix decisions to promote their acceptance. Two examples follow to illustrate these points.

INFLUENCE OF TECHNOLOGY ON FASHION DISTRIBUTION

New technologies such as mass customization and electronic retailing have the potential to radically change the manner in which fashion products are produced and distributed to consumers. Levi Strauss & Company is an example of an apparel manufacturer that is experimenting with mass customization of its product line in its Personal Pair jeans program. A customer's measurements are sent electronically to a Levi's factory that manufactures custom made versions of several basic styles of Levi's mass-produced jeans.[9] A futuristic view of mass customization involves the use of imaging devices capable of scanning an individual customer's body. The image then will be stored and can serve as an electronic paper doll on which garments from racks or in electronic picture form can be superimposed on the body image. Items can then be custom-made by manufacturers who will use the body image as an electronic pattern.[10] These fashions may be sold through both store and interactive electronic retailers. To encourage mass market acceptance of these new manufacturing and retailing methods, companies will need to identify opinion leaders to promote their benefits as well as the innovators and early adopters who will use them.

USE OF CHANGE AGENTS

The U.S. consumers are increasingly value-oriented and have developed a more functional attitude toward their clothing purchases. These social and economic trends create new growth opportunities for discounters such as Wal-Mart and moderately priced department stores such as Sears and JCPenney. A variety of strategies including well-known brands, reputable private label programs, and celebrity endorsements are being successfully used to target new markets and have contributed to a growing apparel business for these retailers at the expense of both department and specialty stores.

UNIQUE CHALLENGES OF RETAILING FASHION

The symbolic properties of fashion goods combined with the complex social interactions that influence their adoption and diffusion create unique challenges for fashion retailers. Among these challenges are managing products with short product life cycles, broken life cycles, and symbolic and aesthetic characteristics that can be difficult to identify.

SHORT PRODUCT LIFE CYCLES

Fashion trends change constantly because they result from social, economic, political, and technological conditions influencing consumer behavior. Therefore, life cycles for fashion products tend to be relatively short. When changes in fashion are gradual or evolutionary, they can be monitored and managed more easily than when changes occur rapidly.

Although fashion goods move through their life cycles at varying rates, there is evidence that fashion, like most other products, is also experiencing increasingly shorter product life cycles. One explanation for more rapid changes in fashion trends is the increased speed at which information on new fashions is disseminated to consumers through mass media and other electronic communication technologies.

Shortened product life cycles mean that retailers must pay careful attention to product demand. If a particular fashion experiences accelerated sales growth, a retailer must not only have sufficient inventory available to meet increased demand, but must also be able to recognize whether the product is a fad or is entering the decline stage of its life cycle. In either case, saturation among consumers will follow quickly. Excess inventory may then be difficult to sell, resulting in a loss to the retailer. Merchandise information systems that use computerized inventory management to effectively manage the time between the manufacturing of a product and its sales, similar to those used by stores such as Dillard's and Sears, are becoming essential for fashion retailers.

Although short product life cycles are generally considered a phenomena reserved for fashion products, business analysts report that virtually all types of businesses are experiencing reduced lead times for new product development and shorter product life cycles. Consequently, all types of retailers may eventually have to become more "fashion-oriented" with respect to their merchandising decisions.

BROKEN PRODUCT LIFE CYCLES

Many classifications of fashion goods are subject to temporary interruptions in their life cycles. There are three distinct reasons for broken cycles including seasonal, catastrophic, and revolutionary. Seasonal breaks that are normally due to changing climatic conditions are the most common reason for a life cycle interruption. Catastrophic events (e.g., wars) and fashion revolutions are not as common and are beyond the scope of this appendix.

For apparel, changing weather patterns create needs for different clothing styles and fabrications. Also, in most regions of the country, custom dictates the use of different colors and fabrics based on the season of the year. Consequently, demand for seasonal fashion products is not continuous throughout the life of the product. For some products, the life cycle can stop at the end of a season and start again the next time the season begins. For others, the life cycle may only span the length of a season. The fashion industry has geared its distribution efforts to these seasonal shifts in demand. For women's apparel, suppliers produce up to five seasonal collections: Spring, Summer or Transition, Fall I, Fall II, and Resort or Holiday. For men's wear, there are typically two to four seasonal lines produced, depending on whether the supplier produces tailored men's wear or sportswear.

SYMBOLIC AND AESTHETIC CONSUMPTION PROPERTIES

Fashion products convey meanings about a user to others in his or her social group that play an important role in the decision to purchase or, for that matter, discard a fashion. The meanings communicated by fashion are based on subjective criteria and emotional responses that come from within an individual. They are not readily observable and may be difficult to identify.

Consumer preferences for products displaying designer names such as Gucci or Dior or licensed cartoon characters such as Mickey Mouse provide evidence of the importance of symbolism and emotional appeal present in fashion goods. That consumers discard usable fashions out of boredom or because they are perceived to be outdated is another indicator of the importance of symbolism. Often, there is little relationship between price and value measured in objective terms such as *quality, dependability,* and *service.*

ADAPTING RETAIL PRACTICES

Although fashion retailers operate in a manner that is substantially similar to nonfashion retailers, they find it necessary to adapt specific practices to address needs created by distinct characteristics of fashion goods. This section describes several of these practices, including identifying consumer segments and creating buying and assortment plans. The impact of technological advances on buying and controlling merchandise is also discussed.

IDENTIFYING CONSUMER FASHION SEGMENTS

The chapter on *Retail Planning and Management* addressed the importance of accurately identifying a viable target market and selecting appropriate retail mix strategies. Because competition among fashion retailers is very intense, effective consumer segmentation is essential to survival.

Research has shown the long-term level of involvement in fashion to be very effective for differentiating segments of fashion consumers.[11] Differences in fashion involvement are related to variations in the importance given merchandise price, quality, service, and fashionability. Demographic and socioeconomic characteristics, preferences for different fashion information sources, shopper orientations, lifestyles, and store choice also vary by level of fashion involvement. In addition, fashion involvement is predicted to be useful for identifying segments of fashion consumers with different attitudes toward the symbolic properties of fashion goods.

Another way to effectively segment fashion consumers is to target segments with unique fashion needs. Special groups such as plus-size women, large men, and maternity are all examples of niches targeted by both fashion retailers and manufacturers.

DEVELOPING ASSORTMENT PLANS

A common goal of retailers is offering a merchandise assortment balanced to consumer demand. Because demand for fashion changes constantly, maintaining a balanced fashion assortment is of major importance to fashion retailers.

Separate assortment plans are developed for both basic and fashion merchandise categories. Basic or staple categories include goods whose product attributes are similar from one selling season to the next, whereas the attributes of fashion categories are highly susceptible to change. Merchandising decisions related to these attributes (i.e., styles, design features, colors, fabrics, etc.) for fashion categories need to be monitored closely and revised to take advantage of new fashion trends.

Technological advances in information systems have greatly enhanced the fashion retailer's ability to plan and maintain balanced assortments. The impact of these information systems on managing fashion elements of a merchandise assortment is discussed in the chapter on retail information systems.

Some fashion retailers are able to augment their traditional merchandise information system with information from their customer databases. Fashion retailers such as Talbot's, Saks Fifth Avenue, and Bloomingdale's use their customer databases to identify and build loyalty among active customers by marketing to their individual needs. In turn, these retailers use purchase profiles developed from their databases to plan and maintain their merchandise assortments.

RETAILER–SUPPLIER RELATIONSHIPS

All retailers are finding that establishing closer working relations with suppliers is essential for survival. Because of keen competitiveness in the fashion business and increased segmentation of consumer markets, fashion retailers are placing increasing importance on developing the supplier relationships pointed out in the chapter on *Channel Behavior*. Partnerships, especially those using quick response (QR) systems, are of particular importance to retailers that sell fashion goods.

For fashion retailers that have adopted QR, the benefits have exceeded initial expectations. Although basic assortments are automatically replenished by the vendor when they reach minimum stock levels, fashion assortments are monitored very closely by buying personnel. This permits detailed analysis of the performance of a product by important attributes such as size, style, and color and enables a buying staff to respond more precisely to consumer demand for changing fashion trends. As a result of using QR, fashion goods retailers report dramatic increases in sales and turnover and decreases in markdowns.

The effectiveness of QR also influences the manner in which some of the large retailers purchase merchandise. Many now have buying teams that are responsible for establishing master basic and model stock plans and developing an approved vendor list. Vendors are now selected not only on factors such as product quality, price, and delivery schedules but also on their capabilities for "partnershiping" by using QR.

The use of merchandise planners or coordinators, a relatively new middle management position created by upscale fashion retailers and manufacturers, provides evidence of the importance of selling partnerships for retailers and vendors. These positions are found either in large department and specialty retailers such as Mervyn's and Macy's or collection manufacturers such as Polo, Nautica, Liz Claiborne, and Perry Ellis. Planners are employed to track collection sales and other merchandise performance information, assist in buying and reordering merchandise, and present selling seminars. They provide suppliers with increased consumer exposure and offer assistance in analyzing their business with a supplier and monitoring fashion trends.

SUMMARY

Fashion retailing is a very dynamic business, due not only to distinct characteristics associated with the product class, but also to complex social interactions that influence fashion adoption and diffusion. Factors related to unique characteristics of fashion products including constant change that results in short life cycles and a tendency to experience broken life cycles were described. Difficulties in identifying the important symbolic and aesthetic properties of fashion goods were also discussed.

Retailers have adapted several practices for identifying target consumers and planning and controlling fashion assortments to address the special problems in merchandising fashion goods. In addition, advances in selling partnerships with suppliers augment a fashion retailer's ability to analyze consumer demand and improve productivity and financial performance.

NOTES

1. George B. Sproles, *Fashion Consumer Behavior toward Dress* (Minneapolis: Burgess Publishing Co., 1979): 5.
2. Ibid, 5–8.
3. "French Fashion Loses Its Primacy as Women Leave Couture Behind," *Wall Street Journal*, August 29, 1995: A1, A9.
4. "Out of Fashion, Many Women Lose Interest in Clothes, to Retailers Dismay," *Wall Street Journal*, February 28, 1995: A10; "Consumers Draw the Line in Fashion," *Fortune*, May 1, 1995: 21.
5. George B. Sproles, "Behavioral Science Theories of Fashion," in *The Psychology of Fashion*, ed. Michael R. Solomon (Lexington, MA: D.C. Heath & Co., 1983): 55–70; Susan B. Kaiser, *The Social Psychology of Clothing* (New York: Macmillan Publishing Co., Inc., 1985): 332–338.
6. "Fashion Knockoffs Hit Stores before Originals as Designers Seeth," *Wall Street Journal*, August 8, 1994: A1, A4.
7. Richard A. Feinberg, Lisa Mataro, and Jeffrey Burroughs, "Clothing and Social Identity," *Clothing and Textiles Research Journal*, Fall 1992: 18–23; Russell Belk, Melanie Wallendorf, and John F. Sherry, Jr., "The Sacred and the Profane in Consumer Behavior: Theodicy on the Odyssey," *Journal of Consumer Research*, 1992: 1–38; Elizabeth C. Hirschman and Morris B. Holbrook, "Hedonic Consumption: Emerging Concepts, Methods, and Propositions," *Journal of Marketing*, Summer 1982: 92–101.
8. Hirschman and Holbrook, 95–97.
9. "Bill Gates, Bill Fields Debate Cyberspace Versus Retail Space," *Women's Wear Daily*, March 20, 1996: 1, 4; "Digital Blue Jeans Pour Data and Legs into Customized Fit," *New York Times*, November 8, 1994: A1, D8.
10. "Garment Scanner Could Be a Perfect Fit," *Wall Street Journal*, September 20, 1994: B1, B6.
11. Jonathan Gutman and Michael Mills, "Fashion Life Style, Self Concept, Shopping Orientation, and Store Patronage: An Integrative Analysis," *Journal of Retailing*, Summer 1982: 64–86; Charles W. King and Lawrence J. Ring, "Market Positioning across Retail Fashion Institutions: A Comparative Analysis of Store Types," *Journal of Retailing* Spring 1980: 37–55; Lawrence J. Ring, "High-End Fashion Positioning," in *Patronage Behavior and Retail Management*, eds. William R. Darden and Robert F. Lusch (New York: Elsevier Science Publishing Co., Inc., 1983): 165–178.

MERCHANDISE PRICING

Old Navy has set its prices to be consistent with its store image and design and promotion which all communicate good value for casual clothing.

OVERVIEW

In this chapter, we examine the retailer's need to make pricing decisions. We begin with a discussion of the impact of a firm's objectives on its policies and strategies. After reviewing several strategies, we look at why initial markups and maintained markups are seldom the same. We also discuss how a retailer establishes an initial markup. We conclude this chapter with a discussion of why and how a retailer takes markdowns during the normal course of business.

LEARNING OBJECTIVES

After reading this chapter, you should be able to

1. discuss the factors to be considered when establishing a retailer's pricing objectives and policies
2. describe the differences between the various pricing strategies available to the retailer
3. describe how retailers calculate the various markups
4. discuss why markdown management is so important in retailing, as well as some of the errors that cause markdowns

LO • 1
Discuss the factors to be considered when establishing a retailer's pricing objectives and policies

PRICING OBJECTIVES AND POLICIES

One of the most frequent decisions facing retailers is, "What is the correct price for this product?" This should not be a difficult decision, however, if retailers have been performing their other activities correctly. Pricing, as we pointed out in our Retail Planning and Management Model (Exhibit 2.3), is an interactive decision made in conjunction with the firm's mission statement, its goals and objectives, its strategy, its operational management (i.e., merchandise planning, promotional mix, building and fixtures, and level of service), and its administrative management.

Pricing does present more difficult decisions for retailers of services. This higher degree of difficulty exists because services are intangible, not easily stored, and cannot be returned to the vendor for credit. A movie theater running a hit movie during a blizzard, will have the same fixed costs for being open as it would on any other night. The theater manager cannot resell the empty seats at a later date or increase attendance on the night of the blizzard by reducing ticket prices.

INTERACTIVE PRICING DECISIONS

As shown in Exhibit 10.1, decisions regarding pricing objectives should be interactive with other retail decisions. Specifically, the decision to price an item at a certain level should interact with the retailer's decisions on lines of merchandise carried, location, promotion, credit, customer services, the store image the retailer wishes to convey, and the legal constraints we discussed in Chapter 6.

MERCHANDISE   Retailers should not set prices without carefully analyzing the attributes of the merchandise being priced. Does the merchandise have attributes that differentiate it from comparable merchandise at competing retailers? What is the value of these attributes to the consumer? Consider, for example, the men's wear retailer who has purchased 100 men's suits for the fall selling season. What are the attributes of these suits (size, color, type of fabric, cut or style, brand label, quality of workmanship, quality of fabric)? How does the consumer value these attributes? Is a Giorgio Armani label more valuable than a Stanley Blacker label or a Hart, Schaffner and Marx label? Is good workmanship worth more? Are better quality fabrics worth more? The answers to these questions are not easily determined; they depend on the retailer's market and how the retailer makes the consumer aware of these differences in the various merchandise lines.

Merchandise selection presents the retailer with another decision: the range of prices to be made available to the consumer. Remember, the retailer's controllable element of price can be either the cost of goods sold or the gross margin that is added to the cost. The retailer, in deciding to buy an item to sell at a specific price, may either purchase lower-cost merchandise and have a high gross margin to offset the higher expenses needed to sell at that price or purchase more expensive goods and reduce the gross margin and expenses to sell at a given price.

LOCATION   The location of the retail store, as we discussed in Chapter 7, will have a significant effect on prices that can be charged. The closer the store is to competitors with comparable merchandise and customer service, the less pricing flexibility the retailer has. The distance between the store and the customer is also important.

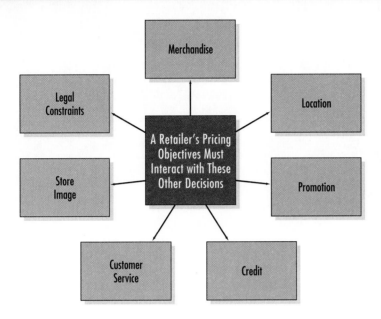

EXHIBIT 10.1 INTERACTION BETWEEN A RETAILER'S PRICING OBJECTIVES AND OTHER RETAIL DECISIONS

Generally, if the retailer wants to attract customers from a greater distance, it must either increase its promotional efforts or lower prices on its merchandise. This is because of the increasing travel costs (expressed in both time and dollar amounts) consumers incur when they are located farther from the store. Travel costs cut into the amount the customer is able or willing to pay for the merchandise, thus forcing the retailer to lower prices to attract those customers. For example, the lowest prices for many brand-name products can usually be found at factory outlet malls, yet these locations usually have the highest travel costs. Thus for many consumers, it is cheaper to purchase the merchandise at a nearby retailer.

PROMOTION   In the next chapter, we illustrate how promotion can increase demand for the retailer's merchandise. This chapter, however, shows how pricing can influence demand. This doesn't mean that pricing and promotion decisions are independent. If the retailer promotes heavily and is also very price-competitive, the result may be an increase in demand greater than the high-promotion and lower-price strategies would produce independently. Imagine, for example, the retailer establishing low prices but not promoting them in the marketplace. How would consumers know of the price cuts? Or imagine heavy promotion but no cut in prices. Obviously, each will generate demand, but the interactive and cumulative effect of both would be much greater.

CREDIT   For a given price level on merchandise, retailers selling on credit, even if they only are using bank cards, will often be able to generate greater demand than retailers not selling on credit. Conversely, retailers selling merchandise on credit may be able to charge slightly higher prices than retailers not selling on credit and still generate

Factory outlets are known for their low prices. However, the typical consumer will incur high travel costs to reach these outlets.

the same demand as noncredit retailers. That credit-granting retailers can charge higher prices can be seen by the action of some retailers offering special discounts for cash-paying customers. This is an attempt to eliminate the 1.5 to 4.5 percent that credit card companies charge retailers on credit card purchases and shift the credit costs back on the customers actually using the credit.

CUSTOMER SERVICES

Retailers that offer many customer services (delivery, gift wrapping, alterations, more pleasant surroundings, sales assistance) tend to have higher prices. A decision to offer many customer services will automatically increase operating expenses and thus prompt management to increase retail prices to cover these additional expenses. However, such a policy may result in higher profits. Consider the case of women's dresses. Customer service used to be common in department stores that took 50 to 60 percent initial markups, but pricing pressure by discounters caused department stores to respond by cutting markups and service. Women purchasing dresses began to feel neglected in department stores, especially when they had to start paying for alterations. Specialty stores have picked up on this and, as a result, offer the consumer greater assistance in selecting and trying on a dress, something unheard of in the "low price" stores. Another example of a retailer justifying a higher price by offering outstanding service is No Kidding. This small toy store in an affluent suburb just west of Boston can't compete with the retail megamarkets on either price or variety. Therefore, it doesn't carry the extremely popular items, such as Barbie or Nintendo, that everybody else discounts, but it does carry many items that can't be found in the bigger stores. However, what enables No Kidding to produce a profit at a time when most small toy shops fail is the makeup and behavior of its sales staff. This well-informed staff is mostly made up of moonlighting teachers who can discuss the finer points of play and inform the purchaser what is developmentally correct for a child of a certain age. In addition, the store wraps gifts at no charge, accepts returns without a receipt, and donates part of its profits to local schools and public television.[1]

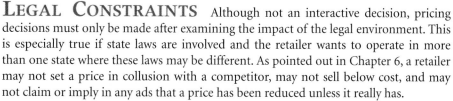

When retailers offer free delivery, the cost of providing this service must be factored into the prices the retailer charges.

In fact, many consumers are willing to pay more for extra service. Consequently, it is important to remember that customer service decisions interact strongly with pricing decisions.

STORE IMAGE

One of the cues that a customer uses in determining a retailer's image is the retailer's prices. If not offset by a poor location with poor service and merchandise selection, prices aid the customer (either consciously or unconsciously) in developing an image of the store. If an exclusive, high-fashion store such as Nordstrom started to discount the merchandise heavily, it simply would not be the same store in the eyes of the customers. The merchandise, store decor, and personnel may remain unchanged, but the change in pricing strategy will significantly alter the overall store image. Thus, pricing policies and strategies interact with store image policies and strategies.

LEGAL CONSTRAINTS

Although not an interactive decision, pricing decisions must only be made after examining the impact of the legal environment. This is especially true if state laws are involved and the retailer wants to operate in more than one state where these laws may be different. As pointed out in Chapter 6, a retailer may not set a price in collusion with a competitor, may not sell below cost, and may not claim or imply in any ads that a price has been reduced unless it really has.

The other environmental factors that we discussed in Part 2 (consumer behavior, competitor behavior, channel relationships, the socioeconomic environment, and the technological environment) should also be considered when the retailer is developing its overall pricing and market strategy. Still, as pointed out in the Global Retailing box, pricing decisions are easy to make in the United States when compared with some other countries' retail environments.

JAPAN'S SAM WALTON:
ISAO NAKAUCHI

After graduating from what is now Kobe University, Isao Nakauchi (pronounced Na-KA-oo-chee) set about visiting the United States before returning home to work at his family's pharmacy. After his trip, Nakauchi was convinced that below-market pricing was the key to retail success.

Mr. Nakauchi opened a discount drugstore in 1957 that carried not only pharmacy products but also health and beauty aids (HBA), food, and household goods. With prices 15 to 20 percent below competition, Nakauchi soon was a hero to the consumers but a villain to his father's business associates.

Four decades later, Mr. Nakauchi's drugstore has grown into The Daiei (pronounced DIE-ay) Inc., the world's ninth-largest retailer, with nearly 400 supercenters and sales approaching $30 billion annually.

However, pricing decisions are not as easy to make in countries such as Japan as they are in the United States. Although reducing prices hardly seems controversial in the United States, it can be in other economic environments. The threat posed by Nakauchi challenged a monopolistic system of distribution that had long been in place.

In the United States, there are laws against vertical monopolies and other restraints of trade to ensure fair competition. American consumers can buy from a full-price retailer or they can use a discounter. American discounters depend on bulk purchase discounts from manufacturers, rapid inventory turnover, inexpensive real estate, and price-conscious shoppers who are willing to perform some marketing channel functions themselves.

However, the densely populated Japanese market doesn't work like ours. The country's distribution system isn't set up for discounters. Japan has the same number of retail stores as the United States does, 1.6 million, but has only half the U.S.'s population. Prior to Mr. Nakauchi, most of the retailers in Japan were small "mom and pop" outlets. Supporting Japan's vast system of retailers is a multilayered network of 500,000 wholesalers who supply their customers with goods and credit. The system is expensive but well-suited to a country whose consumers lack personal transportation and until recently shopped daily for fresh food and used small refrigerators better suited for college dorm rooms. Wholesalers compose a major link in the traditional system of "keiretsu," the vertical monopoly of market distribution used by large manufacturers to suppress competition and keep fixed prices high.

Nakauchi's began its fight against the system by skipping the middlemen and purchasing vegetables directly from farming cooperatives. Later, he began importing foreign products directly, just as Sam Walton was doing in the U.S..

The Daiei continued to undercut competitors' prices by 15 to 20 percent. Mr. Nakauchi was even threatened by Matsushita Electric, the world's largest manufacturer of consumer electronic products, for undercutting other retailers. Matsushita vowed to crush the retailer. Undeterred by the threat, Nakauchi continued slashing prices whenever possible. During one free-for-all price war with a rival store, for example, The Daiei sold sugar for less than four cents a pound.

Today, Mr. Nakauchi has not changed his determination to keep shoppers happy. Recently, a delegation of his customers from one of the islands complained that they had no professional baseball team, so Nakauchi bought a team for a reported $32 million. The purchase delighted his sports fan customers but gave only limited pleasure to Nakauchi.

"To me," he says, "the ring of cash registers is the best music in this world."

SOURCE: Based on conversations with Bob Kahn and "Is Japan's Sam Walton Up to the Job?" *New York Times*, December 4, 1994, section 3, p. 1.

PRICING OBJECTIVES

A retailer's pricing objectives should be in agreement with its mission statement and merchandising policies. Some objectives may be profit-oriented, some may be sales-oriented, and some may be to leave things just the way they are. However, by beginning with the proper pricing objectives, the retail manager can establish pricing policies that will complement the store's other decisions and assist in attracting the desired target customers.

PROFIT-ORIENTED OBJECTIVES
Many retailers establish the objective of achieving either a certain rate of return or maximizing profits.

> TARGET RETURN. A target return objective sets a specific level of profit as an objective. This amount is often stated as a percentage of sales or of the retailer's capital investment. A target return for a supermarket might be 2 percent of sales.
>
> PROFIT MAXIMIZATION. A profit maximization objective seeks to obtain as much profit as possible. Some individuals claim that this pricing policy "charges all the traffic will bear." Retailers know that if they follow such a policy, they are inviting competitors to enter the market. However, in some cases, a retailer may have a temporary monopoly and want to take advantage of it. The first video rental stores, knowing that others would follow shortly, often charged high rental fees, only to lower them when competition, such as Blockbuster Video, did enter the market. This is skimming, or trying to sell at the highest price possible before settling on a more competitive level. Other retailers may take the opposite approach and use penetration, which seeks to establish a "loyal" customer base by entering the market with a low price.

SALES-ORIENTED OBJECTIVES
Sales-oriented objectives seek some level of unit sales, dollar sales, or market share but do not mention profit. Two of the types most commonly used in retailing are growth in market share and growth in dollar sales.

Although both of these objectives are common with retailers today, especially with smaller retailers, the achievement of either doesn't necessarily mean that profits will also increase. After all, if a retailer lowers prices, gross margin will go down, sales may improve, but the retailer may not make more money.

STATUS QUO OBJECTIVES
Retailers who are happy with their market share and level of profits sometimes adopt status quo objectives, or "don't rock the boat" pricing policies. Many supermarkets gave up on the extra profits and increases in market share that "double coupons" might have brought because they were afraid of what competitive actions would have resulted. Such pricing actions as "double couponing" are not always effective and profitable. Many times, especially when other retailers match the promotion, it's only the retailer's regular customers who use them.

Also, some retailers prefer to compete on grounds other than price. Convenience stores, for example, seldom match the prices of nearby supermarkets. Still, sometimes retailers such as McDonald's and Burger King, who want the consumer to focus on factors such as quality of food, service, and locational convenience instead of price, are forced to drop prices in the face of mounting competition just to maintain status quo market share.[2]

Target return objective
is a pricing objective that states a specific level of profit, such as percentage of sales or return on capital invested, as an objective.

Profit maximization
is a pricing objective that seeks to obtain as much profit as possible.

Skimming
is a pricing objective where price is initially set high on merchandise to skim the cream of demand before selling at more competitive prices.

Penetration
is a pricing objective where price is set at a low level on merchandise in order to penetrate the market and establish a loyal customer base.

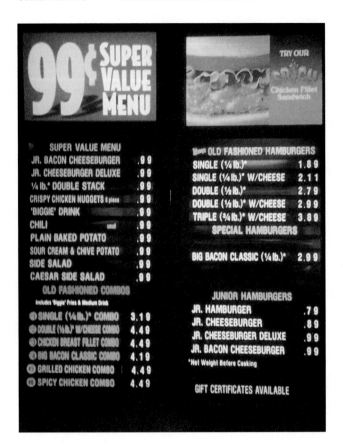

When Wendy's established its 99 cents Super Value Menu, it was attempting to create a below market pricing image.

PRICING POLICIES

Pricing policies

are rules of action, or guidelines, that ensure uniformity of pricing decisions within a retail operation.

Pricing policies are rules of action, or guidelines, that ensure uniformity of pricing decisions within a retail operation. A large retailer has many buyers who are involved in pricing decisions. By establishing the store's overall pricing policies, the top merchandising executives provide these buyers with a framework for adopting specific pricing strategies for the entire organization.

A retail store's pricing policies should reflect the expectations of its target market. Very few retailers can appeal to all segments of the market. Low- and middle-income consumers are usually attracted to low-priced discount stores. The middle-class market often shops at moderate-priced general merchandise chains. Affluent consumers are frequently drawn to high-priced specialty stores that provide extra services. Only supermarkets are able to cross the various income lines, and even then there is some basis for segmentation. Successful retailers carefully position themselves in a market and then direct their specific pricing strategies toward satisfying their target market. Many times, the proper pricing policies influence consumers to patronize one store over another.

In establishing a pricing policy, retailers must decide whether they should price above market levels, at market levels, or below market levels.

PRICING ABOVE THE MARKET

Some retailers, either by design or circumstance, follow an above-market pricing policy. Certain market sectors are receptive to high prices because nonprice factors are more important to them than price. Some retailers such as Nordstrom offer such outstanding service that it has minimal price competition. Other retailers, such as small neighborhood drugstores and hardware stores, are forced to price above the market because of their high cost structure and low sales volume. Some other conditions that permit retailers to price above market levels involve merchandise offerings, services provided, convenient locations, and extended hours of operation.

MERCHANDISE OFFERINGS Some consumers will pay higher-than-average prices for specialty items, for an exclusive line, or for unusual merchandise. Prestige retailers such as Gucci or Neiman-Marcus, carry high-priced specialty items. An exclusive line, such as Christian Dior, permits higher-than-average prices. Unusual merchandise, such as Neiman-Marcus's annual Christmas catalog one-of-a-kind gift, is normally not price compared because no competitor carries similar merchandise.

Above-market pricing policy
is a policy where retailers establish high prices because non-price factors are more important to their target market than price.

SERVICES PROVIDED In many communities, there are service-oriented merchants with a loyal group of customers who are willing to pay higher prices to obtain an array of services ranging from wardrobe counseling to delivery. Nordstrom's clerks have a habit of doing those special things such as dropping off purchases at a customer's home, sending "thank you" notes to customers, or even ironing a newly purchased shirt so the customer can wear it that day. These services put Nordstrom in a nonprice-competitive sector of retailing.

CONVENIENT LOCATIONS The convenient location of gift shops in hotels and airline terminals allows them to charge high prices. Knowing that consumers value time, fast-food retailers select sites adjacent to residential areas. Retailers in metropolitan office buildings often charge premium prices not only because of their accessible locations but because of their higher rents. In addition, consumers have no other place to shop. For example, a stranded, hungry flyer at many airports has to eat lunch there or not eat. There are no alternatives.

EXTENDED HOURS OF OPERATION By remaining open while other stores are closed, some merchants are able to charge higher-than-average prices. Service plazas on interstate highways justify their higher prices by never closing.

PRICING AT MARKET LEVELS

Most merchants want to be competitive with one another. The use of comparison shoppers, that is, having employees visit competitive retail outlets to compare prices, by retailers stems from this basic premise. Competitive pricing involves a price zone, a range of prices for a particular merchandise line that appeals to customers in a certain market segment, such as Kmart selling women's tops for $9.99 to $19.99. Dillard's does not need to match the prices of Kmart. However, Macy's should establish prices that are on a similar level with its competitor, Saks Fifth Avenue. And Kmart should be competitively priced with Wal-Mart and Target.

Price zone
is a range of prices for a particular merchandise line that appeals to customers in a certain market segment.

Although MEIJER, a super-center chain, is open 24 hours, it is still able to offer discount prices at below the market.

The size of a retail store affects its ability to compete on a price basis. Small retailers usually pay more for their merchandise and have higher expenses as a proportion of sales than larger retailers. Although small retailers have joined voluntary cooperative chains to reduce their expenses through quantity discounts, they continue to experience a cost disadvantage. For these reasons, small retailers such as mom-and-pop grocery stores and convenience stores often stress convenience and service strategies rather than price in their retailing mix. Even in this case, the price cannot be too far out of line.

Below-market pricing policy
is a policy that regularly discounts merchandise from the established market price in order to build store traffic and generate high sales and gross margin dollars per square foot of selling space.

PRICING BELOW THE MARKET   Because there is a large market sector buying mainly on a price basis, a below-market pricing policy is attractive to many retailers such as discounters and warehouse clubs. For retailers to consistently price below the market and be profitable, they must concentrate on generating gross margin dollars per square foot of space, not the gross margin percentage. After all, profitability is not directly related to the gross margin percentage of the product sold but the amount of gross margin per unit sold times the number of units sold. Such retailers must always try to increase the sales per square foot of store space because they are compelled to reduce their markups. In addition to buying wisely, which may include closeouts and seconds, these stores stock fast-selling merchandise, curtail customer services, and operate from modest facilities. Some of these retailers such as Kmart and Target are offering apparel and housewares made from the same fabrics and styles as the pricier full service department stores. For instance, Kmart has a line of Martha Stewart bed sheets of 100 percent cotton with a 230 thread count and a sateen finish at very competitive below-market prices.[3] Also, some of them stock private brands extensively and enhance their low-price image by promoting the price differences between their private brands and comparable national brands. That some retailers are successful with such a policy is evident by the fact that many local retailers, especially restaurants, now use Wal-Mart and Sam's as suppliers.[4]

SPECIFIC PRICING STRATEGIES

V arious pricing strategies are adopted by retailers in their effort to achieve certain pricing objectives. The pricing strategies should be in accord with the other components of the store's retail mix: location, promotion, display, service level, and merchandise assortment.

CUSTOMARY PRICING

Customary pricing occurs when a retailer sets prices for goods and services and seeks to maintain those prices over an extended period of time. Candy bars, newspapers, movies, and vending machine products are all items that use customary pricing. For such products, retailers, such as movie theaters with their $6.00 ticket prices, seek to establish prices that customers can take for granted for long periods of time.

Customary pricing is a policy where the retailer sets prices for goods and services and seeks to maintain those prices over an extended period of time.

VARIABLE PRICING

Variable pricing is used when differences in demand and cost force the retailer to change prices in a fairly predictable manner. Flowers tend to be higher priced when demand is greater, around Mother's Day and Valentine's Day. It is a common practice for most resorts to increase their rates on premium rooms in June, a busy wedding time. Tuesday and Wednesday nights tend to have lower demand for movies, so many theaters offer $2 specials on those nights. Fresh fruits tend to sell for less during their growing seasons when the retailer's costs are down.

Variable pricing is a policy that recognizes that differences in demand and cost necessitate that the retailer change prices in a fairly predictable manner.

FLEXIBLE PRICING

Flexible pricing means offering the same products and quantities to different customers at different prices. Retailers generally use flexible pricing in situations calling for personal selling. The advantage of using flexible pricing is that the salesperson can make price adjustments based on the customer's interest, a competitor's price, a past relationship with the customer, or the customer's bargaining ability. Most jewelry stores and automobile dealerships use this pricing policy, although not all customers like it. This policy can increase costs as customers begin to bargain for everything or find that they paid more than a friend did for the same product. That is why the one-price policy is so popular in the United States.

Some retailers vary their prices by giving discounts to special consumer groups such as senior citizens and the clergy. Even some employee groups (e.g., credit unions) have negotiated price discounts with selected retailers.

Flexible pricing is a policy that encourages offering the same products and quantities to different customers at different prices.

ONE-PRICE POLICY

Under the one-price policy, a retailer charges the same price for an item to all customers. A one-price policy may be used in conjunction with customary or variable pricing. All people buying the same blazer at a local retailer will pay the same price. Roland Hussey Macy, the founder of Macy's department store, is credited for adopting the one-price policy. This policy meant efficiency and fairness in handling customer transactions in a large store, where the selling activity is delegated to salespersons who

One-price policy is a policy that establishes that the retailer will charge the same price for an item to all customers.

have varying degrees of loyalty to the retailer. If salespersons were permitted to bargain over price, customers who are shrewd and assertive could conceivably negotiate terms that are unprofitable to the retailer.

A one-price policy, therefore, speeds up transactions and reduces the need for highly skilled salespersons. Most catalog operators adopt a one-price policy because they are forced to retain their prices until the expiration date of the catalog, which can be six months from its issuance.

Today, some automobile manufacturers, such as General Motors (GM), who already has had success with this policy in its Saturn division, are encouraging their dealers to adopt the one-price policy as a means of regaining market share. For example, suppose that GM determines that most buyers of the Pontiac Grand Am SE want an FM/AM radio with cassette player, antilock brakes, dual airbags, air conditioning, tilt steering wheel, and power door locks. By packaging all these options together, the dealers can sell the car for $14,995, which is substantially less than what the buyer would have paid buying all these "extras" separately. Also, GM hopes that the use of this one-price policy gives its dealers a competitive advantage over a similarly equipped Honda Accord LX or Toyota Camry LE.[5] However, such a pricing policy will only work if all the dealers voluntarily agree to stick to the plan. Otherwise, the flexible price dealer will know the price it has to beat.

PRICE LINING

To simplify their pricing procedures and to aid consumers in making merchandise comparisons, some retailers establish a specified number of price lines or price points for each merchandise classification. Once the price lines are determined, these retailers purchase goods that fit into each line. This is called price lining. For example, in men's slacks the price lines could be limited to $29.95, $49.95, and $69.95. The monetary difference between the price lines should be large enough to reflect a value difference to consumers. This makes it easier for a salesperson to either trade-up or trade-down a customer. Trading up occurs when a salesperson moves a customer from a lower-priced line to a higher one. Trading down occurs when a customer is initially exposed to higher-priced lines but expresses the desire to purchase a lower-priced line which may appear to be an especially good buy given the price of the higher price line..

Retailers select price lines that have the strongest consumer demand. By limiting the number of price lines, a retailer achieves broader assortments, which leads to increased sales and fewer markdowns. For example, a retailer who stocks 150 units of an item and has six price lines would have an assortment of only 25 units in each line. However, if the 150 units were divided among only three price lines, there would be 50 units in each line.

When retailers are limited to certain price lines, they become specialists in those lines. This permits them to concentrate all their merchandising and promotional efforts on those lines, thus defining more clearly their store image. In addition, they direct their purchases to vendors who handle those lines. The vendors, in turn, provide favored treatment to their large-volume retailing customers. Other advantages of price lining include buying more efficiently, simplifying inventory control, and accelerating inventory turnover. From the shopper's perspective, it is easy to shop when price lining is used, because differences are perceived among the various price points.

An analysis of a store's best-selling price lines is essential before making any decision to alter them. Generally, the middle-priced lines should account for the majority of sales. When the bulk of sales occurs at the extremes of the price lines, a retailer

Price lining
is a pricing policy that is established to help customers make merchandise comparisons and involves establishing a specified number of price points for each merchandise classification.

Trading up
occurs when a retailer uses price lining and a salesperson moves a customer from a lower-priced line to a higher one.

Trading down
occurs when a retailer uses price lining, and a customer initially exposed to higher-priced lines expresses the desire to purchase a lower-priced line.

ORIGIN OF ODD-NUMBERED PRICING

The effectiveness of the use of certain rather common odd-numbered prices based on the belief that $9.99 sounds lower to the customer than $10 and 49 cents sounds better than 52 cents has never been proven with any conclusive research. Another theory suggests that the use of an odd price means the price is at the lowest level possible, thus encouraging the customer to purchase more units. Still, a more plausible explanation for the adoption of odd-numbered pricing might go back to the early 1900s before there was a sales tax. In those days, when merchandise was priced at even dollars, it was very easy for salesclerks to pocket either an occasional one-, five-, or 10-dollar bill or gold piece because they didn't have to make change for the customer.

When Marshall Field caught on to this, he devised the first odd-numbered pricing system to stop the practice. Field ruled that, "We'll charge 99 cents instead of even dollars. This will force the clerks to ring up the sales, open the cash register, put the money in and give the customer a receipt and change."

Maybe this explains why, despite the lack of supportive research, odd-numbered pricing is such a standard in retailing today.

should take corrective actions. These include altering the assortments in the present price lines, changing the price lines, redirecting the salespersons' efforts, developing more effective promotions, or adjusting the total marketing mix to a new target market.

ODD PRICING

The practice of setting retail prices that end in the digits 5, 8, or 9—such as $29.95, $49.98, or $9.99—is called odd pricing. A quick look at retail advertisements in newspapers will reveal that many retailers use an odd-pricing policy. Retailers feel that odd prices produce significantly higher sales. Supposedly, the consumer perceives these odd prices as substantially lower. That is, the $495 seems more like $400 than like $500, and the $4.98 seems more like $4.00 than $5.00. Whether this is indeed true is debatable.[6] The Behind the Scenes box provides another insight into the historical development of odd pricing as a means to reduce employee theft.

Because odd prices are associated with low prices, they are typically used by retailers who sell either at prices below the market or at the market. Retailers selling above the market, such as Neiman-Marcus and Nordstrom, usually end their prices with even numbers that have come to denote quality. These retailers would likely sell an item for $90.00 rather than $89.99. Prestige-conscious retailers are not seeking bargain hunters as customers.

Odd pricing
is the practice of setting retail prices that end in the digits 5, 8, 9—such as $29.95, $49.98, or $9.99.

MULTIPLE-UNIT PRICING

With multiple-unit pricing, the price of each unit in a multiple-unit package is less than the price of each unit if it were sold singly. Grocery retailers use multiple-unit pricing extensively in their sales of cigarettes, light bulbs, candy bars, and beverages. Apparel retailers often sell multiple units of underwear, hosiery, and shirts.

Multiple-unit pricing
occurs when the price of each unit in a multiple-unit package is less than the price of each unit if it were sold individually.

Odd pricing is a common pricing policy in retailing.

Retailers use multiple-unit pricing to encourage additional sales and to increase profits. The gross margin that is sacrificed in a multiple-unit sale is more than offset by the savings that occur from reduced selling and handling expenses. Generally, multiple-unit pricing can be effectively employed for items that are either consumed rapidly or used together.

BUNDLE PRICING

Bundling
occurs when distinct multiple items, generally from different merchandise lines, are offered together at a special price.

Bundling generally involves selling distinct multiple items offered together at a "special price." Here, the perceived savings in cost and/or time for the bundle justifies the purchase. Many travel agencies use bundling for their vacation packages, by packaging airfare, hotel, transfers, and meals together. The example of GM's one-price policy for its Grand Am discussed earlier could also be an example of bundle pricing. Before Congress recently deregulated the telecommunications industry, consumers had to shop separately for local, long distance, paging, cable television, Internet access, and cellular service. While the so-called major telecommunications companies were busy trying to meet the various state and federal requirements to bundle these services together, the previously unknown Frontier Corp. became an industry leader by being able to offer all these together a year before everybody else.[7]

LEADER PRICING

Leader pricing
is when a high-demand item(s) is priced low and heavily advertised in order to attract customers into the store.

In leader pricing, a high-demand item is priced low and advertised heavily in an effort to attract consumers into a store. The items selected for leader pricing should be widely known and bought frequently. In addition, information should be available that will permit consumers to make price comparisons. National brands of convenience goods, such as Crest toothpaste, Mitchum antiperspirant, Maxwell House coffee, and Coca-Cola, are often designated as leader items.

Leader pricing is usually part of a promotional program that is directed to increase store traffic. A successful program will produce additional sales for all areas of a store. In many instances, the price of the leader item is reduced only for a special promotion. There are retailers, such as supermarkets, however, who regularly feature leader items. Today, many convenience stores use gasoline as a leader. These retailers reduce their gas price by a penny or two, just enough to get the customer into their store. Once in the store, they are exposed to fast-food sandwiches, groceries, fresh produce, beverages, and even fresh flowers. In such stores, the inside operations contribute more than 70 percent of the store's gross margin dollars and subsidize the gasoline business.[8]

A retailer using leader pricing should carefully evaluate its usefulness. If consumers are limiting their purchases to only the leader items, then the policy is ineffective. Because the leader items may be sold at or near a retailer's cost, higher-markup items must also be sold to generate a profit for the retailer. An item that is sold below a retailer's cost is known as a loss leader. For example, every Thanksgiving many supermarkets sell turkeys at a loss in hopes of attracting consumers to their stores and making a profit on the rest of their purchases.

The pricing actions of discounters using below-market pricing have forced manufacturers into changing their pricing strategy, thus endangering another group of retailers' use of leader pricing. The use of "everyday low prices" (EDLP) has propelled below-market pricing discounters such as Wal-Mart and Kmart to the top two spots in U.S. retail sales. These retailers want vendors to offer them EDLP prices as well by phasing out virtually all deep discounts and offering them the same low price every day. For example, instead of selling retailers a case of peanut butter for $20 one week and offering it on sale the next few weeks for $15, they want it priced at $18 every week. This would limit the ability of leader pricers, such as supermarkets, to continue their use of "high-low pricing." High-low pricing involves the use of high everyday prices and low leader "specials" on featured items for their weekly ads.

BAIT AND SWITCH PRICING

The practice of advertising a low-priced model of a shopping good, such as a washing machine or a refrigerator, to lure shoppers into a store is called bait and switch pricing. Once the shoppers are in the store, a salesperson tries to persuade them to purchase a higher-priced model. Bait and switch pricing, which was discussed in detail in Chapter 6, is considered by the Federal Trade Commission to be an illegal practice when the low-priced model used as bait is unavailable to shoppers, or as some in the industry describe as being "nailed to the floor."

PRIVATE BRAND PRICING

A private brand item can often be purchased by a retailer at a cheaper price, have a higher markup percentage, and still be priced lower than a comparable national brand. Private brands also permit the retailer a large degree of pricing freedom because consumers find it difficult to make exact comparisons between private brands and national brands of similar goods. Mervyn's, Sears, Kmart, and other discounters price their private brands below the market. Private labels can be used by a retailer to differentiate itself and its merchandise from competitors. At a time when everybody seems to be selling the same things, retailers are using their own store's image to an advantage by developing their own exclusive private labels. Studio B, one of Bloomingdale's private labels, offers a trouser-and-vest outfit for $116. A look-alike designer-name outfit

Loss leader *is an extreme form of leader pricing where an item is sold below a retailer's cost.*

High-low pricing *involves the use of high everyday prices and low leader "specials" on items typically featured in weekly ads.*

Bait and switch pricing *is a practice where a low-priced model of a shopping good, such as an automobile or refrigerator, is used to lure shoppers into a store and then the salesperson attempts to persuade them to purchase a higher priced model.*

would cost more than $300.[9] Zellers, a division of The Hudson Bay Company, has relied on private labels to respond to Wal-Mart's invasion of its Canadian market. With its motto—"The Lowest Price Is the Law"—Zellers uses private labels to give it exclusivity and quality, especially in apparel, in which 80 percent of its line is private.[10]

LO • 3
Describe how retailers
calculate the various
markups

USING MARKUPS

A retail buyer should be able to calculate rapidly whether a proposed purchase will provide an adequate markup or gross margin. The markup can be expressed in dollars or as a percentage of either the selling price or the cost of the good. There are times, however, when a retail buyer needs to compute the markdown, which is a reduction in the selling price of the goods. Markdowns are made to quickly sell certain merchandise, especially when the color or size assortments are no longer complete.

CALCULATING MARKUP

To calculate the selling price (or retail price), the retailer should begin with the following basic markup equation:

$$SP = C + M$$

where C is the dollar cost of merchandise per unit; M is the dollar markup per unit; and SP is the selling price per unit.

Thus, if the retailer has a cost per unit of $16 on a calculator and a dollar markup of $14, then the selling price per unit is $30. In other words, markup is simply the difference between the cost of the merchandise and the selling price, which is the same as gross margin.

Markup

is the selling price of the merchandise less its cost, which is equivalent to gross margin.

This markup is intended to cover all the operating expenses (wages, rent, utilities, promotion, credit, etc.) incurred in the sale of the product and still provide the retailer with a profit. Occasionally, a retailer will sell a product without a markup high enough to cover the cost of the merchandise to generate traffic or build sales volume. This chapter is, however, only concerned with using markup to produce a profit on the sale of each item.

MARKUP METHODS

Markup may be expressed as either a dollar amount or as a percentage of the selling price or cost. It is most useful when expressed as a percentage of the selling price because it can then be used in comparison with other financial data such as last year's sales results, reductions in selling price, and even the firm's competition. The equation for expressing markup as percentage of selling price is

$$\text{Percentage of markup on selling price} = (SP - C)/SP = M/SP$$

Although some businesses, usually manufacturers or small retailers, express markup as a percentage of cost, this method is not widely used in retailing because most of the financial data the retailer uses are expressed as a percentage of selling price. Nevertheless, when expressing markup as a percentage of cost, the equation is

EXHIBIT 10.2	MARKUP CONVERSION TABLE		
MARKUP PERCENTAGE ON SELLING PRICE	MARKUP PERCENTAGE ON COST	MARKUP PERCENTAGE ON SELLING PRICE	MARKUP PERCENTAGE ON COST
4.8	5.0	32.0	47.1
5.0	5.3	33.3	50.0
8.0	8.7	34.0	51.5
10.0	11.1	35.0	53.9
15.0	17.7	36.0	56.3
16.7	20.0	37.0	58.8
20.0	25.0	40.0	66.7
25.0	33.3	41.0	70.0
26.0	35.0	42.8	75.0
27.3	37.5	44.4	80.0
28.0	39.0	47.5	90.0
28.5	40.0	50.0	100.0
30.0	42.9	66.7	200.0

$$\text{Percentage of markup on cost} = (SP - C)/C = M/C$$

Several problems occur when we attempt to equate markup as a percentage of selling price with markup as a percentage of cost. Because the two methods use different bases, we really are not comparing similar data. However, there is an equation to be used to find markup on selling when we know markup on cost:

Percentage of markup on selling price = Percentage of markup on cost/(100% + Percentage of markup on cost)

Likewise, when we know markup on selling price, we can easily find markup on cost:

Percentage of markup on cost = Percentage of markup on selling price/(100% − Percentage of markup on selling price)

The preceding equations are conversions, converting percentage markup on cost to percentage markup on selling price, or vice versa. Exhibit 10.2 shows a conversion table for markup on cost and markup on selling price. Let's go back to our original example of the calculator and see how easy it is to determine markup on selling price when we know the markup on cost and vice versa.

The retailer purchased the calculator for $16.00 and later sold it for $30.00. The difference between the selling price and the cost is $14.00. This $14.00 as a percentage of selling price (markup on selling price) is 46.7 percent ($14/$30). This same $14.00, however, represents 87.5 percent ($14/$16) of the cost (markup). In this example, if all we knew was that the calculator had a 87.5 percent markup on cost, we could determine that this was the same as a 46.7 percent markup on selling price:

EXHIBIT 10.3	RELATIONSHIP OF MARKUPS EXPRESSED ON SELLING PRICE AND COST

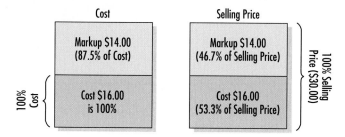

Percentage of markup on selling price = Percentage of markup on cost/(100% + Percentage of markup on cost) = 87.5%/(100% + 87.5%) = 46.7%

Likewise, if we knew we had a 46.7 percent markup on selling, we could easily determine markup on cost:

Percentage of markup on cost = Percentage of markup on selling price/(100% − Percentage of markup on selling price) = 46.7%/(100% − 46.7%) = 87.5%

Exhibit 10.2 gives you the total picture of the relationships between markup on cost and markup on selling price. In Exhibit 10.3, you can see that dollar markup does not change as the percentage changes on cost or selling price. Dollar markup is presented as a percentage of a different base, cost or selling price.

Exhibit 10.4 reviews the basic markup equations.

USING MARKUP FORMULAS WHEN PURCHASING MERCHANDISE

Although simple in concept, the basic markup formulas will enable you to determine more than the percentage of markup on a particular item. Let us work with the markup on selling price formula to illustrate how an interesting and frequently occurring question might be answered. If you know that a particular type of item could be sold for $8 per unit and that you need a 40 percent markup on selling price to meet your profit objective, then how much would you be willing to pay for the item? Using our equation for markup on selling price, we have

$$\text{Percentage of markup on selling price} = (SP - C)/SP$$
$$40\% = (\$8 - C)/\$8$$
$$C = \$4.80$$

Therefore, you would be willing to pay $4.80 for the item. If the item cannot be found at $4.80 or less, it is probably not worth stocking.

Likewise, if a retailer purchases an item for $12.00 and wants a 40 percent markup on selling price, how would the retailer determine the selling price? Returning to our original equation ($SP = C + M$), we know that $SP = C + 0.40SP$ because markup is 40 percent of selling price. If markup is 40 percent of selling price, cost must

EXHIBIT 10.4	BASIC MARKUP FORMULAS

BASIC MARKUP FORMULAS

$$\% \text{ Markup on Selling Price} = \frac{\text{Selling Price} - \text{Cost}}{\text{Selling Price}} = \frac{\text{Markup}}{\text{Selling Price}}$$

$$\% \text{ Markup on Cost} = \frac{\text{Selling Price} - \text{Cost}}{\text{Cost}} = \frac{\text{Markup}}{\text{Cost}}$$

Finding % Markup on Cost when % Markup on Selling is Known:

$$\% \text{ Markup on Cost} = \frac{\% \text{ Markup on Selling Price}}{100\% - \% \text{ Markup on Selling Price}}$$

Finding % Markup on Selling Price when % Markup on Cost is Known:

$$\% \text{ Markup on Selling Price} = \frac{\% \text{ Markup on Cost}}{100\% + \% \text{ Markup on Cost}}$$

Finding Selling Price when Cost and % Markup on Cost Are Known:
Selling Price = Cost + % Markup on Cost (Cost)

Finding Selling Price when Cost and % Markup on Selling Price Are Known:

$$\text{Selling Price} = \frac{\text{Cost}}{(1 - \% \text{ Markup on Selling Price})}$$

be 60 percent because cost and markup are the complements of each other and must total 100 percent. Thus if

$$60\% \; SP = \$12.00$$

(divide both sides by 60 percent), then

$$SP = \$20.00$$

INITIAL VERSUS MAINTAINED MARKUP

Up to this point, we have assumed that we have been able to sell the product at the price we initially set when the product arrived at the store. We have assumed that the initial markup (the markup placed on the merchandise when the store receives it) is equal to the maintained markup or achieved markup (the actual selling price less the cost). Because in many cases the actual selling price for some of the firm's merchandise is lower than the original selling price, the firm's maintained markup is usually lower than the initial markup. Thus, maintained markup differs from initial markup by the amount of reductions:

Initial markup = (Original retail price − Cost)/Original retail price

Maintained markup = (Actual retail price − Cost)/Actual retail price

Five reasons can account for the difference between initial and maintained markups. First is the need to balance demand with supply. Because most markup

Maintained markup *is the actual selling price (not the initial asking price) of the merchandise less its cost.*

formulas are cost-oriented, rather than demand-oriented, adjustments in selling prices will occur. This is especially true when consumers demand changes and the only way for retailers to reduce their inventory and make their merchandise saleable is by taking a markdown or reduction in selling price. A second reason is stock shortages. Shortages can occur from theft by employees or customers or by mismarking the price when merchandise is received or sold. In either case, the selling price received for the goods will be less than the price carried in the inventory records. In fact, clerical error probably accounts for more stock shortages than theft. Third, there are employee and customer discounts. Employees are usually given some discount privileges after they have worked for the firm for a specified period of time. Also, certain customer groups (i.e., religious and senior citizen groups) may be given special discount privileges.

Fourth is the cost of alterations. Some fashion apparel items require alterations before the product is acceptable to the customer. Although men's clothing is often altered free of charge, there is usually a small charge for altering women's wear. Nevertheless, this charge usually doesn't cover all alteration costs, and therefore, alterations are actually a part of the cost of the merchandise.

A fifth and final reason that initial markup may be different from maintained markup is manufacturer's cash discounts. Cash discounts are offered to retailers by manufacturers or suppliers to encourage prompt payment of bills. Cash discounts taken reduce the cost of merchandise and therefore make the maintained markup higher than the initial markup. This is just the opposite of the first four factors.

Some large retailers ignore cash discounts in calculating initial markup because the buyer may have little control over whether the discount is taken. The reason for this is that achieving discounts through prompt payment is thought to be the result of financial operations rather than merchandising decisions, and therefore the buyer should not be penalized if the discounts are not taken.

PLANNING INITIAL MARKUPS

As the previous discussion illustrates, retailers do not casually arrive at an initial markup percentage. The initial markup percentage must be a carefully planned process. Markups must be large enough to cover all the operating expenses and still provide a reasonable profit to the firm. In addition, markups must provide for markdowns, shortages, employee discounts, and alteration expenses (all these together are referred to as total reductions), which reduce net revenue. Likewise, cash discounts taken, which increase net revenue, must be included.

INITIAL MARKUP EQUATION   To determine the initial markup, use the following formula:

Initial markup percentage = (Operating expenses + Net profit + Markdowns
+ Stock shortages + Employee and customer discounts + Alterations costs
− Cash discounts)/(Net sales + Markdowns + Stock shortages
+ Employee and customer discounts)

We can simplify this equation if we remember that markdowns, stock shortages, and employee and customer discounts are all retail reductions from stock levels.

Likewise, gross margin is the sum of operating expenses and net profit. This produces a simpler formula:

Initial markup percentage = (Gross margin + Alterations costs − Cash discounts
+ Reductions)/(Net sales + Reductions)

Because some retailers record cash discounts as other income and not as a cost reduction in determining initial markup, the formula can be simplified one more time:

Initial markup percentage = (Gross margin + Alterations costs + Reductions)/
(Net sales + Reductions)

Regardless of which of the three formulas is used, the retailer must always remember the effect of each of the following items when planning initial markup: operating expenses, net profits, markdowns, stock shortages, employee and customer discounts, alteration costs, cash discounts taken, and net sales.

At this point, a numerical example might be helpful. Assume that a retailer plans to achieve net sales of $1 million and expects operating expenses to be $270,000. The net profit goal is $60,000. Planned reductions include $80,000 for markdowns, $20,000 for merchandise shortages, and $10,000 for employee and customer discounts. Alteration costs are expected to be $20,000, and cash discounts from suppliers are expected to be $10,000. What is the initial markup percentage that should be planned? What is the cost of merchandise to be sold?

The initial markup percentage can be obtained by using the original equation:

Initial markup percentage = ($270,000 + $60,000 + $80,000 + $20,000 + $10,000
+ $20,000 − $10,000)/($1,000,000 + $80,000 + $20,000 + $10,000) = 40.54%

The cost of merchandise sold can also be found. We know that the gross margin is operating expenses plus net profit ($330,000). This gross profit is equivalent to net sales less cost of merchandise sold, where cost of merchandise sold includes alteration costs and where cash discounts are subtracted. Thus, in the problem at hand, we know that $1 million less cost of merchandise sold (including alterations costs and subtracting cash discounts) is equal to $670,000. Because the alterations costs are planned at $20,000 and cash discounts at $10,000, the cost of merchandise is equal to $660,000 ($670,000 − $20,000 + $10,000).

We can verify our result by returning to the basic initial markup formula: asking price minus cost divided by asking price. The asking price is the planned net sales of $1 million plus planned reductions of $110,000 ($80,000 for markdowns, $20,000 for shortages, and $10,000 for employee and customer discounts). The cost is the cost of merchandise before the alteration costs and prior to cash discounts, or $660,000. By using the basic initial markup formula, we obtain ($1,110,000 − $660,000)/$1,110,000, or 40.54 percent. This is the same result we achieved earlier.

The preceding computations resulted in a markup percentage on retail selling price for merchandise lines storewide. Obviously, not all lines or items within lines should be priced by mechanically applying this markup percentage, because the actions of competitors will affect the prices for each merchandise line. Thus the retailer will want to price the mix of merchandise lines in such a fashion that a storewide markup percentage is obtained. To achieve this, some lines may be priced with considerably higher markups and others with substantially lower markups than the storewide average that was planned by using the initial markup planning equation. It will be helpful to explore some of the common reasons for varying the markup percentage on different lines or items within lines.

MARKUP DETERMINANTS In planning initial markups, it is useful to know some of the general rules of markup determination. These are summarized as follows:

1. As goods are sold through more retail outlets, the markup percentage decreases. However, selling through few retail outlets means a greater markup percentage.
2. The higher the handling and storage costs of the goods, the higher the markup should be.
3. The greater the risk of a price reduction due to the seasonality of the goods, the greater the magnitude of the markup percentage early in the season.
4. The higher the demand inelasticity of price for the goods, the greater the markup percentage.

Although these rules are common to all retail lines, there are others that are unique to each line of trade and are only learned through experience in the respective lines, such as how much to markup produce in a supermarket during different seasons.

LO • 4
Discuss why markdown management is so important in retailing, as well as some of the errors that cause markdowns

---

MARKDOWN MANAGEMENT

Although retailers would prefer to have their initial markup (the markup placed on the merchandise when the store receives it) equal to the maintained markup (the actual selling price less the cost), this seldom happens. Markdowns, which are reductions in the price of an item taken to stimulate sales, and other reductions result in a firm receiving a lower price for its merchandise than originally asked. The markup percentage is the amount of the reduction divided by the original selling price:

Markdown

is any reduction in the price of an item from its initially established price.

$$\text{Markdown percentage} = \text{Amount of reduction/Original selling price}$$

Thus maintained markup (sometimes referred to as "gross margin" or just plain "gross") is the key to profitability because it is the difference between the actual selling price and the cost of that merchandise.

For effective retail price management, markdowns should be planned. In principle, they need to be planned because pricing is not a science with high degrees of precision but an art form with considerable room for error. If retailers knew everything they needed to know about demand and supply factors, they could use the science of economics to establish a price that would maximize profits and ensure the sale of all the merchandise. Unfortunately, retailers do not possess perfect information about supply and demand factors. As a result, the entire merchandising process is subject to error, which then makes pricing difficult. Four basic errors can occur: (1) buying errors, (2) pricing errors, (3) merchandising errors, and (4) promotion errors.

BUYING ERRORS

Errors in buying occur on the supply side of the pricing question. They result as the retailer buys the wrong merchandise or buys the right merchandise in too large a quantity. The merchandise purchased could have been in the wrong styles, sizes, colors, patterns, or price range. Too large a quantity could have been purchased because demand was overestimated or a recession was not foreseen. Whatever the cause of the buying error, the net result is a need to cut the price to move the merchandise. Often, the resulting prices are below the actual cost of the merchandise to the retailer. Thus buying errors can be costly. As a consequence, you might expect that the retail manager would wish to minimize buying errors. However, this is not the case. The retailer could minimize buying errors by being extremely conservative. It could buy only what it knew the customer wanted and what it could be certain of selling. Then buying errors would be minimized but at the expense of lost profit opportunities on some riskier types of purchase decisions. Recall that when we reviewed the determinants of markups, we mentioned that the greater the risk of potential price reductions the higher the markup percentage. This is simply another way of recognizing that taking a gamble on some purchases that represent buying errors can be profitable if initial markups are high. Review the most common buying errors made by buyers discussed in Chapter 9.

PRICING ERRORS

Errors in pricing merchandise can be another cause of markdowns. Errors occur when the price of the item is too high to move the product at the speed and in the quantity desired. The goods may have been bought in the right styles, at the right time, and in the right quantities, but the price on the item may simply be too high. This would create purchase resistance on the part of the typical customer.

An overly high price is often relative to the pricing behavior of competitors. Perhaps, in principle, the price would have been acceptable, but if competitors price the same item substantially lower, then the retailer's original price becomes too high.

MERCHANDISING ERRORS

Although many new retailers believe that carrying over seasonal or fashion merchandise into the next merchandising season is the most common merchandise error, it really isn't. Failure by the buyer to inform the sales staff how the new merchandise relates to the current stock, ties in with the store's image, and satisfies the needs of the store's target market is the most common merchandising error. A key merchandising error is the failure to keep the department manager and salesforce informed about the new merchandise lines, so that these goods will be available to the customer. Too many times, the new merchandise is left in the storeroom or the salespersons are not informed on the "key" features of the new item, and thus the customer will never be able to become excited about the new merchandise. Also, another merchandising error is the improper handling of the merchandise by the sales staff or ineffective visual presentation of the merchandise. Mishandling errors could be failure to stock the new merchandise behind old merchandise whenever possible or simply misplacing the merchandise. All too often, a slow seller is a "lost" bundle of merchandise.

PROMOTION ERRORS

Finally, it is often the case that even when the right goods were purchased in the right quantities and were priced correctly, the merchandise fails to move as planned. In this situation, there is most often a promotion error. The consumer has not been properly informed or prompted to purchase the merchandise. The advertising, personal selling, sales promotion activities, or in-store displays were too weak or sporadic to elicit a strong response from potential customers.

MARKDOWN POLICY

Retailers will find it advantageous to develop a markdown timing policy. In almost all situations, retailers will find it necessary to take markdowns; but the crucial decisions become when and how much of a markdown to take. In principle, there are two extremes to a markdown timing policy: early and late.

EARLY MARKDOWN POLICY

Early markdown policy *is when the retailer takes markdowns early to speed the movement of merchandise and thus increase inventory turnover.*

Most retailers who concentrate on high inventory turnover pursue an early markdown policy. Markdowns taken early speed the movement of merchandise and also generally enable the retailer to take less of a markdown per unit to dispose of the goods. One of the author's bosses taught him early in his retailing career that "the first markdown is the cheapest to take. Therefore once you take it, don't look back." In other words, when you as a buyer make a merchandising error, take your loss early and don't look back because taking that early markdown will allow the dollars obtained from selling the merchandise to be used to help finance more saleable goods. At the same time, the customer seems to benefit, because markdowns are offered quickly on goods that some consumers still think of as fashionable and the store has the appearance of having fresh merchandise. For example, the best women's apparel shoppers usually visit their favorite store three to four times a month. Thus, it is important for the retailer to always have the appearance of presenting fresh merchandise. Therefore, many fashion retailers use the following set of rules when taking early markdowns.

- After the third week, mark it down 25 percent from the original price.
- After the seventh week, mark it down 50 percent from the original price.
- After the 11th week, mark it down 75 percent from the original price.
- After the 16th week, sell it to an outlet store or give it to charity.

Another advantage of the early markdown policy is that it allows the retailer to replenish lower-priced lines from the higher ones that have been marked down. For instance, many women's wear retailers will regularly take slow-moving dresses from higher-priced lines and move them down to the moderate- or lower-priced lines. Other retailers mark goods down at regular intervals until the merchandise is sold. In effect, this represents a markdown, even though it is not recognizable by the consumer.

LATE MARKDOWN POLICY

Late markdown policy *is when the retailer allows the merchandise to have a long trial period before a markdown is taken.*

Allowing goods to have a long trial period before a markdown is taken is called a late markdown policy. This policy avoids disrupting the sale of regular merchandise by too frequently marking goods down. As a consequence, customers will learn to look forward to a semiannual or annual clearance, in which all or most merchandise is marked down. Thus the bargain hunters or low-end customers will be attracted only at infrequent intervals.

Regardless of which timing policy a retailer follows, it must plan for these reductions. Markdowns are not always the result of buyer errors. They may simply be the selling of merchandise that is late in the season and before larger markdowns must be

MARKDOWNS AREN'T ALWAYS TOTALLY THE RETAILER'S LOSS

Often, retailers are able to have their suppliers supplement their markdown losses with "markdown money" or some other type of price reductions.

Here's how it works: Let's say Acme Clothing Company delivers 100 sweaters to Judy's Dress Shop at the wholesale price of $40 each. Judy, in turn, plans to take her customary markup of 50 percent on selling price to sell each sweater for $80, thus producing a gross margin of $4,000.

However, after three months Judy still has 50 of the sweaters in stock, which she puts on sale for $50 each to move the merchandise. After selling the remaining sweaters, Judy's gross margin was only $2,500: [(50 × $80) + (50 × $50) − (100 × $40)].

The following month, Judy goes to market and visits the Acme showroom. Judy wants Acme to pay her the $1,500 that she lost in taking the markdowns on their sweaters. Judy threatens Acme with a loss of future orders if it doesn't cover her losses. Does this sound fair to you?

Actually, this type of scenario happens quite frequently when buyers go to market. Buyers maintain that manufacturers should share in the responsibility when the merchandise doesn't sell as promised. Buyers claim that if the supplier cannot deliver the gross margin desired, there is no reason to reorder from that supplier again. From the retailers' standpoint, when the manufacturer contributes markdown money, the manufacturers are really asking for a second chance to prove the salability of their lines. This markdown money could be in the form of cash payment or of a discount on future purchases.

---

taken. Remember, when preparing a merchandise budget the retailer must estimate reductions for that time period.

AMOUNT OF MARKDOWN An issue related to the timing of markdowns is their magnitude. If the retailer waits to use a markdown at the last moment, then the markdown should probably be large enough to move the remaining merchandise. This, however, is not the case with an early markdown. An early markdown only needs to be large enough to provide a sales stimulant. Once sales are stimulated, the retailer can watch merchandise movement; when it slows, the retailer can provide another stimulant by again marking it down. Which is the more profitable strategy depends on the situation. One rule of thumb for markdowns is that "prices should be marked down at least 25 percent for the consumer to notice." However, the markdown percentage should vary with the type of merchandise, time of season, and competition.

The Behind the Scenes box describes how retailers sometimes can regain part of their markdowns from their suppliers.

Now, let's look at how the maintained markup percentage is determined. A retailer purchases the calculator, used in an earlier example, for $16 with the intent of selling it for $25 (an initial markup of 36 percent). However, the calculator did not sell at that price and the retailer reduced it to $20 to sell it. This would result in a maintained markup of 20 percent:

$$\text{Maintained markup} = (\text{Actual selling price} - \text{Cost})/\text{Actual selling price}$$
$$= \$4/\$20 = 20\%$$

The following formula can also be used to determine the maintained markup percentage:

Maintained markup percentage = Initial markup percentage − [(Reduction percentage) × (100% − Initial markup percentage)]

where

Reduction percentage = Amount of reductions/Net sales

In the above example,

Maintained markup percentage = 36% − [($5/$20) × (100% − 36%)]
= 36% − 16% = 20%

STUDENT STUDY GUIDE

SUMMARY

LO • 1 **WHAT ARE FACTORS TO BE CONSIDERED WHEN ESTAB-LISHING A RETAILER'S PRICING OBJECTIVES AND POLICIES?** Pricing decisions are among the most frequent that a retailer must make. They cannot be made independently, because they interact with the merchandise, location, promotion, credit, customer service, store image decisions the retailer has already made, as well as the federal and state legal constraints.

The pricing objectives that the retailer ultimately sets must also agree with the retailer's mission statement and merchandise policies. These objectives can be profit-oriented, sales-oriented, or seek to maintain the status quo.

After establishing its pricing objectives, the retailer must next determine the pricing policies to achieve these goals. These policies must reflect the expectations of the target market.

LO • 2 **WHAT ARE THE VARIOUS PRICING STRATEGIES AVAILABLE TO THE RETAILER?** Among the strategies discussed were customary pricing, variable pricing, flexible pricing, one-price policies, price lining, odd pricing, multiple-unit pricing, bundle pricing, leader pricing, bait pricing, and private brand pricing.

LO • 3 **HOW DOES A RETAILER CALCULATE THE VARIOUS MARKUPS?** The basic markup equation states that, per unit, the retail selling price is equal to the dollar cost plus the dollar markup. Markups can be expressed as either a percentage of selling price or as a percentage of cost to the retailer. Because the initial selling price that the retailer puts on a newly purchased item may not be attractive enough to sell all the inventory of that item, the price may need to be reduced. When we talk of actual selling prices versus initial selling prices, we are discussing the difference between an initial and a maintained markup.

Initial markups should be planned. Next, the initial storewide markup percentage can be determined by using operating expenses, net profit, alterations costs, cash discounts, markdowns, stock shortages, employee and customer discounts, and sales. The retailer must recognize that not all items can be priced by mechanically applying this markup percentage. Some lines will need to be priced to yield a considerably higher markup and others, a substantially lower markup. The initial markup is seldom equal to the maintained markup because of three kinds of reductions: markdowns, shortages, and employee and customer discounts.

LO • 4 **WHY IS MARKDOWN MANAGEMENT SO IMPORTANT IN RE-TAILING?** Because the retailer does not possess perfect information about supply and demand, markdowns are inevitable. Markdowns are usually due to errors in buying, pricing, merchandising, or promotion. Because markdowns are inevitable, the retailer needs to establish a markdown policy. Early markdown speeds the movement of merchandise and also allows the retailer to take less of a markdown per unit to dispose of the merchandise. Late markdown avoids disrupting the sale of regular merchandise by too frequent markdowns. The best policy from a profit perspective depends on the particular situation involved.

TERMS TO REMEMBER

target return objective
profit maximization
skimming
penetration
pricing policies
above-market pricing policy
price zone
below-market pricing policy
customary pricing
variable pricing
flexible pricing
one-price policy
price lining
trading up

trading down
odd pricing
multiple-unit pricing
bundling
leader pricing
loss leader
high-low pricing
bait and switch pricing
markup
maintained markup
markdown
early markdown policy
late markdown policy

REVIEW AND DISCUSSION QUESTIONS

LO • 1 WHAT ARE FACTORS TO BE CONSIDERED WHEN ESTABLISHING A RETAILER'S PRICING OBJECTIVES AND POLICIES?

1. How does a store's location affect the price it can charge?
2. How can promotion decisions influence the demand for a retailer's product line?
3. Is a profit maximization objective fair to a retailer's customers?
4. When should a skimming pricing objective be used?
5. What is the major objection to a retailer using a sales-oriented pricing objective?
6. Is it possible that a retailer could use an above-market pricing policy with private label products?

LO • 2 WHAT ARE THE VARIOUS PRICING STRATEGIES AVAILABLE TO THE RETAILER?

7. Would you prefer to buy a car from a dealer using flexible or a one-price policy? Why?
8. Do you think odd pricing is really effective?
9. What type of store would be most likely to use leader pricing?
10. What is high-low pricing ? What type of retailer is most likely to use this pricing policy?

LO • 3 HOW DOES A RETAILER CALCULATE THE VARIOUS MARKUPS?

11. Compute the markup on selling price for an item that retails for $19.95 and costs $11.20.
12. Complete the following:

	DRESS SHIRT	SPORT SHIRT	BELT
Selling Price	$30.00	$24.95	$12.50
Cost	$18.00	$14.35	$ 7.50
Markup in Dollars	_____	_____	_____
Markup Percentage on Cost	_____	_____	_____
Markup Percentage on Selling Price	_____	_____	_____

13. A buyer buys 28 raincoats at $342/dozen. If the department markup on selling price is 52.5 percent, what should be each raincoat's retail price?

14. Markup on cost is 56 percent, what is markup on selling price?

15. Which is more important to a retailer — initial or maintained markup?

16. Can an initial markup ever be equal to the maintained markup? Explain.

17. Assume that a retailer plans to achieve a net sales of $1.5 million and expects operating expenses to be $375,000. The net profit goal is $100,000. Planned reductions include $88,000 for markdowns, $38,000 for merchandise shortages, and $14,000 for employee and customer discounts. Cash discounts from suppliers are expected to be $30,000. At what percentage should initial markups be planned?

18. Intimate Apparel wants to produce a 12 percent operating profit this year on sales of $460,000. Based on past experiences, the owner made the following estimates:

Net Alteration Expenses	$ 800	Employee Discount	$ 3,400
Markdowns	27,000	Operating Expenses	215,000
Stock Shortages	4,200	Cash Discounts Earned	2,100

Given these estimates, what average initial markup should be asked for the upcoming year?

19. What are some of the key determinants used in determining markup percentage?

LO•4 WHY IS MARKDOWN MANAGEMENT SO IMPORTANT IN RETAILING?

20. Why should a retailer plan on taking markdowns during a merchandising season?

21. Somebody once said, "Good buyers never have to take markdowns." Do you agree with that statement? Explain your answer.

22. Given the following information, what is the maintained markup percentage? Planned sales = $300,000; planned initial markup = 40 percent; planned reductions = $36,000.

SAMPLE TEST QUESTIONS

LO•1 WHAT WORD BEST DESCRIBES THE RELATIONSHIP BETWEEN A RETAILER'S PRICING DECISIONS AND THE MERCHANDISE, LOCATION, PROMOTION, CREDIT, SERVICES, IMAGE, AND LEGAL DECISIONS THAT RETAILERS MUST MAKE?

a. independent
b. separate
c. interactive
d. competitive
e. multifaced

LO•2 IF A RETAILER IS OFFERING THE SAME PRODUCTS AND QUANTITIES TO DIFFERENT CUSTOMERS AT DIFFERENT PRICES, THE RETAILER HAS WHAT KIND OF PRICING POLICY?

a. two-price
b. customary
c. flexible
d. leader
e. variable

LO·3 IF A RETAILER BUYS A PRODUCT FOR $25 AND SELLS IT FOR $45, WHAT IS THE MARKUP PERCENTAGE IF THE MARKUP IS BASED ON THE SELLING PRICE?

a. 44.4 percent
b. 80 percent
c. 75 percent
d. 100 percent
e. 55.5 percent

LO·4 AN ITEM WAS MARKED DOWN TO $19.99 FROM ITS ORIGINAL RETAIL PRICE OF $29.99. WHAT IS THE REDUCTION PERCENTAGE FOR THIS ITEM?

a. 33.3 percent
b. 25 percent
c. 50 percent
d. 41.3 percent
e. 66.7 percent

APPLICATIONS

WRITING AND SPEAKING EXERCISE   You have just been hired to be the merchandise manager of a small chain (four stores) of women's apparel stores. The chain caters to working women, and five of its six buyers have less than one year's experience. In looking over the records, you notice that these buyers have been late in taking markdowns. As a result, the chain's profits have suffered. In talking with the buyers, you detect a sense of fear in taking markdowns. They believe that a markdown is an admission of an error in their buying and that if they make too many errors, their jobs will be in jeopardy. You decide to write the buyers a memo regarding markdowns.

RETAIL PROJECT   On your next trip to a mall, visit all the anchor stores and leading apparel stores. Look around at displays and notice if they are having sales. Now, based on the amount of merchandise on sale and the amount of reductions, determine if each store is using an early or late markdown policy. Explain your reasoning for each store and especially explain the reasoning for differences between the stores. (*Note:* You can also do this project for different web sites.)

CASE LONE STAR DEPARTMENT STORE

PART A The buyer for the women's sweater department has purchased wool sweaters for $37, and she wants to sell them at a 47 percent markup on selling price. At what price should each sweater be sold?

PART B The buyer for men's shirts has a price point of $25 and requires a markup of 40 percent. What would be the highest price he should pay for a shirt to sell at this price point?

PART C The buyer for housewares hopes to achieve net sales of $1,000,000 for the coming year. Operating expenses are $190,000 and retail reductions are $80,000.

Management has set a profit goal of $110,000. What should the initial markup percentage be?

PART D The women's dress department wants to produce an 18 percent operating profit on forecasted sales of $600,000. The divisional merchandise manager has made the following estimates:

Alterations	$1,800	Operating expenses	$150,000
Stock shortages	3,000	Markdowns	55,000
Employee discounts	1,500	Cash discounts earned	400

Based on this information, what initial markup percentage will be needed?

PLANNING YOUR OWN RETAIL BUSINESS

The True Value hardware store you recently opened is doing well, but you are uncertain of your pricing strategy. Currently, the typical customer purchases four items at an average price of $11.71, for an average transaction size of $46.84. The cost of goods is 60 percent of sales, which yields a 40 percent gross margin. You are considering lowering prices by 10 percent across the board so you can better compete with the new Home Depot that is about to open one mile from your store. If you lower prices by 10 percent, you believe that the average items purchased per customer would rise by 25 percent. Assuming that your assumptions are correct, should you lower prices by 10 percent across the board? If not, do you have an alternative pricing strategy to propose?

NOTES

1. "A Small Toy Store Manages to Level the Playing Field," *Wall Street Journal,* December 20, 1996: A1, A8.
2. "McDonald's Falls Back to Price-Cutting Tactics," *Advertising Age,* February 3, 1997: 57.
3. "Discounters Dress Up to Lure the Well-Heeled Shopper," *Wall Street Journal,* December 3, 1997: B1, B13.
4. "Retailers Turn to Wal-Mart, Sam's as Suppliers," *Lubbock Avalanche-Journal,* May 4, 1997: 4E.
5. "GM Expected to Expand 'No Haggle' Pricing Plan," *Wall Street Journal,* April 24, 1996: A3.
6. Zarrel V. Lambert, "Perceived Prices as Related to Odd and Even Price Endings," *Journal of Retailing,* Fall 1975: 13–21, 78; "Strategic Mix of Odd, Even Prices Can Lead to Increased Retail Profits," *Marketing News,* March 7, 1980: 24.
7. "The Bundler," *Forbes,* April 22, 1996: 82–86.
8. "Exxonsafeway," *Forbes,* March 11, 1996: 106; "Convenience Stores That Sell Gas Find Higher Prices a Mixed Blessing," *Wall Street Journal,* May 16, 1996: A1.
9. "Back to Basics," *Forbes,* May 10, 1993: 56–58.
10. "Zellers Fights Back," *DM,* January 1996: 24–30.

ADVERTISING AND PROMOTION

To stay competitive in to-day's retail environment, retailers need to look beyond traditional advertising strategies. One retailer who goes to the customer, as opposed to making the customer come to it, is JCPenney, which attracts customer interest with its sponsorship of the LPGA Skins Game and the mixed-team JCPenney Classic.

OVERVIEW

Promotion is a major generator of demand in retailing. In this chapter, we focus on the role of advertising, sales promotion, and publicity in the operation of a retail business. Retail selling, another important element of promotion, is discussed in Chapter 12. Our discussion is directed at describing how retailers should manage their firm's promotional resources.

LEARNING OBJECTIVES

After reading this chapter, you should be able to

1. name the four basic components of the retailer's promotion mix and discuss their relationship with other retailer decisions

2. describe the differences between a retailer's long-term and short-term promotional objectives

3. list the six steps involved in developing a retailer's advertising campaign

4. explain how retailers manage their sales promotion and publicity

Advertising
is paid, nonpersonal communication through various media by business firms, nonprofit organizations, and individuals who are in some way identified in the advertising message and who hope to inform and/or persuade members of a particular audience; includes communication of products, services, institutions, and ideas.

Sales promotion
involves the use of media and non-media marketing pressure applied for a pre-determined, limited period of time at the level of consumer, retailer or wholesaler in order to stimulate trial, increase consumer demand, or improve product availability.

RETAIL PROMOTION MIX

By making their targeted customers aware of current offerings, retailers use promotion to generate sales. This doesn't mean that sales can't occur without using promotion. Some sales will always take place, even if the retailer doesn't spend any money on promotion. For example, households close to the retailer may shop there strictly for convenience; passersby might occasionally visit the store for an impulse purchase. Most retailers, however, use a combination of location, price levels, displays, merchandise assortments, customer service, and promotion as a means to generate store traffic and sales.

Retailers do make trade-offs between the elements of the retailing mix. Some retailers, such as The Limited, operate in high-rent prime mall locations and seldom advertise. The Limited prefers to use these prime mall locations to generate customer traffic. Most of The Limited's promotional expenses are made in combination with other mall merchants using the mall's co-op promotional campaigns. However, although this has been the policy of The Limited in the past, it is starting to change as the retailer is finding even with its high-rent locations that it needs to advertise more to help enhance the image of some of its private label brands.[1] Wal-Mart is another retailer that spends only a small percentage of its sales on promotion. Wal-Mart believes that lower prices are more effective than location and heavy promotional expenditures in generating traffic levels. Thus, although direct promotional expenditures are not always a prerequisite to generating sales, they are a means of achieving sales above those that could be obtained merely from offering a lower price range, having a better location, or offering outstanding service. After all, without promotion how would the consumers be aware of these retail offerings. Therefore, many of today's high-performance retailers use promotion to bring traffic into their stores, move the traffic to the various selling areas of the store, and entice the traffic into purchasing merchandise.

TYPES OF PROMOTION

There are four basic components of promotion: advertising, sales promotion, publicity, and personal selling. Collectively, these components comprise the retailer's promotion mix. Each component is defined[2] as follows and is discussed from a managerial perspective.

1. **Advertising** is "paid, nonpersonal communication through various media by business firms, nonprofit organizations, and individuals who are in some way identified in the advertising message and who hope to inform and/or persuade members of a particular audience; includes communication of products, services, institutions, and ideas." Retail advertising's function is primarily to inform potential buyers of the problem-solving utility of a retailer's offering, with the objective of developing consumer preferences for a particular retailer. Retailers most commonly use the following advertising media: newspapers, radio, television, and printed circulars. Recently, some of the major retail chains have started using the Internet to support these other media.

2. **Sales promotions** "involve the use of media and non-media marketing pressure applied for a pre-determined, limited period of time at the level of consumer, retailer or wholesaler in order to stimulate trial, increase consumer demand, or

improve product availability." The most popular sales promotion tools in retailing are premiums, frequent buyer programs, coupons, in-store displays, contests and sweepstakes, product demonstrations, and sampling.

3. Publicity is "non-paid-for communications of information about the company or product, generally in some media form." Popular examples are Macy's Thanksgiving Day Parade and local retailers supporting various civic and educational groups.

4. Personal selling is "selling that involves a face-to-face interaction with the consumer." Personal selling and other services provided by retailers, which are discussed in detail in the next chapter, occur when the retailer's promotional efforts cause a shopper to reach a specific selling area.

All four components of the retailer's promotion mix need to be managed from a total systems perspective. That is, they need to be effectively blended together to achieve the retailer's promotion objectives and reinforce each other. If the advertising conveys quality and status, so must the sales personnel, publicity, and sales promotion. Otherwise, the consumer will receive conflicting or inconsistent messages about the retailer, which will result in confusion and loss of patronage.

DOLLAR $ & ¢ENTS

Retailers who integrate their promotional efforts with the other elements of the retailing mix will be higher performers.

The management of promotional efforts in retailing must also fit into the retailer's overall plan. Promotion decisions relate to and must be integrated with other management decisions, such as location, merchandise, credit, cash flow, building and fixtures, price, and customer service. For example,

1. There is a maximum distance consumers will travel to visit a retail store. Thus a retailer's *location* will help determine the target for promotions. Retailers should direct their promotional dollars first toward households in their primary trading area, the area where the retailer can serve customers in terms of convenience and accessibility better than the competition, and then to secondary trading areas, areas where a retailer is still competitive despite a competitor having some locational advantage.

2. Retailers need high levels of store traffic to keep their *merchandise* rapidly turning over. Promotion helps build traffic.

3. A retailer's *credit customers,* such as Neiman-Marcus's InCircle members who charge more than $3,000 a year, are more store loyal and purchase in larger quantities. Thus they are an excellent target for increased promotional efforts. Although the increased use of MasterCard, Visa, and Discover cards has affected this retail advantage in recent years, many retailers have overcome this problem by developing their own co-branded cards.

4. A retailer confronted with a temporary *cash flow* problem can use promotion to increase short-run cash flow.

Publicity
is non-paid-for communications of information about the company or product, generally in some media form.

Personal selling
involves a face-to-face interaction with the consumer with the goal of selling the consumer merchandise or services.

Primary trading area
is the geographic area where the retailer can serve customers in terms of convenience and accessibility better than the competition.

Secondary trading area
is the geographic area where the retailer can still be competitive despite a competitor having some locational advantage.

5. A retailer's promotional strategy must be reinforced by its *building and fixtures* decisions. Promotional creativity and style should coincide with building and fixture creativity and style. If the ads are exciting and appealing to a particular target market, so should the building and fixtures.

6. Promotion provides customers with more information. That information will help them make better purchase decisions, because risk is reduced. Therefore, promotion can actually be viewed as a major component of *customer service*.

The retailer that systematically integrates its promotional programs with other retail decision areas will be better able to achieve high performance results. One retailer even developed a set of basic promotional guidelines that all retailers should follow when using promotion. These guidelines are

- Try to use only promotions that are consistent with and will enhance your store image.
- Review the success or failure of each promotion to help in developing better future promotions.
- Wherever possible, test new promotions before making a major investment by using them on a broader scale.
- Use appeals that are of interest to your target market and that are realistic to obtain. For example, double-couponing offers everybody an award; a sweepstakes has only one winner.
- Make sure your objectives are measurable.
- Make sure your objectives are obtainable.
- Develop total promotional campaigns, not just ads.
- The lower the rent, the higher the promotional expenses generally needed.
- New stores need higher promotional budgets than established stores.
- Stores in out-of-the way locations require higher promotional budgets than stores with heavy traffic.[3]

PROMOTION IN THE CHANNEL

The retailer is not the only member of the marketing channel that uses promotion. Manufacturers also invest in promotion for many of the same reasons retailers do (i.e., to move merchandise more quickly, to speed up cash flow, and to better retain customer loyalty). However, the promotional activities of the retailer's channel partners may sometimes conflict with the retailer's. There are three major differences in the way retailers and manufacturers use promotion:

1. *product image versus availability:* The manufacturer's primary goal is to create a positive image for the product itself and differentiate it from competing products. For example, when introducing a new product, a manufacturer will attempt to explain how the product works. Retailers, however, are primarily interested in announcing to their customers that they have the product available for purchase at a convenient location(s).

2. *specific product benefits versus price:* Manufacturers generally don't care where customers make their purchases, just so they buy their product. That is why they promote the benefits of their products. Retailers, however, don't care which brand the customer purchases. (Remember retailers carry many different manufacturers' brands.) Retailers just want the customer to make the purchase in their store. Thus, in addition to availability, retailers feature the product's price in their ads.

3. *focused image versus cluttered ads:* In comparison with manufacturers, most retailers carry a larger variety and breadth of products, whereas manufacturers produce a greater depth than most retailers carry. Thus, retail ads, which are usually geared toward short-term results, tend to be more cluttered, with many different products, as opposed to the manufacturer's ad, which focuses on a single product theme.

DOLLAR $ & CENTS

Retailers who realize that there are major differences in the way retailers and manufacturers use promotion will be higher performers than those who don't understand these differences.

Sometimes, a lack of promotional harmony by channel members results from other factors. Consider the case of the automobile channel. Assume that an increase in inflation has slowed the country's rate of real economic growth, and as a result the country's auto sales are off 10 percent from last year. The manufacturer believes that this recession will be short-lived and therefore does not want to get into a "price war" by offering any price rebates or other special promotions from the factory. However, the automobile dealers believe that the recession will be fairly prolonged. They think that advertising by the manufacturer should be increased and that special allowances should be given for increased local advertising. They would also like to see the manufacturer tie in this increased advertising program with a cash rebate from the factory. Because the manufacturer and dealer have different beliefs about the economy's future, this could lead to serious problems between them.

A second possible source of problems is when the channel members think that the chain's promotional campaign is a mistake. For example, in 1997, McDonald's, the nation's largest fast-food chain, was forced by it franchisees to cancel its major promotional campaign just one week into the program. "Campaign 55" (McDonald's was founded in 1955) featured 55-cent Big Macs and the promise that customers would get their orders within 55 seconds of paying for them or get a coupon for free merchandise. The franchisees thought that although such a program would guarantee success for the franchisor, which gets a royalty based on sales, it would only lead to hassles with the customers and lost profits.[4]

Another source of problems among channel members over promotional policies is the case in which the manufacturer seeks, through the use of promotion, to attract a high-quality, high-price, high-status image to its brand, whereas the retailer wants to be known as the price leader and advertises that "I will not be undersold!" Or it can be as simple as recently occurred when Nissan introduced a new campaign that sought to develop a positive "brand image" for its line of cars, but dealers said that the campaign didn't help them sell cars.[5] Here, the manufacturer's and the retailer's promotional efforts are not interwoven, and again a serious conflict can develop between them. Such different perceptions show why it is important for retailers to develop the cooperative relationship discussed in Chapter 5 with their suppliers so that the conflict can be resolved.

PROMOTIONAL OBJECTIVES

To efficiently manage the promotion mix, retail managers must first establish their promotion objectives. These promotional objectives should flow from their overall objectives that were discussed in Chapter 2. They should be the natural outgrowth of the retailer's operations management plans. As such, all promotion objectives should ultimately seek to improve the retailer's financial performance, because this is what strategic and administrative plans are intended to accomplish.

Exhibit 11.1 shows how promotion objectives should relate to financial performance objectives. As this exhibit shows, promotion objectives can be established to help improve both long- and short-term financial performance.

LONG-TERM OBJECTIVES

Institutional advertising
is a type of advertising in which the retailer attempts to gain long-term benefits by promoting and selling the store itself rather than the merchandise in the store.

Institutional advertising is an attempt by the retailer to gain long-term benefits by selling the store itself rather than the merchandise in it. By doing this, the retailers are creating a positive image for themselves in the consumer's mind. Retailers using institutional ads generally seek to establish two long-term promotion objectives: creating a positive store image and public service objectives.

CREATING A POSITIVE STORE IMAGE
The first objective is intended to establish or reinforce in the consumer's mind the positive store image that the retailer wants to convey relative to its competitors. Here, the retailer is seeking to gain that differential advantage by providing a clear positive image that is distinctive from other retailers. By providing such an image, the retailer hopes to develop a long-term relationship with the customer. Two of the most successful retailers in this area have been Neiman-Marcus and Nordstrom. Today, when consumers think of these retailers, they perceive elegantly designed store layouts featuring the top names in fashion backed by excellent service and a helpful, knowledgeable sales staff. Promotion directed at fulfilling this objective will have its major effect on improving the retailer's long-term financial performance. However, as you might expect, this type of promotion will also assist the retailer in the short run, such as when a consumer is seeking to purchase a gift for a special friend and the retailer's ad suggests that "perfect" product idea. After all, promotional efforts of a store have been found to be a key predictor of store choice when gift shopping.

PUBLIC SERVICE PROMOTION
The second long-term objective is directed at getting the consumer to perceive the retailer as a good citizen in the community. Retailers may sponsor public service advertisements to honor local athletes and scholars as well as provide cash and merchandise to local charities. For example, some retailers offer meeting rooms for use by local civic organizations; some supermarkets have begun publishing consumer news with health, cooking, safety, and beauty tips; and others provide public service announcements and sponsor programs on public television stations.

SHORT-TERM OBJECTIVES

Promotional advertising
is a type of advertising where the retailer attempts to increase short-term performance by using product availability and/or price as a selling point.

Promotional advertising, however, attempts to bolster short-term performance by using product availability or price as a selling point. The two most common promotional objectives are increasing patronage of existing customers and attracting new customers.

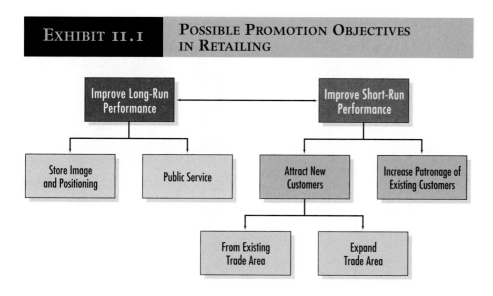

EXHIBIT 11.1 | **POSSIBLE PROMOTION OBJECTIVES IN RETAILING**

INCREASED PATRONAGE FROM EXISTING CUSTOMERS

Increased patronage is probably one of the most common promotion objectives found in retailing. Simply stated, promotion expenditures should be directed at current customers to encourage them to make more of their purchases at the retailer's store. In other words, promotion attempts to make present customers more store loyal.

ATTRACTION OF NEW CUSTOMERS

A second major short-term promotion objective is to increase the number of customers that can be attracted to the store. One approach is to try to attract new customers from the retailer's primary trading area. There are always some households within the primary trading area that, for a variety of reasons, do not patronize the retailer. Perhaps they do their shopping at a retailer close to their place of employment or perhaps they simply do not think that the retailer's store is attractive to their tastes. Maybe they once had a bad experience while shopping there and vowed never to return. A second approach to gaining new customers is to attempt to expand the trading area by attracting customers from the secondary trading area. Here, the retailer might want to consider using different media to expand the geographic coverage of its promotional efforts. A third type of new customer is the customer just moving into the retailer's market area. Mobile consumers, for instance, are generally more prone to use national retailers, because they are familiar with the stores, unless local retailers use promotions to inform them of their offerings.

INTERDEPENDENCE

The two-way arrow in Exhibit 11.1 suggests that although promotion objectives can be established to improve either long- or short-term financial performance, programs designed to achieve either objective will benefit the other as well. Promotion efforts to build long-term financial performance will begin to have an effect almost immediately but also will have a cumulative effect over time. Similarly, efforts to promote short-term financial performance will carry over to affect the long-term future of the retailer.

Wal-Mart sponsors a variety of community and public service programs, which help to promote its role as a good corporate citizen.

LO • 3
List the six steps involved in developing a retailer's advertising campaign

STEPS IN PLANNING A RETAIL ADVERTISING CAMPAIGN

What is involved in planning a retail advertising campaign? As we discussed in Chapter 2, the elements of the retailer's advertising campaign are just a part of the total company's overall strategy. A retailer's advertising campaign is a six-step process:

1. selecting advertising objectives
2. budgeting for the campaign
3. designing the message
4. selecting the media to use
5. scheduling of ads
6. evaluating the results

ADVERTISING OBJECTIVES

The advertising objectives should flow from the retailer's promotion objectives but should be more specific because advertising itself is a specific element of the promotion mix. The objective should be chosen only after the retailer considers several factors that are unique to retailing:

1. *age of store.* New stores or stores seeking to rebuild a poor image need more advertising.
2. *store location.* Stores in poor locations need more advertising.
3. *types of goods sold.* Retailers selling high-image fashion goods generally require more advertising than discounters normally use. These high-fashion retailers also need greater personal selling support to increase inventory turnover.
4. *level of competition.* The greater the level of competition, the more advertising and other promotional activities are needed.

5. *market area size.* The size of the market will often dictate the type and extent of the media that can be used. Also, the larger the market, the greater the need for promotional activities.

6. *supplier support.* Suppliers may provide advertising and other promotional support that will enable the retailer to reduce its expenditures for those activities.

The specific objectives that advertising can accomplish are many and varied, and the one(s) chosen depend on the target market that the retailer is seeking to reach. Examples of common objectives used by retailers include the following:

- Make consumers in your trading area aware that you offer the lowest prices (Wal-Mart's "Always Low Prices").
- Make newcomers in your trading area aware of your existence (The "Welcome Wagon" coupons given to new residents of the area).
- Make customers aware of your large stock selection (Nordstrom promising the shopper a free shirt if they are "out of stock" on the basic sizes).
- Increase traffic during slow sales periods (Subway Sandwiches Shop's "Two-for-One Tuesdays").
- Move old merchandise at the end of a selling season (The "after-Christmas clearance sales" that all retailers use).
- Strengthen your store's image or reputation (Neiman-Marcus's famous Christmas catalog that generates news stories around the world when the catalog is mailed to customers).
- Identify your store with the nationally advertised brands that it sells (Dillard's featuring Tommy Hilfiger clothing in their ads).
- Reposition the image of your store in the minds of consumers ("Softer side of Sears").
- Cultivate new customers (Any of the one-day discounts that a customer gets for opening a charge account with the retailer).
- Make consumers think of you first when a need for your products occurs, especially if they are not commonly purchased (1-800-FLOWERS or the St. Louis service retailer's easy to remember jingle "For a hole in your roof or a whole new roof—Frederick Roofing").
- Retain your present customers (7-Eleven's "Frequent Fill-Up" gasoline program).
- Get customers who previously shopped at your store but no longer do to return to your store ("JCPenney: I Love Your Style").

Although the ultimate goal of every advertising campaign is to generate additional sales, you will notice that increasing sales was not listed above as an advertising objective. That is because other elements of the retail mix, that are outside of advertising's control, could negatively affect sales. The retailer could have, for example, selected the wrong merchandise for its target customers, charged too high a price for the merchandise in comparison with the competition, or improperly displayed the merchandise in the store. Therefore, because increasing sales is usually beyond the total control of the advertising campaign, advertising should not be held solely accountable for increasing total sales.

Regardless of the objective chosen, it must be aimed at a specific market segment and be measurable over a given time period. For example, Holiday Inn recently sought to reposition itself. The object of the chain's "On the Way" campaign is directed at "middle-aged" business travelers and points out that Holiday Inn today isn't the same boring place that their parents took them to when they were kids. The ads conveyed the message that the new Holiday Inn is a completely remodeled operation that caters to the needs of the business traveler. Thus, a good description of this campaign's objective would be "to increase the level of positive feelings among middle-aged business travelers about Holiday Inn by 30 percent over the next six months."

BUDGETING THE CAMPAIGN

A well-designed retail advertising campaign requires money that can be spent on other areas (e.g., more merchandise or higher wages for employees). The retailer hopes that the dollars spent on advertising will generate sales that will in turn produce added profits, which can then be used to finance the other activities of the retailer.

When developing a budget, the retailer should first determine who is going to pay for the campaign (i.e., will the retailer be the sole sponsor or will it get co-op support from other retailers and/or the manufacturer?).

RETAILER ONLY CAMPAIGNS   If a retailer decides to do the campaign alone, the retailer generally uses one of the following methods to determine the amount of money to be spent on the advertising campaign: the affordable method, the percentage-of-sales method, or the task and objective method.

Affordable method
is a technique for budgeting advertising where all the money a retailer can afford to spend on advertising in a given time period becomes the advertising budget.

Percentage-of-sales method
is a technique for budgeting advertising where the retailer targets a specific percentage of forecasted sales as the advertising budget.

1. *affordable method.* Many small retailers use the affordable method by allocating all the money that they can afford for advertising in any given budget period. This may lead to an inadequate appropriation or to a budget that is not related to actual needs. The logic of this approach suggests that advertising does not stimulate sales or profits but rather is supported by sales and profits. However, some retailers have little choice but to use this approach. A small retailer cannot go to the bank and borrow $100,000 to spend on advertising. This is unfortunate, because the small retailer might benefit more from advertising than from more inventory or equipment. Thus, we can see that although the affordable method may not be ideal in terms of advertising theory, it is certainly defensible given the financial constraints that confront the small retailer.

2. *percentage-of-sales method.* In the percentage-of-sales method of budgeting for advertising, the retailer targets a specific percentage of forecasted sales to be used for advertising.

   The percentage of sales that should be used is frequently determined by industry data or the retailer's past experience. Industry data, such as shown in Exhibit 11.2, are often published by trade associations. These figures are averages, however, and do not reflect the unique circumstances and objectives of a particular retailer. A more suitable guide to the level of advertising appropriations is the retailer's past sales experience. The average percentage of advertising expenditures to sales for the past several years can be applied to the current year.

   One of the weaknesses of the percentage-of-sales method is that the amount of sales becomes the factor that influences the advertising outlay. In a correct cause-and-effect relationship, the level of advertising should influence the amount of sales. In addition, this technique does not reflect the retailer's advertising goals. One of the author's early retail mentors said that he never saw business so bad that he couldn't buy all of it that he wanted. By that he meant that when business slowed and all his competitors reduced their ad budgets, this retailer would then increase his ad expenditures. Without the clutter of competitor ads, consumers became more aware of his ads and his sales increased, despite the general sales slowdown affecting the other local merchants.

EXHIBIT 11.2	ADVERTISING EXPENDITURES AS A PERCENTAGE OF SALES

LINE OF TRADE	AD DOLLARS AS PERCENTAGE OF SALES
Apparel and accessory stores	2.4
Auto and home supply stores	1.4
Building materials, hardware, garden	2.2
Catalog, mail-order houses	6.5
Computer and software stores	1.1
Department stores	2.5
Drug and proprietary stores	1.5
Eating places	3.4
Electronic parts, equipment	2.5
Family clothing stores	2.4
Furniture stores	6.5
Grocery stores	1.2
Hardware, plumbing, and heat equipment	4.7
Hobby, toy, and game shops	1.3
Home furniture and equipment stores	3.0
Lumber and other building materials	1.2
Miscellaneous general merchandise stores	4.1
Miscellaneous shopping goods stores	4.1
Radio, TV consumer electronic stores	4.1
Record and tape stores	0.9
Retail stores	3.7
Shoe stores	3.4
Variety stores	1.6
Women's clothing stores	3.1

SOURCE: From *Advertising Ratios & Budgets*, published by Schonfeld & Associates.

Another weakness of this method is that it gives more money to departments that are already successful and fails to give money to departments that with a little extra money could be successful.

Percentage-of-sales does, however, provide a controlled, generally affordable amount to spend, and if spent wisely, it may work out well in practice. Most retailers, especially the smaller ones, do not use ad agencies and lack the sophistication required to adequately implement the task and objective approach. A percentage-of-sales guideline allows the retailer to follow objectives in an affordable, controlled manner. If the dollars are carefully applied in appropriate amounts over the year in such a way that they relate to expected sales percentages in each month, the percentage-of-sales method can work well.

3. *task and objective method.* With the preceding budgeting methods, advertising seemed to follow sales results. With the task and objective method, the logic is properly reversed; advertising leads to sales or some other measure of financial

Task and objective method

is a technique for budgeting advertising where the retailer establishes its advertising objectives and then determines the advertising tasks that need to be performed to achieve those objectives.

EXHIBIT 11.3	TASK AND OBJECTIVE METHOD OF ADVERTISING BUDGET DEVELOPMENT	
	OBJECTIVE AND TASK	ESTIMATED COST
Objective 1:	Increase traffic during dull periods.	
Task *A:*	15 full-page newspaper advertisements to be spread over these dates: February 2–16; June 8–23; October 4–18	$22,500
Task *B:*	240, 30-second radio spots split on two stations and spread over these dates: February 2–16; June 8–23; October 4–18	4,320
Objective 2:	Attract new customers from newcomers to the community.	
Task *A:*	2,000 direct-mail letters greeting new residents to the community	1,000
Task *B:*	2,000 direct-mail letters inviting new arrivals in the community to stop in to visit the store and fill out a credit application	1,000
Task *C:*	Yellow-Page advertising	1,900
Objective 3:	Build store's reputation.	
Task *A:*	weekly 15-second institutional ads on the 10 P.M. television news every Saturday and Sunday	20,800
Task *B:*	one half-page newspaper ad per month in the home living section of the local newspaper	9,500
Objective 4:	Increase shopper traffic in shopping center.	
Task *A:*	cooperate with other retailers in the shopping center in sponsoring transit advertising on buses and cabs	3,000
Task *B:*	participate in "Midnight Madness Sale" with other retailers in the shopping center by taking out 2 full-page newspaper ads—one in mid-March and the other in mid-July	3,000
Objective 5:	Clear out end-of-month, slow-moving merchandise.	
Task *A:*	run a full-page newspaper ad on the last Thursday of every month	18,000
Task *B:*	run 3, 30-second television spots on the last Thursday of every month	14,000
Total advertising budget		$99,020

performance. Basically, the retailer establishes its advertising objectives and then determines the advertising tasks that need to be performed to achieve those objectives. Associated with each task is an estimate of the cost of performing the task. When all these costs are totaled, the retailer has its advertising budget. In short, this method begins with the retailer's advertising objectives and then determines what it will cost to achieve those objectives.

Exhibit 11.3 gives an example of the task and objective method. Notice that the retailer has five major advertising objectives and a total of 11 tasks to perform to accomplish these objectives. The total cost of performing these tasks is $99,020. Although the task and objective method of developing the advertising budget is the best of the three methods from a theoretical and managerial control perspective, it is still not totally adopted by all retailers.

Sometimes accounting errors or errors in forecasting future sales may cause a retailer to exceed its planned advertising spending for a period. McDonald's, for example, in 1996 spent almost $20 million more than planned when an error occurred in its ad agency's media buying department. The agency forgot to account for several weeks of television and radio costs when preparing the retailer's ad budget. Compounding this error was the fact that sales failed to meet the planned goal. This resulted in reduced franchise fees from retailers at a time when the chain was weeks away from its major Summer Olympics campaign.[6]

Many of the major retailers use a combination of the percentage-of-sales method, which they use to keep pace with competitors, and task and objectives, which reflects the different tasks that they must accomplish to reach their objectives. Thus, although the percentages for close competitors are similar, they are still different. For example, in a recent year Circuit City spent 4.9 percent of its sales on advertising whereas rival Tandy spent 5.2 percent; Federated Department Stores spent 3.4 percent whereas May spent 3.8 percent; Sears spent 3.9 percent whereas JCPenney spent 2.8 percent; and Kmart spent 1.5 percent whereas Wal-Mart spent 0.4 percent.[7]

CO-OP CAMPAIGNS

Although most retail advertising is paid for solely by the retailer, sometimes manufacturers and other retailers may pay part of or all the costs for the retailer's advertising campaign.

Vertical cooperative advertising allows the retailer and other channel members to share the advertising burden. For example, the manufacturer may pay up to 40 percent of the cost of the retailer's advertising of the manufacturer's products up to a ceiling of 4 percent of annual purchases by the retailer from the manufacturer. If the retailer spent $10,000 on advertising the manufacturer's products, then it could be reimbursed 40 percent of this amount, or $4,000, as long as the retailer purchased at least $100,000 during the past year from the manufacturer.

There is a strong temptation among retailers to view vertical co-op advertising money as free. Retailers forget, however, that even if the supplier is putting up 50 percent of the expense, they must still pay the other 50 percent. In addition, because the supplier often exercises considerable control over the content of the advertising and its objectives may be different than the retailer's, retailers may be actually paying 50 percent of the supplier's cost of advertising rather than vice versa. Also, suppliers know that it is a common media practice to offer local retailers a discount on rates relative to national advertisers. Thus, suppliers often use local retailers to get them this discount on their ads.

Retailers must, therefore, decide whether they can get a better return on their money with vertical co-op dollars or by total sponsorship of advertising seeking to achieve their objectives.

> **Vertical cooperative advertising**
> *occurs when the retailer and other channel members (usually manufacturers) share the advertising budget. Usually the manufacturer subsidizes some of the retailer's advertising that features the manufacturer's brand(s).*

DOLLAR $ & CENTS

Retailers who realize that it can be more profitable to pass up co-op promotional deals on some product lines will be higher performers.

Horizontal cooperative advertising is when two or more retailers band together to share the cost of advertising. Significantly, this tends to give small retailers more bargaining power in purchasing advertising than they would otherwise have. Also, if properly conducted, it can create substantially more store traffic for all participants. For

> **Horizontal cooperative advertising**
> *occurs when two or more retailers band together to share the cost of advertising usually in the form of a joint promotion of an event or sale that would benefit both parties.*

example, retailers in shopping malls will often jointly sponsor multiple-page spreads in newspapers promoting special events such as "Santa Land" or "Moonlight Madness" sales, whereas downtown merchants usually jointly sponsor "Sidewalk Days" or "Downtown Days" sales. That these events are good traffic generators can be shown by the many malls that have recently turned a very slow shopping night (Halloween) into a very successful "Dead Night." By having a store-to-store program that provides a "safe" place for trick-or-treating, a mall can pull significantly more individuals into each retailer's store than the retailers operating individually could expect to do at the same cost. However, sometimes successful promotions can create too much traffic. This was the case in November 1997 when the rock band Hanson was scheduled for a concert at a new outlet mall in Grapevine, Texas. The concert was scheduled on a Tuesday morning and therefore thousands of teenagers skipped school and created major traffic problems at the mall.[8]

As pointed out in the Behind the Scenes box, sometimes these horizontal co-op programs can produce unexpected negative results.

DESIGNING THE MESSAGE

The next step in developing an advertising campaign is to design a creative message and select the media that will enable the retailer to reach its objectives. In reality these decisions are made simultaneously. Creative messages can't be developed without knowing which media will be used to carry the message to the target market. This text, however, covers media selection after discussing how retailers design their message.

Creative decisions are especially important for retailers because their advertising messages usually are seeking an immediate reaction by the consumer and have a short life span. The development of such messages is one of retailing's major failings. By merely covering up the retailer's name in ads used in your local newspaper or tuning out the retailer's name in a broadcast ad, you will realize that all too often retailers lack originality in their ads, because they will all be the same.

Creative retail ads should seek to accomplish three goals:

1. attract attention and retain attention
2. achieve the objective of the advertising strategy
3. avoid having any errors, especially legal ones

Accomplishing these goals is an extremely difficult task in today's marketplace given the limited time span of the consumer. With newspaper and magazine readership declining and the increased use of the remote control to "surf the tube" during television commercial breaks, it is becoming more and more difficult to first get the consumer's attention and then to hold it.

DOLLAR $ & CENTS

Retailers who realize the importance of creative decisions in their advertising will have higher long-term performance.

MALLS' SALES PROMOTIONS BACKFIRE

Sometimes, the best laid plans of mice and men can go astray. Doral Chenoweth, a nationally recognized consultant on mall promotions, was once asked to list "all the bad mall promotions known to humankind." His response was that it would take a thousand pages just to list them and that wasn't counting his own.

Chenoweth's "three all-time bad mall promotions" all involved animal acts and two resulted in lawsuits.

Number one, and the only one not generating a lawsuit, involved a Michigan mall in the early 1970s, when Flipper was a top children's television show. The mall had Flipper appear in a big pool in the parking lot. Of course, there were many so-called Flippers available for rent at the time, and the mall's marketing director decided to save money and use the cheapest one, a 15-year-old dolphin named Max. You can imagine what happened when, at high noon after the big buildup that attracted thousands of youngsters,

Max flipped into the pool and suddenly died of a heart attack. At least the mall got some publicity out of this sad event when a newspaper columnist suggested that the mall should then have had a sale on fish sandwiches.

An Ohio mall sought to draw customers to its grand opening with a live bear act. A small boy standing too close was mauled and nearly killed in front of everybody. Wire services had a field day with photos. At least everybody in the trading area now knew the mall was open for business.

Even such tame animal acts such as petting zoos are too risky in our present lawsuit-minded society. Consider the Minnesota mall where a billy goat escaped from its pen and ran through the mall. During the chase, two elderly patrons fell into a planter and sued the mall.

Maybe that's why Chenoweth joins David Letterman in saying folks should avoid "stupid pet tricks."

Kmart, for example, recently started using celebrities such as Penny Marshall, Rosie O'Donnell, and Martha Stewart in its ads to attract attention. Small local retailers often use big bold copy offering something exciting in their print ads to get attention. Other retailers use a combination of one or more of the common advertising appeals to gain attention. These appeals are profit, fear, pleasure, vanity, convenience, romance, admiration, and health.

However, even after the retailer gets the consumer's attention, the retailer must hold on to that attention. After all, if consumers have already seen or read the ad, why should they continue to view it again. Some of the common approaches that retailers use to gain repeated viewing include

lifestyle	shows how the retailer's products fit in with the consumer's lifestyle
fantasy	creates a fantasy for the consumer that is built around the retailer's products
humorous	built around humor that relates to using the retailer's products
slice-of-life	depicts the consumer in everyday settings using the retailer's products
mood/image	builds a mood around using the retailer's products

Finally, before using the ad, the retailer should pretest it with both consumer groups and legal experts for errors. For example, Burger King recently ran a national television ad featuring a bookish-looking boy playing a cello badly. After being zapped

This advertisement for Baby Gap stores appeals to the admiration and love parents and grandparents have for their babies and grandchildren.

by a cartoon character, the boy is taken to a Burger King for a Whopper and transformed into a skilled electric-guitar player. Music teachers began complaining to Burger King at once, and some even picketed outside Burger King restaurants.[9] By failing to pretest the ad, Burger King never realized that this ad could offend these teachers. Similarly, Taco Bell ran an April Fool's Day ad claiming that it purchased the Liberty Bell from the government and was going to rename it the "Taco Liberty Bell." Many consumers failed to realize the significance of the date and angrily confronted the company.[10] Likewise, in the Holiday Inn campaign mentioned earlier, the chain's first ad of this campaign was dropped after only one airing. In this ad, a former male, Bob Johnson, returns to his high school reunion as a transsexual and nobody is able to recognize him/her. Holiday Inn hoped this would reinforce the campaign's main message of "the renovations at Holiday Inn." Unfortunately, many viewers found the ad offensive, and it was dropped at once.[11] All of these mistakes could have been detected during a pretest. The Global Retailing box shows that American retailers are not the only ones who sometimes fail to pretest or proof their promotions.

Although these errors are serious enough in nature, they should not present the retailer with legal problems. That does not mean the retailer isn't in danger of violating some laws with its ads, even if it isn't trying to deceive the consumer. Chapter 6 discussed some of the various federal laws governing retail advertising. All too often the retailer runs into trouble with local laws. Some states, for example, limit promotions involving games of chance, others regulate the use of ads with price comparison among retail stores, and others regulate the use of certain words in the description of merchandise. For example, the Pennsylvania Human Relations Commission has issued guidelines against the use of the following words that may tend to discriminate among consumer groups in real estate ads: bachelor pad, couple, mature, older seniors, adults, traditional, newlyweds, exclusive, children, and established neighborhood.

INTERNATIONAL PROMOTION MISTAKES

There are usually significant differences between domestic and foreign retail markets. Nowhere, however, have international retailers had more problems than with regard to promotional activities. However, the real errors in international promotion usually result from retailers trying to write signs and instructions in a foreign language and not checking these signs for errors. Sometimes, poor knowledge of the customer's language results in unintentional but highly "interesting" promotions. Consider the following errors by foreign retailers trying to translate ads into English:

Airline counter in Copenhagen: WE TAKE YOUR BAGS AND SEND THEM IN ALL DIRECTIONS.

Tokyo bar: SPECIAL COCKTAILS FOR LADIES WITH NUTS.

Mexico City discount store: AMERICAN WELL SPEAKING HERE.

Paris dress shop: DRESSES FOR STREET WALKING.

Hong Kong dentist: TEETH EXTRACTED BY LATEST METHODISTS.

Rome laundry: LADIES, PLEASE LEAVE YOUR CLOTHES HERE AND SPEND THE AFTERNOON HAVING A GOOD TIME.

French hotel: PLEASE LEAVE YOUR VALUES AT THE FRONT DESK.

Athens hotel: WE EXPECT OUR VISITORS TO COMPLAIN DAILY AT THE OFFICE BETWEEN THE HOURS OF 9 AND 11 A.M.

Tokyo hotel: THE FLATTENING OF UNDERWEAR IS THE JOB OF THE CHAMBERMAID—TO GET IT DONE, TURN HER ON.

Bangkok dry cleaner: DROP YOUR TROUSERS HERE FOR BEST RESULTS.

Amsterdam hotel: YOU ARE ENCOURAGED TO TAKE ADVANTAGE OF OUR CHAMBERMAIDS.

Swiss restaurant: SPECIAL TODAY . . . NO ICE CREAM.

Hong Kong tailor shop: ORDER YOUR SUMMER SUIT NOW. BECAUSE OF BIG RUSH WE EXECUTE CUSTOMERS IN STRICT ROTATION.

Stockholm furrier: FUR COATS MADE FOR LADIES FROM THEIR OWN SKIN.

Newspaper ad for donkey rides in Thailand: WOULD YOU LIKE TO RIDE ON YOUR OWN ASS?

Still, even native Americans have trouble with English. Consider this sign on a Philadelphia clothing store: SEMI-ANNUAL CLEARANCE SALE! SAVINGS LIKE THESE ONLY COME ONCE A YEAR. And then there was the Concord, California, florist advertising a PRE-GRAND OPENING CLEARANCE.

MEDIA ALTERNATIVES

The retailer has many media alternatives from which to select. In the past, retailers generally categorized media as either print, which included newspaper, magazines, and direct mail, or broadcast, which lumped radio and television together. Now, however, retailers are beginning to classify media from a managerial perspective by recognizing that newspapers and television are mass media alternatives aimed at a total market, whereas radio, magazines, direct mail, and the Internet can be more easily targeted toward specific markets.

NEWSPAPER ADVERTISING   The most frequently used advertising medium in retailing is the newspaper for the following reasons. (1) Most newspapers are local. This is advantageous because most retailers appeal to a local trading area. (2) A low technical skill level is required to create advertisements for newspapers. This is helpful for small retailers. (3) Newspaper ads take only a short time between the time copy is written and when the ad will appear. Because some retailers do a poor job at planning and because they tend to use advertising to respond to crises (poor cash flow, slackening of sales, need to move old merchandise), the short lead time for placing newspaper ads is a significant advantage.

Retail newspaper advertising also has its disadvantages, among them being (1) the fact that a consumer was exposed to an issue of a newspaper does not mean the consumer read or even saw the retailer's ad; (2) the life of any single issue of a newspaper is short—it's read and subsequently discarded; (3) the typical person spends relatively little time with each issue, and the time spent is spread over many items in the newspaper; (4) newspapers have poor reproduction quality, which leads to ads with little appeal; and (5) if the retailer has a specific target market, much of its advertising money will be wasted, because newspapers tend to have a broad appeal. In fact, seldom does the retailer's target market match the circulation of any newspaper. Still, despite these disadvantages, newspapers continue to be the number 1 form of advertising for retailers. Many of the large retailers, such as Wal-Mart, Target, Sears, Mervyn's, and Kmart, use newspapers to deliver their own centrally produced inserts.

TELEVISION ADVERTISING   Today, retailers such as Sears and JCPenney, with their women's apparel, are turning to television advertising as a means of creating an image or position in the marketplace.[12] Research suggests that, over time, pictures retain their effects on consumer memory and evaluations to a greater extent than the verbal messages from media such as radio. However, television advertising is expensive. A half-dozen well-designed television ads may use up the total ad budget. In addition, for the small or even intermediate-sized retailer, a television ad would reach well beyond its trading area. A final disadvantage of television advertising is that competition is high for the viewer's attention. During advertising periods, the viewer may take a break and leave the room, may be exposed to several ads, or use the remote control to "surf" to other channels. "Surfing the tube," however, has become a significant problem recently, as most viewers have remote controls and the number of channels available has increased from three or four in the early 1980s to the more than 500 that are now available on many cable systems. Such an increase in channel availability may cause retailers to view television advertising not so much a mass audience approach but one that can be targeted to specific markets.[13]

Despite the preceding drawbacks, television advertising can be a powerful tool for generating higher sales. The American public spends more time relaxing in front of the television than in any other recreational activity. Television has broad coverage; more than 98 percent of homes in the United States have at least one television set. Most of these sets are color and offer the retailer a vehicle in which both sight and sound can be used to create a significant perceptual and cognitive effect on the consumer.

The widespread development of cable television has made television attractive to small local retailers. Local cable operators have been selling advertising on cable channels, which is quite competitive with that of newspaper advertising. However, retailers just starting to use TV advertising may be hard pressed to find a niche because so many others have already been seeking to fill niches too. The point to remember, as we mentioned earlier, is to sell both the products and store image at the same time. Cable television has also provided a new means of television advertising—the 24-hour shopping channels.

RADIO ADVERTISING

Many retailers prefer to use radio because it can target messages to select groups. In most communities, there are five to 10 or more radio stations, each of which tends to appeal to a different demographic group. Retailers can use radio, through the use of proper variations in volume and types of sounds, to develop distinctive and appealing messages and to introduce a store and its image to current and potential customers. In short, there is a lot of flexibility. Also, many radio audiences develop strong affection and trust for their favorite radio announcers. When these announcers endorse the retailer, the audience is impressed.

Radio advertising also has its drawbacks. Radio commercials, especially the uncreative ones, are not easily saved or referred to again like print media ads. In fact, some media experts claim that radio's lack of creativity is a major shortcoming. All too often, ad agencies and radio stations lack the creativity to help local retailers. The CBS radio network, claiming the last truly great radio campaign was Motel 6's "And we'll leave the light on for you," recently hired top creative individuals to stimulate better radio commercials, at both the national and local levels.[14] In addition, radio is frequently listened to during work hours or driving to and from work (drive time) and tends, over time, to become part of the background environment. Also, because radio is nonvisual, it is impossible to effectively demonstrate or show the merchandise that is being advertised. And, finally, radio signals tend to cover an area much larger than a retailer's trading area. Therefore, a good portion of the retailer's advertising dollars may be wasted.

MAGAZINE ADVERTISING

Relatively few local retailers advertise in magazines, unless the magazine has only a local circulation. Nationally based retailers such as JCPenney will allocate some of their advertising budget to magazines. Usually, the retail ads that these retailers place in magazines are institutional.

Magazine advertising can be quite effective. In relation to newspapers, magazines perform well on several dimensions. They have a better reproduction quality, they have a longer life span per issue, and consumers spend more time with each issue of their magazine than their newspaper. An added benefit is that featured articles in a magazine can put individuals in the mood for a particular product class. For example, a feature article on home remodeling in *Better Homes and Gardens* can put people in a frame of mind to consider purchasing wallpaper, carpeting, tiling, draperies, paint, and other home improvement items.

The major disadvantage of using magazines is that the long lead time requirements prevent price appeal advertising, as well as the lack of urgency in its messages.

DIRECT MAIL

Direct marketing can be a powerful addition to the retailer's promotional strategy. With direct mail, the retailer can precisely target its message at a particular group as long as a good mailing list of the target population is available. Bloomingdale's, for example, uses a customer database to select targeted recipients for each of its roughly 300 annual catalog and promotional mailings. In addition, direct mail provides retailers a personal contact with individual consumers who share certain valued characteristics. Thus, although all Bloomingdale's customers receive the Christmas catalog, only those recently purchasing a men's suit will receive a postcard promoting a sale on shirts and ties. Such messages can reach the consumer without being noticed by the competition. Finally, direct-mail results can generally be easily measured, thus providing the retailer with important feedback information.

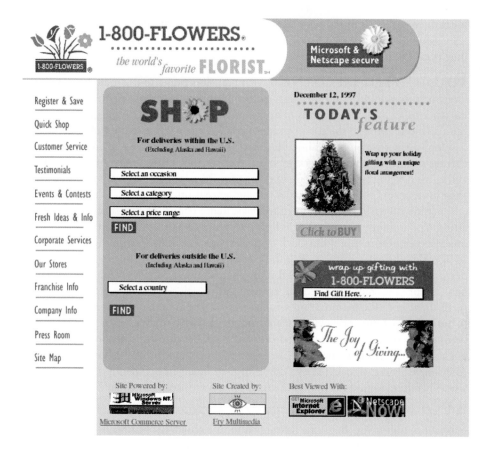

The web site for 1-800-FLOWERS (www.1800flowers.com) provides information on various floral arrangements based on the customer selecting an occasion, category, or price range. Also, the user of this web site can interact with the site to obtain a variety of other relevant information.

On the negative side, direct-mail advertising is relatively expensive per contact or message delivered. Also, the ability to reach the target market depends totally on the quality of the mailing list. If the list is not kept current, advertising dollars will be wasted. A related problem is the incidence of unopened or unexamined mail, especially when it is addressed to "occupant" or is mailed using third-class postage.

INTERNET[15]

Within the next few years, the number of web users is expected to exceed 200 million. Most of the 50 million users in 1997 made their purchases on-line strictly for convenience. After all, the disconnect between seeing a picture of a lamp and then finding a store where that lamp is sold disappears when you can order on-line. The web site for 1-800-FLOWERS (www.1800flowers.com) is a good example. On the web, the customer can get a better idea of the various arrangements available than by calling the florist and asking for a description. In the future, however, the customer is expected to be lured by price. This emphasis on price is already seen in the equipment necessary to go on-line. In 1996, only one-third of American households had invested the $2,000 needed for a PC with the modem and software to shop the Internet. However, within the next few years, the cost for such equipment will likely drop to the $500-to-$700 range. At this time, computers will be as cheap, as dependable, and as simple to use as televisions, and, as noted throughout every chapter in this text, the high-performance retailers will be ready for these shoppers.

Successful retailers, even the small ones, already realize that the cost of setting up and maintaining a commercial web site is minuscule compared with the cost of building additional stores. Thus, as Internet shopping becomes more popular and the technology that enables it becomes cheaper, prices on the Web will drop below prices in traditional stores. In addition, the retailer's web site will help it promote and advertise its business.

MISCELLANEOUS MEDIA The retailer can advertise by using media other than those previously identified: yellow pages, outdoor advertising, transit advertising (on buses, cabs, subways), electronic information terminals, specialty firms such as Welcome Wagon, and shopping guides (newspaper-like printed material, but with no news). Each of these is usually best used to reinforce other media and should not be relied on exclusively unless the retailer's advertising budget is minimal. Most retailers look on these media vehicles as geared more toward particular product advertising by manufacturers. However, that doesn't mean a retailer can't make use of them.

DOLLAR **$** & **C**ENTS

Retailers who understand the advantages and disadvantages of the various media and select the most cost effective ones will be higher performers.

MEDIA SELECTION

To select the best media, the retailer needs to remember the strengths and weaknesses of each medium and needs to determine the coverage, reach, and frequency of each medium that is being considered.

Coverage refers to the theoretical maximum number of consumers in the retailer's target market that can be reached by a medium—not the number actually reached. For example, if a newspaper is circulated to 70 percent of the 20,000 households in a retailer's trading area, then the theoretical coverage is 14,000 households.

Reach, however, refers to the actual total number of target customers who come into contact with the ad message. Another useful term is cumulative reach, which is the reach achieved over a period of time.

Frequency is the average number of times each person who is reached is exposed to an advertisement during a given time period.

Different media can be evaluated by combining knowledge on the cost of ads in a medium and the medium's reach and cumulative reach. The most commonly used method for doing this is the cost per thousand method (CPM). The most appropriate way to compute the CPM is to divide the cost for an ad or series of ads in a medium by the reach or cumulative reach. If a newspaper ad cost $500 and the cumulative reach was 13,860, then the cost per thousand is $36.08 [($500/13,860) × 1,000]. The newspaper may have actually reached 38,200 households in the community, but if only 13,860 were reached in the retailer's trading area, then that is the relevant statistic.

The CPM is useful for comparing similar-sized advertisements in the same media type (e.g., two local newspapers). But, when comparing different media (TV versus newspapers), the CPM can be misleading. A medium such as television may cost more

Coverage
is the theoretical maximum number of consumers in the retailer's target market that can be reached by a medium and not the number actually reached.

Reach
is the actual total number of target customers who come into contact with an advertising message.

Cumulative reach
is the reach which is achieved over a period of time.

Frequency
is the average number of times each person who is reached is exposed to an advertisement during a given time period.

Cost per thousand method (CPM)
is a technique used to evaluate advertisements in different media based on cost and reach or cumulative reach. The cost per thousand is the cost of the advertisement divided by the reach or cumulative reach which is then multiplied by 1,000.

Impact
refers to how strong an impression an advertisement makes and how well ultimately leads to a purchase.

based on CPM, but if it has a significantly greater impact, it may be the better buy. Impact refers to how strong an impression an advertisement makes and how well it ultimately leads to a purchase. As a result of the increase in media alternatives and consumers spending a stable amount of time on the various medias, CPM has had a fivefold increase in the past decade.

SCHEDULING OF ADVERTISING

When should a retailer time its advertisements to be received by the consumer? What time of day, day of week, week of month, and month of year should the ads appear? No uniform answer to these questions is available for all lines of retail trade. Rather, the following conventional wisdom should be considered.

1. Ads should appear on, or slightly precede, the days when customers are most likely to purchase. If most customers shop for groceries on Thursday through Saturday, then grocery store ads might appear on Wednesday and Thursday.
2. Advertising should be concentrated around the times when individuals receive their payroll checks. If they get paid at the end of each month, then advertising should be concentrated at that point.
3. If the retailer has limited advertising funds, it should concentrate its advertising during periods of highest demand. For example, a muffler repair shop would be well advised to advertise during drive time on Thursday and Friday when the consumer is aware of his or her problem and has Saturday available for the repair work.
4. The retailer should time its ads to appear during the time of day or day of week when the best CPM will be obtained. Many small retailers have found the advantages of late-night television.
5. The higher the degree of habitual purchasing of a product class, the more the advertising should precede the purchase time.

Many retailers use advertising to react to crises (e.g., an unexpected buildup of inventory due to slow sales). Of course, if this is the situation, the timing of ads is not planned in advance. This, however, is an ineffective method of scheduling retail advertising.

ADVERTISING RESULTS

Will the advertising produce results? It depends on how well designed the ads are and how well the advertising decisions were made. A consistent record of good retail advertising decision making is achieved only if the retailer effectively plans its advertising program.

Advertising effectiveness
is the extent to which the advertising has produced the result desired or helped to achieve the advertising objective.

Some retailers will try systematically to assess the effectiveness and efficiency of their advertising. Advertising effectiveness refers to the extent to which the advertising has produced the result desired (i.e., helped to achieve the advertising objective). Advertising efficiency is concerned with whether the advertising result was achieved with the minimum effort (e.g., dollars).

Advertising efficiency
is concerned with whether the advertising result was achieved with the minimum financial expenditure.

The effectiveness or efficiency of a retailer's advertising can be assessed on a subjective basis. Simply ask yourself: Are you satisfied with the results produced? Do you believe you achieved those results at the least cost? Most, but not all, ineffective advertising is due to 10 errors:

1. The retailer may be bombarding the consumer with so many messages and sales that any single message or sale tends to be discounted. A retailer that has a major sale every week will tend to wear out its appeal.
2. The advertising may not be creative or appealing. It may be just more "me too" advertising, in which the retailer does not effectively differentiate itself from the competition.
3. The advertisement may not give the customers all the information they need. The store hours or address may be absent because the retailer assumes that everyone already knows this information. Or information may be lacking on sizes, styles, colors, and other product attributes.
4. The advertising dollars may have been spread too thinly over too many departments or merchandise lines.
5. There may have been poor internal communications among salesclerks, cashiers, stock clerks, and management. For example, customers may come to see the advertised item, but salesclerks may not know the item is on sale or where to find it, and cashiers may not know the sale price. Worst yet, for a variety of reasons, the advertised product may not be available when the consumer seeks to purchase it.
6. The advertisement may not have been directed at the proper target market.
7. The retailer didn't consider all media options. A better buy was available, but the retailer didn't take the time to find out about it.
8. The retailer made too many last-minute changes in the advertising copy, increasing both the cost of the ad and chances for errors.
9. The retailer took co-op dollars just because they were "free" and therefore thought to represent a good deal.
10. The retailer used a medium that reached too many individuals not in the target market. Thus too much money was spent on advertising to individuals who were not potential customers.

MANAGEMENT OF SALES PROMOTIONS AND PUBLICITY

LO • 4
Explain how retailers manage their sales promotion and publicity

Retailers also use sales promotion, which provide some type of short-term incentive, and publicity to increase the effectiveness of their promotional efforts. The role of sales promotions and publicity in the retail organization should be consistent with and reinforce the retailer's overall promotion objectives.

ROLE OF SALES PROMOTION

Sales promotion tools are excellent demand generators. Many can be used on relatively short notice and can help the retailer achieve its overall promotion goals. Furthermore, sales promotions can be significant in helping the retailer differentiate itself from competitors. Retailers have long known that consumers will change their shopping habits and brand preferences to take advantage of sales promotions, especially those that offer something special, different, or exciting.

Retailers must remember that because all stores are able to shop the same vendors, that merchandise alone doesn't make a store exciting. In-store happenings of sales

EXHIBIT 11.4	TYPES OF SALES PROMOTIONS

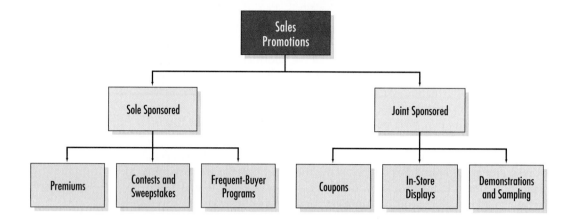

promotion can generate excitement. Many retailers fail to recognize that the role of sales promotion is quite large and may represent a larger expenditure than advertising. They do not recognize this because of their poor record-keeping systems. They know the cost of advertising because most of that is paid to parties outside the firm. However, the cost of sales promotions often includes many in-store expenses that the retailer does not trace to promotion activities. If these costs were properly traced, many retailers would discover that sales promotions represent a sizable expenditure. Therefore, promotions warrant more attention by retail decision makers than is typically given.

TYPES OF SALES PROMOTION

As a rule, high-performance retailers break sales promotions into two categories: those in which they are the sole sponsors and those involving a joint effort with other parties. These are shown in Exhibit 11.4.

SOLE-SPONSORED SALES PROMOTIONS
Just like advertising, sales promotions are an expense to the retailer that may or may not be shared with others. With sole-sponsored sales promotions, the retailer has complete control over the promotion but is also completely responsible for the costs. Although there may be some overlap in the sponsorship of these promotions, retailers generally consider these sales promotions to be sole-sponsored:

1. Premiums are extra items offered to the customer when purchasing a promoted product. Premiums are used to increase consumption among current consumers and persuade nonusers to try their promoted product. Generally, the retailer is solely responsible for such programs, although some exceptions may occur. An example of a successful premium is when McDonald's gives away a free toy (e.g., a Teenie Beanie Baby) with the purchase of a Happy Meal.

2. Contests and sweepstakes, which face legal restrictions in some states, are designed to create an interest in the retailer's product and encourage both repeat purchases and brand switching. Although such programs produce only one grand

Premiums
are extra items offered to the customer when purchasing a promoted product.

Contests and sweepstakes
are sales promotion techniques in which customers have a chance of winning a special prize based on entering a contest in which the entrant competes with others or a sweepstakes in which all entrants have an equal chance of winning a prize.

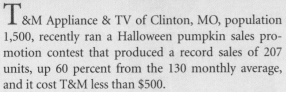

PUMPKIN PROMOTION

T&M Appliance & TV of Clinton, MO, population 1,500, recently ran a Halloween pumpkin sales promotion contest that produced a record sales of 207 units, up 60 percent from the 130 monthly average, and it cost T&M less than $500.

The way the contest worked was that customers came into the store in early October to get a free pumpkin to carve. They came back with their entry on October 26 or 27 and returned once again to see all the entries and vote for their favorite for the People's Choice award. They came back a fourth time after the October 29 judging during the Moonlight Madness costume contest and parade on Main St. to pick up their pumpkin.

The major expense for the contest was $250 in prize money. The store purchased 150 pumpkins for $95. Attractively designed and well-written orange flyers cost $75, and store decorations such as straw bales cost $35, for a grand promotion cost of $455.

The pumpkins made a great display in the store for Moonlight Madness, Decker said. A half-page of the store's full-page newspaper ad was devoted to the contest. T&M plans to make this promotion an annual event.

T&M recommends these helpful hints to retailers considering a similar promotion.

- Have flyers printed in September.
- When all the pumpkins are gone, tell customers they still can enter with their own pumpkin.
- Put finished pumpkins on paper plates when they are on display in the store—they will leak.
- Start giving away the pumpkins early in October—every day they are in a customer's home will remind the customer of the store.
- Take promotional flyers to the local library, day-care centers, and public schools.
- Keep a list of customers who receive pumpkins and those who return them.
- Put the carved pumpkins throughout the store so customers will see all the store's merchandise.
- Coordinate the promotion with other holiday promotions in the store's area.
- Telephone the local newspapers about printing photos and stories about the promotion.

Based on information supplied by Marvin Lurie of the North American Retail Dealers Association.

prize winner, the selection of a prize that will appeal to a large segment of the market and the addition of smaller prizes make such promotions very popular with consumers. Many local restaurants use weekly drawings to not only generate business but also to track their customers. As the Behind the Scenes box shows, one retailer used a simple little Halloween pumpkin decoration contest to generate both awareness and business.

3. Frequent buyer programs are still rapidly growing as retailers begin to appreciate the importance of combining this promotion with their database system to solidify their relationship with the customer. Neiman-Marcus, for example, offers a free trip for two to London when the customer purchases $125,000 on their Neiman-Marcus credit card. In addition, they offer smaller rewards, starting with membership in their InCircle Club when the customer reaches $3,000.

Frequent buyer programs are a form of sales promotion program where buyers are rewarded with special rewards, that other shoppers are not offered, for purchasing often from the retailer.

JOINT-SPONSORED SALES PROMOTIONS
Jointly sponsored sales promotions offer retailers the advantage of using OPM—other people's money. Although in some cases such promotions require the retailer to relinquish

Coupons are a major form of sales promotion as evidenced by the more than 269 billion money-off coupons that U.S. manufacturers offered consumers in 1997. These coupons can be redeemed by shoppers at retailers that stock the manufacturers' products.

Coupons

are a sales promotion tool where the shopper is offered a price discount on a specific item if the retailer is presented with the appropriate coupon at time of purchase.

In-store displays

are promotional fixtures or displays that seek to generate traffic, highlight individual items, and encourage impulse buying.

some control, the co-sponsor's monetary offering to the retailer more than makes up for it. Retailers generally consider these promotions to be jointly sponsored:

1. **Coupons** offer the retail customer a discount on the price of a specific item. In 1997, American manufacturers offered consumers more than 269 billion money-off coupons worth more than $180 billion. Although only 2 percent of these coupons are redeemed, this represents a win-fall worth more than $500 million to retailers because they receive, on average, a 10 cents coupon handling fee from the manufacturers. Recently, Procter & Gamble has been testing various programs to lower everyday prices and discontinue coupons. However, this move has met strong consumer, retailer, newspaper (they make big money on coupons, also), and political opposition.[16]

   Some manufacturers are testing the use of the Internet for coupon delivery. By going to the Cool Savings web site (www.coolsavings.com), consumers can get coupons for a number of major products. The manufacturer benefits by getting vital demographic information on the consumer and is able to track redemptions rates on all coupons issued.

2. **In-store displays** are promotional displays that seek to generate traffic, highlight individual items, and encourage impulse buying. Such displays offer manufacturers a captive audience for their products in the retailer's store. (Remember, the retailer doesn't care which brand the customer purchases, just as long as the purchase is made in its store.) As a result, the manufacturer is willing to pay for the

right to "rent" the space necessary for this display from the retailer. Chapter 13 provides a greater discussion on in-store displays.

3. Demonstrations and sampling are in-store presentations intent on reducing the consumer's perceived risk of purchasing a product. These presentations on the ease, convenience, and/or product superiority are paid for by the manufacturer at a price that is usually higher than the retailer's cost for providing that service.

> Joint demonstrations and sampling promotions don't have to just be with the retailer's suppliers or other retailers. Every spring, retailers, especially malls, invite landscapers and other lawn care experts onto their grounds to promote their own merchandise and services. Consumers are just getting ready to prepare their lawns for the summer and love the convenience of being able to visit with all the lawn experts at one location. In addition to bringing merchandise for sale, many of these lawn professionals also bring samples of their work to place either in the mall hallways or parking lot. This is really a case of using OPM because the retailer and malls don't have to use their money for this promotion, the lawn care folks are willing to do it as a form of promotion for themselves.

> **Demonstrations and sampling**
> *are in-store presentations with the intent of reducing the consumer's perceived risk of purchasing a product.*

EVALUATING SALES PROMOTIONS

Because sales promotions are intended to help generate short-term increases in performance, they should be evaluated in terms of their sales and profit-generating capability. As with advertising, sales promotions can also be evaluated with sophisticated mathematical models. However, the development and use of such models is usually not cost-effective.

A simpler approach is to monitor weekly unit volume before the sales promotion and compare it with weekly unit volume during and after the promotion.

PUBLICITY MANAGEMENT

Publicity was defined at the outset of this chapter as non-paid-for communications of information about the company or products, generally in some media form. This definition is actually misleading. Although the retailer does not directly pay for publicity, it can be very expensive to have a good publicity department that plants the commercially significant news in the appropriate places. It may be even more expensive to create the news that is worth reporting. For example, although Macy's Fourth of July fireworks display in New York, Dominos' sponsoring a car in the Indianapolis 500 race, and McDonald's Ronald McDonald Houses all create favorable publicity, they are expensive. Earlier, we discussed Taco Bell's infamous Liberty Bell ad. Although Taco Bell did spend more than $400,000 on the ad, the April Fool's hoax did generate more than 400 newspaper and television stories across the country.[17] Whether the money could be better spent in other ways is debatable.

Recently, Dallas restaurateur Dee Lincoln, co-founder of Del Frisco's Double Eagle Steakhouse, made great use of publicity when she paid a record $80,000 for a 1,309-pound Maine-Anjou crossbreed at Denver's National Western Stock Show. An opposing bidder said at the time her winning bid was accepted, "Lady, you must either be really crazy or have too much money." Well, Dee Lincoln isn't crazy. What Dee wanted and got was hundreds of thousands dollars worth of publicity for her high-quality steakhouses (that were mentioned in Chapter 2), the newest of which had just opened in Denver. In addition to having her name/picture in all the Denver media, as the

When Dee Lincoln, co-founder of Del Frisco's Double Eagle Steakhouse, paid a record $80,000 for a 1,309-pound Maine-Anjou cross-breed at Denver's National Western Stock Show, she got more than that amount in free publicity.

show's highest bidder she got to perform other highly visible duties for the remainder of the cattle show. And she even got her picture and restaurant in this book.[18]

We will not pursue a detailed discussion of publicity management, because most retailers do not formally have a publicity department or even a person in charge of publicity. Rather, let us mention that publicity (like other forms of promotion) has its strengths and weaknesses. Perhaps the major advantages are that it is objective and credible and appeals to a mass audience. The major disadvantages are that publicity is difficult to control and time. Except for annual events, such as a charity fund-raiser, publicity may be hard to plan, and if it is planned, the cost can become exorbitant. In addition, sometimes retailers can experience bad publicity in the form of events that are beyond its control.

For example, consider how Food Lion failed to properly handle the negative publicity resulting from ABC's November 1992 airing of a "Prime Time Live" segment. This segment featured undercover reporters, hired with the support and training from a union trying to organize the chain, charging that Food Line had altered expiration dates on various meat items, unsanitary conditions causing health risks for both the employee and shopper, and other assorted atrocities. Even though, the courts in 1997 awarded Food Lion $5.5 million from ABC for fraud (the broadcaster admitted to staging certain egregious scenes and to leaving other scenes supporting Food Lion on the cutting room floor), Food Lion was the big loser in the court of public opinion. Food Lion failed to have a plan to counteract this negative publicity. The chain should have expressed concern and outrage at such a story, remember you can express concern without admitting guilt. Such actions caused many to believe that ABC was really telling the truth.[19]

Rumors are a different story. Only in very rare circumstances does one ever find out who started these false stories about successful retailers. In the past, there have been rumors about snakes being found in one discounter's overcoats and about a well-known fast-food chain using worms in its hamburgers. It seems that the events never happen to the individual telling the story, but always to a friend of a friend. There was a false story involving IKEA, the furniture and housewares chain.[20] It went like this: An unsuspecting shopper, usually a woman, brings an IKEA cactus home. After a few days, she notices that the plant is moving and—could it be?—breathing. She calls IKEA, and someone from the store commands, "Get out of the house—now." Later, two men arrive and confiscate the cactus. The reason: It's filled with tarantula eggs and about to explode, spewing deadly insects.

"Every time we open a new store, [the rumor] hits," Pam Diaconis, IKEA's head of PR, notes. "We have yet to have anyone call who actually has one. It's always a friend of a friend."

The truth is, tarantulas just don't camp out in cacti. But it was a great story until the facts got in the way. Still, such examples do point out the need for retailers to plan for the unexpected, in case something goes wrong. For example, supermarkets should be prepared to handle stories (true or false) of someone's having tampered with packaged items. Similarly, a restaurant might need to be prepared to handle a hepatitis outbreak.

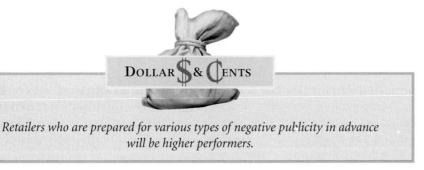

DOLLAR $ & CENTS

Retailers who are prepared for various types of negative publicity in advance will be higher performers.

If publicity is formally managed, it should be integrated with other elements of the promotion mix. In addition, all publicity should reinforce the store's image.

STUDENT STUDY GUIDE

SUMMARY

LO • 1 WHAT ARE THE FOUR BASIC COMPONENTS OF THE RE-
TAILER'S PROMOTION MIX AND HOW ARE THEY RELATED WITH
OTHER RETAILER DECISIONS?   A retailer's promotion mix is comprised of advertising, sales promotions, publicity, and personal selling. All four components need
to be managed from a total systems perspective and must be integrated not only with
each other but with the retailer's other managerial decision areas such as location, merchandise, credit, cash flow, building and fixtures, price, and customer service. In addition, the retailer must realize that its promotional activities may be in conflict with the
way other channel members use promotion.

LO • 2 WHAT ARE THE DIFFERENCES BETWEEN A RETAILER'S
LONG-TERM AND SHORT-TERM PROMOTIONAL OBJECTIVES?   A re-
tailer's promotional objectives should be established to help improve both long-
and short-term financial performance. Long-term, or institutional, advertising is an attempt by the retailer to gain long-term benefits by selling the store itself rather than the
merchandise in it. Retailers seeking long-term benefits generally have two long-term
promotion objectives: creating a positive store image and public service objectives.

Short-term, or promotional, advertising attempts to bolster short-term performance by using product availability or price as a selling point. The two most common
promotional objectives are (1) increasing patronage of existing customers and (2) attracting new customers.

LO • 3 WHAT ARE THE SIX STEPS INVOLVED IN DEVELOPING A RE-
TAILER'S ADVERTISING CAMPAIGN?   A retailer's advertising campaign is a
six-step process: (1) selecting advertising objectives, (2) budgeting for the campaign,
(3) designing the message, (4) selecting the media to use, (5) scheduling of ads, and (6)
evaluating the results.

The advertising objectives should flow from the retailer's promotion objectives
and should consider several factors that are unique to retailing; such as the store's age
and location, the merchandise sold, the competition, size of the market, and level of
supplier support. The specific objectives that advertising can accomplish are many and
varied, and the one(s) chosen depend on the above factors.

When developing a budget, retailers must decide whether they can get a better return on their money with vertical co-op dollars or by total sponsorship of advertising
seeking to achieve their objectives. In budgeting advertising funds, retailers tend to use
the affordable method, the percentage-of-sales method, or the task and objective
method. Although most retail advertising is paid for solely by the retailer, sometimes
manufacturers and other retailers may pay part of or all the costs for the retailer's advertising campaign. For example, vertical cooperative advertising allows the retailer
and other channel members to share the advertising burden whereas horizontal cooperative advertising is when two or more retailers band together to share the cost of
advertising.

Retailers must develop a creative retail ad that accomplishes three goals: attracts
and retains attention, achieves its objective, and avoids having any errors. Some of the
common approaches that retailers use to gain repeated viewing include showing how

the retailer's products fit in with the consumer's lifestyle, creating a fantasy for the consumer that is built around the retailer's products, having the campaign built around humor that relates to using the retailer's products, depicting the consumer in everyday settings using the retailer's products, and building a mood around using the retailer's products. Before using any ad, the retailer should pretest it with both consumer groups and legal experts for errors.

Once the budget is established, it should be allocated in such a way that it maximizes the retailer's overall profitability. In determining allocations, retailers can choose from a variety of media alternatives, primarily newspapers, television, radio, magazines, direct mail, and the Internet. Each medium has its own advantages and disadvantages. To choose among the media, the retailer should know their strengths and weaknesses, coverage and reach, and the cost of an ad.

After the retailer selects a medium, it must decide when the ad should appear. Although no uniform answer to this question is available, conventional wisdom suggests that the ads should (1) appear on, or slightly precede, the days when customers are most likely to purchase, (2) be concentrated around the times when individuals receive their payroll checks, (3) be concentrated during periods of highest demand, (4) be timed to appear during the time of day or day of week when the best CPM will be obtained, and (5) precede the purchase time, especially for habitually purchased products.

Advertising results can be assessed in terms of efficiency and effectiveness. Effectiveness is the extent to which advertising has produced the result desired. Efficiency is concerned with whether the result was achieved with minimum cost.

LO•4 **HOW DO RETAILERS MANAGE THEIR SALES PROMOTION AND PUBLICITY?** Retailers use sales promotion, which provides some type of short-term incentive, and publicity to increase the effectiveness of their promotional efforts. The role of sales promotions and publicity in the retail organization should be consistent with and reinforce the retailer's overall promotion objectives.

Sales promotion tools are excellent demand generators. Many can be used on relatively short notice and can help the retailer achieve its overall promotion goals. Retailers usually break sales promotions into two categories: those where they are the sole sponsors (premiums, contests and sweepstakes, and frequent-buyer programs) and those involving a joint effort with other parties (coupons, displays, and demonstrations and sampling).

Although retailers may not directly pay for publicity, the indirect cost can be quite significant. Most retailers do not have formal publicity departments or directors, but some of the more progressive retailers do. The major advantage of publicity is that it is objective, credible, and appeals to a mass audience. The major disadvantage is that publicity is difficult to control and schedule.

TERMS TO REMEMBER

advertising	secondary trading area
sales promotion	institutional advertising
promotional advertising	affordable method
publicity	percentage-of-sales method
personal selling	task and objective method
primary trading area	vertical cooperative advertising

horizontal cooperative advertising
coverage
reach
cumulative reach
frequency
cost per thousand method (CPM)
impact
advertising effectiveness

advertising efficiency
premiums
contests and sweepstakes
frequent buyer program
coupons
in-store displays
demonstrations and sampling

REVIEW AND DISCUSSION QUESTIONS

LO • 1 WHAT ARE THE FOUR BASIC COMPONENTS OF THE RETAILER'S PROMOTION MIX AND HOW ARE THEY RELATED WITH OTHER RETAILER DECISIONS?

1. Why should a retailer feature price and not product features in its ads for national branded products? Should the same rules be applied for private label products?
2. How could the promotional efforts of other members of a retailer's channel affect the retailer's promotional decisions?

LO • 2 WHAT ARE THE DIFFERENCES BETWEEN A RETAILER'S LONG-TERM AND SHORT-TERM PROMOTIONAL OBJECTIVES?

3. Explain how a long-term promotional objective can affect the firm over the short run.
4. Should the promotional objectives for Neiman-Marcus be the same as those for JCPenney or your hometown's local department store? Explain your answer.

LO • 3 WHAT ARE THE SIX STEPS INVOLVED IN DEVELOPING A RETAILER'S ADVERTISING CAMPAIGN?

5. What factors that are unique to retailing should be considered before selecting an advertising objective? Which one of these factors is most important?
6. From the creative standpoint, it is said that a retail ad should accomplish three goals. What are these goals?
7. Describe the three methods available to the retailer for determining the amount to spend on advertising? Which one is the best one to use? Which one is most commonly used by small retailers?
8. What is cooperative advertising? When should it be used?
9. What methods should a retailer use in making the media selection decision?
10. How should an advertising campaign be evaluated?

LO • 4 HOW DO RETAILERS MANAGE THEIR SALES PROMOTION AND PUBLICITY?

11. What is sales promotion? How is it different from advertising?
12. What is publicity? Isn't this always "free" to the advertiser? How does publicity fit into a retailer's promotional efforts?

SAMPLE TEST QUESTIONS

LO•1 WHICH OF THE FOLLOWING AREAS SHOULD NOT BE TAKEN INTO CONSIDERATION BY A RETAILER WHEN FORMULATING A PROMOTIONAL STRATEGY?

a. the retailer's credit customers
b. the price level of the merchandise
c. merchandise/inventory levels
d. the retailer's building and fixtures
e. the retailer's monthly rent

LO•2 THE TWO OBJECTIVES OF INSTITUTIONAL ADVERTISING INCLUDE

a. creating a positive store image and public service promotion
b. increasing patronage from existing customers and attraction of new customers
c. publicity and sales promotion
d. advertising a sale and generating store traffic
e. using "other people's money" and using "co-op" money

LO•3 WHICH OF THE FOLLOWING SHOULD NOT BE PART OF THE CAMPUS SHOPPE'S ADVERTISING CAMPAIGN'S OBJECTIVES? THE CAMPUS SHOPPE DESIRES

a. to increase awareness of its two locations
b. among incoming freshmen
c. to 40 percent
d. over the next three months.
e. All the above belong in the retailer's advertising objectives.

LO•4 CONSUMER PREMIUMS ARE CONSIDERED TO BE A FORM OF

a. joint-sponsored sales promotion
b. publicity that uses OPM
c. advertising
d. personal selling
e. sole-sponsored sales promotion

APPLICATIONS

WRITING AND SPEAKING EXERCISE   You are doing a summer internship at a new sporting goods super store that is located a couple miles from your campus of 33,000 students. The store is large, 50,000 square feet, and sells all types of sporting goods equipment and accessories. The forecasted sales volume for the first year of operations is $4,750,000.

The store manager wants you to prepare a presentation on how money should be allocated for advertising during the store's first year of operation and what method you used in determining the advertising budget.

RETAIL PROJECT Find two current advertisements using the same media (newspaper, television, radio, Internet, etc.) that you think are effective in achieving their objectives and two that you don't think are effective.

Explain what you think each ad's objectives were and why you categorized them as you did.

In reviewing the ineffective ads, was something wrong with the creative design, did they fail to hold the consumer's attention, did they use the wrong media to reach their intended market, etc.? How would you improve these ads?

CASE To "Co-op" or Not To "Co-op"

While doing your summer internship with P&B Appliances, your boss, Jim Kenderdine, tells you that he has been approached by Sony with a co-op advertising offer on large-screen televisions, but he was wondering if his limited advertising money could better be spent on advertising cell phones, especially with the college students coming back in the fall. He wants you to advise him on his problem.

Kenderdine has $5,000 that he can spend on advertising either the Sony televisions or cell phones. With regard to the televisions, Sony has offered to pay 50 percent of the cost of several television and newspaper ads. This would allow P&B to purchase $10,000 of advertising for a $5,000 investment. No co-op deal is being offered by the supplier of the cell phones, but cell phones are fast becoming a popular item among college students, and Kenderdine believes they could benefit substantially from $5,000 in advertising.

Kenderdine believes that with the additional advertising, sales of the large-screen televisions, which have a 50 percent gross margin, would increase from $80,000 to $110,000 for the month. Cell phones, however, although having a 60 percent gross margin, only are planned to generate sales of $18,000. Kenderdine believes that with $5,000, the amount P&B would have to pay with the Sony deal, of key radio and campus newspaper ads, he could increase cell phones sales volume to $60,000.

Given this information, what should Mr. Kenderdine do?

PLANNING YOUR OWN RETAIL BUSINESS

Your Uncle Nick has agreed to sell you his supermarket where you have worked for seven years after graduating from college. Uncle Nick is 72 years old and is ready to step down from day-to-day management.

After operating Crest on your own for six months, you begin to analyze how you can increase store traffic and consequently annual sales and profitability. During a recent trip to the Food Marketing Institute convention, you ran across several successful grocers. Some of them competed largely on price whereas others competed more on promotion and advertising.

You have decided to pursue a heavy promotion-oriented strategy. Consequently, you have budgeted to increase advertising by $20,000 monthly, or $240,000 annually, and to also have a weekly contest in which you give away $100 in groceries to 25 families. This will cost you (52 × $100 × 25) $130,000 annually.

Currently, Crest Supermarket serves a trade area with a two-mile radius where the density of households is 171 per square mile. Seventy percent of these households shop at Crest an average of 45 times per year. Of those that visit Crest, 98 percent make a purchase that averages $24.45. Crest operates on a 25 percent gross margin.

You estimate that with your new promotion program Crest's trade area radius will increase to 2.5 miles. Assume that all other relevant factors remain constant (171 households per square mile, 70 percent of household shopping Crest, 98 percent closure rate, $24.45 average transaction size, 25 percent gross margin percent). Is the planned promotion program and investment of an additional $370,000 annually a profitable strategy?

HINT: Assume the trade area is circular and thus its size in square miles can be computed as pi (22/7) times the radius of the circle squared. The total square miles of the trade area can be multiplied by the number of households per square mile to obtain total households in the trade area. This, in turn, can be multiplied by the percentage that shop at Crest, which, in turn, can be multiplied by the average number of trips annually to Crest, which will yield total traffic. This traffic statistic can be multiplied by the percentage of visitors who make a purchase, which will yield total transactions. You should be able to figure out the rest of the computations on your own that are needed to determine whether the promotional strategy is profitable.

NOTES

1. "Limited To Boost Ad Spending Tenfold," *Advertising Age,* September 29, 1997: 1.

2. The definitions of the four types of promotion used in this section are from *Dictionary of Marketing Terms* (Chicago: American Marketing Association, 1988) and reprinted with permission of the American Marketing Association.

3. This list was developed by the late Louis Bing, Bing Furniture Company, Cleveland, Ohio.

4. "McD's Gets No Break Today," *Advertising Age,* June 16, 1997: 28; "Hey, McDonald's," *Advertising Age,* June 2, 1997: 30; "McDonald's Pledge of 55-Second Service Ends in a Lot Less," *Wall Street Journal,* May 30, 1997: B12.

5. "McDonald's Dual Ad Campaign Leading to a Single Result: Trouble," *Advertising Age,* March 10, 1997: 24; "Nissan's Ad Campaign Was a Hit Everywhere but in the Showrooms," *Wall Street Journal,* April 8, 1997: A1, A14.

6. "Budgeting Bungle at Leo Burnett Leaves McDonald's in a Pickle," *Wall Street Journal,* July 8, 1996: B2.

7. The above percentages are based on author's calculations of public information contained in annual reports, conversations with key company executives, and *Advertising Age's* "Annual Measure of Media Spending."

8. "Good Band, Bad Plan," *Dallas Morning News,* November 22, 1997: 22A.

9. "Music Teachers Say String Players a Break from Burger King," *Wall Street Journal,* December 16, 1996: B1.

10. "Not Everybody Is Cracking Up over 'Taco Liberty Bell,'" *Wall Street Journal,* April 2, 1996: B6.

11. "Holiday Inn Boots 'Bob Johnson,'" *Advertising Age,* February 3, 1997: 14; "Fleeting Commercial Fame," *USA Today,* March 17, 1997: 6B.

12. "Penney's Touts Fashion to Regain Edge from Sears," *Advertising Age,* March 10, 1997: 6.

13. "Narrowcasting TV Spots by Area No Longer Dream," *Advertising Age,* April 14, 1997: S2; "Making a Stand in Bid for Upscale TV Viewers," *Advertising Age,* April 14, 1997: S24.

14. "King of All Radio," *Fortune,* April 14, 1997: 110–114.

15. The material in the section was developed from "Wired Kingdom," a special section of the January 1997 issue of *Chain Store Age.*

16. "Companies Want to Cut Coupons, but Consumers Demand Bargains," *Marketing News,* May 12, 1997: 15; "Move to Drop Coupons Puts Procter & Gamble in Sticky PR Situation," *Wall Street Journal,* April 17, 1997: A1, A10.

17. "The Quest for Free Ink, Free Air," *USA Today,* May 19, 1997: 3B.

18. Based on an idea from Alan Peppard's column in the February 8, 1997, issue of the *Dallas Morning News* and conversations with Ms. Lincoln and her staff.

19. "Food Lion Injured, Panel Says, but Journalism Takes Bigger Hit," *Advertising Age,* May 12, 1997: 44.

20. "So, Let's Go Hunt Alligators in the Sewers," *Business Week,* February 11, 1991: 32.

CUSTOMER SERVICES AND RETAIL SELLING

Nordstrom, by providing high-quality customer service, has become a leader in relationship retailing and has many loyal long-term customers.

OVERVIEW

In this chapter, we demonstrate how customer services, including retail selling, generate additional demand for the retailer's merchandise. We also examine the determination of an optimal customer service level. We conclude the chapter by looking at the unique managerial problems that retailers of services must address.

LEARNING OBJECTIVES

After reading this chapter, you should be able to

1. explain why customer service is so important in retailing
2. describe the various customer services that a retailer can offer
3. explain how a retailer should determine which services to offer
4. describe the various management problems involved in retail selling, salesperson selection, and training and evaluation
5. describe the retail selling process

Relationship retailing *is comprised of all the activities designed to attract, retain, and enhance long term relationships with customers.*

CUSTOMER SERVICE

The retailers that survive in the 21st century will be those that engage in relationship retailing. Relationship retailing includes all the activities designed to attract, retain, and enhance long term relationships with customers. No longer will retailing be driven by the expansion of large homogeneous chains offering only low prices. Successful retailers in the next century will be those that concentrate on building long-term relations with "loyal" customers by promising and consistently delivering high-quality products, complemented with good service, shopping aids to ease the purchase process, and honest prices. The U.S. Office of Consumer Affairs revealed in a recent study that it takes five times as much money to get a new consumer into your store for the first time as it does to get a "former customer" to come back to your store.[1] As a result, today's retailers are not trying to maximize the profit on each transaction but are instead seeking to build a mutually beneficial relationship with their customers. The operating maxim for high-performance retailers in the 21st century will be, "Proper management of relationships will help you convert consumers into customers, which will produce long-term profits." The Global Retailing box describes how one of Ireland's most successful grocers uses such a philosophy.

High-performance retailers can develop these relationships with their customers by offering two benefits:

1. *financial benefits* that increase the customer's satisfaction, such as the frequent buyer discounts or product upgrades already offered by some supermarkets, airlines, and hotels
2. *social benefits* that increase the retailer's social experience with the customer. For example, Nordstrom's employees not only drop notes to their frequent shoppers; they maintain a file on each customer that lists family members, their birthdays, preferences, and sizes. Thus no customer is a stranger to a Nordstrom salesperson more than once.

The Impact Model of Retailing (Exhibit 12.1) is based on retailing's three most basic tasks: getting consumers from your trading area into your store, converting these consumers into paying customers, and doing so in the most efficient manner possible. Chapter 7 described how retailers determine their trading area, and the earlier chapters of Part 4, Chapters 8–11, discussed the first task: how retailers budget for and then select their merchandise, then price and promote this merchandise. Likewise, Chapter 8 also covered the third task by describing the basic method available to retailers for controlling inventory cost. The next two chapters discuss the second and most important task—converting the consumers from your trading area into customers who are loyal toward your store.

Due to all the cost cutting following the recent span of consolidation and retrenchment by retailers over the past decade, this second task is even more difficult to do. Stores today are so standardized in their physical layout, with each one carrying the same merchandise styles and colors, that customers can't tell them apart. More important, many of these stores are staffed with an indifferent and undertrained salesforce. As a result, there is a complete breakdown of what is essential for a successful retailer: exciting merchandise, backed up by outstanding service, and personal selling that generates loyal customers. In recent years, the intense competition from discounters caused many retailers to lower customer service levels as a means of staying price

WHERE THE CUSTOMER IS KING

GLOBAL RETAILING

In Ireland, when you discuss excellence in customer service, you are talking about Superquinn, a large upscale supermarket chain. The chain's major differentiating point connects directly to what its management calls "The Boomerang Principle" (i.e., it runs its business entirely from the perspective of persuading customers to come back again and again). So, every decision that management makes flows from that philosophy. They ask, "Will this help to bring the customer back next week, and the week after?" If the answer is "No, but it will make us a fast buck now," then they don't do it.

It's the long-term income stream that the chain's management team concentrates on winning. And in addition to being the framework for all the merchandise carried, it provides direction and focus to how management listens to customers, how they seek to serve them, and how they try to meet and even anticipate their needs.

According to Feargal Quinn, the president, "That's what sets us apart. But remember in the fiercely competitive environment we operate in, while being different in this way, we also have to make sure we stay in business long enough for the customers to come back to us. It doesn't mean we take our eye off this week's bottom line."

How difficult is it to maintain such high consistency in customer service? "The sheer difficulty of actually doing it is why the notion of customer service gets so much lip-service rather than action," Quinn responded. "There's no single magic answer, of course. But one facet of the challenge that I'd recommend involves the customers directly. We have this system under which our staff is empowered to reward customers if they find us slipping up—if they catch us making 'goofs,' like giving them a wobbly trolley or if they have to wait behind more than three people in line at the checkout. If you do this with the right blend of good humor and common sense, it becomes a fun game for all concerned, while focusing on keeping those standards up, day in and day out."

Does this sound like an American retailer?

SOURCE: Based on "Where the Customer Is King," *Progressive Grocer*, June 1995: 73.

competitive. These retailers thought that reduced service levels would lower their operating costs, thus allowing increased price competitiveness. No wonder a 1997 study found that department (both conventual and discount) stores tied for 11th in the ranking of customer service providers—well behind the U.S. Postal Service, local telephone companies, and banks.[2]

One notable retailer to go in the opposite direction is Abercrombie & Fitch which has paid particular attention to the responsiveness of its sales staff to customer questions and needs and as a result it is estimated on any given day that 70 percent of Abercrombie & Fitch's merchandise is sold at full price.[3]

Retailers seeking to survive into the 21st century must differentiate themselves by meeting the needs of their customers better than the competition. There is general agreement that a basic retailing strategy for creating this competitive advantage is the delivery of high-quality service.[4] This service must meet or exceed the customer's expectations. Thus, retailers have again come to realize that customer service is a strength. Instead of frustrating the customer by not having the necessary stock on hand or the proper selling support on the sales floor, today's successful retailers realize that customer service is a major demand generator for their merchandise. However, it is important that retailers also remember that when you encourage your customers to establish high expectations, the slightest disappointment in service can be a catastrophe.

EXHIBIT 12.1	THREE BASIC TASKS OF RETAILING

1 Get Consumers into Your Store **2** Convert Them into Customers **3** Operate as Efficiently as Possible

SOURCE: Based on *Management Horizon's* Impact Model of Retailing. Used with permission.

Even Nordstrom, the retailer most famous for its outstanding service, can't please all its customers all the time. One study quoted an unhappy customer as saying: "Never during our visit did she ask me how much money I wanted to spend, who my favorite designers were...or what fashion pet peeves I had."[5] Although Nordstrom really did not make any mistakes, it just failed to live up to the very high expectations that its customer wanted. As the Seattle-based chain has grown into a national retailer, its vendors have become increasingly critical of its decentralized management, which has caused it to be late with many "hot" new items.[6] Not having these "hot" items in stock when customers want them predictably lowers customer service and satisfaction.

Customer service consists of all those activities performed by the retailer that influence (1) the ease with which a potential customer can shop or learn about the store's offering, (2) the ease with which a transaction can be completed once the customer attempts to make a purchase, and (3) the customer's satisfaction with the transaction. These three elements are the pretransaction, transaction, and posttransaction components of customer service. Some common services provided by retailers include alterations, fitting rooms, delivery, bridal registries, check cashing, in-home shopping, extended shopping hours, gift wrapping, charge accounts, parking, layaway, and merchandise return privileges. It must be remembered that none of these services are altruistic offerings; they are all designed to entice the customers with whom the retailer is seeking to develop a relationship.

Retailers should design their customer service program around pretransaction, transaction, and posttransaction elements of the sale to obtain a differential competitive advantage. After all, in today's world of mass distribution, most retailers have access to the same merchandise, and therefore, retailers can seldom differentiate themselves from others solely on the basis of merchandise stocked. The same can be said regarding location and store design advantages. Retailers can, however, obtain a high degree of differentiation through the satisfaction of customers by their customer service programs. In fact, service excellence is a hallmark of America's most successful retailers. Service excellence pays off in greater customer loyalty because such service can actually insulate retailers from price, merchandising, location, and design competition. Some firms are just now beginning to look at customer defections as a means of

Customer service

consists of all those activities performed by the retailer that influence (1) the ease with which a potential customer can shop or learn about the stores' offering, (2) the ease with which a transaction can be completed once the customer attempts to make a purchase, and (3) the customer's satisfaction with the transaction.

targeting areas of the retail mix for improvement to gain greater customer loyalty.[7] After all, a loyal customer in addition to spending a larger share of his or her money at your store will be less susceptible to your competition's temporary price cuts.

A retail shopping experience is more than negotiating your way through the store, finding the merchandise you want, interacting (or not interacting) with store staff, and paying for the merchandise. It also involves your actions before and after the store visit. Therefore, serving the customer before, during, and after the transaction can help to create new customers and strengthen the loyalty of present customers. If customer service before the transaction is poor, the probability of a transaction occurring will decline. If customer service is poor at the transaction stage, the customer may back out of the transaction. And if customer service is poor after the transaction, the probability of a repeat purchase at the same store will decline. The customer who visits a store and finds the service level below expectations or the product "out of stock" will become a transient customer. This transient, or temporary, customer will seek to find a store with the level of customer service that he or she thinks is appropriate. At any given moment, for all lines of retail trade, there are a significant number of transient customers. The retailer with a superior customer service program will have a significant advantage in making these transients loyal customers. Thus customer service can play a significant role in building a retailer's sales volume.

Five research studies illustrate the role of customer service in generating demand. The first study deals with grocery retailing, the second with department store retailing, the third with hotel service, the fourth with handling customer complaints at both retailers and governmental agencies, and the fifth concerns customer satisfaction and dissatisfaction with shopping centers.

In the first study, consumers were asked to weigh the importance of 37 store characteristics.[8] Eleven of these characteristics were found to be crucial in determining store-switching behavior. In other words, when a customer's present store didn't score well on these characteristics, the consumer tended to switch grocery stores. Of these 11 characteristics, seven were directly related to customer service: (1) open late hours, (2) new advertised items are available, (3) good assortment of nonfood merchandise, (4) check cashing service, (5) short wait for check-out, (6) good parking facilities, and (7) good supplies of items on special. In grocery retailing, customer service is a demand generator.

The second study examined consumer attitudes and perceptions about department store shopping. Results of this research indicated that shoppers have 10 common complaints about department store shopping for women's clothing:[9]

1. "Every time you want to try on a new item, you have to get dressed and leave the fitting room."
2. "The department store sells clothes too far in advance, such as selling winter clothes at the end of the summer."
3. "When they have a big sale, they don't have enough help and you have to wait too long."
4. "If I need a different size while I'm in the fitting room, there are no salespersons to get it for me."
5. "You're not allowed to bring enough garments into the fitting room."
6. "Department stores have less and less individuals to serve me."
7. "The lines to pay at department stores are too long for me to shop during lunch hour."
8. "There's no way of telling which size will best fit me without trying the garment on."

Transient customer *is an individual who is dissatisfied with the level of customer service offered at a store or stores and is seeking an alternative store(s) with the level of customer service that he or she thinks is appropriate.*

9. "You have to go from place to place all over the store to get a refund or exchange."
10. "When they have a clothing sale, they don't have enough stock in the most popular items."

This list suggests that department stores can gain a major competitive advantage by upgrading their customer service levels, especially in fitting rooms.

The third study involved a survey of how complaints were handled in various businesses and governmental agencies. The study found that the proper handling of complaints by retailers could increase return on investment in service programs by 35 to 400 percent because 70 percent of consumers who have had their complaints addressed in a satisfactory manner became the retailers' most loyal customers. This is an extremely important study for retailers to remember. All too often, a retailer fails to understand that the extra expense of taking care of an unhappy customer is less than the cost of a single advertisement in the local paper or on the local radio or television. Yet, the results of taking care of that customer can be much more profitable.

DOLLAR $ & CENTS

High-performance retailers invest in customer service programs to increase their return on investment.

The fourth study asked business travelers what their biggest complaints about hotel service were. Their major complaints were poor attitude of employees, rooms not ready, worn facilities/poor maintenance, no record of reservations, and problems with checking in and checking out. As a result of this study, many hotels began to empower employees with the ability to make adjustments on the guest's bill. This, according to one expert, is "the opportunity to make things better for the guest and ensure that they return to our hotel."[10]

The final study asked shoppers visiting shopping centers to identify their top complaints and their best experiences.[11] The top complaints included:

- mall crowding
- parking lots with poor lighting, long walks to shops, or those that charge fees
- groups of teenagers hanging out in the mall making shoppers feel insecure
- no visible security
- poor interior layout, whether it be confusing, unkept, poorly lighted, loud, or laced with bad smells
- shabby treatment and lack of sales help
- shortage of variety
- prices higher than expected

On the other hand the best experiences included:

- pleasant interior—bright, sweet smelling, relaxing, modern, clean, with adequate seating and tidy bathrooms
- a broad variety of merchandise

- polite, helpful and enthusiastic sales associates who had information about not only their stores, but the entire mall
- a variety of food and clean eating areas
- competitive prices
- unusual or distinctive products, beyond the merchandise available in other malls, catalogs, power stores, strip malls, discount warehouses and television
- good parking
- entertainment, with carousels, clowns, book signings, crafts and fashion shows.

Although these five studies have dealt with different industries, their conclusions—good customer service generates demand and builds customer loyalty—are true for all types of retail trade.

Customer service cannot happen all by itself but must be integrated into all aspects of retailing. That is why the high-performance retailers in the 21st century will know that the demand for their merchandise is not just price elastic, as economists would have us believe, but also *service elastic.* This means that an increase in service levels of 1 percent will result in a more than 1 percent increase in sales.

MERCHANDISE MANAGEMENT

One of the best ways a retailer can serve a customer is by having in stock the merchandise that the customer wants. There are few things more disturbing to a customer than to make a trip to a store for a specific item only to discover that the item is out of stock; that is why when Nordstrom opened a store in Dallas, it carried more than 150,000 pairs of shoes. It wanted the customers to be able to find any style or color in their size.[12] Basically, the better the store is at allocating inventory in proportion to customer demand patterns, the better the customer will be served.

BUILDING AND FIXTURE MANAGEMENT

Retailers' decisions regarding building and fixtures can also have a significant effect on how well the customer is served. For example, consider how the following building and fixture dimensions might influence customer service: heating and cooling levels, availability of parking space, ease of finding merchandise, layout and arrangement of fixtures, placement of restrooms and lounge areas, location of check cashing, complaint, and returns desks, level of lighting, and width and length of aisles.

This list is not comprehensive; it is intended merely to provide evidence for the proposition that customer service considerations need to be taken into account in building and fixture decisions.

PROMOTION MANAGEMENT

Promotion provides customers with information that can help them make purchase decisions. Therefore, retailers should be concerned with whether the promotion programs that they develop help the consumer. The following questions can help the retailer assess whether its promotion is serving the customer:

1. Is the advertising informative and helpful?
2. Does the advertising provide all the information that the customer needs?
3. Are the salespersons helpful and informative?
4. Are the salespersons friendly and courteous?

Using Customer Services to Capture a Market

Thirty-six-year-old Chris Zane, who while still a high school student purchased the bike shop where he worked, is now the largest independent bicycle dealer in the New Haven market. How did he do it? By offering the best customer services in the market.

Fifteen years ago, Zane launched his first serious assault on his competitors by offering one-year service guarantees (covering parts and labor on all routine service) when everyone else was only promising 30 days. As they matched this posttransaction service guarantee, he simply increased his until he was offering a two-year guarantee. Then, he learned that some dealers in other markets were offering five-year service guarantees. Figuring that five years is the life of most bikes, he started offering a lifetime of free service.

In reality, this lifetime guarantee was a safe bet for Zane based on percentages. Most customers will use the guarantee during the first year they have the bike. Actually, just 25 percent come back after that. Zane figured that his liability for lifetime free service would be minuscule, even by making it retroactive.

The guarantee soon became the foundation of his business. When an individual came in with a six-year-old pump that had worn out, Zane gave him a new one. Why should Zane do this?

Because he understood what a customer's lifetime of business would be worth. For example, the guy with the $60 pump had a premium model. This was a chance to have him fall in love with his shop. Because Zane had a good relationship with the manufacturer, he knew he could send the broken pump back and get credit, no questions asked—so the cost of the return was zero. The potential payoff, however, was big enough that even if Zane had been forced to absorb the cost of the pump (about $30), it still would have made economic sense for him to take it back.

Within months, the individual had already come back twice and spent $200 on accessories (a $100 net to Zane). And Zane was betting that he'll get first shot at the sale when it came time to buy a new premium bike. At an average cost of $400 for a bike, with a 35 percent margin, he stood to make another $140 and that didn't include the intangibles. Such a customer will probably spread the gospel to other serious and heavy-spending biking enthusiasts—Zane's ideal prospects.

In addition, Zane also found a transaction service that not only made customers happy, but also went straight to his bottom line. A couple of years before, Zane was talking to a customer who was in the

5. Are the salespersons easy to find when needed?
6. Are sufficient quantities available on sales promotion items?
7. Do salespersons know about the ad and what's being promoted and why?

This list also is not comprehensive but is intended only to show that customer service issues need to be considered in designing promotional programs. That is why retailers today are always surveying their customers and use other programs, such as mystery shoppers, to get the answers to the above questions.

PRICE MANAGEMENT

Price management will also influence how well the customer is served. Are prices clearly marked and visible? Is pricing fair, honest, and straightforward? Are customers told the true price of credit? These questions suggest that the pricing decision should not be isolated from the retailer's customer service program.

cellular phone business and learned that although distributors charged approximately $225 for a telephone, the telephone company would actually pay a $250 commission for each activation. Zane called Bell Atlantic immediately, proposing that his bike shop become a retailer. He wanted to give away a telephone to anyone who bought a bike—a "value-added" for customers that would actually earn him a net profit of $25. Bell Atlantic saw the bike shop as an alternative channel of distribution, making him the first retailer in the area to offer free telephones. He activated 500 telephones the first year, which earned him $12,500, plus another $25 a telephone in co-op advertising allowances. His profits are larger today, because the cost of telephones fell to about $165, but commissions have remained the same.

Although Zane's transaction and posttransaction services were his best selling tools, they sometimes make customers suspicious of his prices. Zane knew his prices were competitive, but customers wanted to find that out for themselves. So, he started advertising a 90-day-price-guarantee program (a pretransaction service): find the same bike anywhere in Connecticut for less, and he'll give you the difference plus 10 percent. His sales went up 54 percent the first year, compared with his normal 25 percent growth rate, and he handled 20 percent more customers.

However, such guarantees also present downside. His service guarantee, for example, has limited his opportunity for growth. Shortly, after he initiated the guarantee, he was forced to drop a line of bicycles because the warranty work was killing his profits. Although the manufacturer covered the cost of parts, Zane was obliged to provide free labor, and the number of repairs was too great given his low margins. With a lifetime of free service on every bike sold looming ahead of him, he dropped the brand.

Attention to detail is an integral part of Zane's basic business philosophy, but it's also critical to his survival. Wal-Mart is coming to town, as is Ski Market, a category-killer sporting-goods store. "When a category killer comes in you have to have all your programs in place," says Zane. "You have to work to be as strong as they and kill them where they're weak. And customer service is where they're weakest."

He is not, in fact, comfortable with merely serving his niche, as a good specialty retailer probably ought to be. He wants to lure customers from Wal-Mart and reckons that the giant's presence will actually help him because "there will be more inexpensive bikes out there that need to be fixed." Soon, he'll have a better point-of-sale computer system that will help him track customers more effectively and do more targeted marketing.

SOURCE: Based on information supplied by Chris Zane and used with his permission.

CREDIT MANAGEMENT

The management of credit, both in-house and bank card, should also be integrated into the customer service program. Credit, along with the store's "layaway" plans, is a significant aid in both customers' developing loyalty with a store and helping them purchase merchandise. Retailers' credit policies influence the customers' perception of how well they are being serviced. Some retailers, such as Kmart, Toys "Я" Us, and Planet Hollywood, have recently begun issuing their own co-branded credit cards. They hope that these cards, in addition to increasing store loyalty and generating credit transaction profits, will add to the retailer's database so that the retailer can improve future promotions. For example, Planet Hollywood's Visa card provides card holders a one-year membership in the Planet Hollywood Express Club, which translates to discounts on food, drinks, and merchandise, and immediate first-available seating at the themed restaurant.[13]

A RECAP

Integration with the elements of the store's retail mix is important when retailers develop their customer service programs. Much of what has already been discussed in this book somehow, either directly or indirectly, relates to one of the three broad categories of customer service: pretransaction, transaction, and posttransaction. Successful retailers view customer service as a means of gaining an advantage in competition with other retailers. As a result, even discounters are beginning to empower all their employees, not just management, to do whatever is reasonable to take care of the customer. In our Winners & Losers box, we describe how one small independent bike dealer became a force in the industry by emphasizing customer service.

DOLLAR $ & CENTS

High-performance retailers will integrate customer service decisions with their merchandise, promotion, building and fixtures, price, and credit management decisions.

LO • 2
Describe the various customer services that a retailer can offer

COMMON CUSTOMER SERVICES

Much of the discussion on location, merchandise, pricing, and promotion in previous chapters had implications for serving the customer. However, many of the more popular types of customer services have not been mentioned or have received sparse coverage. Let us review some of them.

PRETRANSACTION SERVICES

Pretransaction services are services provided to the customer prior to entering the store.

The most common pretransaction services, which are provided to the customer prior to entering the store, are convenient hours and information aids. Each of these makes it easier for the potential customer to shop or to learn of the store's offering.

CONVENIENT HOURS   The more convenient the operating hours of the store are to the customer, the easier it is for the customer to visit the store. Convenient operating hours are the most basic service that a retailer should provide to its customers. Retailers must ascertain what their customers want and weigh the cost of providing those wants against the additional revenues that would be generated. If your target customers, because of their work schedules, want longer hours, the retailer should do so provided it is profitable. Some retail entrepreneurs are now serving their time-deprived customers with round-the-clock food service, auto repair services, and medical services. Some merchant groups have started banning together to start a concierge service at the local commuter train station, which, for a fee paid by the merchants, will return video rentals, handle their dry cleaning, pick up prescriptions, and do other shopping chores for the commuter.

A retailer's operating hours also depend on the competition. If a competitor is willing to stay open until 9 P.M. six nights per week to serve customers, it would probably not be wise to close every night at 6 P.M. unless a lease provision requires it.

Retailers must also remember that some states still have blue laws, which were described in Chapter 6, that may restrict the retailer's ability to open on Sundays.

INFORMATION AIDS As we already mentioned, the retailer's promotional efforts help to inform the customer. Many retailers offer customers other information aids that help them enter into intelligent transactions. Today, for example, with the click of a mouse consumers can get information about a retailer's return policies, credit policies, merchandise availability, and even merchandise prices on the web site of most major retailers. There are even cyberspace "malls" (e.g., www.dreamshop.com) on the Internet where consumers experience first-hand a walk through the various stores in the virtual mall. Other web retailers, such as The GAP (www.gap.com), let consumers move images of the latest fashions around on the screen to get a feel for how the different outfits will mix and match if they come to the local Gap to make a purchase.[14]

In addition, retailers regularly offer demonstrations that instruct the customer on how to use, operate, or care for a product. For example, as means of getting away from price competition, the Dorothy Lane Market in Dayton has a reputation for pampering its upscale customer base. One of its stores offers weekly cooking classes. Customers can also pick out recipes off stacks of cards and placards in the wine section that describe the various wines and with which meal to serve them.[15] Not surprisingly, stores that offer these demonstrations can increase their market share because many customers are afraid to buy a new item without first knowing how to use it. If the store offers classes or specific instruction on the use of a product, the customer will be less resistant to trying and ultimately purchasing the product. For many items that are technologically sophisticated or represent significant departures from traditional ways of doing something, the customer will tend to buy from the retailer that offers instruction.

Some firms will also offer booklets that provide useful consumer information. In this regard, Sears provides its customers with many informational booklets including *Floor Coverings: Their Selection and Care; Kitchen Planning Basics; How to Select Furniture; How to Select Hand and Power Tools;* and *Fabric Care Manual.* These booklets can be important sources of pretransaction information to the consumer. During the summer months, nurseries and lawn care retailers provide lawn and gardening tips on local radio and television shows.

Other retailers explain the store policy on returns, matching a competitor's price, and credit in their ads. Some retailers with out-of-the-way locations even use such ads to describe how to reach their stores. Retailers that provide such information are not only serving potential and existing customers but are also building goodwill.

TRANSACTION SERVICES

In the past, retailers believed that transaction services meant having salespersons who would personally take care of an individual customer. But for the high-performance retailers in the 21st century, the term transaction services will mean getting customers out of the store as fast as possible with the conveniences they seek once they have made their purchase. The most important transaction services are credit, layaway, gift

Transaction services are services provided to customers when they are in the store shopping and transacting business.

Many gasoline stations have increased their transaction service by installing gas pumps that can accept debit and credit cards.

wrapping and packaging, check cashing, personal shopping, merchandise availability, personal selling, and the sales transaction itself. These services help to facilitate transactions once customers have made a purchase decision.

CREDIT

One of the most popular transaction-related services offered by retailers is consumer credit. Offering credit can be of great service to the customer because it enables shopping without the need to carry large sums of money. In addition, it allows the customer to buy now and pay later. Credit can be a benefit to the retailer also: It increases sales by increasing impulse buying, as well as the purchase of expensive items. Of course, in-house credit can decrease profits if the credit policy is too lenient.

LAYAWAY

When a layaway service is offered, the customer can place a deposit (usually 20 percent) on an item, and in return the retailer will hold the item for the customer. The customer will make periodic payments on the item and, when it is paid for in full, can take it home. In a sense, a layaway sale is similar to an installment credit sale; however, the retailer retains physical possession of the item until it is completely paid.

A negative issue of using layaways is that many items are not picked up by the customer. This results in the retailer having to return a "dated" item to regular inventory where a markdown, usually larger than the first customer's initial payment, is required.

GIFT WRAPPING AND PACKAGING Customers are typically better served if their purchase is properly wrapped or packaged. The service may be as simple as putting the purchase into a paper bag or as complex as packaging crystal glassware in a special shatterproof box to prevent breakage.

The retailer must match its wrapping service to the type of merchandise it carries and its store image. A discount grocer or hardware store does quite well by simply putting the merchandise into a paper sack. Specialty clothing stores often have dress and suit boxes that are easy to carry home. Some more upscale retailers are even putting the purchased merchandise in decorated shopping bags or prewrapped gift boxes. This reduces considerably the number of packages that must be gift wrapped.

Many larger department stores and most gift shops offer a gift wrapping service. Usually there is a fee for gift wrapping unless the purchase price exceeds some limit, usually $10 or $25. Many other stores also offer a courtesy wrap, which consists of a gift box and ribbon, or a store paper that identifies the place of purchase. This type of wrap is not only a goodwill gesture but a form of advertising.

CHECK CASHING Most retail stores offer some form of check cashing service. The most basic type of check cashing service consists of allowing customers to cash a check for the amount of purchase. Most retailers now have on-line acceptance systems on their registers, which make check cashing as easy as using a credit card. Other retailers provide their customers with an identification card that entitles them to pay for merchandise with a personal check. More liberal check cashing retailers allow qualified customers to cash checks for amounts in excess of the purchase price, usually not for more than $20. This practice has resulted in some supermarket chains becoming the biggest check cashing operators in some cities, bigger than the banks.

PERSONAL SHOPPING The recent changes in family lifestyles have left many Americans without enough time to accomplish all they need and want to do. Other shoppers hate browsing in stores more than they hate doing household chores. Successful retailers have sought to aid these consumers with personal shopping services. Personal shopping is the activity of assembling an assortment of goods for a customer. This can be as varied a service as picking out clothing, filling a telephone order (many retailers now offer key customers an 800 telephone number), assembling a supply of groceries and sending them to the customer's home, or selecting a wedding gift. Personal shopping services are one of the best ways to build a relationship with the customer.[16]

Personal shopping *occurs when an individual who is a professional shopper performs the shopping role for another; very upscale department and specialty stores offer personal shoppers to their clientele.*

MERCHANDISE AVAILABILITY Merchandise availability as a service simply relates to whether the customers can find the items they are looking for in the store. Three causes exist for the customer being unable to find an item: The item can be out of stock, it isn't located where the customer needs it, or the customer doesn't know what is really needed. The retailer can minimize out-of-stock conditions by good merchandise management, although some out-of-stock situations are inevitable. The customer's ability to locate a needed item in the store can be increased by having, in addition to proper in-store signing, displays, and helpful and informative employees, a well-designed layout. The problem of not knowing "what is really needed" is more difficult to overcome. Most major retailers have a bridal registry, for example, the phone number for Chicago's Marshall Field's is 1-800-2-I DO I DO; Sears recently introduced a program covering all its product lines for all occasions, such as Mother's Day, Father's Day, Christmas, and birthdays.[17]

Merchandise availability is an element of customer service that many retailers take for granted, but they shouldn't. When customers do not find items they are looking for in a store—regardless of the cause—they will remember their bad experiences and in all probability tell their friends.

PERSONAL SELLING

Another important transactional service that retailers can offer is a strong, customer-oriented retail salesforce. A good job of personal selling, resulting in a need-satisfying experience, or even the use of suggestive selling, if done well, will greatly enhance customer satisfaction. Personal selling is discussed in detail later in this chapter.

SALES TRANSACTION

The final service to be discussed is the sales transaction itself. Headway is being made by some discount retailers seeking to invoke a positive personal touch with their "greeter" when customers enter the store and specialty retailers, such as Home Depot, Neiman-Marcus, and L.L. Bean, which offer excellent service on the other side. In a similar manner, many older malls are seeking to improve both their sales and their "unsafe" image with their own "greeter" program. North Ridge Mall in Salinas, California, for example, has an Ambassador Corps—a group of employees who greet customers at their cars, drive them around in golf carts, and offer a wide range of other services, including information on merchandise availability, prices, store location, and the names of key employees. These ambassadors contact more than 35,000 customers each month, and as a result these customers spend almost $20.00 more per visit than the mall's other customers.[18] Most retailers, however, do very little to establish a differentiation on which to build customer loyalty. At these stores, good service, at the transaction stage, simply means keeping check-out lines short and accepting credit cards so customers don't leave frustrated. Retail managers that have failed to improve their transaction processes probably view service as a cost to be controlled, so as not to negatively affect their year-end bonus, and not as something that will increase demand.

POSTTRANSACTION SERVICES

The relationship between the retailer and the consumer has become more complex in today's service-oriented economy. The nature of many products, such as computers, automobiles, and travel and financial services, require an extended relationship between the retailer and consumer. The longer this period of time can be extended by taking care of the customer's satisfaction with the product after the transaction is completed, the greater the chances are that future sales will result. The most common posttransaction services, which are provided after the sale has been made, are complaint handling, handling merchandise returns, merchandise repair and servicing, and delivery.

Posttransaction services are services provided to customers after they have purchased merchandise or services.

COMPLAINT HANDLING

Customer dissatisfaction is undoubtedly the major source of customer complaints, and it occurs when the customer's experience with a retailer or a product fails to live up to expectations. The proper handling of customer complaints can mean a big difference in retail performance. Dealing with customers is a sensitive issue because it involves employees who make human errors dealing with customers who make human errors. In essence, this doubles the chance of misunderstanding and mistakes between the two parties. Unfortunately, these mistakes and misunderstandings often lead to a poor image of the retailer.

Therefore, it is essential that retailers try to solve customer complaints. If retailers solve the customer's problem, then the customer is being served.

Computer City in Dallas, Texas, has increased its post-transaction service by offering software training classes.

DOLLAR $ & CENTS

High-performance retailers place a very high emphasis on responsive complaint handling systems. They recognize the cost of fixing mistakes is less than the cost of an unhappy customer.

There are several ways of handling and solving customer complaints. For a large retailer, the central complaint department is most efficient. Here, all customer complaints are heard by a staff that is especially trained for this task. This method leaves the salesforce free to do its job and allows the customer to deal with someone who has the authority to act on most complaints. Many large retailers have even gone to an 800 number so that they may properly handle these complaints with little effort on the part of the customer.

Some retailers use the individual salesperson in handling the complaint. They believe that a friendly, sympathetic attitude exhibited by the salesperson will have a positive effect on future sales, especially if the complaint is about a product, rather than the retailer or salesforce. This method does, however, have several disadvantages. First, the individual salesperson often does not have the authority to settle problems. As a consequence, it is usually necessary to call in someone else to take care of the problem, and usually the customer must state the problem once again. A second drawback of this system is that a salesperson who is listening to a past customer complaining cannot serve present customers, who, incidentally, are overhearing the complaints.

Other retailers are making an all-out effort to stop complaints before they occur. Ohio's Sun Television & Appliances has hired an outside marketing firm to do daily computerized price check on all comparable merchandise. If somebody beats Sun's price within 30 days of any customer's purchase, the customer automatically gets a check in the mail for the difference.[19]

EXHIBIT 12.2	SOME SIGNIFICANT DIFFERENCES BETWEEN HEAVY RETURNERS AND NONRETURNERS

Heavy Returners

- Liberal
- Opinion Leader
- Swinger
- Bargain Seeker
- Action Oriented
- Some College Education
- Large Household
- Marrieds
- High Income

Non-Returners

- Conservative
- Dependent Decision Making
- Home Oriented
- Cautious Buyer
- Less Than High School Education
- Small Household Size
- Singles
- Low Income

SOURCE: Adapted from Barnett Greenberg, Danny Bellenger, Dan Robertson and Ravi Parameswaran, "An Analysis of Return-Prone Consumers." Proceedings of 1979 Southern Marketing Association Meetings, p. 254. Adapted with authors' permission

Regardless of the complaint handling system, the retailer needs to remember three things when handling complaints. The customer deserves courteous treatment, a fair settlement, and prompt action. Remember, even if the sale is lost, the customer need not be lost. The proper handling of complaints has substantial paybacks for the smart retailer.

MERCHANDISE RETURNS   The handling of merchandise returns is an important customer service, sometimes making the difference between making a profit and losing money. The return policy can range from "no returns, no exchanges" to "the customer is always right." Retailers need to decide if they want either of these extreme policies or a more moderate one. Few services build customer goodwill as quickly as a fair return policy. However, the return service is probably the most widely abused service by American consumers. Thus it is important that the store's return policy be consistent with the store's image.

Depending on the item returned, there can be a substantial loss due to the time the item was out of stock. Beach or patio furniture, for example, wouldn't sell as well in the winter, and a returned snow shovel would be in low demand in the summer. Because of this delay, returned merchandise is often stored until the proper season or sold at a reduced price. Reducing the price is also common practice if the merchandise has been used. There is also an opportunity cost—the foregone interest or return on investment dollars. This money is tied up in merchandise that is in the possession of the customer but hasn't been paid for and will be returned.

Some customers, however, are more prone to return merchandise than others. Exhibit 12.2 provides an analysis of the difference between those customers who are prone to returning goods as opposed to those who aren't.

With losses approaching $1 billion due to return fraud, retailers are now beginning to put limits on their return policy because of abuses by consumers. For example, several computer retailers serving college markets now require the product to be returned within 60 days of purchase. This is because a number of college students have been found to want to return laptops at the end of a term. Wal-Mart has abandoned its open-ended return policy and set a 90-day limit. Under their old policy, the store once replaced a thermos that hadn't been manufactured since the early 1950s, 10 years before the first Wal-Mart opened. Nordstrom, which it is said that in the past would accept back hundreds of pairs of shoes during the prom season, is now refusing to take back dresses when the sales tags have been removed. What's more, the chain now puts the tags in conspicuous places where they can't be covered up with a sash, shawl, or belt. Probably the most abused return policy is electronic retailers getting back large-screen television sets the Monday after the Super Bowl.[20]

SERVICING AND REPAIR Any new product with more than one moving mechanical part is a candidate for future servicing or repair. In fact, even items without moving parts, such as clothing, coffee tables, and paintings, are candidates for repair. Retailers who offer merchandise servicing and repair to their customers tend to generate a higher sales volume. And if the work they perform is good, they can also generate repeat business. For example, if the service department of a TV and appliance store has a reputation for doing good work at fair prices, customers will not only purchase a TV at the store but will also tend to purchase radios, stereos, and washers.

Repair servicing, along with delivery, is perhaps one of the most difficult customer services to manage. Although good repair service can stimulate additional sales, many customers will never be satisfied because it is difficult to schedule appointments. In today's urban environment, it is virtually impossible for retailers to schedule a repair call or deliveries even within a three-hour time frame. There's traffic, parking, plus the inability to figure time needed until the repair or service personnel arrive. These factors often make it difficult for today's two-wage-earner families to be home when the retailer's personnel arrive. These disgruntled customers will tell their friends, relatives, and acquaintances of their experiences.

DELIVERY Delivery of merchandise to the customer's home can be a very expensive service, especially because of the high cost of energy. Nonetheless, the benefits derived from providing delivery may be worth the expense if the store, merchandise, and customer characteristics warrant it.

Retailers such as florists can offer free delivery (which is actually absorbed in slightly higher prices) or they can charge the customer a small fee to help offset the cost.

DETERMINING CUSTOMER SERVICE LEVELS

LO • 3
Explain how a retailer should determine which services to offer

It is not easy to determine the optimal number and level of customer services to offer. Theoretically, however, one could argue that a retailer should add customer services until the additional revenue that is generated by higher service levels is equal to the additional cost of providing those services. In the short run, profits can usually be increased by cutting back on costly customer services.

It is also difficult to decide what specific customer services to offer to increase sales volume. Exhibit 12.3 lists six factors to be considered when determining the customer services to offer: the store characteristics, the services offered by the competition, the type of merchandise handled, the price image of the store, the income of the target market, and the cost of providing the service. It is the retailer's job to study these six

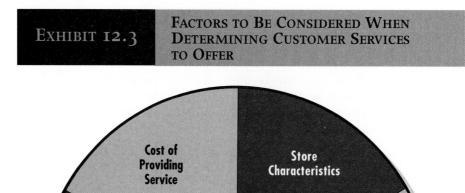

EXHIBIT 12.3   FACTORS TO BE CONSIDERED WHEN DETERMINING CUSTOMER SERVICES TO OFFER

areas to arrive at the service mix that will increase long-run profits by keeping present customers, enticing new customers, and projecting the right type of store image. Above all else, retailers must remember to be realistic and not expect to satisfy the wants and needs of all customers. No strategy could be less profitable than trying to satisfy everybody. What the retailer is really trying to do is to use its sales staff as the conduit between the vendor's expectations and the customer's expectations, as shown in Exhibit 12.4.

STORE CHARACTERISTICS

Store characteristics include store location, store size, and store type. It is especially important to look at these three store characteristics when considering adding a service.

Services offered in the downtown area of a large city would probably be different from those offered by a similar store in a suburban shopping center. For example, a drugstore in the downtown area might offer free delivery of prescriptions as a service to its clientele. This service would be of great benefit to city dwellers without cars and businesspersons who don't want to spend time waiting at the drugstore for a

EXHIBIT 12.4	HOW THE RETAILER'S SALESFORCE MEETS THE EXPECTATIONS OF BOTH VENDORS AND CUSTOMERS

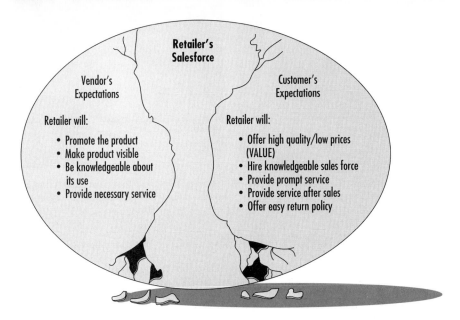

Retailer's Salesforce

Vendor's Expectations

Retailer will:

- Promote the product
- Make product visible
- Be knowledgeable about its use
- Provide necessary service

Customer's Expectations

Retailer will:

- Offer high quality/low prices (VALUE)
- Hire knowledgeable sales force
- Provide prompt service
- Provide service after sales
- Offer easy return policy

prescription. This same service in a suburban shopping center would not be as important. This druggist might get a better return on investment by offering such services as check cashing, credit, and plenty of free parking rather than free delivery of prescriptions.

The size and type of store also determine which services to offer. A major department store would offer a different assortment of services than a supermarket. There would also be a difference between a large and a small store of the same type. The customer would expect more services from a large retailer and probably fewer but more personalized services from the small retailer.

COMPETITION

The services offered by competitors will have a significant effect on the level and variety of customer services offered. A retailer must also offer these services or suitable substitutes or offer lower prices.

Suppose there are three clothing stores of the same general type, price range, and quality within a given area. Store A and store B offer free gift wrapping, standard alterations, bank card credit, and a liberal return policy. Store C, however, offers only standard alterations and has an "exchange only" return policy. Customers who are shopping for gifts will generally prefer stores A and B over store C because they feel confident that whatever they purchase will ultimately be just right. It can even be gift wrapped there at the store. If the gift isn't suitable, the receiver can exchange it or even get a cash refund. In this situation, store C can do two things to compete: add services or lower prices.

Convenience stores that have inadequate merchandise levels project a poor service image.

Convenience stores that have good merchandise availability project a good service image.

TYPE OF MERCHANDISE

The merchandise lines carried can be an indication of the types of services, especially personal selling, to offer. The principal reason is that certain merchandise lines benefit from knowledgeable sales personnel (e.g., would you want a less than knowledgeable salesperson to assist you in purchasing an engagement ring for the woman of your dreams? Or worse yet, would you want your boyfriend buying your engagement ring at a self-service discounter?). In addition, other products benefit from offering complimentary services: bicycles and free assembly, major appliances and delivery, women's suits and alterations, and sewing machines and free instructions.

PRICE IMAGE

Customers will usually expect more services from a store with a high-price image than from a discounter. When a customer perceives a store as having high prices, it also sees the store as possessing an air of luxury. Therefore, the services rendered by this store should also carry the image of luxury or status. Some of the typical high-price image services include personal shopping, a home design studio, free gift wrapping, free delivery, and free alterations.

On the other end of the scale, discount stores needn't offer luxury services, because customers who shop there are seeking low prices and not fancy customer services. A discount retailer or one with a low-price image might offer such basic services as free parking, layaway, bank card credit, and convenient store hours.

TARGET MARKET INCOME

The higher the income of the target market, the higher the price that consumers will pay. The higher the prices consumers will pay, the more services the retailer can profitably provide. Some customers may expect more services than retailers can afford, but retailers must avoid the strong temptation of providing costly services to such consumers. In the long run, the retailer will have to raise prices to pay for the services, and then it will quickly lose its share of low-income customers.

COST OF SERVICES

It is important that retailers know the cost of providing a service so that they have an idea of how much in additional sales they would need to pay for the service. For example, a customer service expected to increase costs by $20,000 per year for a store operating on a gross margin of 25 percent would have to stimulate sales by at least $20,000/0.25, or $80,000. In this sense, customer services are evaluated in a manner similar to promotional expenditures. The key criterion becomes the financial effect of adding or deleting a customer service. As a result, one national retailer recently started charging for its catalog after decades of providing it free. Research determined that while nearly 20 percent fewer customers got the catalog, those that got it thought that they had an investment ($5) in the catalog. As a result, these customers increased their purchases by 25 percent.

Another way of expressing the cost of having poor service is to examine what the costs would be if a store doesn't offer good service. If a 100-store supermarket chain alienated only one customer per day per store, the chain would lose $94.9 million in annual revenue. This is based on the assumption that grocery business is repeat business and that the real cost is the $50 a customer spends weekly.

RETAIL SALES MANAGEMENT

LO • 4
Describe the various management problems involved in retail selling, salesperson selection, and training and evaluation

Retail salespersons and the service they provide are a major factor in consumer purchase decisions. For example, when the retail salesperson is rude or is not helpful, customers will often walk out of the store empty-handed. The salesperson is a major determinant of store image. When the salesperson is available, friendly, and helpful, customers will often be influenced to enter into a transaction with the retailer. The management of the retail salesforce plays a crucial role in the success or failure of retail operations.

TYPES OF RETAIL SELLING

In many retail settings, the employees who are called salespersons are order takers and sell only regular in-stock merchandise. For example, consider the role of salespersons in a typical discount department store such as a Wal-Mart, Kmart, or Target. The employees might show the customer where the merchandise is located in the store or may go to the storeroom to get an item that is not on the shelf, but seldom, if ever, do they attempt to sell the merchandise or demonstrate its use. In fact, one discounter's policy is to provide "next-to-no-sales help." Discounters "don't want to get into the business of person-to-person selling." These stores are appealing to those customers who want value instead of service. Whether these employees should be called salespersons is debatable. Perhaps they should be referred to as retail clerks. Nonetheless, one must recognize that these order takers can influence demand, especially in a negative manner. If you are in a store such as Target and cannot find a retail clerk to assist you when you need help, you may get frustrated and leave the store without making a purchase.

Retail employees who are most appropriately labeled salespersons should be order getters, as well as order takers. Order getters are involved in conversation with

Order takers
are retail clerks that do not actively sell but rather assist the customer in completing a transaction after the customer decides what to purchase.

Order getters
are retail clerks that actively sell merchandise and services by helping the customer decide on what and how much to purchase.

prospective purchasers for the purpose of making a sale. They will inform, guide, and persuade the customer to culminate a transaction either immediately or in the future.

The degree of emphasis that the retailer places on its employees' being order getters depends on the line of retail trade and the retailer's strategy. Retailers that concentrate on the sale of shopping goods (e.g., automobile dealers, furniture retailers, computer retailers, and appliance retailers) will want their salespersons to be both order getters and order takers. In lines of retail trade in which convenience goods are predominantly sold (gasoline service stations and grocery retailers), the role of the salesperson (or what many may call the retail clerk) will be that of an order taker. In terms of strategic orientation, it is generally true that retailers with high margins and high levels of customer service will place more emphasis on order getting. Those with low margins and a low customer service policy will tend to emphasize order taking.

Clearly, however, regardless of the line of retail trade or the retailer's strategic thrust, all retail enterprises must carefully evaluate the role of the salesperson in helping to generate demand.

SALES FORCE MANAGEMENT

Most retailers agree that no matter how it is measured, retail labor productivity has been declining in recent years. Retailers appear to be caught in a vicious circle in which the relatively low wages they offer salespersons have attracted low-quality employees, which tends to continue the low-wage–low-quality cycle.

SALESPERSON SELECTION
Selecting retail salespersons should involve more than casually accepting anyone who answers an ad or walks into the store seeking a job. In fact, the casualness with which many retailers have selected people to fill sales positions is one cause of poor productivity.

CRITERIA   To select salespersons properly, retailers must decide on their hiring criteria. What is expected from retail salespersons? Are retailers looking for a salesforce that has low absenteeism or the ability to generate a high volume of sales? Are they seeking other qualities? Are they seeking a combination of factors? Unless retailers know what they are looking for in salespersons, they will not acquire a salesforce that possesses the proper qualities.

However, good results are not only dependent on the salseperson's characteristics but on how satisfied the salesperson is with the job and how the sales job was designed. Retail selling jobs should be designed to have high levels of variety (the opportunity to perform a wide range of activities), autonomy (the degree to which an employee determines the work procedures), task identity (the degree to which an employee is involved in the total sales process), and feedback from supervisors and customers.

PREDICTORS   Once retailers determine the hiring criteria, they must then identify the potential predictors to meet the chosen criteria. The most commonly used predictors in selecting retail salespersons are demographics, personality, knowledge and intelligence, and prior work experience. We discuss criteria for selecting managerial trainees later in the chapter.

1. *Demographics* Depending on the specific line of retail trade, demographic variables can be important in identifying good retail salespersons. For example, a record and stereo store appealing to teens will probably benefit from having retail salespersons younger than 30 years of age. A high-fashion women's apparel store appealing to 30- to 50-year-old, career-oriented, and upwardly mobile women would probably not desire 18-year-old salespersons from lower-class backgrounds. Interestingly enough, a study by J.D. Power & Associates of more than 33,000 new car buyers has shown that women salespersons scored higher or at least equal to men in 13 of the 15 categories evaluated. The two items in which men scored best were knowledge of "models and features" and "competitive vehicles." Women did, however, score substantiality higher in "sincerity," "honesty," and "concern for the buyer's needs."[21] Obviously, there are exceptions to each of the preceding cases, but the essential point is that retailers can use demographic variables to help screen applicants for sales positions.

2. *Personality* An applicant's personality can reflect on his or her potential as a retail salesperson. The retailer would most likely prefer salespersons who are friendly, confident, consistent, and understanding of others. These personality traits can be identified either through a personal interview with the applicant or by personality inventory tests. In most lines of retail trade, the personal interview will be sufficient.

3. *Knowledge and Intelligence* Many products that retailers sell are technically complex. Consider, for example, microcomputers, solid-state televisions, microwave ovens, 35-mm cameras, and 10-speed bicycles. Salespersons with knowledge of these products will be better able to sell them. Similarly, to be able to respond to customer inquiries in a logical fashion, retail employees will need to possess a level of education and intelligence compatible with the job description.

4. *Experience* One of the most reliable predictors of success as a salesperson is prior work experience, especially selling experience. If applicants have performed well in prior jobs, there is a good chance that they will perform well in the future. Also, many applicants for retail selling jobs will be young and have no prior work experience of any magnitude. These applicants are better assessed on their personal character and apparent ambition, drive, and work ethic.

SALESPERSON TRAINING

After salespersons are selected, they will need some form of training. This is true even if they have selling experience. In these training programs, retailers will have to explain their own store policies to the trainees. Furthermore, retailers may believe that inexperienced salespersons should become familiar with and knowledgeable about the retailers' merchandise, the different customer types they may have to deal with, and the selling strategies available for different customer choice criteria. Even order takers need training in greeting a customer, thanking customers, and using a point-of-sale terminal.

Probably the most important item the retailer can train the new sales staff about is common customer courtesy. One national discounter insists that all its sales staff carry the following "crib sheet" about being customer friendly with them at all times they are on the sales floor.

McDonald's established Hamburger University to train employees and franchisees so it could deliver high and consistent levels of customer service.

CUSTOMER-FRIENDLY MEANS

Smiling
Greeting the Customer
Being as Helpful as You Would Want Somebody to Be to You
Using the Customer's Name (if possible)
Saying "THANK YOU"

The importance of being customer-friendly can be shown from studies from the medical field. These studies found that the physician's competence and prescribed method of treatment play a very small role in determining if a malpractice suit would be filed. Rather it was the interpersonal skills that the physician used with the patient that was the determining factor.[22]

STORE POLICIES   In most situations, the interface between the customer and retailer takes place through the salesperson. It is thus important for the salesperson to become familiar with the store policies, especially those that may involve the customer directly. Some of these policies relate to merchandise returns and adjustments, shoplifting, credit terms, layaway, delivery, and price negotiating. In addition, the retail salesperson should be knowledgeable about work hours, rest periods, lunch and dinner breaks, commission and quota plans, nonselling duties, and standards of periodic job evaluation. Sales employees should also be informed about criteria used for promotion and advancement within the retail enterprise.

MERCHANDISE   If the merchandise includes shopping goods, the retailer will want to familiarize its salespersons with the strengths and weaknesses of the merchandise. This will allow salespersons to assist customers in shopping for the best goods to meet their needs. It also suggests that the salesperson become knowledgeable with the competitor's merchandise offerings and their strengths and weaknesses.

Increasingly, retail salespersons need to be familiar with the warranty terms on merchandise that the retailer handles and also the serviceability of the merchandise. This implies that the salesperson know something about the reputation of each manufacturer that the retailer represents. Exhibit 12.5 lists in greater detail the specific information that a retailer generally expects its salespersons to know about its products.

CUSTOMER TYPES   Retail salespersons can be taught how to identify and respond to certain customer types. Various customer types are described in Exhibit 12.6. By knowing how to handle each of these customers, the salesperson can generate additional sales. Too many times, retailers tend to dwell on handling the technical aspects of a job rather than the feelings of a customer. One car rental clerk was quoted as saying, "The computer training was real good. I know how to do all this technical stuff, but nobody prepared me for dealing with all these different types of people."[23]

CUSTOMER CHOICE CRITERIA   The retail salesperson should also learn how to identify the customer's choice criteria and how to respond to them.[24] There are four choice criteria situations: (1) the customer has no active product choice criteria; (2) the customer has product choice criteria but they are inadequate or vague; (3) the customer has product choice criteria but they are in conflict; and (4) the customer has product choice criteria that are explicit and well defined. For each situation, there is an appropriate selling strategy that the salesperson should learn.

1. *No Active Product Choice Criteria* The best sales strategy when the customer does not have a prior criteria set is to educate the customer on the best choice criteria and possibly how to weigh them. For example, a prospective customer enters an automobile dealership to purchase a used automobile but does not know what criteria to use in selecting the best car. The salesperson may present convincing arguments on why the customer should consider four criteria in the following order of importance: warranty, fuel economy, price, and comfort. Once the salesperson and customer agree on this list, they can work together at finding the used car that best fits the criteria.

2. *Inadequate or Vague Choice Criteria* When the criteria are inadequate or vague, the range of products that will satisfy them is often wide. Perhaps the easiest thing for the salesperson to do is to show that a particular product fits a customer's choice criteria. Because the choice criteria are vague, this would not be difficult, and little actual selling may be involved. However, the customer may have trouble believing that the product the salesperson selected is the best one to meet his or her needs. The customer may therefore choose to shop around at other stores.

   If the sales clerk is interested in building repeat business and customer goodwill and has a wide range of products to sell, a preferable strategy would be to help the customer define his or her problem to arrive at a set of choice criteria. The customer and sales clerk can work together in defining the criteria of a good product and then select the product that best fits the criteria.

3. *Choice Criteria in Conflict* Prospective customers with choice criteria that are in conflict frequently have trouble making purchase decisions. There are two basic ways in which choice criteria can be in conflict. First, the customer may want a product to possess two or more attributes that are mutually exclusive. For example, a person purchasing a 10-speed bicycle may wish it to be of high quality and

Uses of the Product
Primary and secondary uses
Suitability
Versatility

How to Use the Product
How to operate it, wear it, prepare it, eat it, apply it, assemble it, display it, place it

How to Care for the Product
How to handle and adjust the product
How to clean the product
How to store the product
How to oil and grease the product
How to refrigerate the product

Appearance of the Product
Beauty
Style
Ensemble possibilities

Services Available with the Product
Credit terms
Shipping terms
Speed and cost of delivery
Transportation methods

How the Product Will Perform
Durability
Degree of color performance
Shrinkage or stretchage (in case of textiles)
Breaking strength
Resistance to water, wind, wear, heat, light
Cost of upkeep

How the Product Is Made
Size
Weight
Weave (in case of textiles)
Finish
Handmade or machine made
Pressed, molded, stamped, inlaid, etc.
Conditions under which goods are made
Packaging

Background of the Product
History of the article
History of the manufacturer
History of its uses
History of competing articles
Rarity
Prestige

SOURCE: Kenneth H. Mills and Judith E. Paul, *Successful Retail Sales* (Englewood Cliffs, NJ: Prentice-Hall, 1979): 82–83. Reprinted with permission of the publisher.

EXHIBIT 12.6 — VARIOUS CUSTOMER TYPES

Characteristics	Basic Types	Recommendations
Doesn't trust any salesperson. Resists communication as they have a dislike of others. Generally uncooperative and will explode at slightest provocation.	**Defensive** 	Avoid mistaking their silence for openness to your ideas. Stick to basic facts. Tactfully inject product's advantages and disadvantages.
Intense, impatient personality. Often interrupt salespersons and have a perpetually "strained" expression. Often driven and successful people who want results fast.	**Interrupter** 	Don't waste time, move quickly and firmly from one sales point to another. Avoid overkill since they know what they want.
Confident in their ability to make decisions and stay with them. Open to new ideas but wants brevity. Highly motivated by self-pride.	**Decisive** 	No canned presentations. The key is to assist. Don't argue or point out errors in their judgement.
They worry about making the wrong decision, therefore, they tend to postpone all decisions. Want salesperson to make decision for them.	**Indecisive** 	Avoid becoming frustrated yourself. Determine as early as possible the need and concentrate on that. Avoid presenting customer with too many alternatives. Start with making decisions on minor points.
Friendly, talkative types who are enjoyable to visit with. Many have excess time on their hands (e.g., retirees). They usually resist the close.	**Sociable**	You may have to wait out these customers. Listen for points in conversation where you can interject product's merits. Pressure close is out. Subtle friendly close needed.
Quick to make decision. Impatient, just as likely to walk out as they were to walk in.	**Impulsive** 	Close as rapidly as possible. Avoid any useless interaction. Avoid any oversell. Highlight product's merits.

low price. This person will quickly find that these two attributes do not exist in common. The best strategy in this situation is for the salesperson to play down one of the attributes and play up the other. A second way the choice criteria could be in conflict is when a single attribute possesses both positive and negative aspects. Consider a person thinking of purchasing a high-performance automobile. High-performance automobiles have both positive aspects (status, speed, and pleasure fulfillment) and negative aspects (high insurance rates and low mileage per gallon). For this type of conflict, the best selling strategy is to enhance the positive aspects and downplay the negative aspects.

4. *Explicit Choice Criteria* When the customer has well-defined, explicit choice criteria, the best selling strategy is for the salesperson to illustrate how a specific product fits these criteria. "The sales clerk guides the customer into agreeing that each attribute of his product matches the attributes on the customer's specification. If, at the end of the sales talk, the customer does not agree to the sales clerk's proposition, he appears to be denying what he has previously admitted."[25]

EVALUATION OF SALESPERSONS

Evaluation of salespersons seeks to determine each salesperson's value to the firm. That determination is important as a basis for salary adjustments, promotions, transfers, terminations, and sales reinforcement. The retailer should develop a systematic method for evaluating both individual salespersons and the total sales staff. Rather than subjectively evaluating performance, the manager should develop performance standards for its sales staff.

PERFORMANCE STANDARDS   Several standards can be developed to measure a salesperson's performance. Some standards apply only to individual efforts, whereas others assess both individual and total salesforce effort.

Conversion rate
is the percent of shoppers that enter the store that are converted into purchasers.

1. *Conversion Rate* The conversion rate is the percentage of all shoppers who make a purchase (i.e., are converted into customers). This is a measure of the salesforce's performance; not the individual salesperson.

    A poor conversion rate can be caused by a variety of factors. Perhaps there were not enough clerks on hand when customers needed them. This could have resulted in a high degree of unassisted search and long customer waiting times, with many customers exiting the store without making a purchase. Or the number of sales clerks could have been adequate to handle the flow of customers, but the salespersons may not have done a good selling job. A poor selling job could have been caused by a variety of factors, such as the clerk giving inadequate product information to the customer, disagreeing or arguing too strongly with the customer, demonstrating the product poorly, having an unfriendly attitude, or giving up on the sale too early. However, all these factors are really related to poor training, which is the underlying reason for poor sales. Also, a low conversion rate may have been due to factors beyond the salesperson's control, such as inadequate merchandise levels. The important point is that when a substandard conversion rate exists, the retailer should identify the causes and remedy the situation. The Behind the Scenes box shows the impact that a small increase in the conversion rate will have on retail sales.

CONVERSION RATE'S IMPACT ON SALES

Nowhere are the effects of too few salespersons or too little training shown better than in a recent study by Marvin Rothenberg. Rothenberg, a well-known retailing consultant, studied what happened in four chains operating a total of 68 department stores. He found that 131,328,000 sales opportunities a year (i.e., 2.4 million shoppers who averaged 1.9 shopping visits per month going into 2.4 departments per trip) produced only 38 million sales transactions. Thus, 93 million departmental shopping visits resulted in "no sale."

In fact, 49 million of the departmental shoppers who made no purchase didn't even have contact with a salesperson or a cashier. Another 44 million had contact with a salesperson but didn't buy anything. And among these two segments of 93 million shoppers already in the departments, 28 million came into the department with the intent to make a specific purchase! In total, 71 percent of all the departmental shopping visits resulted in shoppers either having no contact with sales personnel or, if they had contact, it was probably the wrong kind, and as a result they made no purchase. No wonder Rothenberg, in another study, found that one-third of customers who entered a store with the expressed intent of making a specific purchase walked out without making any purchase. It is obvious that a small increase in con-

verting these nonpurchasing consumers into customers will increase sales dramatically, even if the shopper is only in the store as a means to combat loneliness.

For example, if these retailers did nothing more than just contact half the 49 million customers who had no sales contact and if the conversion rate among this group was only half what it was among those who had contact, the number of sales transactions, currently 38 million, would increase by 15 percent (half of 49 million who had no contact multiplied by half of the conversion rate for those who had contact equal 5.6 million more sales transactions). That's an opportunity to add 15 percent to sales by doing nothing more than what is already being achieved when customers contact a salesperson. Yet, for many retailers, this is a lost opportunity, as they either do not want to (or do not know how to) train their sales staff in the proper methods of servicing a customer. Worse yet are those retailers who want to cut back on operating expense and therefore don't have the necessary number of sales personnel on duty. Either way, the retailer is missing out on a great opportunity to increase sales.

SOURCE: This above information was provided to the authors by Marvin J. Rothenberg and is used with the permission of Marvin J. Rothenberg, Inc., Retail Marketing Consultants, Ft. Lee, NJ.

DOLLAR $ & CENTS

High salesperson productivity is one of the hallmarks of high-performance retailers. These retailers do a better job selecting, training, and evaluating their salespersons.

2. *Sales Per Hour* Perhaps the most common measure of a salesperson's or salesforce's performance is sales per hour. Sales per hour is computed by dividing total dollar sales over a particular time frame by total salesperson or salesforce hours. A retailer can compute this simple measure for each salesperson, any group of salespersons, or the entire salesforce.

When using this measure, remember that standards should be specific to the group or person being evaluated for a particular time period. For example, in a department store the sales per hour of selling effort cannot be expected to be the same for the toy department as for the jewelry department. Nor could one expect the same sales per hour during July and December, because of the heavy Christmas demand for toys and jewelry. In some lines of retail trade, particularly those selling high ticket items such as automobiles, the key performance measure is gross margin dollars generated per salesperson.

3. *Use of Time* Standards can be developed for how salespersons should spend their time. A salesperson's time can be spent in four ways:

   a. Selling time is any time spent in assisting customers with their needs. This would be time spent talking, demonstrating, writing sales receipts, or assisting the customer in other potentially revenue-generating ways.

   b. Nonselling time is any time spent on nonselling tasks such as marking merchandise or straightening up the store.

   c. Idle time is time the salesperson is on the sales floor but is not involved in any productive work.

   d. Absent time occurs when the salespersons are not on the sales floor. They may be at lunch, in the employee lounge, in another part of the store, or in some inappropriate place.

The retailer may develop standards for each of these ways to spend time. For example, the standard time allocation may suggest that salespersons spend 60 percent of their time selling, 28 percent of their time on nonselling activities, 5 percent idle, and 7 percent absent. Any deviation from these standards should be investigated, and corrective measures should be taken if necessary.

DATA REQUIREMENTS   To establish proper standards of performance, the retailer needs data. What are good standards for the conversion rate? sales per hour? time allocation? Only data will help answer these questions. The data can come from retail trade associations, consulting firms, or the retailer's own experience.

Once the retailer obtains the data on which to base standards, it must collect additional data continually or at least periodically on actual performance. The actual conversion rate, sales per hour, and time allocation must be contrasted to their respective standards. If the actual data differ significantly from the standard, an investigation of the cause is warranted. Both favorable and unfavorable variances should be investigated, because you may learn just as much from unusually good performance as from unusually poor performance.

LO • 5
Describe the retail selling process

THE RETAIL SELLING PROCESS

There are several basic steps that occur during the retail selling process. The length of time that a salesperson spends in each one of these steps depends on the product type, the customer, and the selling situation. Exhibit 12.7 details the process model.

EXHIBIT 12.7	SELLING PROCESS IN THE RETAIL ENVIRONMENT

Step 1 — Prospecting
Who can benefit from your product
a. Finding Prospects.
b. Qualifying prospects, (determining whether a prospect has the ability, buying power, and willingness to make a purchase).

Step 2 — Approach
The first 15 seconds are the key as they set the *mood* for the sale.
a. Never say "May I help you?"
   A single "hello," "good morning," or "what may I show you?" makes the customer realize that you are glad they are in your store.
b. Determine as early as possible the customer's needs.
   Listen – *What you hear* is more important than anything you could possibly tell your customer. Ask a few well-chosen questions — What do I need to know?
   1. Product needed or problem to be solved.
   2. User of the product (tell me about so-and-so).

Step 3 — The Sales Presentation
Getting the customer to want to buy your product/service
a. Pick the right price level.
   If uncertain — ask "Is there a price range you have in mind?" Remember, you can't pick out the *right product* for the uncertain customer if the price is wrong.
b. Pick the right product.
   Match user and need with product. Show the customer at least two items.
c. Show the merchandise in an appealing manner.
   1. Make the merchandise stand out.
   2. Show the item so that its good points will be seen.
   3. Let the customer handle the merchandise.
   4. Stress the features of the product.
   5. Explain the benefits of these features.
   6. Appeal to the customer's emotions.
d. Help the customer decide.
   1. Handle objections.
   2. Replace unneeded items.
   3. Watch for unconscious clues.
   4. Stress features and benefits of "key" product.

Step 4 — Closing The Sale
Reaching an agreement
a. What is going on in the customer's mind.
b. Four effective ways to close.
   1. Make the decision for the customer.
   2. Assume the decision has already been made.
   3. Ask the customer to choose.
   4. Turn an objection around.

Step 5 — Suggestion Selling
Follow-up leads to other sales.

PROSPECTING

Prospecting

is the process of locating potential customers that have the ability and willingness to purchase your product.

Prospecting is the search process of finding those who have the ability and willingness to purchase your product. Prospecting is particularly important when the store is full of customers. A salesperson should be aware that good prospects generally display more interest in the products than poor prospects who are "just looking." Salespersons should take advantage of the behavioral cues shown in Exhibit 12.6.

APPROACH

The salesperson may meet hundreds of customers a day, but the customer is only going to meet the salesperson once that day. Therefore, it is extremely important that the first 15 seconds set the mood for the sale. Never begin the sales presentation with "May I help you?" or any other question to which the customer may respond negatively. A simple good morning (afternoon, evening) or any other greeting acknowledging the customer's presence should do. Nordstrom, long recognized for its outstanding service, has its salesforce use an item that the customer is wearing as an approach if something better isn't evident.

The key to a successful approach is discerning as soon as possible the customer's needs by asking the right questions and listening. What the salesperson hears about the customer's problem or need is more important than anything the salesperson can possibly contribute at this point. Ask a few well-chosen questions to find out more about the need or problem to be solved. The salesperson should also find out if the user of the product is a different individual than the customer. Remember, the salesperson should ask only as many questions as needed and let the customer do the talking.

SALES PRESENTATION

Once the initial contact has been established and the salesperson has listened to the customer's problems and needs, the salesperson is in a position to present the merchandise and sales message correctly. How the salesperson presents the product or service depends on the customer and the situation. The key, however, is to get the customer to want to buy your product or service. Begin by determining the right price range of products to show the customer. A price too high or too low will generally result in a lost sale. If uncertain, ask the customer about the price range desired.

Next, the salesperson should pick out what he or she believes will be the right product or service to satisfy the customer's needs. The salesperson should be careful not to show the customer too many products so as to avoid confusing the customer.

EXHIBIT 12.8	SOME CLOSING SIGNALS THE SALESPERSON SHOULD BE ON THE LOOKOUT FOR

The customer reexamines the product carefully.

The customer tries on the product (i.e., trying on a sports coat or strapping on a wristwatch).

The customer begins to read the warranty or brochure.

The customer makes the following statements:

   I always wanted a compact disc player.

   I never realized that these were so inexpensive.

   I bet my wife would love this.

The customer asks the following questions:

   Does this come in any other colors?

   Do you accept Discover cards?

   Can you deliver this tomorrow?

   Do you have a size 7 in this style?

   Do you accept trade-ins?

   Do you have any training sessions available?

   Do you have it in stock?

   What accessories are available?

   Where would I take it to get it serviced?

   Is it really that easy to operate?

The salesperson should tell the customer about the merchandise in an appealing way, stressing the features that are the outstanding qualities or characteristics of the product. Have the customer handle the merchandise.

Help the customer decide on the product or service that best fulfills the customer's needs. Handle any objection that the customer might have, replace the unneeded items, and continue to stress the features and benefits of the product that the customer seems most interested in. Training and retraining are ongoing activities for all successful retailers.

CLOSING THE SALE

Closing the sale is a natural conclusion to the selling process. However, for most salespersons closing the sale is the most difficult part of the selling process. Remember, the salesperson is there to help the customer solve a problem, so the salesperson should not be afraid to ask for the sale. The key to closing the sale is to determine what is going on in the customer's mind. Exhibit 12.8 lists some of the things a salesperson should be on the lookout for at this stage of the selling process. If the salesperson waits too long or is too impatient in completing this step, the customer will be gone before the salesperson realizes it. There are four effective ways to close a sale: (1) make the decision for the customer, (2) assume that the decision has been made and ask if the sale will be cash or charge, (3) ask the customer to select the product or service, and (4) turn an objection around by stressing a positive aspect of the product. For example, a salesperson might suggest that although the initial cost of a product might be high, its longer life span will reduce total cost.

Closing the sale
is the act the salesperson takes to bring a potential sale to its natural conclusion.

SUGGESTION SELLING

An effective salesperson continues to sell even after the sale has been completed. There is always the possibility of an additional sale. The salesperson should find out if the customer has any other needs or if the customer knows of anybody else with needs that can be solved with the salesperson's product line. A good example of the follow-up would be the salesperson's selling a Valentine's gift to a young college student for his girlfriend and asking if the salesperson can help him with a gift for his mother.

SERVICE RETAILERS AND THE SELLING PROCESS

The teaching of proper selling techniques is even more important in the retailing of services. First of all, it is difficult for retailers of services to attract new customers because they cannot try the product, inspect it, or test it. Second, once they have purchased the service, they only know if it didn't satisfy them or solve their problem. They are generally not happy with a purchase, only dissatisfied if the service was not what they were led to believe it would be. The retailer of services therefore needs to understand what benefit the customer is really buying. For example, it is important for the salesforce to remember that hospitals market health care, not operations, and colleges market educational attainment, not classes.

Third, not only is it important to know what benefit is sought, but the service provider must consider how to help the customer achieve that benefit—a different task from simply providing the service. For example, a plumber is not merely selling the ability to unclog sink pipes but also informing consumers about what they can do to keep the sink pipes running freely. This enables the consumer to become involved and to feel a sense of accomplishment.

Fourth, the retailer should determine how to change the service so as to produce positive customer satisfaction. A consumer might not feel anything if the security firm guarding the household property is merely checking the property daily with routine inspections and nothing bad happens. However, consider the positive customer satisfaction that could be gained if the security firm also involved the customer in the process with a self-defense class.

Finally, the retailer must remember that with services the goal is to preclude dissatisfaction, because that is the best remembered aspect of a service purchase. Here again, it is important for the sales staff to be aware that the end result should match the customer's expectations. Remember, consumers will never forget a poor service job. Research on service selling suggests that future sales opportunities depend mostly on the trust and satisfaction established. The ability to convert these opportunities into sales hinges more strongly on conventional salesperson characteristics such as expertise and similarity.

STUDENT STUDY GUIDE

SUMMARY

LO•1 **WHY IS CUSTOMER SERVICE SO IMPORTANT IN RETAILING?**
This chapter emphasizes that customer service is a key revenue-generating variable for
the retailer. To properly manage the customer service decision area, the retailer needs
to build a relationship with the customer by integrating customer service with merchandise, promotion, building and fixtures, price, and credit management. Only an integrated customer service program will allow the retailer to achieve maximum profits.

LO•2 **WHAT ARE THE VARIOUS CUSTOMER SERVICES THAT A RE-
TAILER CAN OFFER?**   Customer services are classified into pretransaction, transaction, and posttransaction services. Pretransaction services make it easier for a
potential customer to shop at a store or learn about its offering. Common examples are
convenient hours and informational aids. Transaction-related services make it easier
for the customer to complete a transaction. Popular transaction-related services are
consumer credit, gift wrapping and packaging, check cashing, personal shopping, merchandise availability, personal selling, and the transaction itself. Posttransaction services influence the customer's satisfaction with the merchandise after the transaction.
The most frequently encountered are handling of complaints, merchandise returns,
servicing and repairing, and delivery.

LO•3 **HOW SHOULD A RETAILER DETERMINE WHICH SERVICES TO
OFFER?**   Conventional wisdom suggests that in establishing the mix of customer
services the retailer should consider six factors: store characteristics, competition, type
of merchandise, price image, target market income, and cost of the service.

LO•4 **WHAT ARE THE VARIOUS MANAGEMENT PROBLEMS IN-
VOLVED IN RETAIL SELLING, SALESPERSON SELECTION, AND TRAIN-
ING AND EVALUATION?**   This chapter also illustrates the role of managing the
retail salesperson. Regardless of whether sales clerks are primarily order getters or order takers, they play an important role in the demand for a retailer's products. However, the role played by the order getter is obviously more important in this regard.
     The productivity of retail salespersons has been stagnant in recent years. This
problem has been traced to low wages, poor morale, high turnover, and a general inability of retailers to properly manage their salespersons. The criteria to be used in the
selection of a selling staff and its training program was discussed. The section ended by
reviewing performance evaluation of retail salespersons.

LO•5 **WHAT STEPS ARE INVOLVED IN THE RETAIL SELLING
PROCESS?**   The retail selling process consists of five steps: prospecting, approach,
presentation, close, and suggestion selling. The length of time that a salesperson spends
on each step depends on the product type, customer, and selling situation.
     The selling process is even more important for retailers of services because

1. It is difficult to attract customers to merchandise they cannot sample, inspect, or
   test.
2. Usually with services, customers only realize it when they aren't satisfied.

3. Not only is it important to know the benefit sought, but the salesperson must know how to help the customer achieve that benefit.
4. The salesperson determines how to change the service so as to produce positive customer satisfaction.
5. It helps to make sure that the end result matches the customer's expectations.

TERMS TO REMEMBER

relationship retailing	posttransaction services
customer service	order takers
transient customer	order getters
pretransaction services	conversion rate
transaction services	prospecting
personal shopping	closing the sale

REVIEW AND DISCUSSION QUESTIONS

LO•1   WHY IS CUSTOMER SERVICE SO IMPORTANT IN RETAILING?

1. Retailers with high levels of customer service operate on higher gross margins than retailers with low service levels. Agree or disagree and defend your point of view.
2. Why are so many retailers cutting back on service?

LO•2   WHAT ARE THE VARIOUS CUSTOMER SERVICES THAT A RETAILER CAN OFFER?

3. How is a retailer's customer service policy related to other retail management decisions?
4. Some discount stores have a "no layaway" policy and will not accept returns or checks. Will this hinder the stores in the marketplace? Is the trend moving toward or away from increasing service by these types of retailers?
5. What are the significant differences between heavy returners and nonreturners? What do you think accounts for these differences?

LO•3   HOW SHOULD A RETAILER DETERMINE WHICH SERVICES TO OFFER?

6. How would the type of customer affect the level of customer service a retailer should offer?
7. Should a retailer seek to meet or exceed a competitor's level of customer service?

LO•4   WHAT ARE THE VARIOUS MANAGEMENT PROBLEMS INVOLVED IN RETAIL SELLING, SALESPERSON SELECTION, AND TRAINING AND EVALUATION?

8. Develop a list of predictor variables that you would use to screen applicants for a sales position in (a) a jewelry department in a high-prestige department store, (b) a used car dealership, (c) a health club, and (d) an antique shop.
9. How can a small retailer evaluate the performance of its two salespersons?
10. A retail discount department store chain has analyzed the annual sales per salesperson in 20 of its stores nationwide. The sales per salesperson range from a low of $91,000 to a high of $134,000. Develop the list of factors that might help to explain this wide variation.

LO•5 WHAT IS INVOLVED IN THE RETAIL SELLING PROCESS?

11. What should retail salespersons know about consumer behavior?
12. What should retail salespersons know about customer choice criteria?
13. Provide examples of suggestion selling in a discount store.
14. Someone once said that "selling is selling regardless of the product or service being sold." Do you agree with this statement? Defend your position.
15. Why is selling so much more important for retailers of services than it is for retailers selling physical products?

SAMPLE TEST QUESTIONS

LO•1 A TRANSIENT CUSTOMER IS A CONSUMER WHO VISITS A STORE

a. and finds the item desired in a matter of minutes
b. only when his or her regular store is closed
c. that does not meet his or her customer service expectations
d. while on vacation
e. and then visits all the other stores in the neighborhood

LO•2 PERSONAL SHOPPING IS AN EXAMPLE OF A(N)

a. cost of sales
b. pretransaction service
c. operating cost
d. posttransaction service
e. transaction service

LO•3 WHICH OF THE FOLLOWING IS NOT A FACTOR IN DETERMINING THE SERVICE LEVEL TO OFFER?

a. income of target market
b. price image of the store
c. services offered by the competition
d. firm's management structure
e. store characteristics

LO•4 WHICH ONE OF THE FOLLOWING FACTORS IS NOT ONE OF THE ELEMENTS THAT NEEDS TO BE CONSIDERED WHEN DESIGNING A SALES JOB?

a. feedback from supervisors
b. number of complaints a salesperson should have to handle
c. amount of variety involved
d. appropriate degree of autonomy
e. level of task identity present

LO•5 WHAT IS THE FIRST STEP THAT A SALESPERSON SHOULD TAKE DURING THE SALES PRESENTATION?

a. inform the customer about the merchandise in an appealing manner
b. select the right product or service that he or she believes will satisfy the customer's needs
c. greet the customer

   d. help the customer to decide on the product that best fulfills the customer's needs

   e. determine the right price range of products

APPLICATIONS

WRITING AND SPEAKING EXERCISE   Roger Cooper has been involved in appliance retailing since he worked in an appliance store during high school. Five years ago, he opened his first "Ma and Pa" store. In the past several years, the operation has grown to three stores. Because Cooper's business simply "evolved" into its present status, he had never actually provided formal training for his salespersons. Intensifying competition, Wal-Mart has opened at a nearby location, and increased consumer demands has lead Cooper to believe that now is the time for that training. However, Cooper is concerned about the image of his stores. He doesn't want his stores to be known as being "high-pressure" operations. For that reason, he is afraid of using either suggestion selling or being too forceful in handling objections.

Cooper realizes that you are taking a retailing class this semester in addition to being a part-time employee. Therefore, he has asked you to prepare a memo that outlines the basic steps of the selling process. Cooper wants you to include the reason for everything you suggest in your memo.

RETAIL PROJECT   You have just been invited to a wedding next month and you realize that you need a new suit to wear. Because you know what size you need, you decide to put "on-line" shopping to the test.

Determine the difference in the amount of time involved between going to your local mall and purchasing that suit or using the computer to purchase that suit from the same retailer at its web site on your computer. Also, note whether there was a difference in price.

CASE TECH-NO-TRONICS

Tech-No-Tronics is a 10-store retail operation that carries various lines of personal computers, printers, word processing software packages, and related products such as carrying cases and resume paper. Tech-No-Tronics' focus is on meeting the needs of middle-income consumers.

Five Tech-No-Tronics stores are located in areas that are the homes of large community colleges or mid-sized universities. Management believes that approximately 70 percent of the sales in these stores are accounted for by individuals who attend these schools at some level (i.e., traditional undergraduates, continuing education, graduate students, etc.), students' parents, and members of the schools' staffs.

The other five stores are situated in downtown business districts. The downtown stores primarily attract young professionals who work in the area and are technically unsophisticated.

Tech-No-Tronics' philosophy is to help the "average Joe or Jane" purchase their first computer as painlessly as possible. Management wants their stores' image and products to reflect this "user-friendly" objective.

Based on this information, answer the following questions:

1. What factors would management want to consider when selecting potential Tech-No-Tronics salespersons; what kind of a person would Tech-No-Tronics want to employ? Why?
2. Discuss some pretransaction and posttransaction services that may be of particular importance to Tech-No-Tronics customers.

PLANNING YOUR OWN RETAIL BUSINESS

Franklin's Jewelers, a family business that your grandfather started in 1952, had annual sales last year of $453,250. Your parents, who purchased this business from your grandfather in 1981, have asked you to help them develop a strategy to improve sales. Because you plan to open a second Franklin's Jewelers store on graduation, with your family's support, you want to use this opportunity to impress your parents with your business and retail marketing skills.

In reviewing the records of the store, you were surprised to find that a record had been kept of how many shoppers visited the store on a daily basis. For the most recent year, you computed that there were 14,000 visitors and that 2,590 of these made a purchase. You also have spent the past few weeks observing the salespersons (including your parents) make sales presentations. Your observation is that they do a good job on approaching shoppers and making a sales presentation; however, they are quite weak and passive on closing a sale. You also have observed there's little effort made at cross-selling merchandise.

Your recommendation is to have a local professor who teaches a course in personal selling conduct a sales training workshop. This two-day workshop would cost $2,500. After consulting with the professor, you both believe that the training should produce an increase in average transaction size of $25 and an increase in the conversion rate of 5 percent.

Based on the preceding, show the impact on annual sales of the proposed training program.

NOTES

1. "After All You've Done for Your Customers, Why Are They Still NOT HAPPY?" *Fortune,* December 11, 1995: 178–182.
2. "What Happened to Service?" *New York Times,* March 4, 1997: C1.
3. "No Detail Escapes the Attention of Abercrombie & Fitch's Chief," *Wall Street Journal,* October 7, 1997: B1.
4. Pratibha A. Dabholkar, Dayle I. Thorpe, and Joseph O. Rentz, "A Measure of Service Quality for Retail Stores: Scale Development and Validation," *Journal of the Academy of Marketing Science,* Winter 1996: 3–16.
5. "Americans Can't Get No Satisfaction," *Fortune,* December 11, 1996: 186–194.
6. "Service with a Snag," *New York Times,* May 14, 1997: Front Page Business Section & 4.
7. Frederick F. Reichheld, "Learning from Customer Defections," *Harvard Business Review,* March–April 1996: 56–69.
8. "37 Things You Can Do to Keep Your Customers—Or Lose Them," *Progressive Grocer,* June 1973: 59–64.
9. "10 Commandments Aid Department Stores," *Chain Store Age Executive,* September 1980: 10. Reprinted with permission.
10. "Now Hotel Clerks Provide More than Keys," *Wall Street Journal,* March 5, 1993: B1, B2.

11. "Survey Reveals Concerns of Shoppers," *Shopping Centers Today,* September 1997: 82.

12. "Rooted in Success," *Dallas Morning News,* May 22, 1996: 1D, 10D.

13. "Hopelessly Devoted," *Ideations,* Winter 1997: 1, 6.

14. "Cyberstores Overcome Glitches to Post Big Jump in Retail Sales," *Lubbock Avalanche-Journal,* May 4, 1997: 7E.

15. "Finally, Supermarkets Find Ways to Increase Their Profit Margins," *Wall Street Journal,* May 29, 1997: A1, A6.

16. For a more detailed discussion of personal shopping, complete with a list of shopping options, see "One-on-One Shopping," *Fortune,* July 7, 1997: 235–236.

17. "Sears Rolls Out Gift Registry to 800 Mall Stores," *Advertising Age,* February 24, 1997: 3, 83.

18. "Mall 'Ambassadors' Dispel Bad Image," *Shopping Centers Today,* September 1996: 21.

19. "The Latest Weapon in the Price Wars," *Fortune,* July 7, 1997: 200.

20. "Burned Retailers Are Fed Up, Clamping Down," *USA Today,* June 3, 1996: B1, B2; "Without a Receipt You May Get Stuck with That Ugly Scarf," *Wall Street Journal,* November 18, 1996: A1, A6.

21. "Customers Like Buying Cars from Women, Survey Finds," *USA Today,* November 8, 1994: B1.

22. W. Levinson et al., "Physician–Patient Communication. The Relationship with Malpractice Claims among Primary Care Physicians and Surgeons," *JAMA,* February 19, 1997: 553–559; Gerald B Hickson et al., "Obstetricians' Prior Malpractice Experience and Patients' Satisfaction with Care," *JAMA,* November 23/30, 1994: 1583–1587; Stephen S. Entman et al., "The Relationship between Malpractice Claims History and Subsequent Obstetric Care," *JAMA,* November 23/30, 1994: 1588–1591.

23. "Pul-eeze! Will Somebody Help Me?" *Time,* February 2, 1987: 49–53, 55.

24. Much of the following is based on John O'Shaughnessy, "Selling as an Interpersonal Influence Process," *Journal of Retailing,* Winter 1971–72: 32–46.

25. *Ibid.,* 41.

STORE LAYOUT AND DESIGN[1]

Target Greatland stores are designed to be large enough to accommodate a traditional Target discount department store and a full-scale conventional supermarket. The stores, with over 100,000 square feet of space, are able to project a store image of convenience and also generate high-space productivity.

OVERVIEW

In this chapter, we discuss the place where all retailing activities come together—the retail store. The store can be the most meaningful form of communication between the retailer and its customers. Most important, the store is where sales happen or fail to happen. We see that with all its hundreds of elements, the store has two primary roles: creating the proper store image and increasing the productivity of the sales space. We identify the most critical elements in creating a successful retail store and describe the art and science of store planning, merchandise presentation, and design.

LEARNING OBJECTIVES

After reading this chapter, you should be able to

1. list the elements of a store's environment and define its two primary objectives
2. discuss the steps involved in planning the store
3. describe how various types of fixtures, merchandise presentation methods and techniques, and the psychology of merchandise presentation are used to increase the productivity of the sales floor
4. describe why store design is so important to a store's success
5. explain the role of visual communications in a retail store

INTRODUCTION TO STORE LAYOUT MANAGEMENT

The last chapter discussed how customer service and personal selling can be used to develop a relationship with the customer. This chapter discusses another method that retailers can use to initiate and continue this relationship—the retail store itself. Stanley Marcus, the legendary chairperson-emeritus of Neiman-Marcus, once told a group that every morning he expected to see the following headline in the *Dallas Morning News:* "Shopper Found Dead In Local Store; Cause of Death—Boredom."[2] He was trying to get the group to realize the importance of getting customers excited about coming into their store. Allen Questrom, the ex-chairman and CEO of Federated Department Stores, says: "We sell discretionary merchandise. We have to sell theater and excitement."[3]

In fact, no other variable in the retailing mix influences the consumer's initial perception of a retailer as much as the retailer's store itself. High-performance retailers today are spending a great deal of time and effort making sure that the right things happen in their store and that the right customers enter the store, shop, and spend money. Simply put, for retailers the store is "where the action is." Although this chapter is concerned with the physical store, the same factors may be used to develop a "virtual store" for your web site.

Although a store is composed of literally thousands of details, we introduce two primary objectives around which all activities, functions, and goals in the store revolve: store image and space productivity. However, before discussing these two objectives, it is important to identify the elements, which are shown in Exhibit 13.1, that compose the store environment, each of which are discussed in detail in this chapter.

Store image

is the overall perception the consumer has of the store's environment.

Space productivity

represents how effectively the retailer utilizes its space and is usually measured by sales per square foot of selling space or gross margin dollars per square foot of selling space.

ELEMENTS OF THE STORE ENVIRONMENT

DOLLAR $ & CENTS

High-performance retailers, which operate traditional stores or virtual stores, place a heavy emphasis on designing their physical facilities or web site to enhance their image and increase their productivity.

The first decision that the retailer must make in planning a store is how to allocate a scarce resource, space. Next, the retailer must create a store layout, which shows the location of all merchandise departments and the placement of circulation aisles to allow customers to move through the store. The merchandise presentation must be exciting to catch and hold customers' attention, be easy to understand, and encourage shoppers to browse, evaluate, and buy. Therefore, the presentation of the merchandise is a critical factor in the sales power of a store and has a significant effect on the store image. A bookstore with a high percentage of face-outs, for example, can create the image of

| EXHIBIT 13.1 | ELEMENTS THAT COMPOSE THE STORE ENVIRONMENT |

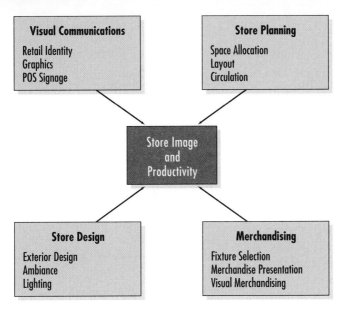

Visual Communications
Retail Identity
Graphics
POS Signage

Store Planning
Space Allocation
Layout
Circulation

Store Image and Productivity

Store Design
Exterior Design
Ambiance
Lighting

Merchandising
Fixture Selection
Merchandise Presentation
Visual Merchandising

being a specialty book boutique that carries a limited selection of exclusive titles and is therefore a rather pricey place to shop. A bookstore with virtually all spine-outs is often perceived as cramming in a huge selection of titles sold at low prices. So, merchandise presentation is a critical factor in determining both store image and productivity. Most shoppers are accustomed to noticing the layout and design of a store, which comprises all elements affecting the human senses of sight, sound, smell, and touch. An effective store layout and design, including storefront, creates a comfortable environment that enhances the merchandise and entices shoppers to browse and buy. Not to be overlooked is in-store lighting, which not only helps create the proper image but draws customers' eyes around the store and onto merchandise. Likewise, in-store graphics such as art, photography, and signs form an important visual communication link between the store and its customers by providing much needed information on how to shop in the store. The Behind the Scenes box gives a description of how supermarket managers have perfected the act of laying out and designing their stores.

Today, even some retailers are also subject to this greed appeal. Many of them ignore their own 25-25-50 rule on endcaps when manufacturers offer money for the right to set up their own displays. Although the supermarket will gain a short-term profit by renting out most of its endcap space, they often destroy the long-term profits that a well-defined endcap policy generates.

OBJECTIVES OF THE STORE ENVIRONMENT

The two primary objectives of creating the desired store image and increasing space productivity amount to a simple description of the Management Horizon's Impact Model described in Chapter 12.

CONSUMER BEHAVIOR: SUPERMARKET STYLE

Although it is doubtful that many supermarket managers ever took a consumer behavior class in college, they sure know how to practice the art. OBSERVE:

Most consumers not only are right-handed, they think right-headed.

■ Thus, because supermarkets make more money on their store brands, due to their higher margins, they stock the store brands to the right of the name brands so that the consumer has to reach across the store brand to get it.

■ Likewise, supermarkets display the higher gross margin merchandise on the right side of an aisle, as gauged from the predominant direction of cart traffic.

■ Because 90 percent of all customers entering a store turn right, that area is the most valuable for the store. Thus it is no accident that produce, a deli, or a bakery is the first section that a customer will reach. That is because they can see, feel, and smell the merchandise. This in turn will get their mouth watering and make them hungry. Any supermarket manager will say that their best customer is a hungry customer.

Most consumers think "neatness" counts.

■ Thus, merchants sometimes try to make their point-of-purchase displays look like a mess. These so-called dump displays, which are affectionately known by some grocers as "organized chaos," are deliberately arranged in a haphazard fashion so the items inside look cheap and are, therefore, a great bargain. The same thought process works for merchants leaving out open cartons piled on top of another. Usually the items aren't on sale, they just look "hot."

■ For the same reason, handwritten (as long as they are legible) signs create the impression of recently lowered prices, thus there hasn't been time to get the printed signs. Thus, even though they don't always look great, handwritten signs move the merchandise faster than standard printed signs.

Most consumers are likely to focus on a large central display.

■ Thus, the point-of-purchase displays at the end of each supermarket aisle that are known in the trade as endcaps are usually the focus of a customer's attention as they wheel their cart through the store. Thus, a smart retailer knows to follow the 25-25-50 rule. That is 25 percent of all endcaps should be advertised "sale" merchandise that the customer will seek out, 25 percent should be unadvertised "sale" items that will cause the customer to be alert when looking at an endcap, and the remaining 50 percent should be regular priced seasonal or impulse merchandise.

Consumers are creatures of habit and when something is out-of-place they become more sensitive to their environment.

■ Thus, every supermarket will make regularly scheduled display changes for staple items such as cake mixes, salad dressings, and cereals. They don't want to move the items to new locations because that may upset time-pressed customers. However, by changing shelf displays of these staples, the grocer draws the attention of the customer and thereby increasing the chances of an impulse sale.

There is a little bit of greed in every one of us.

■ Thus, supermarket managers may put a limit on the purchase of a sale item, say "Limit 4 to a Customer." Not only will consumers think that the limit restrictions mean that it's a great deal, but they will often buy the limit, even if they don't need that many.

■ Similarly, many customers will get so excited by finding a great price on a staple such as peanut butter, they will fail to notice that the item's complimentary products, in this case: jelly and bread, may have had their prices increased.

- get customers into the store (market image)
- convert them into customers buying merchandise once inside the store (space productivity)
- do this in the most efficient manner possible

The retailer must constantly balance the first two elements of the model, as they are sometimes at odds.

DEVELOPING A STORE IMAGE

The starting point in creating this image is, of course, the merchandise carried in the store, along with the retailer's promotional activities, customer service, and salesforce. The store itself also serves a critical role in creating and reinforcing the desired store image.

To illustrate the importance of store image, consider for a moment the words *7-Eleven*. For most people, these words represent more than just two numbers. Together, they form the name of one of the most familiar American retailers, the chain of more than 4,000 convenience stores.

The thoughts and emotions this logo evokes in customers constitute 7-Eleven's store image. Regardless of what its managers would like its market image to be, regardless of what image they have tried to create, the store's actual image exists only in the heads and hearts of consumers. Many factors influence that image.

First, the name itself has a great influence. If the stores were called "8-Twelve," we all might have a different image in our heads. (The name was created in 1946 to stress the stores' operating hours, 7 A.M. to 11 P.M. every day, then unheard of in retailing.)[4] The rhythm and rhyme of seven and 11 allow the name to roll easily off our tongues and be more memorable, even if the customer doesn't shoot craps. (Remember, in craps a 7 or 11 on the shooter's first roll is a winner.) The orange and green colors of the logo suggest to us certain things about the chain's quality. The storefront, historically a large black mansard roof, conveys a heavy, masculine appearance, and the windows plastered with price savings signs suggest a promotional environment. When you walk in the store, a buzzer warns clerks of entering shoppers, suggesting a concern about safety and theft. The smell of cheese nachos and the sight of sausages and hot dogs rolling around on the hot dogger create a certain atmosphere. Even the uniforms worn by the store clerks leave an impression, which joins all other impressions on the five senses to create 7-Eleven's store image in our minds. The consumer's image of a store is, therefore, a combination of out-of-store factors; location (Chapter 7), advertising, and publicity (Chapter 11) plus the dozens of in-store variables perceived by the consumer.

Recently, in fact, 7-Eleven has conducted experiments to change its store image to that of a higher-quality provider of service foods. Managers have altered not only the merchandise mix but such store variables as colors, layout, light levels, and aisle widths to affect the consumer's perception of 7-Eleven's store.

This is why planning the store environment is so important to a retailer. Although advertising and other promotional activities are important in establishing a desired store image, the store itself makes the most significant and lasting impression on our collective consciousness, and it is here that the retailer must focus great energy on creating the right image.

This effort is complicated by the knowledge that consumers are extremely fickle, able to change their feelings about retailers at any time for little substantive reason, and the fact that today there are more stores than ever vying for limited consumer dollars. It is not surprising that image engineering—the ability to create and change a store's image—becomes more important every day for a retailer's survival.

By incorporating a cafe as an integral part of Barnes & Noble bookstores, a very relaxing and casual ambiance is created.

INCREASING SPACE PRODUCTIVITY

The store's image attracts customers, but while they are there, the store must also convince shoppers to make a purchase. Therefore, the store environment must also increase its space productivity, a goal that is summarized in a simple but powerful truism in retailing: *The more merchandise customers are exposed to, that is presented in a orderly manner, the more they tend to buy.* After all, the typical shopper in a department store goes into only two or three shopping areas per trip. Through careful planning of the store environment, the retailer can encourage customers to flow through the entire store, or at least more shopping areas, and see a wider variety of merchandise. The proper use of in-store advertising and displays will let the customer know what's happening in other shopping areas and encourage a visit to those areas. Conversely, however, the store doesn't want to have merchandise pushed into every conceivable nook and cranny of the store so that customers can't get to it.

DOLLAR $ & ¢ENTS

High-performance retailers design their stores to expose shoppers to as much merchandise that is displayed in a safe and orderly manner and creates an uncongested shopping environment.

Many retailers are focusing more attention on in-store marketing, based on the theory that marketing dollars spent inside the store, in the form of store design, merchandise presentation, visual displays, or in-store promotions, should lead to significantly greater sales and profit increases than marketing dollars spent in advertising and other out-of-store vehicles such as public relations and promotions. After all, it is easier to get a consumer who is already in your store to buy more merchandise than planned than to get a new consumer to come into your store. One factor that detracts from space productivity is shrinkage, or merchandise that can not be accounted for due to theft, loss, and damage. It is called shrinkage because you usually don't know what happened to the missing items, only that the inventory level in the store has somehow shrunk. Even stores that move customers through the entire space and effectively use in-store marketing techniques to maximize sales can fall victim to high shrinkage. Remember, when a store sells an item for $1.29, it earns only a small percentage of that sale, perhaps ranging from 15 to 60 cents. When that item is stolen, lost, or damaged, however, the store loses the entire $1.29, and this loss is deducted from the store's overall sales. Shrinkage ranges from 1 to 4 percent of retail sales. Although this may seem like a small number, consider that many retailers' after-tax profit is little more than 4 percent, so high shrinkage alone can make the difference between a profit and a loss.

> **Shrinkage**
> *represents merchandise that can not be accounted for due to theft, loss, or damage.*

Therefore, to enhance space productivity, retailers must incorporate planning, merchandise presentation, and design strategies that minimize shrinkage by avoiding hidden areas of the store that shoplifters can take advantage of and reduce the number of times merchandise must be moved, during which damage and loss can occur.

STORE PLANNING

LO • 2
Discuss the steps involved in planning the store

Planning an effective retail store is like planning an effective piece of writing, and moving through a store as a customer is much like reading through an article or a chapter in a book. The words are like the merchandise, which are there for you to review, understand, and consume. Just as a book needs more than words to make sense, a store needs more than merchandise to be an effective place to shop.

The store's layout and design is like the organization of chapters, sections, and subsections in this book. Grouping the words and thoughts into "mental chunks" makes the book easier to digest and understand. A store that is not broken into departments and categories would be impossible to shop. The pants would be mixed in with the shovels, the socks would be mixed in with the garden plants, and you wouldn't know where to begin.

Signs and graphics are like the headlines and punctuation, which give you cues to understanding the organization of both a book and the merchandise in a store. Without headlines and subheadlines, this chapter would be a stream of words, very difficult, and worse, boring to read and understand. Similarly, without signs, a store would seem like an endless sea of racks and merchandise difficult to understand and shop.

Finally, the illustrations, exhibits, and charts in this book are the retail equivalent of the visual displays and focal points, or areas where the merchandise is pulled off the shelf or racks and displayed in theatrical vignettes, which successful retailers use to break up the store space, illustrate merchandise opportunities in the store, and visually demonstrate how certain merchandise goes together or can work in your life. Like illustrations and exhibits in a book, these visual displays elaborate on the text, or the bulk of merchandise on the racks, to make statements.

More importantly, a retail store and a piece of writing are very similar in the way that they affect the consumer. Many writing coaches teach aspiring writers that each time an uncommon word is used, or a punctuation mark is missing, the reader hits a "speed bump" in the writing and must mentally pause to consider what is meant. After hitting three speed bumps, readers may conclude that the writing is too difficult to understand and quit reading.

It is the same in a retail store. All cues must work subliminally to organize the merchandise and guide the shopper effortlessly through the store. Each time that shoppers become a bit confused as to where they are, where they need to go, how much an item costs, or where certain merchandise is, they become frustrated. The first or second instance may not be noticed, but the shopper quickly becomes frustrated and may walk out, concluding that the store is too hard to shop.

Most shoppers cannot consciously identify the elements of a good store, but certainly they recognize when they are missing. We have all experienced the feeling that a store seems to "really have it together." It's easy to shop, fun, and exciting; the merchandise is easy to understand; the associates seem friendly. You conclude that this store is a "good shop" and, with any luck, are completely oblivious to the thousands of little details that have guided you through the shopping experience.

In retailing, the term floorplan indicates where merchandise and customer service departments are located, how customers circulate through the store, and how much space is dedicated to each department. The floorplan serves as the backbone of the store and is the fundamental structure around which every other element of the store environment takes shape. Therefore, the store's layout and design must be carefully planned to meet the retailer's merchandising goals, make the store easy to understand and shop, and allow merchandise to be effectively presented. The Global Retailing box describes how one American retailer obtained a patent for his store design and how today a Japanese company is taking his idea one step farther.

Floorplan
is a schematic which shows where merchandise and customer service departments are located, how customers circulate through the store, and how much space is dedicated to each department.

ALLOCATING SPACE

The starting point for developing a floorplan is analyzing how the available store space, usually measured in square footage, should be allocated to various departments, and this allocation can be based on mathematical calculation of the returns generated by different types of merchandise. However, before describing this process, we must understand the various types of space in the store.

TYPES OF SPACE NEEDED   Shoppers are most familiar with the sales floor, but this is not the only element in a retail store with which the planner must contend. There are five basic types of space needs in a store: (1) back room; (2) office and other functional spaces; (3) aisles, service areas, and other nonselling areas of the main sales floor; (4) wall merchandise space; and (5) floor merchandise space. The retailer must balance the quest for greater density of merchandise presentation with the functionality of the store and the ability to effectively shop the store. Because space is the retailer's ultimate scarce resource, rarely can the retailer achieve all its desired goals. Rather, most retailers find themselves compromising one or more dimensions, carefully weighing the priorities, strategic goals, and special constraints. In reviewing each of these categories of space, keep in mind that the goal is to make the largest portion possible of the space available to hold merchandise and to make the store an effective place to shop for the consumer.

THE SPIRIT OF CLARENCE SAUNDERS LIVES ON!

Clarence Saunders is the only retailer who ever received a patent for a store design. On October 9, 1917, he was issued U.S. Patent 124872 for his design for self-serving Piggly Wiggly stores. Under Saunders's patented layout, if you were to have entered one of his stores, you would have picked up a basket to the right of the cashier who was facing the door and would then have wandered (Piggly Wiggly fashion) past every product in the store until, once again, you reached the cashier at the entrance of the store. The cashier would have rung up your purchases, taken your payment, and placed the basket to his or her right for another customer to use. Thus, the unique advantage was that each of Saunders' stores was operated by one person!

When he died, Saunders was working on another revolutionary type of self-serving store: the Keydoozle. Using this format, on entering a store, you would have picked up a paper-tape machine to carry while you shopped. If you spotted an item you wished to purchase, you would have inserted the machine in a slot below the item. The item code would then be punched in the paper tape. If you wanted two of a particular item, you would insert the paper punch twice, etc. The cashier would then run the paper tape through a tape reader; and the reader, in turn, would activate a gravity feed that delivered the correct number of each item to the check-out while producing a sales check and computing the total owed.

Today, the spirit of Saunders continues to live on in Japan. Automated convenience stores are now being spread throughout Japan by the AM/PM chain of convenience stores, a sister chain of AM/PM in the United States. By the end of 1997, the chain had 90 stores; and by the year 2000, 500 stores are expected.

And the only employee who is working at each store is a security guard placed outside. Each item of merchandise in an AM/PM store is displayed behind glass with a stock number shown. You must enter into a computerized console the stock number and the quantity of each item you wish to purchase. The console then instructs you to enter the required amount of money for your purchase (there is, of course, a change machine for your convenience). Then, a long mechanized arm picks out the requested item! Within a minute or so, a neat bundle of goods comes sliding down a delivery chute, along with a plastic carrying bag in which you are to pack the items.

The stores provide no human contact. For security, there are surveillance cameras throughout each store, which are brightly lit and equipped with bulletproof glass. This type of setup eliminates the problem of hiring reliable help for a 24-hour-a-day operation and the problems associated with internal and external theft.

U.S. retailers will be watching this operation with interest. Japan now has about 50,000 conventional convenience stores. Trade estimates are that there will be 100,000 by the end of 2000—including several hundred computerized AM/PM stores!

SOURCE: Based on an article in Robert Kahn's *Retailing Today*, April 1997, and used with his permission.

BACK ROOM To operate virtually any type of retail store, some space is required as back room, which includes the receiving area to process arriving inventories and the stockroom to store surplus merchandise. The percentage of space dedicated to the back room varies greatly depending on the type of retailer, but the amount of space is shrinking for all types. Historically, back room percentages have ranged from nearly 50 percent in some department stores to as little as 10 percent in some small specialty and convenience stores. General merchandise stores have historically dedicated about 15 to 20 percent of their store space to the back room. The need to squeeze more sales out of expensive retail space, coupled with new distribution methods allowing smaller, more

Warehouse Clubs, like this Sam's Club, by placing merchandise on warehouse racks, use the floor space to both display and store merchandise and thus the sales floor doubles as the back room.

frequent merchandise deliveries from suppliers (called quick response inventory or efficient consumer response, depending on the industry involved), has allowed retailers to shrink their back rooms, with department stores cutting back to about 20 percent and others cutting back to 5 percent or even less.

Some recent retail formats such as warehouse clubs have only receiving areas but virtually no back room stock capacity. In these stores, the store fixtures are usually large "warehouse racks" that carry inventory at reachable heights (up to 84 inches) and carry large palettes or cartons of excess inventory at higher levels. These racks can go as high as 15 feet.

Warehouse clubs are taking advantage not only of the width and depth of the store, but also the height. In other words, whereas retailers pay expensive rents for their store space, as measured in square footage, the store and the merchandise can be stacked as high as possible at little additional cost, using the *cubic* footage of the store. The ability of shoppers to reach does limit the height at which merchandise can be stacked and retrieved by shoppers, but it does not limit the use of this high space to carry excess inventory. The same inventory carried in the back room would consume additional square footage, either causing higher rent or reducing the amount of space the shopper can effectively shop. Essentially, the sales floor doubles as the back room. Most important, this stocking method visually creates a dramatic low-cost image in the store, which can be advantageous to value-oriented retailers but detrimental to fashion or high-end retailers.

OFFICES AND OTHER FUNCTIONAL SPACES Every store must contain a certain amount of office and other functional space. This often includes a break room for associates, a training room, offices for the store manager and assistant managers, a cash office, bathroom facilities for both customers and employees, and perhaps other areas. Although necessary, the location of such functional spaces receives a lower priority than the location of the sales floor and stockroom. Often they are located on mezzanines over the front of the store or over the back stockroom or in side spaces too small to be stockrooms.

AISLES, SERVICES AREAS, AND OTHER NONSELLING AREAS   Even on the main sales floor, some space must be given up to nonselling functions, the most obvious of which is moving large numbers of shoppers through the store. The retailer's first step, particularly in larger stores, is to create main aisles through which shoppers will flow on their way through the store and secondary aisles that draw customers back into the merchandise. These aisles must be wide enough to accommodate peak crowds and in large stores may be as wide as 15 feet. The amount of space dedicated to aisles can be significant. For instance, a 15-foot aisle running around the perimeter of an 80,000 square-foot store (the size of a typical discount store) may consume 12,000 square feet, or 15 percent of the entire space!

In addition to aisles, space must be given to dressing rooms, layaway areas, service desks, and other customer service facilities that cannot be merchandised. Although the retailer always attempts to minimize the amount of nonmerchandisable space, customer service is an equally important part of a store and should not be short-changed.

FLOOR MERCHANDISE SPACE   Finally, we come to the store space with which we as shoppers are most familiar, the floor merchandise space. Here, many different types of fixtures are used to display a wide variety of merchandise. Generally speaking, retailers use so-called bulk fixtures on the floor to carry large quantities of merchandise. But increasingly, retailers are realizing that the best goal isn't just to cram the largest possible amount of merchandise on the floor but to attractively and effectively display the largest amount customers can understand and shop.

WALL MERCHANDISE SPACE   The walls are one of the most important elements of a retail store. They serve as fixtures holding tremendous amounts of merchandise, as well as serving as a visual backdrop for the merchandise on the floor.

SPACE ALLOCATION PLANNING   To determine the most productive allocation of space, the retailer must first analyze the profitability and productivity of various categories of merchandise. There are several methods for measuring these variables. Regardless of the method used, the results must somehow relate to some type of profitability performance measure (e.g., net sales, net profit, or gross margin) to the amount of space used in the store, to get a productivity figure to use in determining the best allocation of the square footage. There are two different types of situations in which a retailer may have to perform these tasks: revising the space allocation of an existing store and planning a new store.

IMPROVING SPACE PRODUCTIVITY IN EXISTING STORES   When a retailer has been in business for some time, it can develop a sales history on which to evaluate merchandise performance, refine space allocations, and enhance space productivity. One easy measure to use is the space productivity index, which compares the *percent of the store's total gross margin a particular merchandise category generates to its percentage of total store selling space used.* An index rating of 1.0 would be an ideal department size. If the index is greater than 1.0, the product category is generating a larger percentage of the store's gross margin than the percentage of store space it is using, and consideration should be given to allocating additional space to this category. If the index falls

Space productivity index *is a ratio which compares the percent of the store's total gross margin a particular merchandise category generates to its percentage of total store selling space used.*

EXHIBIT 13.2	MERCHANDISE PRODUCTIVITY ANALYSIS						
CATEGORY	TOTAL SALES	SALE AS % TOTAL	TOTAL SQ. FT.	SQ. FT. % TOTAL	SALES PER SQ. FT.	TOTAL G.M. $	G.M. $ % TOTAL	SPACE PRODUCTIVITY INDEX
Juniors	259,645	3.9	1,602	2.9	162.08	211,497	4.57	1.58
Dresses	47,829	0.7	608	1.1	78.67	33,426	0.72	0.66
Misses	512,458	7.7	3,702	6.7	138.43	429,403	9.29	1.39
Womens	170,819	2.6	1,934	3.5	88.33	148,899	3.22	0.92
Boys	184,485	2.8	2,542	4.6	72.58	144,866	3.13	0.68
Mens	751,604	11.3	3,591	6.5	209.30	603,330	13.05	2.01
Infants	204,983	3.1	1,658	3.0	123.63	142,545	3.08	1.03
Toddlers	47,829	0.7	497	0.9	96.24	43,261	0.94	1.04
Girls	191,318	2.9	2,542	4.6	75.27	157,573	3.41	0.74
Lingerie	273,311	4.1	2,431	4.4	112.43	262,548	5.68	1.29
Accessories	245,980	3.7	1,602	2.9	153.55	238,735	5.16	1.78
Jewelry	129,823	1.9	829	1.5	156.60	123,484	2.67	1.78
Total Softlines	3,020,084	45.2	23,537	42.6	128.31	2,539,566	54.92	1.29
Domestics	498,792	7.5	4,531	8.2	110.08	407,745	8.82	1.08
HBA	464,628	7.0	1,989	3.6	233.60	153,153	3.31	0.92
Housewares	457,795	6.8	3,591	6.5	127.48	254,979	5.51	0.85
Cosmetics	75,160	1.1	608	1.1	123.62	55,913	1.21	1.10
Tobacco	140,187	2.1	221	0.4	634.33	37,349	0.81	2.02
Candy	144,944	2.2	387	0.7	374.53	88,179	1.91	2.72
Sporting Goods	184,485	2.8	2,652	4.8	69.56	129,948	2.81	0.59
Stationery	307,475	4.6	2,763	5.0	111.28	254,150	5.50	1.10
Furniture	75,160	1.1	1,547	2.8	48.58	60,333	1.30	0.47
Home Entertainment	601,284	9.0	2,265	4.1	265.47	255,973	5.54	1.35
Toys	300,642	4.5	2,431	4.4	123.67	143,429	3.10	0.70
Seasonal	145,333	2.2	2,652	4.8	54.80	90,168	1.95	0.41
Hardware/Paint	163,986	2.5	2,100	3.8	78.09	111,274	2.41	0.63
Pet Supplies	13,666	0.2	55	0.1	248.47	13,094	0.28	2.83
Auto Accessories	81,993	1.2	1,271	2.3	64.51	29,227	0.63	0.27
Total Hardlines	3,655,480	54.8	29,061	52.6	125.79	2,084,914	45.08	0.86
Non-Selling	—	—	2,652	4.8	—	—	—	—
Total Scores	6,675,564	100.0	55,250	100.0		4,624,480	100.00	1.00

below 1.0, the product category is underperforming relative to other merchandise and should be considered for a reduction in space allocation. The merchandise productivity analysis shown in Exhibit 13.2 indicates that in this store, softlines categories, with an index of 1.29, are performing very well and perhaps should be given more space, and hardlines, with an index of 0.86, are underperforming and should be considered for downsizing.

Of course, as with all financial analysis, the space productivity index is simply a tool to help management make decisions, not a decision-making formula. Even though a certain category may have a low index, senior management may retain its full space because a new buyer has just been hired or because the category is an important image builder. A high-index category might not be given more space if management expects a hot fashion trend to cool off soon and believes the space productivity index for that category will drop accordingly.

SPACE ALLOCATIONS FOR A NEW STORE   When a retailer is creating a new store format, no productivity and profitability data are available on which to base the allocation of space. In these situations, the retailer bases space allocation on industry standards, previous experience with similar formats, or more frequently, the space required to carry the number of items specified by the buyers. Recently, Kroger, for example, used information obtained from existing stores to revamp its beverage section at new locations. In its newer stores, one side of a 48-foot-long aisle was committed to bottled waters and New Age drinks—some 150 different types. At the same time, Kroger reduced the space normally allocated for the traditional colas. Once a detailed assortment plan has been created, typical stock levels are estimated based on minimum and maximum quantities. The retailer can then determine the amount of shelf space required to carry this merchandise. By determining the space for each item, then for each category, and then for each department, the retailer can develop the floorplan for the store. As you can imagine, this is a grueling process. The Winners & Losers box describes a conversation that occurred between Sam Walton and Bob Kahn regarding the allocation of space in new Wal-Mart stores.

CIRCULATION

The circulation pattern not only ensures efficient movement of large numbers of shoppers through the store, exposing them to more merchandise, but also determines the character of the store. Disney Stores, for example, are designed not only to communicate the fun and excitement of the theme parks and famous characters, but also to get customers to walk to the back wall. After all, chances are good that when the customers get to the wall, they will return using a different route. This will expose them to more merchandise and increase the chance of a sale. There are four basic types of layout in use today—the free flow, grid, loop, and spine—each of which is described in the following discussion. Shoppers have been trained to associate certain circulation patterns with different types of stores, so in reading these descriptions, try to think of how they are used in different stores you shop and the store image they evoke in your mind.

FREE FLOW   The simplest type of store layout is a free-flow layout (Exhibit 13.3), in which fixtures and merchandise are grouped into free-flowing patterns on the sales floor. Customers are encouraged to flow freely through all the fixtures, because there are usually no defined traffic patterns in the store. This type of layout works well in small stores, usually smaller than 5,000 square feet, in which customers wish to browse through all of the merchandise. Generally, all the merchandise is of the same type, such as all fashion apparel, perhaps categorized only into tops and bottoms. If there is a greater variety of merchandise (e.g., men's and women's apparel, bedding, and health and beauty aids), a free-flow layout fails to provide cues as to where one department stops and another starts, confusing the shopper.

Free-flow layout
is a type of store layout in which fixtures and merchandise are grouped into free-flowing patterns on the sales floor.

BIGGER STORES; LESS MERCHANDISE

Robert Kahn, the editor of *Retailing Today*, likes to tell the story of when he was a director of and consultant to Wal-Mart. He explained to Sam Walton that one of the problems with retailers was that they thought the best ways to get higher sales per square foot (which they recognized was an important factor in store profitability, because the higher sales would reduce operating expenses as a percentage of sales) were to run more ads and add more merchandise displays. Thus, retailers at the time reduced their aisle space and stacked the merchandise so high that many customers either couldn't reach the top or were afraid to touch the display.

Kahn, however, had his own ideas about the customer's behavior in the store and explained that there was a better formula for higher sales per square foot:

SALES PER SQUARE FOOT = f (NUMBER OF CUSTOMERS) × (THE LENGTH OF TIME THEY SPEND IN THE STORE)

Therefore, according to Kahn's theory, retailers should concentrate on the time customers spend in the store, not how much merchandise they are exposed to. Based on this concept, Kahn outlined four things that Wal-Mart should do:

1. There should not be any aisle in which a customer could not comfortably pass another customer with a cart without having to ask that customer to move.
2. The restrooms should be the best in town so that a woman will never want to rush home to use the bathroom.
3. Forget the old retail adage that if a customer is sitting down, he or she isn't shopping. Put at least one bench in each store, in the alcove at the front door.
4. In all large stores put a coffee stand catty-corner from the snack bar so that customers could recharge themselves to spend more time and money shopping.

All four ideas seemed to agree with Sam Walton's concept that a retailer was a failure if after getting customers to come into the store, the retailer didn't do everything possible to satisfy all their needs and not force them to go elsewhere for merchandise.

As an experiment, Wal-Mart built 10 new 85,000-square-foot stores and 10 new 115,000-square-foot versions. The stores had identical amounts of fixtures and merchandise. The larger stores used the extra 30,000 square feet for wider aisles and extra space at the check-outs and tried to project an open, friendlier image. For example, the new restrooms, which were checked every two hours for cleanliness, had tile, not cement, floors; diaper changing shelves in both the men's and women's restrooms; and easy-to-clean vinyl-covered walls. Also, eight to 10 benches were placed in the main aisles. However, Wal-Mart dropped Kahn's coffee bar idea.

The first indication of the success of the larger store was that their parking lots were always full because shoppers were spending so much more time in the store. Sales figures showed that the larger store not only had higher sales but were also producing higher sales per square foot of store space than the smaller stores, despite all that "wasted" aisle space. Wal-Mart didn't know exactly what the customers were doing in these larger stores, just that they were spending more time and money. As a result, Wal-Mart went with the larger store model and increased from five to six parking spaces per 1,000 square foot of store space.

Recently, Kmart has been following Wal-Mart's example by widening the aisles and adding brighter lights and lower shelving in its 200 "high-frequency" stores. As a result, the same-store sales at these stores have increased 10 to 15 percent, whereas sales in the chain's other stores have increased only by low single digits.

SOURCE: Based on a letter from Bob Kahn and "Will Wider Aisles, Piles of Jeans Bring Customers Back to Kmart?" *Wall Street Journal*, April 8, 1997: B1, B8.

EXHIBIT 13.3	FREE-FLOW LAYOUT

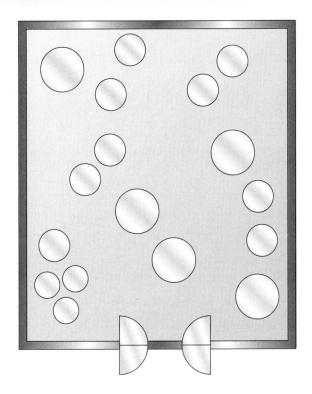

GRID   Another traditional form of store layout is the grid layout, in which the counters and fixtures are placed in long rows or "runs," usually at right angles, throughout the store. In a grid layout (Exhibit 13.4), customers circulate up and down through the fixtures, and, in fact, the grid layout is often referred to as a "maze." The most familiar examples of the grid layout are supermarkets and drug stores.

The grid is a true "shopping" layout, best used in retail environments in which the majority of customers wish to shop the entire store. In supermarkets, for instance, many shoppers flow methodically up and down all the fixture runs, looking for everything they might need along the way. However, if the shopper wishes to find only several specific categories, the grid can be confusing and frustrating, because it is difficult to see over the fixtures to where other merchandise is located (especially today, as fixtures have become higher). For example, Service Merchandise places discounted Black & Decker power tools at the rear of the store to lure customers into purchases of high-margin jewelry located near the entrance.[5] Supermarkets move customers through the entire store by placing the meats, dairy goods, and other high-frequency purchased items at the rear of the store. However, the retailers must be careful, forcing customers to do this when they don't want to, may frustrate customers and lead some to go elsewhere for merchandise.

Grid layout

is a type of store layout in which the counters and fixtures are placed in long rows or "runs" usually at right angles, throughout the store.

EXHIBIT 13.4	GRID LAYOUT

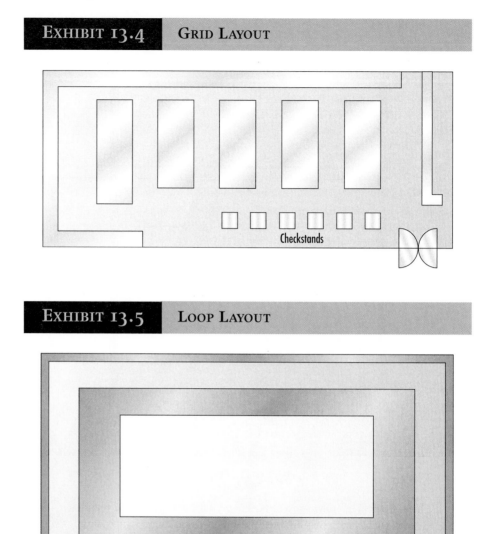

EXHIBIT 13.5	LOOP LAYOUT

Loop layout

is a type of store layout where a major customer aisle that begins at the entrance, loops through the store, usually in the shape of a circle, square, or rectangle, and then returns the customer to the front of the store.

LOOP   Over the past 15 years, the loop layout (sometimes called a racetrack layout) has become popular as a tool for enhancing the productivity of retail stores. A "loop," as shown in Exhibit 13.5, provides a major customer aisle that begins at the entrance, loops through the store, usually in the shape of a circle, square, or rectangle, and then returns the customer to the front of the store. Although this seems like a simple concept, the loop can be a powerful space productivity tool.

The major benefit of the loop layout is that it exposes shoppers to the greatest possible amount of merchandise. An effective circulation pattern must first guide customers throughout the store to encourage browsing and cross-shopping. Along the

EXHIBIT 13.6 | **SPINE LAYOUT**

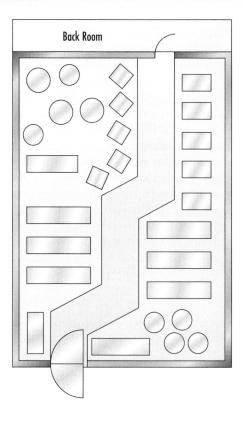

Back Room

way, shoppers must be able to easily see and understand merchandise to the left and right, so ideally the main aisle should never stray more than 60 feet from any merchandise. The way to simultaneously accomplish these two goals is to create a main circulation loop that mirrors the configuration of the outside walls of the store, and is never more than 60 feet from the outside wall. In larger stores, the interior island of the loop can itself be too large to easily see across, and internal walls may be created to shorten sightlines to merchandise.

SPINE The spine layout, which is shown in Exhibit 13.6, is essentially a variation of the free-flow, grid, and loop layouts and combines the advantages of all three in certain circumstances. A spine layout is based on a single main aisle running from the front to the back of the store, transporting customers in both directions. On either side of this spine, merchandise departments branch off toward the back or side walls. Within these departments, either a free-flow or grid layout can be used, depending on the type of merchandise and fixtures in use. The spine is heavily used by medium-sized specialty stores, either hardlines or softlines, ranging in size from 2,000 to 10,000 square feet. Often, especially in fashion stores, the spine is subtly set off by a change in floor coloring or surface and is not perceived as an aisle, even though it functions as such.

Spine layout
is a type of store layout based on a single main aisle running from the front to the back of the store, transporting customers in both directions and where on either side of this spine, merchandise departments using either a free-flow or grid pattern branch off toward the back side walls.

SHRINKAGE PREVENTION

When planning a store's layout and design, the prevention of shrinkage due to theft, damage, and loss must be considered. Some layouts will minimize vulnerability to shoplifters. One of the most important considerations when planning the layout is visibility of the merchandise. Most shoplifting takes place in fitting rooms, blind spots, aisles crowded with extra merchandise, or behind high displays. Fitting rooms, one of the most common scenes of the shoplifting crime, should be placed in visible areas that can be monitored by associates. Historically, display fixtures have been kept no higher than eye level, to allow store associates to monitor customers in other aisles. Recently, mass merchandisers have found that increased sales from the greater merchandise intensity of higher fixtures outweighs the increase in shoplifting due to reduced visibility. This depends greatly on merchandise type, however. Expensive items that are easily placed into pockets and handbags, such as compact discs, are high-theft items and are usually kept on low fixtures to discourage shoplifting. The manager's office and other security windows can be an excellent deterrent to shoplifting if they are placed in an obvious area above the sales floor level, where managers can easily see the entire store. Electronic security systems including sensor tags and video cameras have become very popular and are usually located in a highly visible location to serve as a deterrent.

LO • 3
Describe how various types of fixtures, merchandise presentation methods and techniques, and the psychology of merchandise presentation are used to increase the productivity of the sales floor

On-shelf merchandising *is the display of merchandise on counters, racks, shelves, and fixtures throughout the store.*

PLANNING FIXTURES AND MERCHANDISE PRESENTATION

Retailing is theater, and in no area is that more true than in merchandise presentation. Recently, retailers have been increasing their emphases on merchandise presentation, as competition has grown and stores try to squeeze more sales out of existing square footage. There are two basic types of merchandise presentation, on-shelf merchandising and visual merchandising. In thinking of retailing as "theater," as Federated's Questrom suggested in the chapter's opening paragraph, visual merchandising is analogous to the stage props that set scenes and serve as backdrops.

Merchandise presentation is a complex activity best learned on the retail floor. Although this text does not attempt to teach the art and science of merchandise presentation, you should be familiar with a number of basic components of merchandise presentation and their potential impact on store image and sales, including fixture type and selection and certain techniques and methods of on-shelf merchandising.

On-shelf merchandising, which describes the merchandise that is displayed on and in counters, racks, shelves, and fixtures throughout the store, represents the stars on our theater stage. This is the merchandise that the shopper actually touches, tries on, examines, reads, understands, and, it is hoped, buys. Therefore, on-shelf merchandising must not only present the merchandise attractively, it must display the merchandise in a manner that is easy to understand and accessible to the shopper. Further, it must be reasonably easy to maintain, with customers themselves able to replace merchandise so it is equally appealing to the next shopper. It must not be so overwhelming that the customer is afraid to touch the merchandise. As a result of getting more than 25,000 complaints a year regarding injuries from falling merchandise, Wal-Mart has again sought to reduce the level of merchandise carried in every store.[6] After all, despite

Crate & Barrel makes effective use of lighting to highlight and feature merchandise on display.

the efforts of top management, many mangers still falsely believe the best way to improve sales (and their year-end bonus) is to put as much merchandise as possible into the store.

FIXTURE TYPES

Store fixtures fall into three basic categories: hardlines, softlines, and wall fixtures.

HARDLINES FIXTURES

The workhorse fixture in most hardlines departments is known as the gondola, so named because it is a long structure consisting of a large base, a vertical spine or wall sticking up as high as eight feet, fitted with sockets or notches into which a variety of shelves, peghooks, bins, baskets, and other hardware can be inserted. The basic gondola can hold a wide variety of merchandise by means of hardware hung from the vertical spine. If you think of your last trip to a discount store or supermarket, the long, heavy-duty fixtures fitted predominantly with shelves are gondolas. In addition to the gondola, a few other types of fixtures are in common use today: tables, large bins, and simple flat-base decks. These fixtures are commonly used in promotional aisles to display advertised or other special value merchandise.

SOFTLINES FIXTURES

The bulky gondola is inappropriate for fashion-oriented softlines merchandise. A large array of fixtures have been developed to accommodate the special needs of softlines, which often are hung on hangers. As shown in Exhibit 13.7, the four-way feature rack and the round rack are the two fixtures most heavily used today. These smaller, more specialized fixtures have replaced the straight rack, a long pipe with legs on each end from which rows of apparel were hung, which for generations was the most prevalent softlines fixture. While it held a great quantity of garments and was easy to maintain, the straight rack provided few opportunities to

Gondola

is a common display fixture which is long and consists of a large base, a vertical spine or wall sticking up as high as eight feet, fitted with sockets or notches into which a variety of shelves, peghooks, bins, baskets, and other hardware can be inserted.

Exhibit 13.7	Four-Way Feature Rack and Round Rack

Bulk or capacity fixture
is a display fixture which is intended to hold the bulk of merchandise without looking as heavy as a long straight rack of merchandise.

Feature fixture
is a display fixture which draws special attention to selected features (e.g., color, shape, or style) of merchandise.

differentiate one style or color of garment from another, which merchants have found is the key to selling more. A straight rack is like the hanger rod in your closet, and if you think of what you see when you open your closet, it is nothing more than sleeves. You know your own clothes, so sleeves are enough to tip you off to what the rest of the garment looks like. When you are shopping, however, the more of the garment you are exposed to, and the more varieties of size, silhouette (shape), and color, the more you are going to buy. So, merchants prefer "face-out" presentations over "sleeve-out" presentations. Of course, face-outs take up more space than sleeve-outs, so it is impractical to face-out all or even a high percentage of the total merchandise on the floor.

The round rack is known as a bulk or capacity fixture and is intended to hold the bulk of merchandise without looking as heavy as a long straight rack of merchandise. Although it is smaller than the straight rack, it too allows only sleeve-outs unless fitted with special hardware. The four-way rack, however, is considered a feature fixture, because it presents merchandise in a manner that features certain characteristics of the merchandise (e.g., color, shape, or style). The ingenious design allows it also to hold a large quantity of merchandise on the hanger arms behind the four face-outs. However, to be easily shopped, all the merchandise on one arm must be the same type of garment, with variations only in color and size. When poorly merchandised so that the front garment doesn't match those behind it, the four-way leaves the customer in the same quandary as the straight rack.

WALL FIXTURES   The last type of fixture is designed to be hung on the wall. To make a store's plain wall merchandisable, it is usually covered with a vertical skin that is fitted with vertical columns of notches similar to those on the gondola, into which a variety of hardware can be inserted. Shelves, peghooks, bins, baskets, and even hanger bars can be fitted into wall systems. Hanger bars can be hung parallel to the wall, much like your closet bar, so that large quantities of garments can be "sleeved-out," or they can protrude perpendicularly from the wall, either straight out (straight-outs) or angled down (waterfalls), to allow merchandise to be faced-out. The primary quality to remember about wall systems is that walls can generally be merchandised much higher than floor fixtures. Whereas on the floor, round racks are kept to a maximum of 42 inches so that customers can easily see over them to other merchandise, garments can be hung on the wall as high as customers can reach, which is generally about 72 inches. This allows walls to be "double-hung" with two rows of garments, or even "triple-hung" with smaller children's apparel. Therefore, walls not only hold large amounts of merchandise but also serve as a visual backdrop for the department.

MERCHANDISE PRESENTATION PLANNING

As we have just discussed, there is a large array of fixtures and hardware for use by retailers. This may seem to present an endless variety of ways to merchandise product, but there are essentially six methods of merchandise presentation:

1. *Shelving.* The majority of merchandise is placed on shelves that are inserted into gondolas or wall systems. Shelving is a flexible, easy-to-maintain merchandise presentation method.
2. *Hanging.* Apparel on hangers can be hung from softlines fixtures such as round racks and four-way racks or from bars installed on gondolas or wall systems.
3. *Pegging.* Small merchandise can be hung from peghooks, which are small rods inserted into gondolas or wall systems. Used in both softlines and hardlines, pegging gives a neat, orderly appearance but can be labor-intensive to display and maintain.
4. *Folding.* Higher-margin or large, unwieldy softlines merchandise can be folded and then stacked onto shelves or placed on tables. This can create a high-fashion image, such as when bath towels are taken off peghooks and neatly folded and stacked high up the wall.
5. *Stacking.* Large hardlines merchandise can be stacked on shelves, the base decks of gondolas, or "flats," which are platforms placed directly on the floor. Stacking is easily maintained and gives an image of high volume and low price.
6. *Dumping.* As discussed in the Behind the Scenes box earlier in the chapter, large quantities of small merchandise can be dumped in bins or baskets inserted into gondolas or wall systems. This highly effective promotional method can be used in softlines (socks, wash cloths) or hardlines (batteries, grocery products, candy) and creates a high-volume, low-cost image.

The method of merchandise presentation can have a dramatic impact on image and space productivity. Different merchandise presentation methods have been shown to strongly influence buying habits and cause consumers to purchase more. There is a certain "psychology of merchandise presentation," which must be carefully considered in developing merchandise presentation schemes. Less than 20 percent of department store shoppers make an impulse (unplanned) purchase. And these purchases are made by only 60 percent of the shoppers who actually entered the store with an intent to make a specific purchase. Thus, 40 percent of the shoppers who enter a store to make a purchase are "wasted" because of a failure by the store to use merchandise presentation to generate additional purchases.[7] This is why department store design incorporates a gauntlet of goodies to stimulate impulse buys. For example, cosmetics, usually the store's most profitable department, is always near the main entrance. Typically, the department is leased to cosmetic companies who use their own salespersons to sell the perfume, lipstick, and eye shadow. The other high-impulse items (e.g., hosiery, jewelry, handbags, and shoes) are usually nearby, whereas the "demand" products (e.g., furniture) are on upper floors. After all, these stores would be unprofitable if they failed to induce a significant amount of impulse buying.

The following are a number of key psychological factors to consider when merchandising stores:

1. *Value/Fashion image.* One of merchandise presentation's most important psychological effects is to foster an image in the customer's mind of how trendy, exclusive, pricey, or value-oriented the merchandise is. For each of the merchandise presentation methods mentioned previously, we discussed its effect on price image. By changing the merchandise presentation method, we can change the perception of our towel display from common, high-volume, high-value, to an exclusive selection of high-fashion merchandise, which presumably will be at higher prices.

2. *Angles and sightlines.* Research has shown that as customers move through a retail store, they view the store at approximately 45-degree angles from the path of travel, as shown in Exhibit 13.8, rather than perpendicular to their path. Although this seems logical, most stores are set up at right angles because it is easier and consumes less space. Therefore, merchandise and signage often wind up being at a 90-degree angle to the main aisle. Exhibit 13.8 also shows how four-way feature racks can be more effectively merchandised by being turned to meet the shoppers' sightlines head-on.

3. *Vertical color blocking.* To be most effective, merchandise should be displayed in vertical bands of color wherever possible. As customers move through the store, their eyes naturally view a "swath" approximately two feet in height, parallel to the floor, at about eye level. This is shown in Exhibit 13.9. This visual swath of merchandise will be viewed as a rainbow of colors if each merchandise item is displayed vertically by color (i.e., the vertical columns represent different colors and within these colors could be different sizes). This method of merchandise presentation will create such a strong visual effect that shoppers will be exposed to more merchandise, and this in turn will increase sales. In addition, when shopping for clothing, customers most often think first of color. Thus, they can easily find the column of color on display and locate their size.

SELECTING THE PROPER FIXTURES AND MERCHANDISE PRESENTATION METHODS[8]

Proper fixtures emphasize the key selling attributes of merchandise while not overpowering it. Although it is not always possible to follow, a good guideline for selecting fixtures is to *match the fixture to the merchandise, not the merchandise to the fixture.* This

EXHIBIT 13.8	45-DEGREE CUSTOMER SIGHTLINE

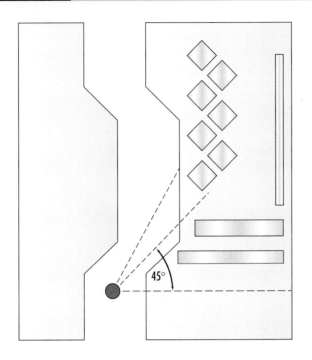

EXHIBIT 13.9	VERTICAL COLOR BLOCKING

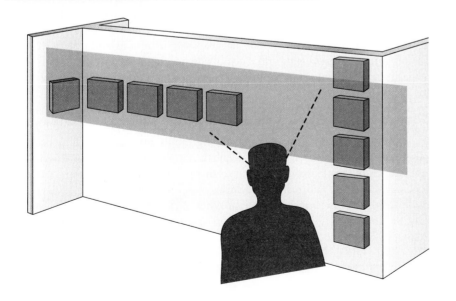

means you should only use fixtures that are sensitive to the nature of the merchandise, but all too often, retailers are forced to put merchandise on the wrong fixture.

Consider intimate apparel, for instance. This is a fast-selling, high-margin merchandise category that can enhance a retailer's image in fashion merchandising. Although retailers entering into this business might be tempted to place intimate apparel on existing shelves of a gondola, they would be well served to consider special fixtures to enhance the delicate qualities of intimate apparel. The large, metal, bulky appearance of the gondola will overpower the small, delicate intimate apparel and therefore reduce sales potential. More delicate fixtures made of softer materials will enhance sales. Similarly, it would not make sense to bulk stack fragile merchandise, because the weight of items might damage those lower in the stack. It would not make sense to peghook large, bulky items because they take up too much room and might be too heavy for the peghook.

VISUAL MERCHANDISING

Visual merchandising is the artistic display of merchandise and theatrical props used as scene-setting decoration in the store.

The second type of merchandise presentation, visual merchandising, is the artistic display of merchandise and theatrical props used as scene-setting decoration in the store. Although on-shelf merchandising must be tastefully displayed to encourage shopping, a store with just on-shelf merchandising would be boring. In fact, many low-price stores contain little visual merchandising, and indeed they do appear more boring than their upscale cousins in fashion retailing, who concentrate heavily on visual merchandising displays, or "visuals," as they are often called.

An effective visual merchandising display has several key characteristics. Visual displays are not typically associated with a fixture that makes the shopping experience easier but are located in a focal point, feature area, or other area remote from the on-shelf merchandising and perhaps even out of reach of the customer. Its goal is to create a feeling in the store conducive to buying merchandise.

Another characteristic of visual merchandising is its use of props and elements in addition to merchandise. In fact, visuals don't always include merchandise—they may just be interesting displays of items somehow related to the merchandise offering or to a mood the retailer wishes to create. It may be a wooden barrel, a miniature airplane, or a mock tree with autumn leaves. Visuals are like the illustrations and design elements in a book that make it interesting and tell you whether this is an upscale, serious shopping experience; a frivolous, fun shopping experience; or a down-and-dirty, low-price shopping experience.

To be most effective, however, visuals should incorporate relevant merchandise. In apparel retailing, mannequins or figure forms are used to display merchandise as it might appear on a person, rather than hanging limply on a hanger. This helps the shopper visualize how these garments will enhance their appearance. Good fashion visuals include more than just one garment to show how tops and bottoms go together and how belts, scarves, and other accessories can be combined to create an overall fashion look. This is called accessorization. When successful, visuals help the shopper translate the merchandise presentation from "garments on a rack" to "fashionable clothes that will look good on me."

The retailer should be careful in setting visuals to make sure that the displays don't create Chinese walls that make it difficult for shoppers to reach other areas of the store.

STORE DESIGN

LO • 4
Describe why store design is so important to a store's success

Store design is the element most responsible for the first of our two goals in planning the store environment: creating a distinctive and memorable store image. Store design encompasses both the exterior and the interior of the store. On the exterior, we have the storefront, signage, and entrance, all of which are critical to attracting passing shoppers and enticing them to enter. On the inside, store design includes the architectural elements and finishes on all surfaces (e.g., wall coverings, floorcoverings, and ceiling). There are literally hundreds of details in a store's design, and all must work together to create the desired store ambiance, which is the overall feeling or mood projected by a store through its aesthetic appeal to human senses.

Ambiance
is the overall feeling or mood projected by a store through its aesthetic appeal to human senses.

STOREFRONT DESIGN

If the retail store can be compared with a book, then the storefront, or store exterior, is like the book cover. It must be noticeable, easily identified by passing motorists or mall shoppers, and memorable. The storefront must clearly identify the name and general nature of the store and give some hint as to the merchandise inside. Generally, the storefront design includes all exterior signage and the architecture of the storefront itself.

In many cases, the storefront includes display windows, which serve as an advertising medium for the store. Store windows must arrest the attention of passing shoppers, enticing them inside the store. Therefore, windows should be maintained in exciting visual displays that are changed frequently, are fun and exciting, and reflect the merchandise offering inside.

INTERIOR DESIGN

Unless you have ever been responsible for redecorating a house or room, you may be unaware of the dozens of design elements that go into a physical space. We can break interior design into two types of elements: the finishes applied to surfaces and architectural shapes. Think of all the elements from the floor to the ceiling. First, we have some type of floorcovering placed over either a concrete or wood floor—at the least paint, but more frequently vinyl floorcovering, carpet, ceramic tile, or marble. Each of these different surfaces leaves a different impression on the shopper. An unpainted concrete floor conveys a low-cost, no-frills environment. Vinyl floorcovering makes another statement, which, depending on its quality, sheen, color, and design pattern, can vary from very downscale to very upscale. Carpet suggests a homelike atmosphere conducive to selling apparel. Ceramic tile and especially marble suggest an upscale, exclusive, and probably expensive shopping experience.

Retailers even have more options for covering the walls: from paint and wallpaper to hundreds of types of paneling. The ceiling must also receive a design treatment, whether it is finished drywall (a very upscale image because it is expensive to do) or a suspended ceiling (very common and economical, although not distinctive), or perhaps even an open ceiling with all the pipes and wires above painted black (which suggests a low-price warehouse approach). Then, there are thousands of types of moldings

Crabtree & Evelyn makes effective use of fragrances and odors to generate smells that reinforce its store ambiance.

that can be applied to the transitions from floor to wall to ceiling, and hundreds of architectural design elements that can be incorporated.

LIGHTING DESIGN

Another important, although often overlooked, element in a successful store design is lighting. Although very little academic research has been conducted on lighting's effects, retailers have come to understand lighting as a science that can greatly enhance store sales. One of the keys to success for Blockbuster Video was said to have been its move away from the boring use of 100 watt bulbs that its competitors used. Department stores, however, have found that raising lighting levels in fashion departments can actually discourage sales, because bright lighting suggests a discount store image. Brighter in-store lighting also influences shoppers to examine and handle more merchandise in a wine store.[9]

Lighting design, however, is not limited to simple light levels. Contemporary lighting design requires an in-depth knowledge of electrical engineering and the effect of light on color and texture. Not only have retailers learned that different types and levels of lighting can have a significant impact on sales, but the types of light sources available have multiplied quickly. Today, there are literally hundreds of light fixtures and lamps (bulbs) to choose.

SOUNDS AND SMELLS: TOTAL SENSORY MARKETING

Effective store design appeals to all human senses of sight, sound, smell, and touch. Obviously, the majority of design activity in a retail store is focused on affecting sight. Research has shown that the other senses can be very important, too, and many retailers are beginning to engineer the smells and sounds in their stores.

Because smell is believed to be the most closely linked of all the senses for memory and emotions, retailers hope that its use as a key in-store marketing tool will put consumers in the "mood." Victoria's Secret has deployed potpourri caches throughout its store, and in fact now sells them, to create the ambiance of a lingerie closet. The Knot Shop, a men's tie store catering to female shoppers buying ties as gifts, uses scent tiles impregnated with leather and tobacco scents to create the ambiance of a men's store, with the goal of making female customers think that the store is the type of store in which their male friend or spouse would buy his own tie.

Retailers have piped music (e.g., Muzak) into their stores for generations, believing that a musical backdrop will create a more relaxing environment and encourage customers to stay longer. Now, Muzak the company that pioneered delivering music in over 50 formats to retail stores and offices is delivering music videos to retailers such as Radio Shack and Foot Locker and also plans to deliver music to internet web sites.[10] Increasingly, music is being seen as a valuable marketing tool, because the right music can create an environment that is both soothing and reflective of the merchandise being offered. For example, a jeans retailer might play hip-hop over baggies and classic rock over the Dockers. Researchers believe that although the tempo of music affects how long shoppers stay in a store, the type of music may be just as influential on how much they purchase.[11] For instance, although classical music is soothing and has been shown to encourage customers to shop longer[12] and select more expensive merchandise,[13] it may be inconsistent with the desired ambiance of a trendy fashion store catering to college-age women. Today, some retailers are experimenting with placing advertisements in with the background music. Other retailers have found a different use for this canned music. 7-Eleven has installed it outside stores in Canada, California, Maryland, and Florida to repel teenagers and vagrants.[14]

DOLLAR $ & CENTS

High-performance retailers use exterior designs that pull shoppers into the store and interior designs that stimulate sales.

VISUAL COMMUNICATIONS

LO • 5
Explain the role of visual communications in a retail store

The last chapter was devoted to the retail selling process. However, sales associates can't always be available to assist customers, particularly in this era of increased competitive pressure and reduced gross margins, which has caused many retailers to cut costs by reducing their sales staffs. Even department stores, which staked their reputations on high levels of personal customer service, have had to reduce their service levels and learn to rely on alternative service strategies. How then, can retailers provide good selling communications and high customer service while controlling labor costs?

The answer is visual communications, in the form of in-store signage and graphics. Retailers can plan the store environment to incorporate signs, large photopanels, and other visual devices that serve as silent salespersons, providing shoppers with much needed information and directions on how to shop the store, evaluate merchandise, and make purchases. Because these visual communications are inanimate objects that stay permanently in place, they require only a one-time installation cost and low maintenance and can always be relied on to perform their function, the same way, for every shopper. Unlike sales associates, visual communications are never late for work, are never in a bad mood, and never mistreat customers. Of course, neither are they as effective as a good sales associate, who provides the personal touch that makes customers feel welcome and comfortable. But when carefully balanced with personal service, visual communications, with their reliability and low cost, can create an effective selling environment and are therefore becoming an important tool in the store designer's toolbox.

Earlier, we likened a retail store to a well-written book. Visual communications are akin to the headlines, subheads, illustrations, and captions that give the reader direction and illustrate the written descriptions. Without visual communications, a store would be like a newspaper full of words but no headlines, a jumbled, incomprehensible mess of merchandise. An effective visual communications program includes a range of messages, from those large and bold in nature, used sparingly to provide cues to the gross organization of the space, to the smaller, more specific and plentiful messages that describe actual merchandise. A visual communications program includes the following important elements.

NAME, LOGO, AND RETAIL IDENTITY

The first and most visible element in a comprehensive visual communications program is the retailer's identity, composed of the store name, logomark, and supporting visual elements. The name and logo are seen not only on the storefront and throughout the store but also in advertising and all communications with the consumers, and therefore they must be catchy, memorable, and most of all, reflective of the retailer's merchandising mission. Historically, many retail companies have taken the name of their founders, as is the case with most department stores. That practice has fallen out of vogue, however, as retailing has become a game of crafty store images and catchy retail identities. A founder's name rarely captures the merchandising spirit of a company as well as names such as Bath & Body Works, Home Depot, and Toys "Я" Us. With advertising messages bombarding customers more than ever and the effectiveness of each message waning, retailers have found it necessary for their names to be highly distinctive, as well as descriptive of their unique offerings.

Once a name has been chosen, a logo is developed to visually portray the name in a creative and memorable manner. Again, the key is to keep the logo simple and easy to understand at a glance, while making it exciting enough to leave a lasting image in the customers' minds. The logo is often accompanied by taglines that provide more description of the store concept, such as "Fashions for the Home." Kmart, for example, changed its logo to the big red "K" in an effort to reflect its move into an upscale environment and away from its old "polyester" and "blue-light" image.

The logo's most prominent placement is on the outside of the store. This is critical to attracting customers and creating high store traffic. Another reason why the store name and logo should be succinct and descriptive is because this important role is often played to motorists passing by at 45 miles per hour.

Wet Seal in Coata Mesa, California, heavily relies on visual communication, including a video wall to help create an effective selling envirnoment.

INSTITUTIONAL SIGNAGE

Once inside the store, the first level of visual communications is known as institutional signage, or signage that describes the merchandising mission, customer service policies, and other messages on behalf of the retail institution. This signage is usually located at the store entrance, to properly greet entering customers, and at service points such as the service desk, layaway window, and cash registers. In addition, some retailers place customer service signage throughout the store, to reinforce special policies several times during the shopping trip. This signage might include messages such as "Lowest Price Guaranteed" or "All Major Credit Cards Accepted."

DIRECTIONAL, DEPARTMENTAL, AND CATEGORY SIGNAGE

Directional and departmental signage serve as the highest level of organization in an overall signage program. These signs are usually large and placed fairly high, so they can be seen throughout the store. They help guide the shopper through the shopping trip and locate specific departments of interest. Not all stores use directional signage, particularly in smaller store environments where it is not necessary, but virtually all stores larger than 10,000 square feet in size use some type of departmental signage. Once a shopper locates and moves close to a particular department, category signage is used to call out and locate specific merchandise categories. Category signage is usually smaller in size, because it is intended to be seen from a shorter distance and is located on or close to the fixture itself. For instance, the departmental sign might say "Sporting Goods" and be two feet high and six feet wide and hang from the ceiling. However, the category signage might be only six inches high and two feet wide, affixed to the top of the gondola, and read "Hunting," "Tennis," or "Fitness."

Directional and departmental signage *are large signs that are usually placed fairly high, so they can be seen throughout the store.*

Category signage *are smaller than directional and departmental signage and are intended to be seen from a shorter distance and are located on or close to the fixture itself where the merchandise is displayed.*

POINT-OF-SALE (POS) SIGNAGE

The next level of signage is even smaller, placed closer to the merchandise, and known as point-of-sale signage, or POS signage. Because POS signage is intended to give details about specific merchandise items, it usually contains more words and is affixed directly to fixtures. POS signage may range in size from 11 by 17 inches to a 3-by-5-inch card with very small words describing an item. Always, however, the most important function of POS signage is to clearly state the price of the merchandise being signed.

POS signage includes a set of sign holders used throughout the store, along with a variety of printed signs that can be inserted into the hardware. Store associates mix and match the signage and hardware as directed by management, so that POS signage changes frequently. Special POS signs for sales, clearance, and "as advertised" are often a different color than the normal price signage to highlight these special values.

LIFESTYLE GRAPHICS

Visual communications encompass more than just words. Many stores incorporate large graphics panels showing so-called lifestyle images in important departments. These photo images portray either the merchandise, often as it is being used, or simply images of related items or models that convey an image conducive to buying the product. In a high-fashion department, lifestyle photography might show a scene of movie stars arriving at a nightclub in very trendy fashions, suggesting that similar fashions are available in that department. In sporting goods, a lifestyle image might show an isolated lake surrounded by autumn colored trees, with mist rising off the water and the sun rising in the background.

Retailers must be careful when choosing lifestyle photography, for as the saying goes, "beauty is in the eye of the beholder." One person's lifestyle is not necessarily another's, so lifestyle photography must be kept very general in nature to be attractive to the majority and offensive to none. Increasingly, photopanels and lifestyle imagery, which can be expensive to create, are being provided free of charge to retailers by merchandise vendors who are looking to gain an advantage for their products on the retail floor.

DOLLAR $ & CENTS

Retailers can use visual communications such as institutional signage, directional and departmental signage, category and POS signage, and lifestyle graphics to communicate more effectively with shoppers and increase space productivity.

STUDENT STUDY GUIDE

SUMMARY

LO • 1   **WHAT ARE THE ELEMENTS OF A STORE'S ENVIRONMENT?**
In this chapter, we focused on the retail store, a key factor influencing the consumer's initial perception of the retailer. It must effectively convey the store image desired by the retailer and provide a shopping environment that is conducive to high sales. The guiding principle in effective store planning, merchandise presentation, and design is that the more merchandise customers are exposed to, the more they tend to buy. This depends largely on planning the name, logo, and visual appearance of the store to convey a desired market positioning image. While retailers work diligently to influence their images, true store image is an amalgam of all messages consumers receive, from advertising, to stories they hear from friends, to the store itself.

LO • 2   **WHAT IS INVOLVED IN STORE PLANNING?**   Store planning refers to developing a plan for the organization of the retail store. First, the retailer must decide how to allocate the available square footage among the various types of space needed. This is usually accomplished by conducting a mathematical analysis of the productivity of various merchandise categories. By comparing the sales and/or gross margin produced by various categories with the space they use, the retailer can develop a plan for the optimal allocation of available space. Next, a floorplan is then created, showing the placement and circulation patterns for all merchandise departments. Finally, thought must be given as to how the floorplan can aid in reducing shrinkage.

LO • 3   **HOW ARE THE VARIOUS TYPES OF FIXTURES, MERCHANDISE PRESENTATION METHODS AND TECHNIQUES, AND THE PSYCHOLOGY OF MERCHANDISE PRESENTATION USED TO INCREASE THE PRODUCTIVITY OF THE SALES FLOOR?**   Fixture selection and merchandise presentation are critical to exposing customers to the maximum amount of merchandise. There are many types of store fixtures, as well as specific methods of merchandise presentation, which have been shown to maximize merchandise exposure and lead to increased sales. Particularly, there is a psychology of merchandise presentation that uses the customer's natural shopping behaviors and adopts merchandise presentation to match them. In addition to maximizing sales, fixture selection and merchandise presentation must conform to operational constraints and be easy to maintain.

LO • 4   **WHY IS STORE DESIGN SO IMPORTANT TO A STORE'S SUCCESS?**   The most visible element of the store is the design of its storefront and interior decor. The storefront or exterior must be eye-catching, inviting, and reflective of the merchandise offering inside. The interior design must be comfortable, put the shopper in the proper buying mood, and provide a backdrop that enhances but does not overpower the merchandise. The store designer must always remember that shoppers are there to look at the merchandise, not the store design.

LO•5 **WHAT IS THE ROLE OF VISUAL COMMUNICATIONS IN A RETAIL STORE?** A successful selling environment is based on effective visual communications with the customers. Because shoppers require information even when sales associates are not available, visual communications must be used throughout the store to provide direction, specific information, and prices. A visual communications program begins with the store name and logo and includes a range of interior signage that walks the customer through the buying experience.

Finally, there are literally hundreds of details in a successful retail store, and all must be carefully coordinated to create a cohesive, targeted store image that reflects the retailer's mission.

TERMS TO REMEMBER

store image	on-shelf merchandising
space productivity	gondola
shrinkage	bulk or capacity fixture
floorplan	feature fixture
space productivity index	visual merchandising
free-flow layout	ambiance
grid layout	directional and departmental signage
loop layout	category signage
spine layout	point-of-sale signage

REVIEW AND DISCUSSION QUESTIONS

LO•1 **WHAT ARE THE ELEMENTS OF A STORE'S ENVIRONMENT?**

1. Discuss the two primary objectives of the store environment and how these are achieved.
2. Discuss some of the constraints retailers face when trying to change their market position.
3. What is merchandise presentation and how does it affect sales?
4. What is the simple but powerful truism in retailing that store planners can use as a guide to increasing the space productivity of a store environment?
5. Why are retailers focusing increasingly on *in-store marketing*? Discuss some in-store marketing strategies and their effect on customers.

LO•2 **WHAT IS INVOLVED IN STORE PLANNING?**

6. What lessons can store planners draw from an effectively written book?
7. Discuss the various types of space in a retail store, describing the role of each.
8. Describe the space allocation planning process. How is this different for a new store as opposed to an existing store?
9. Identify the four main types of store layouts, discussing their differences and impact on customers.

LO•3 **HOW ARE THE VARIOUS TYPES OF FIXTURES, MERCHANDISE PRESENTATION METHODS AND TECHNIQUES, AND THE PSYCHOLOGY OF MERCHANDISE PRESENTATION USED TO INCREASE THE PRODUCTIVITY OF THE SALES FLOOR?**

10. In the theater of retailing, discuss the differences between the "props and visual backdrops" and the "stars."

11. Discuss the different uses of bulk or capacity fixtures and feature fixtures.
12. If retail space is such a scarce resource, why shouldn't an apparel retailer always use the "sleeved-out" approach to stock more merchandise in the limited available space?
13. What is the psychology of merchandise presentation and how is it used.

LO • 4 WHY IS STORE DESIGN SO IMPORTANT TO A STORE'S SUCCESS?

14. What are the goals of interior and exterior design?
15. Why is lighting design important to store planners?
16. Can sounds and smell influence store performance?

LO • 5 WHAT IS THE ROLE OF VISUAL COMMUNICATIONS IN A RETAIL STORE?

17. What are the goals of visual communications?
18. How are the different types of visual communications used and what is their effect on customers.
19. Why isn't the founder's name a good choice for the name of a retail store?

SAMPLE TEST QUESTIONS

LO • 1 THE TWO PRIMARY OBJECTIVES OF THE STORE ENVIRONMENT ARE

a. effective sales management and creating a distinctive ambiance
b. creating the store image and increasing space productivity
c. creative merchandise presentation and effective store traffic control
d. maximizing impulse purchase opportunity and effective shelf space allocation
e. maintaining market share and effective merchandise control

LO • 2 THE GOAL OF STORE LAYOUT AND DESIGN IN STORE PLANNING SHOULD BE TO

a. maximize customer access to high-profit items
b. evenly divide floor space between the five functional areas of a retail store
c. make the store easy to understand and shop and allow the merchandise to be effectively presented
d. allow for the rapid restocking of valuable shelf space in low-turnover merchandise categories
e. design a store that maximizes back room stock capacity

LO • 3 THE PSYCHOLOGY OF MERCHANDISE PRESENTATION REFERS TO THE FACT THAT

a. different merchandising methods can strongly influence the store's image and its sales
b. psychologists should always be hired as merchandisers
c. merchandise presentation teaches consumers how to shop effectively
d. social factors strongly influence shopping behavior
e. shoppers can be classified according to psychological tests

LO • 4   **STORE DESIGN DOES ALL BUT WHICH OF THE FOLLOWING:**

    a. It is responsible for creating a distinctive and memorable store image.

    b. It maximizes sales transactions per customer visit.

    c. It includes the architectural elements and finishes on all surfaces.

    d. It seeks to attract passing shoppers and entice them to enter the store.

    e. It encompasses the store's exterior and interior.

LO • 5   **WHICH OF THE FOLLOWING IS NOT PART OF A VISUAL COMMUNICATIONS PROGRAM?**

    a. store name and logo

    b. institutional signage

    c. directional and category signage

    d. lifestyle graphics

    e. television advertising

APPLICATIONS

WRITING AND SPEAKING EXERCISE   You have just been made the new assistant manager of Value Sports Center. One of your first duties at this "all-sports" equipment retailer is to help the manager design the prototype for the new mega-sized store that you will be moving to next year. Your job is to prepare a memo stating what type of circulation flow the store should use, where the various departments should be located in the box-shaped building of 35,000 square feet, and what can be done to reduce shrinkage. Be sure to include in your memo how the layout might change as the calendar changes.

RETAIL PROJECT   Let's look more closely at some of the attributes that often influence supermarket choice decisions. Nine frequently cited attributes are as follows:

    1. Competitive prices

    2. Choice of national versus private labels

    3. Physical characteristics (including decor, layout, and floor space)

    4. Fast check-outs

    5. Produce quality

    6. Convenience (including hours, location, ease of entrance and parking, ease of finding items)

    7. Services (including credit, delivery, return policy, and guarantees)

    8. Store personnel (including helpfulness, friendliness, and courtesy)

    9. Advertised "specials" in stock

For your assignment, you are to rank these attributes in order of importance to you. After ranking them, take the most important attribute and assign it the value of 10, take the second most important attribute and assign it the value of 9. Continue to do this for your top five attributes, with your fifth attribute getting a value of 6.

Now, visit two supermarkets or supercenters and assign a value (1 being very poor . . . 10 being very good) to the stores' performance on your five attributes. Next, multiply your rank value by their performance value for each attribute and sum the total. Is the store with the highest total points your favorite? If there is a difference, why is it?

If you were planning to shop on the Internet, what "store" attributes would be the most important to you for clothing?

CASE THE IMAGE SHOPPE

The Image Shoppe is housed in a vast warehouse-type building; adjacent to the store is a large suburban mall that is the home of three full-service department stores, a large discount store, and an array of specialty and shoe stores. The Image Shoppe primarily features merchandise for young adults from middle-income families and targets consumers in that age bracket, along with their parents.

Six months ago, Lori Greenly bought The Image Shoppe from John Meyers. Meyers had organized and operated the store in a very haphazard manner. As merchandise arrived, he or other employees simply placed the goods wherever space was available, which led to the dissolution of distinct departments or areas. There is little or no storage space in the building, so Meyers usually placed all stock on the selling floor, even if it meant stacking merchandise to the ceiling or putting goods on the top of shelves or other fixtures.

The display fixtures being used currently had been collected over the years, usually bought from defunct retail operations or discount suppliers. Posters, banners, and sports memorabilia hang throughout the store in attempts to make the young shoppers feel at ease. Meyers had usually piped the local "Top 40" radio station through the store's intercom system.

After several months of observation, Ms. Greenly believes some drastic changes must take place. She sees The Image Shoppe as having become, unintentionally, a discount department store. The image and atmosphere projected by the layout, displays, and merchandise do not sufficiently attract the desired clientele. Ms. Greenly does not think that The Image Shoppe conjures up the picture of up-to-date fashions and current trends in apparel in the minds of the local high school or college students. Actually, a greater percentage of the sales are accounted for by lower-income adults.

Ms. Greenly has found through research that three of the specialty stores in the mall have increased their sales by more than 25 percent in the past year, whereas The Image Shoppe has decreased its sales by at least that much. In addition, one of the full-service department stores has launched a complete promotional campaign and merchandising strategy designed to attract members of The Image Shoppe's desired target market.

In addition to decreasing sales and the declining "quality" of the customers, The Image Shoppe also suffers from a high shrinkage rate due to shoplifting. During the time that Greenly has been at the helm, the percentage of merchandise shoplifted in terms of sales has increased by 2 percent each month. With the store's current setup, it is difficult to "police" all possible areas that may be vulnerable to theft all of the time. The stereo and jewelry sections have been hardest hit. Most of those items are displayed in a self-service style for the convenience of the customers.

Ms. Greenly is firm in her belief that The Image Shoppe should attempt to reestablish itself as a local leader in current fashions, target young adults from the middle-income bracket, and continue to operate as a junior department store. Her vision is that

The Image Shoppe will become the area's department store version of The Limited or The Gap.

1. What other elements of the retail mix will Ms. Greenly want to consider in her attempts to create the appropriate image for the Image Shoppe? Give examples of how selling space layout decisions and decisions concerning other elements of the retail mix might interact.
2. Detail a layout that would help Ms. Greenly achieve her goals. Include descriptions of types of fixtures to be used, space allocations, etc.
3. What actions could Ms. Greenly take when designing a revamped layout to decrease the amount of shoplifting activity that takes place within The Image Shoppe?

PLANNING YOUR OWN RETAIL BUSINESS

After graduation from college, you open a swimwear store on South Padre Island. You call your store the Zig Zag. The building you located is 400 square feet and has been vacant for 18 months. Because of the limited amount of start-up capital you had to invest in the business, you move into the building without remodeling either its exterior or interior.

During the first year, the Zig Zag has 13,400 visitors, of which 3,350 made a purchase. The average transaction size was $38. The Zig Zag operates on a gross margin of 55 percent and has annual fixed operating expenses of $30,000. Variable costs were 15 percent of sales. The two primary fixed expenses are rent of $1,100 a month and salaries of $1,200 a month. You keep all profits in the business to reinvest in inventory and other immediate business needs.

Because your first year was profitable, you are now considering remodeling the store. Your landlord will not help with these expenses. To paint the exterior would cost $1,400. With regard to the interior, you are thinking of tiling the floor in a zig-zag pattern, which will cost $1,600. In addition, new lighting and some new fixtures would cost $4,000.

You believe these changes will increase traffic by 10 percent and that your closure or conversion rate will increase to 30 percent.

Will your proposed changes pay for themselves the first year?

NOTES

1. The authors want to acknowledge the assistance of Randall E. Gebhardt, our co-author on *Retail Marketing,* for his input into this chapter.
2. Stanley Marcus in a speech to the Spring ACRA Meeting, Dallas, TX, April 17, 1993.
3. "Federated, Macy's Head for Alter and Big Alterations," *Wall Street Journal,* November 18, 1994: B4.
4. Alan Liles, *Oh Thank Heaven! The Story of The Southland Corporation,* (Dallas: The Southland Corporation, 1977).
5. "I Screwed It Up," *Forbes,* December 6, 1993: 144.
6. "Caution: Falling Inventory," *Business Week,* April 15, 1997: 8.
7. The above material was provided for the authors' use by Marvin J. Rothenberg of Marvin J. Rothenberg, Inc., Ft. Lee, NJ.
8. For a more detailed discussion of this topic, the reader should consult the latest edition of Martin M. Pegler's *Stores of the Year* published by Retail Reporting Corporation, New York.
9. Charles Areni and David Kim, "The Effects of In-Store Lighting on Browsing," *Stores,* August 1994: RR7–RR8.

10. "Muzak Wafts Tunes into Cyberspace," *Wall Street Journal,* September 25, 1997: B1.

11. Gordon C. Bruner II, "Music, Mood, and Marketing," *Journal of Marketing,* October 1990: 94–104.

12. Ronald E. Milliman, "Using Background Music to Affect Behavior of Supermarket Shoppers," *Journal of Marketing,* Summer 1982: 86–91.

13. Charles Areni and David Kim, "The Influence of Background Music on Shopping Behavior: Classical versus Top-Forty Music in a Wine Store," *Advances in Consumer Research,* 1993: 336–340.

14. "Muzak Once Again Calls the Tune in Retailers' War on the Unwanted," *Wall Street Journal,* December 14, 1992: B1.

RETAILING OF SERVICES[1]

Many service retailers use Walt Disney World as a benchmark of excellence in the delivery of services.

OVERVIEW

Today, more than half of all consumer dollars are spent on intangible services such as dry cleaning, weight loss programs, and medical services. In this chapter, we review the importance of services in our national economy, discuss the unique challenges involved in the retailing of services, and present specific marketing strategies for increasing sales and customer satisfaction for retailers of services. We see that because customers do not distinguish between retailers of services and the services they provide, as they often do between the manufacturers of merchandise and retailers, retailers of services must pay special attention to ensure that they create the appropriate consumer expectations.

LEARNING OBJECTIVES

After reading this chapter, you should be able to

1. describe the key ways in which services differ from physical goods and the implications of these differences for service retailers
2. describe how service retailers are evaluated
3. list and discuss the special strategies service retailers can use to increase sales and customer satisfaction

THE NATURE OF SERVICES AND THE RETAILING OF SERVICES

In the first 13 chapters, we have usually been discussing the retailing of physical products, which are tangible and can be seen, touched, and held by consumers. But not all retailing involves tangible goods. Consumers purchase services and ideas just as they do goods, so the selling of services and ideas must be considered retailing just like the selling of tangible goods.

Recent changes in the nation's economy, lifestyle trends, and a focus on quality and value all call for a special focus on the retailing of services. Some of American business' best known names are service retailers: Hertz and Avis, automobile rentals; Kinder-Care, child care centers; Roto-Rooter, Chemlawn, Merry Maids, and American Maid, home maintenance; Supercuts, hair care; H&R Block, tax preparers; Jiffy Lube and Midas, auto care; Nautilus, fitness centers; Holiday Inn, Hilton, Marriott, Sheraton, and LaQuinta, hotels and motels; and Nutri/System and Jenny Craig, weight control services.

In the past, many other providers of services that have traditionally not considered themselves retailers, such as hospitals, funeral homes, movie theaters, amusement parks, legal and medical clinics, universities, and banks, never worried about developing a retail mix for their offerings. Today's competitive environment, however, has made it necessary and highly beneficial for them to begin using retailing strategies. Our Global Retailing box describes how one service retailer, Service Corporation International, has developed into the world's largest death-care provider by using simple retailing strategies in an industry dominated by "mom and pop" operations.

IMPORTANCE OF SERVICE RETAILERS[2]

Most consumers are unaware of the role service retailers play in their lives. Think about your life during the past 24 hours. Perhaps you began your day by stopping at a fast-food outlet for breakfast. Then you stopped by a laundromat on your way to class and, because you were short of time, left your clothes for cleaning, folding, and pressing if needed. You dropped off a roll of film at the one-hour photo processing center and then stopped by the campus travel agent to begin planning your spring break. After class, you stopped by the post office, went to the copy center to have your term paper copied, and then visited your favorite hair salon to have your hair cut or styled. On your way home, you picked up your developed film, as well as your clothes. Notice that in all these activities, including going to class, you were partaking of a service, which the American Marketing Association defines as

> products such as a bank loan or home security, that are intangible, or at least substantially so. If totally intangible, they are exchanged directly from producer to user, cannot be transported or stored, and are almost instantly perishable. Service products are often difficult to identify, since they come into existence at the same time they are bought and consumed. They are composed of intangible elements that are inseparable, they usually involve customer participation in some important way, cannot be sold in the sense of ownership transfer, and have no title.[3]

THE CHANGING FACE OF FUNERALS

GLOBAL RETAILING

Robert Waltrip is often compared with Ray Kroc and Sam Walton.

The service company he founded three decades ago has been called McFuneral and is increasing sales above Wal-Mart's rate of growth. Waltrip is the founder of Service Corporation International (SCI), the world's largest funeral home company with nearly 3,000 funeral homes, 350 cemeteries, and 150 crematoria in the United States, Canada, Australia, Europe, and the Pacific Rim. In 1997, more than 40 percent of SCI's $4 billion in revenue was foreign-generated and this number was expected to exceed 50 percent by the year 2000.

In an industry marked by staid, conservative, and traditional management, SCI, which trades on the New York Stock Exchange with the symbol SRV, has obtained its high growth by acquiring well-established, usually family-owned, funeral homes in locations across the world. It prefers not to change the acquired home's name and seeks to keep the previous managers in place. Recognizing that one of the most difficult tasks for this type of service retailer is to convey to the public the message that it would like to serve their funeral needs, SCI usually seeks to increase the funeral home's visibility in the community by conducting seminars for physicians, nurses, clergy, and the general public on topics such as dealing with grief. In addition, the "new" home also provides videocassettes and books on grief and sorrow. All these programs are designed to make the home come across as caring and understanding.

With more than 80 percent of all funeral homes in the United States currently owned by small independent operators, there are still plenty of attractive acquisition opportunities domestically. More important, numerous foreign death-care markets remain largely untapped, particularly in Europe and the Pacific Rim.

Like Sam Walton, who used improvements in the distribution system to make Wal-Mart into a retailing power, Waltrip has used distribution to increase profits by 15 to 20 percent a year. Historically, funeral homes are a high fixed-cost retailing operation with widely fluctuating demand. Yet, whereas on some days the funeral home may have three to five funerals, visitations, and/or preparations, most days are spent handling clerical matters, filling out government reports, handling some prearrangements, and waiting. After all, someone must always be on call. SCI has organized its homes into clusters that reduce the need for personnel and equipment by centralizing embalming (which because of Environmental Protection Agency regulations has become a very high fixed-cost operation) and transportation. In one cluster, it might have 15 to 20 funeral homes, 12 to 15 hearses, and 10 to 12 limousines. Night calls to each home are forwarded to a central dispatcher, where a minimum staff is on duty. The firm's Houston office handles all accounting and purchasing.

The firm bases most of its location decisions on demographics. It has maps indicating death rates by ZIP code. As a result, SCI's U.S. operations are heavily represented in Florida and southern California. However, the most promising statistic favoring SCI's continued success is the advancing age of the country's population. Over the next decade, the "older than 75" age segment will grow 25 percent annually in the company's current markets.

Thus, service retailing consists of the sale or rent of an intangible activity, which usually cannot be stored or transported but provides the user some degree of satisfaction even if it can't be owned.

IMPORTANCE OF SERVICES

The retailing of services has become the largest segment of the U.S. economy, representing 75 percent of the nation's gross domestic product when government and

Service retailing
consists of the sale or rent of an intangible activity, which usually cannot be stored or transported, but provides the user some degree of satisfaction even if it cannot be owned.

Copy centers, one of the most rapidly growing services in the United States, have expanded to offer computer rental and other related services which have further strengthened their growth.

business-to-business services are included. More dramatically, more than half of all consumer expenditures today are spent on services.

There are numerous reasons for this growth of services. One key reason is the productivity increase in agriculture and manufacturing over the past century; we simply need fewer individuals in these industries due to automation. Three trends covered in Chapter 3, the "graying of America," changes in leisure time, and an increase in the number of two-career families, have also played a role in increasing the demand for services. The most important of these consumer trends is the amount of leisure time Americans now have compared with past generations. Despite the fact that Americans currently have more free time at their disposal than in the past, an increasing number believe that they have less free time. Various explanations have been offered for this apparent discrepancy between reality and consumer perception. The most plausible seems to be that although each individual worker may be working fewer hours, the family unit, comprising both working parents, may be working more hours. A study comparing the work habits of Japanese and American men, for instance, found that although both work about 56 to 58 hours each week, American men work 44 hours at a job and 14 doing household chores, and Japanese men spend 52 hours on the job and only four doing household chores.[4] With each spouse working, less time is available in the total family unit to complete household maintenance tasks, which have not diminished.

Regardless of the underlying reasons and whether the time poverty is real or imagined, consumers' perceptions of time poverty have created opportunities for retailers of all kinds, especially retailers of services. After all, reality is not always as important as consumer perceptions, because it is perceptions that drive consumer spending activities.[5] Some sociologists credit this perception of decreased time for parents to spend with children as one reason why toy sales have skyrocketed in recent years, tripling the past decade to more than $450 per child. Not only traditional service industries but new ones offering mailing services, such as Box and Mail, pet

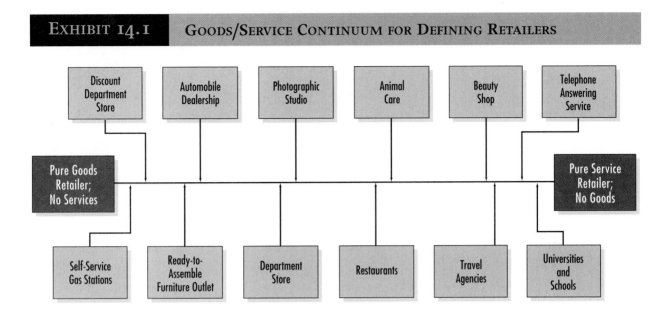

EXHIBIT 14.1 — **GOODS/SERVICE CONTINUUM FOR DEFINING RETAILERS**

care providers such as Home Sitters for Pets, home meal replacement operations such as Eatzi's, and dating services such as It's Just Lunch (the latter two are discussed later this chapter), have taken advantage of changing consumer lifestyle patterns and perceptions.

ALL RETAILING IS A SERVICE

You may recall from your introductory marketing course that it is difficult to classify most marketing transactions as strictly involving goods or services, because most products involve both physical characteristics and some intangible service. This is especially true in retailing, because all retailers are providing services to customers. Therefore all retailers can benefit from the service strategies suggested in this chapter. Retailers of physical goods, such as furniture, really provide time and place value to consumers. They collect products, arrange for their delivery, prepare the goods for use if needed, provide a store for the transaction, and provide information consumers need to make purchase decisions. By performing these services for thousands of consumers, retailers spread the expense and reduce the cost to each consumer. In view of this overlap between retailers of goods offering services and retailers of services offering some physical goods, many people use a continuum like the one shown in Exhibit 14.1 to differentiate between the two types of retailers. However, the emphasis of this chapter is on service retailers, or those operating toward the right on the continuum in Exhibit 14.1. The various types of transaction-aiding services offered by retailers were discussed in Chapter 12.

Services are different from physical products, and accordingly, the retailing of services requires some specialized strategies. Let's review the fundamental differences between goods (or physical products) and services and then discuss some retail implications of the special characteristics of services.

EXHIBIT 14.2	FOUR CHARACTERISTICS OF SERVICES

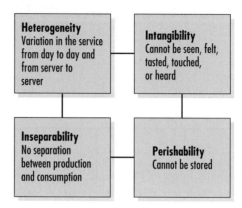

HOW SERVICES AND GOODS DIFFER

To fully appreciate the unique requirements in the retailing of services, we must first review, as shown in Exhibit 14.2, the four ways in which goods and services differ.

INTANGIBILITY   The first and most obvious difference between goods and services is that goods are tangible and services are intangible. Perhaps the most dramatic implication of the intangibility of services is the consumer's inability to perceive them through the five human senses. We can perceive a tangible good through sight, smell, hearing, touch, and taste and can generally agree on what the good is. However, services cannot be directly perceived through the senses and can therefore go undetected by consumers or may be perceived differently by different consumers, thus making it harder to evaluate the quality of the service. As a result, consumers must look for "signals" for indications of the service quality. Thus your insurance agent will use the "goods hands" symbol on his or her business cards as well as on the office door to convey a tangible image for the service.

PERISHABILITY   Perishable services, unlike goods, cannot be produced or manufactured, boxed, stored, and shelved; they don't endure through time and thus can't be inventoried. Goods can be manufactured today, stored tomorrow, and sold to the end consumer next week. Services, however, because they generally have no material qualities are perishable. In fact, services theoretically perish the moment they are produced. This perishability is not a problem when demand is steady. However, when demand fluctuates, service retailers have problems. As a result, service retailers often try to balance their demand and supply by altering their retail mix. Resorts, for example, often charge premium rates in June, a busy wedding season, and low rates during the off-season.

Behind the Scenes describes how Boston Market seeks to balance its supply and demand with the aid of a computer.

Intangibility

is a major characteristic of services meaning that the service cannot be perceived by the human senses.

Perishability

is a major characteristic of services meaning that the service cannot endure through time and thus cannot be inventoried.

RESTAURANTS AND COMPUTERS

Boston Market, one of the stock market's hottest initial public offerings (IPOs) in the 1990s, has seen its stock come down recently as it expanded its menu too fast. However, not to be blamed is the firm's use of the computer.

Boston Market uses a computer program that tracks the sales of every menu item on an hourly basis and sets cooking schedules based on the program. After consulting the printout, the manager can determine how much chicken to cook and when to put it on the rotisserie to meet the expected demand. Although it is not completely accurate, the computer, according to one manager, bats close to 90 percent. The same program can also be used to schedule hourly employees for the restaurant as well as order merchandise. The computer program alone saves the store manager more than 25 hours a week in calculations by hand.

A companion software program tracks waste by translating every menu item into raw ingredients and keeping a tally based on cash register sales. At closing time, all remaining food is weighed and entered into the computer. The computer then compares what should be left over and figures the "waste" for the day. As a result, the average store's waste has dropped to 1 percent from the industry norm of 5 to 7 percent.

Home meal replacements have an even higher waste percentage, because meats aren't cooked ahead of time. One operation has found a unique way of reducing its waste. Eatzi's Market & Bakery, a New York–style gourmet restaurant, is located in an affluent Dallas neighborhood near the Southern Methodist University (SMU) campus. The store, which has limited in-store seating but does have 30 chefs, features sushi and pasta dishes catered to young professionals, as well as fresh produce, pastries, and flowers. Most dishes are in the $8 to $12 range. However, rather than carry the dishes over to a second day, the store offers a two-for-one promotion every night after 9 P.M., and the SMU crowd cleans them out.

DOLLAR $ & ¢ENTS

High-performance service retailers do a superior job of matching the supply of services with the demand for services, because services are perishable and mismatches of supply and demand lower performance.

INSEPARABILITY   Closely related to perishability is inseparability, or the concept that there can be no separation between production and consumption of a service. They occur simultaneously. This is in contrast to a physical product, which can be manufactured days, weeks, even years before it is actually used. Due to inseparability, service retailers do not have the luxury of hiding the messy or unpleasant process of production from the consuming public. For instance, consider hot dogs, a manufactured food product. Although the process of making hot dogs may be perfectly clean

Inseparability
is a major characteristic of services meaning that there can be no separation between production and consumption of a service.

Ocean cruises, a popular vacation alternative, are perishable services.

and natural, many consumers would just as soon not know the many ingredients that go into them. Service providers must often perform the service, with all its potential unpleasantries, in the presence of the purchaser. Some service providers have turned this fact into a differential advantage. To speed service, McDonald's prepares many of its food products in full view of its customers. Realizing that cleanliness is a major concern of customers, McDonald's from its beginning structured its stores with stainless steel and porcelain surfaces that are easily cleaned, do not discolor with age, and shine and sparkle when clean. This design technique emphasizes to viewing customers that McDonald's is health-conscious. *In fact, it is so clean that it is not afraid to expose its kitchen and food preparation areas.* McDonald's turned a potential problem into a differential advantage.

Another important implication of inseparability is that service providers don't get a second chance. All manufacturers expect a certain amount of incorrectly manufactured product—often called scrap—due to human error or deviations in raw materials. They simply discard this scrap or, if possible, recycle it into future product, building the cost into the price of saleable goods. Service providers can't do this. If a service is provided incorrectly, it has by virtue of inseparability already been delivered to the consumer, who is likely already dissatisfied. Have you ever tried a new hair stylist and been disappointed with the results? There is little you can do except wait for your hair to grow back. This situation does, however, present a unique opportunity for the retailer of services by handling the complaint in a positive manner. Although such actions may not save the immediate sale, it can certainly save the customer for the retailer.

HETEROGENEITY Because services are provided by human beings, they are subject to inconsistent performance. This results in heterogeneity, or a variation in the service from day to day and from server to server. Even the most accomplished service providers are occasionally subject to subpar performance. This is known as single-server heterogeneity. In addition, other services are performed not by one but by many different servers, resulting in variations in the way the service is delivered. This is known as multiple-server heterogeneity.

Because services are naturally subject to heterogeneity and yet service providers cannot catch and remove substandard services before they are delivered as manufacturers handle scrap, retailers of services must be even more attentive to creating and maintaining high performance standards. Each step in the service process must be carefully programmed and controlled so that every individual server can perform the process in a similar manner, time after time. In some businesses such as fast-food, this requires simple and clearly defined job duties and an emphasis on discipline rather than creative thinking. To see this concept in action, try ordering a hamburger at Wendy's with onions, catsup, mustard, and pickle. Invariably, the order taker will call out your order as "catsup, onion, pickle, mustard" — precisely in that order — because employees are trained to always call the condiments in a specific order to reduce confusion.

Many service providers have developed elaborate training programs to instill this consistency, direction, and discipline, such as the employee "universities" operated by McDonald's and Walt Disney Company. In fact, Southwest Airlines and Disney have been so successful in empowering employees to provide good customer service that they now offer paid training seminars to other companies.[6]

Because service retailers cannot anticipate and program every service requirement, they instead instill their employees with simple epithets such as "Always do whatever it takes to satisfy the customer." One national chain known for its great customer service reportedly has a simple, three-part code of conduct for its employees:

1. Always satisfy the customer.
2. Don't steal from the company.
3. Never chew gum.

By not burdening its employees with rules and regulations, this retailer empowers them to use their best judgment in satisfying customers. Of course, at times an employee may use poor judgment and give away more than required to a customer, but retailers that are highly focused on customer service will not discourage them. As one Disney executive said:

> It's okay if the customer gets away with something, because the alternative is that we [Disney] might be wrong. And if we're wrong, it might cost us a fortune, because that guest will go away and tell everyone he knows that Disney is cheap.

UNIQUE CHALLENGES IN THE RETAILING OF SERVICES

As a result of these characteristics of services, the retailing of services is more difficult. It is important for service retailers to understand the five unique challenges facing them. We conclude this chapter with strategies for overcoming these challenges.

Heterogeneity is a major characteristic of services meaning that most services are subject to inconsistent performance or a variation in the service from day to day and from server to server.

Southwest Airlines has trained its employees to minimize heterogeneity in service performance. As a result, Southwest is often rated the top U.S. airline in customer satisfaction.

SERVICES, SERVICE RETAILERS, AND THE SELLING ENVIRONMENT ARE INTERTWINED

A key characteristic of retailing of services is that consumers often don't make a distinction between the service, which is intangible, and the retailer of services. When a tangible good is purchased but is unsatisfactory, the consumer often blames the manufacturer and forgives the store where the item was purchased—assuming that the store treated the customer well. This is rarely true for services, which are seen as integral to the stores that provide them. For example, tax preparers such as H&R Block offer services through a retail facility. If a particular preparer makes a mistake on a tax return, most affected customers would not view H&R Block as a generally good tax preparer that just had one bad employee that year. Instead, most customers would be soured on H&R Block in general. Therefore, as we see in this chapter, all messages that retailers of services communicate to consumers are critical to attracting, satisfying, and retaining customers. To a greater extent than is seen in consumer goods, the image and tangible communications of a retailer of services are one and the same as the service itself.

Because consumers identify service retailers with their services, the selling environment becomes integral to the service itself. Consumers will sometimes purchase a name-brand packaged good from a dark, dingy store with a substandard environment, feeling that once they get the product home it will be the same as one purchased at a fancy store. The same cannot be said of services, the use and evaluation of which goes hand in hand with the selling environment. Most individuals, for instance, prefer not to eat in restaurants that have a dated, unkempt appearance, for fear the food will be unclean or low quality. As we see throughout this chapter, service providers must pay careful attention to their selling environment, which helps customers form expectations about the service, encourages them to use more services, and is an integral part of their evaluation of the quality of the service.

INTANGIBLE SERVICES ARE UNDETECTABLE In the retailing environment, the implication of the difference between services and goods is that service products are, by themselves, undetectable by the customer. They have no qualities that can be perceived by the human senses. Therefore, service retailers must create tangible messages that serve as proxies or substitutes for their products in the customer's mind. These tangible cues alert customers to the availability of various service products; describe them, their characteristics, and their potential benefits; and provide details on how customers can order and/or use them. Without these tangible cues, a service retailer would be little more than an empty room with a human sales clerk, through whom all information about the services would come. In fact, this is exactly what many service retailers have historically been. Banks, car rental agencies, airline counters, and tax-preparing retailers were simply rooms with counters and service persons. If customers didn't ask for a service—often because they didn't know it existed—it didn't get sold. If a salesperson suggested an additional service, customers often felt like they were being railroaded into spending more money by high-pressure sales tactics. Today, such retailers have become service stores by creating tangible messages that communicate the full range of services and information about them to customers, who think that they are educating themselves about services and then asking for, rather than being sold, the service. This leads to not only greater sales but greater customer satisfaction.

SERVICES ARE INDISTINGUISHABLE FROM ONE ANOTHER Because services are intangible, they have no physical qualities that customers can use to independently distinguish one from another. Without further explanation, a shoe shine is a shoe shine. Of course, every shoe shiner has a different technique, and some are better than others. Some have created different names for different kinds of shines. A sign in one airport shoe shine shop listed a wax shine for $2, buff and polish for $2.50, and a spit shine for $3. The sign is a good start at creating tangible cues that differentiate various levels of service, for it encourages customers to ask for the higher-priced shine. The prices help you determine that a spit shine must be the best. But without further description about the features and benefits, it is impossible to determine why the spit shine is worth the extra 50 cents, and most important, why this individual's spit shine is better than that of the shoe shine in the other terminal. It is very difficult for consumers to differentiate one service from another, and to be successful, service retailers must communicate specific reasons why their service is unique or somehow offers an advantage over that of a competitor.

DOLLAR $ & CENTS

High-performance service retailers excel at providing strong tangible cues for their services.

EXHIBIT 14.3	PRODUCTION AND CONSUMPTION PROCESS FOR GOODS AND SERVICES

Goods

 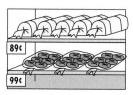 

Services

CUSTOMERS HAVE DIFFICULTY SHOPPING FOR SERVICES

Consumers must identify and learn about options that are available, make decisions regarding the benefits and cost of alternatives, make a purchase decision, and complete a transaction. This is easy for a retailer offering purely tangible goods, because the goods themselves often provide the information necessary to shop. Produce can be squeezed to determine ripeness. Boxes can be read to determine specifications or ingredients. In a store selling services, however, customers often have difficulty shopping. If you have ever entered a service retailer's store and felt awkward because you weren't even sure where to stand to wait for help, you have experienced the difficulty of shopping for intangible services. Therefore, the service retailer must provide not only tangible cues that substitute for services, but they must organize these cues in a manner that provides a rational shopping process for the customer to follow. If a hardware store carried four types of hammers but placed each of them in a different part of the store, customers would find it very difficult to shop. Similarly, if a service retailer hangs four signs about similar services at disparate points in the store, the customer will become confused.

SERVICE DELIVERY OFTEN FORCES CUSTOMERS TO WAIT

The inseparability and perishability of services means that they must be produced simultaneously as they are sold and cannot be stockpiled for later sale. Exhibit 14.3 demonstrates that for purchasers of physical goods, they just have to go to a store to pick up a product that has already been produced and is waiting for them on the shelf. However, customers wanting a service must wait for the service to be performed, and when several customers request a service at the same time, they wind up waiting in line. Further, many services are subject to inconsistent demand. Restaurants obviously have peak demand points during breakfast, lunch, and dinner. Dry cleaning shops have peak pickup times right after work hours, when customers stop on their way home. Beauty salons have demand peaks on Saturdays, and even certain days of the month coinciding with pay days.

To retailers, these peak demand periods and the lines of waiting customers present both difficulties and opportunities. Certainly, it is difficult to economically operate a facility designed for peak crowds but that operates well below peak much of the time. Supermarkets cannot call in extra employees for the two-hour rush and send them home with only two hours' pay or workers would quit. However, lines of waiting customers present an opportunity to communicate many positive messages about the retailers and the goods and services they offer. Many retailers put so-called impulse merchandise in waiting areas or lines where customers have dwell time, or must wait to complete their transaction. Similarly, service retailers can use dwell time to communicate messages about various services, leading to increased sales.

Dwell time *is the amount of time customers spend waiting in line.*

EVALUATING SERVICE RETAILERS

LO • 2
Describe how service retailers are evaluated

Retailers of services must, therefore, understand service quality concepts and apply them in managing their store image, store exterior, selling environment, service assortment, and pricing, to attract and retain customers. Now that we understand some of the key characteristics of services, we next look at how consumers evaluate the quality of those services and then describe how services can be delivered in such a manner as to satisfy the recipient.

DEFINITION OF SERVICE QUALITY[7]

Service quality, which in the retail world equates to customer service and satisfaction, is central to the success of the retailer selling both tangible and intangible products. But how do service retailers achieve this simple goal? How do you know what customers want? How do you ensure that possibly hundreds of different human beings providing the service do it the right way, time after time? And how do you know when customers are really satisfied and dedicated to coming back, especially because some dissatisfied customers may be forced by constraints to "have to" come back?[8]

High-quality service is defined as delivering service that meets or exceeds customers' expectations. In this definition, there is no absolute level of quality service but only service that is perceived as high quality because it meets and exceeds the expectations of customers. For example, suppose a consumer has dinner one night at a restaurant at which he or she expects to have slow service and is served in 10 minutes. The next night, the same consumer eats dinner at a another restaurant that he or she expects to have fast service and again is served in 10 minutes. Even assuming that other factors such as cleanliness, friendliness, and food quality are the same, this consumer might report the service quality to be better in the first restaurant, because the 10-minute service was faster than expected, and report lower service quality in the second restaurant because the 10-minute service was slower than expected. On an absolute basis, the service was the same in each case—good food in 10 minutes—but the customer's evaluation was different due to different expectations.

High-quality service *is service that meets or exceeds customers' expectations.*

Thus, high-quality service entails first knowing what customers expect of your service and then meeting or exceeding these expectations. This has prompted research on how customers form their expectations. Initial research has shown that this task is different for customers of service retailers than it is for manufacturing and retailers of tangible goods.[9]

The way that consumers form expectations of and evaluate the transaction-aiding services, which were discussed in Chapter 12, offered by a retailer to support the sale of another product is similar to how consumers evaluate the end product of service retailers. It is important for two reasons that all retailers, but most especially retailers of services, understand this process. First, expectations can either lead to initial store visits or dissuade consumers from visiting a store. If customers expect they will receive poor service, they obviously will not visit the store except in an emergency. Second, as seen previously in our example of the two restaurants, prior expectations of service have a dramatic effect on the consumer's evaluation of the service once it is provided, which naturally influences whether he or she will return in the future or recommend the store to others.

HOW CONSUMERS FORM EXPECTATIONS

Customers can form expectations before they have ever tried the service or after using the service. Not surprisingly, customers have some difficulty forming expectations before their first use of a service, because they have no direct prior experience. Research has shown that consumers have more trouble forming first-time expectations with services than they do with goods[10] and that they form prior expectations about services by using slightly different inputs than for tangible goods.

Consumers often base their decision whether to try a new service retailer on images they have formed from many messages. Although advertising and the selling environment, which is the most tangible form of communication between a service retailer and consumers, can be important, service retailers must also be concerned with not only "word-of-mouth" comments by others but also the interaction that occurs among patrons while purchasing the service.[11]

Purchasing a service, however, is often more risky than purchasing a packaged good. A good can usually be returned or exchanged; but a service is consumed as it is produced, and it is generally too late to return it. Therefore, consumers rely more heavily on personal information sources, such as recommendations from friends and family, than on nonpersonal sources such as promotional material and advertising, which they are not sure whether to trust. They also are influenced by their personal observations of external tangible cues of the service retailer, such as corporate identity and physical facilities.[12]

The decision to visit a particular service retailer is partially driven by customer expectations. But customers have trouble forming expectations prior to their first visit, and therefore, many retailers of services attract first-time users by offering free trials. Movie theaters often hand out free passes, amusement parks offer discounts, and professionals such as chiropractors and lawyers offer free consultations to determine how they can help. These trial offers allow customers to form positive expectations through personal experience at little risk and encourage both initial visits and continued patronage. Because consumers tend to be more loyal in their use of services than in the purchase of goods, the minimal cost of the initial giveaway is quickly offset by ongoing patronage.

Consumers also form expectations of services retailers based not just on characteristics of that retailer but also on where that retailer fits on a continuum of other firms that consumers consider to be competitors. So, consumers' expectations can be influenced not just by the retailer's own image but by how it stacks up against other competitive firms. Retailers are therefore wise to be fully cognizant of competitors' market images and position themselves to play off these images positively.

Finally, as the perceived risk of a service purchase decision goes up, so does the consumer's reliance on personal knowledge and observations. For this reason, corporate image can be more important for a service firm than for a goods manufacturer,

EXHIBIT 14.4	FACTORS USED BY CONSUMERS TO EVALUATE SERVICE

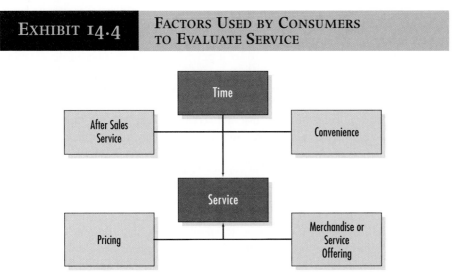

because it serves as a key factor in consumers' formation of expectations regarding not just the company but also the services it provides. Corporate image, of course, can be influenced by the external visual cues that a company communicates—such as its name, logo, corporate colors, slogans, and advertising—as well as by uncontrollable communications such as news articles and word of mouth.

HOW CONSUMERS EVALUATE SERVICE IN THE RETAIL ENVIRONMENT

High quality service was defined as meeting and exceeding customer expectations, and because we have already discussed how consumers form expectations, we now look at how services are evaluated by consumers once they have been used. This process is somewhat different for services than for tangible goods, and research has shown that it is more difficult for consumers to form evaluations of services than goods.[13]

Customers who were satisfied by a service were shown in one study to be more likely to describe the service in emotional rather than functional terms.[14] In other words, customers reported positive feelings in terms of how they felt about the retailer's service process rather than just the technical quality or functionality of the service. It appears that the process of receiving the service is just as important as, or perhaps more important than, the outcome of the service itself. It is almost as though customers view satisfaction of their functional needs as a prerequisite of the service rather than an advantage. The difference between different service providers as seen through the eyes of the consumer, then, is often the satisfaction with the service process that they provide, not so much the service outcome.

An easy way to think of the factors that consumers consider when evaluating the quality of service retailers is to think of all the types of expectations that consumers form about retailers. These factors are shown in Exhibit 14.4. Customers come to expect a shopping visit to take a certain amount of time and to be convenient. They expect the right selection of goods and services to be available, appropriate prices, and the right amount of after-sale service such as money-back guarantees. We look at these key factors in more detail.

TIME

Waiting, or the amount of time needed to order, receive, and use the service is a pivotal factor in the evaluation of service satisfaction and quality.[15] Whether it is the number of minutes waiting to see a physician or the number of days waiting for a car to be repaired, customers have specific expectations of how long a service should take. For many retailers, one of the most critical aspects of a customer's quality evaluation is the time customers must wait in the check-out lane. Most retailers use this as a critical gauge of their customer service, and in fact, the supermarket industry spends millions of dollars on research and technology to streamline its checkout operations.

Interestingly, one study found that customers' perceptions of the waiting time can be influenced by how quickly they are moving through the line or by activities they can perform while in the line.[16] As a result, some service retailers now follow the example of amusement parks and employ clowns or other simple entertainment to occupy the minds of customers waiting in long lines. The implication is that consumers don't mind the actual wait but rather the notion that service is being provided slowly. As long as they have a sense that service is being provided quickly, as evidenced by a fast-moving check-out line, customers are willing to wait a little longer before becoming frustrated.

Other service retailers use this concept to create an image of fast service. Banks, fast-food restaurants, and airlines use centralized check-out lines that feed to many different service points. Although any number of stations may be open, the entire line moves each time a new window comes open, as opposed to the slower movement of separate lines. This gives the impression of rapidly provided service, even though the total waiting time may be the same. Of course, although the single serving line emphasizes fast-moving service, it can just as easily emphasize slow service. Recall how infuriating it is to wait in an airline counter line during a holiday weekend, when the line never seems to move.

In the previous chapter, the use of music in stores selling physical goods was discussed. Some service retailers have experimented with music also. It was thought that music could be effective in alleviating the negative impact of waiting. Research, however, has found that although music doesn't always act as a distractor to reduce the customer's perceived wait duration, it can positively influence the customer's mood and emotion. For example, although music may, in fact, increase the perceived wait duration, the music may be an effective tool to minimize any of the negative consequences of that waiting.[17]

Convenience
relates to how easy it is for the customer to order, receive, and use the service.

CONVENIENCE

Closely related to time is convenience, or how easy it is for the customer to order, receive, and use the service. Factors in the consumers' perception of convenience may include location of the store, ease of parking, length of walk, ease in locating and selecting merchandise or services, ease of payment, ease of delivery, and ease of use. Customers form expectations regarding each of these factors, and much of their satisfaction with a particular shopping trip depends on how the trip stacks up against these expectations.

To encourage sales during times that are less convenient, service retailers often offer special values that offset the inconvenience. Movie theaters offer lower ticket prices for weekday matinees, telephone companies offer reduced late-night rates, restaurants have "specials" for dinners before 6 P.M., and motels and hotels have special weekend rates. These are all examples of service providers trading off price for convenience.

The consumer's demand for convenience sometimes conflicts with the reality of providing services, which by virtue of inseparability can be less predictable and therefore less subject to planning than manufacturing goods. Although a few service retailers, such as Cox Cable, may because of the nature of their service calls guarantee to arrive within 20 minutes of their scheduled time, many home repair retailers do not know the exact nature of a repair problem before arriving at the home and therefore can only estimate the time required to make the repair. After several of these unpredictable repair calls, a service person's schedule can vary by minutes or hours, causing delays in arriving at later appointments. As a result, most repair services will not schedule an exact time for a repair or home delivery, often specifying only a morning or afternoon appointment. Consumers are obviously frustrated by having to wait for several hours, particularly when both spouses have jobs outside the home, but repair services have found this system frustrates customers less than showing up two hours late for a set appointment. By creating only expectations they can be sure to meet, such as showing up within a four-hour period, repair services are attempting to maximize their service quality.

MERCHANDISE OR SERVICE OFFERING

Not surprisingly, consumers' evaluations of whether they receive good service in a store depends on whether they found the merchandise or services that they were seeking. Again, the critical factor in this evaluation is not just what merchandise or services were available but what the customer was expecting. Today, many young professionals have been too busy with school and their fast-track careers to date seriously. The traditional dating services don't offer them the service they want. After all, who wants to spend an evening with someone when after just 30 minutes they already have figured out that their date for the evening is not "right" for them. Besides, there is also that "goodnight kiss" problem if the meeting involves an evening activity. It's Just Lunch has solved this problem by arranging its introductions over lunch in popular locations. In addition, these introductions were based on a hour-long personal interview with a staff member, not some computer test score. Finally, an assistant at the company made the lunch reservations so that even if the other party wasn't what an individual expected, the lunch made up for it.[18] Likewise, service customers can be disappointed when they find a necessary piece of equipment, such as a shoe resoler, is broken.

Retailers of services must constantly change their merchandise offering, creating new reasons for customers to shop there. Retailers should establish a core merchandise mix on which customers can depend and then experiment with new and exciting offerings that keep their businesses exciting and fresh. If we know nothing else about retail customers, we know that their needs, desires, and expectations constantly change, and a stale outlet is a sure way to lose your customer franchise. For example, today video rental retailers are now allowing fast-food operators to set up telephones in their stores. Now, when someone comes in to pick out a video, he or she can order a pizza and have it delivered to their home in time for the movie's opening credits.

PRICING

Although pricing is one of the most obvious expectations that customers form about stores and probably is the primary reason that 20 percent of customers might pick a particular retailer,[19] it is not always appreciated for its role in service quality. Consumers probably have strong expectations regarding price levels in most stores that they enter, and how actual prices compare with these expectations can play a critical role in the consumer's evaluation of service quality. Therefore, retailers must always be aware of customer's expectations regarding their pricing, as well as their actual pricing and that of their competitors.

The amount of time customers wait in line to receive a service is a key determinant of customer satisfaction with the service.

The physical facility and selling environment can make a dramatic contribution to achieving high customer service by creating the appropriate price image. If the retailer's image, store exterior, layout, design, merchandising, and graphics create the appropriate image, customers will develop price expectations in line with the retailer's actual pricing levels. Some banks, for example, shy away from expensive decor because they create an inappropriate price image regarding fees that may intimidate selected customers.

In some special cases, the selling environment can be used to create a deceptively high-price image. It is then easy for the retailer to meet and exceed the customer's price expectations. For instance, the Metropolitan Museum of Art stores use expensive ceiling soffits, sophisticated lighting, and rich design finishes including dark wood to create a high-price image. The merchandise is displayed in recessed shelving, much as it would be in a museum. This creates the illusion that the merchandise includes rare highly priced art pieces, when in fact most items are moderately priced reproductions. Customers are pleasantly surprised to find the prices well below the expectations fostered by the selling environment, and they often purchase out of a sense of relief. This is sometimes referred to as "reverse sticker shock." Of course, creating the illusion of higher prices can be a risky venture, as it may scare away rather than entice customers in many merchandise lines.

AFTER-SALES SERVICE
Whether consumers are purchasing goods or services, they generally expect certain after-sale assurances from the retailer. These may include warranties or guarantees to ensure the product or service will be replaced if defective, a method for repairing a good if it should fail later, delivery or installation, follow-up service, and more often these days, a price-matching guarantee should

NEW RULES FOR ESPs

Today, most independent retailers, especially those selling appliances, are relying on third-party administrators (TPAs) to administer and back their service contracts on older products and their in-house extended service protection (ESP) programs. These ESPs, which are sold on 20 percent of all new major appliances and 25 percent of all consumer electronics, have long been a source of extra profits for the retailer, especially because competition from discounters has lowered the margins on many of the products. Historically, almost 60 percent of such contracts was a profit to the selling retailer.

However, after the failure of EWC Corp., a major underwriter of such programs, in the early 1990s, state governments have taken a greater interest in protecting the public from underfinanced service contract programs.

Most states now require that all service contracts be backed by insurance. If escrow accounts are used as alternatives to insurance, some states require that the proceeds from contract sales after paying expenses, such as commissions and administration fees, be deposited in a bank for up to 10 years before sellers can realize the profit from the sale.

These rules especially hit hard the in-house programs of appliance retailers, who in the past usually placed just 50 to 75 percent of each contract sale after expenses in escrow accounts.

Funds for these and other policies sold at the same time remained in such accounts for the duration of the contracts to pay the claims. However, as contracts expired, dealers withdrew the remaining funds as profits.

The states thought that these escrow systems had two weaknesses. For example, if contract prices were not kept current with actual service costs and the frequency of covered product failures, the escrow account could be depleted easily. Likewise, if contract sales on new products declined but renewals on older policies remained high, the fund would not have enough money in escrow for the length of the service contracts to cover the more failure-prone older products' claims. In both cases, the contract program could become bankrupt.

These government remedies to ensure that all ESP claims would be fulfilled created new problems for small retailers' in-house programs. With relatively low contract sales, small dealerships could not get insurance coverage priced to allow continued contract sales at competitive prices. Additionally, the 10-year escrow requirement in use by most states not only prevented retailers from immediately claiming earned profits, it also created cash flow problems. The Internal Revenue Service (IRS) demanded immediate tax payments on sales revenues that the retailers could not touch legally for years!

SOURCE: This Behind the Scenes was suggested by Marvin Lurie, North American Retail Dealer Association, and used with his permission.

---

the customer find the service for less money elsewhere. Consumers don't always demand each of these items, but they certainly form expectations about a store relative to each of them. If a retailer's representative meets or exceeds a customer's expectations on one or more of these after-sale service items, the store is able to maintain a loyal customer.[20]

Behind the Scenes describes how recent legal changes have reduced the profits that many automobile and appliance dealers earned by selling extended service protection (ESP) warranties.

LO • 3
List and discuss the special strategies service retailers can use to increase sales and customer satisfaction

STRATEGIES FOR ENHANCING SERVICE RETAILERS' OFFERINGS

In the preceding discussions of how customers form expectations about and evaluate retailers, there are many hints about how retailers of services can enhance their quality by helping shoppers form appropriate expectations. We look at a number of key strategies that service retailers should use.

USING THE ENVIRONMENT TO CREATE CUSTOMER EXPECTATIONS

A common theme in this section is the consumer's use of outward, tangible cues to form expectations about intangible offerings of service retailers. One of the most important of these tangible cues is the physical facility through which the service is simultaneously retailed and produced. The retailer can therefore plan the physical appearance of a store, especially its exterior (which customers frequently see before their first use), to be a key tangible cue that helps form appropriate customer expectations. The store provides information that helps consumers form a perception of the service retailer's image and the types of services provided.[21] In addition to the exterior and interior design or appearance, the store location and layout can provide important tangible cues that customers use to form expectations about a service provider.

One service industry that has prospered in recent years is weight loss guidance centers. Many such centers, including Physician's Weight Loss Centers based in Akron, Ohio, offer medically supervised diets in which routine checkups by physicians and registered nurses and an implied sanctioning by the medical community serve as the differential advantage. Although a doctor may be present as little as two hours a week, Physician's Weight Loss Centers designs and locates its facilities to mimic a physician's office. Centers are often located in medical or professional buildings alongside physicians and dentists, and even when located in strip centers, they are designed with a patient waiting room in front and private examination rooms in the back. Service associates often wear white smocks such as those found in physicians' offices.

Bob Evans Restaurants has successfully built a chain that offers "down-home cooking" and traditional dishes. The restaurants themselves are an architectural representation of this service offering. The dramatic red and white wood siding with Chippendale facade creates an eye-catching exterior that suggests traditional, high-quality service.

CREATING TANGIBLE EVIDENCE OF SERVICES

Customers cannot see and touch services, because they are intangible. However, to form expectations of and evaluate services, a process central to customer satisfaction, customers must be able to sense their availability and performance through the five human senses. Therefore, retailers should strive to create tangible cues that describe their services. By developing tangible cues for their services, retailers can make more customers aware of their existence, create and influence customers' expectations regarding them, and to some extent influence customers' perceptions about their performance.

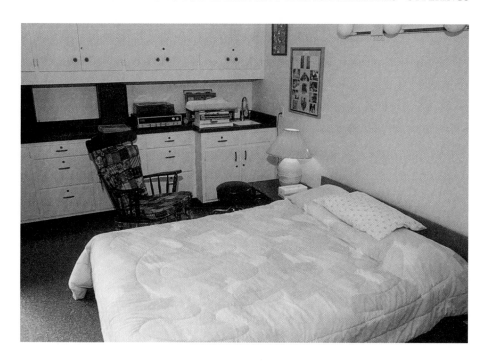

Many hospitals have remodeled their maternity units to provide home-style rooms that create tangible cues that the hospital and staff care for the new mother and her baby.

For example, deregulation made the financial services industry dramatically more competitive, and many banks turned to traditional retailing principles to gain a competitive advantage. Although most banks offer many services, most customers use only two or three, and these are often the bank's less profitable transaction-related products such as check cashing. Banks needed to find ways to entice their regular transaction-based customers to use more profitable services such as loans, financial planning, and investment assistance. By creating elaborate signage systems that advertised these services in appealing ways, banks exposed their intangible products to more customers, thereby increasing sales. By creating tangible cues for their services, banks became more successful retailers.

Retailers can make their service more tangible by dramatizing their products (i.e., showing consumers the benefits of using it). For example, Carnival Cruise Lines uses television ads showing happy passengers dining, dancing, and enjoying the pleasure of travel. American Express uses a famous actor to point out the dangers of traveling on that same cruise without the convenience and safety of using their travelers' checks.

MERCHANDISING A DIFFERENTIAL ADVANTAGE

All service retailers enjoy some advantage over competitors in one or more specific attributes. Perhaps their check-out lanes are quicker, their location or parking more convenient, their pants pressing more crisp, or their paint-mixing ability more complete. In many cases, this differential advantage is an intangible service that cannot be directly sensed by shoppers. Retailers should create tangible cues of this service and merchandise their differential advantage.

In a simple yet powerful example, Fuller O'Brien Paints faced the challenge of creating a store that attracted not only the professional painters who were a strong customer franchise for Fuller O'Brien, but also retail customers. Fuller O'Brien, a premier paint manufacturer, knew that one of its key selling attributes was the store's ability to mix thousands of shades of paint almost instantly. Rather than placing the paint-mixing equipment in the backroom, as is done in many paint stores to hide the mess, Fuller O'Brien created a new store prototype that featured a glass-enclosed "Pro Shop" behind the check-out counter. In this Pro Shop, associates mix many different paint colors on demand, putting on a show at the same time. Although not all customers have paint mixed each visit, the Pro Shop creates a lasting visual image, and the next time customers need paint, this image reminds them of Fuller O'Brien. By merchandising its differential advantage, an advantage that was an intangible service rather than a tangible good, Fuller O'Brien created a competitive advantage.

Similarly, many one-hour photo-finishing stores now place the photo-finishing equipment in plain view of customers, often in a storefront window for passersby to see as well. Although the photo-finishing process is not all that exciting, the brightly colored machine creates a lasting visual impression that merchandises the store's key differential advantage over competitors that don't have one-hour service. In an effort to gain a differential advantage with services that have indistinguishable differences to certain groups of consumers; retailers have introduced frequent-buyer programs to develop the most desirable of all customer categories — the loyal customer.

CREATING A HIERARCHY OF MERCHANDISING INFORMATION

Customers must not only be aware of available goods and services; they also must be able to understand what they are, why they should use them, and how to buy them. Successful retailers create a hierarchy of merchandising information that leads the customer through the shopping and buying process. This is important in all retail stores, but especially in those that offer predominantly services, because it is the primary way by which customers become aware of the services available.

To create the hierarchy of merchandising information, retailers must understand the way that human beings sense and evaluate their environment. Individuals entering a facility usually look at high levels and great distances to obtain an overall orientation to the space. Once they understand how it is organized, they look for specific messages as to the merchandise opportunities available. They then make a choice and begin heading in a particular direction, at which time their sightlines often drop to lower levels, and they begin looking for closer messages. As they move through the space and choose a specific area to shop, their eyes drop farther, and they look for very close messages regarding goods or services available in the immediate area. The rest of the store is now unimportant to them, but as soon as they are done with the immediate good or service, they will look high and far once again to find messages about where to go next.

To communicate effectively, messages must be not only in the right place, but in the right form. Generally, the farther the message is from the customer, the larger the message — whether words, pictures, or merchandise — must be. Messages placed high in the store need to be visible from long distances and must be very large. As messages drop down in the hierarchy, they tend to become smaller, because customers will be reading them from shorter distances. Signage on a fixture explaining merchandise right next to it is often very small.

Another merchandising concept is to understand that words are often not the most effective way to communicate with human beings, who see so many words that

Hierarchy of merchandising information

is strategically placed in-store messages that lead the customer through the shopping and buying process beginning with the customer entering the store and ending with them looking at specific merchandise.

they begin to ignore them. Often, the merchandise itself, or a picture of the merchandise, is a more effective way to communicate. Imagine, for instance, a hardware store that identified its paint department either with a two-foot by six-foot sign that said, "Paint," or a 20-foot-high by 10-foot-wide stack of paint cans. Most customers would more quickly notice the stack of paint cans, which just as effectively communicates the location of the paint department.

Finally, effective merchandisers understand that customers do not really want to buy the good or service itself but rather the benefits it brings them. If they are buying paint, customers are really seeking a different color house or room. If they are buying dry cleaning services, they really want clean clothes. Messages in the merchandising hierarchy are often pictures depicting the benefit of the service or good. This helps customers visualize how the good or service can enhance their lives.

To use these merchandising strategies, retailers should create a systematic hierarchy of merchandising information, which is translated into physical messages such as signage, pictures, and merchandise displays. These messages are placed strategically throughout the facility to draw customers through the store, help them stay oriented to the space and find the goods and services they seek, provide information required to make purchase decisions, and actually enter them into the transaction process.

USING DWELL TIME

As we discussed earlier, even customer waiting time can influence expectations and evaluations of service quality. Although customers understand that certain waiting periods are required in service retailing, they must be kept busy so as not to perceive that slow service is being provided. Retailers can use dwell times as prime opportunities to communicate messages regarding services available in the store and at the same time entertain waiting customers. Dwell time messages can be used to provide tangible cues for services, merchandise differential advantages, and show elements of the hierarchy of merchandising information.

Citibank has developed very effective merchandising systems that use dwell time in the lines at many of its branches. Instead of simple velvet ropes or other queuing guides, Citibank installed structured mini-merchandising walls to guide customers through the line. These mini-walls were lined with photographs and brochures describing many available services and showing how they could enhance a shopper's life. By providing tangible cues for these services and placing them in the line, Citibank uses dwell time to merchandise its services and increase sales. Similarly, CoreStates Bank in Philadelphia placed large graphic panels in its 24-hour automatic teller areas that alert waiting ATM customers to service offerings available inside.

STUDENT STUDY GUIDE

SUMMARY

LO•1 **WHAT ARE THE KEY WAYS IN WHICH SERVICES DIFFER FROM PHYSICAL GOODS AND WHAT ARE THE IMPLICATIONS OF THESE DIFFERENCES FOR SERVICE RETAILERS?** Although much of this text has focused on the retailing of tangible goods, the retailing of intangible services is also an important part of the retail industry. Retailing of services has become more important in recent years. In fact, service retailers touch most of our lives everyday, among them restaurants, health clubs, shoe shine stands, and dry cleaners.

Services, however, differ from goods in four significant ways — intangibility, perishability, inseparability, and heterogeneity — that present unique challenges for retailers of services to overcome. Because services are intangible and cannot be produced in advance of consumption, the service, service retailers, and the selling environment are really one in the same. The intangibility of the services makes them difficult to detect. As a result, consumers often do not distinguish between a service and the retailer providing it, as they sometimes do between goods and a store. This makes shopping for services difficult. In addition, the delivery system for services often causes customers to have to wait. It is also important to remember that all retailers are really providing services (time and place value) to their customers and are therefore retailers of services that can benefit from the strategies outlined in this chapter.

LO•2 **HOW ARE SERVICE RETAILERS EVALUATED?** The retail environment plays a critical role in the retailing of services by helping consumers form expectations about services and evaluate the process in which they are received. This process in which consumers form expectations about services and then evaluate their performance is the essence of high service quality, which is defined as meeting or exceeding customers' expectations. Providing high-quality service leads to increased patronage, sales, and profit for retailers of services, partly because consumers tend to be more loyal in their use of services than in their purchase of goods. Consumers form expectations about services based primarily on personal information they have received from personal observation or through friends and family and evaluate retailers of services based on factors such as time, convenience, merchandise or service offering, pricing, and after-sales service.

LO•3 **WHAT ARE THE SPECIAL STRATEGIES THAT SERVICE RETAILERS CAN USE TO INCREASE SALES AND CUSTOMER SATISFACTION?** Based on the unique characteristics of services and the manner in which consumers form expectations and make evaluations, retailers of services can use their retail environment to use specific marketing strategies that increase sales and customer satisfaction. The retail environment must first be carefully planned to create an image and expectations that are consistent with a merchandise and service offering that the retailer can deliver. Graphics and visual displays can be used to tangibly represent intangible services, which helps customers become aware of and shop for additional services. Visual displays and store design can also be used to merchandise the retailer's differential advantage, which is often an intangible service rather than a tangible, and therefore self-evident, good. The signage and other visual communications must create a hierarchy of merchandising information that leads the customer through the shopping process. Finally, service environments often require waiting times by customers, and the retail environment should be planned to take advantage of such dwell time to both occupy customers' minds and make them aware of additional services.

TERMS TO REMEMBER

service retailing
intangibility
perishability
inseparability
heterogeneity

dwell time
high-quality service
convenience
hierarchy of merchandising information

REVIEW AND DISCUSSION QUESTIONS

LO • 1 WHAT ARE THE KEY WAYS IN WHICH SERVICES DIFFER FROM PHYSICAL GOODS AND WHAT ARE THE IMPLICATIONS OF THESE DIFFERENCES FOR SERVICE RETAILERS?

1. Why is the retailing of services an important consideration in the study of retailing?
2. Try to name at least 20 retailers of services that you have seen or patronized in the past few days.
3. Describe the four ways in which services differ from goods.
4. Describe some of the unique challenges faced by service retailers.
5. If services are indistinguishable from each other, what can a retailer do to increase sales?

LO • 2 HOW ARE SERVICE RETAILERS EVALUATED?

6. Define high service quality. Is high-quality service easier for a service retailer or a goods retailer to deliver?
7. Why does high service quality depend on a retailer's image relative to its competition?
8. List and describe some of the factors that consumers use to evaluate the service performance of retailers?

LO • 3 WHAT ARE THE SPECIAL STRATEGIES SERVICE RETAILERS CAN USE TO INCREASE SALES AND CUSTOMER SATISFACTION?

9. Describe how tangible cues for services can be created and give an example that you have noticed recently in a retail store offering goods, services, or both.
10. Describe the concept of merchandising a differential advantage and give an example that you have noticed recently in a retail store offering goods, services, or both.
11. What is a hierarchy of merchandising information and how does it function to increase a store's sales and customer satisfaction?
12. Discuss examples of how retailers can use dwell time. Discuss the potential effect of this practice on both sales and customer satisfaction.

SAMPLE TEST QUESTIONS

LO • 1 ALL RETAILERS CAN BENEFIT FROM SERVICE RETAILING STRATEGIES BECAUSE

a. advertising costs are rising
b. there are more and more service retailers

    c. all retailers are really service providers
    d. consumers are less price-sensitive when buying services
    e. retailers cannot afford to expand their facilities

LO•2 RETAILERS SHOULD CONSIDER USING A CENTRALIZED CHECK-OUT LINE THAT FEEDS TO MANY DIFFERENT SERVICE POINTS BECAUSE

    a. it costs less money
    b. it takes less space
    c. dwell time is eliminated
    d. the line will move faster and customers will perceive a shorter wait
    e. it merchandises a key differential advantage

LO•3 THE CREATION OF PHYSICAL CUES TO DESCRIBE A SERVICE AND INFLUENCE CUSTOMER EXPECTATIONS IS CALLED

    a. making services concrete
    b. creating tangible cues for services
    c. first-person service retailing
    d. cue-based service retailing
    e. physical service retailing

APPLICATIONS

WRITING AND SPEAKING EXERCISE You have just taken a summer job at your uncle's pest control firm. On your first day on the job, your uncle asks you to help him solve a major problem that has been bothering him for some time.

No-Pest, the name of your uncle's firm, has been a successful family-run business operating in a midwestern city of 75,000 for more than 50 years. In fact, most of the city's mortgage bankers insist on using No-Pest for their termite inspections before granting a mortgage. In addition, a poll in the local newspaper cited No-Pest as the Reader's Choice Award winner for being the best exterminator in the city. Still, although many consumers use No-Pest for their termite problems, less than one-third take advantage of the firm's extended warranty. And the vast majority of those drop the warranty after the first or second year.

At a recent trade meeting, your uncle heard that the national average for the extended service guarantee was more than 50 percent and that most of those users kept their warranty for more than five years.

Your uncle provided you with these facts to aid you in solving his problem. The No-Pest termite control process, which cost $1,000 for a typical house, involves drilling holes for chemicals completely around the house and in the house where water pipes emerge from the ground. For a smaller fee, usually about $200, No-Pest will just treat the infected area and hope the termites don't return or spread throughout the house. The warranty plan involved annual visits to the house to look for termites, and the charge was 10 percent of the original cost, usually $100 per year. The two other services that No-Pest performs are spraying the lawn for fleas and ticks, $60, and spraying the interior of the house for insects, $40.

That first afternoon, you went with your uncle while he made his first warranty check at the home of Ms. Joyce Moore. Your uncle arrived at Ms. Moore's home just after 1 P.M. and spent approximately 10 minutes looking over her home, inside and outside, for possible signs of termites. After he was sure that there were no signs of infestation, he presented Ms. Moore with an updated warranty covering the next 12 months and collected her check. Ms. Moore made some comment about paying $100 for such a little bit of time and while writing out the check asked about what would happen if she discontinued the warranty and termites later appeared. Your uncle explained that there would be no need to completely re-do the entire house, just the infected area for the $200 fee. When you and your uncle got into the truck, he said that he expected that Moore would drop the service next year.

Given what you learned in this course, you decide to prepare a memo discussing the advantages and disadvantages of several alternative strategies he could use, indicating their short-term and long-term impact on profit and their likely effect on customer satisfaction.

RETAIL PROJECT

One of the major providers of services in the United States is the federal government. Best of all, most of the information is free. Below are several easy projects using the Internet for you to complete.

1. You have just started a new retail firm (the type of firm is not important for this project) and you want to know if the name of the firm needs trademark protection. By going to the government's web site (http://www.uspto.gov), you can answer these three questions:

   What is a trademark?
   How does one register a trademark?
   Where is the closest trademark depository to your university?

2. By going to the Census Bureau's site (http://www.census.gov:90/stat_abstract), you can find which city in your state has the most and which has the highest percentage of one-person households.

3. By going to the Bureau of Labor Statistics site (http://www.stats.bls.gov), you can find which occupations are expected to grow the fastest over the next decade.

CASE | COMPETITECH LEARNS TO USE TELEMARKETING

by William A. Staples, University of Houston
and John I. Coppett, University of Houston

Brenda Johnson, vice-president of marketing, was confronted with a major problem. Her company, Competitech, a retailer of computer supplies, was considering setting up a web page on the Internet. However, before setting up the web site, Ms. Johnson was to review the profitability of the toll-free 800 number that the firm was using in all its advertisements, direct-mail pieces, and catalogs. The public was responding very well to this easy-to-use, economical method of ordering products. Response rate reports indicated that sales should have been up by 12 to 15 percent. Actual sales, however, were just about the same as before Competitech started using telemarketing. As Ms. Johnson studied the report, she saw that her three telemarketing service representatives had received approximately 4,000 calls during the last 20 working days. Although Ms. Johnson was pleased to note that about 50 percent of the callers had never previously purchased anything from Competitech, the fact that the telephone was ringing but the cash register wasn't, caused deep concern.

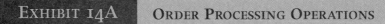

EXHIBIT 14A   ORDER PROCESSING OPERATIONS

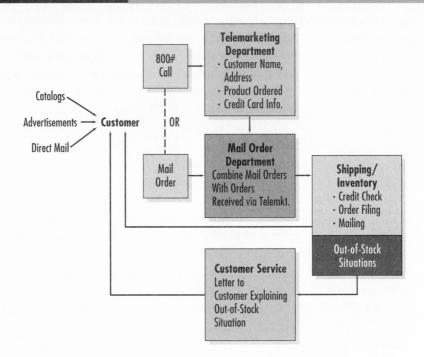

Later that day, Ms. Johnson called a meeting of the managers of the telemarketing operation, the shipping and inventory management group, the mail-order department, and customer service department. The meeting focused on determining where and how business was being lost. The managers spent most of the time discussing the steps of order processing as depicted in Exhibit 14A.

The telemarketing personnel, when they received a call for a computer part or a software package, recorded the customer's name, address, product identification information, and credit card information, and then they asked the caller where he or she had seen a Competitech advertisement or other promotional information. This last bit of information was considered vital by Ms. Johnson to learn which media were stimulating the most responses. At the end of the workday, the telemarketers forwarded all orders to the mail-order department, where that day's orders were totaled. The orders were then passed on to the shipping and inventory management department. Shipping and inventory verified credit-worthiness if necessary and then order pickers filled each request and prepared the products for shipment.

If the requested merchandise was out of stock, a written notice of the shortage and the customer's name and address were forwarded to customer service. Customer service sent a letter apologizing for the temporary delay in completing the order and indicated when Competitech anticipated the back-ordered product could be shipped.

The telemarketing group was beginning to receive calls from customers stating that they did not want to wait for back orders and wished to cancel their orders. Some customers angrily said that if they had known about this delay, they would have never done business with Competitech.

Ms. Johnson realized that Competitech was not only losing an opportunity to capitalize on the new business, but, even worse, was alienating some customers. She wondered whether telemarketing might hold the solution to some of the problems.

1. What could the telemarketers do if they had on-line computer access to inventory status information?
2. How could telemarketing be used to more efficiently support the customer service function?
3. What information does Ms. Johnson need to determine where the problem(s) is in Competitech?
4. Assuming that the telemarketing representatives knew what the inventory status was of every product Competitech sold, how could Ms. Johnson motivate the telemarketing personnel to sell more?

PLANNING YOUR OWN RETAIL BUSINESS

Your brother and you opened a health club near an upscale residential neighborhood two years ago. Initially business was good, and many households or individuals purchased six-month memberships. A consultant whom you hired has recommended you do three things: (1) open up a fresh juice bar, (2) decorate the gym with photo murals showing individuals exercising and involved in physically active exercise such as jogging, hiking, tennis, swimming, and so on, and (3) provide a hierarchy of merchandising information that clearly communicates where different weight lifting stations are and what the machines can accomplish and how to use the machines. If you do these things, the consultant advises you that 70 percent of visitors to the gym who inquire about membership will sign up (right now, only 50 percent sign up) and that the average member will stay with the gym for 1.5 years (currently, the average member stays for nine months). A member pays $30 per month. Compute the expected value of a potential visitor if you implement the suggested changes versus if you keep the status quo.

NOTES

1. The authors want to acknowledge the assistance of Randall E. Gebhardt, our co-author on *Retail Marketing*, South-Western Publishing Company, 1993, for his input into this chapter.
2. For a more detailed discussion of this topic, see the special issue of the *Journal of Retailing*, Spring 1997, on services marketing.
3. *Dictionary of Marketing Terms* (Chicago: American Marketing Association, 1988): 184. Reprinted with the permission of the American Marketing Association.
4. "If the U.S. Work Ethic Is Fading, Alienation May Be Main Reason," *Wall Street Journal*, February 7, 1992: A1.
5. Kenneth E. Clow, Dave L. Kurtz, and John Ozment, "How Customers Form Expectations of Service Quality Prior to a First Time Purchase," in *The Cutting Edge II*, William R. Darden, Robert F. Lusch, and J. Barry Mason, eds. (Baton Rouge, LA: Louisiana State University, 1992): 99–110.
6. "Southwest's Love Fest at Love Field," *Business Week*, April 28, 1997: 12E4.
7. For a more complete discussion of service quality, see A. Parasuraman, Valerie A. Zeithaml, and Leonard L. Berry, "A Conceptual Model of Service Quality and Its Implications for Future Research," *Journal of Marketing*, Fall 1985: 41–50; "Reassessment of Expectations as a Comparison Standard of Measuring Service Quality: Implications for Further Research," *Journal of Marketing*, January 1994: 111–124; J. Joseph Cronin, Jr., and Steven A. Taylor, "Measuring Service Quality: A Reexamination and Extension," *Journal of Marketing*, July 1992: 55–68.

8. For a more complete discussion of this topic, see Neeli Bendapudi and Leonard L. Berry, "Customers' Motivations for Maintaining Relationships with Service Providers," *Journal of Retailing,* Spring 1997: 15–37.

9. Valerie A. Zeithaml, "How Consumer Evaluation Processes Differ between Goods and Services," in *Marketing of Services,* James H. Donnelly and William R. George, eds. (Chicago: American Marketing Association, 1981): 186–190. Also, Keith B. Murray, "A Test of Services Marketing Theory: Consumer Information Acquisition Activities," *Journal of Marketing,* January 1991: 10–25.

10. Zeithaml, *Ibid.*

11. Stephen J. Grove and Raymond P. Fisk, "The Impact of Other Customers on Service Experiences: A Critical Incident Examination of 'Getting Along,'" *Journal of Retailing,* Spring 1997: 63–85.

12. Clow, Kurtz, and Ozment, *Ibid.*

13. Robert F. Young, "The Advertising of Consumer Services and the Hierarchy of Effects," in *Marketing of Services,* James H. Donnelly and William R. George, eds. (Chicago: American Marketing Association, 1981): 196–199; Keith B. Murray, "A Test of Services Marketing Theory" in *Marketing of Services,* James H. Donnelly and William R. George, eds. (Chicago: American Marketing Association, 1981): 10–25.

14. John E. Swan and Linda J. Combs, "Product Performance and Consumer Satisfaction: A New Concept," *Journal of Marketing,* April 1976: 25–33.

15. Shirley Taylor, "Waiting for Service: The Relationship between Delays and Evaluations of Service," *Journal of Marketing,* Summer 1994: 56–69.

16. "Retailing Excellence: The Customer's Perspective," a study commissioned by the International Mass Retail Association and conducted by Ambassador Cards division of Hallmark, Kansas City, May 1989.

17. Michael K. Hui, Laurette Dube, and Jean-Charles Chebat, "The Impact of Music on Consumers' Reactions to Waiting for Services," *Journal of Retailing,* Spring 1997: 87–104.

18. "Yuppie Yenta," *Forbes,* March 25, 1996: 102–103.

19. Michael J. O'Connor, "Almost Anyone Can Buy a Crowd, but Few Can Be 'Reason Why' Retailers," *International Trends in Retailing,* Summer 1993: 19–26.

20. Susan Keaveney, "Customer Switching Behavior in Service Industries: An Exploratory Study," *Journal of Marketing,* April 1995: 71–82.

21. Mary Jo Bitner, "Servicescapes: The Impact of Physical Surroundings on Customers and Employees," *Journal of Marketing,* April 1992: 71–84.

RETAIL ADMINISTRATION

MANAGING HUMAN RESOURCES

Starbucks Coffee has experienced explosive growth over the last five years and thus has had to put considerable effort into planning for and recruiting human resources at all levels in the organization. In fact, Starbucks was the first American retailer to provide its part-time employees (65 percent of its workforce) full health care benefits and stock options.

OVERVIEW

In this chapter, we examine the role that human resources plays in retail firms. We show that to carry out a retail strategy successfully, it is necessary to have not only the proper number and mix of human resources, but to have them empowered to serve the customer. Thus, retail managers must plan for human resources, they must acquire human resources, they must train and develop human resources, they must evaluate the employees' performances, and finally, they must compensate human resources.

LEARNING OBJECTIVES

After reading this chapter, you should be able to

1. list and explain the steps involved in planning human resources
2. describe the process involved in hiring employees
3. discuss how retailers manage existing employees
4. describe the various methods that retailers can use in compensating their employees

PLANNING FOR HUMAN RESOURCES

In our discussion of retail planning (Chapter 2), we described the role of administrative management as acquiring, maintaining, and controlling of retail resources. In this chapter, we are going to look into one, if not the most important, of those retail resources, human resources. Human resources makes things happen. After all, customers don't care who owns a retail store, they just want their questions answered, their problems solved, and their money for their purchases taken by the "first person they see." For many retailers, labor productivity has been declining over the past two decades. These retailers appear to be caught in a vicious circle in which the relatively low wages that they offer salespersons have attracted low-quality employees, which tends to perpetuate the low-wage–low-quality cycle. In fact, it might even be argued that "Americans have developed utter contempt for the retail clerk." Not all retailers are in this vicious circle; many have gotten out by investing time and money in their employees.

Empowerment

occurs when employees are given the power in their jobs to do the things necessary to satisfy customers and make things right for them.

Nordstrom employees, for example, who are known and respected for their service around the world, make a great deal of money on commission by both knowing their merchandise and how to take care of the customer. Home Depot employees, although not on commission, are paid an above-average wage to provide outstanding customer service. However, what really sets these two retailers' employees, as well as the employees of other high-performance retailers, apart from their counterparts, is that they have been "empowered" by their employers to take care of the customer. Empowerment simply means that the employee has the "power to make things right for the customer." An empowered retail employee

1. seeks to understand the customer's problem
2. desires to develop a relationship with the customer
3. understands the value of customer loyalty
4. is encouraged by management to solve the customer's problem

DOLLAR $ & C ENTS

High-performance retailers empower their employees to solve customers' problems.

The profit impact of empowering employees in retailing is dramatic. Providing good customer service or using suggestion selling can often be the difference between success and failure for many retailers. Because retailers operate on very low net profit margins even a small increase in salesforce productivity, be it measured in sales per employee-hour or gross margin per employee-hour, would, in most part, directly translate into an improvement in store profits. Consequently, retailers are now trying to improve labor's productivity, especially that of the salesforce, by training and using empowerment. An additional benefit of empowerment is that it leads to greater customer satisfaction and higher self-esteem among employees, which in turn reduces employee turnover. Before being able to empower their employees, retailers must first decide what human resources will be needed to achieve their firm's goals and objectives. Next, retailers must make sure that only the right types of employees are hired, that they are managed properly, and that they are fairly compensated for their efforts. These activities are the focus in this chapter.

TASK ANALYSIS

The starting point for a retailer's human resources planning is task analysis. Task analysis involves simply identifying all the tasks that the retailer needs to perform and breaking those tasks into jobs. Four steps should be followed: identifying the functions within the marketing system that retailers need or wish to perform; identifying the tasks that need to be performed within each function; mapping the tasks into jobs; and developing the job description and job specifications.

Task analysis
is the process of identifying all the tasks that the retailer needs to perform and breaking those tasks into jobs.

MARKETING FUNCTIONS
In Chapter 5, it was stressed that retailers need to view themselves as a part of a larger marketing system. Retailers are but one institution in a marketing channel that, as a system, must perform eight marketing functions: buying, selling, storing, transporting, sorting, financing, information gathering, and risk taking. Because the eight functions can be shifted and divided, no single institution in the marketing channel will typically perform all the functions.

The starting point for good human resource planning is for the retailer to decide which and how much of the eight marketing functions it will perform. As retailers assume more functions, they will require more human resources. For instance, the large chain retailer may

1. perform more of the buying function by having buying offices in major cities throughout the world
2. perform more of the selling function by heavily advertising and promoting merchandise on television and radio and in the newspapers and magazines
3. perform more of the storage function by operating its own warehouses
4. perform more of the transportation function by having its own trucks
5. perform more of the sorting functions by buying in large quantities and breaking bulk and in some cases doing its own packaging
6. perform more of the financing function by establishing a subsidiary to finance consumer purchases or by helping to finance small manufacturers
7. perform more of the information-gathering function by tracking customer purchases and developing a department of consumer research and long-range planning
8. perform more of the risk-taking function by designing and developing specifications for products and then contracting with manufacturers to produce them

IDENTIFYING TASKS
Once retailers have established the amount of each marketing function to perform, they must identify all the tasks that will need to be performed. Functions are broad classifications of activities; tasks are specific activities. For example, selling is a function that may involve the tasks of customer contact, customer follow-up, advertising in newspapers, and pricing merchandise.

Exhibit 15.1 provides a list of typical tasks that most retailers perform, ranging from transporting goods to cleaning the floor and windows of the store.

EXHIBIT 15.1   TYPICAL TASKS PERFORMED BY RETAILERS

Searching for merchandise	Following up on customers	Contacting customers	Doing customer reasearch
Packaging	Handling customer complaints	Transporting inbound merchandise	Preparing press releases
Gift wrapping	Cleaning store	Transporting outbound merchandise	Preparing financial statements
Advertising	Controlling inventory	Paying bills	Storing merchandise
Purchasing supplies	Hiring and firing employees	Handling cash	Preparing merchandise statistics
Purchasing merchandise	Training employees	Altering merchandise	Maintaining the store
Granting credit	Selling	Repairing merchandise	Providing store security
Billing customers	Supervising employees	Forecasting sales	
Building merchandise asssortments	Displaying merchandise		
Pricing merchandise			

MAPPING TASKS INTO JOBS

The third step involves the mapping of tasks into jobs. Retailers want a job to be comprised of a relatively similar set of tasks. Because most retail tasks are not similar, retailers will need to find those tasks that are most similar and group them together. The smaller the retail firm, the less this will be possible. In a "mom and pop" store, the owner does everything from purchasing supplies and merchandise, preparing financial statements, contacting customers, to even washing windows.

As stores grow in size and add more employees, specialization can occur. As a retailer grows, the tasks of granting credit, billing customers, paying bills, and preparing financial statements will be placed in the hands of an accounting or financial clerk. Similarly, the tasks of handling customer complaints, repairing and altering merchandise, and gift wrapping may be placed in the hands of a director of customer services. When the retailer was smaller, these two sets of tasks may have been handled by the same person, even though they weren't similar in nature. At the other extreme, if the retailer gets large enough, each task may be performed by a separate individual and ultimately there may be many employees handling a single task. For instance, Sears needs hundreds of employees just to bill customers, and thousands more just to purchase merchandise.

DEVELOPMENT OF JOB DESCRIPTIONS AND JOB SPECIFICATIONS

Once the tasks have been mapped into jobs, job descriptions and job specifications should be developed so that human resource managers know what the job applicant should be able to do, the skills required to do the job, and the kind of training that should be provided to the employee. Employees prefer working for employers with explicit job descriptions. Research has shown that if an employee's code of conduct states that theft of any type from the firm is a misdeed and the employee's job description makes it a responsibility to report such theft by others, then employees will be more willing to report such incidences than if it was not listed as a responsibility.[1]

Job descriptions and specifications also can help determine the sources that should be used to recruit applicants, the selection procedures that should be used in evaluating applicants, and the training and development that should be given new employees to maximize performance.

LONG-RANGE AND SHORT-RANGE ANALYSIS

Retailers generally use two different time frames in planning their human resource needs. On a long-range time horizon (one to five years), the major focus will be on the retailer's projected growth in sales volume and number of stores. Frequently, the growth in sales and number of stores depends on the availability of good human resources. In analyzing long-range growth trends, retailers should pay particular attention to the speed and predictability of sales growth, the geographic dispersion of growth, and the amount of growth related to line-of-trade diversification.

Most retailers, however, are more concerned with the short-range time frame. This is anything less than one year and in many cases may be weekly, monthly, or seasonal. Historically, for example, one of the most time-consuming and difficult jobs for retail managers was the weekly labor schedule, which took 6 to 10 hours a week to complete. Today, with the aid of computer programs such as Labor Day from Timecorp Systems, SuperSked from Management Robotics, Smart Scheduler from Kronos, and People-Planner from Information Marketing Businesses, most retailers have reduced this chore to less than an hour. The use of these programs frees managers to make better use of their time.

It is also wise for the managers to analyze any recurring seasonal trends. If retailers always do a strong business during the Christmas season, they should plan to have adequate human resources during this period each year. Periodic and predictable increases in short-run demand for human resources can be handled either by using part-time employees or by having existing employees participate in job sharing. Part-time employees for peak periods such as Christmas or weekends can help retailers serve more customers. One way of attracting good part-timers is to send out stuffers to your charge account holders, those customers who already use and probably like the store, offering part-time employment for the Christmas season with the standard employee's discount privileges. The peak business can often be handled by having existing employees share jobs, such as having managers waiting on customers, or by having some employees work overtime. However, using overtime is not a long-term solution. At 60 hours a week, a worker's performance declines by 25 percent.[2]

Dollar $ & Cents

Retailers that best schedule employees (supply of labor) to match the flow of shoppers (demand) will achieve higher performance levels.

LO • 2
Describe the process
involved in hiring
employees

HIRING THE RIGHT PERSON FOR THE JOB

Retailers must remember that human resources are acquired in a competitive marketplace. Good employees are not waiting around to be hired, and seldom will they come pounding at your door. In fact, when good workers or managers are looking for employment, they will seldom think of contacting retail firms, simply because of the reputation many retailers have for low starting wages. Therefore, retailers must aggressively seek out and recruit good employees; in so doing, they must compete with other industries for labor resources.

SOURCES

What are the sources from which retailers can obtain human resources? The seven sources shown in Exhibit 15.2 are the most common: competitors, walk-ins, employment agencies, schools and colleges, former employees, advertisements, and recommendations.

Retailers sometimes have to resort to using a different type of labor pool to match personnel with business demand. For example, several years ago, when Best Western International was faced with a shortage of reservation takers, it turned to a most unconventional source of employees—the Arizona Department of Corrections, which was seeking to find productive and profitable work for its inmates.[3]

SCREENING AND SELECTION

Regardless of the specific source, all job applicants should be subject to a formal screening process to sort the potentially good from the potentially bad employees. As with any judgment process, some mistakes will happen. But fewer errors occur when screening is used.

Retailers tend to vary in the amount of screening they use. In principle, there are four screens that retailers use: application blanks, personal interview, testing, and references. The total applicant pool for a particular job is progressively reduced as the applicants are subjected to each screen.

Screening

is the process that is used to sort the potentially good from the potentially bad employees and typically involves four screening devices: application blanks, personal interviews, testing, and reference checks.

APPLICATION BLANKS
As a matter of procedure, all applicants should be asked to fill out an application blank. The application blank should capture conveniently and compactly the individual's identity, training, and work history that will relate to his or her performance of the job tasks. Title VII of the Civil Rights Act of 1964 prohibits employers from discrimination in employment on the basis of race, color, religion, sex, or national origin; the Age Discrimination in Employment Act of 1967 (ADEA) prohibits employers from discrimination in employment on the basis of age; and the Americans with Disabilities Act of 1990 prohibits employers from discrimination in employment on the basis of handicap/disability. Moreover, laws and regulations in many states also prohibit discrimination on other bases, such as marital status, ancestry, arrest record, credit record, prior accidents on the job, disabilities unrelated to ability, weight, height, etc. Thus, the employer is effectively prohibited from asking any questions whose answer could be used to discriminate between two different groups of applicants. For example, if it could be shown that certain minorities have a higher

EXHIBIT 15.2   SOURCES OF RETAIL EMPLOYEES

Competitors. Competitors are the most common source for middle to upper management personnel, particularly when the retailer does not have someone to promote from within the firm due to geographic or line- of-trade conditions.

Walk-ins. Often a source for clerical, sales, and custodial positions, but seldom for managerial or supervisory employees. Walk-ins are most frequent during periods of high unemployment, when retailers need additional human resources least.

Employment Agencies. All states provide public employment services, which are typically available free of charge to both job seekers and employers. They are a reasonable, if not good, source for unskilled employees. At the same time, they are an excellent source for minority, handicapped, and veteran employees. This can help retailers meet their commitment to help achieve a specific policy of equal employment opportunities for all persons.

Private employment agencies, which may charge either the hiring company or the applicant a fee, are generally a much better source for managerial and white-collar employees, especially top executives. Two examples are Retail Executive Search, Inc., based in Chicago and Retail Recruiters based in New York City. Both are good sources for suitable candidates for top management retail positions.

Schools and Colleges. High schools that have Distributive Education Clubs of America (DECA) chapters provide an excellent source for operating-level employees. Many such employees have the basic talent, skills, and ambition to become shift managers or assistant department managers within a one- or two-year period.

Junior-college graduates, because of their college training, can begin in some low-level supervisory roles, such as assistant night manager of a store.

Four-year college graduates, and in some cases MBAs, expect and receive higher starting salaries due to educational experiences that enable them to move quickly into management positions.

Former Employees. Since retail organizations are always changing, there may come a time when a position is open for which a former employee would be excellent. It is not uncommon for a person to leave one retail organization as an assistant buyer to take a job as a sales rep for a supplier or as a buyer at another retail organization and then return to the initial retailer several years later as divisional merchandise manager.

Advertisements. Advertisements are a good source for sales clerks, cashiers, and janitors and occasionally buyers and managers. This is especially true when a retailer is entering a new geographic area and wants to make sure that employees at other retail firms in the area are aware that the new retailer is really interested in obtaining personnel with knowledge of the local market and not merely transferring existing personnel.

Recommendations. Current employees and vendors may have acquaintances or friends with an interest in applying for the jobs that are open. This source is good for filling jobs at all levels in the organization. Sales clerks as well as store managers, vice-presidents, and sales reps may know others seeking employment at a variety of ranks or positions.

Some potential male employees have complained about Hooters only hiring females of a certain age and type to serve customers.

Bona fide occupational qualification
is a qualification that potential employees should have in order to be able to perform certain narrow job functions for a particular retailer.

arrest record or that they change residences more often than nonminorities, then questions concerning such information would be illegal; they could be used to discriminate and normally do not elicit data indicative of likely job performance. Very rarely, exceptions may be made in which religion, sex, or national origin (but never race or color) is a bona fide occupational qualification (BFOQ) that is reasonably necessary to the narrow operation of a particular enterprise.[4] Our Behind the Scenes box describes how the issue of what can be a BFOQ problem area for retailers. As a matter of precaution, many retailers now check the Equal Employment Opportunity Commission's (EEOC) web site (http://www.eeoc.gov) or a commercial web site (http://www.smartbiz.com) before revising their employment applications or making other employment decisions. After all, this is generally not an area in which they have a high level of expertise.

Based on a study of the existing laws, the court interpretations thereof, and current practices of a national sample of National Retail Federation (NRF) department store retailers with regard to development and use of employment application blanks, 98 percent of retailers responding were using "suspect" questions on their application blanks.[5] Exhibit 15.3 shows some examples of legal and illegal questions that retailers in this study were found to be using. Retailers should make every effort to avoid using such questions.

From the list of qualified applicants who filled out applications, the retailer must select the best possible subset of candidates for each job.

WHEN CAN A RETAILER LEGALLY DISCRIMINATE?

BEHIND THE SCENES

In *Dothard v. Rawlinson,*[6] the court ruled that good examples of a BFOQ were a restaurant on the Mexican border hiring bilingual personnel or a women's apparel store hiring only females as dressing room attendants. However, recently the EEOC argued that Lillie Rubin Affiliates, an upscale women's clothing retailer that sells sequined creations in private dressing rooms, should use men as salespersons. The EEOC ruling came after an otherwise qualified male in Arizona was turned down when he applied for a job.

Lillie Rubin, where the average garment sells for nearly $400, contended that if it is forced to hire men, then it would then have to discriminate against its female salespersons by making them assist salesmen to ensure the customer's privacy. The retailer also pointed out that just two years earlier, the EEOC's Tampa office followed the Dothard's ruling and would not support a Florida man who claimed similar discrimination.

The EEOC acknowledged that the need for customer privacy raised special concerns for designer salons such as Lillie Rubin. However, the EEOC pointed out that it had been willing to work out practical accommodations with employers, especially with individuals whose bodies may be in various states of undress (i.e., coaches for sports teams). Therefore, why couldn't the male salesperson wait outside the dressing room until invited in by the customer?

Lillie Rubin, however, contended that maintaining the privacy of its customers was essential to its goal of encouraging the purchase of expensive garments in a relaxed fitting room atmosphere. As a result, the retailer and the EEOC have begun what will be a lengthy legal battle.

You be the judge. What should be done in this case?

SOURCE: Based on Patrick Dunne, Alan Levin, James Wilcox, and Roy Howell, "Avoid Discrimination Hassles When Recruiting New Personnel," *Narda News,* October 1991, p. 16, 58–60.

PERSONAL INTERVIEW Those applicants who possess the basic characteristics needed to perform the job should be personally interviewed. This important step allows the retailer to assess how well qualified the applicants are for the job. By its very nature, an interview is subjective, but in a well-structured interview one can obtain information or at least gain insight into the attitudes, personality, motives, and job aspirations of the interviewee.

Many interviewers overlook the fact that the interview should be a two-way communication process. Not only does the retailer want to gather information about the applicant, but the applicant may desire information about the retailer. Allowing time for the applicant to ask questions is essential if the retailer is competing for the talents of highly desired applicants. In fact, part of the interview time may actually be used by the interviewer to try to sell the applicant on working for the retailer as well as honestly explaining what the job entails so as not to lead to job dissatisfaction or possible legal complications based on misunderstandings.[7]

A new trend is to use the computer for gathering information about the applicant during the interview phase. Research has shown that more correct information is obtained this way and that it is cheaper.[8] Also, because the responses were to the computer directly rather than on paper or given to the interviewer, respondents thought that the information was more readily subject to instant checking and verification with other databases. Thus, to avoid potential embarrassment, applicants were more truthful.

EXHIBIT 15.3	LEGAL AND ILLEGAL QUESTIONS FOR EMPLOYMENT APPLICATIONS

LEGAL SCREENING DEVICES

Are you over 18?

Is there anything that would prevent you from being transferred to another city? (If the job entails a transfer.)

Do you currently use, or have you in the past used, another name?

What do you feel are your major strengths (weaknesses)?

Are you a U.S. citizen or an alien authorized to accept permanent employment in the United States?

Where do you live?

Can you perform the functions involved with or without reasonable accommodation?

Do you have any physical disability that would prevent you from performing this particular job? If so, what, if any, reasonable accommodations could be made to enable you to perform the job?

Where have you worked previously?

Do you drink alcohol?

ILLEGAL SCREENING DEVICES

How old are you?

Are you over 18 and under 70?

List the names and dates of all schools attended. (Start with high school)

Do you prefer being called Miss, Mrs. or Ms.?

What is the name of your pastor or rabbi?

How many days were you sick last year?

Are you married?

Does stress ever affect your ability to be productive?

How many dependents do you have?

What languages, besides English, do you speak fluently?

What social organizations are you currently a member of?

Other than the usual holidays, would you be absent for any religious holidays?

What medications are you currently taking?

Do you have any relatives working for the firm?

Where does your spouse work?

How long have you lived at your current residence?

Have you ever been arrested?

Have you ever filed for workmen's compensation?

Do you have a disability?

Have you ever had a serious illness?

How much alcohol do you drink per week?

SOURCE: Based on Patrick Dunne, Alan Levin, James Wilcox, and Roy Howell, "Employment Application Blanks: Are Retailers Using Them Correctly?" working paper, Texas Tech University, 1991.

Retailers use application blanks to obtain relevant data to help screen potential employees for jobs that are available.

TESTING Sometimes, formal tests will be administered to those applicants who received favorable ratings in their personal interviews. These tests may look for certain characteristics such as intelligence, interests, leadership potential, personality traits, or honesty. Since 1989, retailers have not been permitted by federal law to use lie detector tests. Although most retailers never used polygraph tests, some, especially in the jewelry business, relied heavily on their results. Many retailers have switched to other types of tests. For example, research has shown that pencil-and-paper tests to measure integrity have an excellent record at picking out the low-integrity population and that employers using these tests have substantial success in screening out the kind of irresponsible and counterproductive behavior that drives bosses crazy: disciplinary problems, disruptiveness on the job, chronic tardiness, and excessive absenteeism.[9] Other types of tests used by retailers include credit checks with local credit bureaus, checks of prior worker's compensation claims, drug tests, and even handwriting analysis. However, because each state has different laws on the use of these types of tests, especially drug tests, the retailer should consult with an attorney before using them. In addition, some tests could violate the applicant's rights if he or she isn't advised of such inquiries ahead of time and given the opportunity to consent or if the tests run afoul of the antidiscrimination laws' protections for minorities and the handicapped. Besides, in many cases these tests have been found not only to violate the applicant's rights but also to give error-ridden information about the applicant.[10]

REFERENCES As a general rule, retailers should not ask for or check the references the applicant has provided until the applicant has been screened or filtered through the preceding stages. If references were obtained and verified on all initial applicants, the cost would be excessive.

Negligent hiring is one of the hottest issues in current employment law. The premise is that an employer can be held responsible for an employee's unlawful actions if it did not reasonably investigate an employee's background and then placed the employee in a position where he or she caused harm to a customer.[11] When references are

AN AMBIGUOUS LEXICON FOR JOB RECOMMENDATIONS

Every once in a while, a person requests a letter of recommendation from a previous employer, professor, or family friend about whom the letter writer has serious reservations. Does the writer send a moderately favorable letter and live with his conscience or write a frank, unfavorable letter and risk a lawsuit when the person finds out about it. (Remember, under certain circumstances, such letters are no longer confidential.)

Professor Robert J. Thornton at Lehigh University has developed the following guidelines for handling such a dilemma.

To describe a candidate who is not particularly industrious:

"In my opinion you will be very fortunate to get this person to work for you."

To describe a candidate who is not worth further consideration:

"I would urge you to waste no time in making this candidate an offer of employment."

To describe a person who is woefully inept:

"I recommend this person with absolutely no qualifications whatsoever."

For someone who has had trouble getting along with others.

"I am pleased to say that he is a former student of mine."

For the person who is not even worth serious consideration:

"I would urge you to waste no time making this person an offer of employment."

For the student who will most surely get sacked at his first job:

"I have little doubt you will find him fired with enthusiasm."

For the person who has lackluster work habits or credentials:

"I cannot recommend this person highly enough." OR "All in all, I cannot say enough good things about this candidate or recommend him highly."

For the person who has difficulty telling the truth:

"His (or her) true ability is deceiving."

For the student who is so unproductive that the position would be better left unfilled:

"I can assure you that no person would be better for this job."

In addition, Thornton also demonstrates the use of the "questionable" or "missing" comma.

For example, the person who was a lazy, unproductive employee, looking for a new position:

"He won't do anything, which will lower your high regard for him."

OR

"He won't do anything which will lower your high regard for him."

"The job required very few skills, which he lacked."

OR

"The job required very few skills which he lacked."

SOURCE: The above was used with the written permission of Robert Thornton.

obtained and checked, the retailer should try to assess the honesty and reliability of the applicant. The reason for leaving the prior place or places of employment should also be investigated. The retailer should be interested in finding out what type of person will vouch for the prospective employee. Although most references provided by the applicant can be expected to give a neutral or favorable recommendation (if they give one at all), the reference check does give the retailer a means to verify the accuracy and completeness of the application. Also, as a point of information, many retailers have found greater success by using telephone interviews instead of asking for written replies. This method enables retailers to gather more complete and honest evaluations than do written replies, even if it is only in what the reference doesn't say about the applicant. Our Behind the Scenes box points out one of the major problems faced by writers of such letters of recommendation.

One final comment on checking references: the retailer must tread carefully here to avoid breaking federal and state laws. The personnel manager will be well advised to visit the firm's legal staff yearly to determine the firm's and the applicant's legal rights. New laws are regularly being made in the courts, Congress, and state legislatures.

MANAGING EXISTING EMPLOYEES

LO • 3
Discuss how retailers manage existing employees

Once an employee is hired, the retailer must prepare programs for training the employee to meet current or future job requirements, evaluating employees, and motivating them. However, the most critical job for retailers entering the 21st century is developing a teamwork attitude among its employees.

TEAMWORK APPROACH

Many high-performance retailers have been reengineering their staff to stress the importance of overall department (store, division, or company) performance by working toward team versus individual achievements. Federated Department Stores has taken the approach that teams don't need bosses to lead them. The chain believes that the employees can work better leading themselves, managing their own time, functions, and responsibilities. After all, the individuals who know the business best are the empowered employees. Team members, working in merchandising, store management, marketing, finance, and logistics, work in concert with each other to define their roles based on the knowledge and talent of each member. Members are compensated based partly on the overall team's performance, the individual's contribution to the team, and the individual's value based on his or her knowledge and skills to the team.[12]

DOLLAR $ & ¢ENTS

Retailers that are able to develop a team-oriented attitude among their employees and management will achieve higher levels of performance.

Self-service Best Buy, which is engaged in a heated battle with Circuit City, with its highly trained commission-oriented salesforce, recently changed its incentive program. Best Buy, as an experiment, is now testing the use of "team" commissions in its appliance department.[13] Wal-Mart has long used such a teamwork approach by offering

WAL-MART'S PARTNERSHIP WITH ITS ASSOCIATES

Sam Walton followed a simple philosophy with his Wal-Mart associates—take care of them, treat them well, and involve them in the business. By sharing the profits (in the beginning, profits were just shared with the management; however, he later corrected this admitted mistake by covering all associates), he reasoned—whether it's in salaries or incentives or bonuses or stock discounts—the more profits would accrue to the company. After all, if the associates were happy and involved, they would give the customers that little extra and the customers would return again and again. And this was better than dragging strangers into your store based on splashy sales or expensive advertising. As a result, Wal-Mart has developed a partnership with its associates that goes beyond just sharing profits.

In his autobiography, Sam Walton noted that there is one more aspect to a true partnership: executives who hold themselves aloof from their associates, who won't listen to their associates when they have a problem, can never be true partners with them. Often, this is an exhausting and sometimes frustrating part of the management process, but folks who stand on their feet all day stocking shelves or pushing carts of merchandise out of the back room get exhausted and frustrated too. And occasionally they dwell on problems that they just can't let go of until they've shared it with somebody who they believe is in a position to find a solution. That's why as big as Wal-Mart got to be, Sam really tried to maintain an open-door policy at Wal-Mart. It got to be a common sight for a Wal-Mart hourly associate to drive to Bentonville just to see Mr. Sam and he WOULD see them. In addition, all the time he was alive, Sam Walton's telephone number was listed in the Bentonville telephone directory. Never mind that some calls would be in the middle of the night.

The fact that this partnership, or teamwork, was so unique to Wal-Mart in its early days can be attested by a story told by Gordon Grender, a mutual fund manager. In the early 1970s, Grender spent a day with Sam Walton. On visits to Wal-Marts in those little southern towns, he saw Walton carp unceasingly at the associates about their work. And the associates carped to him about the incompetent head office. As a result, Grender avoided buying the stock, which was the greatest stock market performer for the next two decades.

Now, Grender realizes that the strength of Wal-Mart was the ability of the associates to complain to Sam and his ability to complain to them.

SOURCE: Based on excerpts from Sam Walton, *Made in America: His Story,* conversations with Wal-Mart executives, and "Diogenes in Search of a Smart Stock Picker," *Forbes,* October 7, 1996: 153.

bonuses to all employees based on their store's profits and shrinkage total. In fact, many retail experts credit Wal-Mart's partnership program, as discussed in our Winners & Losers box, as a major contributing factor behind its success.[14]

In fact, the first two things David Novak did when he took over Tricon, the spin-off of PepsiCo's three restaurants (KFC, TacoBell, and Pizza Hut) in 1997, was enlarge the menu and follow Wal-Mart's approach by dramatically lifting the morale of the persons who matter most in a retail operation—the in-store employees and franchisees who interact with customers.[15]

TRAINING AND DEVELOPING EMPLOYEES

Retailers wanting the best return on their human resource investment should provide training and development for both new and existing employees. Training and development are consistent with the concept of human resource planning.

Training is not a "one-time happening," however. Retailers today view training as a process of continuing education. Thus, as an individual's responsibilities increase so does the training and development. Employees are taught not just technical skills but administrative and people skills as well. Each phase of development is built on the training that has preceded it and includes training in merchandising, operations management, motivation, decision making, problem analysis, and time management.

In addition to developing a pool of future managers and assisting employees with present duties, training and development programs enable the employees to know where they are and how they are doing. Remember, a career in retailing is different from careers in other business fields. In the beginning, it is like a pyramid, with the employee becoming increasingly specialized toward the goal of being a buyer—the ultimate specialist. Afterward, the goal is to increase breadth, not specialty, so as to become a store or division manager.

Remember, the best training and development program devised is useless unless management adopts a philosophy of complete support. In the past, many retail executives got so tied up in merchandising concerns, they forgot about human resources.

EVALUATING EMPLOYEES

Performance appraisal and review is the formal systematic assessment of how well employees are performing their jobs in relation to established standards and the communication of that assessment to employees. Employees place a great deal of importance on appraisals, and the way the appraisal system operates affects morale and organizational climate in significant ways. Moreover, the appraisal system also has an impact on other human resource processes, such as training and development, compensation, and promotion.

Informal appraisals tend to take place on an ongoing basis within the retail firm as supervisors evaluate their subordinates' work on a daily basis and as subordinates appraise each other as well as their supervisors. However, the formal systematic appraisal of an individual is likely to occur at certain intervals throughout the year or when the employee is being considered for a wage increase, a promotion, a transfer, or an opportunity to improve job skills.

Retailers of all sizes should try to use objective criteria for the appraisal and review process wherever possible. A form for the objective review and appraisal of salespersons is shown in Exhibit 15.4. However, not every item that the retailer might want to evaluate can be quantified. Larger retail operations use a committee, frequently consisting of the vice-president of human resources and one or two other executives, to evaluate each employee. Some retailers, especially smaller ones, sometimes forego the formal evaluation process and judge a salesperson on the basis of dollar sales, number of transactions, errors, on-time performance, ratio of returned merchandise, and customer complaints.

It is important to recognize several key factors in conducting performance appraisals. First, the process should be an ongoing affair, not just a periodic review. Regularly scheduled review times should not keep supervisors from appraising or coaching their subordinates whenever necessary. Second, employees seek feedback, or information about how well they are doing their jobs, and this feedback should be provided on a timely and relevant basis. Third, the person doing the review should know what the job being reviewed entails and what the performance standards are. Many times, employees can become upset with the review process when the reviewer is not aware of problems and limitations of the job under review. Fourth, different supervisors are

Performance appraisal and review
is the formal systematic assessment of how well employees are performing their jobs in relation to established standards and the communication of that assessment to employees.

EXHIBIT 15.4	CRITERIA USED IN THE APPRAISAL AND REVIEW PROCESS

Merchandise Procedures:
Employee's accuracy in counting and inventorying merchandise.

Prevents merchandise shrinkage due to mishandling of merchandise.

Keeps merchandise in a neat and orderly manner on sales floor.

Knows the design and specification of warranties and guarantees of the merchandise groups.

Gets merchandise on sales floor quickly after merchandise arrival.

Customer Service Ability:
Provides courteous service to customers.

Handles customer complaints and/or service problems as indicated by store procedure.

Follows proper procedure concerning merchandise returns and lay-aways when conducted through credit transactions.

Suggests add-on or complementary merchandise to customers.

Sales Ability:
Has strong ability to close the sale.

Promotes sale of merchandise items having profit margins.

Acts as a resource to other departments or other salespeople needing assistance.

Works well with fellow workers in primary merchandise department.

Product-Merchandise Knowledge:
Knowledgeable of design, style, and construction of merchandise group.

Knowledgeable of special promotions and/or advertised sale items.

Knowledgeable of material (fabrics), color coordination, and complementary accessories related to returned merchandise.

Provides accurate and complete paperwork related to returned merchandise.

Store Policy:
Provides accurate and complete paperwork related to work schedules.

Provides accurate and complete paperwork for cash and credit transactions.

Shows up on time for work, sales meetings, and training sessions.

Accurately follows day-to-day instructions of immediate supervisor.

Employee's overall job-related attitude.

SOURCE: Robert P. Bush, Alan J. Bush, David J. Ortinau, and Joseph F. Hair, Jr., "Developing a Behavior-Based Scale to Assess Retail Salesperson Performance," *Journal of Retailing,* Spring 1990: 119–136.

Retail managers will often consult with and seek the input of employees before delegating authority and responsibility to them.

likely to rate personnel with different degrees of leniency or severity. Therefore, not only should the person making the review understand the performance standards, but at least two people should make the review. Finally, research has shown that the particular method of reviewing the employee doesn't matter. Retailers have found success in various types of measures including the rating scale, checklist, free-form essay, and rankings.

MOTIVATING EMPLOYEES

Human resource management goes beyond selecting, training, and compensating the employees. It also involves motivating them to improve current performance. A successful retailer today must constantly motivate all employees to strive for higher sales figures, to decrease expenses, to communicate company policies to the public, and to solve problems as they arise. This is achieved through the proper use of motivation.

Motivation is the drive that a person has to excel at the activities it undertakes such as a job. Several theories on motivation have been developed. These can be divided into content theories, which ask "What motivates an individual to behave," and process theories, which ask "How can I motivate an individual." Among the content theories we discuss are Maslow's Hierarchy of Needs, Herzberg's Two-Factor Theory of Motivation, and McGregor's Theory X and Theory Y. In our discussion of the process theories, we look at two of the most widely used: Expectancy Theory and Goal Setting.

Motivation
is the drive that a person has to excel at activities, such as a job, it undertakes.

CONTENT THEORIES
Abraham Maslow, a noted psychologist, developed a Hierarchy of Needs Model, which is shown in Exhibit 15.5, that suggests that individuals have different types of needs and that they satisfy lower-level needs before moving to higher levels. The first level is the basic physiological need, which can be satisfied by the employee's cash wages. Once a salesforce becomes content at this level, they become concerned with safety and security needs. Retailers have satisfied these needs with such benefits as security-patrolled parking locations. The third level of needs, that of belongingness and social needs, can be satisfied with "employee or

Hierarchy of Needs Model
theorizes that individuals have lower level physiological and safety and security needs which are first satisfied and then higher level needs of belongingness or social esteem and self actualization are pursued.

EXHIBIT 15.5	HOW RETAILERS CAN USE MASLOW'S HIERARCHY OF NEEDS

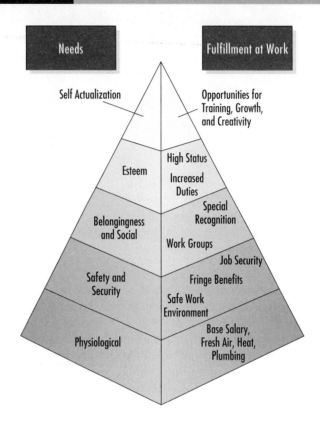

salesperson of the month" awards. A similar approach can be used at the fourth level of needs, esteem, with fancier offices and job titles. The highest need level is self-actualization or "becoming all you can be" in this life. Here, retailers can provide seminars to help broaden the horizons of salespersons. Maslow's hierarchy thus provides retailers with ideas that can appeal to the basic needs of their employees.

Offering another perspective on motivation was Herzberg's Two-Factor Theory, which suggested that two factors operate to encourage people to work hard: hygiene factors and motivators. Hygiene factors are extrinsic to the individual and can be organizationally determined. Examples of hygiene factors in a retail setting are pay, verbal praise, and special name badges. Motivators are intrinsic to the individual and include the feeling of self-accomplishment or the desire to excel.

Thus, Maslow's and Herzberg's theories as to what motivates an individual to behave are quite similar. Herzberg's hygiene factors are basically Maslow's two lower levels of need (physiologic and safety), and motivators are his top two levels (esteem and self-actualization). Maslow's third level of need, belonging, can fit into either of Herzberg's two categories depending on the situation.

A third content theory was McGregor's Theory X and Theory Y. Theory X assumes that employees must be closely supervised and controlled and that economic inducements (salaries and commissions) will provide the means of influencing employees to perform. This theory assumes that employees need to be induced or coerced to work

Herzberg's Two-Factor Theory
argues that two factors encourage people to work hard: hygiene factors which are extrinsic to the individual and motivators which are intrinsic to the individual.

Theory X
is a theory of management that views employees as unreliable and thus must be closely supervised and controlled and given economic inducements to perform properly.

because they are inherently lazy. Theory Y, however, assumes that employees are self-reliant and enjoy work and can be delegated authority and responsibility. Over the past decade, many different retailing employee groups have foregone wage increases for a share of management. These "employee-managed" retail stores have generally experienced an increased organizational effectiveness, thus supporting Maslow's, Herzberg's, and the Theory Y contention that money alone is not a primary motivator.

PROCESS THEORIES

On the other side of content theories are process theories, which are concerned with how to motivate a salesperson to behave in the retailer's best interest.

Expectancy Theory addresses the relationship between effort, performance, and organizational outcomes. It assumes that employees know this relationship and that this knowledge influences them to behave in one way or another. More specifically, expectancy theory states that a salesperson's motivation to expend effort on some task depends on whether (1) the salesperson expects that the effort will lead to a sale (performance), (2) the sale will likely lead to a reward or bonus (outcome), and (3) the reward or bonus is desirable (valued). Obviously, the critical consideration is how much value the salesperson attaches to the reward or bonus, be it cash, prizes, promotions, fancier offices, increased job status, better conditions, or a greater sense of achievement.

Expectancy theory appears to provide a logical answer to the question "how to motivate a sales staff." If a salesperson likes to travel and thinks he or she can reach quota, he or she will work hard to win a trip.

Goal setting is a way to obtain the firm's objectives that depend on inducing a person to behave in the desired manner. The goals must be attainable; too difficult a goal, such as an increase in sales of 50 percent, will not motivate a salesperson because the chances of achieving the target are slim. Likewise, too easy a goal, such as a 1 percent increase, is often demotivating and unchallenging. The time frame is also important. Too long a time frame is generally demotivating. Just as you would put off a term paper due in four months, the salesperson might do the same with a year-long sales goal. A 10 percent increase in yearly sales might be broken down into either the two seasons or 12 separate months, with changes made at stated intervals based on market conditions.

Remember, it is the retail manager's job to motivate employees in a manner that yields job satisfaction, low turnover, low absenteeism, and high performance results.

Theory Y
is a theory of management that views employees as self-reliant and enjoying work and thus can be empowered and delegated authority and responsibility.

Expectancy Theory
suggests that an employee will expend effort on some task because the employee expects that the effort will lead to a performance outcome which will lead to a reward or bonus which the employee finds desirable or valued.

Goal setting
is the process where management and employees establish goals which become the basis for performance appraisal and review.

HUMAN RESOURCE COMPENSATION

LO • 4
Describe the various methods that retailers can use in compensating their employees

As all businesspersons know, human resources are not free goods. They are expensive, and in retailing their cost typically represents 50 percent of operating expenses. We do not discuss here how to control labor expenses but merely highlight some important aspects about compensating human resources.

Compensation is one of the major variables in attracting, retaining, and motivating human resources. The quality of employees that can be attracted, whether as sales clerks or executives, is directly proportional to the compensation package offered. The better the human resource, the higher the price. Naturally, other things besides compensation are important to employees. A recent Gallup Poll found that good health insurance is the most important aspect of their job. Interesting work and job security were second and third.[16]

Competitive compensation is just as important to retaining good employees as it is to attracting them. In this regard, the retailer needs to realize that if it invests more money in training and developing employees, these employees will actually increase in value, not only to the retailer, but also to competitors who may try to hire them. Thus, as the retailer invests money to train and develop employees, it must also make a commitment to provide them with more compensation, or the retailer will be training and developing employees for its competitors.

Here, the term compensation includes direct dollar payments (wages, commissions, and bonuses) and indirect payments (insurance, vacation time, retirement plans). Compensation plans in retailing can have up to three basic components: a fixed component, a variable component, and a fringe benefit component. The fixed component typically is composed of some base wage per hour, week, month, or year. The variable component is often composed of some bonus that is received if performance warrants. Sales clerks may be paid a bonus of 10 percent of sales above some established minimum; department managers may receive a bonus based on the profit performance of their department. Workers in restaurants often receive tips, a variable component that the retailer does not control. Finally, a fringe benefit package may include such things as health insurance, disability benefits, life insurance, retirement plans, the use of automobiles, and financial counseling. Each of the three components helps the retailer to achieve a different human resource goal. The fixed component helps to ensure that employees have a source of income to meet their most basic financial obligations. This helps to fulfill the employees' physiologic needs. The variable component allows the retailer to offer employees an incentive for higher levels of effort and commitment, which helps to fulfill a belongingness and social need among employees for special recognition in return for high performance. The fringe benefit component allows the retailer to offer employees safety and security. Retail employees have a need to be protected and cared for when they are faced with difficult times or when they become too old to provide for themselves. Also, certain employees (especially executives) have a need for prestige and status.

The best combination of fixed, variable, and fringe compensation components depends on the person, the job, and the retail organization. There is no set formula. Some top retail executives prefer mostly salary, others thrive on bonuses, and still others would rather have more pension benefits. The same holds for sales clerks. Therefore, the compensation package needs to be tailored to the individual. We now focus our attention on compensation of the salesforce, but the same principles will apply to managers.

COMMON TYPES OF COMPENSATION PROGRAMS FOR SALESFORCE

Retail salesforce compensation programs can be conveniently broken into three major types: (1) straight salary, (2) salary plus commission, and (3) straight commission. Each of these methods has its advantages and disadvantages.

STRAIGHT SALARY
In the straight salary program, the salesperson receives a fixed salary per time period (usually per week) regardless of the level of sales generated or orders taken. However, over time, if the salesperson does not help

---

Compensation
includes direct dollar payments (wages, commissions, and bonuses) and indirect payments (insurance, vacation time, retirement plans).

Fringe benefit package
is a part of the total compensation package offered many retail employees and may include health insurance, disability benefits, life insurance, retirement plans, child care, use of an auto, and financial counseling.

Straight salary
is a compensation plan where the individual receives a fixed salary per time period regardless of the level of performance.

generate sales or take enough orders, he or she will likely be fired for not performing adequately. Similarly, over time, if the salesperson helps to generate more than a proportionate share of sales or fills more than a proportionate number of orders, the retailer will be unable to retain the employee without a raise.

Many small retailers use this compensation method because they typically assign stock rearranging, merchandise display, and other nonselling duties to their salespersons. Therefore, if the employees were paid on a commission basis they would spend little if any time on their nonselling duties, and the retail organization would suffer. Many promotional and price-oriented chain stores whose salespersons are merely order takers will use the straight salary method because the salesperson is not much of a causal factor in generating sales. Also, most clerks and cashiers, as well as other lower-level retail personnel, are almost always paid straight salaries.

The salesperson may view this plan as attractive because it offers income security or as unappealing because it gives little incentive for extraordinary effort and performance. Thus, for this method, which is also the easiest plan for the employee to understand, to be effective, it must be combined with a periodic evaluation so that superior salespersons can be identified and singled out for higher salaries.

SALARY PLUS COMMISSION

Sometimes, the salesperson is paid salary plus commission which consists of a fixed salary per time period plus a percentage commission on all sales or on all sales over an established quota. Because merchandise lines and items can vary in terms of gross margins, some retailers pay commissions on gross margin dollars generated. The fixed salary is lower than that of the salesperson working on a straight salary plan, but the commission structure gives one the potential to earn more than the person on the straight salary plan. In fact, most salespersons on the salary plus commission program earn more than their counterparts on a straight salary program.

This plan gives the employees a stable base income—and thus incentive to perform nonselling tasks—but it also encourages and rewards superior effort. Therefore, it represents a good compromise between the straight salary and the straight commission programs. In many cases, top management generally receives a salary and a bonus based on overall store or department performance.

Salary plus commission is a compensation plan where the individual receives a fixed salary per time period and a commission which is usually based on sales the individual generates.

STRAIGHT COMMISSION

Income of some salespersons is based on straight commision, for example, a percentage commission on each sale they generate. The commission could be the same percentage on all merchandise or it could vary depending on the profitability of the item. Retail salespersons working on a straight commission typically receive commissions of 2 percent to 10 percent of the selling price.

The straight commission plan provides substantial incentive for retail salespersons to generate sales. However, when the general business climate is poor, retail salespersons may not be able to generate enough volume to meet their fixed payment obligations (mortgage payment, auto payment, food expenses). Because of that problem, most retailers slightly modify the straight commission plan to allow the salesperson to draw wages against future commissions up to some specified amount per week. For instance, the employee may be able to draw $200 per week, which will be paid back with future commissions.

A major problem with the straight commission plan is that it may provide the retail salesperson with too much incentive to sell. The employee as a result of the income insecurity features of this plan may begin to use pressure tactics to close sales, hurting the retailer's image and long-run sales performance. Similarly, the employee may not

Straight commission is a compensation plan where the compensation is limited to a percentage commission on each sale generated.

Close and frequent conversations between a retail manager and his or her staff can help clarify goals and objectives.

be willing to perform other duties such as helping customers with returned merchandise or helping to set up displays. Because, after all, compensation is paid to sell and not to handle customer complaints or displays. Generally, sales personnel for high-price merchandise, or high ticket items such as automobiles, real estates, jewelry, and furniture, as well as those items requiring the sales personnel to prospect or seek out potential customers (e.g., insurance and door-to-door selling), are paid this way.

An Ernst & Young survey reported that 51 percent of the retailers polled used a salary plus commission plan and 38 percent used straight commission.[17] Exhibit 15.6 summarizes the attributes of each of these plans. During the early 1990s, many retailers began to reduce the commission portion of employee compensation plans and increase the salary portion. This was an attempt to reduce consumer distaste for what was perceived to be "high-pressure selling" and was highlighted by Sears's problems with its auto repair centers, where service representatives were paid a commission on the amount of service work they wrote up.[18] Recently, however, the trend has begun to reverse.

SUPPLEMENTAL BENEFITS

In addition to regular wages (salary, commission, or both), retail employees also can receive four types of supplementary benefits: employee discounts, insurance and retirement benefits, child care, and push money (or spiffs).

EMPLOYEE DISCOUNTS   Almost all retailers offer their employees discounts on merchandise or services that they purchase for themselves or their immediate family. About the only line of trade in which these discounts are not offered is

EXHIBIT 15.6	ATTRIBUTES OF COMPENSATION PLANS

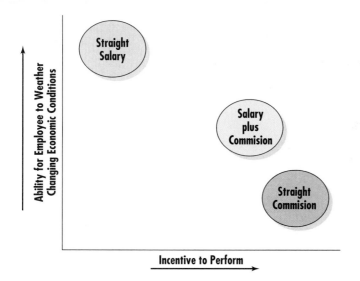

grocery retailing, because grocery retailers operate on relatively thin gross margins. In other lines of retail trade, the discounts can range from 10 to 40 percent.

INSURANCE AND RETIREMENT BENEFITS Historically, retail personnel were not provided any insurance or retirement benefits. In some situations, this is still the case. However, many retailers are providing their employees with either free or low-cost group health and life insurance. Still others are making profit sharing, stock ownership, and retirement programs available to long-tenure employees. These benefits are valued between $50 and $190 a month per individual.

CHILD CARE In an effort to attract employees from two-wage-earner families or single parent households, some U.S. businesses have begun to provide child care for employees' offspring during working hours. Retailers have just started providing child care, a program that experts agree will become a necessity over the next decade. However, with health care costs rapidly increasing, some retailers have delayed plans to add child care due to the added expenses. Hardee's Food Systems, for example, recently eliminated its successful pilot child care subsidy at six Raleigh, N.C., restaurants.[19]

PUSH MONEY A final type of supplementary benefit is "push money," which some may call "prize money," "premium merchandise," or just plain "PM." Retailers commonly call it by another name "spiffs." The PM, paid to the salesperson in addition to base salary and regular commissions, is said to encourage additional selling effort on particular items or merchandise lines.

PMs can be either retailer- or supplier-sponsored. A retailer may give a PM to get salespersons to sell old or slow-moving merchandise. The salesperson who sells the most may win a free trip to Hawaii or some other prize, or everyone who sells an established quantity of merchandise may get a prize or premium. Or the retailer may simply offer an extra $10 bonus for the sale of a specific product (e.g., a dining room table). Suppliers, however, tend to offer PMs to retail salespersons for selling the top-of-the-

PM
is also called push money or spiff and is a payment made to salespersons in addition to their base salary and regular commisisons to encourage additional selling effort on particular items or merchandise lines.

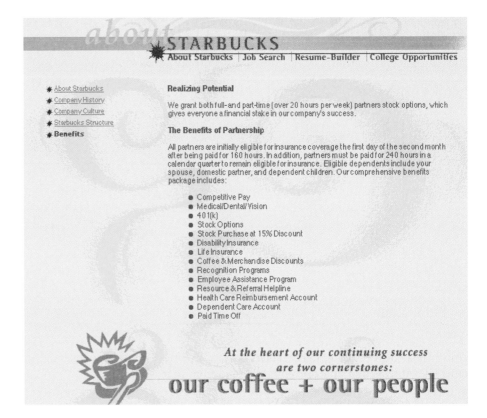

Starbucks was the first American company to offer benefits to part-time employees.

line or most profitable items in the suppliers' product mix. These supplier-offered PMs are common in the appliance, furniture, jewelry, and floorcovering industries.

Occasionally, there may be a conflict between the supplier and the retailer over the offering of PMs. This conflict arises because the supplier may be offering the retailer's salespersons an incentive to push an item or merchandise line that may not be the most profitable line for the retailer or the best for the customer, although it may be highly profitable to the supplier. Some retailers prefer to keep all PMs for themselves, because they believe they are already paying a fair wage to their salespersons.

COMPENSATION PLAN REQUIREMENTS

Regardless of what method a retailer ultimately determines to use in compensating its employees, the method should meet the following general requirements:

1. *fairness:* The plan does not favor one group or division over any other group or division or enable such a group to receive disproportionate rewards in relation to contributions. It must also keep wage costs under control so that they do not put the store at a competitive disadvantage.
2. *adequacy:* The level of compensation should enable the employee to maintain a standard of living commensurate with job position and to maintain job satisfaction.
3. *prompt and regular payments:* Payments should be made on time and in accordance with the agreement between employer and employee. In incentive plans, greater stimulation is provided when reward closely follows the accomplishment.

4. *customer interest:* The plan should not reward any actions by an employee that could result in customer ill-will.
5. *simplicity:* The plan must be easy to understand so as to prevent any misunderstandings with the resultant ill-will. This should also enable management to minimize the man-hours needed to determine compensation levels.
6. *balance:* Pay, supplemental benefits, and other rewards must provide a reasonable total reward package.
7. *security:* The plan must fulfill the employee's security needs.
8. *cost-effective:* The plan must not result in excessive payments, given the retailer's financial condition.

Although none of the three plans we discussed above satisfies all these requirements to the maximum level, awareness of these requirements will aid in the selection of the best plan given the individual circumstances. In fact, it is not uncommon for the same retailer to use more than one plan in the same store as different divisions or departments have different needs or as different types of employees, for example, office personnel vs. salespeople or store managers are motivated by different compensation programs.

JOB ENRICHMENT

A planned program for enhancing job characteristics is typically called job enrichment. Job enrichment is the process of enhancing the core job characteristics for the purpose of increasing worker motivation, productivity, and satisfaction. There are five core job characteristics that should be increased:

1. *skill variety:* the degree to which an employee can use different skills and talents
2. *task identity:* the degree to which a job requires the completion of a whole assignment that has a visible outcome
3. *task significance:* the degree to which the job affects other employees
4. *autonomy:* the degree to which the employee has freedom, independence, and discretion in achieving the outcome
5. *job feedback:* the degree to which the employee receives information about the effectiveness of his or her performance[20]

Job enrichment programs have their base in motivation theory, which suggests that job factors themselves (e.g., job challenge, independence, and responsibility) are powerful motivators.

Retail management has long recognized that paying attention to job characteristics and descriptions, work scheduling, job sharing, and employee input programs will have a positive effect on employee productivity and satisfaction. Retailers using the job enrichment program must be careful in presenting it to the employees, otherwise the employees may think that they are being asked to do too many tasks without being compensated for the extra work load.

Finally, by following the guidelines discussed in this chapter, retailers will be able to avoid the expenses associated with employee turnover, which are shown in Exhibit 15.7. A recent study has revealed that only half of all retail associates attempting to service customers have the 10-plus months experience deemed necessary to achieve adequate product and service knowledge.[21] Turnover is even worse in specialty stores, which typically hire part-timers at entry-level positions.

Job enrichment
is the process of enhancing the core job characteristics of employees to improve their motivation, productivity, and job satisfaction.

EXHIBIT 15.7	VARIOUS TYPES OF EMPLOYEE TURNOVER COSTS

Direct: These costs are reflected on the retailer's financial statements.

- Cost of recruiting applicants
- Cost of evaluating applicants (including interviews, reference checks, and any testing)
- Cost of training classes (including management's time)
- Pay (including benefits) during period when new employee is taking training course
- Part of supervisor's pay (including benefits) to cover costs spent helping new employee during first few weeks of job

Indirect: These activities cause a reduction in the firm's revenue. Thus, while they are not shown on the retailer's financial statements, they are still a cost.

- Loss of customers that were "loyal" to former employee
- Lost sales resulting from the lack of product knowledge during the initial time of job
- Lost sales and potential profits missed from alienated customers resulting from inexperience in retail selling
- Decrease in employee morale caused by the departure of an employee
- The effect of the employees' lower morale on customers

As Exhibit 15.7 points out, there are two categories of turnover expenses: direct and hidden. Although it is impossible to measure the indirect costs, the direct costs average nearly $1,000 per employee.[22] Therefore, it is to the retailer's advantage to reduce these expenses by training, compensating, and empowering their employees to the fullest extent.

STUDENT STUDY GUIDE

SUMMARY

LO•1   WHAT STEPS ARE INVOLVED IN PLANNING HUMAN RE-SOURCES?   Our discussion of human resource planning and management focused on four major dimensions: planning for human resources, employee hiring, managing existing employees, and human resource compensation.

To properly plan for human resources, retailers should attempt to empower their employees so that both they and the customer are satisfied. However, to gain the benefits of empowerment, the retailer must first identify the myriad of functions that employees need to perform. A useful frame of reference is the marketing functions. Which functions and how much of each does the retailer desire to perform? Each function can then be broken into tasks, which are grouped together into jobs. Finally, a job description must be developed.

In long-range planning, the retailer should carefully examine its projected speed of growth, the predictability of this growth, and geographic and line-of-trade diversification. In short-run human resource planning, the retail executive should attempt to forecast any weekly, monthly, or seasonal swings in sales activity and then adjust human resource inputs appropriately.

LO•2   WHAT IS THE PROCESS FOR HIRING EMPLOYEES?   Human resources acquisition occurs in a competitive labor market. There are many available sources of applicants; the more common ones include competitors, walk-ins, employment agencies, schools and colleges, former employees, advertising, and recommendations from existing employees. Once the applicants are obtained, they must be properly screened. We suggested a four-step screening process: application blanks, personal interview, testing, and reference check.

LO•3   HOW DO RETAILERS MANAGE EXISTING EMPLOYEES?   Once an employee is hired, the retailer must still be concerned about continuing to train and develop the employee, evaluating the employee, and motivating the employee.

Expenditures on training and development are an attempt by the retailer to increase the productivity of human resources. These programs are ongoing as the employee's responsibilities first become specific and then increase in breadth.

The employee's performance should be subjected to an ongoing formal systematic review process. This process will enable the employer to make better decisions concerning wage increases, promotions, transfers, or improvement in job skills.

Employee motivation is also a topic of great importance. In our discussion, we looked at two schools of thought: content theories and process theories. Although the content theories are older, retailers have made more use of the process models in that they have tried to link together the task, the outcome, and the reward.

LO•4   WHAT METHODS CAN RETAILERS USE IN COMPENSATING THEIR EMPLOYEES?   Compensation is crucial to attracting, retaining, and motivating retail employees. A good compensation program includes a fixed component to provide income, a variable component to motivate employees, and a fringe benefit component to provide security and prestige. Special attention was paid to the advantages and disadvantages of the three types of compensation plans: straight salary; straight commission, and a combination of both.

Job enrichment is the process of increasing the skill variety, task identity, task significance, autonomy, and feedback from the job in an effort to improve worker motivation, productivity, and satisfaction and thereby reduce turnover.

TERMS TO REMEMBER

empowerment
task analysis
screening
bona fide occupational qualification
performance appraisal and review
motivation
Hierarchy of Needs Model
Herzberg's Two-Factor Theory
Theory X
Theory Y

Expectancy Theory
goal setting
compensation
fringe benefit package
straight salary
salary plus commission
straight commission
PM
job enrichment

REVIEW AND DISCUSSION QUESTIONS

LO•1   WHAT ARE THE STEPS INVOLVED IN PLANNING HUMAN RESOURCES?

1. Are the problems facing a personnel manager in a retail firm any different from the problems confronting a personnel manager in a factory?
2. Why is a job description necessary if the employee has been told the tasks to be performed?

LO•2   WHAT IS THE PROCESS INVOLVED IN HIRING EMPLOYEES?

3. Why is it so important for a retailer to screen the applicant before hiring the individual?
4. If you were a personnel director for a large department store chain, what traits or characteristics would you look for in a college student under consideration for your management training program?
5. Should a small retailer have a training program or is this just for large retailers like Kmart and Sears?
6. Develop a list of predictor variables that you would use to screen applicants for a sales position in (1) a jewelry department in a high-prestige department store, (2) a used car dealership, (3) a health club, and (4) an antique shop.

LO•3   HOW DO RETAILERS MANAGE EXISTING EMPLOYEES?

7. Why must training be an ongoing operation?
8. Why should a retailer institute an employee performance appraisal plan? What factors make such a plan fair to both employee and employer?
9. Is money the best motivator for every employee?

LO•4 WHAT ARE THE METHODS RETAILERS CAN USE IN COMPENSATING THEIR EMPLOYEES?

10. What are the various methods of compensating retail employees?

11. What are the advantages and disadvantages of paying salespersons in a furniture store strictly on a commission basis?

12. If you were the manager of a department store, would you have the entire sales-force under the same compensation plan? Explain your reasoning.

13. If you were to go to work for a retailer today, what would be the most important supplemental benefit the retailer could offer you? Would this benefit change as your lifestyle changed?

14. Why would an increase in task significance enhance a job and increase job productivity.

15. What factors in the retailer's control have a positive effect on employee productivity.

SAMPLE TEST QUESTIONS

LO•1 WHEN RETAILERS GRANT THEIR EMPLOYEES "EMPOWERMENT," THEY ARE

a. giving them the power to set their own hours
b. giving them the power to kick improperly dressed customers out of the store
c. giving them the power to determine what products should be featured in the retailer's weekly ad
d. giving them the power to make things right with the customer
e. giving them all the above powers

LO•2 WHICH OF THE FOLLOWING QUESTIONS CAN A WOMEN'S APPAREL STORE ASK ON AN EMPLOYMENT APPLICATION?

a. What is your marital status?
b. What is your age?
c. Have you ever been arrested?
d. Are you handicapped?
e. The retailer is not allowed to ask any of the above questions because each of them can be used to discriminate against a minority or group of minorities.

LO•3 TRAINING AND DEVELOPMENT PROGRAMS SHOULD

a. only be concerned with new employees
b. get rid of the least productive employees at the end of the first two years
c. be an ongoing process
d. rely heavily on senior management's teaching skills
e. only focus on operational skills

LO•4 FOR AN INDIVIDUAL WHO DOESN'T CARE ABOUT SECURITY, BUT ONLY WANTS TO MAXIMIZE HIS OR HER CURRENT EARNINGS, THE _____ COMPENSATION PLAN WOULD BE BEST.

a. straight commission
b. straight salary
c. salary plus commission
d. fringe-plus salary
e. teamwork salary

Applications

Writing and Speaking Exercise A vendor has approached your firm, a single-unit furniture store, wanting to know if it can pay push money to your salespersons. At the present time, your store has no set policy on the subject, because no other vendor has ever offered to pay push money or spiffs. The owner has asked that you prepare a memo on the subject for next week's board meeting. Be sure to include the pros and cons of spiffing in your statement.

Retail Project Because retailers often lack legal expertise when making human resource decisions, it is a good idea to review the current laws before doing anything in this area. For your assignment, go to the EEOC's web site (http://www.eeoc.gov). Now, list five circumstances in which sexual harassment may occur. Also, how may an individual waive his or her rights under the Age Discrimination in Employment Act?

CASE Harold's Fried Chicken[23]

High employee turnover has always plagued the fast-food industry. After being trained, the employee quits for one reason or another. Harold's is taking steps to reduce their turnover rate.

Harold's hires prospective employees at minimum wage for a 28-day period. If the employee remains with the company after the trial period, the employee receives a pay increase of five cents per hour. The training program at the store level includes working for badges that are earned for demonstrated skill in cutting, cooking, and counter service. Employees are given a manual and audiovisual aids to help them learn. A badge and another five-cent-per-hour raise is awarded following the successful completion of both a written and physical test of skills.

When an employee earns three badges, he or she qualifies as a team leader. Team leaders are eligible to attend one of the five training schools. The training school is a three-week program that combines academic training with the maintenance of management/customer relations.

Because many of Harold's units are located in lower-income areas, the vast majority of the students attending the classes are from the ghettos and not necessarily well educated. To train and motivate the students, they are paired up with students of comparable ability. They work together and test one another on the concepts and skills they learn. The program uses several steps to teach them how to study. The program is self-paced. A student must master the first step before going on to subsequent steps. Each student is awarded points for every accomplishment, and these points are graphed on a daily basis. Discussion groups are held at the end of the day, and students receive feedback for their work and validation for their accomplishments. Problems are also reviewed at this time.

After the successful completion of the training program, the students return to their respective areas as assistant managers. They hold the position for a minimum of two years before becoming store managers. Harold's also provides store managers with an opportunity for store ownership.

1. How would you improve Harold's program?
2. Do you think the employee turnover rate will still be high? Why?

PLANNING YOUR OWN RETAIL BUSINESS During the planning process for starting a gift shop in a local resort town, you began to question and consider different compensation plans for the retail clerks. It was fairly standard in the area to pay retail clerks $6.25 an hour. However, as you visited gift shops that were paying these rather low wages you noticed that the clerks simply took orders and did not sell or try to answer any questions for customers. In a visit to a gift shop in Ft. Lauderdale last Spring you struck up a conversation with the owner. She was more than willing to share her experiences about retail clerks. In fact, after a lot of trial and error she decided to pay upper-quartile compensation. This consisted of a base wage of $7.50 an hour and a 3 percent commission on all sales. She mentioned that when she went to this type of system her average transaction size increased by 20 percent and that closure went from 28 to 40 percent. More important, she found that her bottom line profit rose by 32 percent. In short, by paying more for retail clerks, she increased employee productivity and the profits of her store.

For the gift shop that you are planning, you initially estimated that traffic would be 25,000 visitors annually and that closure or conversion would be 25 percent. You estimated your average transaction size at $32. Your gross margin percentage would be 60 percent, and fixed operating expenses would be $60,000 annually. Variable operating expenses would be 20 percent of sales. Under this plan, you would pay two full-time clerks $6.25 an hour and you would fill in when things got busy.

Your new plan that you want to evaluate calls for paying the clerks $7.00 per hour plus 4 percent commission on all sales. Thus your fixed operating expenses would go up by $3,000, and variable operating expenses would rise to 24 percent of sales. You believe that closure or conversion would rise to 32 percent and average transaction size would rise to $36. Which compensation strategy should you pursue?

NOTES

1. "To Prevent Theft, Make Ratting Part of the Job." *Wall Street Journal,* April 2, 1993: B1.
2. "Letter from a Productive Lover of Leisure," *U.S. News & World Report,* August 5, 1991: 6.
3. "Dial 800-Prison," *Sales & Marketing Management,* February 1991: 34.
4. Section 703(e) of Title VII.
5. Patrick Dunne, Alan Levin, James Wilcox, and Roy Howell, "Avoid Discrimination Hassles When Recruiting New Personnel," *NARDA NEWS* (October 1991): 16, 58–60; "Employment Application Blanks: Are Retailers Using Them Correctly?" a working paper, 1991.
6. 433 U.S. 321, 15 FEP 10 (1977).
7. "Employers Face New Liability: Truth in Hiring," *Wall Street Journal,* July 9, 1993: B1, B2.
8. "A Job Is Just a Phone Call Away at Belk Stores," *Chain Store Age,* September 1996: 74.
9. "Searching for Integrity," *Fortune,* March 8, 1993: 40.
10. "Credit Bureaus: Consumers Are Stewing—And Suing," *Business Week,* July 29, 1991: 69, 70.
11. Joseph Ambash, "Knowing Your Limits: How Far Can You Go When Checking an Applicant's Background?" *Management World,* March/April 1990: 8–10.
12. "Teams, Not Titles," *Chain Store Age,* September 1994: 49–50.
13. "Electronics Giants Use Different Battle Plans," *Shopping Centers Today,* May 1997: 64, 70.
14. Sam Walton, *Sam Walton, Made In America: My Story* (New York: Doubleday, 1992): 126–142.

15. "Pepsi's Eateries Go It Alone," *Fortune,* August 4, 1997: 27.

16. "What Workers Want," *American Demographics,* August 1992: 30–37.

17. *An Ernst & Young Survey: People in Retail,* September 1990: 11.

18. "How Did Sears Blow This Gasket?" *Business Week,* June 29, 1992: 38; "Sears's Brennan Accepts Blame for Auto Flap," *Wall Street Journal,* June 23, 1992: B1, B12.

19. "Employers Report Gains from Babysitting Aid," *Wall Street Journal,* July 22, 1991: B1.

20. J. Richard Hackman and Greg R. Oldham, *Work Redesign* (Reading, MA: Addision-Wesley, 1980): 77–80.

21. "Turn Down Turnover to Turn Up Profits," *Chain Store Age,* November 1996: 64–68.

22. *Ibid.*

23. This case was prepared by Roger Dickinson, University of Texas-Arlington, and used with his permission.

RETAIL INFORMATION SYSTEMS

Do you know which sizes have been slow sellers this week and why? A high-performance retailer with a retail information system does.

OVERVIEW

The purpose of this chapter is to illustrate the role of information in retail planning and management. Information plays a role in all types of retail planning and management, and its availability in a usable form is a pervasive force in retail decision making.

LEARNING OBJECTIVES

After reading the chapter, you should be able to

1. describe what a retail information system (RIS) is

2. explain why an RIS is divided into a problem identification and problem solution subsystem

3. discuss what types of information are useful to retailers developing an RIS

LO • 1
Describe what a retail information system (RIS) is

INTRODUCING THE RETAIL INFORMATION SYSTEM

One of the ways retailers can achieve high performance results is by having a better understanding of the "whys" and "hows" of the marketplace than their competition. Therefore, successful retailers are preparing for the 21st century by investing in retail information systems (RIS) capable of providing this knowledge as a means of gaining a differential advantage in future competitive wars.

Throughout this text, we have noted that good ideas can, and will, be copied by competitors. Only a retail strategy based on a detailed understanding of what is happening and what may happen in the highly competitive environment can produce highly profitable results before the competition is able to react. In fact, every retailer would like to develop a strategy so good that the only way it can be copied by the competition is with a lot of time and money. Thus, the purpose of this chapter is to focus attention on how a retailer can use an RIS to gather the necessary knowledge about the marketplace so that strategic plans can be made and executed.[1]

In addition, an RIS can be used to monitor existing operations so that they may be modified as conditions warrant. This is especially true today. Successful retailers in the 21st century, especially those working in partnerships with their suppliers, need an RIS that provides them with timely, accurate, effective, and reliable information. Thus, merchandising performance data can only be useful if the data can be acted on. The more detailed and the finer the merchandising data, the more effectively someone, such as a store manager or buyer, can be assigned responsibility to act on them. Exhibit 16.1, for example, shows the six levels of data aggregation on which a chain's merchandising performance can be analyzed: total chain, region, store, department, merchandise line, and stock-keeping unit (SKU). The higher the level of aggregation, the more the truth is hidden. Let's see how this can be the case. If a retailer were to examine this week's chainwide sales, the retailer would see they were $13,784,000. This is useful information, especially if it were compared with chainwide sales for the previous year. However, if the retailer looks at a finer breakdown, he or she might study sales by geographic area, and in this example, the retailer would see that sales in the southeastern region were the highest at $5,917,000. Of course, the retailer might wish to know at which store in the southeast sales were the best. The third level of analysis would show that the highest sales occurred at the Lenox Square store in Atlanta, which had sales of $36,445. The analysis can still become more refined by noting that the best performing department was men's suits, with weekly sales of $4,478,000, and that the sports coat merchandise line, with weekly sales of $781,000, performed best. Finally, the finest analysis is the SKU. The highest-performing SKU was the Ralph Lauren size 40 regular in hunter green, with weekly sales of $4,934.

At its simplest level, an RIS might just be a store owner regularly reading retail trade association magazines, talking with customers to determine how satisfied they are with the store's merchandise and services, and regularly studying quarterly income statements and balance sheets. At a higher level, an RIS can be much more extensive, such as analyzing vendor reports, conducting marketing research studies, and using scanning equipment to track both products and customers with automatic identification programs. We, however, do not wish to define such a system in terms of what it might be for a typical retailer, but in terms of what it should be (i.e., we want to give a normative definition). Thus, the retail information system is a blueprint for the

Retail information system (RIS) *is a blueprint for the continual and periodic systematic collection, analysis, and reporting of accurate and relevant data about any past, present, or future developments that could or already have influenced the retailer's performance.*

EXHIBIT 16.1	SIX LEVELS OF ANALYZING MERCHANDISE PERFORMANCE

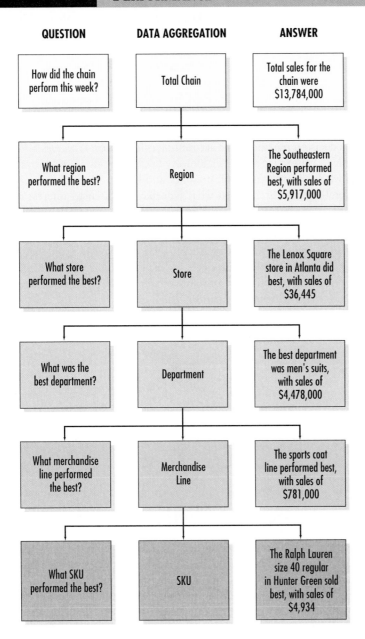

QUESTION	DATA AGGREGATION	ANSWER
How did the chain perform this week?	Total Chain	Total sales for the chain were $13,784,000
What region performed the best?	Region	The Southeastern Region performed best, with sales of $5,917,000
What store performed the best?	Store	The Lenox Square store in Atlanta did best, with sales of $36,445
What was the best department?	Department	The best department was men's suits, with sales of $4,478,000
What merchandise line performed the best?	Merchandise Line	The sports coat line performed best, with sales of $781,000
What SKU performed the best?	SKU	The Ralph Lauren size 40 regular in Hunter Green sold best, with sales of $4,934

continual and periodic systematic collection, analysis, and reporting of accurate and relevant data about any past, present, or future developments that could or already have influenced the retailer's performance. Several prominent features of the RIS are

1. Both continual and periodic collection of relevant data should occur. Data should be continually collected on those activities that are always in a state of flux such as the retailer's financial performance or competitor behavior. Data should be

periodically collected when a nonrecurring problem arises, such as the need for extra cash to fund a new building or inventory.

2. The data collection activities should be systematic and relevant. The world is drowning in data. Retailers must decide what information they need and collect only that information in an orderly fashion.

3. Analysis and reporting of data are important parts of the RIS. The data cannot merely be dumped on the executive's desk. To be useful, they must be analyzed and put in a reportable format. A computer file with 3,000,000 bits of data is not usable information until it is analyzed and placed in a reportable format for the manager to use.

4. The data can be about the past, present, and/or future, all of which can be relevant for retail decision making. Most accounting information is historical: it tells where the retailer has been (in the past). However, point-of-sale (POS) terminals provide data on what is happening now (present), and six-month monetary projections by the Federal Reserve System tell what will likely happen to interest rates (in the future).

The high-performance retailer should strive to develop an RIS that incorporates the above features. This chapter elaborates on what an ideal RIS should look like. It will not, however, discuss the many procedures for the systematic collection and analysis of data. These topics are best covered in many of the fine books on marketing research, accounting, and management information systems.

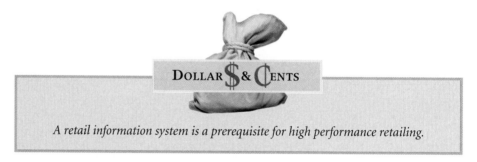

DOLLAR $ & CENTS

A retail information system is a prerequisite for high performance retailing.

NEED FOR INFORMATION

In the previous 15 chapters, the need for useful information that can be acted on by retailers has been demonstrated repeatedly. The fact can clearly be seen by referring to the retail planning and management model, Exhibit 2.3. This model clearly shows that strategies can only be developed after management has used its RIS to conduct a strengths, weaknesses, opportunities, and threats (SWOT) analysis. The exhibit also points out that the management of a retailer's operations and the management of the retailer's resources can only be accomplished after proper strategies, which are based on the SWOT analysis discussed in Chapter 2, are developed. Finally, only by the continuous monitoring of the business can management achieve the high performance results that this text has stressed.

AMOUNT OF INFORMATION

Unfortunately, an RIS that provides complete or perfect information is extremely expensive if not impossible to develop; for example, the net profit of a privately held

Since fast-food restaurants, such as Taco Bell, face very intense competition, they need to invest heavily in information to help them decide on the best retail locations.

competitor who doesn't have to report its earnings to shareholders is an example of the type of information that is beyond reach. Although the area of "competitive intelligence" is one of the fastest growing business activities in the modern world, the expense of such an activity would not only be in terms of direct dollar outlay to secure the best estimate of such information but also in the time needed to gather and analyze it.[2] This extended period of time can represent an opportunity cost of postponing a decision. For example, if you own and operate a car wash and you want to open a second outlet somewhere else in the city, you may decide to gather data on the best location for the new store. The longer you take to gather the information on the best possible site, the longer you will put off opening a potentially profitable outlet. Moreover, if you wait too long, a competitor may open a car wash, which could saturate your proposed new market area and lower the likelihood of your success.

SOURCES OF RETAIL INFORMATION

The two major sources of retailing information are internal and external. Both need to be used and properly integrated into one retail information system.

INTERNAL INFORMATION

Internal information is found within the retailer's records. Retailers are able to generate databases from a wide range of information in the normal course of their business (operating or income statements, sales records, credit reports, shipping records, purchasing invoices, inventory records, customer charge account records, employee personnel records, accounts payable and receivable, and past merchandise budgets). All the questions answered in Exhibit 16.1 are examples of this type of information. By applying certain statistical and analytical procedures, retailers can generate information on a number of different topics.

One of the ways that retailers can make use of their internal information is with the automatic identification systems equipment such as bar codes and scanners.

Internal information is information that is within the retailer's records and thus is already available for analysis.

www.
TradeDimensions
.com

At Trade Dimensions we track *many* different types of information on *various classes* of retailers. However, the majority of our products are tailored to meet the needs of two specific industries. So that we can better guide you to the products that meet the needs of your business, enter our site using one of the three links below. The best description of my company would be:

Consumer Packaged Goods Manufacturer OR Supplier of CPG-Related Products or Services

Shopping Center Industry-Related (Leasing, Development, Store Design, etc.)

All Other Companies that do Business with Retailers

Retailers can obtain a considerable amount of information from external sources such as Trade Dimensions.

Electronic data interchange (EDI) consists of a set of protocols for computer-to-computer communication between a retailer and its suppliers.

Bar coding, and other types of source marking by vendors such as preticketing, prelabeling, or any markings desired, provides savings to retailers because they do not have to individually price mark merchandise. In addition, many retailers experience lower personnel costs as a result of needing less-skilled employees to operate scanners. Scanner information, which for years wasn't used to its fullest potential by retailers,[3] now offers substantial inventory savings by enabling retailers to develop an automatic inventory replacement system in partnership with their vendors.[4] By using electronic data interchange (EDI), a computer-to-computer communication system, retailers are able to manipulate scanner data to plan consumer-driven merchandise mixes by being advised about inventory levels, the status of deliveries, and projected reorder points. These systems have changed the shape and function of the retailer's distribution centers. Retailers such as Wal-Mart and Kmart, which require all their major vendors to be electronically connected to their distribution system, now have the opportunity to improve inventory turnover by using quick-response (or efficient consumer response) delivery programs, which has come to mean later ordering in smaller quantities, thus reducing inventory costs; accelerating the movement of the goods through the channel, and getting the merchandise on the sales floor as quickly as possible.[5] As the year 2000 approached, however, retailers that used EDI worked very closely with their vendors to help insure that their computer software programs and computers would be able to continue to accurately communicate. This was because some retailers and vendors in the 1900's wrote computer programs, when computer memory was very expensive, with the year indicated by two digits and thus the year 2000 or 2001 could be read as 1900 or 1901.[6]

Internal data, as shown in Exhibit 16.2, can also be a source of useful information for retailers monitoring the performance of their use of labor. Exhibit 16.2 shows the actual payroll summary for a 13-week period. A closer look at this exhibit will show that 12 outlets are underbudget. This should be as much a concern for the retailer as being overbudget, because either the budget was wrong or the service at these stores could be poor due to a lack of employees.

EXHIBIT 16.2	PAYROLL SUMMARY, 13 WEEKS, ENDED SEPTEMBER 24

STORE	SPVSR	ACTUAL HOURS	BUDGET HOURS	ACTUAL DOLLARS	BUDGET DOLLARS	DOLLARS (OVER)/UNDER BUDGET	ACTUAL SALES	ACT % TO SALES	AVG HRLY RATE
Americana	DB	6,120	6,760	31,698	37,047	5,349	547,000	5.79%	5.18
Bayside	DB	2,605	2,600	13,601	13,601	0	119,400	11.39%	5.22
Brooklyn	DB	4,650	4,810	27,103	28,048	945	191,700	14.14%	5.83
Cedarhurst	DB	2,661	2,340	14,780	13,000	(1,780)	130,700	11.31%	5.55
Centereach	SC	3,496	4,030	18,235	20,501	2,266	237,500	7.68%	5.22
Commack	SC	3,776	4,160	20,750	23,829	3,079	277,800	7.47%	5.50
Forest Hills	DB	4,411	4,160	23,974	22,256	(1,718)	264,600	9.06%	5.44
Green Acres	DB	5,569	5.200	28,498	28,402	(96)	350,200	8.14%	5.12
Hicksville	SC	4,039	5,070	23,205	26,390	3,185	294,600	7.88%	5.75
Holbrook	SC	3,822	3,900	23,041	24,248	1,207	261,900	8.80%	6.03
Madison	DB	4,588	4,680	27,364	28,002	638	266,300	10.28%	5.96
Riverhead	SC	2,669	2,860	14,763	16,192	1,429	173,400	8.51%	5.53
Roosevelt	DB	11,472	14,300	67,280	81,868	14,588	1,168,700	5.76%	5.86
Sands	SC	3,628	3,900	19,761	20,722	961	248,300	7.96%	5.45
S. S. M.	SC	5,455	6,760	27,960	34,710	6,750	516,900	5.41%	5.13
Walt Whitman	SC	6,485	8,190	34,711	43,521	8,810	633,900	5.48%	5.35
Wheatley	DB	4,116	3,965	26,771	26,332	(439)	280,200	9.55%	6.50
Total		79,562	87,685	443,495	488,669	45,174	5,963,100	7.44%	5.57

EXTERNAL INFORMATION

External information is obtained from sources outside of the firm. This information includes

> External information *is information that is obtained from outside the retail enterprise.*

1. *published statistics.* A vast amount of statistical data is published by a variety of public and private sources. The major public source is the federal government. Among the reports most often used by retailers are *County Business Patterns,* the *Standard Industrial Classification (SIC) Manual,* and *Current Industrial Reports.* Private publishers, such as *Sales and Marketing Management's Survey of Buying Power* and those publications listed in Exhibit 16.3 are also widely used.
2. *standardized retailing information services.* Many research agencies compile data on market trends and consumer behavior and sell the data in standardized form to interested retailers. Included here is the *Nielsen Retail Index,* which every two months from a sample of 1,600 supermarkets, 750 drugstores, and 150 mass merchandisers, tracks data on individual brands and their price, market share, and promotion.
3. *research reports.* Publicly circulated research reports are usually found in the various trade and business journals.
4. *Internet.* Today, the Internet is fast becoming the tool of choice by retailers for gathering external data. Thousands of databases and other sources of information are currently available in cyberspace. Caudra's *The Directory of Online Databases* is

EXHIBIT 16.3	SOURCES OF RETAIL INFORMATION FROM PUBLICATIONS

Advertising Age	International Trends in Retailing
Ad Week	International Journal of Retail &
American Fabrics and Fashion	Distribution Management
Auto Merchandising News	Juvenile Merchandising
Beverage World	Luggage and Leather Goods
Business Week	Marketing & Media Decisions
Chain Store Age	Mart Magazine
Clothing and Textiles Research	Merchandising Week
Journal	Modern Jeweler
Clothes	Office Products Dealer
Discount Merchandiser	Office Products News
Distribution	Progressive Grocer
Drug Topics	Retail Advertising Week
Dun's Business Month	Retail Control
DYI Retailing	Retail Technology
Floor Covering Weekly	Sales and Marketing Management
Florist	Sports Merchandiser
Fortune	Stores
Furniture News	Supermarket Business
Hardware Age	Supermarket News
Hardware Merchandising	Visual Merchandising
Hardware Retailing	Volume Retail Merchandising
Harvard Business Review	Wall Street Journal
Home Furnishing Daily	Women's Wear Daily
Journal of Retailing	

a great place to start any search. Exhibit 16.4 provides a guide to on-line sources of external data. The Behind the Scenes box presents a great example of how one individual conducted such a database search.

LO • 2
Explain why an RIS is divided into a problem identification and problem solution subsystem

Problem identification subsystem
is the part of the retail information system that monitors and scans changing trends in behavioral, environmental, and operating performance.

RIS SUBSYSTEMS

Exhibit 16.5 shows a model RIS as it relates to our Retail Planning and Management Model (Exhibit 2.3).

An inspection of the RIS in Exhibit 16.5 will show that the problem identification subsystem monitors and scans changing trends in behavioral, environmental, and operating performance areas. It is directed at the identification of problems or potential problems confronting the retailer. This subsystem should be designed to compile information continuously on constantly changing events affecting the retailer's SWOT analysis, as well as how these environmental trends are effecting the retailer's

EXHIBIT 16.4	SOURCES OF ON-LINE RETAILING INFORMATION

Government Data Sources

- U.S. Census Bureau (http://www.census.gov/) – This site provides free access to many census data reports and tables. Also available are international census data from many countries.
- Small Business Administration (http:/www.sbaonline.sba.gov/) – This site is the federal advocate for all small businesses and provides all sorts of information.
- U.S. Bureau of Economic Analysis (http://www.bea.gov/) – This site provides national and regional economic information by industry.
- U.S. Bureau of Labor Statistics (http://stats.bls.gov/) – This site gives access to the BLS survey of consumer expenditures, including a report on how U.S. consumers spend their money.
- Department of Commerce/STAT-USA (http://www.stat.usa.gov/) – This subscription-based site provides access to hundreds of government-sponsored marketing research studies and other statistical information.
- FedWorld (http://www.fedworld.gov/) – This site provides central access point for locating government information. If you need data from the government but don't know where to find it, start here.

Private Data Sources

- Knight-Ridder (http://www.dialog.com/) – This extensive database provides access to thousands of marketing research reports, industry and competitor information, and trade publications. Although it is an excellent source for secondary data of all types, a typical search can be expensive. Knowledge Index, available on CompuServe, provides access to many of the Knight-Ridder databases for an hourly fee.
- Lexis-Nexis (http://lexis-nexis.com/) – This is another extensive, and expensive, database of directories, trade publications, and legal information.
- Chain Store Age (http://chainstoreage.com/) – This contains all the features of the monthly magazine. It is updated twice daily with breaking retailing news, and has stock quotes on all publicly traded retailers.
- Smart Business Supersite (http://www.smartbiz.com/) – This site has thousands of free how-to resources geared specifically to help businesses run better.

Search Engines (These search engines can help track down online information on a variety of topics)

- Search.com (http://www.seasrch.com/) – This site gives access to over 300 specialized indexes and search engines.
- Metacrawler (http://www.infoseek.com.) – This service submits your question to all of the top search engines at once.
- Altavista (http://altavista.digital.com/) – This service is one of the largest search indexes on the Web.
- Info Guide (http://www.infoseek.com/) – Ths search index includes millions of listings.
- Yahoo! (http://www.yahoo.com/) – This useful search index divides reference sites into logical groups.

EXHIBIT 16.5   RELATIONSHIP BETWEEN A RETAILER'S PLANNING MODEL AND RIS

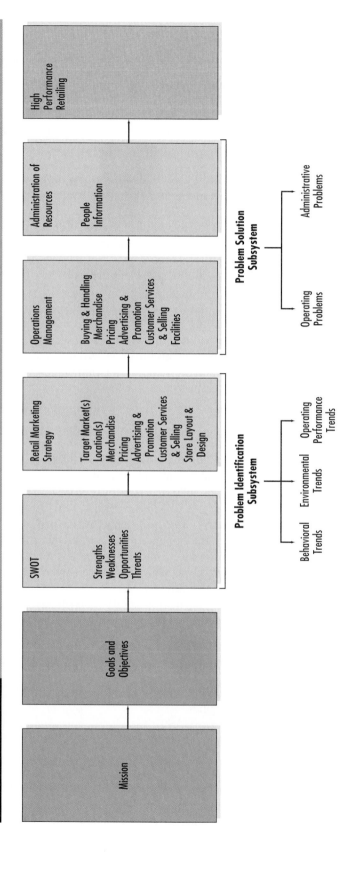

USING CYBERSPACE TO GATHER SECONDARY DATA

Suppose that a household goods buyer at the local department store is wondering whether there is a demand for left-handed cooking gadgets. Given that as baby boomers age they spend more time entertaining at home, the buyer assumes that the 13 percent of Americans who are left-handed will want special equipment to match that of their right-handed counterparts to aid in developing their gourmet skills. However, before making any rash merchandising decisions, the buyer decides to "surf the net" for some more information.

The buyer begins with on-line newsgroups. Before leaving the office one Friday night, the buyer searches the Usenet listings by using the keywords *food, cooking, left,* and *gourmet.* Finding no groups for *gourmet,* only four for *cooking,* but nearly 80 for *food,* the buyer posts a short message on a busy discussion group called "rec.food.cooking," asking readers what left-handed cookware they would like to see sold at local stores. Under *left,* the buyer finds several possible information sources, with the busiest being "alt.lefthanders." Here, the buyer posts the same message.

Next, the buyer goes to the Yahoo! search engine. One of the five matches under the word *left-handed* is for Southpaw Pineapple, a gift store catering to left-handers. The buyer spends the next 15 minutes before heading home visiting this store's web site to check out what this retailer is offering.

On returning to work the following Monday morning, the buyer finds only six responses to her messages from the "rec.food.cooking" group. One of the replies is from a woman who used to own a left-handed specialty store in St. Louis. The women lists what items were "hot-sellers" and what items were "slow-movers." She also provided the names and telephone numbers of seven other stores carrying such cookware across the country. The five other replies ask for combinations of cooking mitts, cheese grater, a can-opener, and scissors for left-handers. There were no other responses to the message.

Based on this quick cyberspace search, the household buyer decides to rethink her idea about stocking left-handed cookware.

strategy. In the behavioral area, for example, three patterns can be monitored: consumers, channels, and competitors. In the environmental domain, three environments can be scanned: legal and ethical, socioeconomic, and technological. Finally, in the area of operating performance, asset, revenue, and expense trends can be monitored.

The problem-solving subsystem, which seeks to provide solutions for problems that the retailer faces as a result of these changing trends, obtains information on several areas. These problems can either be recurring or nonrecurring problems for the retailer. These problem areas coincide with the retailer's operations management and its administration of resources. Operating management problems will either be related to assets or involve revenue and expense management. Administrative problems involve capital structure and generation, organization structure and human resources, or location analysis.

Problem solving subsystem
is the part of the retail information system that provides information to help solve problems that may arise in the retail enterprise.

LO • 3
Discuss what types of information are useful to retailers developing an RIS

TYPES OF INFORMATION NEEDED BY AN RIS

The remainder of this chapter discusses each component of the model RIS, allowing you to obtain a fairly broad and general understanding of the information requirements of retailers.

PROBLEM IDENTIFICATION SUBSYSTEM

The central goal of this problem identification subsystem is to highlight for the retailer, on a continuing basis, the major problems that the retailer is about to encounter or is presently encountering.

BEHAVIORAL TRENDS **MONITORING CONSUMERS** Most retailers scan the behavior of their customers in a casual manner. Some retailers may read the trade press or business magazines or search the Internet to obtain information on future consumer trends. Small retailers may simply listen to customer complaints or informally converse with regular customers about their needs, wants, and level of satisfaction. This can be quite cost-effective for the small, single-outlet retailer. Others do as the local barber or hair stylist does—they merely look at local economic forecasts. If the economy gets worse, they know their customers will let their hair grow longer and vice versa. They realize that although some other methods may provide a better monitor, they may not be worth the additional expense involved. While he was alive, Sam Walton claimed to use the MBWA (management by walking around) method to spot future trends. Larger retailers might use more formal methods to foresee the future. Some of these methods include the analysis of purchases, tracking customers' charge accounts, and using consumer panels.

The larger the retailer, the more likely it is to use more formal and/or sophisticated methods to monitor consumer behavior trends. This is because as the retailer grows, retail decision makers become increasingly removed from regular face-to-face contact with the consumer. Consider Weight Watchers International, which leases space for up to 20,000 meetings a week. Because its business is so sensitive to economic downturns that reduce the consumer's disposable income, Weight Watchers monitors consumer confidence indexes from the University of Michigan and the Conference Board before booking rooms for the following month.[7] Our Winners & Losers box describes some of the other activities retailers have done in monitoring consumer behavior.

If the retailer decides that a continual monitoring of consumer behavior patterns would be valuable—and we believe that it would be for most large-scale retailers—then regular data collection is needed on three crucial consumer behavior variables: purchase probabilities, attitudes, and consumer satisfaction.

Information on purchase probabilities (how likely a consumer is to purchase a particular product within the next six months) will allow the retailer to keep apprised of the products that it should stock and promote. For example, on the national level, the Survey Research Center, at the University of Michigan, reports quarterly on the future plans of American consumers to purchase such major durables as automobiles. On the local level, many larger city newspapers provide continuing consumer surveys of their market areas as a service to advertisers. One retail consultant has developed a probabilities model to say that if a consumer pays X dollars for an item, he or she will

Weight Watchers monitors consumer confidence indexes from the University of Michigan and the Conference Board before booking rooms for meetings the following month.

then purchase a companion product costing Y dollars. For example, if a consumer pays between $71 and $129 for a blazer, she will want to purchase a skirt costing $69 to $99 and shoes costing $59 to $89. This model enables the retailer to know what price ranges should be used and what inventory levels must be maintained given previous purchases.[8] Likewise, Wal-Mart has discovered, with the aid of its computer system, that shoppers who buy Huggies on Thursday buy more items than the retailer's other consumers do, leading to a decision to cut the price of Huggies on Thursdays.[9]

Consumer attitudes toward the retailer's store and operation can be a significant determinant of patronage behavior. Changing attitudes can forewarn the retailer of problems on the horizon.

Some retailers find it useful to break consumer attitudes down in terms of the store's attributes by measuring the importance of each attribute in the eyes of the consumer and how well the consumer thinks the store performed on that attribute. The result of such a study might resemble the four quadrants in Exhibit 16.6. The exhibit's upper-right corner represents attributes of above-average importance in which the retailer is doing an above-average job. Here, the retailer wants to continue as is. The bottom-right quadrant addresses attributes that are important to the customers, but the retailer is failing in performance. Here, improvement is needed in the areas of informative advertising and convenient store hours and parking. The lower-left corner is an area of below-average performance and importance. Usually, retailers leave this area alone and work on the other areas. Finally, in the upper-left quadrant, the retailer has above-average performance in areas of below-average importance. Here, management should consider deemphasis or reallocating some effort to more important attributes.

Information on customer satisfaction with both the retailer's service and the merchandise will indicate whether the customer's visit to the store was rewarding (a good experience) or unsatisfying (a bad experience). After all, it is four to five times more expensive to obtain a new customer than to retain an existing one. In a recent survey, retailers scored worst out of six industries in customer satisfaction. This is especially dangerous when the retailer doesn't know, can't identify, or can't understand the

SUPERMARKET SPYS: WE GOT OUR EYES ON YOU

Astute retailers need to know not only which sections of a store are most heavily traveled, but which products, by being placed together, increase store profits. Nowhere is this more important than in the supermarket industry with its low margins. Supermarket managers will go to any length to get an advantage over their competition. Consider the following examples of the extent that some supermarkets will go.

A Texas grocer used shopping carts with infrared sensors in the ceiling to track the carts' movement. It found out that customers were more prone to move in a circle near the peanut butter section than at any other location in the store. Realizing that the customers were probably looking for the jelly, the store moved the jelly next to the peanut butter and saw sales increase 18 percent.

An Arkansas operator used the same sensor system to note that shoppers heavily shopped the store's periphery, starting with the produce, moving to the dairy, then the meat. However, they spent only a fraction of the time in the store's inner section with its higher-margin packaged groceries. The store has since redesigned its layout.

An Ohio supermarket found that although 90 percent of shoppers entering the store went through the grocery section on the store's right side and more than half of the shoppers visited the HBA (Health & Beauty Aids) section on the extreme left wall, less than one-fifth of all shoppers went down the aisle selling some of the store's highest margin merchandise: greeting cards, candy, and toys/gifts. As a result, greeting cards were moved near the floral section at the beginning of the store's power alley (the far right wall). The candy was moved across from the ice cream, and gifts were moved across from baby things.

A New York supermarket has taken this cart movement information and assigned "rents" to various locations in the store. For example, if some package-good manufacturer wants a promotional display located near the bakery, an area that nearly every cart goes through but only one-third make a purchase, it will have to pay a higher rent than if the display was located in the center of the store, near the greeting cards.

SOURCE: Discussions with Paul Adams, Director of Retail Education Services, Fleming Companies, and the authors' industry knowledge.

---

reasons that it lost a customer. Therefore, many experts believe today's high-performance retailers are doing a better job of monitoring their customers.[10]

If there is dissatisfaction with both the service and merchandise, then the customer is less likely to choose that store in the future, thus decreasing sales. Retailers have found that customer dissatisfaction is usually the result of discrepancies between

1. what the consumer actually expected and what the retailer thought the consumer wanted in terms of service and merchandise
2. what the retailers thought the consumer wanted and what the store actually delivers in terms of service and merchandise
3. what the retailers promise in their promotional messages and what is delivered

In an effort to eliminate, or at least reduce, these discrepancies, retail managers must spend time "on the floor," interacting with customers and checking to see if their expectations of what customers want is correct. When placing top management "on the floor" is impossible, the management should at least visit regularly with the customer-contact personnel to have management's expectations of customers' wants shaped by the personnel with the hands-on experience. One of the major contributors to

EXHIBIT 16.6	IMPORTANCE/PERFORMANCE ATTITUDINAL ANALYSIS

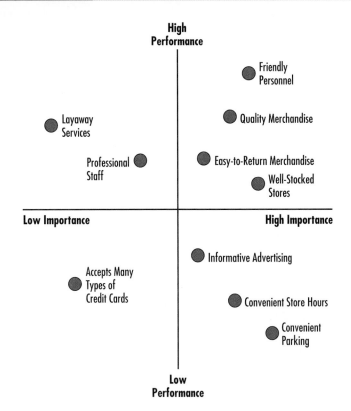

Wal-Mart's early success, for example, was Sam Walton visiting every store at least once a year and getting a feel for what his customers really wanted.[11] This is another reason executives at Sears headquarters are often seen waiting on customers in the various Chicago-area malls.

The second type of discrepancy is the result of a lack of management's commitment to the customer. By making the customer secondary to profits, gross margin, market share, price points, or cost reduction, management tells employees that the expected service or merchandise shouldn't be delivered unless the other objectives are first achieved. Many restaurants and motels ask their patrons to fill out a brief questionnaire on how satisfied they were with their visit or meal. Also, many auto dealers and furniture retailers send recent customers a letter encouraging them to call a toll-free number if they are dissatisfied with their recent purchase. These retailers are able to obtain information on customer satisfaction at a relatively low cost and take corrective actions if dissatisfaction is seen to be rising.

The final discrepancy occurs when retailers exaggerate the quality of their merchandise or services, resulting in customers expecting more than the retailers provide. This exaggerated promise could come from the retailers ads, in-store displays, or even the salesforce. Retail managers can become aware of this type of discrepancy by doing the same things recommended for handling the first type of discrepancy and spend more time on the floor.

Historically, retailers lose half their customers every five years. Most of these losses are due to dissatisfaction with the retailer's services or merchandise. As a result, many high-performance retailers are now monitoring why these customers were dissatisfied. After all, such defections are the clearest sign that customers see a deteriorating value from shopping with that retailer. Also, an increasing defection rate will soon mean a decreased cash flow for the retailer.[12] This doesn't mean that all satisfied customers will be loyal to your store; many satisfied customers may become more satisfied elsewhere.[13] It just means that successful retailers must know why they lose a customer.

MONITORING THE MARKETING CHANNEL   The retailer is part of a larger marketing channel system, which few retailers can totally control. Most retailers must adapt to the behavior of other organizations in the channel. Therefore, the behavior of channel members should be monitored.

In Chapter 5, we discussed some of the intricacies of adapting to the marketing channel. Here, let us focus on obtaining information on alternative merchandise supply sources, alternative facilitating agencies, financial performance of channel partners, and channel conflicts.

If retailers become too dependent on a few sources of merchandise, then their ability to bargain and negotiate with suppliers will be hampered. The suppliers may even try to dictate how the retailers should conduct their business. The best way to avoid this unfortunate circumstance is to be continually aware of alternative supply sources. Even if retailers have found that supplier X always has the best merchandise for the lowest price, they should not become complacent and stop looking for a better deal.

High priority should be placed on designing an ongoing system of information collection to alert the retailer to the best deals. For instance, many supermarkets constantly evaluate their present wholesale sources of supply against alternative sources. This helps them assess the terms of their present suppliers. Also, present suppliers will be more cooperative if they know that the retailer is always keeping abreast of the terms being offered by their competitors. Customer surveys are an effective tool when retailers use vendors to supply services such as housekeeping and/or food services.

Today, some vendors are taking advantage of their partnerships with retailers to use the retailer's RIS to avoid costly mistakes. Book publishers are often unsure of the number of books to print in the first printing. Today, by using shared information from retailers such as Barnes & Noble, the publishers are able to instantaneously spot sales and determine if the book's jacket cover, merchandising, or price should be changed or if more books should be quickly published.[14]

Most retailers rely on a number of facilitating agencies (banks, ad agencies, brokers, insurance firms, etc.) to assist them. Just as retailers should monitor alternative merchandise supply sources, they should also monitor the availability and strengths and weaknesses of alternative facilitating agencies. Are there public warehouses or advertising agencies that can do a better job at a more competitive price? Retailers should have access to any information that can help answer such basic questions.

As much information as possible should be obtained about the financial performance of channel partners. What is happening to their profit margins, inventory turnover, credit policy, cash flow, labor productivity, and sales growth? Whenever any member of a marketing channel begins to have financial problems, it will start to squeeze its channel partners (e.g., attempting to cut credit terms, increase minimum order quantity size, or raise prices) to increase its performance at the expense of the retailer. By monitoring channel member performance, the retailers can have countermoves developed to minimize any unfair pressure that the poorly performing supplier may try to exert. If your channel partner is a publicly held corporation, it must file a

Bookstores constantly analyze sale trends and share this with publishers so they can quickly adjust production schedules in order to keep best sellers in stock.

10K report with the Securities & Exchange Commission (SEC). This report is available free through the company or the SEC. Many other data-gathering firms will provide information on other firms for a small fee.

A final area of behavior that should be monitored is the level of conflict. For every significant channel interface, retailers should identify any sources of conflict. Specifically, it must be regularly able to answer such questions as: To what extent do the channel partners have goals that are not compatible with mine? To what extent does each channel partner try to unduly control various aspects of my business? To what extent do channel partners perceive significant events in the economic, social, legal, and technological environments differently than we do? To what extent do channel members trust each other with their shared information.[15] It is better to know of potential conflict than to learn after the conflict has become manifest and more difficult to resolve.

MONITORING COMPETITORS   Almost any retail executive will tell you that they are more interested in what their competitors are doing than in how channel partners or consumers are behaving, but all three behaviors are equally important.

All executives (whether small or large) have some means of monitoring competitors' activities. At the simplest level, this may consist of reading or listening to competitors' ads and shopping their stores personally to inspect merchandise, prices, displays, and store decor. More sophisticated monitoring may involve systematic collection and analysis of data on over or understoring, pricing, merchandise mixes, promotion, market shares, and trading areas.

As discussed in Chapter 4 when a particular market area, typically a town or city, is overstored competitors will compete more aggressively for consumer expenditures. When a market is understored, the opposite occurs. Not surprisingly, therefore, over or understoring is a good indication of potential profits in a particular market area. The more understored a market is, the greater the profit potential and visa versa.

The retailer should determine a bundle of goods on which it desires to be most competitive with regards to pricing. For example, a grocery store may identify 135 items out of the 12,000 SKUs it stocks that it wants to be visibly price competitive on.

Wal-Mart founder Sam Walton would visit Wal-Mart stores weekly, in his red pickup, to obtain firsthand knowledge of what customers wanted and disliked. He would also visit the local competition to assess their strengths and weakneses.

Once the bundle has been established, the retailer should compute price indices that show its price for each item compared with the price that each of its major competitors is charging. These indices should be constructed regularly, probably weekly or monthly. When analyzed on a longitudinal basis, trends in these price indices will vividly demonstrate the extent to which the retailer is continuing to be price-competitive.

How strong is the retailer's merchandise mix in relation to key competitors? Is it deeper, wider, and of a lower or higher quality? How has this changed over time? In short, are the retailer's assortments of merchandise competitive? Only ongoing data collection can provide a meaningful answer to this important question. Therefore, retailers must systematically and regularly send out employees to shop competing retailers to provide the needed answers.

There are two fundamental questions retailers will want their information system to answer regarding competitor's promotional efforts. First, how much are competitors spending on promotion in relation to themselves? Second, what is the quality of competitors' promotional activities.

Neither question is easily or inexpensively answered. A detailed analysis would be needed of competitors' advertising, sales promotion activities, publicity efforts, and personal selling. Because such a task would be a burden, most retailers may decide to collect data on a regular basis on only competitor's advertising and, in some cases, on their sales promotion activities. For example, many apparel retailers will develop an ongoing file of competitors' newspaper advertising. Ads of competitors are clipped daily and placed in this file, and then once a month the intensity and quality of competitors' advertising will be analyzed. This simple process will allow the retailer to spot any significant deterioration in its advertising in relation to competitors.

What are the respective market shares of the retailer and its competitors, and how are these changing? One of the best indicators of future profit performance is market share.[16] If retailers observe their market share slipping, then they should be forewarned of future profitability problems.

Retailers that sell a wide range of merchandise will ideally want to obtain market share data by merchandise line. Rather than only comparing competitors' market shares as a whole, a department store manager may find it most useful to have market share data on particular departments: household furnishings, men's wear, women's apparel, children's clothes, sporting goods, jewelry, toys, and lawn and garden equipment. However, the collection of such information may be extremely expensive and may not be worth the cost. Also, in many cases, it may be almost impossible to secure.

Is the retailer's trading area (the geographic area from which it draws its customers) stable, shrinking, or expanding? A shrinking trade area is a bad omen; an expanding one is good. Many of the previously discussed items—overstoring, competitive pricing, competitive merchandise assortments, and competitive promotional strength—will affect trading area size. The less competitive the retailer's pricing, merchandise assortment, and promotion, the more its trade area will shrink. Again, the more overstored the market, the more the trade area will shrink.

It is relatively easy to obtain information on the trade area. If the retailers have the addresses of store patrons, the retailer can easily construct a trade area map. Many retailers continually hold contests asking for business cards or have customers fill out entry blanks with their names and addresses to qualify for a weekly drawing. At the end of each month, the owner could go back and plot on a map where patrons came from, enabling him or her to observe quickly any change in the size or nature of his or her trading area by comparing one month's map to the previous month's.

Although most retailers will admit that monitoring a competitor is important, many will reluctantly admit to not having visited a competitor's store within the past week or even checking out the competitor's web site to see its new offerings. (The web sites for each of the nation's largest 25 retailers are listed inside the front and back covers of this text.)

DOLLAR $ & CENTS

Retailers that regularly monitor consumers, marketing channels, and competitors will be higher performers.

ENVIRONMENTAL TRENDS MONITORING THE SOCIOECONOMIC ENVIRONMENT

Events in the socioeconomic environment, which were discussed in Chapter 3, that should be monitored can be categorized into demographic, psychographic, and economic trends.

Major demographic trends that may be particularly useful to monitor are changing household size, educational levels, age distribution of household members, population growth, and geographic migration. Psychographic trends that may be particularly insightful are changes in leisure-time activities, work habits, and religious, family, and cultural values. Economic trends that should be followed are changes in disposable personal income, in household expenditure patterns, in discretionary income, and in the use of credit.

If retailers desire highly personalized continuing data on demographic, psychographic, and economic trends in their trade areas, the price will not be cheap. National data tell retailers little about the socioeconomic dynamics of their trade area, but some secondary data on their area may be available. Many local newspapers in large cities conduct regular surveys of the geographic area of their readership, and this geographic area may closely approximate a retailer's trade area, especially if the retailer sells shopping goods. These surveys collect data on a large number of demographic, economic, and in some cases, psychographic variables.

As noted earlier, the U.S. Census Bureau can also provide a wealth of demographic data on-line. Also, the various trade associations and publications described earlier are a great source for these data.

MONITORING THE LEGAL ENVIRONMENT   Although a disquieting fact to most retailers, the legal environment is always in a state of flux. To avoid costly legal errors, the retailer should design its RIS to keep it alerted of changes in that environment. In fact, the larger the retailer, the higher priority this area should receive.

No retail manager or store owner can be expected to monitor all the relevant changes in the legal environment. Fortunately, all the major retail trade associations devote a fair amount of space in their publications to the retail implications of pending legislation at both federal and state levels.

Probably, the legal area of most immediate practical concern to the retailer is tax law. Changes in tax laws will generally have a significant effect on most major retail decisions. For example, a favorable change in the investment tax credit can make store remodeling or expansion an attractive plan. Tax laws can influence other decisions such as inventory valuation methods, executive compensation plans, or recording of credit sales. As a result, retailers need to monitor tax legislation continually.

Recently, the cigarette industry has come under fire, not only by public health groups but also by Congress. The Behind the Scenes box takes a look at some of the changes that might occur for retailers selling tobacco products.

Retail corporations that are publicly held should also stay informed of the regulations of the SEC and the accounting standards established by the Financial Accounting Standards Board (FASB). All publicly held retailers must abide by the SEC guidelines in reporting to stockholders. The FASB develops generally accepted accounting principles (GAAP), which are not legal requirements. However, retailers that want their financial statements to receive an unqualified opinion by a certified external auditor will follow the GAAP.

MONITORING THE TECHNOLOGICAL ENVIRONMENT   Technology is the application of science to develop new methods of doing things. It is always at work slowly but continually to change the nature and scope of retailing.

The retailer can monitor the technological environment at two stages: the basic science stage or the applied science stage. In either case, the retailer will want to monitor technology as related to four areas of innovation: management techniques, merchandising techniques, equipment and fixtures, and construction and building.

A retailer desiring to monitor any of the four areas at the basic science stage could read the academic journals in the underlying disciplines. For example, to monitor management and merchandising at the basic science level, the retailer might read such periodicals as the *Journal of Finance, Journal of Retailing, Journal of Marketing,* or *Administrative Science Quarterly.* Unfortunately, most topics and concepts discussed in the academic, business-related journals take a long time to get to the applied science stage,

THE CHANGING FACE OF TOBACCO RETAILING

Over the past half century, Americans have become accustomed to the idea of being able to buy cigarettes from vending machines in a variety of retail outlets such as bars, restaurants, airports, supermarkets, convenience stores, gas stations, and discount stores. However, federal legislation may soon change the way that tobacco is sold in the United States.

Wal-Mart was one of the first major retailers to face the tobacco issue. In 1991, Sam Walton announced the banning of smoking on all Wal-Mart property, including the stores, as well as the removal of any vending machines. At the time, Walton wasn't aware of any vending machines, but as a precaution, he issued the "ban" order. Later, when Wal-Mart expanded into Canada by purchasing 127 Woolco stores, Walton met with the pharmacists from the newly acquired stores. They informed Walton that their job involved helping people get well, not causing health problems, which tobacco did. At their request, Wal-Mart dropped the sale of tobacco in its Canadian stores.

At the same time, various state and local agencies began to enforce age restrictions on the sale of cigarettes and other products such as firearms, spray paint (which was used for painting gang slogans), and even glue. Wal-Mart introduced a program into its scanners that froze the cash register when the SKU for one of these products was recorded until the clerk ascertained the age of the purchaser. As a result of this increased enforcement of the laws regulating the sale of tobacco, some retailers, especially supermarkets and drug stores, began to drop tobacco. How would this affect the sale of these legal products, which accounted for $45 billion in sales in 1997?

If such a charge were to occur, what retailers would benefit? Some experts think that one of the retailers best prepared for cigarettes being dropped by the mass sellers is John Roscoe's family-owned Cigarettes Cheaper chain. This is a 400-store operation already doing $50 million in sales each year.

Cigarettes Cheaper, which only sells cigarettes in 1,200-square-foot outlets located primarily in strip malls, is a spin-off of Roscoe's Customer Company convenience store chain. The name Customer Company was a reflection of Roscoe's appreciation for his consumers, and as a result he offered the lowest prices on everything in the store. His tobacco stores follow the same philosophy by charging 20 percent less on the average pack or carton of cigarettes.

The chain is able to charge such prices by taking advantage of every manufacturer discount available and realizing that its customers are not apt to buy just a pack or even a carton but more likely to purchase 10 to 12 cartons at a time. But low prices aren't the only thing. Roscoe's store, and others like his—there were almost 4,000 at the end of 1997—have a broader range of brands and packaging than other retailers, a regular diet of promotions, and a welcoming attitude toward smokers that is not always the case elsewhere.

Many retail experts think this might be the way all cigarettes are sold in the future. What do you think?

SOURCE: Conversations with Bob Kahn, editor, *Retailing Today*.

---

because many practical problems of implementation remain to be worked out. Similarly, the retailer could read the academically oriented publications in engineering, computer science, and architecture to obtain a glimpse of future technology in equipment and buildings. But again, the lead time between the basic science stage and the application would probably be too great to be of any practical value.

Generally, it will be more beneficial for the retailer to monitor technology at the applied level. To do this most effectively, retailers should regularly attend industry trade shows and read business trade-related publications. For example, the annual meeting of the National Retail Federation has hundreds of vendors displaying the latest technological advances in retailing.

Exhibits 16.3 and 16.4, for example, list some of the publications and on-line sources that report on innovations that can be or are being applied to retailing, as well as on other facets of the retail business.

It is easy to see why the interest in technology is increasing. Importantly, just keeping up with the advancing use of scanners beyond inventory control or as a means of scheduling employees can make the difference between achieving or not achieving profitable results.

DOLLAR $ & ¢ENTS

Retailers that regularly monitor the socioeconomic, legal, and technological environments will be higher performers.

OPERATING PERFORMANCE TRENDS   MONITORING ASSETS

The accounting system should be designed to be part of the RIS, because it can be an important vehicle for portraying financial operating performance trends.[17]

An RIS should have the capability to monitor the retailer's assets continually. At the most basic level, the retailer may design the RIS to construct a balance sheet at the end of each operating period (typically, a month or a quarter) for assessing the magnitude and composition of its assets. By comparing the current balance sheet with prior ones, retailers can examine the growth of their asset base and the extent of changes in the composition of their assets. More detailed analysis of period-to-period balance sheets and the general ledgers used to construct them will provide information on the sources and uses of capital. The balance sheet is one of the most useful pieces of information available to retailers because "problems show up on the balance sheet first, and then percolate to the income statement." For example, an excessive amount of inventory or accounts receivable usually forewarns of trouble because that excess merchandise will probably have to be sold at a discount or customer receivables will have to be written off due to nonpayment.

Two service providers that do an excellent job of using an RIS to monitor their assets are Avis and American Airlines. Avis uses what it calls a rate-shoppers' guide. The specifics remain secret, but in general, the Wizard system (Avis' Reservation System) allows agents to quote up-to-the-minute prices that change with the availability of the fleet at a particular location. If the cars aren't moving, a lower price will kick in. If the fleet is tight, the price stays up.[18] American Airlines uses a computerized information and planning system to predict demand for hundreds of flights a day based on the various fare strategies to maximize revenues.[19] Retailers are now developing similar systems by using the creative powers of their RIS. For example, the major discounters such as Target and Wal-Mart are now using micromarketing to tailor the merchandise mix differently for each store in the same city. Thus, 15 to 20 percent of each store's products are catered to the ethnic makeup of the neighborhood.

MONITORING REVENUES AND EXPENSES   By monitoring revenues and expenses, retailers are able to readily identify any significant gaps in planned profit levels and develop appropriate remedial actions. Probably no retailer does this better than Wal-Mart, which monitors sales and labor costs on a daily basis at over 3000 stores and immediately takes corrective action if performance is sub-standard. It also has 24 terabytes of storage (second only to the U.S. Government) which enables it to store historical data for future analysis.[20]

All the revenues and expenses data that the retailer needs to be kept informed about can be presented in a detailed income statement. Thus, at the most fundamental level of analysis, retailers will want to design their RIS to regularly generate a detailed income statement.

Because the magnitude of dollars on a retailer's income statement can change from period to period, it is best to have the income statement constructed in both dollars and percentiles (in which total sales are equated to 100 percent). The percentile income statement facilitates the comparison of operating periods over time. Thus, a retail executive can quickly read if the cost of merchandise, advertising, utilities, wages, or any expenses is behaving differently in relation to sales than it has historically.

The percentile income statement will also allow us to compare current performance with our plan or standard. A standard income statement can be developed in which each expense is programmed to be a standard percentage of sales. Percentages on the actual income statement can then be compared with the standard to gauge performance and identify any significant problem areas.

Many retail trade associations, such as the National Retail Federation, conduct annual studies of operating results, which show the average operating performance of the retailers that belong to the trade association. These studies can help the retailer develop standards.

It is important that retailers give careful consideration to the frequency with which their RIS generates income statement data. The income statement should be prepared often enough to allow management to take corrective action if an expense is out of control or if revenues are below standard. An annual income statement will not suffice; monthly or bimonthly statements would be much better. Such analysis is especially important for the managers of many of today's category killers such as Home Depot, Office Depot, and Barnes & Noble. In the past, they only had to compete with small "mom-and-pop" operations; today as they are now forced to compete head-on with each other, their expense ratios are undergoing major changes.[21]

DOLLAR $ & ¢ENTS

Retailers that continually monitor revenue and expense data, compare these to budgets, and take corrective action when necessary, will be higher performers.

THE PROBLEM SOLUTION SUBSYSTEM

Once the problem identification RIS subsystem has been used to spotlight key problems, the problems must be solved if the retailer is to effectively manage its operations and administer its resources. Frequently, this problem solving requires additional information, and it is the role of the problem solution subsystem to gather that information. There are two broad categories of problems, which parallel the two types of retail planning and management: operations management and administration of resources.

OPERATIONS MANAGEMENT PROBLEMS

Operations problems are those that are related to operations planning and management as illustrated in the retail planning and management model (Exhibit 16.5). Operations problems involve day-to-day management activities. Most can be quickly and effectively solved by an experienced and talented retail manager. However, for the occasional unique problem, special information is needed. Most operations problems are related to assets, revenues, or expenses. Let us briefly examine these problem areas.

Operations problems may be related to any of the individual assets that the retailer must manage on a day-to-day basis. Consider the following problems:

- Inventory is disappearing from the stockroom daily.
- There has been a significant slowdown in customers paying their bills.
- The store roof has developed a leak.
- The air conditioning system repeatedly breaks down.

To solve these problems properly, the manager may require information that is not readily available; he or she will thus need to use the RIS.

Let us illustrate a typical problem in more detail. Assume that you are a store manager, and the air conditioner regularly breaks down. Would you conclude that all that needs to be done is to replace the old air conditioner with a new unit? We hope not. Careful analysis of the technological environment will reveal that there is a wealth of new air conditioning technology, which can have a significant effect on operating costs. At the same time, these lower operating costs must be compared with the higher initial cost of a technologically superior air conditioning system. Also, there may be other, less tangible costs and benefits. What will be the effect of a new air conditioning system on employee morale and customer loyalty? Therefore, the apparently simple problem of whether to replace an air conditioner cannot be properly solved in the absence of substantial information.

Other operating problems that arise can be related to various revenue and expense items. And the ability to solve these problems may require more information than the manager has at his or her disposal. What might be some of these problems? Consider the following:

- Sales of a previously popular merchandise line drop 8 percent.
- Employee overtime hours rise by 14 percent in a single month.
- Gross margin declined by 3 percent.

Retail managers would probably have only a few good hunches of the causal factors unless the preceding situations had been closely studied. However, even if the managers had a few hunches, additional information would be required to help determine which hunch was correct. In one particular case involving the above problem areas, the retailer was a fast-food (chicken) restaurant chain and sales of new products—fried catfish and chicken nuggets—(with a 40 percent gross margin as opposed to the 50 percent gross on regular fried chicken) accounted for the decline in the previously popular items (breasts, wings, and drumsticks) and the gross margin. The overtime was caused by employees inexperienced with handling the new lines. However, management when presented with all the information developed a new in-store operation procedure, and the new products, even though reducing the sales of the previously popular regular chicken, drew additional customers, resulting in a profit increase of more than 10 percent the next year.

When we earlier discussed monitoring operating performance trends in the problem identification subsystem, we provided a framework for comparing standard with actual performance. This framework can be a good source for identifying significant revenue and expense problems. The problem solution subsystem can then be used, if needed, to gather additional information to solve these problems.

ADMINISTRATIVE MANAGEMENT PROBLEMS Administrative problems arise in relation to the acquisition and management of the resources that the retailer needs to carry out its strategy. In this regard, three types of resources are especially important: financial, human, and locational.

The problem identification subsystem of the RIS can help retailers identify financial resource problems that the problem solution subsystem of the RIS can help them to solve. For example, monitoring of economic trends by using the problem identification subsystem may alert a retailer to the fact that interest rates are rapidly rising and are expected to remain high for at least a year. At the same time, monitoring of the balance sheet may alert the retailer to the fact that a $10 million bond issue is maturing in six months. This pair of events should trigger problem recognition. The problem, which must be solved with the help of the problem solution subsystem, is how to generate $10 million in capital to retire the bond issue and subsequently restructure the balance sheet. Obviously, additional information will need to be collected to solve this perplexing problem. In the past, although many manufacturers and utility firms have shown an uncanny ability to issue bonds just before interest rates increased, retailers haven't always monitored rates as well as they have the consumer market.[22]

The problem solution subsystem should also be used to help solve the retailer's human resource problems. Although the problem identification subsystem may have been instrumental in calling to the retail executive's attention the presence of a human resource problem—such as low or deteriorating employee satisfaction—it is the problem solution subsystem that must obtain the necessary information to solve this problem. After all, a recent study of Sears' employees has shown that an increase in employee satisfaction results in an increase in customer satisfaction.[23]

Human resource problems can have many forms, including morale problems, motivation problems, productivity problems, turnover problems, conflict problems, and organizational design problems.

Often, human resource problems can best be solved by using the talents of external consulting organizations, which provide an independent analysis and opinion of the cause. People in the retail organization are often personally too close to the human element to be objective researchers. Nonetheless, the practice of having outside consultants conduct the research should still fall within the domain of the RIS. Basically, the retail manager is freely admitting that information is needed, but it can obtain the most valid information by contracting with an independent consulting agency to conduct the research and analyze the results.

A retailer's store location, whether it is a physical store or a site on the Internet, is one of the most valuable resources in its arsenal. But this resource can change in value as the retailer's trade area changes. When this happens, the retailers may discover that their location is no longer optimal.

To solve a location problem, retailers need information to help them evaluate alternatives. Reasonable alternatives may be to close the store, modify its merchandise mix, modify the store image, or keep the store operating as is but seek a new location.

ORGANIZING THE RIS

How should the RIS be organized for a retailer? The answer depends on the scope of the RIS. If the RIS is nothing more than a beefed-up accounting system, then the retail controller is probably the best person to manage it. However, if it is the comprehensive system that has been proposed, one consisting of both problem identification and problem solution subsystems, then the controller may not be the appropriate person. He or she would not have the time to manage such a comprehensive system.

We propose an RIS manager who would manage both RIS subsystems. This manager would need inputs from the controller, the legal counsel, the store or department managers, the buyers, and anyone else in the firm who would be either a potential user or a potential provider of information to the RIS. The RIS manager would have to be a very special and talented individual. To interact with a wide range of individuals on a broad array of topics, over which he or she had little authority, the manager would have to be persuasive and diplomatic; also, he or she would need to be knowledgeable in all aspects of retailing. The RIS manager must be just as comfortable conversing with a store manager, warehouse manager, buyer, or corporate lawyer.

Don't be misled into believing that an RIS manager is a necessity. The manager's contribution to the organization must justify the cost. If the RIS manager—or even the RIS itself—won't help decision makers make more profitable decisions, then the position is an unnecessary luxury.

Obviously, the retailer with only a few employees cannot justify a comprehensive RIS, much less an RIS manager. Nonetheless, small retailers should embrace the notion that they should remain cognizant of changes in consumer, competitor, and channel behavior; of changes in the socioeconomic, legal and ethical, and technological environments; and of changes in asset, revenue, and expense performance. Further, when significant problems occur, even small retailers should try to get the best data available within their established cost constraints to solve the problem.

STUDENT STUDY GUIDE

SUMMARY   In this chapter, we delineated the nature and scope of an RIS.

LO • 1   **DESCRIBE WHAT AN RIS IS.**   An RIS was defined as a blueprint for the continual and periodic systematic collection, analysis, and reporting of relevant data about past, present, or future developments that could influence or have influenced the retailer's performance.

LO • 2   **EXPLAIN WHY AN RIS IS DIVIDED INTO TWO SUBSYSTEMS.** An RIS should have two major operating subsystems. The problem identification subsystem should provide constant feedback on behavioral, environmental, and operating performance trends to identify current or potential problems. The problem solution RIS subsystem should be designed to generate information to help solve special management problems dealing with operations and how to get the most effective administration of its resources.

LO • 3   **DESCRIBE THE TYPES OF INFORMATION THAT ARE USEFUL TO RETAILERS USING AN RIS.**   The behavioral monitoring problem identification subsystem should involve scanning the behavior of consumers, competitors, and channel members. Environmental monitoring should involve scanning the socioeconomic, legal and ethical, and technological environments. Monitoring operating performance should involve regular analysis of the retailer's assets, revenues, and expenses.

The problem solution RIS subsystem should be designed to generate information to help solve problems spotted by the identification subsystem. Operation problems can be those that are primarily asset-related or primarily revenue- and expense-related, but which in either case require special data collection for proper solution. The types of administrative problems that will involve an RIS may be categorized as financial resources, human resources, and location problems. Special research may be necessary for effective problem solving.

TERMS TO REMEMBER

retail information system

external information

internal information

problem identification subsystem

electronic data interchange

problem solving subsystem

REVIEW AND DISCUSSION QUESTIONS

LO • 1   **WHAT IS AN RIS?**

1. Why is it important for a retailer to have an RIS in today's turbulent environment?
2. Discuss the concept that some information, while being very valuable, may be too expensive for the retailer to obtain in relation to its value toward improving the retailer's performance. Can you think of an example of such information?
3. Why should a small retailer pay between $20,000 and $40,000 for automatic identification equipment? Can this retailer ever hope to recover its investment? How?

4. What are the major differences between external and internal information sources? Which one is the best one to use for retailers?

LO•2 WHY IS AN RIS DIVIDED INTO TWO SUBSYSTEMS?

5. How is the problem identification subsystem different from the problem solution subsystem?

LO•3 DESCRIBE WHAT TYPES OF INFORMATION ARE USEFUL TO A RETAILER USING AN RIS?

6. Is it more crucial to monitor the consumer or the marketing channel?
7. How much information should retail decision makers have at hand when making decisions? Does your answer vary depending on the type of decision being made?
8. If you were the owner-manager of a local furniture store, how would you obtain information on your competitors?
9. What are the various external information sources available to all retailers?
10. Who should manage the RIS?

SAMPLE TEST QUESTIONS

LO•1 INTERNAL INFORMATION IS FOUND

a. within the retailer's own records
b. in the Internal Revenue Service's file
c. by buying statistical studies
d. through studying competitors
e. inside trade journals

LO•2 THE TWO SUBSYSTEMS OF THE RIS ARE THE

a. problem identification subsystem and data analysis subsystem
b. accounting subsystem and environmental scanning subsystem
c. problem identification subsystem and problem solution subsystem
d. internal subsystem and external subsystem
e. accounting subsystem and environmental scanning subsystem

LO•3 THE HOUSEWARE BUYER IS ATTEMPTING TO DETERMINE HOW MANY OF ITS CUSTOMERS ARE LIKELY TO BUY LEFT-HANDED COOKING WARE. THE BUYER NEEDS INFORMATION ON

a. customer attitudes
b. competitors' behavior
c. purchase probabilities
d. market saturation
e. market share

APPLICATIONS

WRITING AND SPEAKING EXERCISE A major manufacturer of grocery products, with whom your firm does more than $25 million a year in business, has proposed that it be allowed to hook-up with your computer. In return, the manufacturer would eliminate the need for your firm to carry warehouse inventory for their best selling products. The manufacturer will use your scanner data to develop a quick-response delivery system for these products. However, store managers are concerned that by allowing the manufacturer to hook-up, your firm will be giving away important information. As the newest member of the Operations Department, you have been asked to prepare a memo on the subject.

RETAIL PROJECT

One of the best on-line sources for current retail happenings is Chain Store Age's web site (www.chainstoreage.com). Go to this web page and click on the site map. Chain Store Age's site map has several important sites that all retailers should review weekly.

Select what you believe is the most important current news story on this site, state why you believe this is the most important, and list the retailers involved in this story. Finally, go to the financial site and look up the most recent sales figures and stock quote for the retailers involved in the news story.

CASE LEIGHTON'S

Leighton's is a 12-store operation that carries fishing, hunting, and other outdoor sporting equipment. The stores are located throughout upstate Maine and cater, primarily, to the "serious" sports men and women but also serve "recreational" sports men and women. The geographic area in which the stores are located is heavily trafficked by vacationers and tourists who tend to be repeat visitors.

For the past six months, Anne Curley has been involved in the classroom training portion of Leighton's management development program. Yesterday, Anne and the five other trainees took part in the last classroom session to be held before they are placed in a permanent position in one of the stores or on the buying staff. The presenter was Robert Disbennett, who is general manager of Leighton's.

Mr. Disbennett spoke on Leighton's current methods of operation and its future direction. Originally, Leighton's was a one-unit, corner-store operation that was run by Jack Leighton and generated $30,000 a year in sales. Over the past 15 years, Mr. Leighton has passed ownership of the business on to his daughter and son-in-law, 11 more stores have been added, and annual sales now total nearly three quarters of a million dollars.

Traditionally, the stores have merchandised their goods in a "no frills" manner, using simple tables and series of shelves for display purposes. In-store decorations and exhibits have been fairly primitive (usually created internally), and their selection has been left up to the discretion of each store's manager. In addition, individual stores maintain their own inventory warehouses or storage spaces and write their own re-orders for basic items, when needed, for buyers' approval.

Mr. Disbennett told the trainees that Leighton's upper-level executives have decided that it is now the appropriate time to formalize the stores' operations. It is their belief that standardized and centralized accounting, inventory, merchandising, and management systems will increase Leighton's efficiency and, therefore, its profitability. In this regard, Mr. Disbennett explained that he and the other executives are currently researching and developing an RIS for Leighton's.

Today, Anne has been asked to answer the following questions as part of her pre-placement evaluation. If you were in Anne's place, how might you answer the questions?

1. Do you support Mr. Disbennett's belief that Leighton's methods of operations should become more formalized? Why? What is the advantage/disadvantage of having a formal RIS?
2. What are the basic components that should be covered by Leighton's RIS?
3. How might the impending changes (positively and negatively) effect Leighton's current situation and level of performance?

PLANNING YOUR OWN RETAIL BUSINESS

After graduating at the end of this semester, you plan on joining your uncle operating the family clothing store in a West Coast city with a population of 400,000. You believe that given the type of merchandise the store stocks and the store's price lines, the store should appeal to 40 percent of the population of the city. However, only about 8 percent of current residents shop at your family's store on an annual basis. Based on prior internal research, you know that about 90 percent of store visitors actually purchase something. This research also found that customers shop an average of 2.5 times a year and that they spend an average $67 on each shopping trip to the store.

You are convinced that the $140,000 that your uncle spends each year on advertising must not be very effective. Over a recent break from school, you met with a local retail consultant. After this meeting, your feelings were reinforced. The consultant stated that if the family store is designed to appeal to 40 percent of the population, yet only gets 8 percent to shop there on an annual basis, then either the store's merchandising, store atmosphere, pricing, location, or advertising must be wrong. Both you and your uncle believe the merchandising, atmosphere, pricing, and location are in tune with the market and not in need of change. The consultant, based on a quick visit to the store, shared your impressions. In fact, the consultant proposed that she conduct a marketing research study of the community by randomly sampling 1,200 households in the store's target market. This study would assess the media habits of the respondents and also ask them the probability they would purchase new clothing for each family member over the four seasons of the year. The consultant would then use this information to develop a new advertising schedule (using the same $140,000 annual budget) targeted at different media over the year to maximize residents of the community shopping at your store.

The proposal sounded great until you received the formal plan, which involved an upfront payment of $20,000 and an additional $30,000 on completion of the research study. You were reluctant to ask your uncle to spend $50,000 for this information even if it sounded great. When you asked the consultant what type of results you could expect from conducting the research and following the recommendations to be developed, she stated that you could easily expect that between 12 and 15 percent of residents of the community would shop the store based on a new more targeted and effective advertising campaign. Because currently only 8 percent of residents shop at the store, you again got excited about the research project. However, your uncle wants you to show him precisely what the financial impact of the $50,000 expenditure would be. Incidentally, the store operates on a 40 percent gross margin.

NOTES

1. "Making Sense out of the Data," *Progressive Grocer*, June 1995: 75–77.
2. "They Snoop to Conquer," *Business Week*, October 28, 1996: 172–176.

3. "Making Information Pay," *Chain Store Age,* November 1996: Section 2, 4A.

4. "A New, Networked Point of Sale Puts the Retailer in Charge," *Chain Store Age,* August 1997: Section 3, 3B–11B.

5. "The Next Frontier for Leading Retailers," *Chain Store Age,* November 1995: 62–68.

6. "A Dry Run For Year 2000-Compliant EDI," *Chain Store Age Executive,* December 1997: 145.

7. "Need an Economic Forecast?" *Business Week,* September 13, 1993: 38.

8. Based on a model developed by Marvin J. Rothenberg, Marvin J. Rothenberg, Inc., Retail Marketing Consultants, Ft. Lee, N.J., and used with his permission.

9. "21st-Century Data," *Forbes ASAP,* April 8, 1996: 16. For a more detailed description of how Wal-Mart uses it computer to track merchandise performance, see "Believe in Yourself, Believe in the Merchandise," *Forbes,* September 8, 1997: 118–124.

10. "Moving to Customer Category Management," *Progressive Grocer,* April 1997: 69–72.

11. "Off the Wal-Mart," *Forbes ASAP,* August 26, 1996: 18.

12. Frederick Reichheld, "Learning from Customer Defections," *Harvard Business Review,* March–April 1996: 5669.

13. "A Satisfied Customer Isn't Enough," *Fortune,* July 21, 1997: 112–113.

14. "Book Chains' New Role: Soothsayers for Publishers," *New York Times,* August 12, 1997: A1, C5.

15. "Categorical Imperatives," *The Economist,* May 17, 1997: 75.

16. Sidney Schoeffler, "Nine Basic Finding on Business Strategy," *PIMS Letter,* No. 2, 1977.

17. Robert Stevens, "Using Accounting Data to Make Decisions," *Journal of Retailing,* Fall 1975: 23–28.

18. John Grossmann, "Vittoria in the Driver's Seat," *American Way,* August 1988: 44–52.

19. "Did Northwest Steal American's Systems? The Court Will Decide," *Wall Street Journal,* July 7, 1994: A1.

20. "Believe in Yourself, Believe in the Merchandise," *Forbes,* September 8, 1997: 118–124.

21. "Superstore Inflation," *The New York Times Magazine,* April 6, 1997: 66–68.

22. "Some Firms Rush to Offer Debt, Sparking Rate Fear," *Wall Street Journal,* August 18, 1997: C1, C17.

23. "The Checkoff," *Wall Street Journal,* August 12, 1997: A1.

APPENDIX

ANSWERS TO SAMPLE TEST QUESTIONS

CHAPTER ONE

1. C is the correct answer. A is wrong because retailing includes credit card purchases. B is wrong because, as shown in our Global Retailing box, retailing is different in each country. D is wrong because retailing involves selling to the final consumer, not the wholesaler. E is wrong because retailing is a valued sector of the economy and it does increase economic growth.

2. A is the correct answer, as we have pointed out that retailing is changing, challenging, and exciting and certainly not the other possible answers.

3. E is the correct answer, as the other four answers were among the five ways of categorizing retailers listed in the chapter. The fifth way, which wasn't listed as a possible answer, was Census Bureau's SIC codes. The manager's gender should have no impact on a store's performance, besides federal sex-discriminating laws would make this an illegal means for categorizing retailers.

4. B is the correct answer because we would certainly hope that a retailer possesses the other four characteristics as well as being decisive.

5. B is the correct answer. The ability to conceptualize and be imaginative, which is the description of a creative person, is not required of an analytical person (A) or detectives (D), although it would improve their thinking process. Nor is this ability required for all retail managers (C) or of "A" students (E).

CHAPTER TWO

1. B is the correct answer because market performance objectives seek to establish the retailer's dominance against the competition. A and C are wrong because they are made-up terms. D is wrong because societal performance is concerned with the broader issues of the world, and E is wrong because financial objectives are internally number oriented, dealing with profit or productivity.

2. C is the correct answer. A and B are wrong because price is the poorest way to differentiate yourself. D is wrong because this action would restrict you from selling many of the top brands. E is wrong because the customers really don't see planning, only the results of planning.

CHAPTER THREE

1. C is the correct answer. The "boomerang effect" is a relatively new phenomenon that describes something many of today's students will face that previous generations did not have to face—returning home to live with their parents. A, B, and D are at least true statements, but they have nothing to do with the "boomerang effect." E could be true or not at the time you are reading this, but it also has nothing to do with the question asked.

2. D is correct because too rapid a growth in GDP will produce inflation and too slow a growth will result in a no-growth environment. That is why E is wrong. A is wrong because underemployment also reduces buying power and increases the retailer's costs. B is wrong because our economy is characterized by change. C is wrong because this isn't an economic factor discussed in the text, and besides, there is no correlation between number of college students and short-term sales projections.

3. B is the only false statement. Fifty-one percent of Americans say that they would rather have more free time even if it meant less money.

4. E is the correct answer. Passive information gathering, which consists of receiving and processing information regarding the existence and quality of merchandise, stores, shopping convenience, pricing, and any other factors that a consumer might consider in making a purchase, is at the center of our consumer behavior model because this learning subsequently influences all other stages or steps in the buying process. A, the need recognition stage, occurs when the consumer recognizes a need or desire for a product or service after passive information has been gathered. B, the active information-gathering stage, occurs later when consumers gather and evaluate information that will eventually lead to a decision either to not purchase or which item to purchase and where to purchase the item. C and D are wrong because they are made-up terms not discussed in the text.

CHAPTER FOUR

1. B is the correct answer. E is true in rare cases, but the question asked for what structure MOST retailers are involved in. D, although it is a type of market structure, is wrong because retailers don't operate in environments with horizontal demand curves. A and C, although sounding good, are made-up terms.

2. D is the correct answer because this involves different types of retailers competing with each other with similar products. B is wrong because intratype refers to cases in which the same types of retailers compete with each other and Wal-Mart is a general merchandise store and not a full-line grocer, such as Kroger. C (scrambled merchandising) can be used to describe what Wal-Mart is doing, but this term does not refer to a type of competition. E refers to a situation in which a retailer dominates a single line of merchandise, not many lines as Wal-Mart is doing with its supercenters. A is wrong because it is a made-up "nonsense" term.

3. D is the correct answer. Some might say that the Retail Accordion Theory could be used by saying that the small original hamburger stand expanded to the large McDonald's and Burger Kings of today and will get smaller as customers rebel. However, this isn't entirely accurate. Nevertheless, we didn't include the Accordion Theory as a possible answer. B is wrong because it describes stage of growth that institutions pass through and not why they change formats. The other three possible answers used made-up terms.

4. D is the correct answer as all the others are expected to be successful new retail formats, especially shopping via the computer, which is also called Internet shopping. Door-to-door shopping has been with us for centuries.

5. D is the correct answer. A is wrong because retailing is more diverse around the world. B is wrong because success in one country doesn't guarantee success in other countries; witness the hypermarkets in the United States. C is wrong because private labels are different in other countries. E is wrong because other countries have also developed successful new retailing formats; witness IKEA.

CHAPTER FIVE

1. C is the correct answer because location analysis is not one of the marketing functions discussed in the text.

2. E is the correct answer because facilitating institutions aid the channel by performing tasks at which they are more capable than the current channel members are of doing. A is wrong because some facilitating institutions may take possession of the merchandise, but none of them take title. B is wrong because facilitating institutions don't take title to the goods. C is wrong because they don't manage the channel, and

besides, the goal of a channel is to minimize "suboptimization" because they can't operate at 100 percent efficiency. D is wrong because they can't do all eight functions without taking title, and besides, the text mentions that no one firm would want, or be able, to perform all eight functions.

3.
E is the correct answer. A and C are wrong because conventional channels, because of their loose alignment, are by their very nature not efficient. B is wrong because contractual channels are not loosely aligned because the contract directs each member's duties and responsibilities. D is wrong because there isn't any feeling of partnership and cooperation in a conventional channel.

4.
B is the correct answer. A is wrong; even though it may be true that each member wants all the power, a channel member is still dependent on the other members. C is wrong; no member can perform all eight functions. D is wrong because a partnership should be committed to the life of the channel. E is wrong because if everybody wants to work independent of each other, there would not be a channel in the first place.

CHAPTER SIX

1.
E is the correct answer because the major price discrimination law, the Robinson-Patman Act, is meant to protect competition by making sure that retailers are treated fairly by suppliers. The act doesn't apply to retail sales to consumers. The possible other answers pertain to laws covering other situations.

2.
E is the correct answer because it involved a deceitful action (using another firm's trademark) that cause damage to the other firm. A is wrong because it did not cause damage to the competitor. B is wrong because it wasn't deceitful; the retailer told the truth. C is wrong because it involves deceptive pricing. D is perfectly legal because you didn't do anything wrong.

3.
A is the correct answer because an implied warranty of fitness for a particular purpose arises when the customer relies on the retailer to assist or make the selection of goods to serve a particular purpose. B is wrong because an implied warranty of merchantability means that the retailer implies that the merchandise is fit for the ordinary purpose for which the product is usually purchased. C is wrong because it is a made-up answer. D and E are wrong because no verbal or written guarantee was mentioned in the question.

4.
B is the correct answer because the purchase of the cat food was tied to the purchase of the unpopular product—litter. The other answers have nothing to do with the question.

5.
B is the correct answer. Although there are federal laws governing franchise operations, the most stringent laws are usually state laws because the state government wants to protect its citizens and locally owned franchise businesses, as well as voters, from unfair practices of out-of-state franchisors.

6. A is the correct answer because it is a merchandising decision regarding the success or failure of merchandise. The other four answers pertain to the ethical decisions discussed in the chapter.

CHAPTER SEVEN

1. C is the correct answer. It is not essential that a market segment create high sales; however, it should be profitable. A, B, D, and E are all criteria used to successfully reach a target market and thus are incorrect answers.

2. A is the correct answer. Because free-standing retailers are not part of a shopping center or CBD, they do not have direct competition. B is not correct because it is an advantage of retailers in shopping centers. C is incorrect because shopping malls have higher traffic than free-standing stores. D is incorrect because free-standing retailers are not able to share advertising costs with other retailers as in a shopping center. E is incorrect because free-standing stores do not necessarily have longer store hours.

3. E is the correct answer, A, B, C, and D are all purposes of GISs, and thus any one of these answers is not the single best choice.

4. B is the correct answer. The three steps presented are exactly as discussed in the textbook. A is wrong because the first step is incorrect. C is wrong because the second step is incorrect. D is wrong because all three steps are incorrect. E is wrong because the third step is incorrect.

5. A is the correct answer. B, D, and E are factors to consider in the final site selection and not the earlier site analysis. C is incorrect because how a site is financed is not a part of either site analysis or deciding the final site.

6. C is correct because return on equity implicity takes into account financial leverage (total assets divided by equity) which is a top management decision that represents how much debt the retail enterprise is willing to assume and is irrelevant in evaluating any particular retail site. A, B, D, and E are incorrect because they are all important considerations in selecting the best site.

CHAPTER EIGHT

1. B is the correct answer because current liabilities are listed on the balance sheet but are not included in the merchandise budget. The other answers are all included in the merchandise budget.

2. D is the correct answer because the income statement is a summary of the sales and expenses for a given time period. A is wrong because an expense report, although not mentioned in the chapter, only would cover expenses. B is wrong because although the inventory valuation will affect the retailer's expenses, it also doesn't include sales. C is wrong because the cash flow statement only deals with the inflow and outflow of cash. E is wrong because gross margin only considers sales and cost of goods sold and doesn't include operating expenses.

3.   C is the correct answer because the cost ($120,000) divided by sales ($200,000) is 0.6 which is equivalent to 60 cents of each sales dollar.

CHAPTER NINE

1.   A is the correct answer because $425,000 \times \frac{1}{2}[1 + (\$170,000/\$142,000)] = \$466,901$. E would be the correct answer if question asked for the basic stock method and not the PVM. D is the average stock for the season but not the correct answer. The other two answers are made-up numbers.

2.   Because the key feature of OTB is that it can be determined at anytime during the merchandise period, D is the correct answer. The other answers are wrong because they are time-specific.

3.   C is the correct answer as the other four are the constraints listed in the text.

4.   B is the correct answer because it best describes what is involved in a vendor profitability analysis statement, which was defined in the text as "the record of all purchases you made last year, the discounts granted you by the vendor, transportation charges paid, the original markup, markdowns, and finally the season-ending gross margin on that vendor's merchandise." A is wrong because it is about the vendor's financial statements, which are seldom provided to retailers. C is wrong because it deals with new lines of merchandise. D is wrong because it deals with the retailer's line of credit granted by the vendor. E is wrong because it covers only one factor (discounts) covered by the vendor profitability analysis statement.

5.   B is the correct answer. A is wrong because it describes a noncumulative quantity discount. C is wrong because it assumes that the discount period started when you began dealing with the vendor. D is wrong because it describes a different type of discount. E is wrong because it is based on a specific quantity that may be too high or too low given the circumstances of the sale.

6.   B is the correct answer because it is the combination of vendor and retail employees that are most often involved in collusion. A and D are wrong because customers are not involved in vendor collusion. C and E are wrong because although the sales representative or accountant may be involved, the individuals involved with the delivery person must also be included.

CHAPTER TEN

1. C is the correct answer because the retailer's pricing objectives must be interactive with all the other decision areas of the firm. A is incorrect because pricing can't be independent of these other decision areas. B is incorrect because pricing can't be separate from these other areas. D is wrong because the retailer's pricing objectives should not be in competition with these other areas. E is incorrect because multifaced has nothing to do with the question.

2. C is the correct answer because in this case the retailer offered the same merchandise to different customers at different prices. E is incorrect because variable pricing means that the prices for all customers may change as differences in either demand or costs occur. Nevertheless, all customers will pay the same price unless the retailer also uses a flexible policy. A is wrong because there is no such policy as "two-price." B is incorrect because with customary pricing, the retailer seeks to maintain the same price for an item over an extended period of time. D is incorrect because leader pricing involves taking a popular item and offering it for sale to everybody as a means of drawing these consumers into a store.

3. A is the correct answer because markup on selling price is $[(SP - C)/SP]$ ($45- 25)/$45 = 44.4 percent. B is incorrect because the question asked for markup on selling price and 80 percent is the markup on cost. The other answers are merely made-up numbers.

4. This question was chosen because many students get confused about reduction percentage. C is the correct answer because reduction percentage is the amount of the reduction ($29.99 − $19.99 = $10) divided by the new selling price ($19.99). A is the markdown percentage, which is the amount of the reduction divided by the original selling price ($10/$29.99). The other answers are made-up numbers, although E is the result of dividing the new selling price by the original selling price.

CHAPTER ELEVEN

1. E is the correct answer. Even though the retailer's rent will affect the retailer's advertising expenditures (the lower the rent, the higher the promotional expenses generally needed), it should not be a major consideration when developing a promotional strategy. After all, the customer doesn't care what the retailer's rent payments are. The other four alternatives (credit customers, price level, merchandise, and building and fixtures) are managerial decisions that must be integrated into the retailer's overall plan.

2. A is the correct answer. Institutional, or long-term, advertising tries to create a positive store image and provide public service. B lists the objectives for short-term, or promotional, advertising. C lists the two other types of promotion. D lists how a retailer might seek to obtain short-term results. E lists two other topics covered in this chapter that have nothing to do with the question.

3.
E is the correct answer, as all four of the alternatives belong as part of an ad's objectives.

4.
E is the correct answer. Premiums are the extra items offered to customers when they purchase the promoted items. When in a limited number of cases premiums could be joint-sponsored sales promotions (alternative A), such promotions would not be beneficial to the retailer because the consumer could purchase the product from another retailer. The other three alternatives (B, C, and D) are other forms of promotion.

CHAPTER TWELVE

1.
C is the correct answer because the text explained that a transient customer is an individual who visits a store and finds the service level below expectations or the product "out of stock." This transient, or temporary, customer will seek to find a store with the level of customer service he or she thinks is appropriate. A is wrong because, even though the dictionary defines *transient* as short-lived or not long lasting, the term doesn't refer to length of time spent shopping. The other choices are wrong because they have nothing to do with a transient customer.

2.
E is the correct answer because personal shopping is a transaction service that helps build the relationship with the customer, thus making B and D wrong. A and C are wrong because personal shopping is a service not a cost, despite the fact that there might be some additional cost involved.

3.
D is wrong because, as shown in Exhibit 12.3, the other alternatives are factors that must be considered when determining the service levels to offer.

4.
B is the correct answer because a well designed sales job is not dependent on the number of complaints a salesperson should have to handle but on how satisfied the salesperson is with the job and how the sales job was designed. Retail selling jobs should be designed to have high levels of variety (C), autonomy (D), task identity (E), and feedback from supervisors (A).

5.
E is the correct answer because once the approach has been completed, the salesperson is in a position to present the merchandise and sales message correctly. The key to the presentation, however, is to get the customer to want to buy your product or service. Therefore, you must have the right price range of products to show the customer. A is wrong because if the price too high or too low, the sale will be already lost. B is wrong because you can't select the right product unless you know the right price. C is wrong because the greeting occurs in the approach stage. D is wrong because helping the customer to decide is the last step of the presentation.

CHAPTER THIRTEEN

1. B is the correct answer because the two primary objectives around which all activities, functions, and goals in the store revolve are store image and space productivity. Alternatives C and D have two worthwhile activities (merchandise presentation and traffic control; opportunities for impulse buying and shelf management), but by themselves they will not produce high-performance results. A and E are wrong because although its activities are also good traits, sales management (A) and maintaining market share (E) are not objectives of the store environment.

2. C is the correct answer because the store's layout and design must allow the shopper to easily shop the store and for the merchandise to be effectively presented. A is wrong because even though the retailer would like all the customers to see every high-profit items, this is not always possible, and nothing was said about presentation of the merchandise. B is obviously wrong because it would be foolish to give offices, the back room, wall, and aisles as much space as the selling floor because this is not where sales are generated. D is wrong because why would a retailer care to have rapid replacement in a low-turnover area. E is wrong because retailers today want to minimize the space given to back rooms.

3. A is the correct answer because the method of merchandise presentation has an impact on the store's image and space productivity. B is obviously wrong because it would be foolish to hire a psychologist to do the store's displays. C is wrong because by shopping effectively, the customer might not make any impulse purchases. D is wrong because although social factors may influence our behavior, this alternative has nothing to do with the question. E is another obviously wrong choice because it would be foolish for this to be done.

4. B is the correct answer because store design is most responsible for developing a store image, which the other four alternatives are concerned with doing. A store design will not however necessarily maximize sales transactions per customer visit.

5. E is the correct answer because visual communications is concerned with messages within the store, which are covered by the other four possible answers, and not those external to the store.

CHAPTER FOURTEEN

1. C is the correct answer because as explained throughout the chapter, all retailers are service providers. B is wrong because more and more implies less than 100 percent. D is wrong because even though consumers might be less price sensitive when purchasing services because service offerings may be more difficult to compare, it doesn't mean that this will benefit all retailers. A and E are wrong because they have nothing to do with the question.

2. D is the correct answer because centralized check-outs are faster and let consumers perceive a shorter wait. C is wrong because dwell time is never completely eliminated from services. E is wrong because centralized check-outs are not a merchandise method. Although A and B could be right in a few limited cases, they are not universal rules for using centralized check-outs.

3. B is correct because although services are intangible by their very nature, retailers try to provide tangible cues for the services they offer. A is wrong because if you made services concrete, they would be tangible and thus be a physical good and not a service. The other three alternatives are made-up terms.

CHAPTER FIFTEEN

1. D is the correct answer as empowerment gives the employee the power to make decisions so that the customer is taken care of. A is wrong because it is the concept of teamwork, not empowerment, that lets the employees adjust their hours. B is wrong because empowerment is concerned with satisfying customers' problems, not enforcing dress codes. C is wrong because although the employees may make suggestions for featuring products in the weekly ads, this decision is made by the buyer and department manager.

2. E is the correct answer. As noted in the text, none of these would be a valid reason for not hiring an applicant.

3. C is the correct answer because training and development must be viewed as a process of continuing education. A is wrong because existing employees must also undergo training to remind them of how things are done and to teach and inform them of new items. B is wrong because even though employee turnover is expensive, it is better to get rid of unproductive employees as soon as possible. D is wrong because senior management should not be involved in the training process; their time will be more efficiently spent doing the things they are an expert in, such as store management, buying, and finance. E is wrong because training should cover all retail activities.

4. A is the correct answer because straight commission offers the greatest potential for instant income. B is wrong because straight salary can't be influenced in the short run by an individual's performance. C is wrong because the commission in a salary plus commission plan will be lower than the "straight" commission to compensate for the employer taking some of the risk. D is wrong because it isn't a compensation plan. E is wrong because a "teamwork" salary is based on the entire team's performance, not just an individual's.

CHAPTER SIXTEEN

1. A is the correct answer because in the text we define internal information as that which is found within the retailer's records. All the other answers are examples of secondary or external data, although it is not legal to get information from the Internal Revenue Service (IRS) files. The IRS does, however, provide general information for use by all businesses.

2. C is the correct answer. All the other answers contain made-up names of sub-systems.

3. C is the correct answer as purchase probabilities seek to determine how likely a consumer is to purchase a particular product within the next six months and allow the retailer to keep appraised of the products that it should stock and promote. This question is based on the Behind the Scenes example used in the text. A is wrong because consumer attitudes are concerned with how a customer feels about the retailer's store and operation. These attitudes can be a significant determinant of store choice but not product choice. B, D, and E are wrong because they have nothing to do with the question, even though they could each influence the retailer's future sales of the cookware.

CREDITS

All other photos:

12   © Bonnie Kamin/PhotoEdit
25   © Don Bryan
37   © Amy C. Etra/PhotoEdit
39   © Jean-Marc Giboux/Gamma Liaison
42   © Evan Agostini/Gamma Liaison
143 © Michael Schwarz/Gamma Liaison
145 © Tom Benoit/Tony Stone Images
158 © Mark Peterson/SABA
194 © Ferguson & Katzman/Tony Stone Images
213 Courtesy of Business Information Technologies Inc., Richard M. Byers, Vice-President (800-533-7742).
281 © Michael Newman/PhotoEdit
301 © Michael Newman/PhotoEdit
311 © Spencer Grant/PhotoEdit
327 © Jeff Greenberg/PhotoEdit
342 © Mark Peterson/SABA
358 © Spencer Grant/PhotoEdit
364 © Michael Newman/PhotoEdit

383 Ken Geiger/Time Inc. Picture Collection
408 © David R. Frazier/Tony Stone Images
410 Courtesy of Del Frisco's Double Eagle Steak House
442 © Mark Peterson/SABA
497 © John Neubauer/PhotoEdit
504 © CLEO/PhotoEdit
506 © Mark Richards/PhotoEdit
514 © Michael Newman/PhotoEdit
517 © D. Young-Wolff/PhotoEdit
536 © Spencer Grant/PhotoEdit
539 © Jim Leynse/SABA
545 © Jon Riley/Tony Stone Images
550 © Eric Futran/Gamma Liaison
552 Used with permission of Starbucks Coffee Company.
565 © Spencer Grant/PhotoEdit
573 © PhotoEdit
578 © Marc Francoeur/Gamma Liaison

COMPANY INDEX

NAME INDEX

SUBJECT INDEX

613

TOP 25 Retailers

1 **Wal-Mart Stores, Inc. (NYSE / WMT)**
702 Southwest 8th Street   www.wal-mart.com
Bentonville, AK 72716
3-Year Sales History:
Fiscal 1995 $ 93,627,000,000
        1996 $104,859,000,000
        1997 $113,428,000,000

2 **Sears Merchandise Group (NYSE / S)**
3333 Beverly Road   www.sears.com
Hoffman Estates, IL 60179
3-Year Sales History:
Fiscal 1995 $34,995,000,000
        1996 $38,236,000,000
        1997 $40,363,000,000

3 **Kmart Corporation (NYSE / KM)**
3100 West Big Beaver Road   www.kmart.com
Troy, Michigan 48084
3-Year Sales History:
Fiscal 1995 $31,713,000,000
        1996 $31,437,000,000
        1997 $30,122,000,000

4 **JCPenney Company, Inc. (NYSE / JCP)**
6501 Legacy Drive   www.jcpenney.com
Plano, TX 75024
3-Year Sales History:
Fiscal 1995 $21,419,000,000
        1996 $23,649,000,000
        1997 $28,951,000,000

5 **Dayton Hudson Corporation (NYSE / DH)**
777 Nicollet Mall   www.shop-at.com
Minneapolis, MN 55402
3-Year Sales History:
Fiscal 1995 $23,516,000,000
        1996 $25,371,000,000
        1997 $26,971,000,000

6 **The Kroger Co. (NYSE / KR)**
1014 Vine Street   www.kroger.com
Cincinnati, OH 45202
3-Year Sales History:
Fiscal 1995 $23,937,795,000
        1996 $25,170,909,000
        1997 $26,257,000,000

7 **The Home Depot, Inc. (NYSE / HD)**
2727 Paces Ferry Road   www.homedepot.com
Atlanta, GA 30339
3-Year Sales History:
Fiscal 1995 $15,470,358,000
        1996 $19,535,503,000
        1997 $23,383,000,000

8 **Costco Companies, Inc (NASDAQ / COST)**
999 Lake Drive   www.pricecostco.com
Issaquah, WA 98027
3-Year Sales History:
Fiscal 1995 $18,247,286,000
        1996 $19,566,456,000
        1997 $22,421,404,000

9 **Safeway, Inc. (NYSE / SWY)**
5918 Stoneridge Mall Rd.   www.safeway.com
Pleasanton, CA 94588
3-Year Sales History:
Fiscal 1995 $16,397,500,000
        1996 $17,269,000,000
        1997 $20,185,000,000

10 **American Stores Company (NYSE / ASC)**
709 East South Temple
Salt Lake City, UT 84102
3-Year Sales History:
Fiscal 1995 $18,308,894,000
        1996 $18,678,129,000
        1997 $19,068,000,000

11 **Federated Department Stores, Inc. (NYSE / FD)**
151 West 34th Street   www.federated-fds.com
New York, NY 10001
3-Year Sales History:
Fiscal 1995 $15,048,513,000
        1996 $15,228,999,000
        1997 $15,643,000,000